THIS BOOK BELONGS TO

MARTHA STEWART'S

Encyclopedia of Sewing and Fabric Crafts

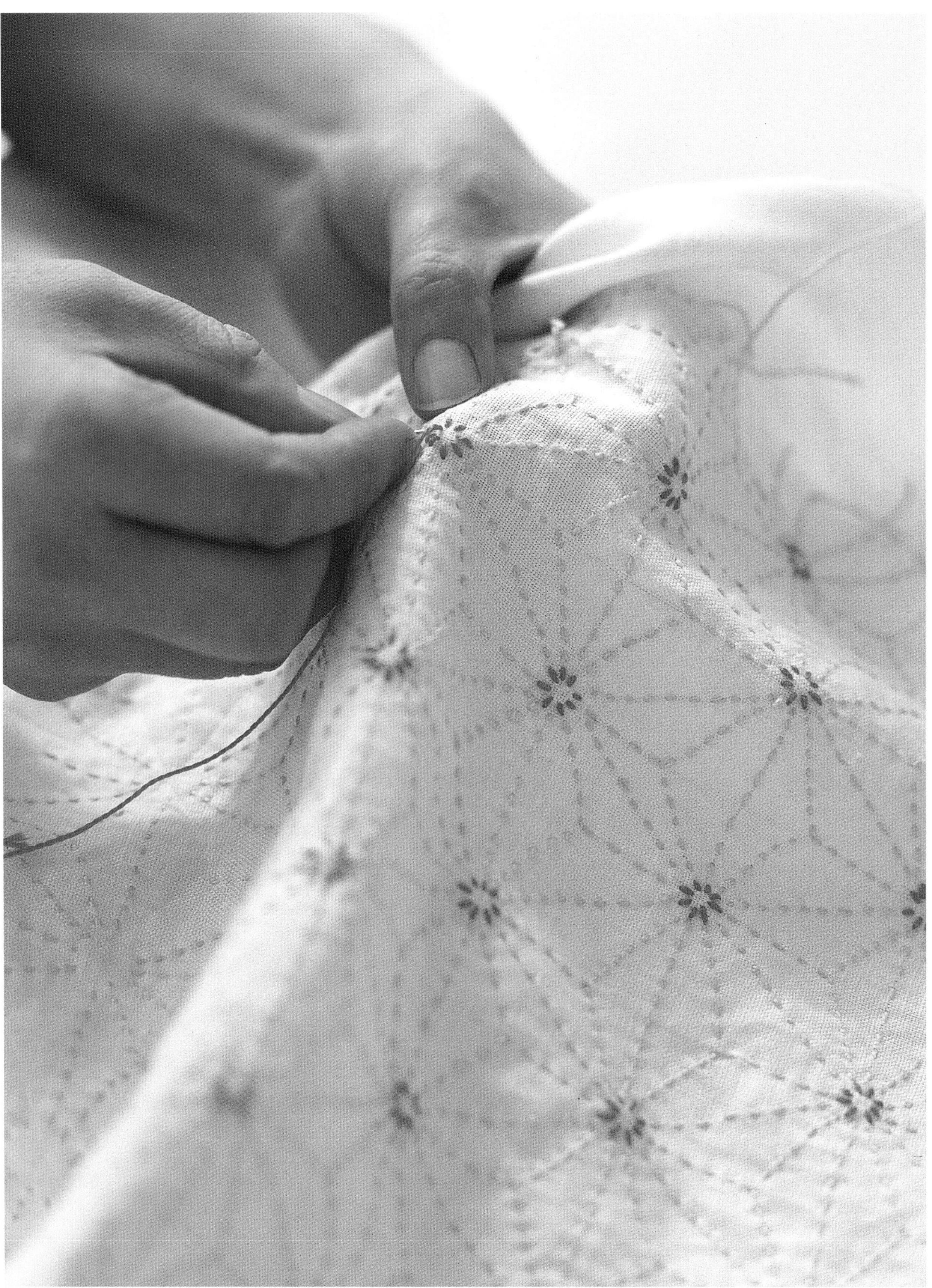

MARTHA STEWART'S
Encyclopedia of Sewing and Fabric Crafts

Basic techniques for sewing, appliqué, embroidery, quilting, dyeing, and printing, plus 150 inspired projects from A to Z

POTTER
CRAFT
NEW YORK

To our mothers and teachers who instilled in us a love for a needle and thread.

Published in the United States by Potter Craft,
an imprint of the Crown Publishing Group,
a division of Random House, Inc., New York.
www.crownpublishing.com
www.pottercraft.com

Potter Craft and colophon is a registered trademark of
Random House, Inc.

Library of Congress Cataloging-in-Publication Data

Stewart, Martha.
[Encyclopedia of sewing and fabric crafts]

Martha Stewart's encyclopedia of sewing and fabric crafts: basic
techniques for sewing, appliqué, embroidery,
quilting, dyeing, and printing, plus 150 inspired projects from
A to Z. — 1st ed.

p. cm.
ISBN 978-0-307-45058-6
1. Textile crafts. 2. Sewing.
I. Title.
II. Title: Encyclopedia of sewing and fabric crafts.
T699.S7334 2010
746--dc22
2009040548

Printed in China

Design by Yasemin Emory

For product information on the Singer sewing machines used in this book, and a special offer exclusively for you, please visit www.singerco.com/martha.

A list of photography credits appears on page 400.

10 9 8 7 6 5 4 3 2 1

First Edition

acknowledgments

This book was created by a team of talented and very hard-working individuals. Our brilliant crafts editors deserve great thanks and praise, not only for their handiwork with a needle and thread, but for their ability to impart their skills to our readers. Their primary goal, and the aim of all of us at Martha Stewart Living Omnimedia, is to inspire and to teach. The editors continually create beautiful crafts projects, then support those projects with clear, detailed instructions, so that anyone can learn how to make them at home.

Silke Stoddard, deputy crafts editor, and Nicholas Andersen, senior crafts editor, worked tirelessly to create this book, thoughtfully selecting our very best sewing and fabric crafts content, creating new projects, and vetting every word. They were guided in their efforts by Marcie McGoldrick, editorial director of crafts. We are also grateful to executive editorial director of crafts Hannah Milman. We'd like to thank current members of the crafts department, including Corrine Gill, Morgan Levine, Athena Preston, and Blake Ramsey, as well as past crafts editors whose contributions appear in these pages, including Anna Beckman, Shannon Carter Goodson, Bella Foster, Katie Hatch, Megen Lee, Jodi Levine, Sophie Mathoulin, Laura Normandin, Charlyne Mattox, Shane Powers, and Kelli Ronci. And thank you to all of the editors and art directors of *Martha Stewart Living,* who continue to produce such great work in the crafts arena, as well as in all areas of "living."

Just as on *Martha Stewart's Encyclopedia of Crafts,* the special projects group, headed by editor in chief Ellen Morrissey and art director William van Roden, compiled many years of content into one concise, carefully organized, and well-written book. We are especially grateful to editors Christine Cyr, Stephanie Fletcher, and Sarah Rutledge Gorman for their diligence and care with the voluminous material; they spent countless hours making sure that everything was worded perfectly, and that no detail was overlooked. Thank you to writer Bethany Lyttle for her contributions to the text and for her guidance. A million thanks are due as well to associate art director Yasemin Emory, who designed the beautiful book, and to Catherine Gilbert, who helped to organize and compile the hundreds of pieces of artwork that grace its pages. The special projects group is indebted to interns Jessica Blackham, Lauren Piro, and Megan Rice, and to original *Crafts Encyclopedia* designer Amber Blakesley. Thank you as well to editorial and creative director Eric A. Pike for carefully stewarding all of our book projects, as well as to Gael Towey, Dora Braschi Cardinale, Denise Clappi, Lawrence Diamond, and George D. Planding.

Johnny Miller and Raymond Hom deftly shot the bulk of the new photography, and John Huba photographed the lovely cover portrait. Many other photographers (too many to name here) also contributed their fine work (a complete list appears on page 400). Thank you as well to Heloise Goodman, Mary Cahill, Alison Vanek Devine, and Sara Parks of our photography department, and to stylists Julie Ho and Robert Diamond.

A heartfelt thank you to our partners at Singer Sewing Company for their very generous assistance with the production of the CD of patterns and templates included with this book.

We are grateful for our partnership with Potter Craft, an imprint of Random House. Thank you to the editors, production managers, and designers, including Victoria Craven, Derek Gullino, Caitlin Harpin, Chi Ling Moy, Marysarah Quinn, Brian Phair, Erica Smith, and Kim Tyner, as well as to Jenny Frost, President and Publisher of The Crown Publishing Group, and Lauren Shakely, Senior Vice President and Publisher at Potter Craft.

CA 02776
Gütermann
100 m - 110 yds/vgs
100 % Viscose
100 % Polyester

CONTENTS

INTRODUCTION 8

GETTING STARTED 10

fabric glossary 12 — *thread glossary* 18 — *setting up a sewing area* 20 — *good things for sewing* 22

BASIC TECHNIQUES

SEWING 26

APPLIQUÉ 38

EMBROIDERY 44

QUILTING AND PATCHWORK 62

DYEING 74

PRINTING 84

PROJECTS A TO Z

ANIMALS 92

APRONS 102

BAGS 112

BATH LINENS 128

BED LINENS 138

BIBS 152

BLANKETS 156

BOOKS 164

CLOTHING 172

COASTERS 188

COZIES 192

CURTAINS 196

DECORATIVE PILLOWS 208

DOLLS 234

FLOWERS 238

HANDKERCHIEFS 244

NURSERY 248

ORGANIZERS 256

PETS 268

PINCUSHIONS 276

POT HOLDERS 282

QUILTS AND PATCHWORK 286

SHADES 298

SLIPPERS 308

TABLE LINENS 312

UPHOLSTERY 332

WALL DÉCOR 350

TOOLS AND MATERIALS 356

TIPS AND EXTRA TECHNIQUES 368

CD PATTERNS AND TEMPLATES 374

SOURCES 378

BUYER'S GUIDE 380

INDEX 388

PROJECTS BY TECHNIQUE 398

PHOTOGRAPHY CREDITS 400

introduction

As a child, I was fascinated with sewing. Mother always sewed—her own clothes, the clothes for her three daughters, Halloween costumes for all six of her children, and random gifts and objects for family and friends. She had an old Singer machine in a wooden carrying case given to her by her mother, but that was put away when she bought a new White machine. The White, in its maple wood cabinet table, occupied one wall of our large eat-in kitchen. It was always open, with a project or two neatly folded on the worktable or on the ironing board next to it.

It was inevitable that I, my sister Kathy, and the youngest sibling, Laura, would all become proficient seamstresses. Buying fabrics in specialty stores Mother discovered in Passaic, Rutherford, and Belleville, New Jersey, and later in the myriad fabric shops on West 39th Street in New York City, was another favorite pastime. I learned all about weaves, textures, fibers, and which fabrics and threads were best for which projects and for specific patterns. The pattern books by Vogue and Butterick and Simplicity were like great art books to all of us, and we pored over them for hours, dreaming up lavish costumes that of course we could not afford but desired to wear. We all made small projects like aprons, scarves, and some decorative household objects, but we were primarily interested in the creation of clothing for every day as well as special occasions. I took sewing courses in the Nutley public schools and learned to make a blouse with set-in sleeves and yoke and collar, a circle skirt, a simple jacket, and a pair of cuffed shorts with zippered-fly front. Mother taught me all the rest of what I know—tailoring, interfacing, bias cutting, bound buttonholes, handmade buttonholes—and she instilled in me the basic good habits that make one a good sewer for life.

I can remember so many of the projects we made together: the white Swiss organdy First Communion dress with wide tucks and short puffy sleeves, my first "formal" of blue silk Shantung with pale pink tulle overskirt, my graduation dress with pale blue embroidered flowers on imported white cotton, my prom dress of sophisticated dark brown voile with a sweetheart neckline, and of course, my wedding dress, of embroidered Swiss organdy, with a peau de soie lining and cotton voile interfacing.

Throughout college, I continued to sew, and all of my fancy clothes were made from designer patterns from my friend Ann Boswell's aunt, who owned a couture shop called Chez Ninon. I wore Balenciaga and Dior and Givenchy to class and fell in love with great couture. When I married, my first sewing machine was a Singer, with the most advanced technology and features of the 1960s models. I learned a lot on that machine, and I sewed with it for many years, experimenting with construction and design. Even today, with construction so much more relaxed, I still examine seams and fabrics and the way things are made, and I still sew all the time.

This book is meant to be both a primer for new sewers and a refresher for those of us who know how to sew and want to get some new ideas and projects. Sewing is, of course, not just fashion. It incorporates appliquéing, embroidery, quilting, and fabric crafts, such as dyeing and printing, as well as many other things. We at *Martha Stewart Living* hope this volume fills voids in your knowledge and inspires you to try new things. Enjoy!

Martha Stewart

how to use this book

This book is divided into four sections. First, you will find Getting Started, with glossaries of fabrics and threads, which are central to everything contained in this book. In addition, the information on the following few pages will help you get started, with suggestions on how to set up a sewing area, and clever tips and tricks for organizing your supplies.

The chapters in the Basic Techniques section provide an overview of six essential fabric-crafting techniques: sewing, appliqué, embroidery, quilting, dyeing, and printing. They include illustrated how-to instructions as well as detailed descriptions of the tools and materials you will need. While you will want to peruse them before you begin sewing and fabric crafting, you may also find it useful to refer to them as you work.

In Projects A to Z, the content is organized alphabetically into 27 chapters. Each project includes a description of the materials needed, as well as by step-by-step instructions. Most projects call for "basic sewing supplies," which refer to the contents of a sewing box as described on page 28. Many projects are meant to be sewn by hand, or require no sewing at all; others require a sewing machine. All projects vary in style and skill level, and incorporate one or more of the six basic techniques covered in the previous section.

Toward the end of the book, you will find a section called XYZ, with a glossary of essential tools and materials, a handful of supplemental sewing and mending techniques, and lists of trusted vendors and other sources to help you find everything you need. You will also find miniature versions of the patterns and templates on the enclosed CD (see below).

how to use the accompanying CD

All the patterns and templates you will need to make the projects in this book are included on the enclosed CD (you will need Adobe Acrobat Reader, which can be downloaded online at http://get.adobe.com/reader, to view the PDF files). The patterns and templates are organized by chapter; each PDF file name corresponds to the project name as it appears in the book. In most cases, the patterns will print at their actual size on 8 ½-by-11-inch (21.5cm × 28cm) paper. Alternatively, you may want to use a photocopier to enlarge or reduce the size of a template to fit your project size. A few full patterns may require you to tape multiple sheets of paper together; assemble the patterns by matching the numbers on each corner of the pages.

GETTING STARTED

FABRIC GLOSSARY . . . 12

Solid Cottons . . . 12

Patterned Cottons . . . 13

Silks . . . 14

Linens . . . 15

Wools . . . 16

Specialty Fabrics . . . 17

THREAD GLOSSARY . . . 18

SETTING UP A SEWING AREA . . . 20

GOOD THINGS FOR SEWING . . . 22

fabric glossary

SOLID COTTONS

The fibers of the cotton plant can be woven into a variety of fabrics; they can also be combined with other natural or synthetic fibers to create blended fabrics. In general, cotton is durable, comfortable, and easy to care for.

1. **DENIM** Denim is a coarse twill (see below) used primarily for work clothes, jackets, and jeans. Its tight diagonal weave, along with the thickness of its yarn, produces a strong and durable cloth. Traditionally, the warp, or lengthwise, threads are dyed blue and the weft, or crosswise, threads are left natural or white.
2. **COTTON VELVET** Rich and opulent, velvet has long suggested luxury. Its soft pile is formed by warp threads that are looped over thin metal rods on a loom. When the rods are removed, the loops remain. Sometimes, the loops are cut, resulting in cut velvet. Cotton velvet comes in many weights and is appropriate for upholstery, clothing, and decorative accessories; silk, rayon, or blended-fiber velvet is also available. Clean velvet with a soft, dry brush, or dry-clean. To avoid crushing the pile, steam (do not iron) to remove wrinkles.
3. **TWILL** The term "twill" refers to a specific type of weave in which the weft threads pass over one and then under two or more warp threads (as opposed to a plain weave, in which the threads interlace evenly); the result is a distinctive diagonal pattern. Cotton twill is often used to make khaki pants, military wear, and work clothes.
4. **CORDUROY** Like velvet, corduroy features a lush pile. It is characterized by vertical pile ridges, which can be wide or narrow. The width of the ridges is known as the wale; while often referred to as "fine" or "wide," wale can also be denoted by a number that indicates the number of ridges per inch.
5. **CANVAS** Also called duck cloth or sailcloth, canvas is extremely tough and is commonly used to make tote bags or outdoor upholstery. Its thick fibers—usually cotton, but sometimes linen or synthetic—are tightly woven in a plain weave.
6. **MUSLIN** An inexpensive plain-weave cotton, muslin is usually undyed. It is often used as a lining or to make a practice version of a garmet or slipcover, to test for fit.
7. **TERRY CLOTH** Most commonly used to make bath towels and robes, terry cloth is absorbent because of its looped pile of thick cotton yarns. It can have a pile on one or both sides.
8. **FLANNEL** Flannel can be made from cotton, wool, or a wool blend. Although it is popular for baby clothes and bedding, its softness makes it a nice choice for lining winter garments.
9. **CHAMBRAY** Made of cotton or cotton-synthetic blends, chambray is a plain-weave fabric. The warp threads are dyed and the weft threads are left white, as they are for denim. It is used for making clothing, especially shirts.
10. **POPLIN** Durable cotton poplin has a tightly woven plain weave and slight horizontal ribs. It is a good choice for children's and lightweight adult clothing.
11. **COTTON VOILE** Lightweight, sheer cotton voile is perfect for clothing and for breezy curtains.

PATTERNED COTTONS

When sewing with fabrics that feature large patterns, be sure to align the pattern at the seams. You may need to purchase an extra 1/4 yard (23cm) or 1/2 yard (45.5cm) to cut and match the fabric correctly.

1. **LACE** Developed in Europe in the fifteenth century, this textile was traditionally made by looping and twisting threads by hand to create ornamental motifs; modern lace is machine-made. In the early days of hand-crafted lace, different regions became famous for their distinctive patterns; many of those patterns are still used. Venise lace (at right; also called *guipure*) features heavy, raised motifs joined by connecting threads called "brides." *Alençon* lace, a thicker, more sculptural fabric, consists of floral designs that are outlined by a fine silk cord. Chantilly lace is characterized by botanical motifs worked into a mesh background. Lace is usually white or off-white, but colored lace can also be found.
2. **POLKA DOT** To capitalize on the popularity of the polka in the late nineteenth century, one enterprising American textile manufacturer coined the term "polka dot" to describe the dots on one of his fabrics. The name stuck, and today the term refers to round, evenly spaced dots of identical size.
3. **TICKING** Traditionally used to make mattress covers, ticking is a sturdy, tightly woven cloth made of cotton or linen, which gets its strength from having more warp, or lengthwise, yarn than weft, crosswise.
4. **DOTTED SWISS** Also called Swiss dot, this pattern features raised polka dots on a background of light, sheer cotton. Dotted Swiss can be used for making curtains and clothing, including children's garments.
5. **GINGHAM** A distinct two-tone-over-white checkered pattern characterizes gingham fabrics. It can be made of cotton or blended fibers and is well suited to lightweight summer clothing and household linens.
6. **SHIRTING** This fabric is often used to make men's and women's shirts. It is made of cotton or cotton-synthetic blends, and can be a solid color or patterned. Yarn-dyed patterns do not fade; printed patterns often do. Choose the type that best suits the appearance you hope to achieve.
7. **CALICO** In the United States, "calico" refers to inexpensive, lightweight cotton with a small printed pattern. It is used to make quilts, craft projects, and clothing. (In the United Kingdom, "calico" refers to what is known as muslin in the United States; see opposite.)
8. **SEERSUCKER** A lightweight cotton or synthetic blend that features alternating puckered and smooth stripes or checks. The puckers in the fabric are thought to allow air to circulate under the fabric, making it ideal for summer clothing.
9. **EYELET** Although it looks like lace, the method for making eyelet is quite different. Sections of fabric are cut away from a piece of cloth; the cutouts are then embroidered with thread, which keeps the cloth from unraveling. Eyelet comes in many patterns and is available both as yardage and trim.

SILKS

Spun from the delicate threads of silkworms (caterpillars of the moth *Bombux mori*), silk originated in China and has been treasured the world over for thousands of years. Used for interior decoration as well as in fashion, it is strong, lightweight, and takes dye well, allowing for brilliantly colored fabrics with a natural luster. Because it takes many silkworms to produce even a small amount of silk—12 pounds of silkworm cocoons produce 1 pound of silk—pure silk fabric can be costly. However, blended fabrics such as linen-silk or cotton-silk often retain many of silk's desirable qualities, but are less expensive. Some silks may be gently hand-washed, although dry-cleaning is recommended for most. Do not wring wet silk, as the fibers become weaker when wet; to dry, roll the fabric inside a towel to absorb excess water. Never spot-clean silk, as water may leave a mark.

1. **ORGANZA** Organza is a very fine, crisp sheer silk that has a slight sheen. It is often used for formalwear and formal home décor, such as table linens.
2. **SATIN** Satin has a glossy shimmer on one side and a dull surface on the other. To achieve its perfectly smooth finish, the fabric is usually made from very high-quality silk, which can be expensive. Less costly satin is made from cotton or synthetic fibers.
3. **VELVET** Silk velvet has a greater luster and warmth than velvets made of cotton or synthetic materials; it is also more expensive.
4. **SHANTUNG** Shantung is a form of slub silk—fabric with a rough, nubby texture—that originated in China's Shangdong Province. It is often used to make elegant women's suiting, pillows, and other home accessories.
5. **RAW SILK** Also called silk noil, raw silk is made from shorter silk fibers and has a dull sheen, loose weave, and rough texture. It is slightly bulky and has a gentle drape. It is excellent for home décor.
6. **DAMASK** Damask has a reversible pattern woven into the cloth; it is commonly used for upholstery, drapery, and table linens. It features subtle tonal motifs and has a soft sheen. It can also be made from linen (see opposite).

LINENS

Made from flax, linen is one of the oldest textiles in human history. It is extremely strong and durable, and can be fairly heavy, yet feels light and cool against the skin. Its properties and beautiful drape make it ideal for warm-weather wear, bedding, and table linens. You will find it in natural hues such as wheat-colored or silvery white, or dyed to brilliant shades, including solids and patterns. Linen softens if machine-washed, a trait some people find desirable; if you prefer your linen crisp, dry-clean it. Wash, dry, and press (or dry-clean) linen before sewing it.

1. **UPHOLSTERY** Heavyweight upholstery linen will stand up to years of wear and tear. Use it to cover furniture such as chairs, sofas, ottomans, and headboards.
2. **HOMESPUN** As its name suggests, homespun linen is loosely woven with a textured surface, made to resemble hand-made cloth.
3. **DAMASK** Damask is woven in such a way that the pattern on one side is the inverse of the other, so it has no "wrong" side. It is often woven from threads in similar shades, although you can find all kinds of color combinations. Linen damask is especially popular for tablecloths and napkins.
4. **MESH** Linen mesh has a loose weave that makes it easy to fringe. It is a good choice for table linens or curtains.
5. **HANDKERCHIEF** This lightweight, fine linen is ideal for making blouses and other warm-weather garments, baby clothes, and handkerchiefs. It feels smooth to the touch and is slightly sheer. It makes a pretty background for embroidery.
6. **COATED LINEN** This fabric is treated with a layer of plastic or vinyl to make it water-resistant and easy to clean. Coated linen is similar to oilcloth (page 17).

WOOLS

Warm and insulating, wool is manufactured in many weights and styles, from lightweight suiting to heavy blanket cloth. Fuzzy, textured fabrics are generally called woolens, while worsted wools—used for suiting—are smoother and finer. True wool comes from sheep; other similar woolly fibers come from animals such as goats (cashmere and mohair), llamas and alpacas, and rabbits (angora). Wool will last a long time if it is properly cared for; most wool fabrics should be dry-cleaned, although some can be hand-washed in cold water. When machine-washed in hot water and tumbled in a dryer, wool can shrink and become felted (see page 96).

1. **MOHAIR** This lustrous fabric comes from the hair of Angora goats. The fibers can be either straight or curly, and can be dyed to brilliant shades.
2. **FLANNEL** Wool or wool-cotton blend flannel is extremely soft and warm—ideal for overcoats and blankets. Wool flannel is also used to make men's suits and women's clothing. It can be made with a plain or twill weave, and sometimes has a nap—fuzzy, slightly raised fibers—on one or both sides.
3. **WINDOWPANE** Windowpane is a classic menswear pattern characterized by horizontal and vertical pinstripes. The fabric is worsted wool, which is smooth and lustrous, and most often used for suiting.
4. **HERRINGBONE** Typically made from wool, herringbone refers to a twill-weave fabric with a distinctive V pattern, so named because it resembles the skeleton of a herring fish. It is a popular choice for suiting.
5. **TWEED** Originally from Scotland, tweed is characterized by its coarse weave, slubby texture, and flecks of color. It comes in a range of colors, from dark or neutral shades to bright hues, and patterns. Tweed can be found in a plain or twill weave.
6. **CASHMERE** Known for its luxurious texture, cashmere is exceptionally lightweight and soft. Like mohair, it comes from goats, not sheep. Because the goats produce usable hair in small quantities, the finished product can be costly. Cashmere blended with other fibers is a less expensive alternative than pure cashmere.

SPECIALTY FABRICS

These fabrics are in a category all their own; each has a special use. Leather and Ultrasuede® allow you to experiment with texture, while felt is wonderfully easy to work with, making it the go-to choice for a multitude of crafts. These fabrics won't fray or unravel when cut because there are no woven fibers. Oilcloth does have woven fibers, but they are bonded to a vinyl topcoat.

1. **OILCLOTH** Originally made from heavy canvas or cotton coated with linseed oil and paint, modern oilcloth is made from a vinyl top layer bonded to a woven cotton under side. It's durable and easy to clean—just wipe with a sponge or cloth—and is available in a variety of patterns or solid colors. Use it for aprons and bibs, as well as tablecloths.
2. **POLAR FLEECE** Polar fleece was invented as a synthetic alternative to wool; it is made in part (and often completely) from recycled materials. Like wool, it is warm and breathable. It is also machine washable and can be somewhat stretchy when blended with Lycra. It's commonly used to make blankets, cold-weather clothing, and sportswear.
3. **FELT** This thick, durable fabric is made when wool fibers are matted together instead of woven. The felt pictured is 100 percent wool, but synthetic blends are also available. Felt is available in many colors and thicknesses.
4. **ULTRASUEDE** Ultrasuede is a synthetic microfiber fabric with the look and feel of suede. It is available in different weights and is machine washable.
5. **LEATHER** Leather is typically sold by the hide and is priced per square foot; look for it at leather stores, online retailers, and some fabric shops. The most common types are cowhide, lambskin, and suede (which can come from a variety of animals). Leathers that are 1⁄16 inch (1.5mm) or thinner can be fed through a sewing machine; use a leather needle, sturdy poly-cotton thread, and a nonstick presser foot. To prevent the leather from tearing, use long stitches and adjust the tension according to your machine's instructions. When using a pattern, secure it to the leather with tape, not pins, then trace around it with a ballpoint pen; cut it out using scissors for curves and a rotary cutter and ruler for straight lines. Instead of ironing seams open, smooth flaps with a bone folder (a bookbinding tool available at crafts stores and online), and secure with leather glue.

Gütermann
Güterm
1
2
% Polyester
CA02776
3
100% Polye
4
200 m – 220 yds
5
CA027
6
Dekor
20 Mètres
40
7
8

thread glossary

To accommodate the vast array of sewing techniques and fabric weights, there are many types of thread. Threads vary in weight, strength, elasticity, and appearance, and these characteristics determine which thread to use for what project. All-purpose thread, as its name implies, is suitable for most uses; however, embroidery, quilting, and upholstery projects may call for other, more specialized threads. Most are available at fabric and crafts stores; others may be found at specialty shops or from online retailers. When buying thread, consider the fiber content and weight of the fabric you will be sewing with it: A lightweight fabric should be sewn with finer thread; heavy cloth requires heavy-duty thread. Thread weight is typically denoted by a number (the higher the number, the finer the thread; 50 is a medium, all-purpose weight), or in some cases, a letter (A is the finest and D is the thickest). In general, use cotton thread when sewing natural fabrics such as cotton or linen, and synthetic thread when working with man-made materials such as polyester. It's worth buying good-quality thread, which will stitch smoothly; lesser-quality threads may tangle, break, or leave lint buildup in your machine.

1. **COTTON ALL-PURPOSE** Made of natural fibers, cotton all-purpose thread is a good choice for hand- or machine-sewing medium-weight, natural woven fabrics. It is of medium thickness (50 weight). Most is mercerized, a process that results in thread that is stronger, more lustrous, and better able to absorb dye. Because cotton thread has no give, it is not appropriate for sewing knits or other stretchy fabrics.
2. **POLYESTER OR BLENDED ALL-PURPOSE** Durable polyester is stronger than cotton and slightly elastic; use it with synthetic fabrics and knits. You'll find all-polyester thread and cotton-wrapped polyester thread, both in 50 weight. Polyester thread is usually treated with wax or silicone to help it glide easily through fabric. Cotton-wrapped polyester thread has a heat-resistant finish that will stand up to the friction that occurs during machine sewing.
3. **METALLIC** A metallic thread will add shine or sparkle to embroidery, quilting, or other decorative stitching. Choose a high-quality thread, as the sheen on inferior threads may rub off. The best metallic threads have a durable core, such as nylon or polyester, and a protective coating, which reduces friction in the machine.
4. **INVISIBLE** Nylon monofilament is transparent, resulting in nearly invisible stitches. It comes in clear and smoke (nearly black). Use invisible thread for machine quilting, appliqué, and other fabric crafts.
5. **QUILTING** Hand-quilting thread, which can be cotton or cotton-wrapped polyester, is heavier than all-purpose thread, usually 30 or 40 weight. It has a smooth finish that helps prevent tangling; however, this finish makes it unsuitable for machine quilting. For machine quilting, choose mercerized cotton or cotton-wrapped polyester machine-quilting thread. Threads in variegated colors blend easily with patterned fabrics. You can also use nylon monofilament (or invisible thread) for transparent stitching, or metallic threads for decorative effects. For piecing patchwork together, any medium-weight cotton or cotton-wrapped all-purpose thread will do.
6. **MACHINE EMBROIDERY** Used for decoration only, machine-embroidery thread is typically made of rayon or polyester, although you will also find cotton and silk threads sold for this purpose. The standard weight is 40, but other weights are also available; 30 and 50 are common. Rayon machine-embroidery thread is soft, with a high sheen, and comes in many colors. Polyester thread is stronger than rayon and stretches more; it can be matte or shiny and won't shrink, fade, or bleed when washed. Neither rayon nor polyester will break or fray during sewing. Mercerized cotton machine-embroidery thread is available in many weights, including exceptionally fine thicknesses for delicate work. Silk versions are lustrous, with bold color and a high sheen.
7. **UPHOLSTERY** Usually made of a synthetic material such as polyester or nylon, upholstery thread is heavier and stronger than all-purpose thread. Some is treated to be UV protected and weather-resistant for outdoor upholstery projects.
8. **HEAVY-DUTY** Use heavy-duty thread when sewing fabrics such as canvas or denim, or for upholstery and outdoor projects. It is slightly thicker than all-purpose thread (usually 40 weight), and can be made of nylon, polyester, cotton, or cotton-wrapped polyester. Like upholstery thread, it is sometimes treated to resist moisture and sun exposure. The thread pictured is for hand-sewing, but you can also find heavy-duty thread on spools, for machine-sewing.

ABOUT THREAD COLOR

In general, choose thread that is the same shade or one shade darker than your fabric. When sewing patterned fabric, use thread in the predominant color. In addition, you may want to keep threads in several common colors in your sewing box for mending or spur-of-the-moment projects: If you find yourself turning to the same palette again and again, stock your sewing box with these colors, as well as black, white, navy, and medium gray.

setting up a sewing area

A well-equipped sewing space encourages creativity. Arrange your space in a way that is convenient, comfortable, and easy to navigate. This will make your sewing experience more fun, encourage you to start new projects, and help motivate you to finish those in progress.

Shallow porcelain dishes offer a streamlined approach to organizing a sewing drawer. Pull out the drawer completely and affix the dishes with double-stick mounting tape in a pleasing pattern. Don't use regular double-sided tape; the thick, foamy mounting tape will form a tighter bond.

For a harmonious sewing area, all you need are a few tools and some free space. Whether you can designate an entire room, a closet, a nook, or simply a kitchen or dining room table to your sewing projects, following these few guidelines will help create a space that works best for you.

CONSIDER YOUR SEWING STYLE

How and where you designate the space will partially depend on what you like to sew. If you're a quilter, for example, you need a larger area where you can work on patchwork pieces for several weeks at a time, without having to fold everything up and store it away between crafting sessions. If you generally work on smaller projects, or sew infrequently, a smaller space makes more sense. Or, you might simply store supplies in a closet and move them temporarily to a kitchen or dining room table.

ANALYZE SPACE CONSTRAINTS

If you have the luxury of a spare room, or even an alcove in another part of the house, you can keep your sewing area set up all the time. But even small apartments can be outfitted with a permanent sewing area. An armoire, computer desk with doors, or a spare closet can all make pleasing spaces for sewing, as long as they are well lit and have a comfortable chair (see box, right). If you don't want to establish something permanent, consider storing sewing equipment and other tools in rolling plastic carts that can easily be moved to a work surface, then tucked away when not in use.

GET ORGANIZED

However you set up your space, keep all of your sewing equipment together, so that you'll be able to easily find what you need when you need it. Stackable clear plastic bins are excellent for organizing fabrics, thread, notions, and other supplies, and are available in a variety of sizes. Label the bins with their contents. You may also want to store fabrics destined for the same use—quilter's cotton or canvas for making bags, for example—in the same bins. If you have drawers in your sewing table or desk, use small trays to individually compartmentalize thread, needles, scissors, and other tools and materials. Tackle boxes make good portable sewing boxes. Keep your equipment and materials organized by straightening up drawers, bins, and other storage areas periodically and getting rid of items you no longer need.

ESSENTIAL FURNISHINGS AND EQUIPMENT

You don't need much to get started—a table for sewing, a space for cutting, an ironing station, a chair, and a light source. To prevent a sore neck and back pain, choose a chair and table that are ergonomically appropriate to your stature. When considering furnishings and equipment, keep the following criteria in mind.

SEWING TABLE The height of your sewing table should be level with your bent forearms when seated. This will keep you from bending over or scrunching your shoulders while sewing, both of which can result in sore neck and back muscles. If necessary, you can raise or lower your work height with an adjustable office chair.

CUTTING AREA Use a table or other surface that is large enough to spread out your fabric. If you don't have a large table, spread the fabric to be cut on a cardboard pattern sewing cutting board on the floor. These boards, available at sewing stores and from online retailers, have grids for precise measuring (up to 36 inches by 60 inches [0.9m X 1.5m]), and protect floors and other surfaces from scissor blades and pins.

IRONING STATION An ironing board should come to a height just below your bent forearms while standing. This will keep you from bending over as you press. Save space by hanging your ironing board and iron from hooks or store-bought hardware on the back of a door or inside a closet.

CHAIR Choose a chair that is comfortable and has adequate lumbar support. You should be able to rest your feet squarely on the ground. An adjustable office chair is particularly useful, and one on wheels is handy for moving around the sewing area.

TASK LIGHTING To keep from straining your eyes, use lamps and other task lighting to illuminate your work area. Even if you have good overhead lighting or natural light, there will be times when you'll need more. A desk lamp that can shine directly on your work is particularly helpful.

TIP Take a break from your sewing projects every hour or so and walk around. This will help stretch your legs and refresh your mind. Most sewing mistakes happen when you are tired or lose focus.

good things for sewing

Follow these additional organizing tips to help make your sewing space more functional and to keep your supplies tidy.

designated cushions

Different types of fabric require different needles (for a glossary of types, see page 356). You'll need heavy, stronger, longer needles for denim, leather, or oilcloth, while finer needles are best for delicate fabrics. Unless you've memorized sewing-machine manufacturers' numbering systems, you won't always know which needle to use with specific types of fabric. Make designated pincushions to keep track: a denim cushion for denim needles, a woven-fabric one for woven-fabric needles, and so on. With just a glance, you'll know which needle to reach for.

measuring table

Any table or countertop used for crafts or sewing projects can be outfitted with a measuring tape along the edge, just like the ones you see in fabric stores. Purchase a metal measuring tape backed with peel-off adhesive from a home center, hardware store, or crafts shop, then apply the tape around the perimeter of the work surface, as pictured, uncovering the adhesive as you go. Snip excess tape with utility scissors. The table should be tall enough that you can cut fabrics easily without hunching over. To gauge the appropriate height, bend your arms to a 90-degree angle while standing; the table should come just below your forearms.

magnetic pin dish

A magnetized dish is a great alternative to a pincushion. To make one, affix a slim, powerful magnet to the underside of a small, shallow dish. Use epoxy for the strongest bond.

hanging tin organizers

Magnetic racks are sold in kitchen-supply stores to hold knives on the wall, but they also work well as organizers for sewing supplies. Mount the magnetic rack on a bulletin board above your sewing area. Place small essential items, such as buttons and safety pins, in round tins or steel boxes with tight-fitting lids. Use superglue to affix a sample of the contents to the top of each tin so you'll know what's inside; place the bottom side of the tin on the magnet. Hang larger metal objects, such as scissors or a stainless-steel ruler, directly on the magnet.

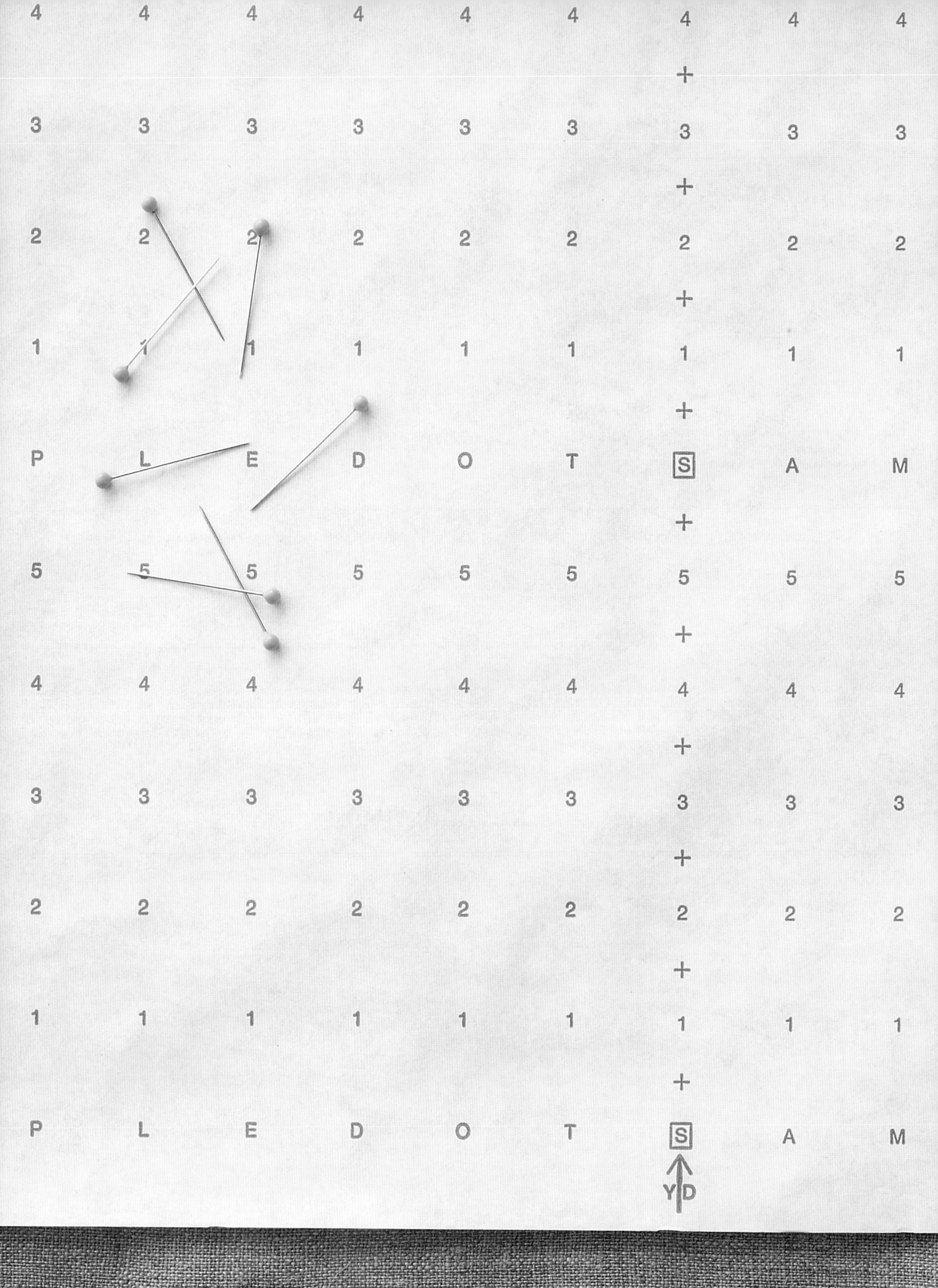
4 4 4 4 4 4 4 4 4
+
3 3 3 3 3 3 3 3 3
+
2 2 2 2 2 2 2 2 2
+
1 1 1 1 1 1 1 1 1
+
P L E D O T S A M
+
5 5 5 5 5 5 5 5 5
+
4 4 4 4 4 4 4 4 4
+
3 3 3 3 3 3 3 3 3
+
2 2 2 2 2 2 2 2 2
+
1 1 1 1 1 1 1 1 1
+
P L E D O T S A M
Y D

BASIC TECHNIQUES

TECHNIQUE:

sewing

Whether you are new to sewing or have years of experience under your belt, this craft grows more satisfying over time. Each new skill mastered builds confidence, and every new fabric discovered fosters creativity. Suddenly, you can look at almost anything made of fabric and begin to understand—or at least guess—how it was constructed, and to imagine yourself making something just like it.

Sewing lets you be creative in three dimensions: think pillows and toys, clothing and tote bags. So, not only is there the thrill of poring over fabrics in an endless variety of weights, textures, colors, and patterns, there's also the satisfaction of transforming something flat into an object you can put to good use.

In the following pages, you'll find instructions for essential stitches, both hand and machine, as well as tips for sewing basic seams. You'll also learn the best way to prepare fabric for sewing, and the indispensable finishing techniques that will help make your projects look more polished. Tools and materials are identified and described here, too, so if you're a beginner you'll know what to look for (and why), and if you've been sewing for years (but have perhaps taken a break), your memory will be refreshed.

Think of this section as a trusted reference, a place to turn in the course of embarking on any of the sewing projects in this book. Using it as a guide will allow your projects to unfold in easy-to-follow steps that are sure to encourage and delight you in the process.

IN THIS CHAPTER:

+ BASIC SEWING SUPPLIES
+ PREPARING FABRIC FOR SEWING
+ ESSENTIAL HAND STITCHES
+ ANATOMY OF A SEWING MACHINE
+ ESSENTIAL MACHINE STITCHES
+ HOW TO SEW A BASIC SEAM
+ HOW TO SEW CURVES AND CORNERS
+ SEAM-FINISHING TECHNIQUES
+ HOW TO SEW A HEM

basic sewing supplies

What's in your sewing box? The list can be as simple or as elaborate as you like. The key is to gather the necessary supplies in one easy-to-find spot. After all, nothing puts a project on hold like hunting for scissors or realizing that you don't have the right thread. Here is a checklist of essentials needed for most hand- and machine-sewing projects. For a detailed glossary of tools and materials, see page 356.

1. **PINKING SHEARS** These scissors have a sawtooth rather than straight blade. They are used to prevent cut fabric edges and seams from unraveling.
2. **ACRYLIC GRID RULER** This clear ruler is particularly helpful when measuring and marking straight lines on fabric.
3. **SEWING SHEARS** Use these smaller scissors for cutting notches, clipping curves, and snipping thread.
4. **FABRIC SHEARS** These large scissors are designed specifically for cutting fabric; to keep the blades sharp, do not use them to cut paper or other nonfabric materials (this is true of all the shears pictured).
5. **THREAD** All-purpose thread is appropriate for most sewing. Use extra-thin on particularly fine fabrics, heavy-duty on thick fabrics.
6. **SEWING MACHINE NEEDLES** A package of machine needles in assorted sizes allows you to work on a variety of fabrics. The smaller the number, the finer the needle. Sharps are best for everyday stitching and mending; ball points are designed for knits.
7. **HAND NEEDLES** Needles vary in type, length, eye shape, point, and width. They are categorized by name and number—the larger the number, the shorter and finer the needle. Choose a needle fine enough to pass easily through your fabric, yet sturdy enough not to bend or break.
8. **BEESWAX** To stiffen a length of thread, run it over this disk to coat it with wax. When hand sewing, this will make it easier to push the thread through a needle's eye, and help prevent tangling.
9. **NEEDLE THREADER** To use, slip the flexible wire loop through the eye of a hand needle, feed the thread through it, and pull the wire back out, bringing the thread with it.
10. **THIMBLE** When hand-sewing, wear this pitted cap on your middle finger to help push the needle through the fabric.
11. **PINCUSHION** To keep pins organized and easily accessible, stick them in a small cushion. Pincushions are often filled with emery, which helps keeps points sharp.
12. **PINS** Pins are available in different lengths and gauges; all-purpose pins are fine for general sewing. Glass-head pins won't melt when ironed, and are easier to spot when sewing a seam than metal-tipped ones.
13. **SEAM RIPPER** This tool has a sharp edge and hook that snip through stitches to remove them. Use it with care to avoid ripping the fabric.
14. **POINT TURNER** After turning pillows and other square or rectangular projects right-side out, this tool helps to sharpen corners and crease seams.
15. **TWEEZERS** Look for tweezers with a curved point for pulling loose threads and picking up small items.
16. **CHALK PENCIL** This tool can be used to mark fabric before cutting or altering, and will wipe off easily; it is an alternative to tailor's chalk (see below).
17. **DISAPPEARING-INK FABRIC PEN** Look for a pen with water-soluble ink that can be wiped away with a damp cloth, or ink that disappears within a few days. You may want to test the pen on a scrap of fabric before drawing, as it may leave permanent marks on some fabrics.
18. **SEAM GAUGE** A short ruler with an adjustable flange, a seam gauge is designed to measure and mark seam allowances to keep seams and hems even.
19. **TAPE MEASURE (EXTRA LONG)** Compact and flexible, a tape measure is an essential tool for measuring curved objects and taking body measurements. (When measuring fabric on a flat surface, use a yardstick.)
20. **TAILOR'S CHALK** This is used to mark fabric before cutting or altering; the marks from tailor's chalk brush off easily when you're done.

Nearly any compact container will do for keeping sewing supplies organized. Here an old cigar box houses threads, needles, and notions. Glue a double piece of grosgrain ribbon to the lid for storing pins and easy-to-lose buttons.

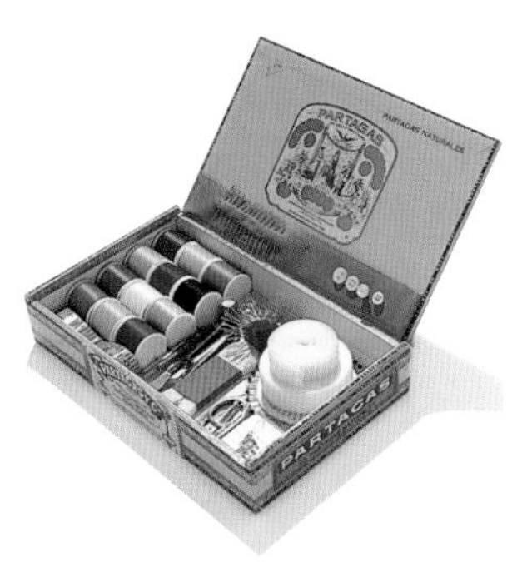

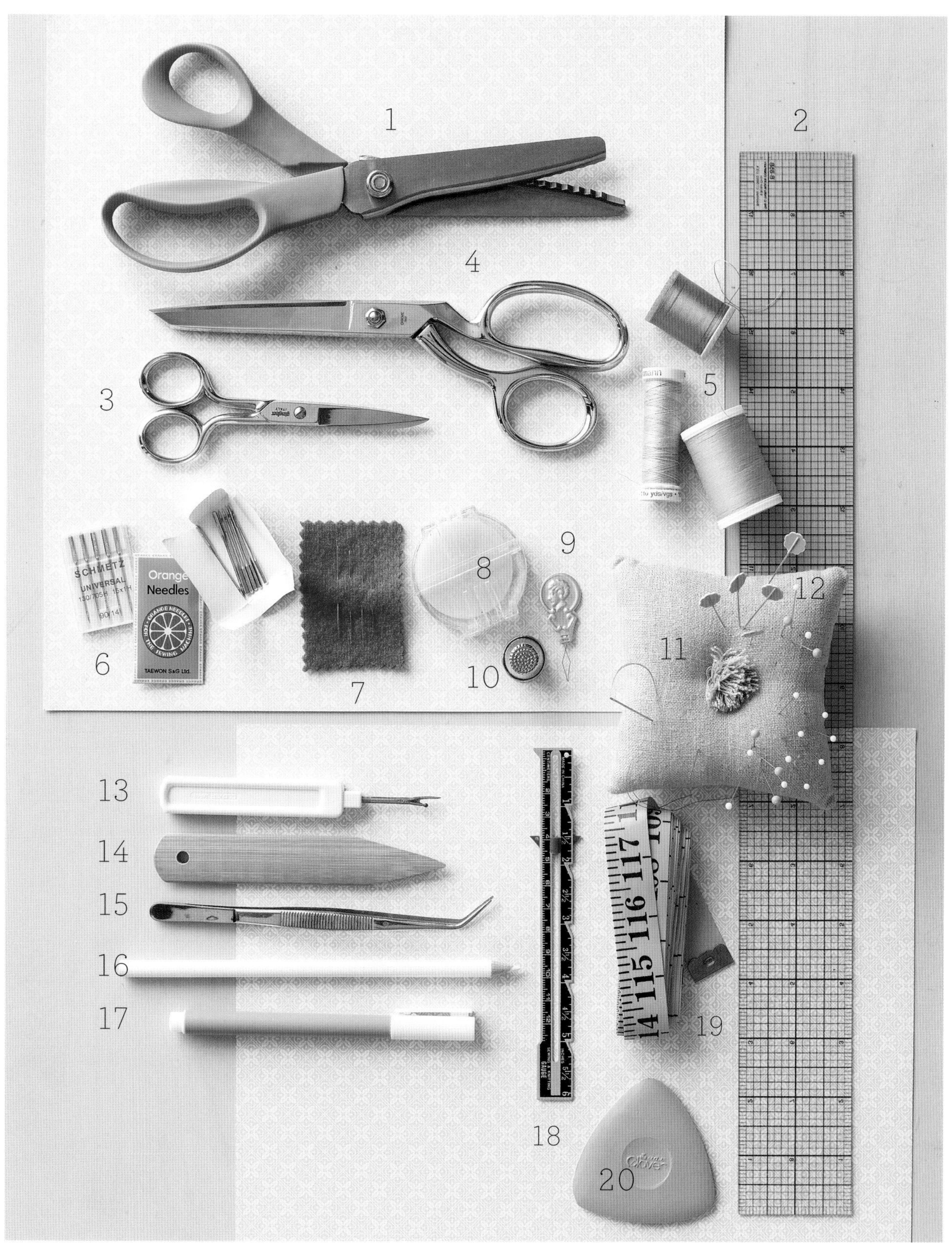
1
2
4
3
5
9
8
12
11
6
10
7
13
14
15
16
17
19
18
20
SCHMETZ
UNIVERSAL
Orange
Needles
TAEWON S&G Ltd.
Clover

preparing fabric for sewing

All set to sew? The following tips and guidelines for preparing your fabric will ensure great results.

WASH AND DRY Prewashing and drying the fabric will prevent your finished project from shrinking in the wash after it is sewn and prevent puckering along seam lines. Some fabrics have care symbols on the selvage, which is the smooth, uncut border on the left- and right-hand edges of the fabric. Other yardage will come with care instructions; if not, ask a salesperson for suggestions. Certain fabrics, such as silk, wool, and wool felt, should not be prewashed; after sewing, dry-clean anything made from these fabrics. You don't need to prewash fabrics that will not be washed after sewing or assembling—for example, if using linen to cover a bulletin board.

PRESS Even if the wrinkles look insignificant, they will distort the fabric enough to throw off sizes and shapes when it comes time to sew. Smoothing wrinkles and creases makes it easier to cut the fabric properly.

FIND THE GRAIN The grain of woven fabrics influences both the drape and durability of a finished project, so it's very important to identify it before you cut out pieces. Woven fabric is made up of threads that run lengthwise (warp) and crosswise (weft). To find the grain, look at the direction the fabric fibers run: The warp always runs parallel and the weft perpendicular to the selvage. Even if you can't immediately see these threads, tugging on the fabric will give you a hint. If you are tugging with the crosswise or lengthwise grain, there will be no stretch. If you tug at a 45-degree angle ("on the bias," typically from corner to corner) you'll feel the fabric stretch. Some types of patterns, particularly for clothing, are cut on the bias, which will give a garment or other project a graceful drape. Other patterns or templates are better cut with the grain. An arrow on the pattern piece will direct the pattern placement.

PIN FABRIC AND PATTERNS Lay out your pressed fabric on a hard, flat surface. With your hands, smooth out any ripples (double-check that there are no folds or wrinkles). When pinning two pieces of fabric together, insert pins perpendicular to the stitch line, inside the seam allowance. This will prevent puckering and protect your fabric from undue tension or accidental snags. When pinning patterns to your fabric, insert pins on the diagonal in relation to the stitching lines. Cut out pattern or template pieces (with paper or all-purpose scissors, not fabric shears) before pinning. If you are using a store-bought pattern, consult the accompanying placement diagram; it will show you where on your fabric to pin the pattern pieces. (The diagram will also tell you whether your pattern pieces should be placed on the fold, or placed upside down or right-side up on the fabric.)

CUT THE FABRIC Use sharp sewing shears, and make long, smooth cuts. The same goes for pinking shears—make long cuts. If you are cutting notches or clipping curves, small sewing shears cut more precisely, making them more accurate.

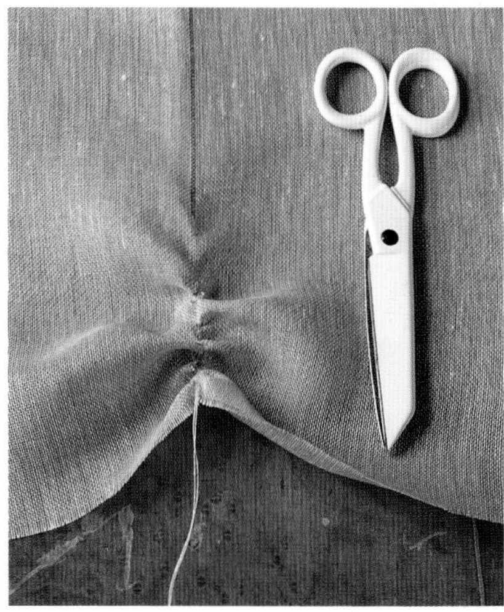

The easiest way to cut a straight line in loose-weave fabric, such as linen, is to pull a few threads from the warp or weft. The resulting small gaps will provide a perfect line to use as a guide.

RIGHT AND WRONG SIDES OF FABRIC

The side of the fabric that will face out is referred to as the right side; the other side is called the wrong side. Identifying the right and wrong side of the fabric will help you successfully cut out and sew pieces together. Many fabrics have sides that do not match. Patterned cotton, for example, may be darker on one side than on the other. Pick the side of the fabric that you want to face out, and be consistent in cutting all pattern or template pieces so that, once sewn, they face out. If you are working with fabric that looks identical on each side, such as linen or felt, it doesn't matter which side faces out.

essential hand stitches

Three hand stitches will get you through just about any basic sewing task. Begin by threading a needle with an 18- to 24-inch (45–61cm) length of thread and knotting it at one end. As you stitch, gently pull the thread—never tug, or the fabric will pucker. Secure the stitches with a knot on the wrong side of the fabric (see box below).

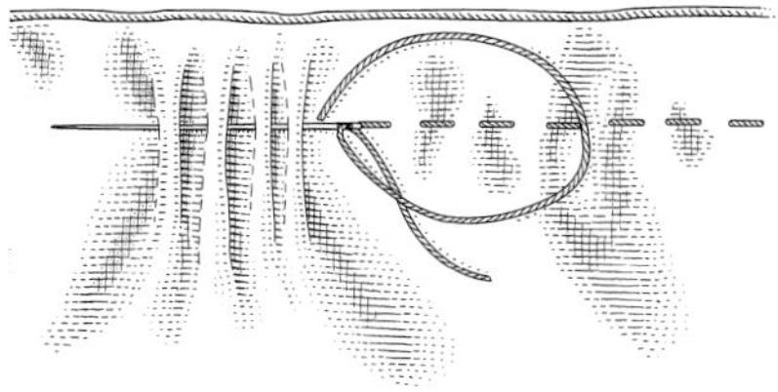

RUNNING STITCH This simple straight stitch is often used to baste—to sew with long, loose stitches that will hold fabric in place temporarily before applying a permanent stitch. When used for basting, the stitch is temporary, so the thread needn't be knotted to begin. Insert the needle at evenly spaced intervals into the fabric several times, then pull the needle and thread through. Repeat. The running stitch can also be used as a decorative stitch for embroidery projects (see page 54).

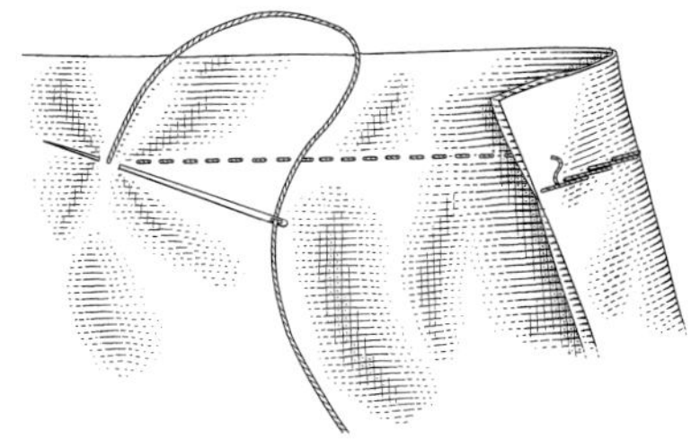

BACKSTITCH This strong stitch is commonly used to make a permanent seam. With right sides of the fabric together, bring the threaded needle through the two layers of fabric. Pass the needle back down through the fabric, about ⅛ inch (3mm) to the right; bring it back up at about the same distance to the left of where you started. Repeat.

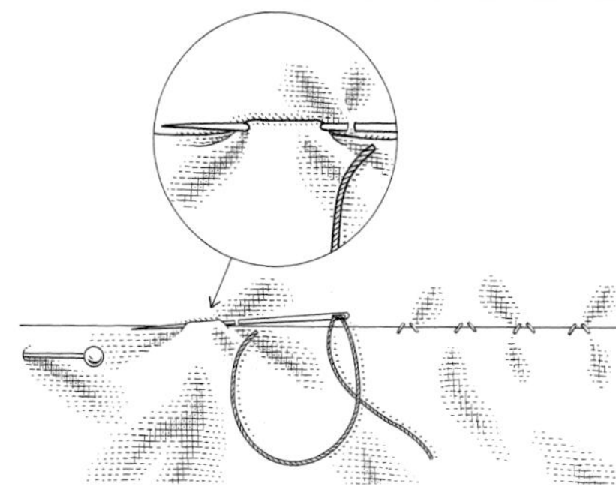

SLIPSTITCH This stitch is used to make an invisible seam between folded edges or between one folded edge and a flat piece of fabric (it is used for hand-turn appliqué; see page 41). Because the thread is hidden inside a fold of fabric, it is virtually invisible. Insert the needle through the fold and pass it through the top single layer of fabric; pick up a thread or two from the top of the opposite fold or flat piece of fabric. Pass the needle back into the fold, and repeat.

FINISHING KNOTS

Secure a row of stitches, using either of these methods, to make a finishing knot: For a basic knot (figure a), wrap the thread around the needle three times; pull the needle through the wrapped thread to form a knot (figure b). For a backstitch knot, simply make three small backstitches (see above) at the end of the seam.

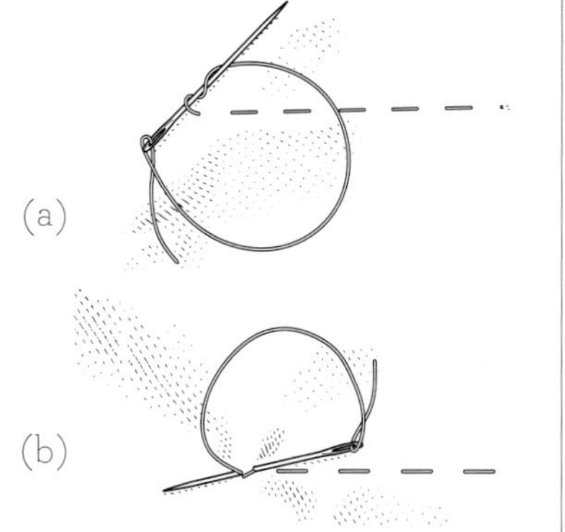

anatomy of a sewing machine

All sewing machines differ, but most have basic features that are similar from model to model. Here's a quick reference to identify the different components on most machines. You probably have a manual that provides similar information specific to your model. If you've lost it, or if you're using a vintage machine, you can find many manuals online.

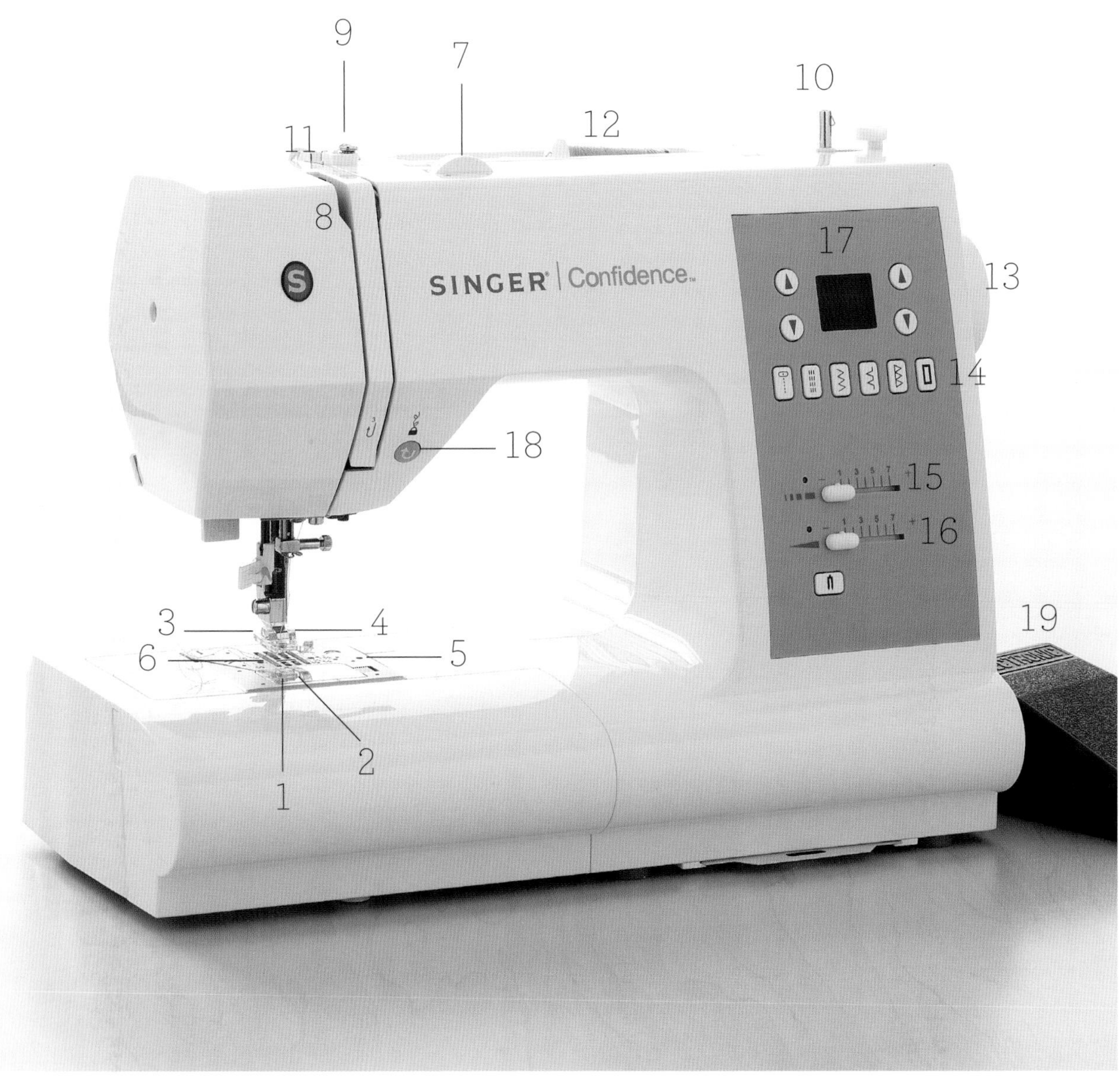

1. **BOBBIN AND BOBBIN CASE** The bobbin is wound with the thread that will make up the underside of a machine stitch. Machines have either a top drop-in style of bobbin (like the one shown), or a front-loading bobbin. The bobbin case holds the bobbin. It is usually not interchangeable between machines. Use only bobbins recommended by the manufacturer for your particular model, or the machine may not work properly.
2. **SLIDE PLATE OR BOBBIN COVER** Depending on the machine, a slide plate or hinged bobbin cover allows access to the bobbin.
3. **PRESSER FOOT** This removable foot keeps fabric in place as you sew. Different feet are appropriate for different sewing techniques or fabrics. For example, a zipper foot is used to install a zipper, and a roller or nonstick foot for sewing leather and oilcloth smoothly.
4. **NEEDLE AND NEEDLE CLAMP** Sewing-machine needles are removable and come in a variety of sizes. (For more on machine needles, see page 357.) As its name implies, the needle clamp holds the needle in place.
5. **THROAT PLATE** This metal plate, sometimes called a needle plate, sits below the needle and presser foot. A small opening in the plate allows the bobbin thread to come out and the needle to pass through to make stitches. Most throat plates have small lines notched to the right of the presser foot; these serve as guides for seam allowances and for sewing straight lines. The plate can be removed to clean underneath.
6. **FEED DOGS** These small metal or rubber teeth pull the fabric between the presser foot and throat plate. The feed dogs also regulate the stitch length by controlling how much fabric passes through at once. As you guide the fabric, always allow the feed dogs—not your hands—to move the fabric. Manually pulling or pushing may cause the needle to bend or break.
7. **TENSION REGULATOR** This dial controls the tension on the top thread. With proper tension the top thread and bobbin thread will join together in uniform stitches. If the tension is set too tight, the stitch will pucker and break; if set too loose, the stitches will not hold. For machines with a manual dial, turn the dial counterclockwise to decrease tension, and clockwise to increase tension. For machines with computerized tension, which displays digitally, press the control to a higher setting to increase tension and a lower setting to decrease it.
8. **TAKE-UP LEVER** The top thread passes through this metal lever, which moves up and down in tandem with the needle. Depending on the machine, the take-up lever may protrude from the front or be hidden inside the plastic casing (as it is on the machine shown). Before placing fabric under the presser foot, raise the lever completely (the needle will be at its highest point); this will keep the needle from snagging the fabric.
9. **BOBBIN WINDER TENSION DISK** On machines that have an external bobbin winder, the tension disk helps guide the thread between the spool and the winder.
10. **BOBBIN WINDER** An empty bobbin is placed on this winder to be filled with thread from the spool. To ensure that the thread winds evenly, always start with an empty bobbin.
11. **THREAD GUIDES** From the spool pin, thread passes through these metal loops to help regulate the tension of the thread.
12. **SPOOL PIN** This small dowel holds the thread. Some machines come with several spool pins for various types of thread spools and for decorative or twin-needle sewing. Spool pins can be horizontal or vertical, but horizontal ones provide smoother thread feed.
13. **FLYWHEEL** This knob, also called a handwheel, raises and lowers the take-up lever. Always turn the flywheel toward you (it will also turn toward you as you press the foot controller).
14. **STITCH SELECTOR** On older machines, a dial allows you to choose between different machine stitches. Newer machines have buttons to select stitches (as shown).
15. **STITCH-LENGTH SELECTOR** Use this dial or lever to set the length of the stitches on manual and some electronic machines. Stitches are measured differently, depending on the machine. The stitches may be measured per inch, usually ranging from 0 to 20 (by metric scale, from 0 to 4 stitches per millimeter), or simply numerically from 0 to 9. For general sewing, use medium-length stitches; for fine fabrics, shorter stitches; for heavier fabrics, or when basting or gathering, use long stitches.
16. **STITCH-WIDTH SELECTOR** On manual machines, as well as some electronic machines, this dial or lever controls the width of decorative stitches, such as the zigzag stitch.
17. **MENU SCREEN** On newer electronic and computerized machines, the menu screen allows you to adjust functions and stitches, sometimes replacing the separate stitch, stitch-width, and stitch-length selector dials.
18. **REVERSE-STITCH BUTTON** Pressing this button will reverse the direction of the stitches, allowing you to secure the thread at the beginning and end of a seam. (Some manuals call this a backstitch button.)
19. **FOOT CONTROLLER** The speed of the stitches is partially controlled by pressing on this pedal.

SAFETY TIPS Needles are sharp, so it's important to heed a few precautions when working with your machine. When guiding fabric over the throat plate, keep your fingers an inch or two away from the presser foot at all times. If you pause between stitches, take your foot off the foot controller so that you don't accidentally set the needle in motion. If you are taking a longer pause, turn off the machine completely. In addition to preventing accidental stitches, this will prolong the life of any small light bulbs that illuminate your work.

essential machine stitches

While many machines, particularly modern ones, allow for multiple stitching options and effects, the following basic stitches are the only ones you'll need to complete the projects in this book—and many other machine-sewing jobs.

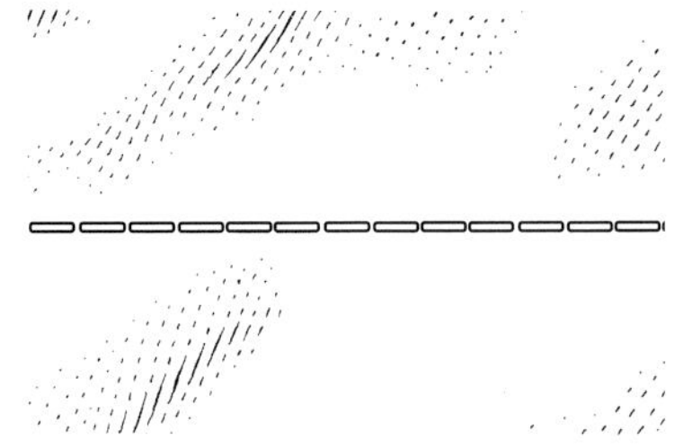

STRAIGHT STITCH This stitch is the one used most to make most seams and hems. Use a short stitch length for sewing seams on lightweight fabrics, medium stitch length for general sewing, and long stitch length for basting and making ruffles (use the stitch-length selector dial or lever to alter the length).

ZIGZAG STITCH Used to prevent the fraying of raw edges on seams, as well as for edging, attaching elastic, and adding trim, this stitch binds threads while allowing for movement, something that prevents the thread from snapping and seams from opening. This stitch may also be used to join pieces of fabric, and as a decorative stitch in machine embroidery (page 60).

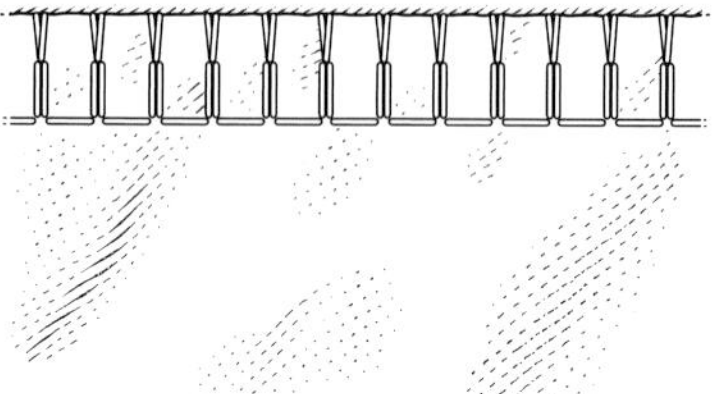

OVEREDGE STITCH Sometimes called an overcast stitch, this is used to produce neat, durable seams on bulky fabrics and to prevent the edges of woven fabrics from fraying. The overedge stitch essentially forms and finishes a seam at the same time. It can be used to sew jersey and other knit fabrics.

ABOUT EDGE STITCHES AND TOPSTITCHES

Edge-stitching and topstitching are both straight stitches worked close to a folded edge. The edge stitch is often used to finish hems, and is sewn anywhere from 1/16 to 1/8 inch (2–3mm) from the folded or sewn edge. The topstitch is typically a decorative element, sewn between ¼ inch and a few inches (6mm–7.5cm) from the folded or sewn edge. Before starting either stitch, pin or baste the stitching line so that it lays flat. Sew with a long straight stitch. Use matching thread and a regular stitch length if you are using either an edge stitch or topstitch to strengthen or close a seam or hem. Use a contrasting thread if topstitching is meant to be decorative.

how to sew a basic seam

There are many different types of seams, but the flat seam, described here, is the most widely used. It is always sewn with the right sides of the fabric together. Before you begin, make sure the needle and thread are appropriate for the weight and texture of the fabric you are using.

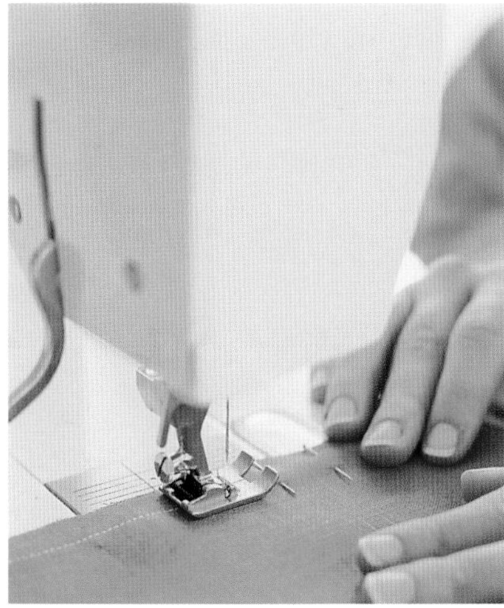

PIN Right sides facing, place pins at each end of the seam line, then at regularly spaced intervals in between. The seam will depend on the instructions of the project or pattern. Common seam allowances range from 1/4 to 1/2 inch (6–13mm).

STITCH Using the markings on your throat plate as a guide, stitch along the seam line, as shown. About 1/2 inch (13mm) from where you began, use the reverse-stitch button to stitch back to the edge, then stitch forward; this will secure the thread. Continue stitching the seam to the end, then reverse-stitch again about 1/2 inch (13mm).

FINISH Raise the needle to its highest position and lift the presser foot. Withdraw your work by pulling it back and away from the needle. Leaving a short length, cut both threads. Trim ends.

how to sew curves and corners

Curves and corners are easy to sew, but they require a few steps to create even seams and to prevent puckering, creasing, and bulk.

STITCHING CURVES The key to stitching hems or seams on a curve is to use your hand to guide the fabric, gliding it across the machine in a fluid motion, as you stitch. Try to stitch slowly and deliberately, without "forcing" the curve by stretching or pulling on the fabric. It may take a bit of practice to get it right.

CLIPPING CURVES When curved work is turned right-side out, the fabric bunches and puckers along the curve of the stitching line, and it no longer looks curved. To help it lay flat and retain its rounded appearance, snip into the seam allowance in several places along the curve (as shown, right). You can also trim the width of the seam allowance; this will result in less bulk.

STITCHING CORNERS To stitch corners, "pivot" the fabric: Stitch to a turning point, with the needle lowered in the work. Raise the presser foot and pivot the fabric on the needle. Then lower the presser foot and continue. Reinforce the corners by shortening the stitch length just before and after the point of the corner.

CLIPPING CORNERS Before turning projects right-side out, clip the tips off any corners at a 45-degree angle. Be careful not to snip into the stitching. Clipping this way reduces bulk and ensures that, when turned right-side out, the angles are sharp and the corners are pointed. Using a point turner (page 28) also helps.

seam-finishing techniques

To keep seam allowances from unraveling, professional sewers use a serger—a specialty machine that simultaneously sews and finishes the raw edge. If you don't have one, any of the following methods should do the trick.

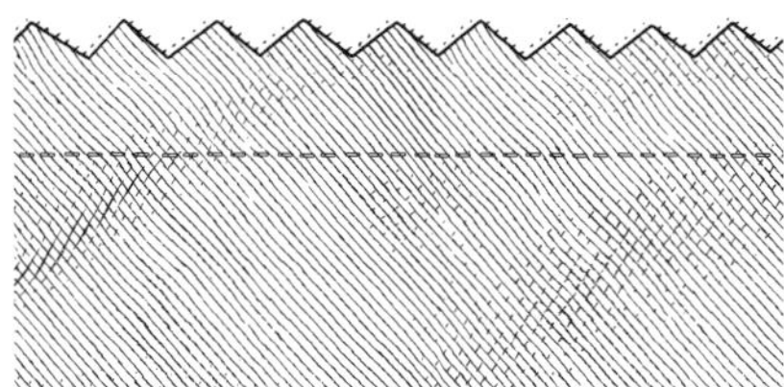

PINKING SHEARS The easiest way to finish a seam is to trim the seam allowance with pinking shears. The zigzag cut produces a nearly ravelproof edge. If your pinking shears are sharp, and your fabric is not too thick, you can cut through both layers of the seam allowance (take care not to cut through the seam) and then press the seam open. But if you are working with a thick fabric, such as denim, press the seam allowance open first, and then cut each unfinished edge.

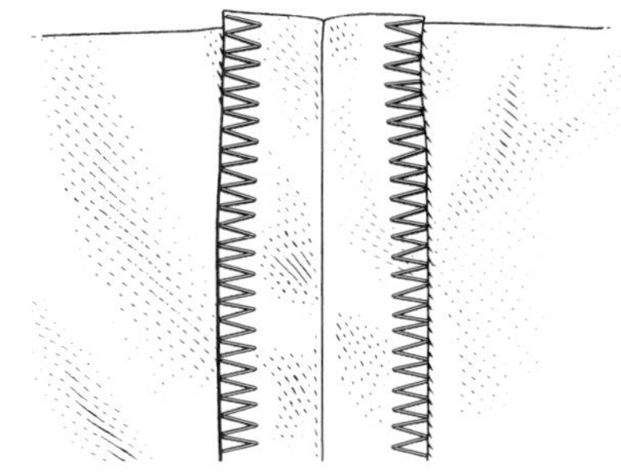

ZIGZAG-STITCH FINISH This method wraps the raw edges of your seam with a row of zigzag stitches. After sewing the seam, press open the seam allowance. Set your machine to the zigzag stitch. Adjust the stitch width to about 1/4 inch (6mm) and the length to about 3/8 inch (10mm; a 3 or 5 on your machine); a long stitch length keeps the edge from getting bulky, and helps the seam lay flat. Align the right edge of the seam allowance so that part of the stitch catches the fabric and the other goes slightly off the edge; this will enclose the loose threads, preventing fraying. Repeat with the remaining seam allowance, then press the seam open once more.

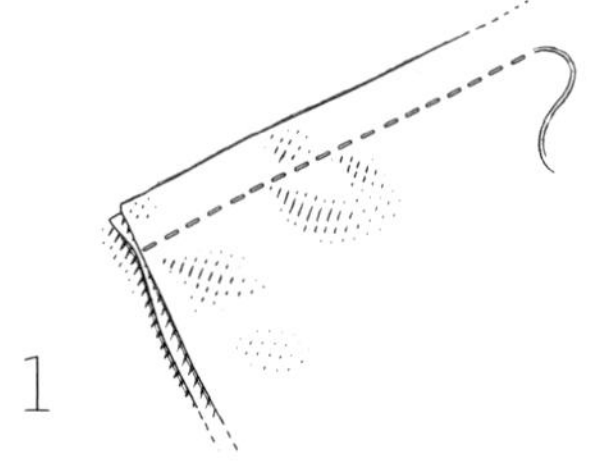

1

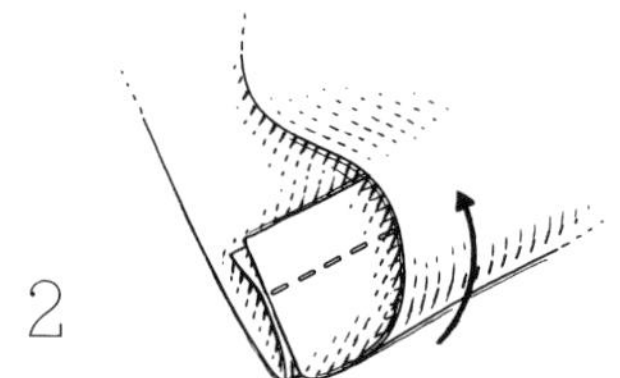

2

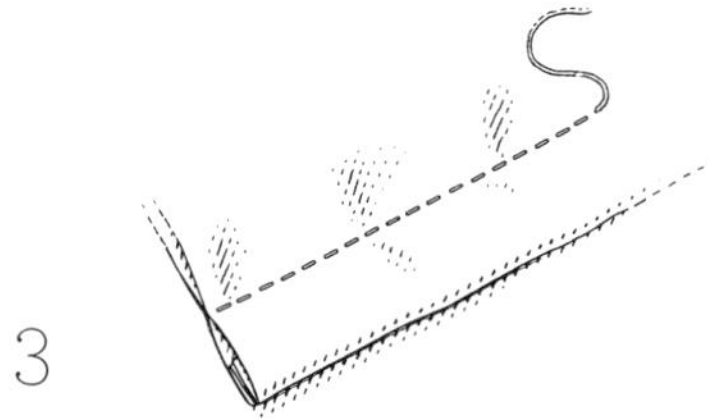

3

FRENCH SEAM FINISH This is the most professional, advanced, and clean-looking seam-finishing technique. A French seam encloses raw edges in a fabric casing that creates a strong edge. French seams are often used on finely tailored clothing—or anything made from thin and delicate material, such as chiffon or organza. They're also recommended for seams that will be seen from both sides, such as on a shower curtain. French seams are not appropriate for most curved seams, or thick fabrics, such as denim (the seam will get too bulky). **1.** To make a French seam, first align the fabric or pattern pieces together, wrong sides facing, and sew close to the raw edge. **2.** Flip the fabric back the other way over the seam, so that the right sides are facing. **3.** Sew another seam with a slightly larger seam allowance to enclose the first seam.

how to sew a hem

Hemming prevents the edges of fabric from fraying and creates weight so that fabric drapes properly. The single-fold hem is the simplest: the edge is folded over, pressed, then edge-stitched at the top of the fold. Yet most of the projects in this book rely on a double hem—the edge is folded over twice—to produce a ravelproof edge.

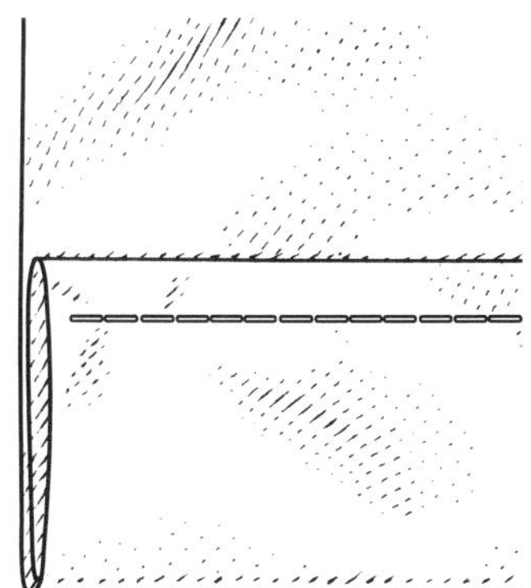

MARK HEM With a seam gauge and tailor's chalk or a disappearing-ink fabric pen, mark a dashed line the distance you want the first fold to be from the unfinished edge of the fabric; continue along the entire hem. Use a clear ruler to make sure the hem is even as you make the marks. Repeat this process for making a second dashed line where you want the second fold. To make an even ½-inch (13mm) double hem, for example, make the first marks ½ inch (13mm) from the unfinished edge, and the second set of marks 1 inch (2.5cm) from the unfinished edge. Some projects will call for an uneven double fold; for example, the hem of a curtain may be turned over ½ inch (13mm), then turned over again 2 inches (5cm). In this case, your marks would be ½ inch (13mm) from the unfinished edge and 2½ inches (6.5m) from the unfinished edge.

TURN UP EDGES AND PRESS Fold the fabric over at the first mark, and press. Then fold the fabric over at the second mark, press, and pin. For an even double hem (see illustration, left), the first fold will be exactly the same size as the second. For an uneven double hem, the first fold will be smaller than the second.

SEW HEM Edge-stitch ⅛ inch (3mm) from the top fold, removing the pins as you sew. Use the markings on your machine's throat plate to ensure a straight seam.

alternative hems

BOUND HEM To keep hems from becoming bulky, bind unfinished fabric edges with seam binding or bias tape. For straight edges, sandwich the unfinished edge in seam binding and machine-stitch close to the edge, making sure to catch the bottom layer. (You can pin the seam binding to the fabric first, but, depending on the weight of your fabric, it may be easier to skip this step.) For curved edges, follow the same directions, but use bias tape, which will curve with the hem. Do not pull on the bias tape, and never use seam binding on a curved edge, or the hem will pucker.

INVISIBLE HEM For this hand-sewn hem, the needle picks up just a few threads from the fabric, so the seam is barely visible. After pressing the hem, make the smallest possible stitch in the wrong side of the fabric; it will show on the right side. Bring the thread down and to the right on a diagonal, and make a stitch in the hem, piercing only the top layer of fabric (if working with a double-fold hem), again pushing the needle from right to left to create tiny Xs. Repeat, working left to right, every ⅓ inch (8mm). Press to crease.

HAND-ROLLED HEM Best for lightweight fabrics, a hand-rolled hem is often used to finish the edges of handkerchiefs and lightweight scarves. For a smooth finish, this hem should be as narrow as possible. Deep hems are bulky and prevent the fabric from laying flat. To begin: Lay the fabric on a flat surface with the wrong side up. Roll ¼ inch (6mm) of the top edge of the fabric toward you (you may want to moisten your finger on a damp sponge to help catch the fabric). Roll the hem tightly, so that it won't unravel during future washings. (For larger projects, it may help to pin the rolled hem at this point.) Insert a threaded needle into the end of the rolled edge, guiding the needle out near the base of the rolled hem, about ½ inch (13mm) from where you inserted the needle. Catch a few threads of the fabric near the edge of the rolled hem. Pull the thread through the fabric and insert the needle back into the roll slightly left of where the thread first came out. Repeat stitches; knot the thread several times just under the rolled hem to finish (for an illustration of this technique, see page 247).

TECHNIQUE:

appliqué

Although appliqué probably has roots in the practical need to patch holes, it has long been celebrated in textile design for its decorative possibilities. And it's no wonder: the two-dimensional surface of appliquéd pieces are pleasing to the eye and variable in texture, inspiring you to consider small patches of material in new ways.

With a name that derives from the French *appliquer* ("to apply"), the technique involves placing shapes that have been cut from one fabric onto another fabric background to create a picture or pattern. Usually the fabrics contrast with one another, whether in color or texture, but you can also appliqué pieces of the same fabric for a subtle effect. Sometimes the decorations are used to embellish the top layer of a quilt, or are finished with embroidered details. In all cases, these fabric shapes—or motifs, as they're called—can be as playful or elegant as you like, and can be cut from almost any type of fabric. Close-woven linens and cottons are easy to work with, as are nonwoven, nonfraying fabrics such as felt and Ultrasuede. After you've practiced with these, you may want to experiment with looser-woven materials.

Once applied, the motifs bring visual and textural interest to all manner of household items, including pillows, bed linens, and curtains, as well as to apparel and accessories, such as shirts, scarves, and tote bags.

The three basic appliqué methods—hand-turn, machine-sewn, and iron-on—are all easy to tackle. In this chapter, you'll be introduced to each technique, with step-by-step photographs to illustrate them. Throughout this book, there are several attractive projects that make good use of appliqué, including one on page 353 that includes a special technique for attaching precise shapes such as circles. Look for inspiration in bits and pieces—patches of fabric, small amounts of yardage, or remnants—and remember that any imperfections in your appliquéd motifs will only enhance their handmade appeal.

IN THIS CHAPTER:

+ BASIC APPLIQUÉ SUPPLIES
+ HOW TO APPLIQUÉ BY HAND
+ HOW TO APPLIQUÉ WITH A SEWING MACHINE
+ HOW TO IRON ON APPLIQUÉ

basic appliqué supplies

1. **FUSIBLE WEB** Made of adhesive backed with removable paper, fusible web is used to attach designs by the iron-on appliqué technique.
2. **TRANSFER PAPER** Once you've determined where to place appliqué designs, you can use this paper to outline the motif onto the background fabric. This method is particularly useful when working with templates that have multiple pieces.
3. **THREAD** Any all-purpose thread may be used for appliqué. For more decorative stitches, use a thread color that contrasts with your fabric, or try thread with a glossy finish.
4. **TRACING WHEEL** Used in conjunction with transfer paper, the pressure from the thin wheel helps trace outlines onto fabric to mark the placement of appliqué motifs.
5. **DISAPPEARING-INK FABRIC PEN** This water-soluble pen can be used to trace around templates, or as an alternative to transfer paper to mark the placement of appliqué pieces.
6. **HAND-SEWING NEEDLES** Short needles are best for basting as well as for the fine hand-turn stitches required to attach appliqué pieces to the background fabric. Specialty appliqué needles are also available (see page 356).
7. **SMALL POINTED SCISSORS** Appliqué pieces are often small or intricate, and small pointed scissors—such as embroidery shears—help to accurately clip sharp corners and curves. They can also be used to snip stray threads from appliquéd designs.

ABOUT TEMPLATES

COPYING AND SIZING In most cases, an existing template will include information regarding how much you will need to resize it (if at all). This may require enlarging it using a photocopier or computer; most of the ones on the CD enclosed with this book, however, are included at 100 percent.

CREATING TEMPLATES Practically any flat object can be used to create a template. From an online source, download, print, and cut out copyright-free art. If desired, make it smaller or larger with a photocopier or computer. From clip art or typography books, such as those published by Dover Press (see Sources), trace or photocopy the design onto tracing paper, altering the size as needed. Of course, shapes can also be drawn by hand, then cut out to make templates.

CARDSTOCK VS. PAPER If you will be tracing the templates onto fabric, cut them from heavy cardstock. If you will be pinning them to fabric and cutting around them, regular-weight paper should do. (Some crafters like to print onto regular-weight paper and then trace the template with tracing paper, which is easier to pin to fabric.)

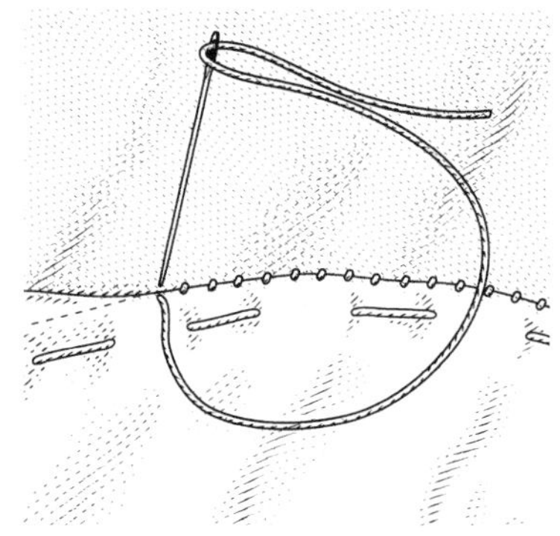

APPLIQUÉ STITCH

how to appliqué by hand

Hand-turn appliqué is not the only hand-worked method, but it is quick, easy, and well suited to most pieces. You will use a sewing needle to turn under the seam allowance, and the slipstitch (sometimes called the blind stitch) to secure the motif to the background fabric (the finished pillow is shown on page 229). Choose a thread color that matches the appliqué piece. Don't worry if the edges of your appliqué aren't even; slight variations are part of the charm of this technique.

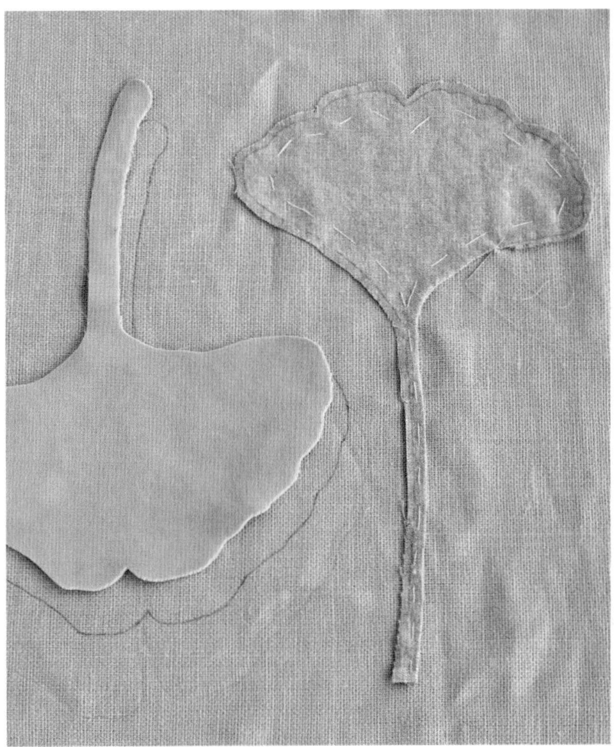

CUT OUT MOTIF Place wrong side of template on the right side of the appliqué fabric, and trace with a disappearing-ink fabric pen. If the template does not include a seam allowance, add a ¼-inch (6mm) allowance all around the motif; cut out. (For a template with seam allowance included, mark the allowance on the appliqué piece with the fabric pen.) For felt and other nonwoven appliqué pieces that don't fray, cut pieces to the exact size of the outline (do not add seam allowance), and slipstitch in place.

MARK PLACEMENT Position appliqué piece or template on fabric; trace with a disappearing-ink fabric pen.

BASTE OR PIN PIECES Baste large motifs in place ½ inch (13mm) from raw edge (above right); this will leave room to turn under edge. Pin smaller appliqué pieces in place.

STITCH IN PLACE Thread appliqué needle and knot thread; with the tip of the needle, turn under the seam allowance at the starting point of the motif. Slipstitch to the background fabric: Bring the needle up through the background fabric in line with the motif's folded edge; catch a few of the threads on the motif's edge and pull until stitch is taut. Insert the needle into the background fabric beside the stitch in the appliqué fold. Repeat stitches ⅛ inch (3mm) apart. Use the point of the needle to turn under the edge (see illustration, opposite), following the marked seam-allowance line. Continue to stitch around the motif. Secure the thread on the underside of your work with a knot or backstitch. Remove basting thread or pins.

how to appliqué with a sewing machine

This method allows you to apply a motif without turning under its raw edges. The zigzag or satin stitch on a sewing machine is used to bind the edge while attaching the appliqué piece at the same time. Machine appliqué can be done quickly, making it a better choice for large appliquéd areas, such as the duvet cover shown here and on page 150.

CUT OUT MOTIF Place wrong side of template on the right side of the appliqué fabric, and trace with a disappearing-ink fabric pen; cut out.

MARK PLACEMENT Position the appliqué piece or template on the background fabric. Use a disappearing-ink fabric pen to outline the design. For a large motif or multiple pieces in a pattern, use transfer paper and a tracing wheel to transfer the template design (as shown, above left).

BASTE OR PIN PIECES Pin or baste the appliqué piece to the background fabric. If you are pinning, keep the head of the pin a safe distance from the edge of the motif to prevent catching it in the seam. If appliquéing multiple pieces, secure and sew one piece before moving on to another; this will cut down on handling, which may fray the fabric edges.

MACHINE-STITCH IN PLACE With your machine set to the zigzag stitch or satin stitch, sew around the perimeter of the motif (above right). (Use a short zigzag or satin stitch for smaller pieces; for larger ones, use longer stitch lengths.) To finish, tuck the thread tail back under the stitches by hand with a needle. Trim any loose threads with small pointed scissors. Repeat with remaining appliqué pieces.

how to iron on appliqué

There are two advantages to the iron-on appliqué method: The adhesives in the fusible web prevent fabrics from fraying (so edges do not need to be turned under or machine-sewn), and you can apply designs quickly. However, this method is best for projects that will not be washed often—such as curtains (shown below and on page 204) or tote bags—and clothes that aren't machine-dried.

CUT OUT MOTIF Cut a piece of fabric that is larger than the appliqué piece or pieces that you plan to cut out. Then cut a piece of fusible web slightly smaller all around than the fabric piece. Using an iron on the wool setting, press the web onto the back of the fabric; the rough side of the web should be facing the wrong side of the fabric. Allow the paper backing to cool completely. With the right side of the template facing the paper backing, use a pencil to trace your template shape. Cut out the shape, and peel off the paper backing.

POSITION AND PRESS MOTIF Position the appliqué piece or pieces, fabric side up, on your background fabric, and pin. If you are working with sheer fabric, place a pressing sheet on your ironing board (this will keep the fabric from sticking to the board). Press with steam for about 10 seconds, or according to the fusible web manufacturer's instructions. Make sure to press down on the motif; do not move the iron back and forth, as this will cause the fabric to shift, permanently creasing or wrinkling it.

TECHNIQUE:

embroidery

The impulse to embellish fabric with decorative stitches dates back thousands of years—even before woven cloth—yet at least one thing about embroidery hasn't changed: No matter how complicated the result looks, the technique is remarkably simple. If you can use a needle and thread, you can embroider. The stitches are versatile enough to create a variety of lovely, personalized designs.

An array of basic hand-embroidery stitches is described in detail in the following pages, including favorites such as the cross-stitch, running stitch, and French knot. In addition, you will learn about embroidery that is produced using basic sewing-machine stitches, as well as specialty computer-aided embroidery machines.

One of the most inviting aspects of this fabric craft is that it is not limited to a "flat" canvas. A framed sampler exhibits old-fashioned charm, but clothes, linens, and tote bags look modern when adorned with just a few artful stitches. Fabrics with a visible weave, such as linen, cotton, and wool, are the best choices; felt, while dense, is also suitable, because it is sturdy and easy to work with.

Any image that can be drawn with a pencil can also be embroidered. Crafts and fabric stores stock ready-to-use iron-on transfers, but leafing through clip-art or vintage picture books can provide additional ideas. Calligraphy primers, coloring books, and old greeting cards are rich sources for letters and numbers, and field guides can be helpful if you want to embroider birds, trees, leaves, or flowers. And finally, remember: Nothing compares to the moment when you realize that your carefully wrought stitches have resulted in something beautiful and all your own.

IN THIS CHAPTER:

+ BASIC EMBROIDERY SUPPLIES
+ HOW TO EMBROIDER BY HAND
+ ESSENTIAL HAND-EMBROIDERY STITCHES
+ THE CROSS-STITCH
+ THE FRENCH KNOT
+ THE RUNNING STITCH
+ ABOUT JAPANESE SASHIKO
+ ABOUT RIBBON EMBROIDERY
+ ABOUT MACHINE EMBROIDERY
+ ABOUT COMPUTER-AIDED EMBROIDERY

basic embroidery supplies

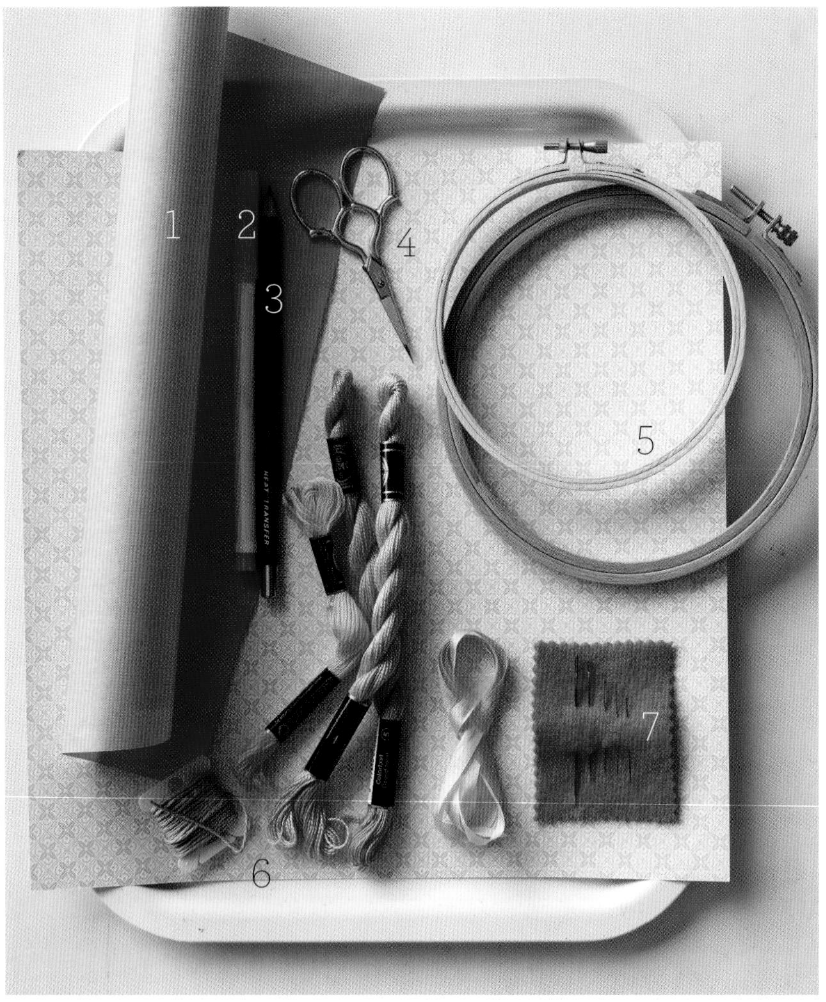

1. **TRANSFER PAPER** Traditionally, embroidery patterns were transferred by sandwiching this paper between the design and the fabric, then bearing down on the lines with a pen, tracing wheel, or knitting needle. Many crafters still use paper; others prefer fabric pens or heat-transfer pencils.
2. **DISAPPEARING-INK FABRIC PEN** You can draw a design directly onto fabric with one of these. Water-soluble inks will wash out (or can be gently sponged off); others are air soluble and will disappear after about an hour (redraw your design before the lines disappear, if necessary).
3. **HEAT-TRANSFER PENCIL** This tool is used to trace a design onto tracing paper, then the paper is placed image-side down onto fabric and ironed. The pattern will be the reverse of the design. If you want to keep the original orientation, trace the design using a regular pencil, then flip the paper and trace pencil lines with the heat-transfer pencil.
4. **EMBROIDERY SCISSORS** These small, sharp scissors give you precise control when snipping threads.
5. **EMBROIDERY HOOPS** A hoop holds fabric taut to keep stitches even and prevent the weave of a fabric from becoming distorted. The hoop is actually made of two interlocking frames; a screw on the outer one loosens or tightens the hoop.
6. **EMBROIDERY FLOSS** Cotton floss, made up of six strands, is the standard choice; you will also find threads and yarns of different materials and thicknesses (see box, left), and embroidery ribbon.
7. **NEEDLES** Embroidery needles have sharp tips and large eyes to accommodate floss or ribbon. Other types include crewel and chenille needles, whose sharp tips are best for embroidering tightly woven fabrics like cotton, and blunt-tipped tapestry needles for loose-weave fabrics like linen. Choose a needle size that corresponds to the weight of your thread—a fine needle for a strand of embroidery floss, a larger one for ribbon or heavy yarn.

ABOUT EMBROIDERY FLOSS, THREAD, AND YARN

The most common material for embroidery is cotton floss, a glossy thread that consists of six strands that can be separated from one another to create lighter weights. Silk and rayon threads also come in divisible strands. (Two or three strands are standard for most woven fabrics; a single strand will do for lightweight fabric.) Perle cotton is a heavy single strand that has a high sheen and distinct texture; it is available in several thicknesses. Wool yarn comes in three- or four-ply weight and cannot be separated into strands, so it is best suited to heavy fabrics such as canvas, wool felt, or the thickest linen. Be careful about bending the rules here: Bulky thread on fine fabric will pucker the material; light threads embroidered on heavy cloth can be difficult to see. A thread must be the suitable weight for a particular material to create the desired appearance: gently raised stitches—the kind you want to touch—with a satin finish on a smooth background. Pictured above, left to right: silk floss, stranded floss, perle cotton (a single-strand mercerized cotton thread), and embroidery ribbon, which can also be used to great effect (see page 58).

how to embroider by hand

Once you've selected a design and chosen your fabric and thread, you're ready to begin. First, transfer the image to your fabric using one of the methods described below. Then embroider, using any of the basic stitches on the following pages.

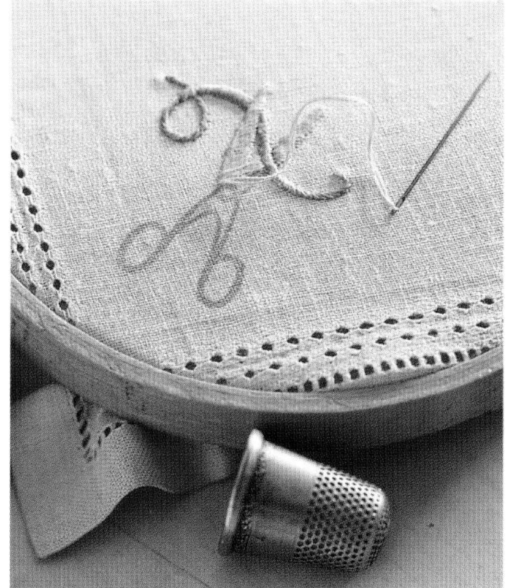

BEFORE YOU BEGIN Make sure your hands are clean when handling fabric or thread. Transfer your selected design onto the right side of fabric (see below).

SECURE FABRIC IN HOOP Loosen the screw on the side of the hoop. Lay the fabric flat and right-side up with the area you want to embroider over the inner ring. Slip the outer ring over the inner ring, and pull the fabric evenly taut; tighten the screw. You may not need a hoop for all projects; exceptionally thick or stiff fabric will not fit into one. To hold delicate fabrics in place, wrap the inner circle in seam binding. As you work, stop periodically to tighten the fabric and the screw again. When you take an extended break from stitching, remove the hoop so it doesn't leave a mark on the fabric.

THREAD THE NEEDLE Use lengths of floss, thread, or yarn no longer than 18 inches (45.5cm) to avoid knotting, twisting, or fraying.

STITCH THE DESIGN Begin stitching, using the transferred design as a guide. Finish all stitches in one color, or an entire component of your design (such as leaves in a floral motif), before beginning the next color or component.

FINISH ENDS Don't knot the ends of the floss, as this will leave marks. Instead, secure each length of floss at the start and end by stitching a few tiny backstitches (page 48). Alternatively, pull the loose ends of the floss through at least 1 inch (2.5cm) of existing stitches on the back side of the fabric, then snip the ends of the floss carefully. To change colors, secure and finish the end of the thread or floss, then thread the needle with a new color. If your design extends beyond the edges of the embroidery hoop, finish stitching within the hoop, then reposition and stitch a new section of fabric.

---

transferring designs

If you are comfortable drawing freehand, you can mark directly on the fabric using a disappearing-ink fabric pen. To use transfer paper, lay it facedown on right side of fabric, and place a template on top, face up. Using a ballpoint pen, retrace the design (as shown, right). The pressure from the pen will transfer a carbon outline onto the fabric. Store-bought iron-on transfers are also widely available. You can also copy an existing copyright-free image or motif—from a book, magazine, or any other source that inspires you, such as a postcard or a scrap of wallpaper. Trace the design onto sheer tracing paper, then transfer the image to fabric using a heat-transfer pencil and plain paper (see "Heat-Transfer Pencil," opposite). Remember that any marks you make on your fabric will eventually be covered by stitching, and iron-on transfers designed for embroidery wash out.

essential hand-embroidery stitches

Learning the following stitches will allow you to embroider a range of designs, whether bold and graphic or delicate and flowery. The simple backstitch, for example, forms a neat outline, while the satin stitch smoothly fills in an open area. Combining multiple stitches imparts dimension. A few other basic, easy-to-master embroidery stitches, including the cross-stitch and French knot, are illustrated and explained in detail on the following pages.

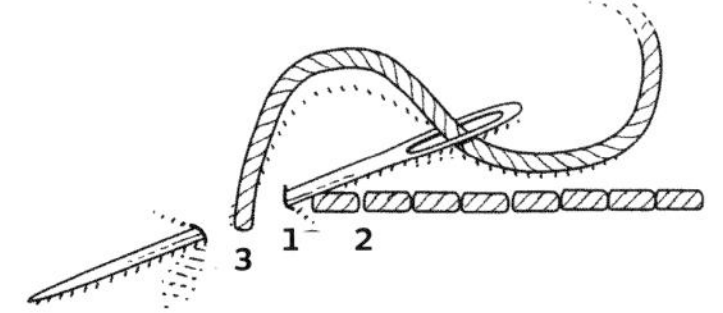

BACKSTITCH Insert the needle from the wrong side of the fabric, coming out at **1.** Insert needle at **2,** pull back out at **3,** and pull thread tight. Insert needle again at **1,** and pull it out past **3** at a distance equal to the length of the previous stitches. This is the first step for the next stitch; insert needle into **3,** and continue.

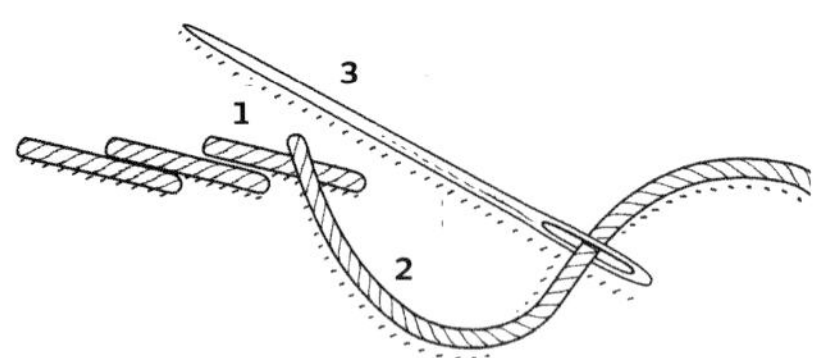

STEM STITCH A cousin to the backstitch, this stitch creates a ropelike effect. Insert needle from wrong to right side, coming out at **1.** Insert the needle at **2** at a slight diagonal, and pull through at **3** (halfway between **1** and **2**). Repeat stitching, keeping the thread on the left side of the needle and making sure stitches are all the same length.

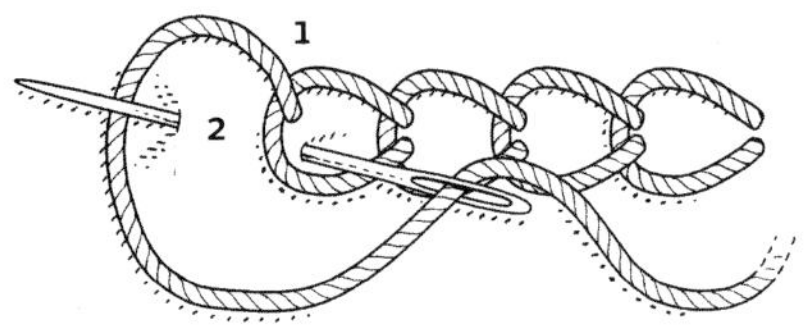

CHAINSTITCH With your thread, insert the needle from the wrong to the right side, coming out at **1.** Making a loop, insert next to **1.** Come out again at **2,** holding the thread under the needle as you pull tight. Insert the needle again next to **2** (inside the new link), and continue.

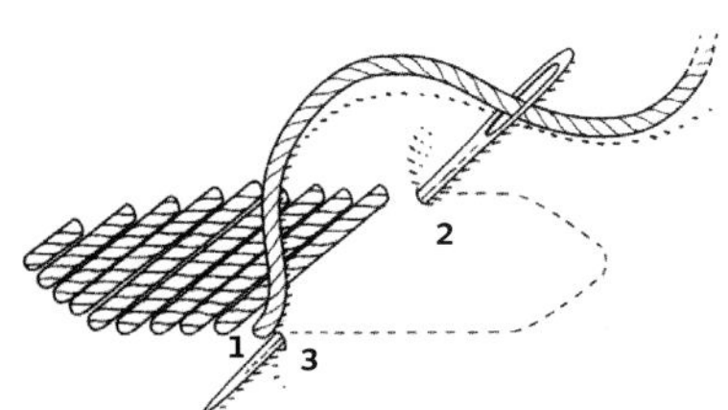

SATIN STITCH Made at an angle or straight across, these side-by-side stitches fill in the outlines of a design that incorporates shape or width. Insert the needle from the wrong to the right side, coming out at **1.** Insert the needle at **2,** and pull it back through at **3,** right next to **1.** Keep the stitches tight and flat to ensure a smooth finish.

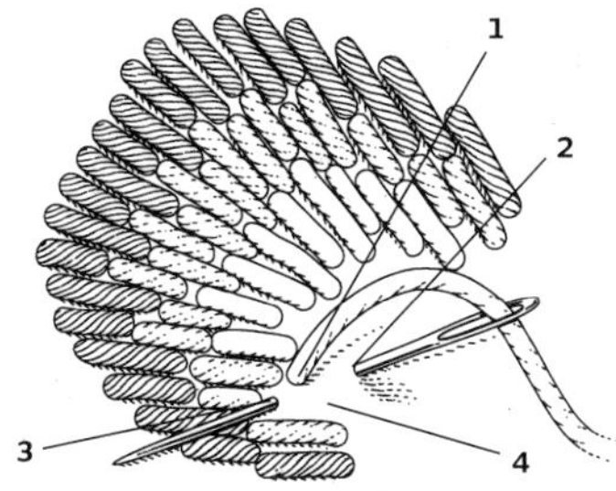

LONG AND SHORT STITCH Use this stitch to blend colors or create a feathery texture. Insert the needle from the wrong to the right side, coming out at **1,** insert at **2,** come out at **3,** and insert again at **4.** Repeat for next tier. If desired, change colors and use the same technique for subsequent tiers, piercing the stitches in the previous tier.

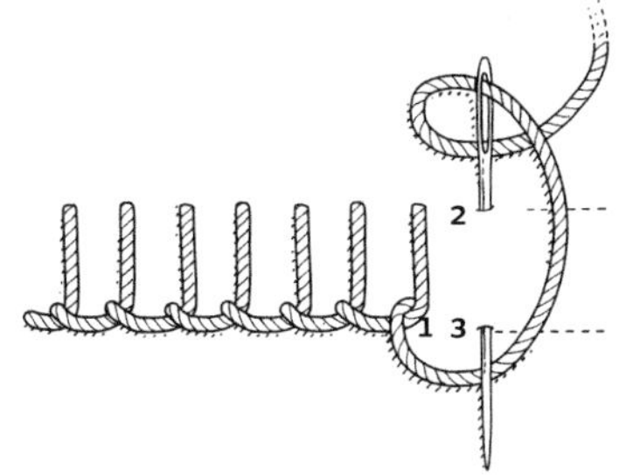

BLANKET STITCH This is a common finishing stitch for blanket edges (see page 158). If using as a decorative edge, work so that the base of the U goes along the edge of the fabric. For lightweight fabrics, stitch along the finished edge. Insert the needle from the wrong to the right side, coming out at **1.** Insert at **2.** Come out again at **3;** hold the thread under the needle with your thumb as you pull tight.

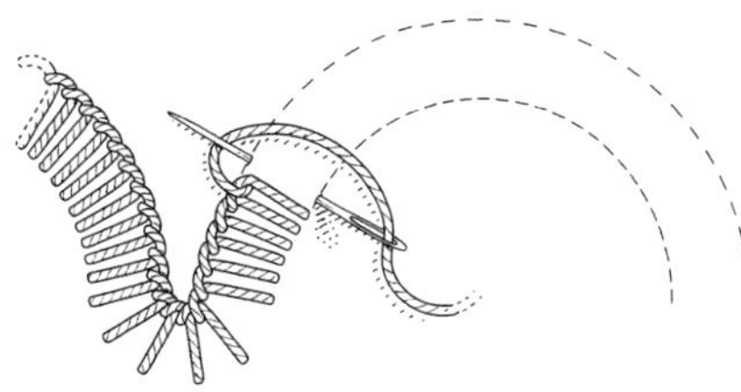

SCALLOPED BLANKET STITCH Draw a scallop pattern near the fabric edge. Vary the blanket stitch by keeping spoke ends close together. Spread spokes wider when moving into an outward curve. Make the same number of stitches for each scallop. For a decorative edge, trim fabric edge carefully when finished stitching.

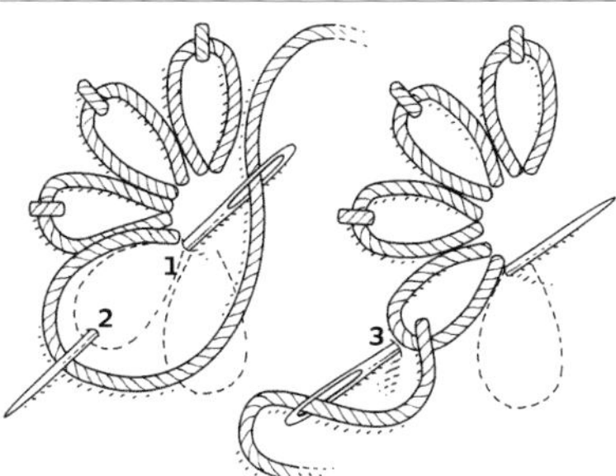

LAZY-DAISY STITCH Anchored chain stitches are used to create a flower. Pull the needle through to the front at **1.** Making a loop, insert again right next to **1.** Come out again at **2,** holding thread under needle as you pull tight. Insert needle at **3** to anchor stitch, and move on to next petal.

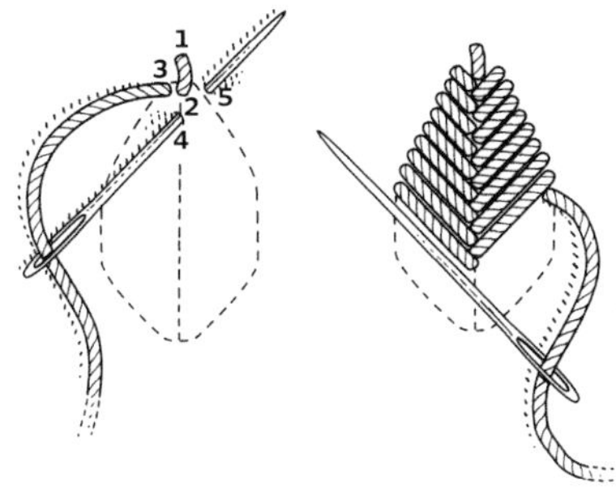

FISHBONE STITCH Perfect for making leaves, the ends of this filling stitch alternate where they meet at the center of the design. For leaf tip, pull the needle through to front at **1** and insert at **2.** Come out at **3,** and insert again (just below **2**) at **4.** Bring the needle out at **5** to make next stitch on the other side of the leaf. Alternate sides as you finish stitching.

the cross-stitch

Counted cross-stitch—a series of handstitched Xs—is one of the easiest and most well-known embroidery techniques. Delightfully simple, they lend surprisingly sophisticated style and rich texture to almost any fabric. The symmetry of these evenly spaced Xs is immensely pleasing; you can also try your hand at the variation known as herringbone cross-stitch, which results in a zigzag pattern that is often used to embellish borders.

To keep the Xs uniform, use the weave of the fabric as a guide, or grid, counting threads as you stitch (the height and width of each X should be equal). To start a row of 3-by-3 cross-stitches, for example, count up 3 threads from where your needle emerges through the fabric and then over 3 threads, re-entering diagonally across from where you started (as shown below). Work a row of diagonal strokes in one direction (\\\); then, working in the other direction, add the second diagonal (///) to complete the Xs. Move to the row above. When your thread runs out, do not knot it. Instead, weave the end through the back of five or six stitches on the wrong side of the fabric.

Loose-weave fabrics such as burlap and heavy linen make it simple to position and space counted cross-stitches (the loose weave of the cloth provides a built-in grid, much like gingham [see box, right]). If you're new to cross-stitch, practice on scraps of fabric before launching into a project. You can use embroidery floss or any of the threads described on page 46; perle cotton is comfortable to work with and complements the weave of heavier fabrics. If you choose thread of a weight that is similar to that of the fabric you're using, the crosses will appear to be woven right into the cloth.

CROSS-STITCH ON GINGHAM With its neat, uniform checks, gingham makes an excellent background for cross-stitching. Instead of counting threads, use the squares as a grid for your pattern, keeping your stitches inside the boxes.

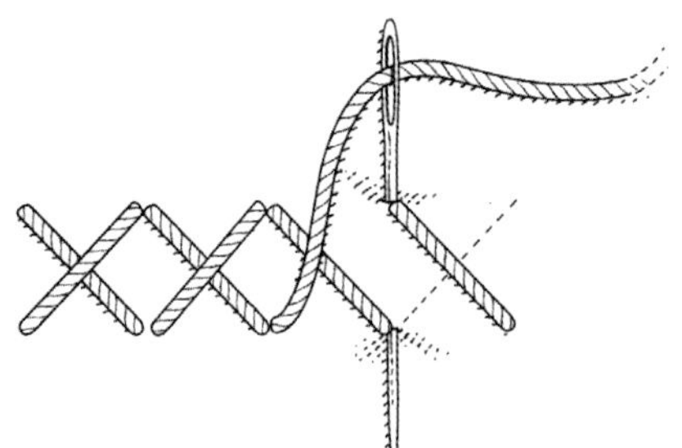

CROSS-STITCH First, stitch a row of evenly spaced parallel diagonal lines. Then stitch diagonally back over the first row, creating crosses as you go. When you can, insert the needle where Xs meet in the same holes. For the entire pattern, the bottom stitches on each X should all slant one way and the top stitches the other way.

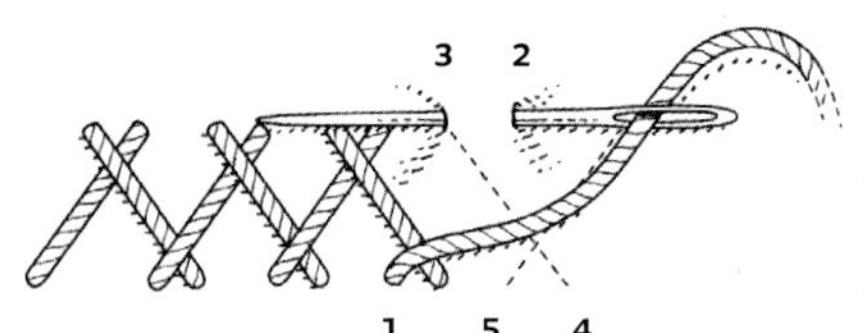

HERRINGBONE CROSS-STITCH In this variation on the counted cross-stitch, threads overlap at the end rather than the center. Pull needle through to front at **1.** Insert at **2,** pulling it back out at **3,** and pull thread tight. Cross over stitch and insert needle at **4** and pull back through at **5.**

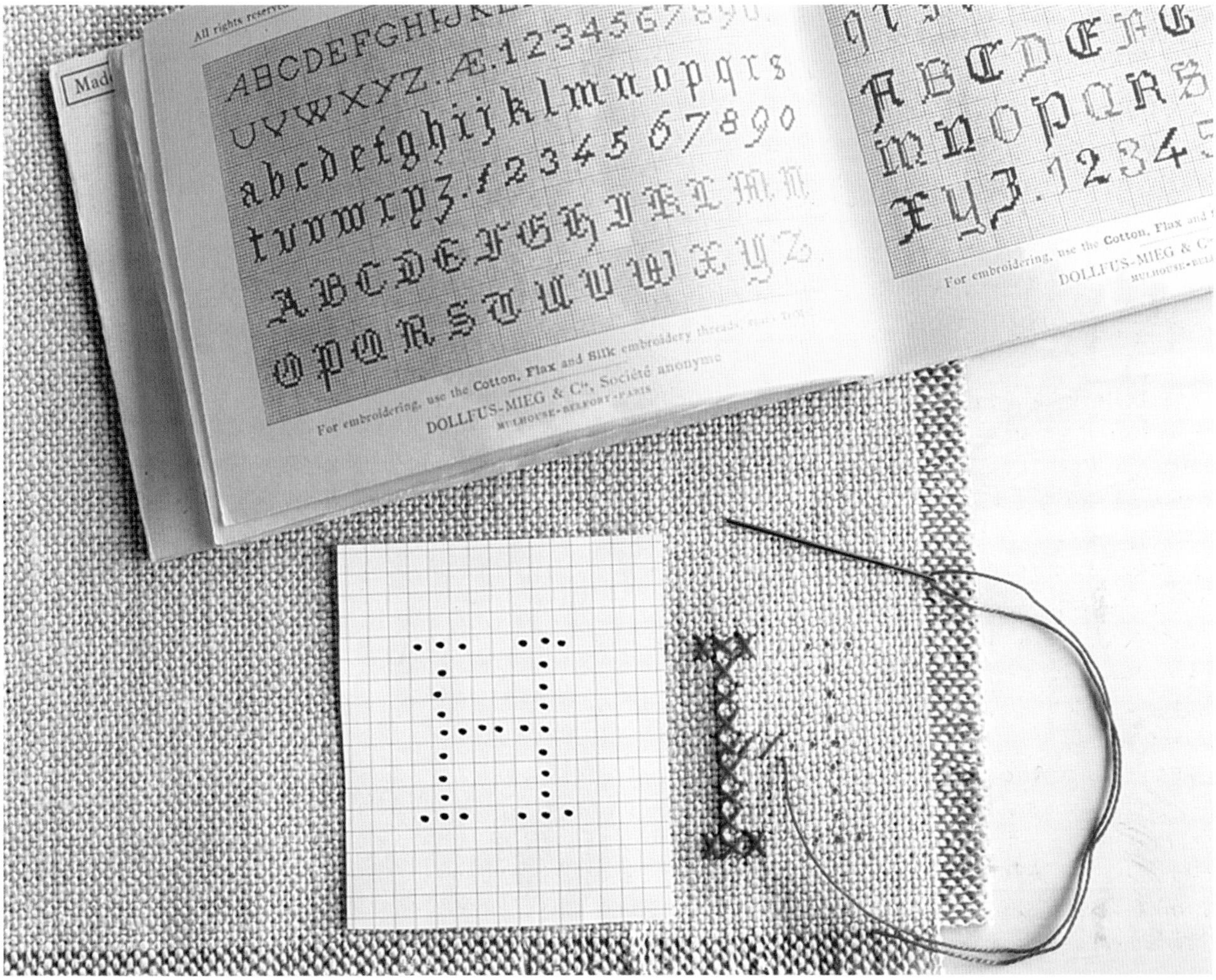

choosing cross-stitch patterns

Counted cross-stitch patterns are usually printed on graph paper; a dot inside a square indicates where a stitch should be made on the fabric. You can draw your own patterns on graph paper, or use preprinted designs. To make your own pattern, refer to an old sampler, lettering book, or any eye-catching imagery for inspiration (in the photo above, the letter being stitched is copied from a cross-stitch book). Photocopy letters to desired size, then trace onto graph paper. Use dots—one per square—to mark out the letter on the graph paper. If you prefer, you can use a disappearing-ink fabric pen to make dots directly on the fabric. Then, working bottom to top and left to right, cross-stitch the letter one row at a time. Most patterns can be completed by using the row-by-row technique described on the opposite page. When making solid images without a pattern or graph paper, start by stitching the outline in individual Xs, then fill in using the row technique.

Refer to cross-stitch books or old samplers to find lettering you like. Here, linen napkins are monogrammed with embroidered cross-stitch in several typography styles.

the French knot

French knots are created by wrapping floss, thread, or yarn around a needle as you stitch. The resulting pearl-shaped dots can be sprinkled across fabric like confetti, made one right after the other to create lines and circles, or stitched in dense clusters to produce raised, nubby shapes. French knots can be worked onto any fabric, including woven cotton, wool, and linen, or dense felt and flannel.

Embroidered knots of red yarn are worked on a piece of red-orange felt for a tone-on-tone effect that emphasizes texture. Using wool yarn instead of embroidery floss creates a homespun look and is appropriate for heavy fabrics such as wool felt.

Once you master the technique, you can use it to create borders on bedding, add charming details to clothing, or enliven a plain tablecloth or blanket. Think of the knots as polka dots and embroider dozens of them on one piece, either in a gridlike pattern or randomly. Each knot will look a little different: Some will be round, like grains of barley; others will be elongated, resembling grains of rice. Both results are fine. It is this variety in shape and size that creates an appealing texture.

Use a heat-transfer pencil or disappearing-ink fabric pen to draw a design, or photocopy or print out a template. Then, punch out dots at desired intervals along the template's lines with a large needle; the dots represent the knots you will stitch. Lay the template on the fabric. Using the pen, mark the fabric through the holes in the paper.

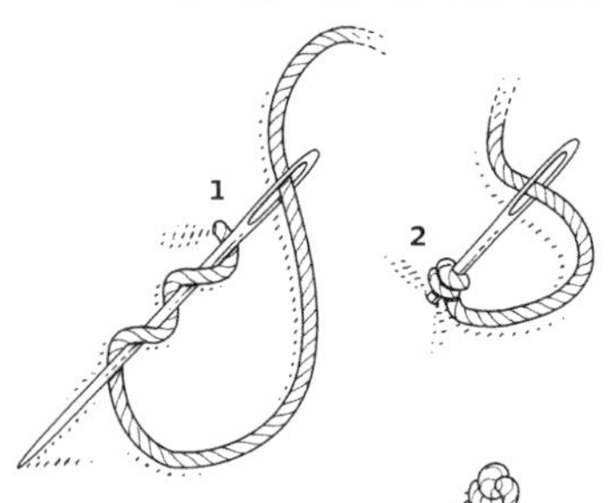

FRENCH KNOT Insert the needle from the wrong to the right side of the fabric at **1.** Keeping the thread taut with one hand, use your other hand to wind it over the needle twice. Reinsert the tip of the needle into the fabric at **2,** as close as possible to where it first emerged. Before passing the needle through the fabric, pull the thread tight so that the knot is flush with the material. Pull the needle through the fabric, continuing to hold the thread tight until you have a 3- to 4-inch (7.5–10cm) loop, then let go, and finish the knot. For larger knots, wrap more than two times.

FRENCH KNOT PATTERNS

Design and texture come from the knots' placement. Here, a ladybug (1) and a twig with acorns (2) are worked in clusters: The design is sketched onto the fabric with a disappearing-ink fabric pen and filled in with knots. You can use the pen to draw grids (3), circles (4), dots (5), monograms (6), or outlined designs, such as the leaf (7), onto fabric, and then stitch a series of French knots close to one another along those lines.

1

2

3

4

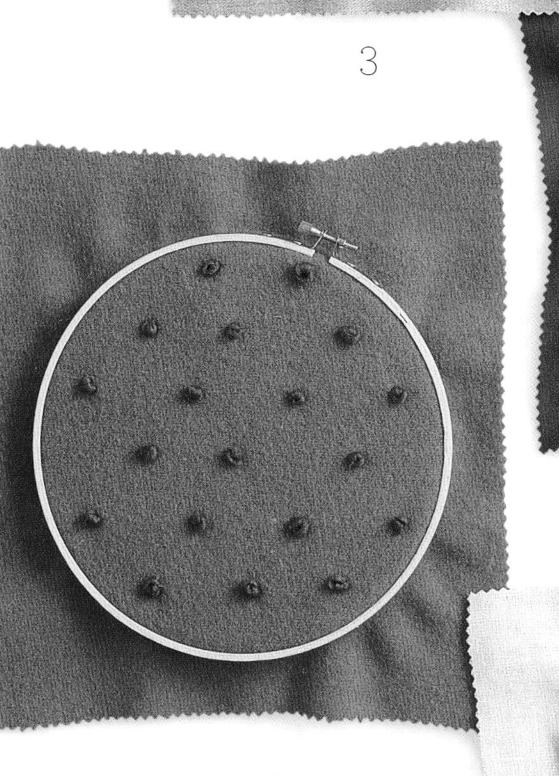

5

6

7

the running stitch

Although the running stitch is, in the strictest terms, a practical hand-sewing stitch (see page 31), it can also be used to embroider details on almost any material, including striped and other patterned pieces. By combining threads and fabrics in a variety of colors and textures, experimenting with the scale of the stitches, and playing with their spacing, you can create an array of effects.

Use the running stitch as you would any other embroidery stitch: Plan a design and transfer it to fabric (or follow the lines of a patterned fabric without first transferring a design), then choose a length of floss, thread, or yarn, and start stitching. Work the stitches in precise rows for a graphic simplicity that complements a minimalist aesthetic, or make them more freestyle to bring a stylish yet hand-worked effect to even the most basic attire and home accessories.

GLOSSARY OF STITCHES

The same basic running stitch takes on different guises when you vary the direction of the stitch, the type of thread, and the weight of the fabric.

1. **INTERSECTING GRID** in cotton ribbon on burlap
2. **CIRCLE** in metallic embroidery floss on canvas
3. **FREESTYLE** rows in variegated floss on linen
4. **DIAGONAL STITCHES** in embroidery floss on checked cotton
5. **QUILT** in sewing thread on padded cotton
6. **BRICK PATTERN** in embroidery floss on striped cotton
7. **BIG STITCHES** in wool yarn on wool blanket (you can also use silk)
8. **CHICKEN SCRATCH** (zigzag) in floss on cotton bedding

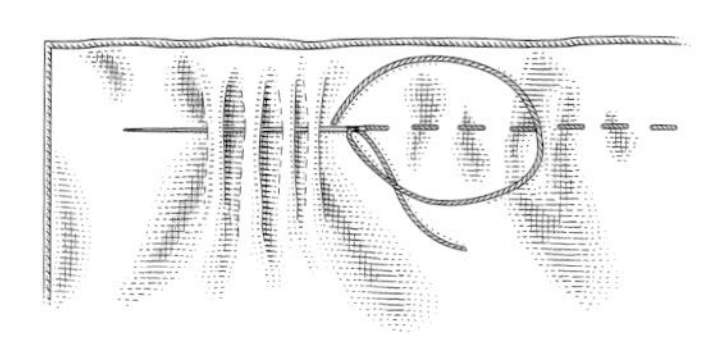

RUNNING STITCH Insert the needle several times at evenly spaced intervals, then pull the needle and thread through. Repeat.

about Japanese sashiko

In the Japanese embroidery tradition known as *sashiko,* fine, evenly spaced running stitches are sewn into repeating geometric shapes to create intricate patterns. Hundreds of years ago, fishermen's wives used this technique to add strength and beauty to their cotton garments; the motifs were imbued with symbolic meaning—patterns to encourage strength or long life, for example.

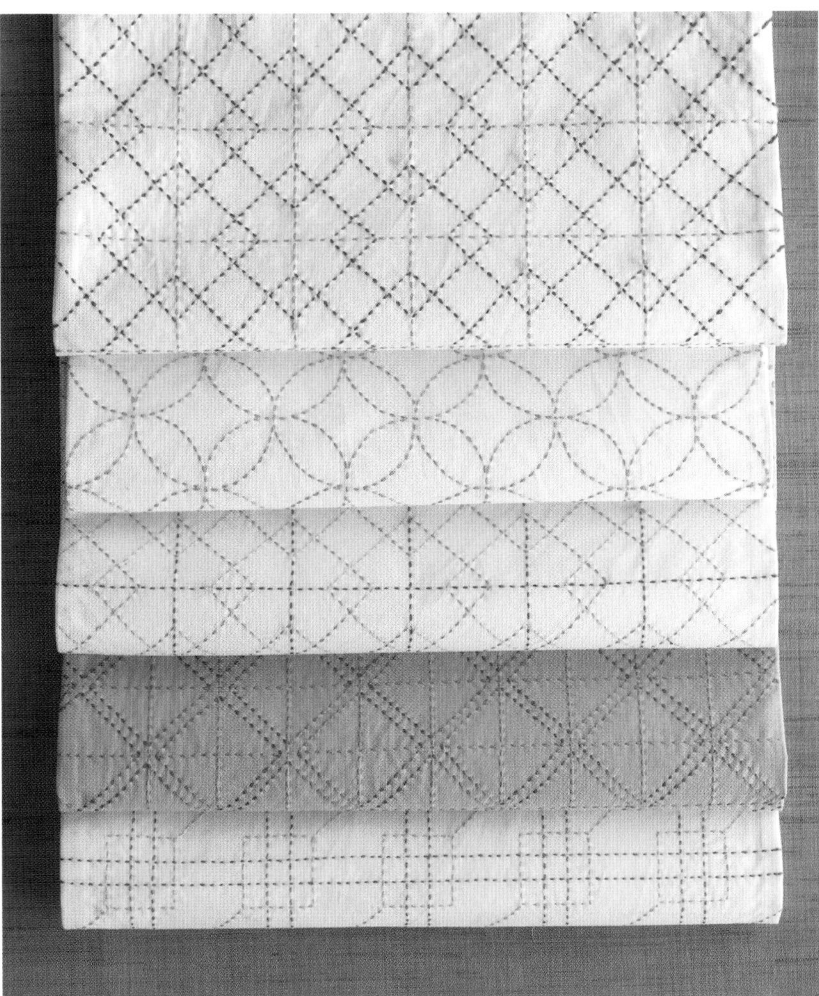

Tiny running stitches create sashiko's gridlike patterns. Pictured on the placemats above, from top to bottom, are hiyokuigeta, shippoutsunagi, hiyokuigeta, koushiawase, and koushitsunagi. For additional traditional sashiko motifs, see pages 56–57; templates for all of the motifs shown above are included on the enclosed CD.

Today, the traditional patterns endure, their understated appearance perfectly suited to any modern setting. While it may look complicated, sashiko is merely a collection of running stitches (see illustration, opposite). To embroider, collect all the stitches along one line onto your needle (or as many stitches as you are comfortable with), then pull the needle through the fabric (see illustration, opposite). A sashiko needle (see page 356), which is longer than a regular embroidery needle, works best for carrying multiple stitches; you can find one at some sewing and quilting stores or from online retailers. Sashiko thread is similar to perle cotton; it is a single strand that is thinner and more tightly twisted than embroidery floss. Work all parallel lines first, then change directions and work another set of parallel lines. Plot your design on graph paper for a neat, uniform look (in addition to square graph designs, you'll also find triangular and hexagonal versions); use a ruler to draw straight lines and a compass for curved ones. Refer to the glossary on the following pages for a sampling of traditional Japanese patterns, or create your own. After you've drawn your pattern on graph paper, transfer it to fabric using transfer paper (see page 46). Premade sashiko templates and patterns, which allow you to transfer designs directly to fabric without having to first draw your own grid, are also available from specialty stores and online retailers.

1
4
5
6
7
8

GLOSSARY OF SASHIKO PATTERNS

You can use a ruler and compass to plot these designs onto graph paper, or see the enclosed CD for design templates. In addition, premade sashiko templates and kits are available from specialty stores and online retailers (see Sources).

1. TORTOISE SHELL/ HANAKIKKOU
2. JUJITSUNAGI
3. KOUSHITSUNAGI
4. HISHIMOYOU
5. KOUSHIAWASE
6. HANAHISHIGATA
7. LINEN LEAF/ASANOHA
8. FUNDOUTSUNAGI
9. SEVEN TREASURES/ SHIPPOUTSUNAGI
10. HIYOKUIGETA
11. STRIPE

about ribbon embroidery

Embroidering with ribbons instead of floss, yarn, or thread creates designs with a distinctive three-dimensional quality. The stitches, although as simple as those made with floss, appear more elaborate, and work particularly well for rendering flowers and vegetation. As the wide strands are tugged through the fabric, they twist and fold, resulting in lifelike petals, stems, and leaves. Keep the stitching loose for a soft, crinkled effect, or pull the ribbon tight to produce sleek, straight lines. For ribbon-embroidered fruits and vegetables, see page 169.

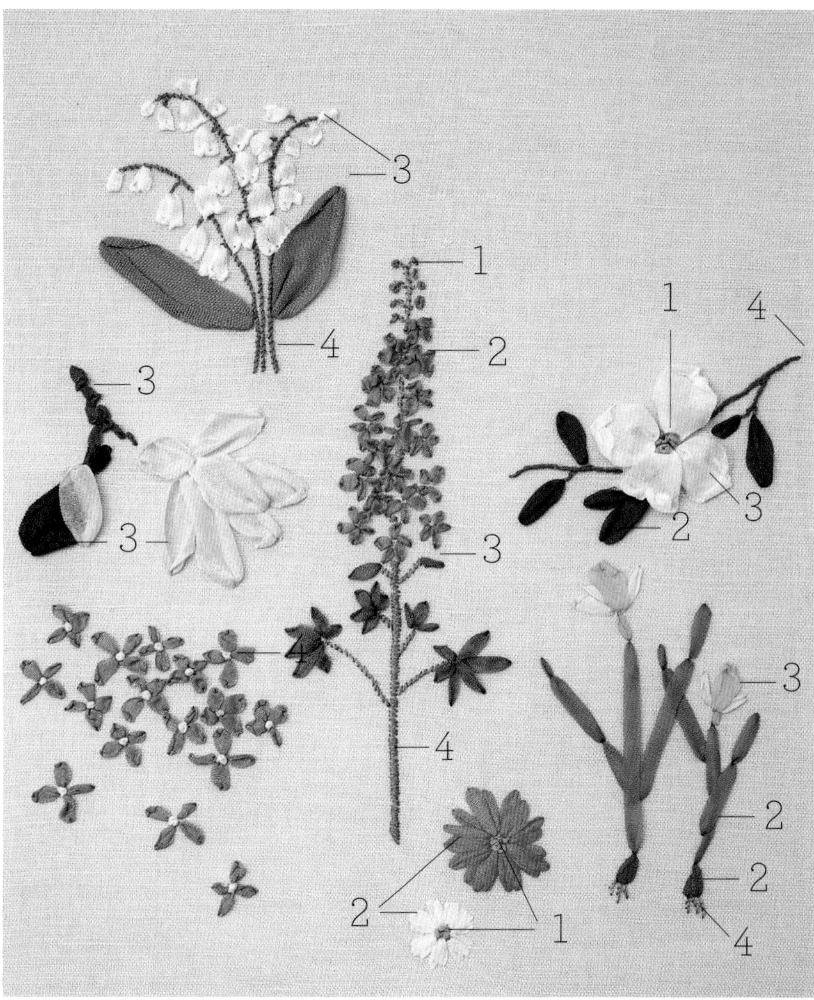

Using a variety of ribbon embroidery stitches creates lifelike flowers and foliage. 1. French knots create tiny buds and flower centers. 2. Straight stitches are used to make simple leaves and petals. 3. Ribbon stitches have curled edges that create textured petals. 4. Stem stitches make straight lines that resemble stems and roots.

Other than basic embroidery supplies (page 46), all you need is embroidery ribbon, which is fine silk ribbon that is available in a variety of widths. Sketch a design onto the fabric with a disappearing-ink fabric pen, then fit fabric into an embroidery hoop. Thread the needle using the following technique, which lets you use most of a length of ribbon: Insert about 2 inches (5cm) through the eye. Pierce ribbon with needle; tug on long end until the ribbon is secure in the eye (see illustration below). Knot the long end. Work with 10- to 12-inch (25–30.5cm) lengths of ribbon to avoid fraying. When the ribbon runs out or you want to change colors, pass it through a few stitches on the back of your work and knot. (For an example of a project featuring the ribbon-embroidered flowers shown at left, see page 351.)

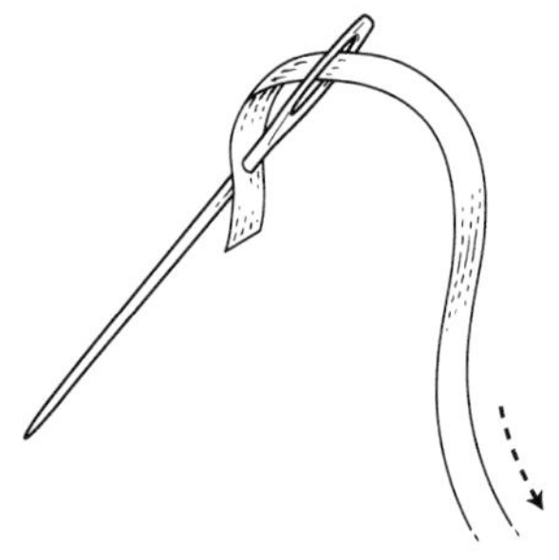

THREADING THE RIBBON

ribbon-embroidery stitches

A few basic stitches can imitate the appearance of flower petals, leaves, and other nature-inspired designs. The French knot (page 52) is also a popular ribbon-embroidery stitch; following the instructions on page 52, use it to create flower centers, or to plump up ribbon or straight stitches to create padded stitches.

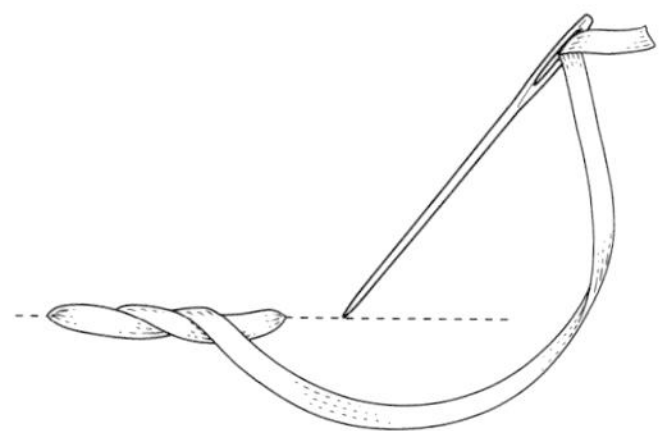

STEM STITCH Pass the needle up through the back of the fabric just to the left of the line you've sketched for the stem or root; reinsert needle just to the right of the line, and pull through fabric. Repeat, working from left to right, overlapping the successive stitches slightly. To create a wider stem or root, start and end your stitches farther away from the line.

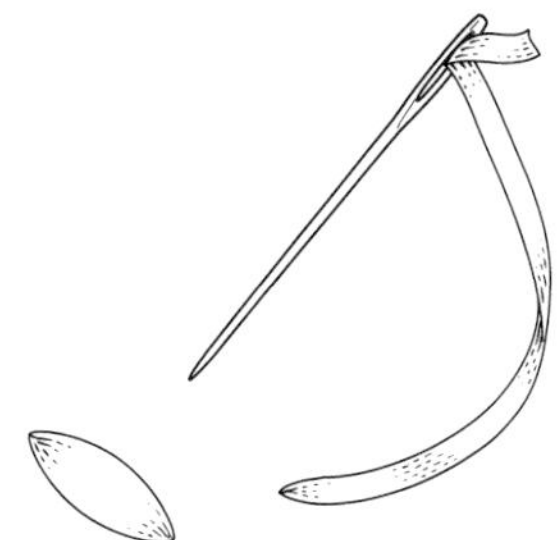

STRAIGHT STITCH Pass the needle up through the back of the fabric and down through the front, using your fingers to prevent the ribbon from twisting. Pull gently to keep the stitch flat.

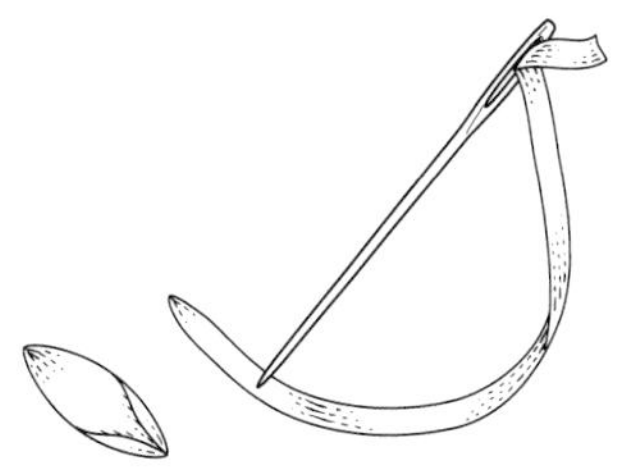

RIBBON STITCH Pass the needle up through back of fabric. Flatten ribbon on surface of fabric; reinsert needle, through ribbon, at far end of stitch. Pull gently, allowing sides of ribbon to curl and form a point. Use your fingers to make ribbon curl inward or outward.

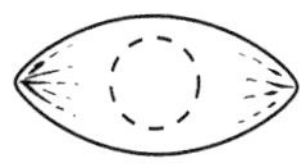

PADDED STRAIGHT STITCH To make plump shapes, stitch one or more French knots (indicated by the dotted lines in the illustration), and then cover them with a straight stitch. Stitch French knots in a row, a triangle, or a rectangle to achieve different shapes. This stitch is used to create the eggplant and mushroom cap shapes shown on the garden journal on page 168.

PADDED RIBBON STITCH To add volume to shapes, stitch one or more French knots (indicated by the dotted lines in the illustration); cover them with a ribbon stitch. This stitch is used to make the radish shown on the garden journal page 168.

about machine embroidery

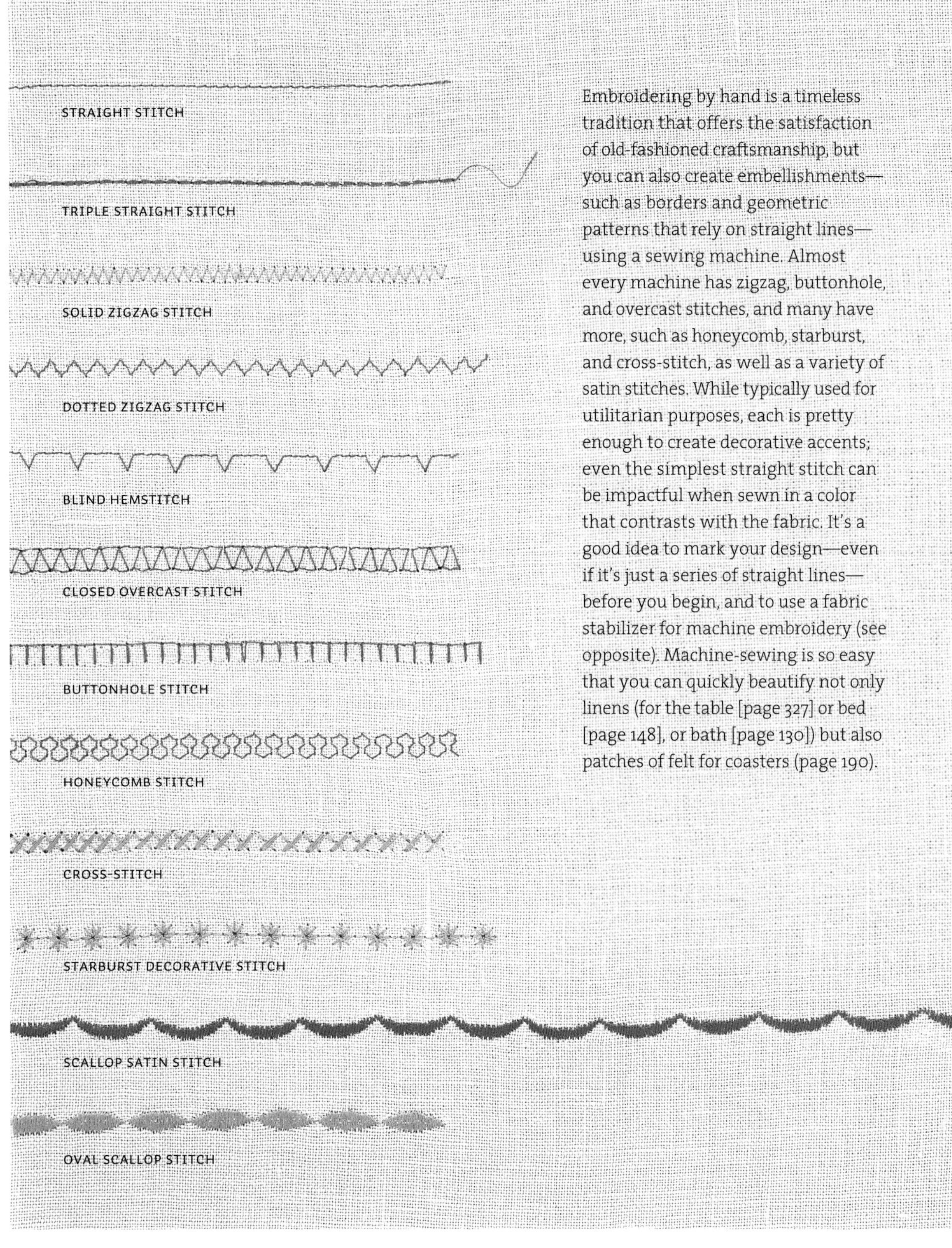

Embroidering by hand is a timeless tradition that offers the satisfaction of old-fashioned craftsmanship, but you can also create embellishments—such as borders and geometric patterns that rely on straight lines—using a sewing machine. Almost every machine has zigzag, buttonhole, and overcast stitches, and many have more, such as honeycomb, starburst, and cross-stitch, as well as a variety of satin stitches. While typically used for utilitarian purposes, each is pretty enough to create decorative accents; even the simplest straight stitch can be impactful when sewn in a color that contrasts with the fabric. It's a good idea to mark your design—even if it's just a series of straight lines—before you begin, and to use a fabric stabilizer for machine embroidery (see opposite). Machine-sewing is so easy that you can quickly beautify not only linens (for the table [page 327] or bed [page 148], or bath [page 130]) but also patches of felt for coasters (page 190).

about computer-aided embroidery

Computer-aided embroidery machines can stitch intricate imagery much more quickly than human hands, with impressive results: With just the touch of a button, you can create a richly detailed flower or a curlicued monogram.

While they vary in price and features, even the most basic embroidery machine comes with a selection of preprogrammed patterns and fonts as well as accompanying software for your computer. You can then purchase additional patterns on a CD or download them from the Internet—more advanced software will help you create your own designs. When you're ready to embroider, import a design from the computer onto the machine. Then watch as professional-looking embroidery appears, as if by magic, on your fabric. In addition to a computer, you'll need to gather a few additional basic supplies. Embroidery machines come with one or two hoops, which hold fabric in place while you stitch. You can buy additional hoops to suit various projects; be sure to buy a hoop designed for your specific machine. A stabilizer creates a stable foundation for stitching, and keeps fabric from shifting out of place, which could compromise the design (see below left). For stitching, use polyester, rayon, or cotton thread; a thickness of 30 or 40 weight will work for most projects. Machine-embroidery needles are made to withstand the speed and constant motion of an embroidery machine. They are usually labeled "universal needles" or "embroidery needles."

ABOUT FABRIC STABILIZERS

Whether you're using a standard sewing machine or a computer-aided embroidery machine, placing a piece of stabilizer underneath (or sometimes on top of) the fabric creates a stronger foundation for the embroidery, ensuring neat results. Here are the four most common types:

CUTAWAY This is used to hem embroidery for denim, sweatshirts, or other stretchy materials. The stabilizer remains attached to the wrong side of fabric, keeping the embroidery from stretching when the garment is worn; once the design is complete, cut away excess stabilizer.

TEAR-AWAY Use tear-away stabilizer for densely stitched patterns on medium-weight fabric. After stitching, gently tear the stabilizer away from the design.

WATER-SOLUBLE Used on lightweight fabrics such as tulle or cotton batiste, stabilizer can be dissolved by submerging the fabric in water after the machine has finished stitching.

IRON-AWAY While stabilizer is usually placed on the wrong side of fabric, iron-away stabilizer is used on the right side when embroidering on pile fabrics such as terry cloth or velvet. It will disintegrate when pressed with a hot iron.

TECHNIQUE:

quilting and patchwork

Like many traditional handicrafts, quilting deftly marries function and form—the same mosaic of pieced fabric that lends a patchwork quilt its appeal also allows it to hold heat and makes efficient use of sewing remnants. Over centuries, different cultures have developed their own customs and styles for quilting and patchwork. Yet in all cases, there is something universally pleasing about the process: the stitching and layering, and the experiments with design and embellishment that these methods entail.

In this chapter, you will learn the basic steps for a handful of quilting and patchwork projects. (For more such projects, see page 286.) To understand the distinction between the two, it helps to consider their definitions. Patchwork, or piecework, is composed of pieces of fabric, often squares, sewn together (usually in columns and rows) to form a larger piece. Because a patchwork piece often becomes the top layer of a quilt, many people identify any patchwork as a quilt. But by definition, a quilt comprises three parts—a top layer, an insulating layer, and a backing. The top layer may be made of a patchwork piece, of course, but it could be just a single swath of fabric (the tablecloth quilt on page 293 is one such example), or one adorned with an appliquéd pattern (many examples of folk-art quilts include such tops, as do Hawaiian quilts, pages 70–71). What matters is that the top and backing are sandwiched with batting, and that the layers are secured with hand or machine stitches, or a series of tufted knots created with yarn, ribbon, or embroidery floss. Each finishing method lends its signature texture and design to a quilt. And, along with the choice of fabrics and threads, each presents an opportunity to make a quilt distinctly your own.

IN THIS CHAPTER:

+ BASIC QUILTING SUPPLIES
+ CHOOSING FABRICS
+ HOW TO MAKE A BASIC PATCHWORK QUILT
+ HOW TO MAKE A STAR-PATTERN PATCHWORK
+ HOW TO APPLIQUÉ AND ECHO QUILT
+ HOW TO REPAIR A PATCHWORK QUILT

basic quilting supplies

1. **QUILTER'S RULER** This clear acrylic ruler allows you to mark placement accurately due to multiple measuring indicators that run both horizontally and vertically. Use it with a rotary cutter. A ruler that measures 24 1/2 inches (62.2cm) long is best for cutting 45-inch-wide (114cm) quilter's fabric.
2. **ROTARY CUTTER** Fitted with a rotary blade, this sharp tool can slice through several layers of fabric at once. Look for one with a retractable blade, and lock it in the safety position when not using. Always cut away from yourself on a self-healing mat, and replace blades as soon as they are dull.
3. **EMBROIDERY YARN AND FLOSS** Use either to tuft—or secure—layers of fabric and batting to one another.
4. **QUILTING THREAD** Stronger than all-purpose thread, this type is best for hand- and machine-quilting through fabric and batting.
5. **SELF-HEALING MAT** Its soft surface and durable core will withstand repeated cutting from a rotary blade or craft knife.
6. **SMALL POINTED SCISSORS** For snipping small threads, keep a pair of embroidery scissors on hand.
7. **FABRIC SHEARS** These make it easy to quickly and accurately cut patchwork pieces and bindings.
8. **SAFETY PINS** To keep fabric and batting from shifting, bind with safety pins before quilting.
9. **BIAS TAPE** Use 100 percent cotton tape to bind edges, or as trim. Bias tape conforms to curves on rounded corners. (Seam binding may cause the edges of your quilt to pucker.) To make your own bias tape, see page 369.
10. **GLASS-HEAD PINS** These pins are so thin that they usually won't leave marks in fabric, and their glass heads won't melt under a hot iron.
11. **HAND NEEDLES** Keep a variety of sizes of needles on hand for different needs: sharps for general sewing; shorter needles for small appliqué stitches; and a tapestry needle with a large eye for tufting.

ABOUT BATTING

When choosing batting for a quilt, consider its loft (thickness). It is often easier to quilt by hand and machine with a thinner batting, but quilts that are merely tufted (tied with yarn or embroidery thread) look better when made with a higher loft. Batting is made from a variety of materials, including the following:

COTTON Cotton batting softens over time, and is the most breathable. It drapes nicely and tends to result in a flatter, more traditional quilt. One hundred percent cotton batting is a particularly nice choice for a baby or small child's quilt.

POLYESTER This inexpensive batting is the most commonly available option. It will not shrink when washed, and comes in a range of lofts. Keep in mind, however, that polyester is the least breathable type of batting.

POLY-COTTON BLENDS Poly-cotton batting is also widely available and inexpensive. Although the fiber content may vary, you'll generally find a blend of 50 percent cotton, 50 percent polyester. The loft of blended batting is usually higher, or fluffier, than 100 percent cotton.

WOOL Washable wool batting is extremely warm, yet light enough to insulate a quilt that will be used all year round. Wool batting is also more expensive than polyester or cotton varieties. (Some people are allergic to wool.)

choosing fabrics

Of all fabric crafts, quilting and patchwork projects offer some of the best opportunities for experimenting with color, pattern, and texture. For the most pleasing results, keep the following guidelines in mind when selecting fabrics.

PICK A PALETTE Color is an important consideration when designing a quilt. Whether harmonious or contrasting, the colors can seem soothing and peaceful, or bold and energetic. Mix patterns and prints in the same palette for more visually dynamic results. If making a quilt as a gift for a friend or family member, think about where and how will it be used.

STICK WITH NATURAL FABRICS One hundred percent cotton is typically used for quilts, you can find fabric labeled "quilter's cotton" at most fabric stores and online in 45-inch (114cm) width. Some silk, wool fabrics, as well as blends, are also options for quilting. The fabrics for a patchwork should be the same weight; sewing very thin to very thick fabrics can cause them to pucker. Make sure to wash and dry fabrics before sewing together to account for shrinkage.

SHOP WITH SWATCHES If you have a swatch or a combination of fabrics that appeals to you, take it with you as you shop for complementary fabrics. Buy more new yardage than you think you may need; you don't want to run out part way through the construction of your quilt.

ARRANGE THE PIECES Lay out patchwork pieces on a table, or as many experienced quilters do, arrange them on a piece of felt hung on a wall. Move pieces around and decide which colors and patterns you like adjacent to one another before pinning and sewing. (It's helpful to do this in a space where you can keep the pieces out for a while.) Your plan for the design of the quilt will evolve as you shift pieces around; this is part of what makes quilting and patchwork especially creative and engaging.

THE QUILTING STITCH

The quilting stitch helps secure layers of a quilt together, often in a decorative pattern; you can also use a machine for the same purpose (see box, page 68). As a hand-sewing technique, it is very similar to the running stitch (page 31). You may want to work with a quilting hoop or quilting frame (similar to an embroidery hoop, but deeper, to hold the quilt layers taut), and wear a thimble to help push the needle through the layers. Start by threading a needle with approximately 15 inches (38cm) of quilting thread, and make a small knot at the end. To hide the knot, insert the needle through the quilt top, the top layer of the batting, and back through the quilt top (do not stitch through the back fabric layer). Gently tug the thread until the knot pulls through the quilt top and wedges in the batting. Insert the needle through the quilt top and batting just until the needle pierces through the bottom layer of fabric; catch a few threads, and then push the needle back up through the batting and quilt top. As you work, you may want to stack two or more stitches on the needle before pushing the needle through the layers. When you have only 4 or 5 inches (10–12.5cm) of thread left, make a small in the knot ¼ inch (6mm) from where the thread emerges from the top layer. Stitch through the top layer, batting, and back up through the top layer; lightly tug the thread until the knot pulls through the top layer and snip the thread close to the top layer.

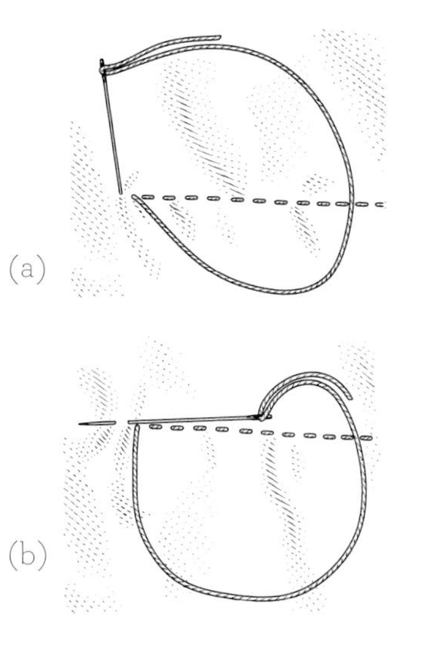

how to make a basic patchwork quilt

Making a patchwork quilt is easy. Cut a backing. Cut a layer of batting. And create a top by cutting smaller pieces, usually squares, and stitching them together. The quilt shown here is for a baby, so the project is small and manageable. To bind the layers, pass short bits of ribbon down through the layers and back up again, then tie these with knots. And instead of finishing the edges with sewn-on bias tape, which requires making mitered corners, simply sandwich the bias tape between the layers when the edges are sewn, to mimic the effect of piping.

Almost any fabric of significance can work in a memory quilt: clothing, blankets, vintage fabrics, hand towels, sheets, or pillowcases. Avoid knits, stretchy material, and thick textiles that will pull and wear differently than other pieces. The finished quilt is sure to become an heirloom that will be appreciated for many generations to come.

1. CUT OUT PIECES With a quilter's ruler, disappearing-ink fabric pen, rotary cutter, and self-healing mat, measure and cut squares of fabric. The patches shown here are 4½-inch (11.4cm) squares—4 inches (10cm) with a ¼-inch (6mm) seam allowance on each side; the finished quilt is 12 by 18 squares. Arrange squares into a pattern.

2. SEW PATCHWORK Pin the squares together, right sides facing, to form rows, then sew with a ¼-inch (6mm) seam allowance. There is no need to secure your sewing by backstitching, as each of the quilt's seams will be crossed by another seam. Press all seam allowances in one direction (rather than open). Pin together the rows, lining them up and measuring an exact ¼-inch (6mm) seam allowance. Sew rows together, pressing the seams in one direction.

3. QUILT PATCHWORK TO BATTING Lay the patchwork, right side up, onto preshrunk 100 percent cotton batting, leaving 3 inches (7.5cm) of excess batting on every side. To avoid slippage, safety-pin each square to the batting, starting in one corner, continually smoothing layers as you go. Sew the two pieces together by "stitching in the ditch," or sewing exactly over the seams to outline each square. Trim excess batting. Remove safety pins.

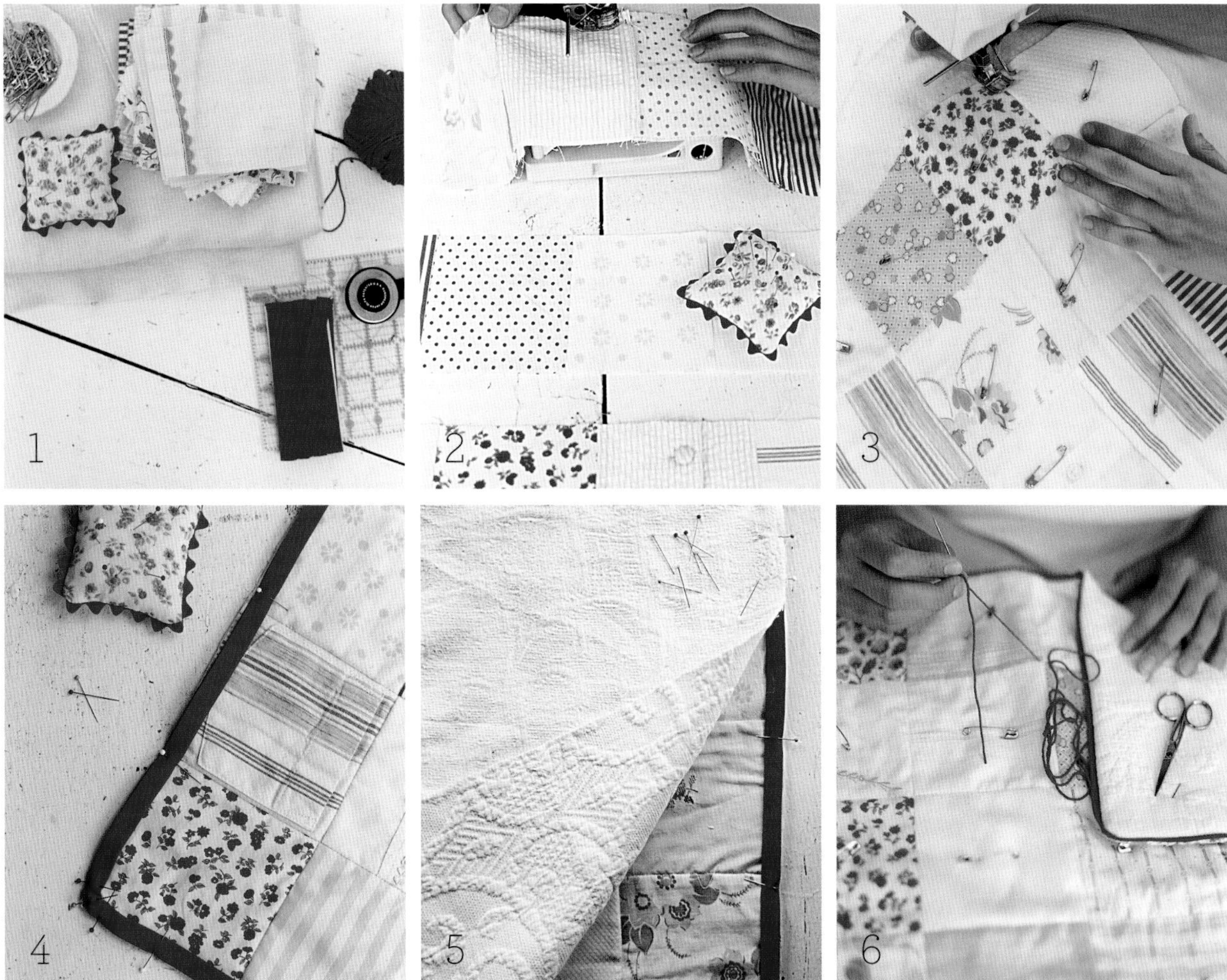

4. ADD TRIM Lay ½-inch-wide (13mm) double-fold bias tape around the perimeter, with the double edge flush with the raw edge of the quilt, and the folded edge of the tape facing inward. Pin, stretching around each corner to prevent puckering.

5. ATTACH BACKING Cut the backing (a piece of vintage mattelassé bedspread is shown) the same size as the top layer, plus ¼ inch (6mm) for a seam allowance. Leaving the straight pins in the trim, place the backing over the patchwork, right sides facing; pin around the perimeter. Sew edges through all layers, leaving a 12-inch (30.5cm) opening on one side; turn right-side out. Slipstitch opening shut; press sides and edges with a steam iron.

6. TUFT LAYERS Safety-pin the layers together so the backing doesn't slip. Using yarn, embroidery floss, or thin (⅛-inch [3mm]) ribbon make a ¼-inch (6mm) tufting stitch across each intersection of four squares: Stab needle straight through quilt along one seam, ⅛ inch (3mm) to either side of intersecting point. Tie square knot; trim ends. Remove safety pins.

MACHINE QUILTING

Machine quilting has been an integral part of quilting for decades and is no longer viewed as a less valid expression of this centuries-old handicraft. Some prefer machine quilting to hand quilting (see "The Quilting Stitch," page 65) because it saves time, particularly for piecing. Others feel its precision allows for creative expression. You do not need a computerized machine for this craft, although these exist and allow for dependable results. Rather, you can machine quilt by using a specialty presser foot (called a walking foot) and a different machine setting. Most newer machines include tips in their manuals. Like hand-quilting, machine quilting requires practice. Begin with a small project, such as a pillow. This will allow you to master machine quilting before launching into something bigger.

how to make a star-pattern patchwork

To experience the pleasure of patchwork, try your hand at an eye-catching eight-pointed Lone-Star pattern. The star's points are formed by diamond-shaped pieces of fabric, and the background is made up of squares and triangles. Traditionally made with tiny calico or solid-color diamonds, the designs shown below are made more contemporary with striped shirting and speckled prints (all pieces are 100 percent cotton).

A star pattern that suggests origami begins as eight diamonds and six squares, two of which are cut in half to form triangles. Pieced together, the diamonds resemble petals. Striped fabrics produce a pinwheel effect. The basic patchwork directions for the 18-inch pillow cover shown here can be adapted to make multiple stars for a quilt. Later in this book you'll find the same technique applied to a wool coverlet (page 296) and wall art (page 355).

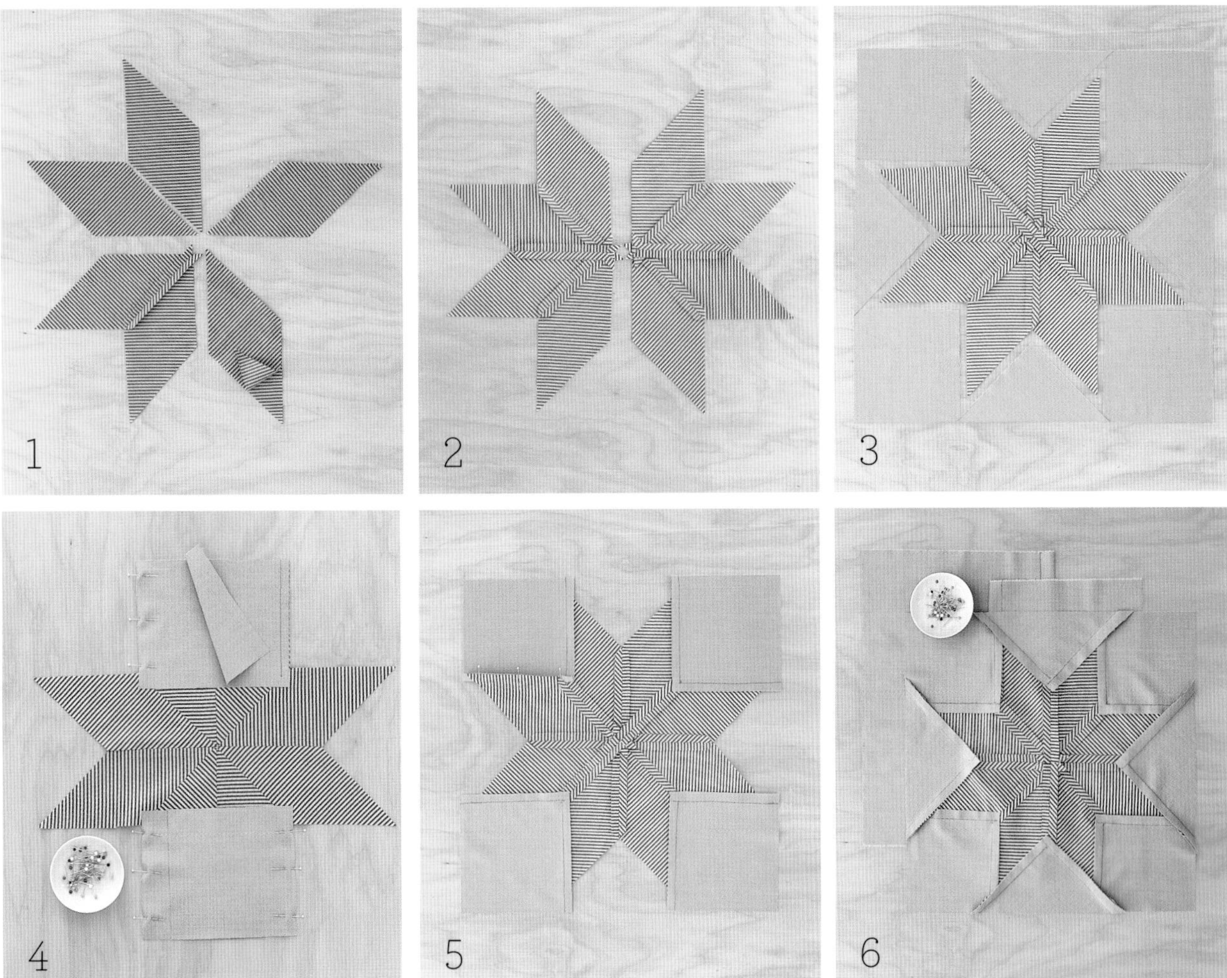

1. CUT DIAMONDS AND STITCH INTO SETS Using the star-pattern patchwork template (see the enclosed CD), a rotary cutter, and a cutting mat, cut 8 diamonds from 1/3 yard [30.5cm] fabric (or a variety of patterns). Stripes can parallel one side of the diamond or run perpendicular, as shown. Arrange diamonds to form a star. Stack 2 diamonds, right sides facing; pin and stitch along one edge, with a 1/2-inch (13mm) seam allowance. Repeat to create 4 sets of stitched diamonds. Press seams open.

2. STITCH SETS TOGETHER Stack 2 sets of stitched diamonds, right sides facing. Pin; stitch together, with a 1/2-inch (13mm) seam allowance. Repeat to create 2 sets of 4 diamonds. Pin and stitch together, with a 1/2-inch (13mm) seam allowance, to complete the star. Press all seams open.

3. CUT AND ARRANGE SQUARES AND TRIANGLES To square off the star, cut six 6-inch (15cm) squares from 3/4 yard (68.5cm) contrasting fabric. Cut two of them in half on the diagonal to create 4 triangles. Lay out star, squares, and triangles.

4. ALIGN SQUARES Turn star right-side up. Align 1 square, right side of fabric facing down, with outer edge of top left-hand point of star; pin. Repeat in reverse on top right-hand point. Stitch in place, as shown. Using 2 more squares, repeat on the bottom of the star. Press seams toward center of star.

5. FINISH ATTACHING SQUARES After attaching one edge of each of 4 squares, pin and turn right-side down. Stitch along a second side of each.

6. FILL IN GAPS AND FINISH PILLOW COVER Fill the remaining gaps with triangles; pin and sew in the same manner. Press seams toward center of star. For envelope-style backing, cut two 13-by-18-inch (33cm × 45.5cm) rectangles from remaining fabric used for squares and diamonds. Hem one long side of each. Overlap them, right sides up. Pin pillow cover front, right-side down, to back pieces; stitch perimeter. Turn right-side out; insert an 18-inch (45.5cm) pillow form.

how to appliqué and echo quilt

Traditional Hawaiian quilts incorporate two unique methods: the appliqué of large pattern pieces, and a hand-quilting style known as echo (or "contour") quilting, so called because the quilting stitches echo the shape of the appliquéd motif as they secure the fabric and batting. A small project, like a pillow cover, offers a lesson in this style of quilting before committing to a larger bed covering.

CUT OUT PIECES From 1 yard (0.9m) light-green 100 percent cotton or linen quilting-weight fabric, cut one 24-inch (61cm) square, one 23-inch (58.5cm) square, and 4 strips that each measure 5 by 23 inches (12.5cm × 58.5cm; for borders). Cut two 24-inch (61cm) squares from 1 yard (0.9m) of pale-blue cotton of similar fiber and weight. Fold the 24-inch (61cm) green fabric square as described in the box below. Lay the Hawaiian template of your choice (see the Upholstery section of enclosed CD; adjust size as needed.) on top of the folded fabric triangle, aligning the V of the template with the bottom-left corner (photo 1). Trace the template with a disappearing-ink fabric pen, then remove template. Pin fabric layers together inside the traced outline. Cut along the traced outline using sharp, pointed fabric shears. For best results, turn the fabric as you cut, holding the scissors as stationary as possible. Unfold the fabric to reveal the complete motif. Fold one blue fabric square

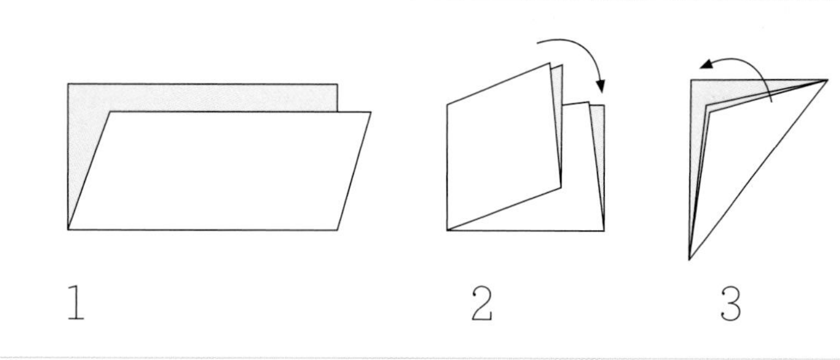

PREPARING TO CUT THE APPLIQUÉ MOTIF

1. Fold the bottom edge to the top edge; press.
2. Fold the left edge to the right edge; press.
3. Fold the bottom-right corner to the top-left corner; press. (The bottom-left corner will become the center when the fabric is unfolded.)

in the same manner described below, pressing after each fold. Unfold fabric. Center the green motif on the blue fabric, aligning the fold lines, as shown. Secure the motif to the fabric by pinning along the folds and inside each petal or leaf. Baste ¼ inch (6mm) inside the motif's perimeter with a ½-inch (13mm) running stitch (page 31). Remove the pins, and smooth the motif as you go.

APPLIQUÉ THE MOTIF Using an appliqué needle, turn one edge of the motif under ⅛ inch (3mm), and secure with appliqué stitches (page 40): Bring needle up through base fabric and motif at its folded edge, then down through base fabric only. Repeat, turning under and appliqué-stitching entire motif. (To appliqué curved areas, turn under less fabric, and work the stitches closer together.) Remove the basting stitches. Press motif and base fabric.

QUILT THE PILLOW'S TOP LAYER From 1 yard (0.9m) of wool batting, cut a 24-inch (61cm) square. Lay the second blue fabric square on a flat surface, and place batting on top. Then lay the appliquéd square face-up on the batting. Baste through all 3 layers along the horizontal and vertical axes with a ½-inch (13mm) running stitch (page 31). Then baste in parallel lines, about 6 inches (15cm) apart, to make a grid. Put fabric in a quilting hoop. Thread a quilting needle with blue quilting thread, knotting at one end. Quilt the layers with the quilting stitch (page 65): Starting near the center of motif at an edge, quilt around the motif's perimeter, closely following its contours. Complete the area within the hoop, and then shift the hoop to work around the entire perimeter of the motif.

ADD ECHO QUILTING AROUND MOTIF About ½ inch (13mm) outside the first quilted line, quilt a second line echoing the first. Continue quilting a third echo line ½ inch (13mm) outside the second, and so on, stopping about 1 inch (2.5cm) from the edges, which will be covered by a border. (You can also start 3 needles at each of these ½-inch [13mm] intervals [photo 2], to have the echo lines progressing simultaneously to help save time.) Tie off knots as needed at the back. When quilting is complete, remove basting stitches.

ADD ECHO QUILTING INSIDE MOTIF Using green quilting thread, follow the step above to quilt echo lines at ½-inch (13mm) intervals inside the motif as well as to delineate the flower contours in motif's corners. Trim ½ inch (13mm) off all sides of quilted fabric square so that it is 23 inches square (58.5cm).

ADD BORDERS AND FINISH PILLOW If edges are frayed, trim them. Sew first two borders: Lay one strip on top of one edge of the quilted fabric, appliqué side up, aligning the fabric's and strip's edges. Machine-stitch lengthwise along the strip, 2 ½ inches (6.5cm) in from edge. Repeat to attach a second strip on the opposite edge of the quilted fabric. Fold back each strip at the machine-stitched lines so that both edges of the strip align with fabric edge; press each. Sew remaining two borders: Attach the third and fourth strips along the remaining edges of the quilted fabric, following the directions above and overlapping the already sewn strips at corners. Fold back remaining 2 strips, and press, following the directions above. Pin remaining green fabric square right side down on top of quilted fabric. Machine-stitch along each edge, with a ½-inch (13mm) seam allowance, leaving a 15-inch (38cm) opening on one side. Turn pillow cover inside out. Insert 22-inch (56cm) pillow. Slipstitch (page 31) the opening closed.

how repair a patchwork quilt

If a well-worn quilt needs repair, tend to it sooner rather than later; frayed edges, tears, and holes will only get bigger with time. These instructions will show you how to patch a hole or tattered area (while leaving the original fabric underneath intact), and how to replace worn or ripped binding. Make the patch templates in the shapes you need to mimic—squares were cut for the colorful postage stamp–pattern quilt pictured. Always prewash new fabric before sewing.

Keep in mind that the restoration and repair techniques demonstrated here are for patchwork quilts to be used and enjoyed at home. Quilts of more than sentimental value should be treated by a professional conservator.

1. MAKE A PATCH PATTERN
To create a template for your quilt's shapes, measure a piece and draw the shape on card stock, then mark 3⁄16 inch (5mm) all around it; use a craft knife to cut out along both lines. Trace template (outer and inner edges) onto a piece of the new fabric's back with a disappearing-ink fabric pen; cut out around outer edge. Repeat, cutting as many pieces as you need. Use a running stitch (page 31) to sew two together, right sides facing, along marked inner lines (as shown). Press this seam to one side. Continue sewing units of 2 pieces, then attach 2 to make units of 4, and sew 4-square units together; depending on the shape and size of the hole, you may need to add single pieces to the edges of the patch.

2. PATCH THE BACK If holes extend through the quilt's backing, create a second patch. Lay the pieced patch (for front of quilt) onto cotton in a color that matches the back. Trace patch onto cotton, mark 3⁄16 inch (5mm) all around it, and cut out around outer line; pin this patch over hole and, turning edges under 3⁄16 inch (5mm) as you go, sew using a slipstitch (page 31): Insert needle through a folded edge, and pull thread up through it. Pick up a thread or two from quilt fabric. Insert needle back into folded edge of patch 3⁄16 inch (5mm) from previous stitch; pull thread through. Continue around perimeter of pattern.

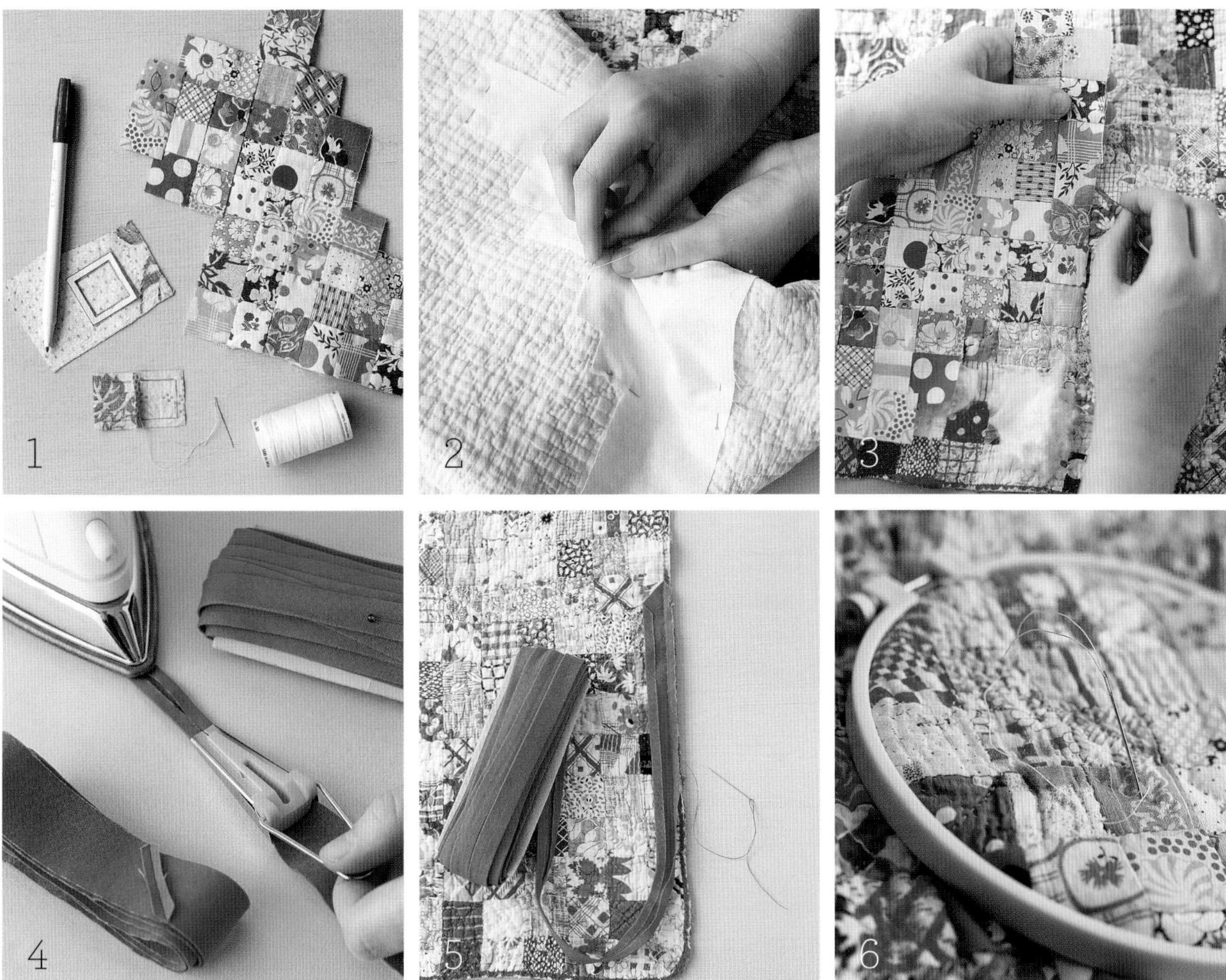

3. PATCH THE FRONT If the damaged area isn't as fluffy as the rest of the quilt, tuck a little batting in the hole, pulling it out around the edges to thin. Slipstitch (see step 2) pieced patch onto the front of quilt, matching seams. Remember to leave the tattered fabric remnants underneath the patch.

4. MAKE BIAS TAPE It's a good idea to custom-make bias tape to rebind a vintage quilt, as packaged tapes are often starchy polyester blends. Cut 100 percent cotton fabric on the bias into 1 1/8-inch (2.9cm) strips. Sew ends of strips together, right sides facing, until you have a strip a few inches longer than the perimeter of your quilt; press seams open. Pass fabric strip through a bias-tape maker (for more on making your own bias tape, see page 369).

5. REBIND THE EDGES Frayed edges are a common problem; many vintage quilts will have had two or three different bindings during their lifetimes. To rebind a quilt, make your own bias tape (see step 4) or look for bias tape in the same color as the original. To attach the bias tape, open it and place it on top of the quilt, wrong side up. Line up the edge of the quilt with the tape's outer fold. Using cotton thread in a matching color and a running stitch (page 31), sew along the inside of this fold. Once you have stitched the tape to the quilt's front, wrap it over the edges and use a slipstitch (step 2) to tack it to the back.

6. QUILT THE PATCHES Give the repaired area the same texture and appearance as the rest of the textile by quilting over the patch. Place the quilt loosely in an embroidery hoop or quilting frame. Using cotton hand-quilting thread and a small needle, copy the length and design of the original quilting stitches (here, an X through each square), sewing through all the layers.

TECHNIQUE:

dyeing

Fabrics are available in an endless assortment of hues and shades, so why bother to dye them yourself? The sheer wonder of watching the gradual—and often unpredictable—transformation of cloth from one color to another is a very good reason.

Hand-dyeing produces gorgeous, one-of-a-kind fabrics that are rarely found in a store. And the appearance of the finished fabric is less uniform than any mass-produced material, something that very often makes it more, not less, appealing. What's more, the patterning and embellishment you impart with dyeing techniques are truly distinctive, the direct result of being crafted by your hand.

Dyeing is eventful in a grand sort of way. You get to stir fabric in big bins and pots of liquid, then transfer them, dripping, from one spot to another. As you experiment with the process of adding color to natural fibers, you elevate simple cloth items and yardage to become heirloom-worthy keepsakes.

Inspired by dyeing practices from around the world, the techniques included in this chapter guarantee wide-ranging and truly satisfying results. Learn to tint solid or patterned fabrics with the basic hand-dyeing technique; the dyed fabrics find their way into a number of delightful projects in this book. You'll also learn about batik, albeit a simpler method than is conventional; use it—and a steady supply of everyday household items—to add playful designs to any fabric. Ombré introduces you to a way of applying dye with an emphasis on tone. Fading fabric and overdyeing are reliable methods that make it easy to transform even the newest yardage or store-bought home goods into something that appears charmingly vintage.

Flip through these pages to see what catches your eye. Then set aside a weekend afternoon to play with color in your kitchen or backyard.

IN THIS CHAPTER:

+ BASIC DYEING SUPPLIES
+ HOW TO HAND-DYE FABRICS
+ HOW TO BATIK
+ HOW TO FADE AND OVERDYE FABRIC
+ HOW TO CREATE AN OMBRÉ PATTERN

basic dyeing supplies

1. **FIBER-REACTIVE DYES** These specialized powder dyes produce vivid colors that resist fading. Mixed with soda ash fixer, also known as sodium carbonate, and warm water (to set the color), fiber-reactive dyes can be used for dyeing by hand and in washing machines.
2. **NONIODIZED SALT** As its name implies, noniodized salt does not contain iodine, making it a better choice to use with dye. Mixing this salt into a dye solution helps keep the fabric from repelling the pigment, ultimately helping it to absorb more color. Some dyes do not require the addition of salt; read the dye manufacturer's label for specific instructions.
3. **MEASURING SPOONS** To make sure you are adding the right amount of dye or other ingredients, always use measuring spoons designated for this task.
4. **ALL-PURPOSE DYES** Widely available in powder and liquid forms, all-purpose dyes are used with hot water. The colors of these dyes are usually not as vibrant or as long-lasting as fiber-reactive dyes; they are a good choice when you want more subtle shades or if the fabric will not be washed often. All-purpose dyes are appropriate for hand-dyeing and in washing machines. Again, follow the dye manufacturer's instructions.
5. **NONREACTIVE BASINS OR BINS** Choose enamel or brand-new porcelain bowls to mix small dye batches and to soak fabric by hand (dye can stain plastic, fiberglass, or worn porcelain containers). Designate a few plastic storage bins that you won't mind staining to use for larger dye batches.
6. **RUBBER GLOVES** To protect hands, always wear protective gloves when working with fabric dyes, bleach, soda ash fixer, and other chemicals.
7. **KRAFT PAPER, PLASTIC COVERING, OR DROP CLOTHS** Before mixing dyes, cover work surfaces with paper, plastic, or drop cloths to protect tables, countertops, and floors.

GETTING STARTED

Following these four guidelines will ensure better results for any fabric-dyeing project.

CHOOSE THE RIGHT FABRIC The best options are natural-fiber fabrics with no treatments or finishes, such as 100 percent cotton, hemp, linen, or silk (wool requires a stovetop dye method not covered in this book). Some untreated synthetic fabrics will also dye nicely.

PREWASH FABRIC Always prewash to remove starch, sizing (a chemical treatment used to strengthen and smooth fabric), and other coatings that may resist dyes, as well as oils and dirt that can accumulate. Professional textile detergent is the preferred choice for washing, as it leaves no residue, but regular detergent may also be used. Machine- or air-dry, depending on the fabric that you choose.

PROTECT CLOTHING AND SURFACES Wear old clothes and shoes, and use a dust mask whenever working with powdered dyes and chemicals. Cover work surfaces with drop cloths, plastic sheeting, or kraft paper.

MAKE A TEST BATCH Before dyeing fabric, test a piece in a small dye batch to learn how the fabric reacts with the dye and whether to add more or less dye in the larger bath.

how to hand-dye fabrics

Hand-dyeing fabric is a simple process with results that vary slightly, depending on the types of dyes and fabric. The amount of dye solution you'll need to mix is based on fabric weight; the instructions here are for ½ pound (226.8g) of fabric. If you don't have a scale, compare the fabric with a T-shirt (about ½ pound [226.8g]) or a pair of jeans (about 1 pound [453.6g]). Experiment with different amounts of dye in the solution to achieve the desired color.

The colors pictured above were added to cotton ticking with all-purpose dye, but the technique can be used on any patterned or solid-colored fabric, or with fiber-reactive dyes (follow manufacturer's instructions).

SOAK FABRIC In a hot-water bath, soak the fabric until you are ready to begin dyeing. This will help the fabric absorb the dye evenly.

PREPARE DYE BATH Fill another basin or bin with 6 quarts (24 cups [5.7l]) of very hot water. Pour in 6 tablespoons (90g) salt so that it covers the bottom of the bowl. Pour in all-purpose dye (the amount will vary depending on the color you want to achieve and can range from ¼ teaspoon [1.25ml] to 6 teaspoons [29.5ml]; use one color of dye, or combine colors for custom shades). Stir well with a nonreactive enameled or metal spoon (the dye will stain wood and plastic).

DYE FABRIC Wring the fabric, smooth it, and slowly submerge it in the dye bath; make sure the fabric is not bunched. To create the colors shown (see photo, left), leave the fabric in the dye bath for about 30 minutes and move it around every 10 minutes. If you're experimenting with tints, inspect shade after 30 seconds, and keep checking every few minutes. Remember that the fabric will look darker when wet.

RINSE FABRIC To remove excess dye and salt, rinse the fabric in cold water until the water runs clear. Machine- or air-dry, depending on the fabric.

ABOUT NATURAL DYES

Before synthetic dyes were invented in 1856, natural dyes were used to color many of the world's most beautiful textiles, from the Persian carpets that decorated Versailles to the red and blue of the first American flag. Natural dyes still offer a bright alternative to synthetic versions, and are now much easier to use than when raw materials had to be gathered, dried, sorted, ground, boiled, and strained before they could be used to color fabric. Now powder dyes made from safflowers, madder root, lichens, and mushrooms, to name just a few substances, yield beautiful results. Even loose tea leaves, wrapped in cheesecloth, can be used to color fabrics (try chamomile for acid yellow; gunpowder green for a mild green; or orange pekoe, Darjeeling, or oolong for beiges and creams). Bear in mind that natural dyes are more volatile than synthetic ones; they are far more likely to bleed, fade, or shift when exposed to light or water. And they require a lot of trial and error. To prevent naturally dyed textiles from discoloring and fading, a mordant is used to help the pigment bond with the fiber. Most mordants are produced from the water-soluble salts of common minerals, and some work better on certain fibers than on others. If you would like to experiment with the process, a prepackaged natural-dye kit is a great place to start; look for such kits from online retailers.

how to batik

Batik is a resist-dye technique in which the overlaying of wax and dye create graphic designs on fabric. The craft, which originated on the Indonesian island of Java, is traditionally quite labor intensive; a single yard of intricate Javanese pattern might take up to a year to produce. The quick method included here isn't nearly as involved, but it allows you to experience the pleasure of using wax and dye to fashion vivid patterns. Here, household items, such as cookie cutters, dowels, icing tips, and a pastry cutter serve as simple wax-stamping tools.

1

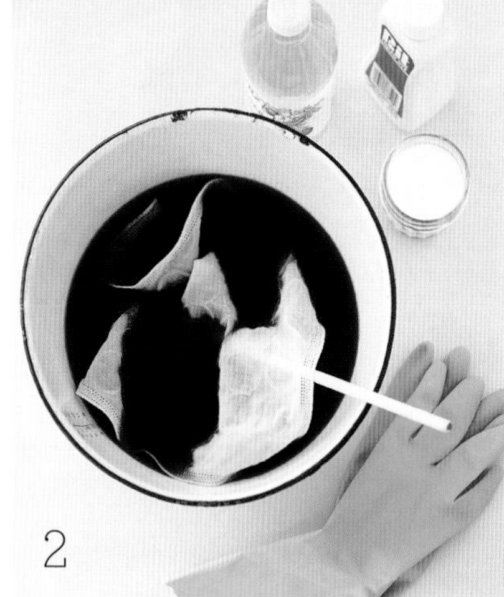
2

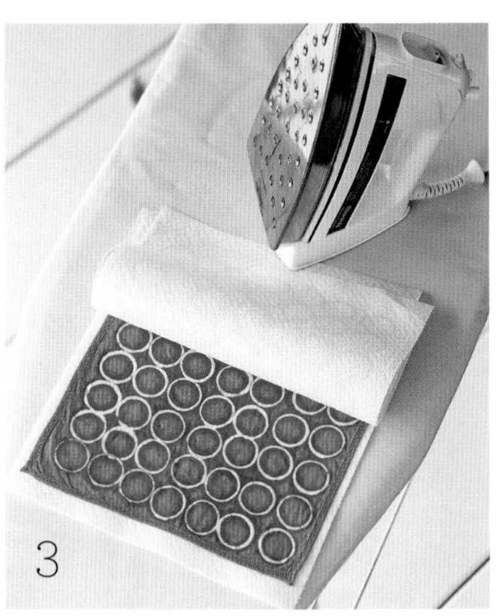
3

1. MELT WAX AND STAMP PATTERN The amount of wax you'll use will depend on the pattern to be created; intricate or dense patterns need more wax, while sparse patterns will require less. Use beeswax for sharp lines; avoid paraffin, which would produce a crackle effect. Place a small amount of wax in top of double boiler, and set over boiling water until melted; simmer, keeping wax hot. If the wax begins to smoke, remove it from the heat. There should be enough melted wax to coat ¼ inch (6mm) of the bottom edge of your stamping tool. Warm the stamp in hot wax for 30 seconds; use pliers or a clothespin to lift out shallow objects. Lightly drag the stamp across the rim of the pot to remove excess wax. Stamp fabric in your desired pattern, catching drips on kraft paper.

2. MIX DYE BATH AND DYE FABRIC In a large nonreactive bowl, mix a dye bath of ½ cup (118ml) liquid all-purpose dye per 4 quarts (3.8l) of hot water (the very hot water required for powdered dyes would melt the wax). For colorfastness, add ½ cup (120g) noniodized salt to the dye bath and stir to dissolve. Submerge fabric for a few seconds or up to 20 minutes, depending on the shade desired; stir periodically with a nonreactive utensil. Remove fabric from bowl, blot with paper towels, and hang or lay flat to dry; the color of the fabric will lighten considerably as it dries.

3. REMOVE WAX When fabric is dry, press it on the hottest setting (no steam) between layers of paper towels, plain newsprint, or kraft paper. Change paper frequently, until all wax is lifted. Wax that is particularly hard to remove can be dry-cleaned (this works well for silk). Batik-dyed fabric should be carefully hand-washed (never use bleach) and air-dried.

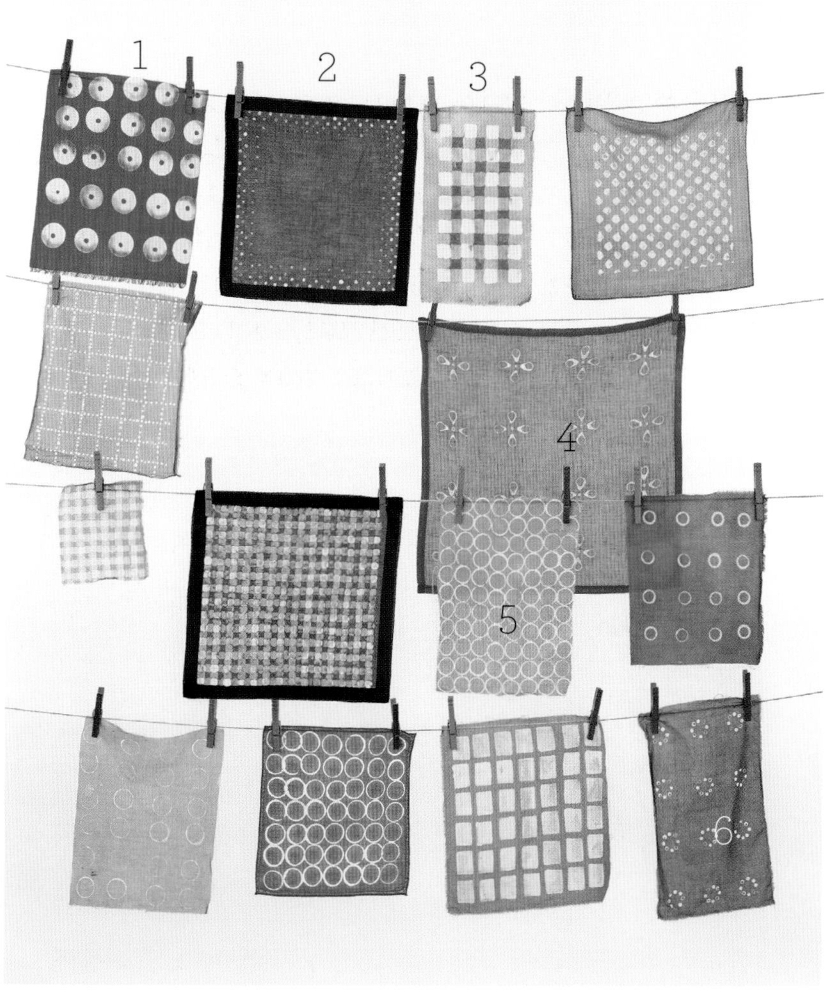

STAMPING TOOLS

Kitchen drawers and sewing boxes are good sources of shapes to use in making batik.

1. WOODEN SPOOL for wide ring shapes

2. WOODEN DOWEL for polka dots

3. WOOD BLOCK for squares (including gingham)

4. COOKIE CUTTER for teardrops or other shapes

5. PASTRY CUTTER for thin rings

6. HOLLOW ICING TIP for small circles

GINGHAM BATIK HOW-TO

A checked pattern can be created with any size square wooden block.

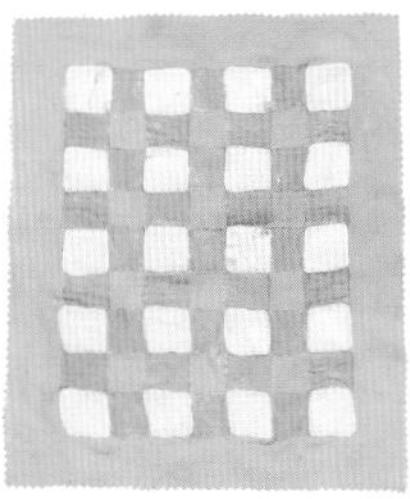

1. Place a sheet of graph paper beneath white fabric to use as a guide. Apply a grid of waxed squares, making equal-size squares and spaces, and then dip fabric briefly, about 20 seconds, into dye.

2. Without removing the wax, stamp a second grid of waxed squares that is vertically and horizontally aligned with squares of the first grid. Immerse fabric in dye again for 20 minutes.

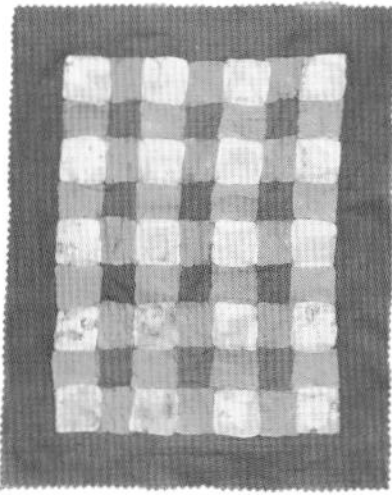

3. Remove the piece from the dye, wax still in place; follow instructions on opposite page for removing wax. The first dye bath is the key to the checks, creating the pale squares that contrast with the white and dark blocks around them.

how to fade and overdye fabric

Simple bleaching and overdyeing techniques transform vibrant printed fabrics into vintage-looking treasures. To soften the color of a piece of fabric, soak it in a bleach-and-hot-water solution, then a chlorine neutralizer. Afterward, overdye the fabric to add a boost of a different color, if you wish. Use 100 percent natural fabric; even a small amount of polyester will prevent fabrics from fading. Choose fabrics in bright or medium tones, and wash and dry before treating.

fading fabric

PREPARE BATHS You will need 3 large plastic storage bins. Wearing rubber gloves and an apron, and working outside or in a well-ventilated area protected with a drop cloth, combine 1 part chlorine bleach with 10 parts very hot water in the first bin; there should be enough liquid in the bleach bath to totally submerge the fabric. Fill a second bin with cold water. In the third bin, mix a chlorine neutralizer (available from pool companies or online) with water, following the manufacturer's instructions. The neutralizer stops bleach from continuing to fade fabric and eliminates chlorine odors.

BLEACH FABRIC Saturate the fabric under hot water, then submerge it in the bleach solution. Watch it closely, keeping in mind that it will look brighter when wet than when it has dried. The fading process takes anywhere from 10 seconds to 15 minutes. If you are unsure how long to soak the fabric, err on the side of caution. Add a little more bleach if you don't see desired results after 15 minutes. Do not use more than 1 part bleach to 5 parts water.

RINSE AND WASH FABRIC Submerge the fabric in the cold-water bin and swish it around, rinsing thoroughly. Wring it out until it is no longer dripping. Transfer the fabric to the chlorine-neutralizer bin and soak according to the manufacturer's instructions. Wash and machine- or air-dry, depending on the fabric.

overdyeing fabric

PREPARE DYE BATH Fill a large plastic storage bin with hot water, all-purpose liquid fabric dye, and noniodized salt; for ½ pound (226.8g) fabric, use 6 quarts (5.7l) water, ½ teaspoon (2.5ml) dye, and ½ cup (120g) salt. (If you are dyeing a larger piece of fabric, double or triple the amounts.) Fill a second large plastic bin with cold water.

DYE FABRIC Run the faded fabric under hot tap water. Referring to the dye manufacturer's instructions, soak the fabric in the first bin until it absorbs the desired amount of color, anywhere from 10 to 45 minutes. To intensify the color, add a few more drops of dye.

RINSE AND WASH FABRIC Thoroughly rinse the fabric in the bin of cold water. Wash and dry the fabric according to the dye manufacturer's instructions.

TIP

If possible, dye small swatches to test them at different time intervals. To get the same shade as your favorite swatch, wet the swatch, then monitor the material in the bleaching or dyeing solution, removing it when it matches the wet swatch. Change the solution in the bin before you start a new dyeing project.

fabrics before and after bleaching

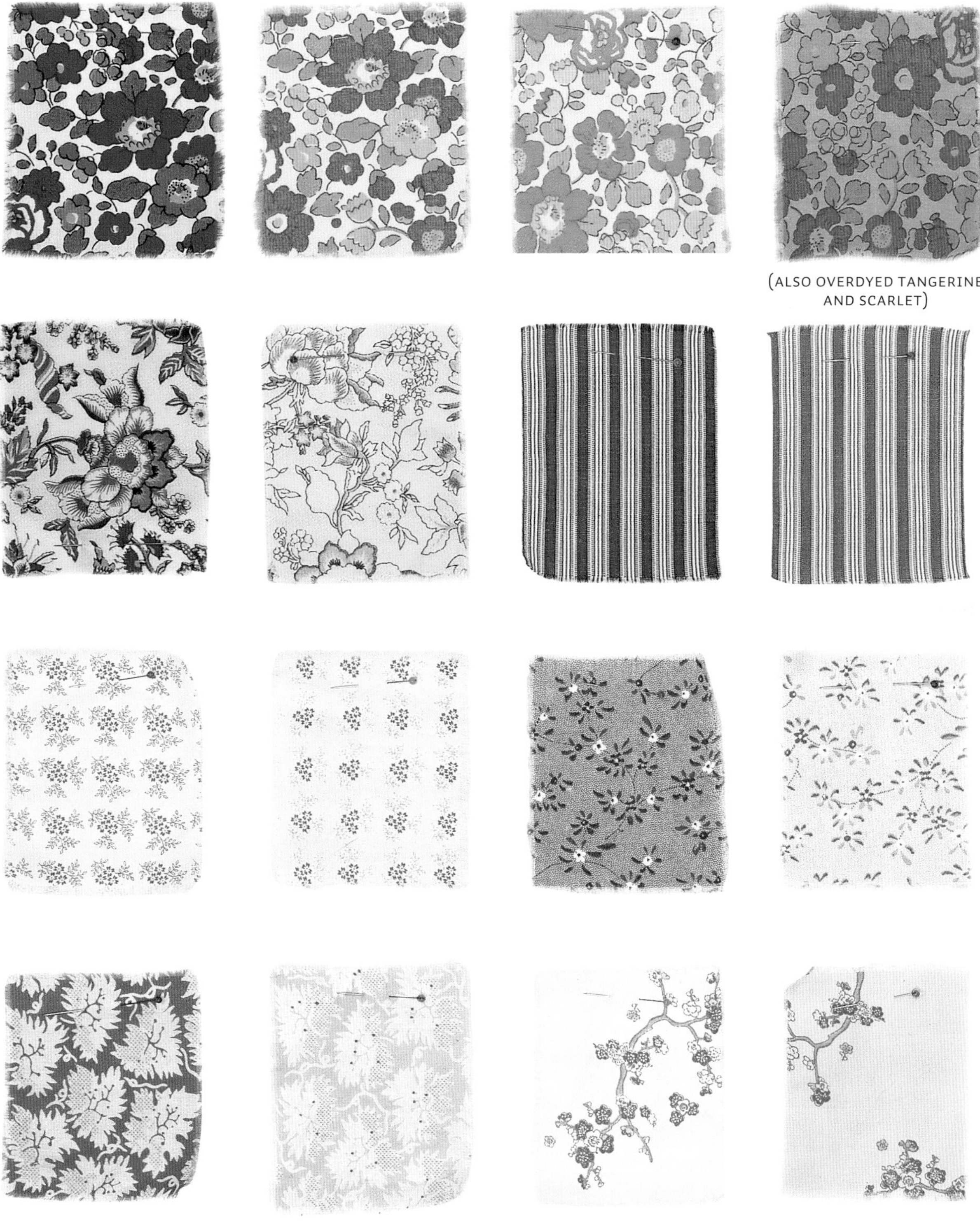

(ALSO OVERDYED TANGERINE AND SCARLET)

(ALSO OVERDYED PINK)

how to create an ombré pattern

Ombré (French for "shaded") is a method of dyeing fabric that renders subtle gradations of color from light to dark. The varying intensity of color is the technique's hallmark, and its beauty is defined by its inexact outcome. By blending hues, you can create a near-limitless array of signature colors. White or tinted yardage and premade items work well for ombré projects.

A quartet of dyed linen panels creates a captivating display. All four panels share a pale-blue base, yet each stands boldly independent given its overlay of color. To make a similar panel, cut fabric six inches longer on all sides than a stretcher bar (available at art-supply stores). Fold fabric in half horizontally to produce identical gradations at top and bottom. Pin through all layers to mark shade levels, and dye as directed on the opposite page. Press dried fabric, then use a staple gun to attach to the stretcher bar.

Fiber-reactive dyes are used here to achieve brighter colors; these dyes require the addition of soda ash fixer—also known as sodium carbonate—to make the dye bath more alkaline and help set the dye color. Soda ash fixer is usually added at the end of the dye process, but here it is added at the beginning because the fabric is not uniformly soaked. Keep in mind that with each washing, the color will fade slightly. The instructions that follow are for ½ pound (226.8g) of fabric; double the quantities of salt, water, dye, and soda ash fixer for 1 pound (453.6g) of fabric.

SOAK FABRIC Wash 100 percent natural-fiber fabric with professional textile detergent; dry. Cover work surface and floor with plastic drop cloths. Saturate ½ pound (226.8g) fabric with water; wring it until it is no longer dripping. Smooth fabric.

PIN FABRIC Decide how far you want the dye to extend, and mark that line with straight pins on right and left sides of the fabric (be sure to measure the placement, for accuracy). Divide area to be dyed into five even segments and mark intervals with pins; more segments will create more subtle gradation, fewer will create more distinct lines between hues.

PREPARE DYE BATH Position a wide nonreactive plastic storage bin for the dye solution near a basin or tub. Dissolve 1½ cups (362g) noniodized salt in 5¼ quarts (5l) warm water in the bin (you'll want the liquid to reach a minimum depth of 4 inches [10cm]). Wearing rubber gloves and a protective mask (some dyes can be toxic), measure 1½ teaspoons (7.5ml) fiber-reactive dye and place it in a small nonreactive bowl. Add 1 to 2 teaspoons (5–10ml) warm water, stirring with a nonreactive utensil to make a paste. Slowly add 1 cup (236ml)of warm water, and stir until dye dissolves completely and mixture forms a slurry. Add the slurry to the bin, stirring until mixed. Measure 2 tablespoons plus 2 teaspoons (40g) soda ash fixer, and place it in a second nonreactive bowl; add 2 cups (473ml) warm water slowly, stirring until dissolved. (Avoid splashing, as fixer is caustic.) Add the soda-ash-fixer mixture to the dye solution, mixing well for about 30 seconds, or according to manufacturer's instructions. The solution will remain effective for about 1 hour and cannot be reused.

DYE FABRIC Lower prepared fabric into dye solution, immersing it to the topmost pins; hold in place for 30 seconds. (The damp fabric will draw dye up, creating blurred gradations.) Raise fabric until solution's surface aligns with second set of pins; hold for 1 minute. Raise fabric to third set of pins; hold for 5 minutes. Repeat at remaining 2 pinned levels, holding for 5 minutes each. Remove pins.

RINSE AND WASH FABRIC Carefully transfer dyed fabric to a wide nonreactive basin or tub. Fill with cold running water, swishing gently to rinse. Drain. Repeat until liquid remains clear. Machine-wash fabric in hot water with professional textile detergent to remove excess dye. Machine- or air-dry.

TECHNIQUE:

printing

Transferring graceful designs to textiles to enhance their surfaces with patterns and borders speaks to an age-old desire for decoration. Imperfections and variations in tone, the inevitable results of simple tools and materials, only add to the fabric's beauty. Evidence of the human hand is plainly revealed, not disguised. In fact, it's the irregularity of printing methods that makes them so appealing.

The techniques included in this chapter—stamping, block-printing, and stenciling—rely on basic materials and washable pigments. Use them to add contrast and embellishment to store-bought cloth items, such as curtains, or to customize yardage intended for a sewing project.

When choosing fabric to print, focus on natural fibers. Be sure to wash the fabric to remove any sizing (a finish that temporarily seals the cloth and gives it a slight sheen), which can prevent pigments from being absorbed.

Press the fabric, too, before printing by any of the methods in this chapter; even tiny wrinkles can distort a design. And look for fabrics with a flat weave; this allows for the crispest, most predictable stamped, printed, or stenciled designs.

Hand-printed fabrics are beloved for their subtle variations in color and intensity, in part because these elements suggest the artistry that produced them. Still, don't be surprised if, once you are finished and ready to show off your handiwork, no one believes that you created it yourself.

IN THIS CHAPTER:

+ BASIC FABRIC-PRINTING SUPPLIES
+ HOW TO STAMP ON FABRIC
+ HOW TO BLOCK-PRINT ON FABRIC
+ HOW TO STENCIL FABRIC

basic fabric-printing supplies

1. **SELF-HEALING MAT** Use this soft but sturdy surface when cutting out stencils and templates.
2. **DRAFTING TAPE** Durable and strong, drafting tape is used to affix templates, stencils, and fabric to one another or to a work surface. Unlike masking tape, it won't leave any residue behind.
3. **TEMPLATES** Use templates to make a fabric stencil or to create a design to be carved on a linoleum block. For more on creating and using templates, see page 40.
4. **WATERPROOF PAPER** To make a fabric stencil from a template, use this specialty paper (Mylar® also works).
5. **CRAFT KNIFE** Sharp and easy to maneuver, a craft knife is great for cutting out delicate stencil designs and templates.
6. **FABRIC PAINT** Water-based fabric paints come in a variety of colors, and can be used to stamp, block print, and stencil. See box, below left, for more information.
7. **RUBBER STAMPS** Used to add accents to fabrics, rubber stamps are available in an endless variety of designs. Botanical images, such as leaves, look particularly elegant on fabric. For best results, choose stamp designs with clearly defined ridges.
8. **FABRIC INKPAD** Designed specifically for fabric stamping, the ink in these pads is set with an iron.
9. **NATURAL SEA SPONGE** A soft, textured sea sponge efficiently soaks up paint to be dabbed on fabric to create stenciled patterns.
10. **CRAFT PAINTBRUSHES** Bristled brushes are best for applying paint to a carved linoleum block for block printing.
11. **PALETTE KNIFE** Use this to add paint to or to mix colors.
12. **FOAM TOOLS** Foam paintbrushes and rollers are handy for applying paint to objects for printing.
13. **PALETTE** This pad of heavy white paper coated with plastic holds paints as you mix colors and print.

ABOUT FABRIC PAINTS

Good-quality fabric paint and ink can make the difference between a short-lived printed design and one with enduring appeal. Most fabric paints for home use are water-based, and are heat-set by ironing on the reverse side of the fabric. Once set, the paints are permanent. At full strength, the paints tend to produce opaque colors that are effective for printing on dark fabrics. But the paints can also be diluted with colorless extender (available at art-supply stores) to make them translucent. Available in standard, metallic, and glow-in-the-dark varieties, fabric paints may also be mixed to create custom colors. If you mix paints on a palette, keep them from drying out between sessions by wrapping the palette with plastic wrap or sealing it in an airtight container. While mixing paint, add colors sparingly until you get the precise tone you want. In general, colors shift in intensity or brightness as they dry, so experiment with a small amount in an inconspicuous area before you begin printing. Look for good-quality paints at crafts stores and from online retailers.

how to stamp on fabric

Printed designs can be applied to any natural-fiber fabric, woven or otherwise. For a breezy summer look, try the technique on diaphanous Indian cotton or voile. For a more substantial effect, print on wool felt. Washable, color-safe fabric paint will ensure your creation retains its beauty. For design options, consider all-over patterns, borders, or, for impact, single shapes.

BEST FABRICS FOR PRINTING

In general, natural, untreated materials are best for fabric printing. Make sure there are no stain-resistant coatings on the fabric or other treatments that could prevent paint from adhering. Synthetic fabrics—such as rayon or polyester—aren't suitable for printing because they can't be ironed at a high enough temperature for the fabric paint or screening ink to set without damaging the material.

COVER WORK SURFACE Before you begin, cover a work surface with towels or kraft paper. If you are printing with three-dimensional objects (such as the seashells shown), use a few layers of towels. If you are printing with a flat-surfaced object, such as a cut potato or apple (see page 125), use a few layers of paper. The goal in both cases is to create a firm, but not hard, surface that has enough give to "receive" the printed design.

PREPARE PAINTS AND FABRIC Set out your fabric paints. If you want to mix colors to create a new shade, do so on the palette. For larger amounts of paint, use a mixing jar. Lay a piece of practice fabric flat on the towels or paper.

BRUSH OBJECT WITH PAINT Using a foam roller or paintbrush, cover part or all of the object with which you will print.

PRINT Press flat objects—such as carved potatoes, carved apples, and leaves—onto the fabric as if they were rubber stamps. If working with a three-dimensional object, such as a shell, you may need to roll the object slightly to ensure that all of the details are captured. Once you're satisfied with the prints on the practice fabric, lay the fabric on the towels and print. If working with a very detailed three-dimensional object, such as a rubber form, you'll get a better print by laying the fabric over the object and pressing with your fingers. With both methods, each time you print, the object will be less vivid, so be sure to reapply paint. Let paint dry according to manufacturer's instructions and follow directions for setting paint. Wash the objects with warm water and detergent and dry them thoroughly before reusing.

how to block-print on fabric

Although traditional block printing relies on inks to create designs on paper, fabric paint makes this craft adaptable for use on yardage or fabric items. Block-printed fabric has a wonderful hand-crafted appearance. The primary tool—a soft block—lets you create any design you like. A linoleum cutter is used to carve the design into the block. The effects can be elegant and intricate, or bold and graphic. Use this method on any flat-weave or nonwoven natural-fiber fabric.

1. TRANSFER TEMPLATE Print the block print branch template (see enclosed CD), or create your own, and cut out. (For more on creating and using templates, see page 40.) Lay a sheet of tracing paper over the template. Trace the design with a graphite pencil. (You may also want to shade the areas that you want to carve away as a guide.) Place the soft-carve block on a flat surface. Position the tracing paper, design-side down, on top of the block; use drafting tape to hold in place. With a bone folder (a bookbinding tool available at crafts stores), rub the entire surface of the tracing paper against the block. Remove paper and tape.

2. CARVE BLOCK Holding a linoleum cutter with the hollow side of the blade facing up, carve the marked areas. Work slowly and begin with shallow cuts. Use a cutter with a V-shaped attachment to outline the design and add intricate details. Switch to a U-shaped attachment to carve out larger areas. As you carve with one hand, use your other hand as a guide, keeping it clear of the blade's path.

3. PRINT With a small bristled paintbrush, apply fabric paint to coat the uncarved surface of the block. Paint with uniform strokes: brushstrokes will be visible on fabric and add interest to the design. If paint pools in crevices, soak up excess with the corner of a paper towel. Practice printing on scrap paper first, then print on fabric. Apply fresh paint each time you use the block. If using a new paint color, clean block first with a damp cloth and, if necessary, a mild, alcohol-free detergent. Let dry, about 15 minutes. Set paint with an iron, according to paint manufacturer's instructions. Machine-wash and -dry, provided the fabric allows.

how to stencil fabric

There are as many ways to integrate stenciling into your sewing and fabric craft projects as there are sources of inspiration. Natural sponges are excellent tools for controlling the amount of pigment applied. Dab the paint-filled sponges lightly with vertical pressure; this will prevent paint from bleeding under the edges of the stencil, which can result in a blurred effect.

1

2

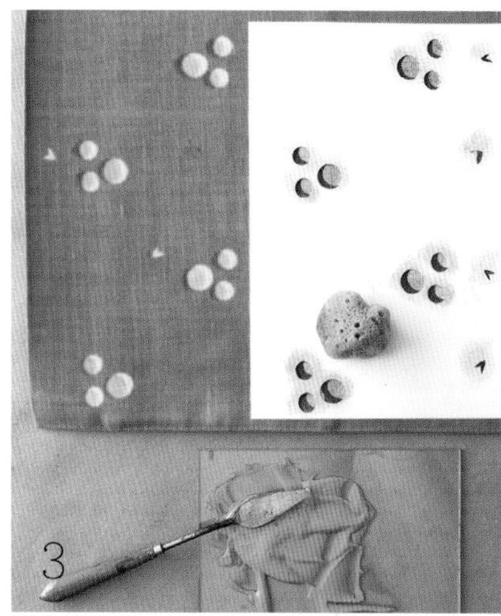
3

1. CREATE STENCIL Tape a template to a sheet of waterproof paper; secure with drafting tape to a self-healing cutting mat. (Pictured above are linen pillow covers stenciled with a series of superimposed dots in white and bluish pink, as well as black leaves; the finished pillows are shown on page 305.) Cut out template designs; here a craft knife is used for leaves and V shapes, and a Japanese hole punch (with attachments for different-size perforations) to punch graduated dots. Remove template and discard; the waterproof paper will serve as the stencil.

2. STENCIL OPAQUE PATTERNS Cover a work surface with kraft paper, and tape the fabric on top. Lay the stencil on the area of the fabric you wish to embellish. Secure with tape. Add fabric paint to your palette. If you wish to mix colors to create a custom shade, do so on the palette. With a clean natural sea sponge, dab the paint inside the stencil. In general, it's best to work left to right and top to bottom. Let dry about 3 minutes. Repeat on other areas of fabric, as desired. Here, white dots were first stenciled, and allowed to dry, then the fabric was stenciled with a design of black leaves and graduated dots. Once you finish stenciling, set paint with an iron, according to paint manufacturer's instructions.

3. STENCIL TRANSLUCENT PATTERNS To give designs a semitransparent, layered effect, fabric paint can be diluted with colorless extender. Here, soft pink dots are stenciled over opaque white ones. (For this look, mix 1 part pink paint—with just a touch of orange for vibrancy—with 3 parts colorless extender on the palette.) If printing over other stenciled designs, align the stencil over the design, then shift slightly for an off-register look. Use a new sponge to apply paint over stencil. Let dry 3 minutes. Shift stencil, and repeat until pattern is complete. Set paint with an iron, according to paint manufacturer's instructions. Machine-wash and air-dry.

PROJECTS

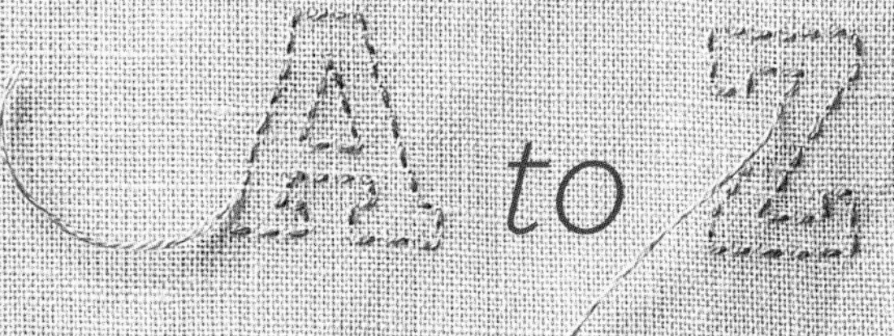

PROJECT:
animals

Handmade stuffed animals are a welcome change from the world of mass-produced toys and novelties. Big on personality—but small on materials—these weekend-friendly sewing projects are quick and fun to put together. Try your hand at a pair of adorable bunnies constructed from menswear fabrics or one-of-a-kind creatures inspired by kids' drawings. Or give new life to castoff clothes: near-forgotten sweaters can be machine-felted and cut up to create fuzzy farm animals, and stray socks are easy to turn into winsome dogs of any breed.

Equally at home in a stroller, on bunk beds, or at sleepaway camp, these cuddly critters make super gifts for someone special. Think they will be difficult to sew? Think again. Many of these projects are simple enough for kids to create. And all of them look decidedly more charming for any quirky imperfections. So heed the instructions that follow—but feel free to bend the rules a bit. Exaggerate facial features. Mix fabrics with abandon. And most of all, let whimsy be your muse.

IN THIS CHAPTER: MENSWEAR BUNNY — FELTED-WOOL ANIMALS — HAND-DRAWN STUFFED CREATURES — SOCK DOGS

MENSWEAR BUNNY (OPPOSITE): *A darling pair of stuffed bunnies is crafted from wool flannel in traditional menswear pinstripe and herringbone patterns; their ears are lined with coordinating cotton shirting. Each eye and nose is easily sewn with a few strands of embroidery floss and a single stitch.*

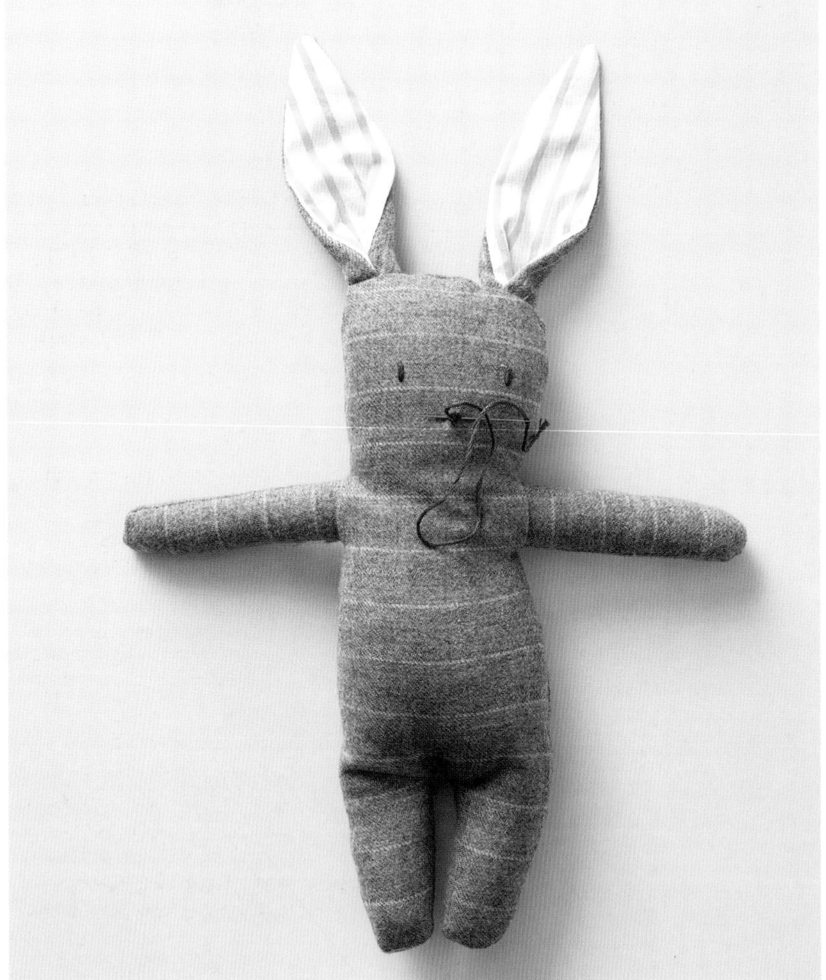

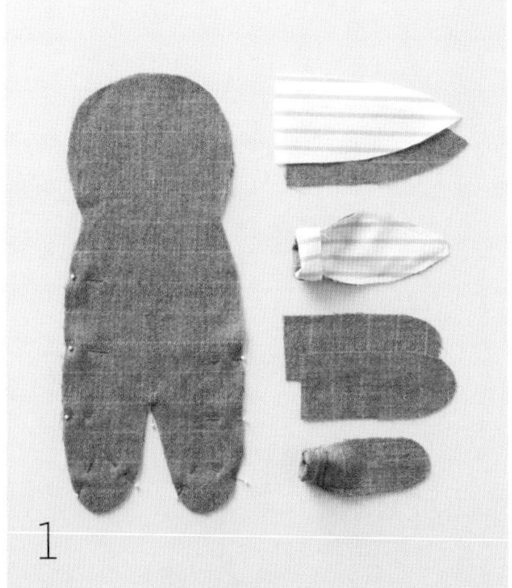
1

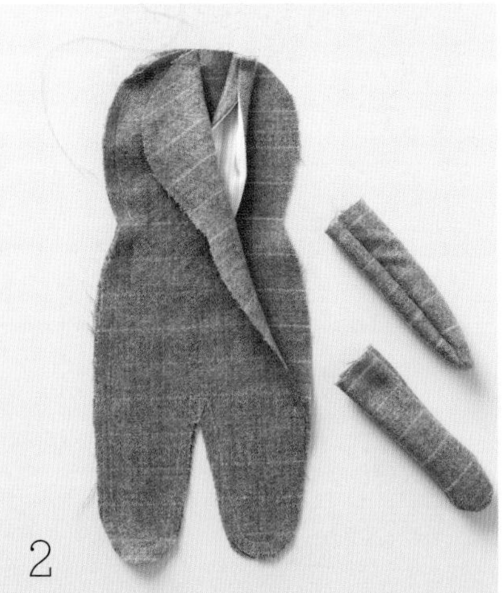
2

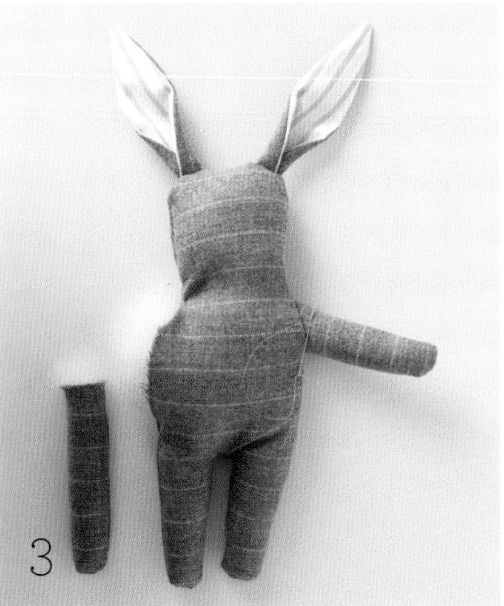
3

menswear bunny SEE PHOTO, PAGE 93

Old-fashioned suiting fabrics are an unconventional but charming choice for making sweet toy bunnies; bright cotton shirting adds a surprising pop of color inside the ears.

MATERIALS basic sewing supplies; menswear bunny pattern; menswear fabrics, such as wool flannel and cotton shirting; fill; embroidery floss; embroidery needle

HOW-TO 1. Print pattern pieces (see enclosed CD), and cut out. From wool flannel, cut out 2 body pieces, 4 arm pieces, and 2 ear pieces. Cut 2 more ear pieces from cotton shirting. Pin 2 arm pieces together, right sides facing; stitch with a ¼-inch (6mm) seam allowance, leaving base open. Repeat for remaining 2 arm pieces, and for ear pieces, using one wool piece and one shirting piece for each ear and leaving base open. Turn arms and ears right-side out. Press so edges lay flat. Pin body pieces together, right sides facing, below the neckline, leaving a 1-inch (2.5cm) opening on one side and a 2-inch (5cm) opening on the other, for arms.

2. Sew lower portion of body (below neckline) with a ¼-inch (6mm) seam allowance. With scissors, notch area where legs meet. Fold base of ears in so edges overlap slightly, and pin in place between body pieces. Pin and sew around head.

3. Turn body right-side out. Stuff body and arms with fill. Hand-sew arms to body and slipstitch to close larger opening.

4. Mark placement of eyes and nose with pins; create each feature with embroidery floss and a single running stitch (see above).

felted-wool animals

If your favorite wool sweater gets a hole or shrinks in the wash, machine-felt it, then stitch it into a stuffed barnyard animal or two. See page 96 for machine-felting how-to; turn the page for instructions on making the pig and chicken.

FELTED LAMB

A fuzzy Fair Isle lamb makes a great gift for a baby or young child.

MATERIALS basic sewing supplies, felted lamb pattern, machine-felted wool sweater(s), fill

HOW-TO 1. Print pattern pieces (see enclosed CD), and cut out. Cut out the underbelly piece from felted wool. To make the legs stand up, fold back at solid lines, and stitch at dotted lines. Cut out a side piece; flip the template, and cut out another side piece (a mirror image). With right sides facing and a ⅛-inch (3mm) seam allowance, stitch one side to underbelly along lower portion, from neck to tail, curving underbelly piece to fit. Stitch the other side piece to the other edge of the underbelly, sandwiching the underbelly between the side pieces. Cut out 2 tail pieces; stitch, right sides facing, leaving the base open. Turn the tail inside out and stuff with fill.

2. Sew a dart at the mouth. Pin the tail, facing inward, between the side pieces. Sew the side pieces along the top portion of the lamb, leaving a gap at the back and at the top of the head. Cut out 4 ear pieces and the head piece. Sew together 2 sets of ear pieces, right sides facing, leaving the base of each open; turn right-side out. Cover the head: Pin one ear to the head piece, with the pointed end facing forward between the layers of the head. Starting in front, sew around the top of the head, stopping when you get to the back. Pin on the other ear, and continue sewing around the head. Turn lamb right-side out. Pull fill into small pieces to prevent lumps from forming, and stuff lamb. Slipstitch the back opening closed. Steam-iron the finished animal to refine its shape and loosen the fill.

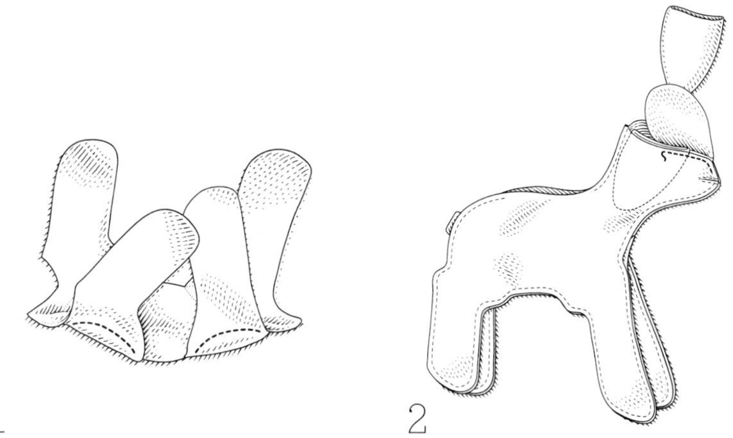

FELTED CHICKEN

Transform any old sweater into a delightfully plump little hen; the one shown on page 95 was stitched from a machine-felted cable-knit sweater. You should be able to make two hens from one small sweater; a larger garment will accommodate more animals.

MATERIALS basic sewing supplies, felted chicken pattern, machine-felted wool sweater(s) (see below right), dried beans, fill

HOW-TO 1. Print the pattern pieces (see enclosed CD), and cut out. Cut out a side piece from felted wool; flip the pattern, and cut out another side piece that's a mirror image of the first. Cut out the underbelly piece. With right sides facing and a 1/8-inch (3mm) seam allowance, stitch one side to the underbelly along the lower side portion, from the neck to the tail, curving the underbelly piece to fit.

2. Stitch the other side piece to the other edge of the underbelly piece, sandwiching the underbelly between the 2 side pieces. Cut out the wattle and the comb pieces.

3. Pin the wattle and the comb, facing inward, between layers of the head and neck. Stitch around the top, leaving an opening for the fill.

4. Turn the chicken right-side out. Cut out 4 wings from felted wool. With right sides facing, stitch 2 wings together, leaving a small opening at the top. Turn right-side out; hand-stitch the opening closed, then hand-stitch to the body. Repeat for the other wing. Make a small sack from a sweater scrap; sew a handful of dried beans inside. Place the sack in the bottom of the chicken to weight and balance it. Pull fill into small pieces to prevent lumps, and stuff the chicken. Slipstitch the opening closed. Steam-iron the finished animal to refine its shape and loosen the fill.

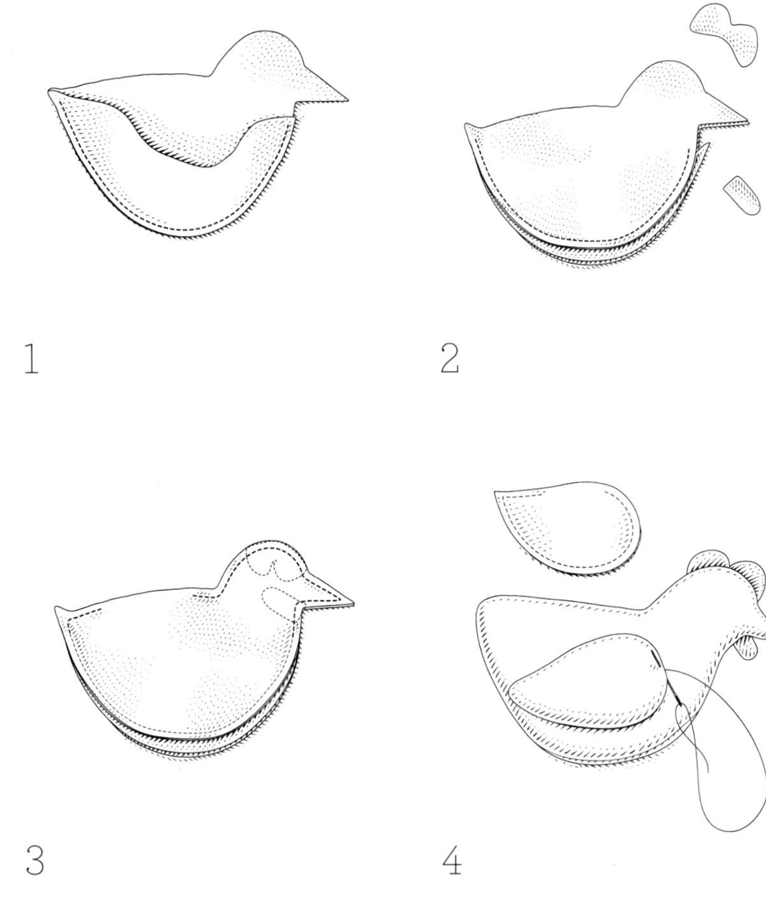

ABOUT MACHINE FELTING

When wool is machine-washed in hot water and then machine-dried, the fibers pull together to produce soft, thick felt. A machine-felted sweater becomes a wonderful crafting medium; use your own worn sweaters or find castaways at thrift shops. To begin, machine-wash a wool garment in hot water, and toss it in a dryer set to a high temperature. To prevent damage to your washer and dryer, place the garment in a lingerie bag. (You may need to wash and dry it more than once.) Once you can snip the fabric with scissors and it doesn't fray, it's felted. If the sweater has a pattern, incorporate it into your project.

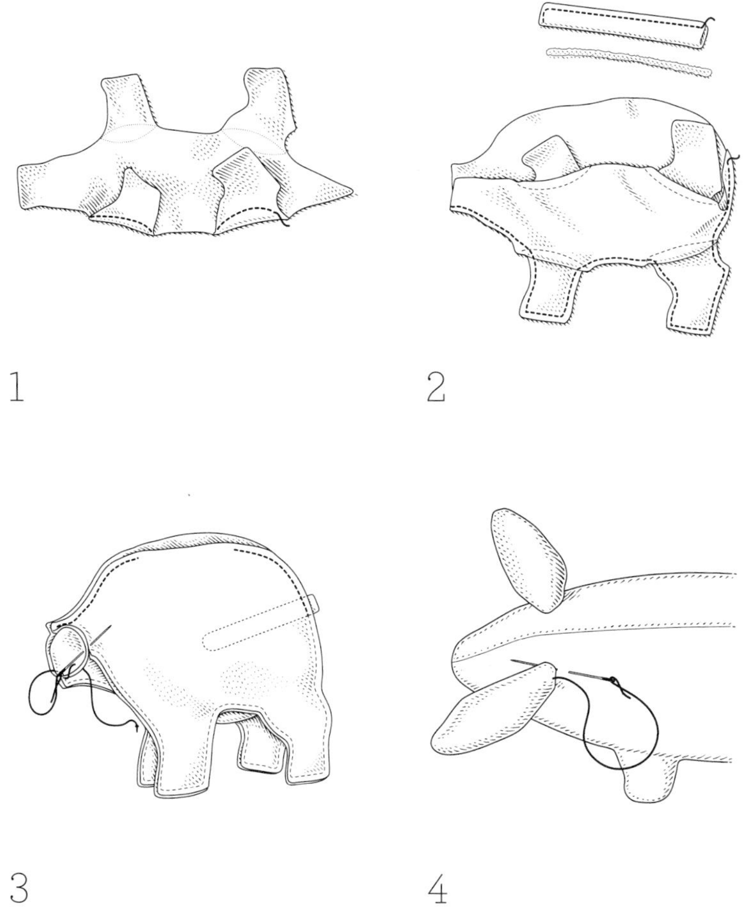

ABOUT FILL

A stuffed animal is incomplete without a plump, cuddly body. You'll find fill for animals (and other stuffed projects, such as pillows) at crafts and fabric stores, as well as from online retailers. The most common type is polyester fill, which is inexpensive and machine-washable. If you prefer natural materials, look for cotton or wool fill. Cotton is firmer than polyester fill, and is also machine-washable; wool fill is especially good for making children's toys, as it is naturally warm, flame-retardant, and antibacterial. Hand-wash animals made with wool fill in cold water, then air-dry.

FELTED PIG

The red-and-gray argyle pig pictured on page 95 is sure to stand out from any herd. A pipe cleaner is used to shape its distinctive curlicue tail.

MATERIALS basic sewing supplies, felted pig pattern, machine-felted wool sweater(s) (see box, opposite), pipe cleaner, fill, pencil

HOW-TO 1. Print the pattern pieces (see enclosed CD), and cut out. Cut out the underbelly piece from felted wool. To make the legs stand up, fold them back at the solid lines, and stitch at the dotted lines.

2. Cut out a side piece; flip the template, and cut another side piece that's the mirror image of the first. With right sides facing and a ⅛-inch (3mm) seam allowance, stitch one side to the underbelly along the lower portion, from snout to tail, curving the underbelly piece to fit. Stitch the other side piece to the other edge of the underbelly, sandwiching the underbelly between the 2 side pieces. Cut out the tail; fold lengthwise, and, with right sides facing, stitch down one side and across one end. Turn right-side out. Place a pipe cleaner inside the tail; stitch the open end closed.

3. Pin the tail, facing inward, between the 2 side pieces. Sew along the top portion of the pig, leaving openings at the snout and at the back. Cut out the nose piece, and hand-stitch it to the snout, right sides facing.

4. Turn the pig right-side out. Pull fill into small pieces to prevent lumps from forming, and stuff the pig. Slipstitch the back closed. Cut out 4 ear pieces. Sew together 2 sets of ear pieces, right sides facing, leaving an opening at the base of each one; turn right-side out and stitch the holes closed. Fold the base of each ear in half, and tack to secure. Hand-stitch the ears to the head. Twist the tail around a pencil to make a curl. Steam-iron the finished animal to refine its shape and loosen the fill.

hand-drawn stuffed creatures

Any character—real or imaginary—that can be drawn on paper can be made into a stuffed toy. Children especially love making 3-D versions of their artwork. An adult can sew a creature based on a toddler's sketch; an older kid can draw and hand-sew all by himself. This project makes great use of fabric scraps.

MATERIALS basic sewing supplies; paper; pen or pencil; an assortment of cotton and felt fabrics; fill; pipe cleaners, yarn, ribbon, and buttons (optional)

HOW-TO Sketch a creature; photocopy it to make it larger or smaller. Cut out only the parts that will be stuffed; ears and limbs can be made from other material and sewn on, if desired. Pin the pattern, facedown, to two pieces of fabric. Trace with a fabric pencil, adding 1/4 inch (6mm) all the way around for the seam allowance; cut out both layers. Unpin pattern. Sew features to one piece of fabric (this will be the front). Repin the fabric pieces together with features on the inside. Hand- or machine-sew the pieces together, using a 1/4-inch (6mm) seam allowance and leaving an opening for fill. Turn right-side out. Stuff with fill. Hand-sew closed. Finish by adding ears, limbs, or other details using felt, pipe cleaners, yarn, ribbon, or buttons.

SOCK DOGS

for instructions, turn the page

sock dogs

It only takes an afternoon and some basic sewing supplies to turn a pair of stray socks into a friendly canine. Different types of socks suggest different breeds: Brown knee socks become a Dachshund; a polka-dotted pair is naturally transformed into a Dalmatian. A few adjustments can change your puppy's features: Experiment with shorter legs, longer tails, or floppy ears. Pipe cleaners will help ears or a tail stand up. To make your dog sit, fold the hind legs forward and stitch them to the underside of the body.

MATERIALS basic sewing supplies, socks, fill, pipe cleaners (optional), buttons

HOW-TO 1. Turn one sock inside out. The ankle will become the back legs. Cut off the cuff: The more you cut off, the shorter the legs will be.

2. Flatten the sock, with the heel on top. Cut the ankle in half from the edge to the heel. Stitch the open sides to make the back legs, leaving a small opening near the heel for fill.

3. Turn the sock right-side out, and add fill. Stretch and shape as you stuff to form the body and legs.

4. Bend the neck back, and stitch the fold in place. Sew the feet shut; bend the paws and stitch the folds in place. Sew the fill opening shut from side to side.

5. Cut the second sock into five sections, following the diagram. Adjust the lines as desired to make the ears, legs, and tail longer or shorter.

6. Slip the head piece over the neck, and sew it in place. Pull fill into small pieces to prevent lumps from forming, and stuff the dog through the opening at the nose.

7. Sew snout shut: Turn edges in, making a curve, and stitch.

8. Flatten out the ear piece, and cut, following the diagram. Turn each ear inside out and stitch, leaving the bottom open. Turn each ear right-side out, stitch it shut, and sew it to the head.

9. Turn each leg piece inside out and stitch, leaving the bottom open. Turn each one right-side out, stuff, and sew it shut. Sew the front legs to the body. Bend the front paws and stitch the folds in place.

10. Turn the tail piece inside out and stitch the sides, leaving the bottom open. Turn it right-side out and stuff, or insert a pipe cleaner to make a tail that stands up straight. Stitch it to the backside.

11. Buttons with two holes are perfect for eyes; sew on using a different color thread for the pupils. Use a shank button or a button with two big holes for a nose.

BULLDOG VARIATION

(PAGE 99, TOP RIGHT)

Sew the head piece, with toe still attached, to the body with the heel in front; the heel will be the snout, and the toe will become the ears. Cut around edge of toe to make an ear shape: You should have two pointed ears attached to the head. Stuff the head, adding extra fill for the jowls. Stitch shut around the ears. Push the snout in and stitch the center fold in place. Finish the dog as described at left.

DACHSHUND VARIATION

(PAGE 99, BOTTOM LEFT)

Because its long body is cut from the leg of a knee sock, a Dachshund is cut differently through step 4: First, trim off the sock's cuff. Cut off the toe end at about the middle of the sock's foot. The remaining foot will become the hind legs. Cut the foot in half, stopping at the base of the heel; sew the open sides to make the legs. Stuff the body through the opening. Make the head as described in step 5, at left. In step 6, slip the head over the open edge of the body and stitch. Finish the dog as described. To make floppy ears, cut two long ovals from a sock toe. Fold each ear in half, right sides together. Stitch, leaving the bottom open. Turn right-side out, stitch shut, and sew the ears to the head. Finish the dog as described at left.

DALMATIAN EAR VARIATION

(PAGE 99, TOP LEFT)

Cut off sock toe, and cut in half; stitch together along straight edge (leave bottom edge open). Sew ears to head. Finish the dog as described.

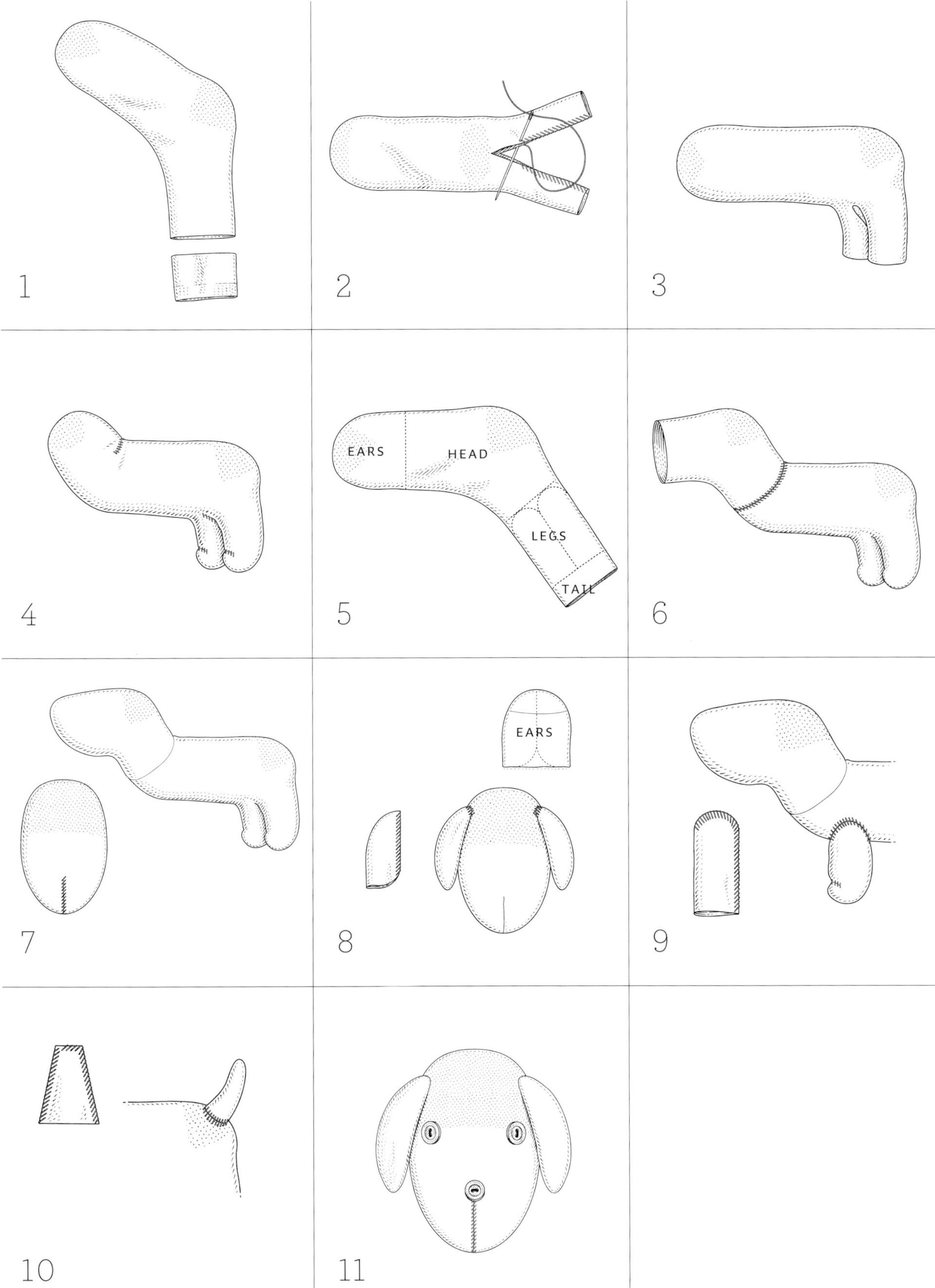
1
2
3
4
EARS
HEAD
LEGS
TAIL
5
6
7
EARS
8
9
10
11

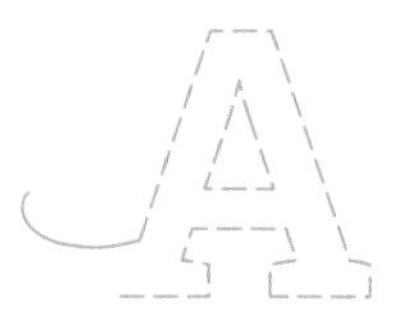

PROJECT:

aprons

Aprons whip up stitchity-quick, leaving you plenty of time for all sorts of creative pursuits. Most of the aprons that follow were designed with practical pockets to hold essential tools and materials, such as wooden spoons, seeds and spades, or paintbrushes. And they all rely on simple lines and basic construction, so you don't need a lot of experience to make one.

The basic linen apron shown on the opposite page makes a great first project. Its form is deliberately foolproof, and allows for easy embellishments; consider adding an embroidered or appliquéd initial or other shape. Actually, you can adapt any of the aprons in this chapter as you please, adding (or removing) pockets or sewing in loops to accommodate an adjustable tie.

For fabrics, look to washable favorites, such as sturdy canvas or cotton, or wipe-clean options, like oilcloth. Or consider starting with a proven kitchen taskmaster, a dish towel. Make one for a seasoned gardener, a junior cook, a crafter, or yourself—the endlessly adaptable apron is always ready to serve.

IN THIS CHAPTER BASIC LINEN APRON — CRAFTER'S APRON — CHILD'S OILCLOTH APRON — DISH-TOWEL APRON — ADJUSTABLE APRON — BAKER'S APRON — FAUX-BOIS GARDENER'S APRON

BASIC LINEN APRON (OPPOSITE): *A pocketed apron makes a handy cover-up in the kitchen, but this design can easily be adapted for crafting, gardening, or even woodworking.*

basic linen apron SEE PHOTO, PAGE 103

The instructions here are for a calf-length apron, but you can customize it by cutting the pattern shorter or longer.

MATERIALS basic sewing supplies, basic linen apron pattern, clear tape, 2 yards (1.8m) medium-weight fabric (such as linen, cotton, or denim)

HOW-TO 1. Wash, dry, and press the fabric. Print the pattern pieces (see enclosed CD), tape together, and cut out. Fold the fabric, right sides facing, and pin the pattern pieces to it; cut out.

2. Unfold the apron piece, and sew double hems to finish the armhole edges: Fold over 1/4 inch (6mm), press, fold over again 1/4 inch (6mm), press, and edge-stitch. Finish the sides with double hems: Fold each side over 1/2 inch (13mm), press, fold over again 1/2 inch (13mm), press, and edge-stitch.

3. Double hem the top edge of the apron: Fold the edge over 1/2 inch (13mm), press, fold over 1 inch (2.5cm), press, and edge-stitch.

4. To make the ties, cut two 2-by-27-inch (5cm X 68.5cm) strips for the neck straps, and two 3-by-32-inch (7.5cm X 81cm) strips for the waist straps. Fold over and press 1/4 inch (6mm) on the short ends of each strap piece. Fold long edge in 1/2 inch (13mm) and press (figure a); repeat on other long edge. Fold the strips in half lengthwise and edge-stitch 1/8 inch (3mm) from the pressed edges. Pin the neck straps 1 inch (2.5cm) below the top corners of the back side of the apron, so that the ends of the straps align with the bottom edge of the top fold (figure b). Make a boxstitch to attach the straps to the apron. Make a boxstitch to attach the waist straps just below the curve on the back side of the apron, so that the ends of the straps align with the side folds (figure c).

5. Double hem the top of the pocket: Fold the top edge 1/2 inch (13mm), press, fold 1/2 inch (13mm), press, and edge-stitch (reversing the stitch at both ends to secure). Fold and press the sides and the bottom of the pocket 1/2 inch (13mm), and pin them onto the apron. Edge-stitch the sides and the bottom onto the apron, leaving the top edge open. Reinforce the upper and lower corners with reverse stitches. Measure and mark a line down the center of the pocket with tailor's chalk or a disappearing-ink fabric pen. Stitch along the line to create 2 compartments.

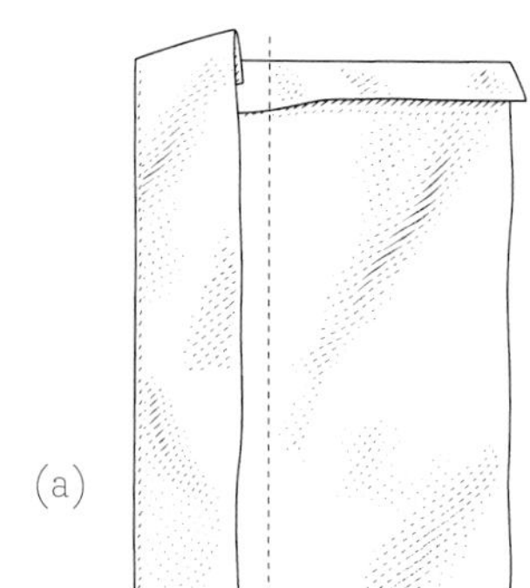

(a)

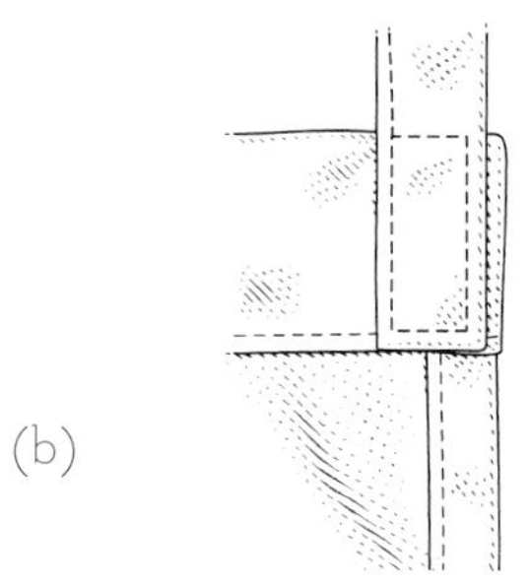

(b)

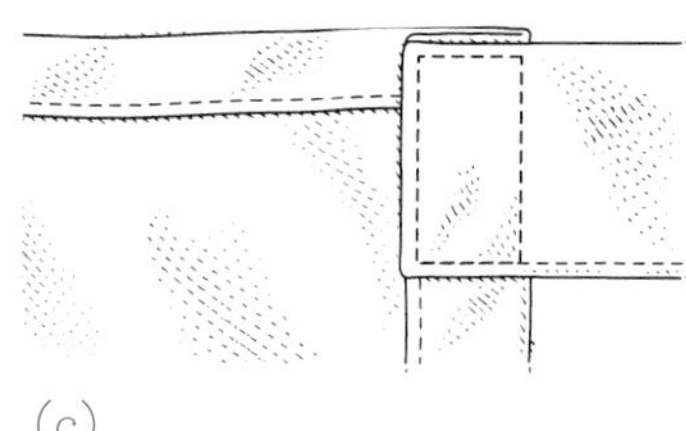

(c)

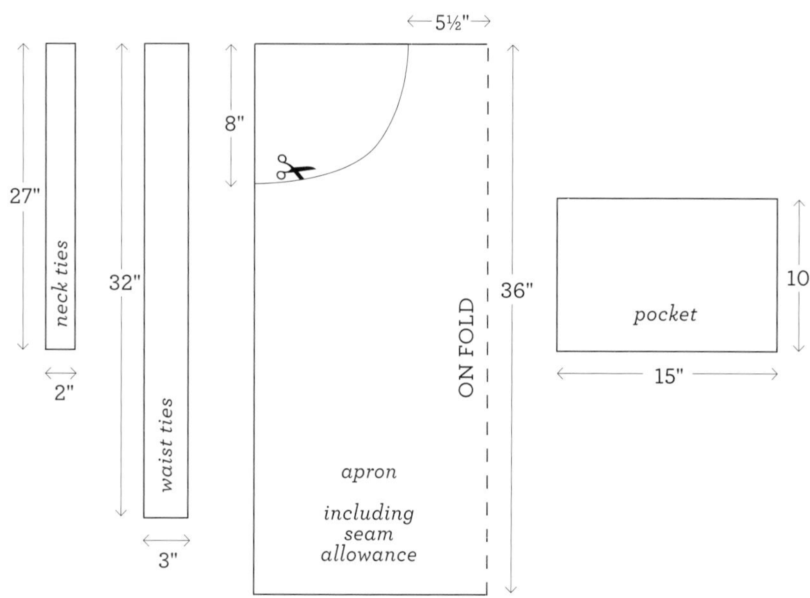

TIP

Customize aprons to fit your style by adding colored twill tape for straps, using a different fabric for the pocket, or appliqué-ing a motif onto the front.

crafter's apron

A series of pleated pockets on a half apron gives a little more room for the myriad supplies needed by dedicated crafters, including Megen Lee, design director of Martha Stewart Living Omnimedia's crafts merchandising team.

MATERIALS basic sewing supplies, crafter's apron and pocket patterns, clear tape, 1/2 yard (45.5cm) 50-inch-wide (127cm) canvas, 1 2/3 yards (1.5m) 5/8-inch (16mm) bias tape, loop turner

HOW-TO 1. Wash and dry the fabric. Print the pattern pieces (see enclosed CD), tape together, and cut out. Pin the pattern pieces to the canvas, and cut out. Use a disappearing-ink fabric pen to transfer the stitch and pleat lines from the pocket pattern to the fabric. Pin 1/4-inch (6mm) pleats, and sew along the bottom of the pocket piece. Sew a double hem to finish the top of the pocket: Fold over 3/4 inch (2cm), press, fold over again 3/4 inch (2cm), press and edge-stitch 1/8 inch (3mm) from the bottom fold. Sew pocket to apron; add compartments by sewing along the pen lines. Slip bias tape over the outer edge of the apron; stitch 1/8 inch (3mm) in from the tape's edge, making sure the needle passes through the underside of the tape. Continue to trim apron with bias tape.

2. Make the waist straps: Cut two 2½-by-34-inch (6.5cm × 86cm) strips of canvas. Fold the strips in half lengthwise, right sides facing. Sew a 1/4-inch (6mm) seam along the long, open edge and one short edge of each strip. Turn the pieces right-side out with a loop turner. To finish strips, tuck 1/4 inch (6mm) of the unfinished end into the strip; hand-stitch closed. Place each waist strap just below the top trim, so that it overlaps apron by 2 inches (5cm). To secure, topstitch the strap where it overlaps the apron to create a boxstitch (see opposite, figure b).

child's oilcloth apron

A simple, functional apron is an essential kitchen uniform for even the youngest home cook. This one is made of oilcloth, which is widely available in bright, cheerful patterns. Because the material is water-resistant, any spills or spatters are easy to wipe off.

MATERIALS basic sewing supplies, ¾ yard (68.5cm) oilcloth (or other sturdy fabric, such as denim or canvas), about 3 yards (2.75m) bias tape

HOW-TO 1. For the main apron piece, fold the oilcloth so that right sides are facing and cut a 23-by-11-inch (58.5cm × 28cm) rectangle against the fold (the full rectangle will measure 23 by 22 inches [58.5cm × 56cm]). On the long side of the fabric, use tailor's chalk to mark 12 inches (30.5cm) from the bottom edge and 5 inches (12.5cm) from the top short edge. Draw a curve between the 2 lines and cut as shown below.

2. To create the pocket, fold the remaining fabric so that the right sides are facing. Cut a 13-by-11-inch (33cm × 28cm) rectangle against the fold (the full rectangle will measure 13 by 22 inches [33cm × 56cm]). Make a 1-inch (2.5cm) hem at the top of the pocket panel; sew the sides and the bottom of the pocket to the apron, with a ¼-inch (6mm) seam allowance.

3. Make compartments by machine-stitching down the front of the pocket panel, about one-third of the way in from each side.

4. Sew a 1½-inch (3.8cm) hem at the top of the apron. Trim the curved edges of the apron with bias tape; first pin the tape to each edge, leaving about 12 inches (30.5cm) extra at the top of each side for the neck ties and about 24 inches (61cm) at the bottom for the waist ties; zigzag-stitch over the entire length of the tape.

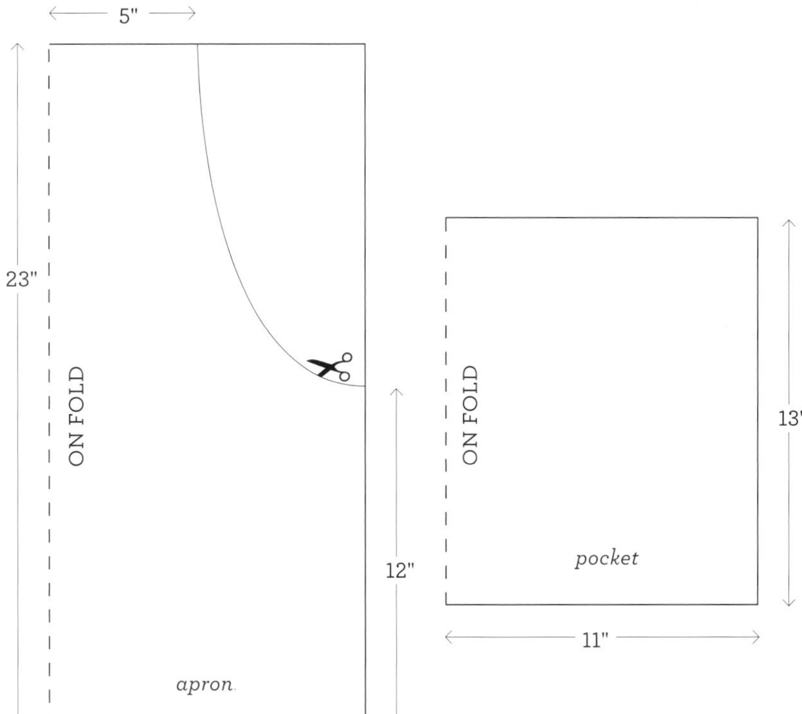

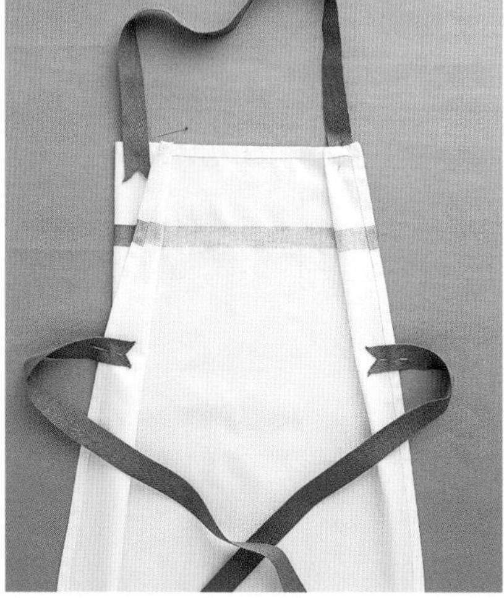

dish-towel apron

Fashion an easy, patternless apron in minutes with just a dish towel and some wide twill tape. No hemming is required, so this project is particularly well suited to someone just learning to sew.

MATERIALS basic sewing supplies, 16-by-24-inch (40.5cm × 61cm) dish towel, about 2 yards (1.8m) 25mm-wide twill tape

HOW-TO Cut 3 pieces of twill tape (one 20 inches [51cm] long for the neck loop; two 24 inches [61cm] long for the waist ties); notch the ends of each. Fold in the right and left sides of the towel 3 inches (7.5cm). Put each end of the neck loop 1/4 inch (6mm) from a folded edge. Fold the excess fabric back over the ends; pin in place. Pin one end of each waist tie to each long side, 9 inches (23cm) from the top. Stitch over the tape ends.

adjustable apron

This one-size-fits-all apron cinches at the waist and neck to fit anyone. You can either remove the existing ties from a standard store-bought apron, as shown, or customize a handmade one, such as the Basic Linen Apron on page 104.

MATERIALS basic sewing supplies, apron, 4 yards (3.6m) 1-inch-wide (2.5cm) cotton twill tape

HOW-TO Cut off the neck strap from the apron. Cut ten 2 1/2-inch (6.5cm) pieces of twill tape for the loops; make a 1/4-inch (6mm) hem at both ends by folding the fabric under and pressing. Pin five evenly spaced pieces to each side of the apron's back, about 1/8 inch (3mm) from the edge. Machine-sew the short ends in place. To make the strap, sew a double 1/4-inch (6mm) hem at each end of the remainder of the twill tape; feed the tape through the loops.

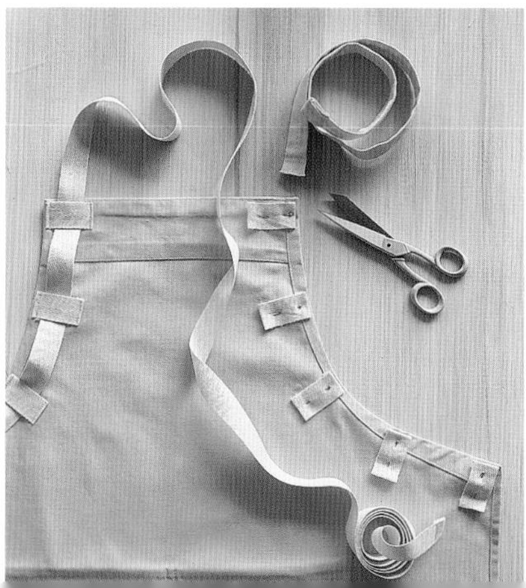

baker's apron

This striped apron is cut extra long to create a deep pocket by folding the fabric up and stitching it in place under the waist ties. It was originally designed for Sarah Carey, food editor at *Martha Stewart Living* and an avid baker.

MATERIALS basic sewing supplies, baker's apron pattern, clear tape, 2 yards (1.8m) heavy cotton fabric (such as canvas), loop turner, two 1-inch (2.5cm) D-rings, zipper foot

HOW-TO 1. Print the pattern pieces (see enclosed CD), tape together, and cut out. Pin the pattern pieces to the fabric, and cut them out.

2. With a disappearing-ink fabric pen, mark 2 lines parallel to the bottom edge, as indicated by the notches on the pattern (one 20 ¼ inches [51.5cm] from the bottom, the other 16 inches [40.5cm] above the first). Fold the apron so the marked lines meet, creating a pocket. Press.

3. Use the disappearing-ink fabric pen to mark 2 vertical lines 10 ⅝ inches (27cm) in from each side. Sew to the left and right of each line (about ⅛ inch [3mm] apart) to create compartments.

4. Make a double hem on all edges of the apron except the bottom: Fold the edges over ¼ inch (6mm), press, fold over again ¼ inch (6mm), press, and edge-stitch ⅛ inch (3mm) from the folded edge. Make a double hem along the bottom: Fold the hem up 2 inches (5cm), press, fold up again 2 inches (5cm), press, and edge-stitch ⅛ inch (3mm) from the top edge.

5. To make the neck and waist straps, cut four 2 ½-inch-wide (6.5cm) strips from the fabric: one 10 inches (25.5cm) long (for the neck D-ring strap), one 33 ½ inches (85cm) long (for the long neck strap), and two 34 inches (86cm) long (for the waist straps). Fold strips in half lengthwise, with right sides facing. Sew a ¼-inch (6mm) seam along the long open edge and one short edge of each strap. Turn all the pieces right-side out with a loop turner. To finish the straps, tuck ¼ inch (6mm) of the unfinished ends into the strips; hand-stitch closed. Thread two D-rings on the neck D-ring strap. Fold the strap in half, so that the D-rings are centered. Using a zipper foot, sew the strap just below the D-rings to secure. Sandwich the top of the apron between 2 sides of the neck D-ring strap, so that the strap overlaps the apron by 2 inches (5cm). To secure, make a boxstitch over the part of the strap that overlaps the apron (see page 116, figure b). Place the long neck strap parallel to the neck D-ring strap, an equal distance from the edge, so that it overlaps the apron by 2 inches. Make a boxstitch to secure. Measure and mark the placement of the waist straps on each side of the apron (make sure they are at an even height); pin them so that they overlap the apron by 2 inches (5cm). Make a boxstitch to secure the straps to the apron on each side.

faux-bois gardener's apron

Although this apron is made from oilcloth with a faux bois (wood grain) pattern, any oilcloth or other durable fabric, such as heavy canvas or denim, will do. The nature motif was inspired by Andrew Beckman, editorial director of gardening at *Martha Stewart Living*.

MATERIALS basic sewing supplies, faux-bois gardener's apron and pocket patterns, clear tape, 1 ½ yards (1.4m) oilcloth, 1 ½ yards (1.4m) cotton broadcloth, about 6 yards (5.5m) ¼-inch-wide (6mm) bias tape, ½ yard (45.5cm) canvas, masking tape, loop turner, four 1-inch (2.5cm) D-rings

HOW-TO 1. Print the pattern pieces (see enclosed CD), tape together, and cut out. Cut one main apron piece from the oilcloth and one from the cotton broadcloth for lining. Stack the apron and lining, wrong sides facing, and sew them together ⅛ inch (3mm) from the edge. Sandwich the apron edge with bias tape. Stitch ⅛ inch (3mm) in from the tape's edges, making sure the needle passes through all the layers (including the underside of the tape). Continue to attach the tape until all edges of the apron are covered.

2. Using the pocket pattern, cut a pocket piece from the canvas. With a disappearing-ink fabric pen, mark lines where each compartment (and any pleats for roomier pockets) will fall. Pin ¼-inch (6mm) pleats in place, and sew along the bottom. Attach bias tape to the bottom and sides of the pocket, as shown, and then add bias tape to the top of the pocket. Snip off any excess.

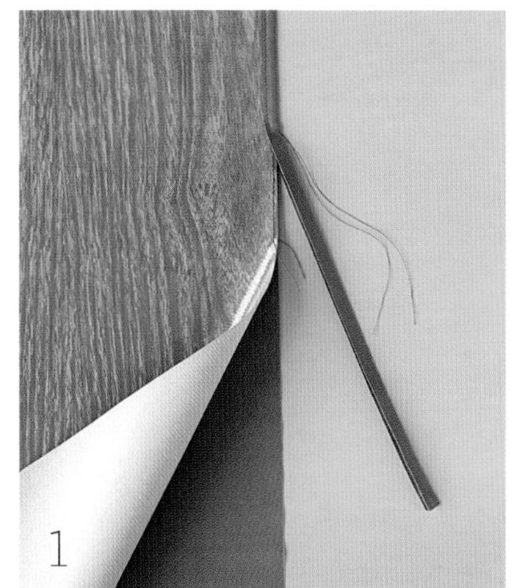

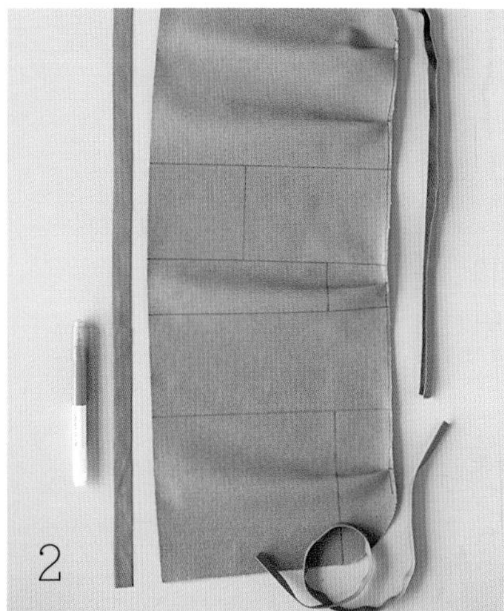

3. Use masking tape to position the pocket on the apron. Sew the sides and bottom of the pocket to the apron. Remove the tape as you work. Sew along the pen lines to create compartments.

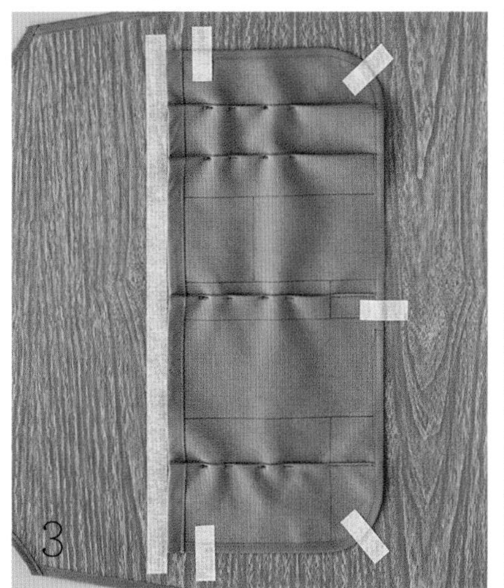

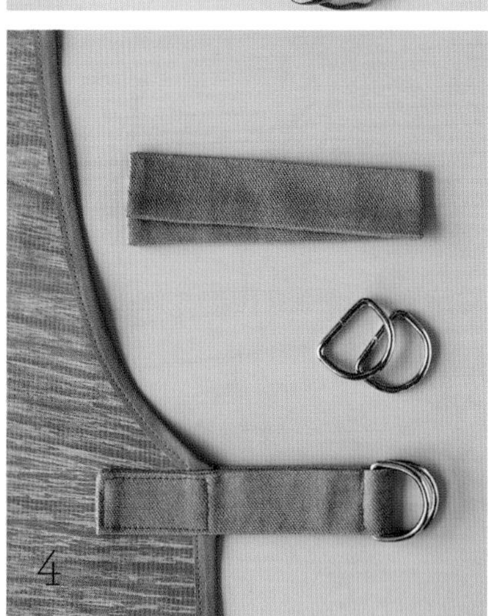

4. To make the straps and the belt loops, cut 2 ½-inch-wide (6.5cm) strips of canvas: one 8 ½ inches (21.5cm) long (for the waist D-ring strap), one 40 inches (101.5) long (for the long waist strap), one 10 inches (25.5cm) long (for the neck D-ring strap), one 33 ½ inches (85cm) long (for the long neck strap), and two 3 ½ inches (9cm) long (for the belt loops). Fold the strips in half lengthwise, right sides facing. Sew a ¼-inch (6mm) seam along the long open edge and one short edge of each strap; sew a ¼-inch (6mm) seam only along the long edge of the 2 belt loops. Turn all the pieces right-side out with a loop turner. To finish the straps, tuck ¼ inch (6mm) of the unfinished ends into the strips; hand-stitch closed. To finish the belt loops, fold the strips in half widthwise, and sew a ¼-inch (6mm) seam across the open ends to join. Turn the loops inside out, so that the sewn edges are on the inside. Attach the D-ring straps: Thread a pair of D-rings on the waist D-ring strap. Fold the strap in half, so that the D-rings are centered. Using a zipper foot, sew the strap just below the D-rings to secure. Sandwich the apron, as shown, between 2 sides of the waist D-ring strap, so that the strap overlaps the apron by 2 inches (5cm). Topstitch the part of the strap that overlaps the apron on 4 sides to create a box, as shown, to secure. Repeat to add the neck D-ring strap to the top of the apron. Place the long waist strap across from the waist D-ring strap, so it overlaps the apron by 2 inches (5cm). Sew to apron to secure, using a boxstitch as described above. Place the long neck strap parallel to the neck D-ring strap, an equal distance from the edge, so it overlaps the apron by 2 inches (5cm). Sew to apron to secure. Slide the belt loops onto long straps so the seams fall behind the straps.

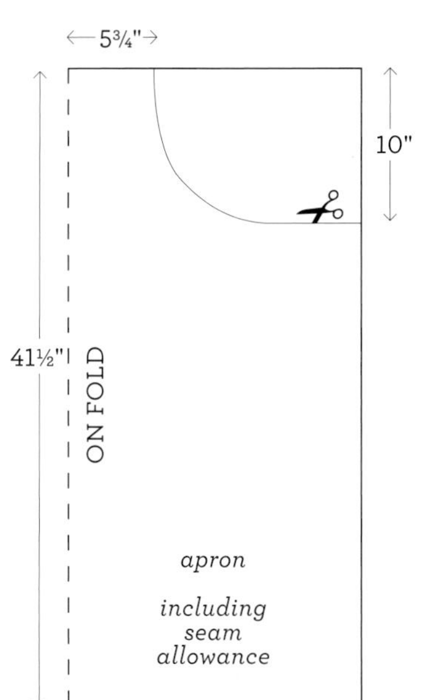

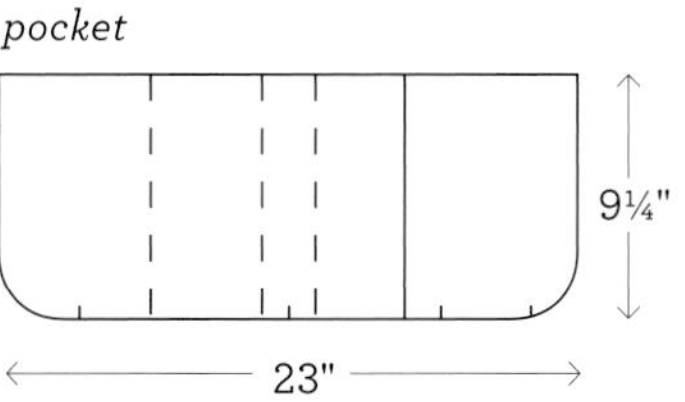

PROJECT:

bags

A tote bag's interior may be purely functional, but its exterior allows plenty of room for creative expression. Whether you begin with a bag that's handmade or store-bought, the possibilities are endless—feel free to add as much or as little pizzazz as you like to make it your own. Experiment with decorative details such as raffia embroidery, appliqué, or stamping. Or simply iron on labels or monograms that identify the bag's contents or its carrier. Roomy totes with multiple compartments are indispensable for trips to the market, library, and playground, so add pockets to the inside or outside—or both.

Looking for another good reason to create a new cloth bag? Because they're reusable, they're better for the environment than plastic bags from the grocery store. In short, carry on!

IN THIS CHAPTER: FABRIC-POCKET TOTE BAG — RAFFIA-EMBROIDERED TOTE — BASIC CANVAS TOTE — APPLIQUÉD SEA-PRINT TOTE — MINIATURE FELT PURSES — EMBROIDERED FELT HANDBAG — FOUR EMBELLISHED-BAG PROJECTS: IRON-ON SILHOUETTES; LABELS AND MONOGRAMS; EMBROIDERED CIRCLES; OMBRÉ — DRAWSTRING POUCHES — CROSS-STITCH SILHOUETTE TOTE — OILCLOTH LUNCH BAG — APPLE-PRINT BAG — PILLOWCASE BAG — MULTICOMPARTMENT BAG

FABRIC-POCKET TOTE BAG (OPPOSITE): *Multiple pockets—inside and out—can accommodate numerous small objects and bring order to a roomy tote. This one is embellished with patterned fabric and twill-tape handles.*

fabric-pocket tote bag

This store-bought canvas bag features dividers added with one clever trick: a row of pockets from a children's apron sewn inside. Additional roomy outer pockets, made from fabric pieces sewn to one side, provide quick access to necessities. Finally, the handles are spruced up, too, with replacement twill tape in a shade that coordinates with the outer fabric.

MATERIALS basic sewing supplies, 12 1/2-by-19-inch (32cm × 48.5cm) canvas tote bag, 1/2 yard (45.5cm) fabric for outside pocket, fabric glue (or pins), 1 1/4-inch-wide (3cm) twill tape or grosgrain ribbon, child's apron with pockets

HOW-TO 1. Remove the existing bag handles with a seam ripper. To make the outer pockets, cut 2 pieces of fabric 6 inches (15cm) narrower than the width of bag. Cut one of these pieces 2 inches (5cm) shorter than the height of the bag, and the other piece 5 inches (12.5cm) shorter. Fold over 1/4 inch (6mm) of each top edge; hem. Stack the small piece onto the large piece, aligning at bottom. Center on the bag; glue or pin in place. Machine-stitch along the bottom. For handles, cut 2 pieces of twill tape twice the height of the bag plus 20 inches (51cm). Attach with glue or pins, covering the sides of the pocket. Attach the other handle. Stitch along both sides of each tape. Reinforce the handles at the top and bottom of the bag.

2. Attach the inner pockets: Cut off the apron top and discard. Fold over the top edge by 1/4 inch (6mm). Glue or pin to the top edge of the bag on one long side; stitch into place.

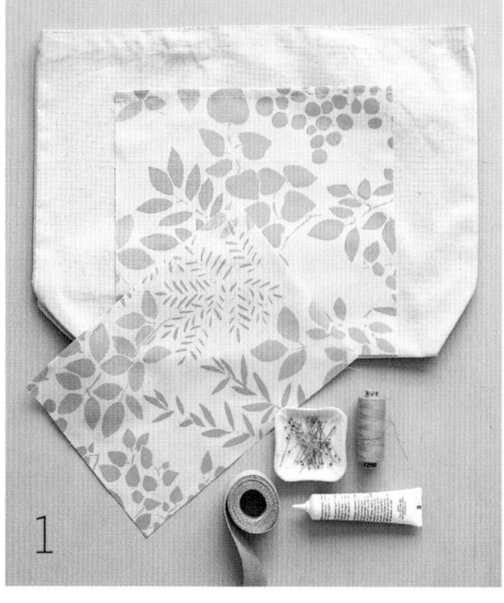

1

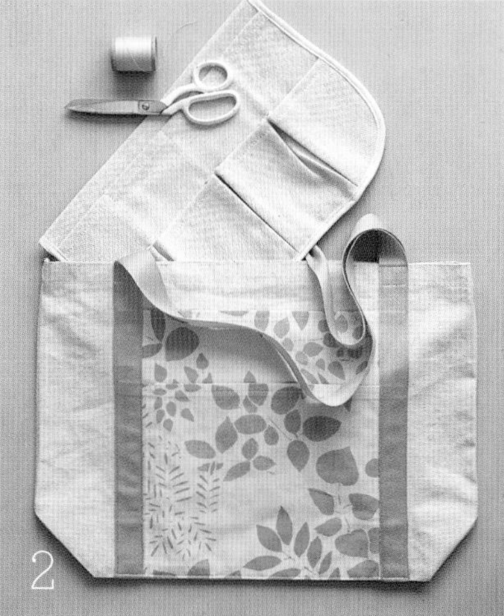

2

raffia-embroidered tote

Raffia is the leaf of *Raphia,* a genus of more than twenty palm trees that includes some of the largest specimens in existence. The threads are available at many crafts stores, as is synthetic raffia, which comes in a wide range of delightfully flashy hues. Here they deliver unexpected whimsy to a canvas tote bag. The hat pictured is embellished with colored-raffia pom-poms, attached with embroidery floss. The pom-poms are made with a 1 ½-inch (3.8cm) pom-pom maker; once formed, their centers are wrapped with floral wire that is twisted with pliers to secure, then trimmed to ½ inch (13mm).

MATERIALS basic sewing supplies, large canvas tote bag, compass (optional), tapestry needle, raffia in 3 shades

HOW-TO 1. Using a disappearing-ink fabric pen, draw circles on the tote, one for each sunburst (the ones shown are 1 ½ to 5 inches [3.8–12.5cm] in diameter; you can use a compass to make the circles, or trace round household objects such as biscuit cutters or drinking glasses).

2. Mark the center point of a circle (A) and one point anywhere along the circle's edge (B; see far left illustration). Thread a large-eyed needle with raffia in the desired color, knotting it before embroidering the design using a French-knots-on-stalks stitch: Draw the needle up through A, as shown in far left illustration. Wrap raffia around the needle 3 times. Holding the wrapped portion together, gently draw the needle down through B, forming a French knot (for more on the French knot, see page 52).

3. Repeat step 3, always coming up through A but moving B ¼ inch (6mm) over (see near left illustration), until the sunburst is complete.

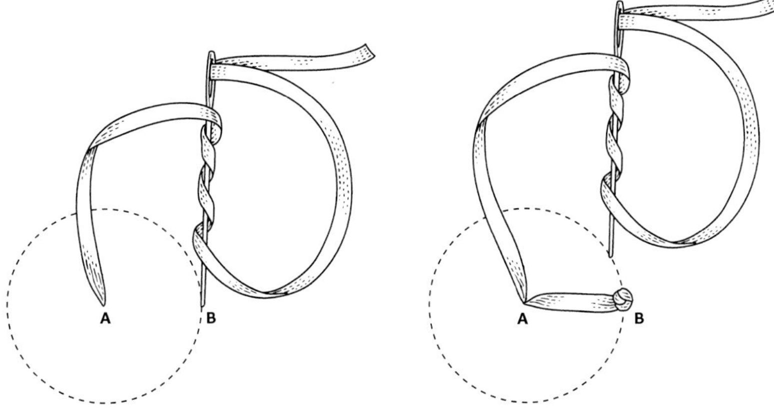

basic canvas tote

Many of the projects in this chapter involve customizing a store-bought canvas tote bag. Here are instructions for sewing a bag yourself.

MATERIALS basic sewing supplies; 1 yard (0.9m) medium-weight canvas (or linen or denim)

HOW-TO 1. Cut 2 pieces of canvas that measure 18 by 20 inches (45.5cm × 51cm) and 2 strips that measure 26 by 4 1/4 inches (66cm × 11cm). Fold one strip in half lengthwise; press. Open the strip, then fold each long side in toward the center to meet at the middle. Fold in half again lengthwise, and edge-stitch along each long side. Finish short ends with a zigzag stitch. Repeat with the other long strip.

2. Pin the two larger pieces of fabric together on the short sides and one long side. Sew pinned sides with a 1/2-inch (13mm) seam allowance. Press seams open, and finish with pinking shears or a zigzag stitch (page 36).

3. With the bag still inside out, open up one corner so that the bottom seam is aligned with the adjacent side seam. Pin along the seam to keep the alignment in place. Mark a point 2 1/2 inches (6.5cm) in from the corner point, then draw a line perpendicular to the seam at that point. Machine-stitch along the perpendicular line, then trim off the resulting corner with pinking shears 1/2 inch (13mm) from the perpendicular stitch (figure a). Repeat on the opposite corner.

4. Make a double hem at the top: Fold the edge over 1/2 inch (13mm), press, then fold again 1 inch (2.5cm). Press, pin, and edge-stitch all the way around. Lay the bag flat (still inside out), then measure and mark a spot 6 inches (15cm) from the outer edge on both sides. Align the short ends of one handle with the marks on one side, and pin it in place (make sure the handle is not twisted). Attach with a boxstitch (figure b). Repeat with other handle. Turn bag right-side out.

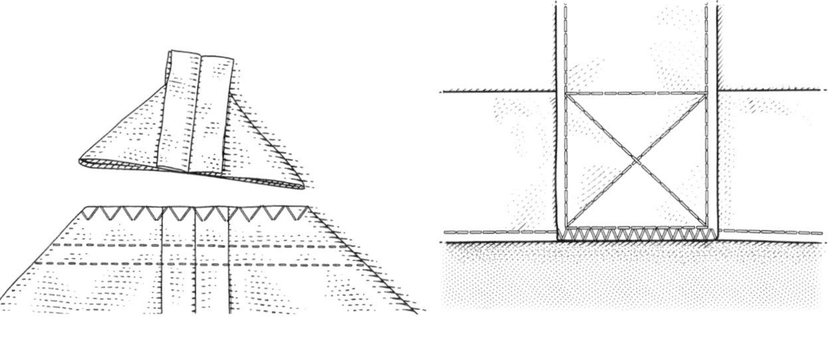

(a) (b)

appliquéd sea-print tote

Printed sea stars (more commonly known as starfish) float across a boxy, natural-hue tote. Because the bag is too thick to print on, a lighter weight canvas was used for the impressions (muslin also works) then appliquéd in place for a pleasing sense of dimension. You can print with rubber forms, available from crafts and art-supply stores, or actual seashore finds, such as shells or stones (see the pillows on page 216 and the sarong on page 178 for other examples of sea prints). The finished bag is perfect for the beach, but it would also look chic on any city street.

MATERIALS basic sewing supplies, fabric paint, 1/4 yard (23cm) lightweight canvas or muslin (for printing), canvas tote, sea stars or other items to print, sponge brush, old towels or paper (to protect surfaces)

HOW-TO Print a few sea stars in various sizes on lightweight canvas or muslin using the fabric-printing technique on page 88. (If the sea star's underside is concave, the details may be hard to capture. Instead, lay the star upside down, and use the rubber-form technique, pressing with your fingers.) Cut out the printed star, leaving a 1/2-inch (13mm) border all around, for seam allowance. Pin a sea-star cutout on the bag. Appliqué the cutout (for more on hand-turned appliqué, see page 41): If it is large, you may want to baste it in place first; otherwise, starting at the end of one of the cutout's arms, tuck the edge of the cutout under 1/4 inch (6mm). Using a needle and thread, sew along the fold, securing with small stitches. Repeat, tucking the next section of the edge under 1/4 inch (6mm) and sewing to secure. Continue along the edge until the cutout is attached. Repeat with additional cutouts.

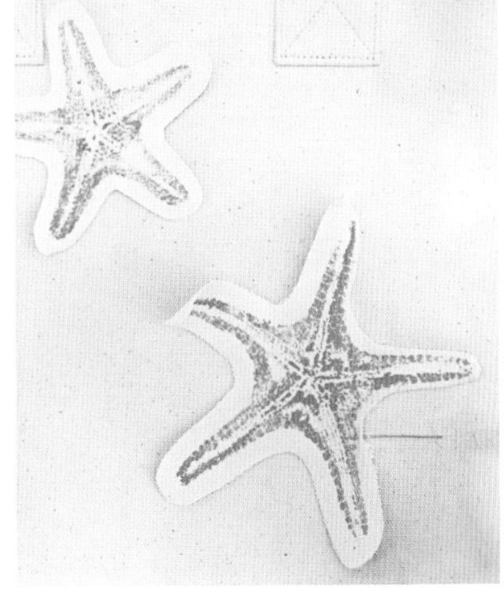

miniature felt purses

Fashionistas of all ages will delight in making pint-size purses for themselves and their friends. The adorable, easy-to-assemble bags (opposite) are just the right size for holding a few small necessities—mini pencils, hair clips, cell phones, MP3 players, keys, loose change, and the like. Each bag starts as two layers of felt (or one long rectangle folded in half).

MATERIALS basic sewing supplies, 2 pieces of wool felt (each about 5 by 7 inches [12.5cm × 18cm]) or one long strip (about 5 by 14 inches [12.5cm × 35.5cm]), wool felt scraps and buttons (for details), embroidery floss, embroidery needle, 1 yard (0.9m) yarn or store-bought cording (for handle)

HOW-TO 1. Using pinking shears, cut out the felt with either a square or rounded bottom. To customize the purses with an original drawing, use a disappearing-ink fabric pen to sketch shapes onto the felt scraps in complementary or pleasantly contrasting colors, then cut them out and attach them to one or both side pieces with a running stitch and embroidery floss.

2. Pin handle in place, and add any other details, such as pretty buttons, before stitching the 2 layers of felt together (or attaching the folded long sides), also with the running stitch and embroidery floss.

embroidered felt handbag

Embroidery doesn't have to be hand-worked to be appealing; the whimsical coils on this ivory-colored wool felt handbag were made with a decorative stitch on a sewing machine. The French knots that dot the seams were done by hand. The ruby-red felt purse was hand-embroidered in chainstitch after a child's drawing. Both bags have simple grosgrain-ribbon handles.

MATERIALS basic sewing supplies, a wide strip of wool felt (you want a long rectangular shape that can be folded in half to form the handbag), embroidery floss, embroidery needle, grosgrain ribbon (for handles)

HOW-TO With pinking shears, trim the short sides of the strip of felt. Fold the bag in half to align pinked ends and pin to hold. With a disappearing-ink fabric pen, mark the pattern you wish to embroider on one or both sides. Unpin, and machine-embroider (or hand-embroider, if you prefer). Fold the bag again and pin; machine-stitch 1/4 inch (6mm) from the edge to secure; working from the inside, hand-embroider evenly spaced French knots along the seams. Attach two pieces of grosgrain ribbon as handles by stitching in place a couple of inches in from the right and left sides.

FOUR EMBELLISHED-BAG PROJECTS

iron-on silhouettes

Sleek silhouettes turn a modest bag into an artful accessory. Scan copyright-free clip art from books or download it online or from a CD. Buy iron-on transfer paper for your tote; choose paper for light cotton fabrics and for dark cotton fabrics, depending on your project. Print the images on transfer paper, following the manufacturer's instructions, and cut them out. Cut around the images cleanly (use a craft knife, for precision) to avoid making jagged edges. Arrange the images on the bag, faceup, for a preview (keep in mind this is a mirror image of the final design). When you're ready to iron, place the images facedown. Press on top of images, starting at the edges of each one and using even pressure so that the image doesn't slide; do not move the iron back and forth, or image will blur or pucker. When iron-ons have cooled, remove the backing paper. Replace the bag's handles with equal lengths of colorful twill tape or cover them with ribbon, if desired.

labels and monograms

The addition of a bold initial or vivid pattern can make a plain canvas bag instantly eye-catching—and personalize it, too. The transformation relies on just one easy technique: ironing on a design (no embroidery is required; see Iron-On Silhouettes, left, for instructions). Vary the art or lettering to customize totes for different family members or specific activities. Large initials identify the totes' keepers, while labels (such as "Books" or "Knitting") designate bags for particular hobbies.

embroidered circles

This carryall is as stylish as it is sturdy, thanks to a simple running-stitch pattern in threads of varying colors and textures. To make one like it, use a disappearing-ink fabric pen to trace circles (a drinking glass makes a good template) onto a cotton-canvas bag; cover the entire bag, arranging the circles randomly. Make running stitches (page 31) along the circles, using a different thread for each one (the bag shown features a variety of lightweight, luminous yarns, including those made from silk, linen, bamboo, and metallic floss).

ombré

A canvas tote dip-dyed to produce shades of orange becomes a vibrant accessory for the beach—or anywhere. Start with a plain canvas tote, and follow the instructions for the ombré technique on pages 80–81. To begin, pin through both layers to mark shade levels. Secure the handles to the top of the bag with binder clips to keep them out of the dyeing solution. Dye as directed. When using heavy fabrics, such as canvas, you may need to hold the fabric in the dye longer at each level than you would for thinner materials.

drawstring pouches

Even a beginner can easily master sewing a drawstring bag. It requires just a few straight seams, and introduces the method of sewing a channel at the top (in this case, for a pair of ties used to cinch the bag closed). The pouches themselves are extremely versatile, and can be sewn in a wide range of sizes to hold everything from laundry to tiny baby shoes. Menswear fabrics were used for the pouches shown, but you can use any fabric.

MATERIALS basic sewing supplies; assorted fabric (amount will depend on desired size of bag; wool suiting and cotton shirting are shown); ½-inch-wide (13mm) or thinner bias tape, twill tape, or cord (optional)

HOW-TO 1. Cut out 2 rectangles from complementary fabrics (one for outside, one for lining). Dimensions for different size bags are: laundry bag (not shown) 19 by 55 inches (finished size: 17 by 26 inches [43cm × 66cm]), shoe bag 15 by 37 inches (finished size: 13 by 17 inches [33cm × 43cm]), lingerie bag 10 by 28 inches (finished size: 8 by 11 inches [20.5cm × 28cm]), jewelry bag 9 by 17 inches (finished size: 7 by 7 inches [18cm × 18cm]). Pin rectangles, right sides facing, along long sides; sew with a ½-inch (13mm) seam allowance. Turn right side out; iron flat. For channels, double-hem short sides: fold over ½ inch (13mm), then 1 inch (2.5cm), and edge-stitch ⅛ inch (3mm) from inner edge. Fold bag in half so hems meet at top. Stitch long sides with a ¼-inch (6mm) seam allowance, stopping 1½ inches (2.5cm) from hems (to accommodate channels).

2. For ties, use store-bought bias tape, twill tape, or cord. If you prefer, you can make your own: Cut 2 strips 2 inches (5cm) wide by twice the length of top of bag plus 3 inches (7.5cm). Fold edges in lengthwise so they meet in the middle; press. Fold strip in half lengthwise again; press again. Make an ⅛-inch (3mm) edge-stitch. Attach safety pin to one tie and thread through both channels, working left to right. Do the reverse with the other tie, threading from right to left. Knot ties and cinch bag to close.

1

2

cross-stitch silhouette tote

A bag with a decorative silhouette is more than a useful carrier; it's a conversation piece. Any profile—your child's, your own, or a friend's—can be enlarged and used as the template. Start with a store-bought burlap tote, or make one and add twill-tape or twig handles. This bag is embroidered with perle cotton, a thick, glossy thread akin to embroidery floss. It's easy to work with, and because the weight of the thread is similar to that of the thread used to make the burlap, the design will appear as if it were woven right into the cloth. The head and necklace were drawn with a disappearing-ink fabric pen and filled in with cross-stitches. The bird and branch are stitched in two different colors; you could embroider both parts in black for a Victorian look.

MATERIALS basic sewing supplies, camera, marker, thin cardboard, burlap tote (or burlap fabric, if making your own), twill tape or twig (for handles, optional), perle cotton (in black and blue), tapestry needle, embroidery hoop, beads and pendant (optional)

HOW-TO 1. Photograph the profile of the chosen person. Photocopy the picture, darken the silhouette with a marker, enlarge to the desired size, and cut out. Trace it onto thin cardboard; cut out. Lay the cardboard template on the tote bag or fabric; trace the image with a disappearing-ink fabric pen. Indicate any details, such as a necklace.

2. Using black perle cotton, a tapestry needle, and an embroidery hoop (if desired), cross-stitch (page 50) the outline of the profile with 2-by-2 stitches. Working left to right, and bottom to top, fill in the profile with black cross-stitches; then cross-stitch the necklace with blue perle cotton. Sew a bead pendant on the bag to finish, if desired. Follow the same instructions for making a bird; make a template to trace the shape, or draw the bird (and branch) freehand.

1

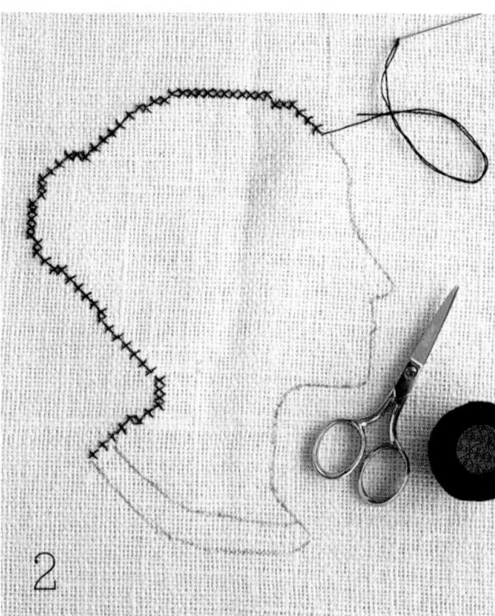

2

Simon

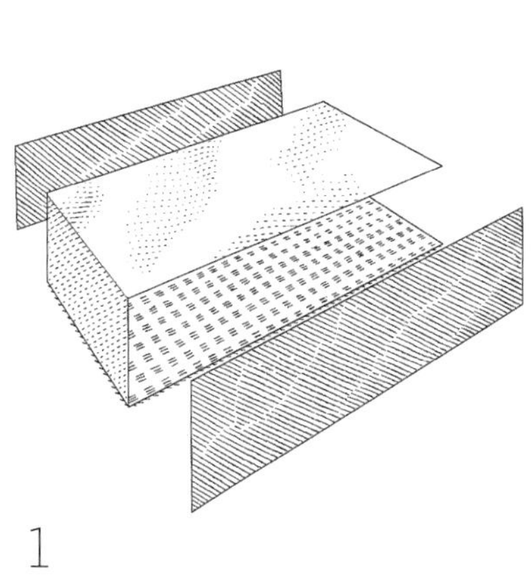
1

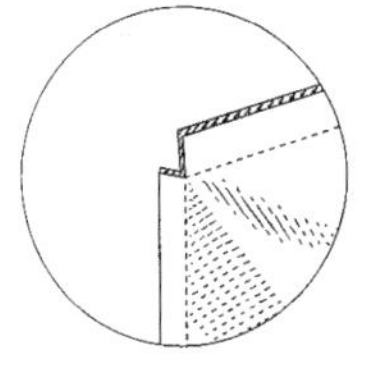

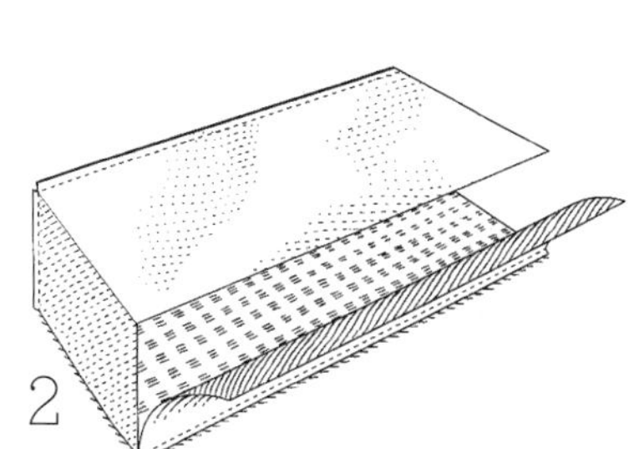
2

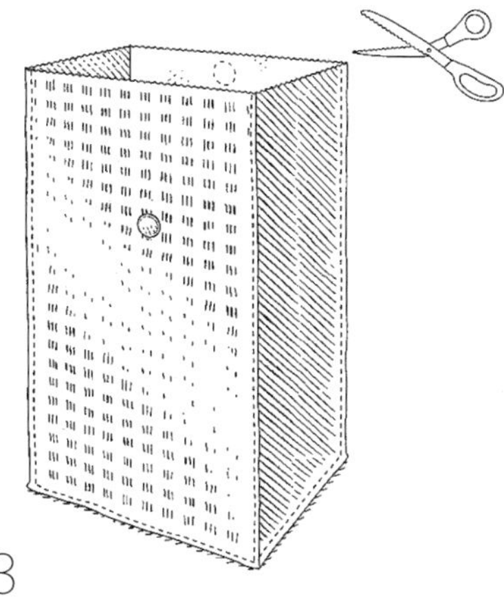
3

oilcloth lunch bag

The same oilcloth that covers kitchen tables can be used to transport a child's lunch to school (or an adult's lunch to the office). These reusable bags will cut back on waste; they can be simply wiped clean with a damp sponge (do not machine-wash). Use a single pattern for the whole bag, or cut out complementary patterns or solid colors for the side panels. Attach small Velcro® tabs to hold the bags closed, or clip the tops with clothespins.

MATERIALS basic sewing supplies, 1/2 yard (45.5cm) oilcloth, Velcro tabs (optional), clothespin (optional)

HOW-TO 1. Cut one main piece 29 1/2 by 8 inches (75cm × 20.5cm), and 2 side panels, each 12 1/4 by 5 inches (31cm × 12.5cm). Fold the long panel, inside out, into a U shape with a 5-inch (12.5cm) bottom.

2. Make a 1/4-inch (6mm) cut at the bottom corners of the side and middle pieces so the bag folds smoothly. Sew on both side panels as shown, with a 1/4-inch (6mm) seam allowance.

3. Turn right-side out and topstitch all around, 1/8 inch (3mm) from the edge. Add Velcro tabs where indicated by dotted circles, if desired.

apple-print bag

The cut side of an apple half can be dipped in paint and stamped onto fabric to produce a charming, cheerful pattern.

MATERIALS apple; knife; medium-size paintbrush; acrylic paint (red and orange are shown); canvas lunch bag, backpack, or tote; colored markers or fabric paint

HOW-TO Cut an apple in half from top to bottom; make sure the cut is smooth and flat. Use a paintbrush to apply the paint evenly over the cut side of the apple. With the apple half cut-side down, stamp the surface of the bag. The more you stamp, the less vivid the print will be, so reapply the paint, or use the other apple half. Use additional apple halves to print with different colors, if desired. Draw stems and leaves with black and green markers.

pillowcase bag

Pillowcases are available in so many pleasing, colorful patterns, and they make wonderful materials for sewing projects. Here an orphaned pillowcase is given a new home—over the shoulder. You can use a stray from a set you already own, or buy new ones just for this purpose. The carefree summer bag is a perfect project for a beginning sewer, requiring only basic supplies and skills.

MATERIALS basic sewing supplies, pillowcase

HOW-TO 1. Trim 1/4 inch (6mm) off the closed end of the pillowcase, and cut the case in half on the diagonal, as shown. Make double hems: Turn the fabric of each of the four diagonal cut edges over by 1/4 inch (6mm), then 1/4 inch (6mm) again, pin, and edge-stitch.

2. Place one pillowcase half inside the other, lining up the bottom edges; pin, and sew (by hand or machine) at the front, where the fabrics overlap, with a 1/4-inch (6mm) seam allowance. Repeat on the other side. Turn the fabric inside out, and hem the case's cut bottom. Trim hem with pinking shears. Turn the case right-side out, and tie the top ends into a knot to secure.

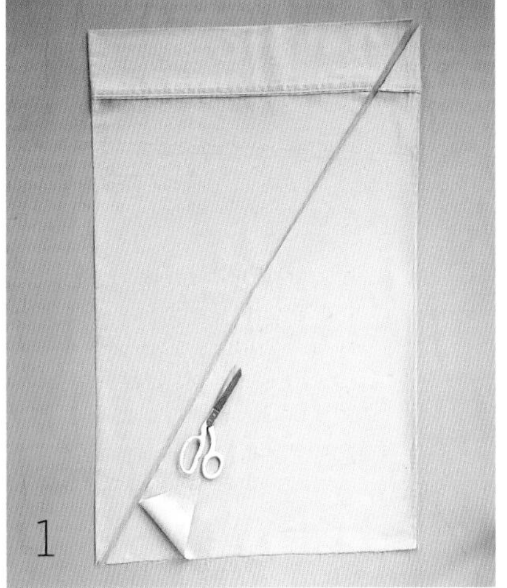

1

2

multicompartment bag

This handmade bag provides a proper place to stash a fine assortment of essentials. The individual pockets are stitched together using bias tape, which binds the edges and creates a colorful contrast to the fabric pieces.

MATERIALS basic sewing supplies, multi-compartment bag template, medium-weight cotton canvas (you will need 1 yard [0.9m] total, either a single piece or pieces of different colors and patterns), 6 yards (5.5m) bias tape (store-bought or handmade; for instructions on making your own, see page 369).

HOW-TO 1. Print the template pieces (see enclosed CD), and cut out. From fabric, cut out 2 handle pieces, 2 bag pieces, one small pocket, and one large pocket.

2. Bind both long edges of each handle, the edges of the large and small pockets, and the top edges of both bag pieces. Finish ends, following bias-tape instructions on page 369.

3. Press under ½ inch (13mm) of both ends of each handle and pin the pressed ends to each bag piece, the folded edge of the handle facing the right side of the fabric, 4 ½ inches (11.5cm) from the top edge and 4 inches (10cm) in from each side of the bag. (The handle will twist, as shown.) Machine-stitch the handles to the bag using 2 horizontal stitches, ⅛ inch (3mm) and ½ inch (13mm) from the folded edge; backstitch for reinforcement.

4. For the front of the bag, stack a small pocket on top of a large one, with side edges aligned; pin both to the right side of one bag piece. Starting at the bag's bottom and machine-stitching through all the layers, sew up the center front of the pockets; backstitch to reinforce.

5. Stack front and back bag pieces, wrong sides facing and edges aligned. Bind the front of the bag to the back with bias tape, stitching in place and beginning and ending with a fold-over finish (page 369).

PROJECT:

bath linens

It's amazing how much brighter a bathroom looks when you introduce a few hand-worked touches. To enliven a powder room or family bath, sew and embellish luxurious soft goods in your favorite colors. When it comes to bathroom décor, even small changes will refresh the space, making it look—and feel—brand-new again.

Add bold stripes to bath towels and other accessories with bias tape, ribbon, or basic sewing-machine stitches. For shower curtains, don't overlook the appeal of novelty fabrics; a lace curtain can be stitched quickly from eyelet lace yardage. Elsewhere, linen panels make a breezy, three-tone example, and a pocketed panel of waterproof yellow fabric creates a shower cover with rain-slicker appeal.

As you shop for materials, keep an eye to washable, color-safe trims and fabrics. Or opt for all-white accessories; you can never go wrong with their crisp, clean look.

IN THIS CHAPTER: MACHINE-EMBROIDERED BATH SET — LINEN SHOWER CURTAIN — BIAS TAPE–EMBELLISHED TOWELS — WASHCLOTH PUPPETS — HOODED TOWEL — RAIN SLICKER SHOWER CURTAIN — RIBBON-BORDERED BATH MAT — REVERSIBLE-BORDER SHOWER CURTAIN — EYELET SHOWER CURTAIN

MACHINE-EMBROIDERED BATH SET (OPPOSITE): *Add six rows of color to a shower curtain with a zigzag stitch, set to the shortest stitch length and the widest width, across its bottom. The stitches will be so close together that they'll resemble an embroidered satin stitch. Use embroidery thread to give the stripes extra sheen. You can add similar stripes to towels or a border to a bath mat, too. Work inside the dobby (the flat surface of the towel or mat) so that the needle doesn't get caught in the loops.*

linen shower curtain

A vibrant three-tier shower curtain is both beautiful and practical. The linen, which is stronger and heavier than cotton, drapes well and will withstand multiple washings. Here two shower curtains were made to fit all the way around a claw-foot tub; you will need only one panel in each color to make a single curtain.

MATERIALS basic sewing supplies, 2 panels of 48-by-74-inch (122cm × 188cm; about 4 ¼ yards [3.9m]) orange linen, 2 panels of 18-by-74-inch (45.5cm × 188cm; about 4 ¼ yards [3.9m]) hot-pink linen, 2 panels of 23-by-74-inch (58.5cm × 188cm; about 4 ¼ yards [3.9m]) brown linen, 1-inch (2.5cm) grommet kit

HOW-TO 1. Using a French seam (page 36), join an orange panel to a pink panel: Align long sides of the fabrics, wrong sides facing, and sew a ¼-inch (6mm) seam. Flip the fabric the other way over the seam, so that right sides are facing; and sew a ⅝-inch-wide (16mm) seam that encloses the first seam. Join the brown and pink panels along long sides in the same way.

2. At left and right sides of the curtain make a double hem: Fold each edge over ½ inch (13mm), press, then fold 1 inch (2.5cm), press, and edge-stitch. Make a double hem along the bottom of the curtain (brown linen): Fold over ½ inch (13mm), press, and then fold 3 inches (7.5cm); press and edge-stitch. Make another double hem at the top of the curtain (orange linen): Fold ½ inch (13mm), press, fold 1 ½ inches (3.8cm); press and edge-stitch. Following the instructions in the grommet kit (or on page 370), make holes at 6-inch (15cm) intervals in the top hem, beginning and ending 1 inch (2.5cm) from the sides; install grommets. Repeat with remaining fabric to make another curtain. Hang curtains with waterproof liners.

bias tape-embellished towels

Colorful bands of handmade bias tape allow you to add a personal touch to an assortment of solid-colored bath towels. A stacked set, tied with a length of tape in the same pattern, makes a stylish housewarming gift.

MATERIALS basic sewing supplies, towels in various sizes, 1 yard (0.9m) medium-weight woven fabric (such as quilting cotton or linen), 2-inch (5cm) bias-tape maker

HAND TOWEL HOW-TO 1. Cut off each towel's hem. Use the bias-tape maker to create two strips of fabric that span the width of the towel, allowing ½ inch (13mm) on each end for finishing (for instructions on making bias tape, see page 369).

2. Slip the bias tape over the edge of the towel, leaving a ½-inch (13mm) overhang on each end. Pin to secure. Starting about 1 inch (2.5cm) from the tape's end, stitch ⅛ inch (3mm) in from the tape's edge, making sure the needle passes through the underside of the tape. Stop stitching about 1 inch (2.5cm) before the tape's end.

3. On each end of the towel, open the bias tape like a book; fold the end over the edge of the towel (see page 369). Close the bias tape, and stitch it in place.

BATH TOWEL HOW-TO 1. To make wider bias tape, cut on the bias two 8-inch-wide (20.5cm) strips of fabric that span the width of the towel, allowing ½ inch (13mm) on each end for finishing.

2. Fold the unfinished long edges of the fabric so they meet in the center, and press. Fold in half lengthwise again, and press.

3. Bind edges as for the hand towel, starting with step 2.

washcloth puppets

A pair of handy terry-cloth animals make charming bath-time pals. For the animal features, look for washable felt, which is made of 100 percent acrylic and won't shrink.

MATERIALS basic sewing supplies, washcloth puppets pattern, clear tape, hand towel (in pink or white), washable felt, fabric glue, embroidery floss, embroidery needle

HOW-TO Fold the hand towel in half, finished end to finished end. Print the pattern (see enclosed CD) and photocopy to adjust size, if desired. Trace puppet shape onto a folded towel, and cut out. Cut the pig's snout or the dog's spot from washable felt; attach them with fabric glue. Embroider features using a satin stitch (page 48). Slip the felt ears between the towel layers (fold in the sides of the pig's ears first). Sew around the perimeter of the puppet with a zigzag stitch.

ribbon-bordered bath mat

Pretty ribbon provides a simple way to transform a store-bought mat into one designed with your bathroom in mind. You'll need a bath mat that has an interior border and no rubber backing. Choose a ribbon that flatters your décor and is the same width as the border.

MATERIALS basic sewing supplies, bath mat, ribbon (washed and dried), washable, clear-drying fabric glue

HOW-TO Measure the length of ribbon you'll need to cover the interior border of the bath mat. Starting at one corner of the border, attach the ribbon with fabric glue; for mitered corners, fold the ribbon back onto itself and turn (as shown at left). Continue gluing and folding all the way around (you may want to pin the ribbon in place as you work). To finish, trim the ribbon, fold the end under at a 45-degree angle for a neat corner, and glue in place. Let dry, then machine-stitch around both edges of the ribbon and diagonally at the corners.

reversible-border shower curtain

A reversible border added to a store-bought shower curtain allows you to change a bathroom's look with the seasons. One side is gingham, for spring and summer; the other, corduroy, for fall and winter. Buttons sewn directly on the curtain fit the buttonholes at the top of the border. You will need a machine with a buttonhole stitch and a buttonhole presser foot to sew the buttonholes.

MATERIALS basic sewing supplies, 2 ½ yards (2.3m) corduroy, 2 ½ yards (2.3m) gingham (or other lightweight patterned fabric), standard 72-by-72-inch (183cm × 183cm) store-bought shower curtain, buttonhole presser foot, 19 buttons

HOW-TO 1. Cut two 73-by-19-inch (185cm × 48.5cm) rectangles, one from corduroy and one from gingham. Pin the corduroy and gingham rectangles together, right sides facing, and machine-stitch along all of the edges with a ½-inch (13mm) seam allowance, leaving 12 inches (30.5cm) open on one edge. Clip the corners and turn the border right-side out. Use a point turner or a closed pair of scissors to push the corners out. Press the edges of the border, turning the unfinished edges of the opening under ½ inch (13mm). Use a slipstitch (page 31) to sew the opening shut. Using the buttonhole stitch on your machine, sew buttonholes ½ inch (13mm) from the top edge of the reversible border every 4 inches (10cm), starting at an outer edge.

2. Sew buttons 17 ½ inches (44.5cm) above the hem of the shower curtain every 4 inches (10cm) to align with the buttonholes, starting at an outer edge. Button the reversible border onto the shower curtain.

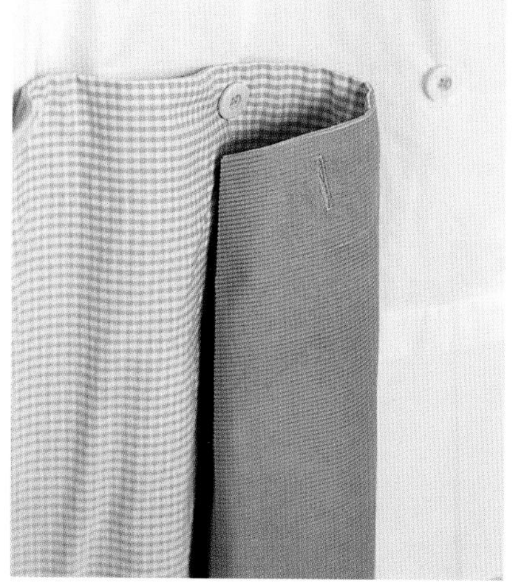

EYELET SHOWER CURTAIN

Airy lengths of eyelet create an elegant shower curtain that also filters light from a nearby window. Use as many panels as you need; cut them to the desired length, and hem if necessary. With some patterns (including the one shown), you can simply cut the fabric so the embroidery stands in as an already-bound edge. Slip shower curtain rings through the holes at the top to hang it, and use a waterproof liner to protect the fabric.

PROJECT:

bed linens

Turn any bedroom into a restful escape with bedding that you design yourself. The simple flat surfaces of plain sheets, duvet covers, pillowcases, and shams make wonderful blank canvases that can be adorned in countless ways. Style your bedding in colors and textures inspired by the season. Or, instead, consider the feeling you want the room to convey. You can even think of bedding as you do apparel, focusing on a favorite style, whether classic, romantic, or modern. If you want a large-scale fabric project that requires only small-scale embellishments, a bedding makeover is a lovely place to begin.

Most of the designs on these pages start with ready-made bedding. You can dress up linens with shell prints, easy rickrack borders, hand-embroidered French knots, or appliquéd geometric cutouts. Whether the bedding you create is for your own room or a guest room, distinctive touches like these create a sense of calm, inviting anyone who enters to instantly unwind.

IN THIS CHAPTER: FADED SHEET SET — EYELET OVERLAY — EYELET PILLOWCASES — FOUR EASY BEDDING EMBELLISHMENTS: ZIGZAG EMBROIDERY; SHELL-STAMPED; FRENCH-KNOTTED BORDERS; RICKRACK TRIM — LINEN PILLOWCASES — MENSWEAR BEDDING SET — COORDINATED-SHEET DUVET COVER — FLAT-SHEET DUVET — RUNNING STITCH–EMBROIDERED BEDDING — SASHIKO-EDGED PILLOWCASES — APPLIQUÉD DUVET COVER AND PILLOWCASES

FADED SHEET SET (OPPOSITE): *A brand-new cherry blossom–strewn flat sheet and matching pillowcase were first faded with a diluted-bleach solution, then tinted with pink fabric dye for a vintage look. Patterned throw pillows and simple curtain panels can be similarly customized to appear gently timeworn. For instructions on fading and overdyeing fabrics, see page 82.*

david sedaris
naked
The Shipping News
ANNIE PROULX

eyelet overlay

Pale-gray eyelet in a honeycomblike pattern, with its embroidered edges neatly cut, makes a serene overlay for a coverlet. You may be able to cover a twin bed without having to sew (use 60-inch-wide [152.5cm] fabric); larger beds will require sewing pieces together. Look for eyelet with a continuously embroidered design, so that the edges won't fray. Dark brown eyelet covers a boudoir pillow. For pillow-cover instructions, see page 210.

MATERIALS basic sewing supplies, coverlet, eyelet fabric (the amount will depend on bed size)

HOW-TO Measure the length and width of your existing coverlet; the eyelet overlay should be slightly shorter on all sides. Carefully cut around the edges of the eyelet, making sure not to cut into the embroidered design. To make a full-, queen-, or king-size covering, sew lengths of fabric together, making sure seams line up with the top edges of the mattress. Match the pattern at the seams and they'll be almost invisible.

eyelet pillowcases

Decorating store-bought pillowcases with eyelet gives them a pretty, fresh appearance sure to brighten any room. Here bands of eyelet trim accent the cuffs of two pillowcases, and eyelet sleeves cover two whole cases.

1. The cuff of this pillowcase is embellished with three bands of 2-inch-wide (5cm) eyelet trim. Measure around the pillowcase opening, adding ½ inch (13mm), and cut three bands of the eyelet trim to this length. Pin each to cuff, overlapping ends, and turning top end under ¼ inch (6mm). Machine-stitch the trim onto the cuff directly down the center of each piece of eyelet.

2, 4. Both of these pillowcases are covered in sleeves made of eyelet fabric that has a scallop on one edge. The sleeves are slightly shorter than the pillowcases, so the eyelet edge is highlighted. Start by measuring the width of your pillowcase. Double the measurement and add 1 inch (2.5cm) for seam allowance. For length, subtract 2 inches (5cm) from the pillowcase length. Cut an eyelet rectangle to this measurement, with the scalloped edge as one of the long sides. Fold the rectangle in half, aligning the scalloped edges, wrong sides facing. Machine-stitch the bottom and side edges ½ inch (13mm) from the unfinished edge.

3. Two bands of eyelet trim, which have one straight and one scalloped edge, are sewn onto the cuff of this pillowcase. Measure and cut the trim you'll need for 2 bands (about 48 inches [122cm] each). Pin the eyelet bands to the pillowcase cuff, straight edge to straight edge, and sew each along the eyelet edge.

FOUR EASY BEDDING EMBELLISHMENTS

zigzag embroidery

A machine-sewn zigzag stitch is one of the easiest ways to adorn store-bought sheets and pillowcases. Here multicolored rows of stitching add subtle detail to a flat sheet and pillowcases. Re-create the look shown here or choose other colors of thread that suit your linens.

MATERIALS basic sewing supplies, pillowcases and flat sheet, embroidery thread in four colors (green, pink, yellow, and mocha are pictured)

HOW-TO For each pillowcase, measure and mark three sets of four stripes crosswise with a disappearing-ink fabric pen. Thread your machine with green embroidery thread, and stitch one row in each set, using a zigzag stitch (or another whimsical, decorative stitch). Repeat, adding a row of pink to each set. Then stitch rows in yellow and, finally, in mocha. To embellish the flat sheet, repeat the machine-stitched design, creating rows in the given order twice (making 8 rows, rather than 4).

shell-stamped

In summer, crisp white sheets look inviting when edged with prints made from seashells. Scallop shells have a naturally beautiful shape, and beachcombing for the perfect candidates is half the fun. For best results, use 100 percent cotton sheets, which absorb the paint better than blended fabric. For more on fabric printing, see page 87.

MATERIALS towel, practice fabric, fabric paint, scallop shells, sponge brush, matching pillowcases and flat sheet

HOW-TO Cover a work surface with a towel. Lay a piece of practice fabric on the towel. Apply fabric paint directly to a shell's surface with the sponge brush, but do so sparingly; you don't want it to fill in the grooves. Press the shell onto the fabric, rolling it slightly if necessary to apply the entire shape. Make practice prints until you can line up several shell prints neatly in a row. Lay the sheet or pillowcase on the towel and print. (Follow the paint manufacturer's instructions for colorfastness.)

French-knotted borders

A border of leafy vines, made from French knots, gives store-bought sheets a romantic, vintage look. For detailed French knot instructions, see page 52.

MATERIALS French-knotted borders template (optional); disappearing-ink fabric pen; linen, cotton, or flannel sheet set; cotton embroidery floss in desired colors (green, orange, and brown are pictured)

HOW-TO Print the template (see enclosed CD), and cut out, or draw a design freehand. Punch out dots at intervals along template's lines with a large needle. Lay the template on the fabric, and use a disappearing-ink fabric pen to mark the dots onto the hems of each pillowcase and the flat sheet. Using 6 strands of embroidery floss, make French knots for stems, leaves, and flowers in desired colors. For the tidiest results, pass the needle and thread between the 2 layers of fabric that make up the hem of a pillowcase. If your pillow-cases or sheet hems are not double layered, simply carry the thread neatly across the back of your work.

rickrack trim

For quick-to-stitch bed accessories, consider widely available—and affordable—rickrack. Use it to trim the inside of a standard pillowcase opening or add a jaunty border to a sham. A set of matching pillow covers makes a great gift.

MATERIALS basic sewing supplies, pillowcase or sham, rickrack

HOW-TO For the pillowcase opening: Measure and cut the length of rickrack you'll need to trim the pillowcase opening, plus ½ inch (13mm) extra to overlap the ends (a standard pillow will require about 45 inches [114cm]). Pin the rickrack to the inside edge of the pillowcase and sew in place. For the sham: Measure one long piece of rickrack that will go around each edge of the pillow. Pin the rickrack on to the seam of the sham, folding the rickrack at a 45-degree angle at the corners; sew in place. Measure another long piece of rickrack that will go around the inside edge of the flange, plus ½ inch (13mm) extra to overlap the ends. Pin over the existing seam, then stitch in place.

linen pillowcases

Add a burst of color to an otherwise neutral bedding ensemble with soft linen pillowcases in ripe shades of watermelon, tangerine, or any other bright shade. Choose one color for the body of the pillowcase, and another for the cuff. The dimensions given here are for a standard-size case.

MATERIALS basic sewing supplies, 1 yard (0.9m) 50-inch-wide (127cm) linen (for the body of the pillowcase), ½ yard (45.5cm) 50-inch-wide (127cm) linen in another color for the cuff

HOW-TO Wash, dry, and press the linen. With a ruler and tailor's chalk, measure a 24-by-40-inch (28cm × 101.5cm) rectangle on the wrong side of the larger piece of linen (for the body piece); cut it out. Measure an 11-by-40-inch (28cm × 101.5cm) rectangle on the wrong side of the smaller piece (for the cuff); cut it out. Pin the cuff fabric to the body fabric, right sides facing, aligning fabrics along one 40-inch (101.5cm) edge. Sew together along this side, ½ inch (13mm) from the raw edge. Open up fabric, and press hem against the cuff fabric. Sew a zigzag seam along the raw 40-inch (101.5cm) edge of the cuff fabric. Fold the piece in half, right sides facing, so short ends meet; leaving the cuff end open, sew along the two sides. Fold the cuff over so that its zig-zagged edge overlaps by ½ inch (13mm) the seam joining the two pieces. Press and pin in place. Turn the pillowcase right-side out, and stitch directly over the seam that joins the two fabrics to secure the cuff.

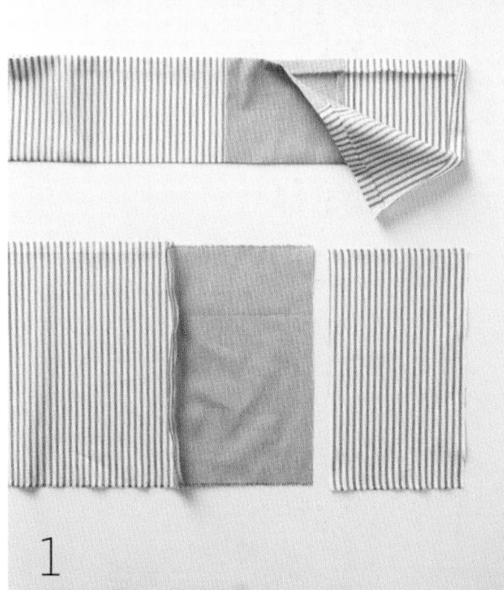

1

2

menswear bedding set

Menswear shirting fabrics come in a variety of handsome hues and subtle patterns that beautifully complement solid-colored bed linens. Here, a band of different fabrics is sewn to the top of a flat sheet, and similar bands create cuffs on the pillowcases. To make the tuxedo pillow cover pictured, see page 233; for the hot-water bottle cozy, see page 108.

MATERIALS basic sewing supplies, rotary cutter, ruler, self-healing mat, assorted striped-cotton shirting fabric, store-bought sheet and standard pillowcases

HOW-TO 1. With a ruler, the rotary cutter, and the self-healing mat, measure and cut an assortment of 8-inch-wide (20.5cm) fabric rectangles. (The lengths can vary.) For the sheet: You will need enough rectangles to create a strip that's as wide as the sheet plus 1 inch (2.5cm). Pin the rectangles together, then sew, right sides facing, with a ½-inch (13mm) seam allowance. Press seams open. Turn long edges under ½ inch (13mm) and press; repeat for short edges. Fold the strip in half lengthwise; press.

2. Fit the folded and pressed strip over the top edge of the sheet; pin in place. Sew along all 3 sides ⅛ inch (3mm) from the folded edge of the strip, making sure that the needle catches the bottom layer of fabric. For pillowcase: Sew an 8-inch-wide (20.5cm) fabric strip whose length is equal to the circumference of the pillowcase opening, plus 1 inch (2.5cm). Stitch the short edges together, right sides facing, with a ½-inch (13mm) seam allowance, creating a loop, and press. Turn the long edges under ½ inch (13mm) and press, as at left. Turn the loop right side out, fold in half, and press. Fit over the edge of the pillowcase. Pin around the opening and edge-stitch to finish.

coordinated-sheet duvet cover

Blocks of subtle color make for an understated beauty that is at once elegant and simple. Here a perfectly coordinated duvet cover made from extra flat sheets (mushroom brown, off-white, and a muted violet-blue are pictured) pulls the bed together with stacked pillowcases in the same shades. It would look just as lovely paired with all-white or all-blue sheets and pillowcases, for example, as it does with the arrangement shown here. You will need to determine the size of the squares before purchasing and cutting the sheets.

MATERIALS basic sewing supplies, 4 twin or full flat sheets in different colors (depending on the size of your squares), comforter, twill tape

HOW-TO 1. Wash, dry, and press the sheets. Cut the sheets to make 8 equal-size patchwork pieces, depending on your comforter's dimensions. To determine the size of the pieces, measure the size of the comforter you want to cover; divide that measurement by 2, adding 1 inch (2.5cm) to each dimension for the seam allowance. (For example, if you have a queen comforter that measures 88 by 90 inches [223.5cm × 229cm], you will need to cut eight 45-by-46-inch [114cm × 117cm] rectangles.) Depending on the measurements, you may be able to cut each sheet in half.

2. For the front of the duvet cover, sew 2 sets of rectangles together, right sides facing, with a ½-inch (13mm) seam allowance. Press the seam allowance open, then finish the edges with pinking shears (page 36). Pin the left and right panels together, right sides facing, making sure that the seams match up. Sew together with a ½-inch (13mm) seam allowance. Press the seam allowance open and finish with pinking shears. Repeat to make the back piece of the duvet cover, using 4 squares in the same or a different color combination.

3. Pin the front and back pieces together, right sides facing, and sew around the perimeter on three sides with a ½-inch (13mm) seam allowance. On the fourth side, sew 24 inches (0.6m) in from each corner, leaving an opening in the center. Press the seams open and finish edges with pinking shears. Turn the duvet cover right-side out. Turn under the unfinished opening ¼ inch (6mm), press, and then turn under again ¼ inch (6mm); press and edge-stitch ⅛ inch (3mm) from the inner edge. For fasteners, cut 5-inch (12.5cm) lengths of twill tape (you'll need enough pairs to sew every 6 to 8 inches [15-20.5cm] along the duvet cover's opening). Sew the pieces of twill tape to the inside edge of the opening, one across from another. Tie them together to fasten the duvet.

flat-sheet duvet

Ready-made duvet covers can be pricey, and you may not be able to find one in just the right color or pattern. One way to remedy this is to sew two flat sheets together to make your own cover.

MATERIALS basic sewing supplies, 2 flat sheets the same size as your comforter, twill tape

HOW-TO Wash, dry, and press the sheets. Place the sheets right sides together, and on the bottom edge, make a mark 24 inches (0.6m) in from each corner. Sew around the perimeter with a ½-inch (13mm) seam allowance, leaving the space between the two marks open. Turn the duvet right-side out. For fasteners, cut 5-inch (12.5cm) lengths of twill tape (you'll need enough to sew every 6 to 8 inches [15-20.5cm] along the duvet's opening). Sew the pieces of twill tape to the inside edge of the opening, one across from another, and tie them together to fasten the duvet.

running stitch-embroidered bedding

One simple stitch made in a few different colors and patterns can unify any assemblage of bed linens. Here the running stitch is used to accentuate the existing patterns on a few pillow covers. It's also used to create homey designs on solid-colored bedding, including the flat sheet, pillowcases, and wool coverlet. For a glossary of running-stitch patterns, see page 54.

DECORATIVE PILLOWS

Pillow covers made of striped or checked material work best for creating the brick designs shown. To make heavier stitches, use all 6 strands of the embroidery floss; use fewer strands for finer stitches.

MATERIALS basic sewing supplies, embroidery floss in a few colors, embroidery needle, decorative pillow covers made of striped or checked fabric

HOW-TO 1. Thread the embroidery needle with about 18 inches (45.5cm) of floss; double-knot one end. For the pillow shown in the back, make a brick pattern: Pass the needle from the back of the fabric to the front, stitching perpendicular to the fabric's stripes at regular intervals, and working over and under contrasting colors (here the red floss is worked over the white stripes and under the blue ones). Don't tug on the needle, or the fabric will pucker.

2. For the middle pillow: Stitch at a 45-degree angle to the fabric's checked pattern, working from one corner to the other, again stitching in even intervals.

3. For the front pillow: Separate three strands from the embroidery floss and use them to stitch thin lines perpendicular to the stripes to make 3-inch (7.5cm) bands at each short end of the pillow.

BEDSPREAD

Long rows of white running stitches brighten a plain red coverlet. Use silk or wool yarns in a color that contrasts with the blanket.

MATERIALS tailor's chalk, ruler, wool coverlet, tapestry needle, silk or wool yarn

HOW-TO With tailor's chalk and a ruler, mark evenly spaced rows on the blanket. Thread the tapestry needle with a length of yarn that is a little longer than the length of the blanket, and knot one end. Pass the needle from the back of the blanket to the front to make a stitch. Rock the needle up and down along the chalk line to pick up bits of the blanket at regular intervals, allowing a few stitches to collect on the needle before pulling it through the blanket. (Gently pull on the needle; don't tug, or the blanket will pucker.) At the end of each row of stitches, knot the yarn and clip off any excess.

ZIGZAG-PATTERNED SHEET SET

A running stitch doesn't need to be worked in straight lines; here a zigzag pattern is used to embellish the pillowcases and flat sheet. You can vary the length of the stitches.

MATERIALS sheet set, contrasting color embroidery floss, embroidery needle, ruler (optional)

HOW-TO Stitch along the hem of the pillowcases and flat sheet in a zigzag pattern, rather than a straight line. Space the stitches about 1/4 inch (6mm) apart. If you like, you can use the existing stitches on the case or sheet as a guide to make even stitches. This stitch can also be used to embellish a blanket.

sashiko-edged pillowcases

In this serene bedroom setting, bands of fabric are covered with intricate sashiko embroidery, then used to decorate a pair of standard-size pillowcases. For more on Japanese sashiko, see page 55.

MATERIALS basic sewing supplies, sashiko-edged pillowcases template, 1 yard (0.9m) white or off-white 45-inch-wide (114cm) smooth cotton or linen, ½ yard (45.5cm) blue or brown linen-cotton blend fabric, sashiko needle, sashiko or perle cotton thread

HOW-TO Wash, dry, and press the fabrics. Print the template (see enclosed CD), and cut it out. From the white fabric, cut two 21-by-29-inch (53.5cm × 74cm) rectangles. From the colored fabric, cut one 21-by-17-inch (53.5cm × 43cm) rectangle. Follow the directions on page 55 for embroidering the colored-fabric rectangle, using one the sashiko template as a guide. Pin one white rectangle to the embroidered rectangle, 21-inch-long (53.5cm) sides together, right sides facing; machine-stitch ½ inch (13mm) from the unfinished edge. Repeat on the opposite side of the embroidered fabric with the second rectangle of white fabric. Press both seams open, and finish the edges with a zigzag seam (page 36). Fold the sewn panel in half, right sides facing. Pin the long edges together and sew ½ inch (13mm) from the unfinished edge. Press the seams open and finish the edges with a zigzag seam. Make a double hem along the unfinished edge of the pillowcase: Fold the fabric over 1 inch (2.5cm), press, then fold over 1 inch (2.5cm), and press again. Edge-stitch the hem. Turn pillowcase right-side out.

appliquéd duvet cover and pillowcases

Adorn a store-bought duvet cover and matching shams with an exuberant machine-appliquéd starburst pattern. (You could also make your own duvet cover, following the instructions on page 147.) Because the duvet is large and the pattern detailed, this project may take a while to complete. But don't be intimidated—the work is quite fun, and it's okay to work at your own pace. Rather than folding it up and putting it away between crafting sessions, keep the duvet out in your workspace so that you can easily pick up where you left off.

MATERIALS basic sewing supplies, appliquéd duvet cover and pillowcases template, clear tape, store-bought linen duvet cover and shams, transfer paper, tracing wheel, cardstock or cardboard, 2 yards (1.8m) lightweight linen (for appliqué pieces)

HOW-TO 1. Print out template pieces (see enclosed CD), and tape together. Lay the duvet cover on a flat surface and place the transfer paper on top; you will need to tape together several sheets. Lay the template on the paper, arranging so that part of the starburst extends past the edge. Trace the teardrops onto the duvet cover with the tracing wheel (don't worry if your marks are slightly off; they will just act as a guide to place the template pieces). Next, print the individual teardrop templates onto cardstock, or trace paper templates onto cardboard, and cut out. (You'll be tracing the templates many times so you want them to be sturdy.) With a disappearing-ink fabric pen, trace the templates onto the appliqué fabric; cut out.

2. Pin, then sew each teardrop, following the machine-appliqué technique on page 42. (Working with one piece at a time is easier than pinning everything at the start and reduces handling, which can cause fraying.) Repeat with remaining teardrop shapes until the design is complete; decorate shams with additional machine-appliquéd teardrop shapes in desired sizes.

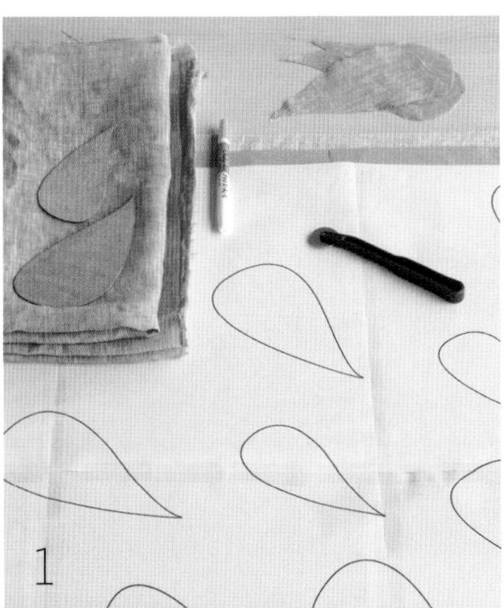

1

2

QUICK DUVET TIE

A duvet cover protects a comforter from spills, stains, and general wear and tear. To make it easier to slip the comforter into the cover (and to keep it from shifting around once inside), try this slight modification: Sew two pieces of 2-inch-long (5cm) fabric tape to all four inside corners of the cover; at each corner of the comforter, push the filler toward the center, and tie the fabric tape around the bunched fabric.

PROJECT:

bibs

Bibs make classic baby-shower and first-birthday gifts. And they are all the more meaningful when hand-sewn or -embellished. If you've been wanting to try out basic embroidery or other quick-sew techniques, a bib is an ideal first project: its small surface area means just one or two carefully stitched shapes and decorative details can make a big impression. Create a one-of-a-kind bib as a keepsake, or sew a whole stack to keep in the kitchen cupboard, diaper bag, stroller, or nursery. Here you'll find fabric and embellishment options to suit every taste, and nearly every stage of a little one's growth: Plain white bibs, made of cotton—soothing on an infant's skin—get cheerful pops of pattern and color with embroidery or bias-tape trim. For toddlers just learning to feed themselves, try oilcloth bibs with pockets that catches missed bites before they hit the ground. These water-resistant examples can also be wiped clean—a bonus for busy parents.

IN THIS CHAPTER: APPLE-EMBROIDERED BIB — BIAS TAPE–EMBELLISHED BIB — OILCLOTH POCKETED BIB

APPLE-EMBROIDERED BIB (OPPOSITE): *A is for apple...and adorable. Satin stitches and backstitches (page 48) create the apples and letters shown, and are strong enough to withstand repeated washings. Print the apple-embroidered bib templates (see enclosed CD), and cut out. Trace onto tracing paper with a sharp heat-transfer pencil (make thin marks). Place the transfer facedown, then iron the design onto the bib. With embroidery floss, satin-stitch the apples and backstitch to make the letters.*

a
IS FOR

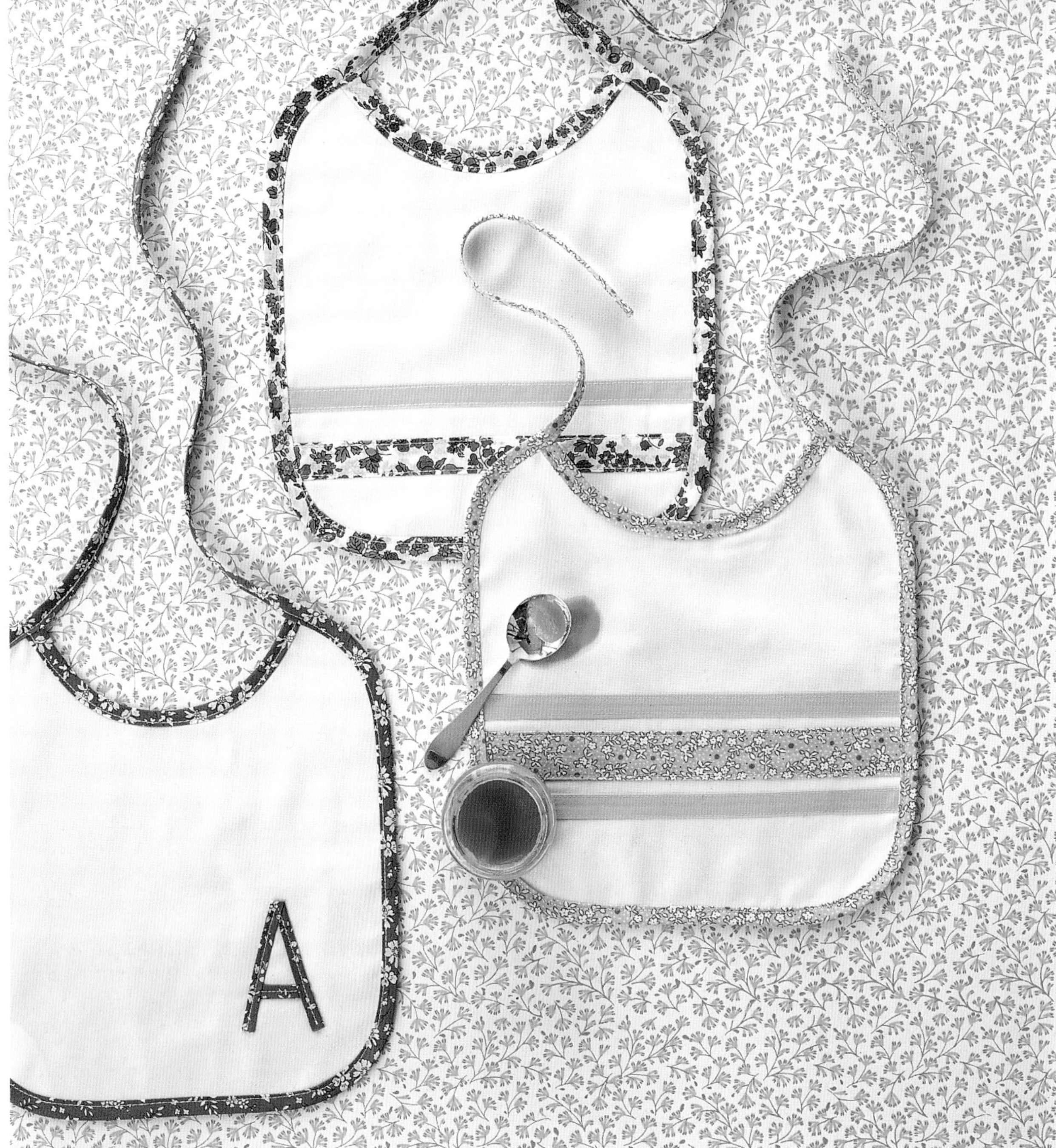

bias tape-embellished bib

Bias tape made from calico, gingham, polka-dot, or striped fabrics quickly dresses up a plain white bib. You can make bias tape (see page 369), or use store-bought versions. A few strips of tape also make easy appliquéd monograms.

MATERIALS basic sewing supplies, bias tape-embellished bib pattern, clear tape, white cotton fabric, 2 yards (1.8m) single-fold bias tape of any width (plus extra for stripes, monograms, or other embellishments)

HOW-TO 1. Print the pattern pieces (see enclosed CD), tape together, and cut out. Cut out bib from white fabric. For stripes, stitch tape in place on the bib, 1/8 inch (3mm) from the tape's upper and lower edges. For a monogram, form letter and stitch the pieces of tape to the bib, folding under the ends to prevent fraying. Stitch bias tape around the neckline, and trim any excess.

2. To cover the outer edge of the bib and make ties, cut the tape to 50 inches (127cm). Measure 11 1/2 inches (29cm) from the end of the bias tape, leaving it loose (this will be a tie). Attach the tape at one outer edge of the neckline, and stitch around the bib 1/8 inch (3mm) from the tape's edge, stopping at the opposite edge of the neckline. Measure 11 1/2 inches (29cm) for the second tie, and snip off any excess. Stitch the entire length of the tie, ending with a fold-over finish (page 369).

oilcloth pocketed bib

Stain-resistant oilcloth is an ideal material for bibs (and aprons; see page 106). It is available in a bounty of cheerful patterns, as well as solid colors. Pair two different patterns of fabric—one for the bib and one for the pocket (or forgo the pocket altogether). For durability, sew the bias tape to the oilcloth with quilting thread or a poly-cotton blend.

MATERIALS basic sewing supplies, bib and bib pocket patterns, clear tape, oilcloth, ½-inch (13mm) single-fold bias tape, quilting or all-purpose thread, snaps, Velcro tabs (optional)

HOW-TO 1. Print the pattern pieces (see enclosed CD), and cut out. Trace onto the right side of the oilcloth; cut out. Sew bias tape around the edges of each piece ⅛ inch (3mm) from the tape's edge, folding under the ends to prevent fraying.

2. Align the pocket with the bottom of the bib, and machine-stitch the pieces together along the bottom seam. Attach a snap to each side of the pocket (this will allow you to unsnap and fold down the pocket to rinse it out after meals), then close the neck hole with a snap, or sew on pieces of Velcro.

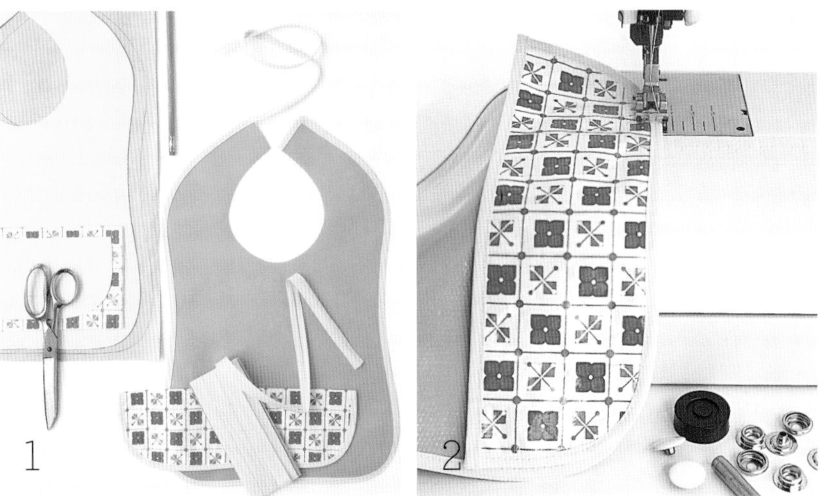

PROJECT:

blankets

Think of a blanket as comfort with four corners. Whether draped over a chair in easy reach or tucked beneath the chin, its warmth is always welcome. You can make a blanket quite easily, so don't let the large scale of such a project fool you. Start with a soft but sturdy swath of wool or cotton fabric, then embellish it to your heart's content.

In these pages, you'll find blankets of all kinds, including a receiving blanket for a newborn baby and a Melton cloth coverlet designed to last for generations. Whatever project you choose, the results will satisfy thanks to their eye-catching color and texture. And whether you choose to curl up in your creation or give it away, you'll have several square feet of beauty as proof of your handiwork.

IN THIS CHAPTER: EMBROIDERY-EDGED BASIC BLANKET — RIBBON-BORDER BLANKET — FRINGED THROW — FRENCH-KNOT BLANKET — FELTED-SWEATER PATCHWORK BLANKET — DOUBLE-SIDED RECEIVING BLANKET

EMBROIDERY-EDGED BASIC BLANKET (OPPOSITE): *For a warm, classic-looking coverlet, use the blanket stitch and worsted-weight cotton yarn to edge Melton wool or other medium-weight fabric.*

embroidery-edged basic blanket

SEE PHOTO, PAGE 157

Most fabric is not wide enough to make a full-, queen-, or king-size blanket, so you'll likely need to connect two lengths of fabric with a flat-felled seam; the raspberry wool-and-cashmere blanket on page 157 is constructed this way.

MATERIALS basic sewing supplies, 2 equal-size pieces of Melton wool or other medium-weight wool blend (together, these should measure 3 inches [7.5cm] longer and wider than your desired blanket dimensions), large embroidery needle, worsted-weight cotton yarn

HOW-TO 1. To connect 2 lengths of fabric, join them with a flat-felled seam: Lay one piece of fabric on top of the other, right sides facing, and pin along one long side. Machine-stitch 1 1/2 inches (6.5cm) in from the edge. Press the seam open, then to one side. Trim the concealed seam allowance to 1/4 inch (6mm). Press under the edge of the top seam allowance 3/8 inch (10mm), then position it evenly over the trimmed edge, and pin in place. Machine-stitch the folded edge to the blanket 1/8 inch (3mm) in from edge, parallel to the previous seam. Press flat.

2. Using a tapestry needle and the yarn, cross-stitch (page 50) over the seam. Hold the blanket right-side up, seam facing you. At one end, pull the needle through from the wrong side to the right, so that it emerges on the left side of the seam at the edge. Insert the needle diagonally down through the right line of the stitching and out horizontally through the left. Make a second diagonal stitch parallel to the first one, with space between the stitches equal to the width of the seam. Continue to create an entire row of diagonal "floats," or stitch backs, across the seam. When you reach the end, reverse directions.

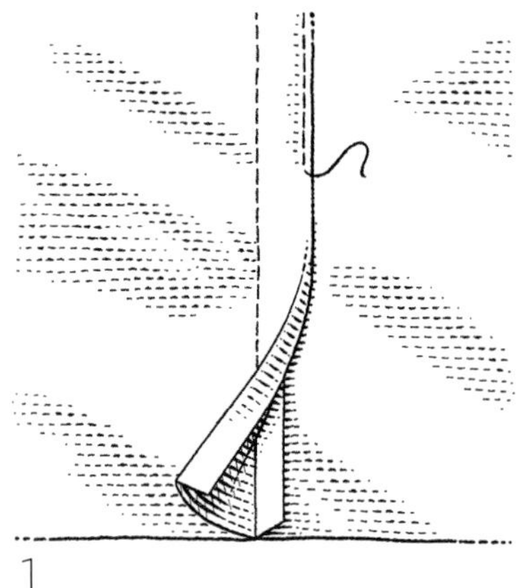

1

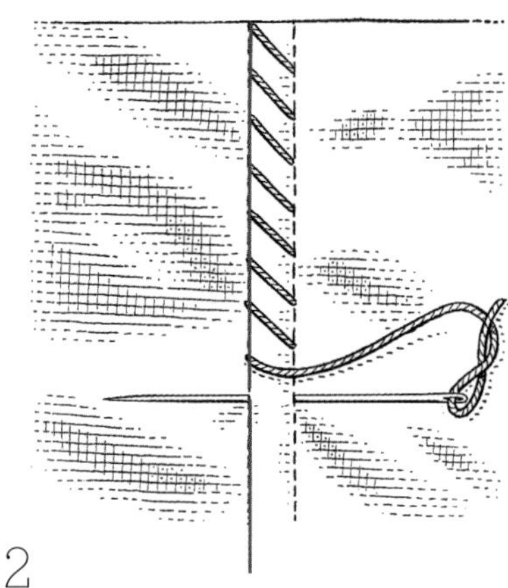

2

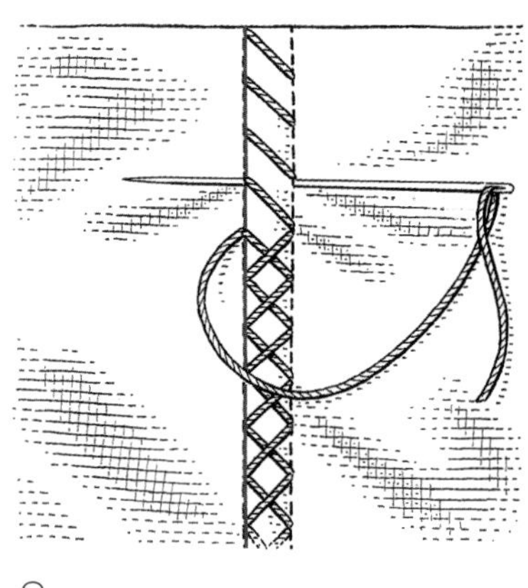

3

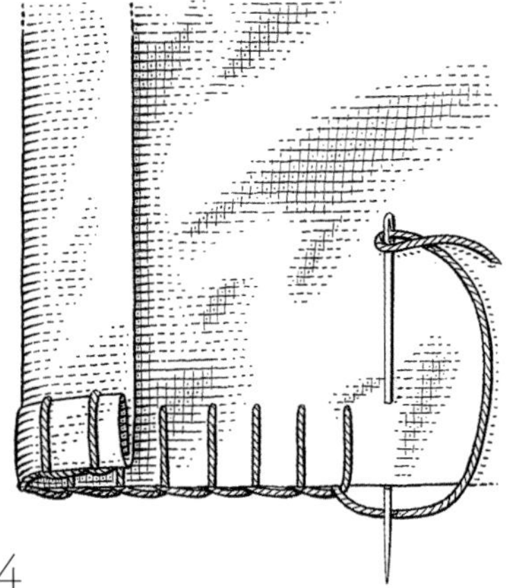

4

3. Work the same stitch heading away from you, still moving from the right to the left. The new floats will cross the old, forming a series of Xs.

4. Double-hem all edges: Turn and lightly press all edges under 3/4 inch (2cm), then 3/4 inch (2cm) again, overlapping the corners. Pin or baste in place. Use the embroidery needle and cotton yarn to finish the edge with a blanket stitch (page 49). Work the stitches so that they encase the 3/4-inch (2cm) hem and are spaced 1/2 inch (13mm) apart, as shown. At each corner, make one stitch on a diagonal. Continue stitching, working left to right, until all sides are finished.

BASIC BLANKET SIZES:

Blanket sizes aren't universally standardized, but here are general dimensions:

THROW 60 inches (152.5cm) wide by 54 inches (137cm) long

TWIN 60 inches wide (152.5cm) by 90 inches (229cm) long

DOUBLE 80 inches (203cm) wide by 90 inches (229cm) long

QUEEN 90 inches (229cm) wide by 90 inches (229cm) long

KING 105 inches (266.5cm) wide by 90 inches (229cm) long

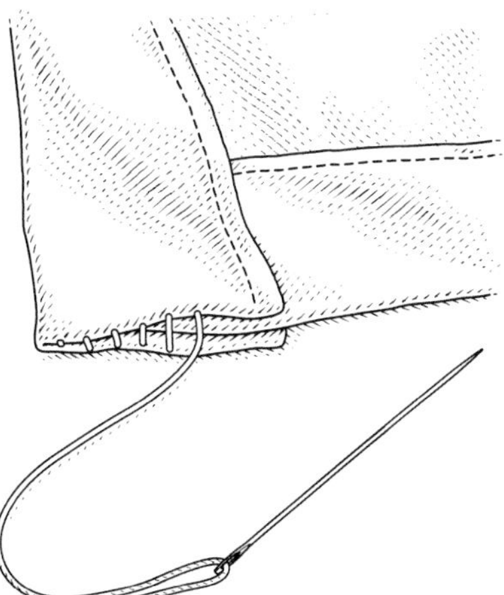

ribbon-border blanket

A ribbon hem visually frames a blanket and gives it a smooth edge. Start with a large piece of wool fabric. If you need to sew two pieces together to get the blanket dimensions you want, use the flat-felled seam method (opposite, step 1).

MATERIALS basic sewing supplies; Melton wool or other medium-weight wool blend; contrasting color of grosgrain, satin, or twill ribbon (at least 4 inches [10cm] wide)

HOW-TO Cut 4 pieces of ribbon: two to the length of a short side plus 1 inch (2.5cm), plus two to the length of a long side plus 1 inch (2.5cm). Press the ribbons in half lengthwise, wrong sides facing. Mark the width of the folded ribbon at both short sides of the blanket with chalk lines. Flip the blanket over, and repeat. Sandwich the blanket with the ribbon on the short sides so that each edge lines up with the tailor's chalk lines, and the ribbon extends ½ inch (13mm) past the blanket at each end. Pin. Fold under the excess at each end flush with the blanket edges. Pin in place, making sure that the hem is the same width on both sides of the blanket. Edge-stitch through all 3 layers, about ¼ inch (6mm) from the edge of the ribbon. Repeat for the long sides of the blanket. Hand-stitch the corners shut, as shown at left.

fringed throw

One easy way to make a blanket is to fringe the edges of a piece of soft, loosely woven fabric. This throw is made of mohair. A wide band of cross-stitches gives it graphic appeal.

MATERIALS basic sewing supplies, 1 ½ yards (1.4m) 60-inch-wide (152.5cm) mohair fabric, embroidery needle, mohair yarn in contrasting color (white yarn is shown)

HOW-TO For fringe, pull out some threads along the cut edges of the fabric, and zigzag-stitch along the top of the fringe (see illustration, right) to prevent the edge from unraveling. Using mohair yarn and an embroidery needle, cross-stitch three rows of large Xs (up and over 8 threads; see page 50 for instructions).

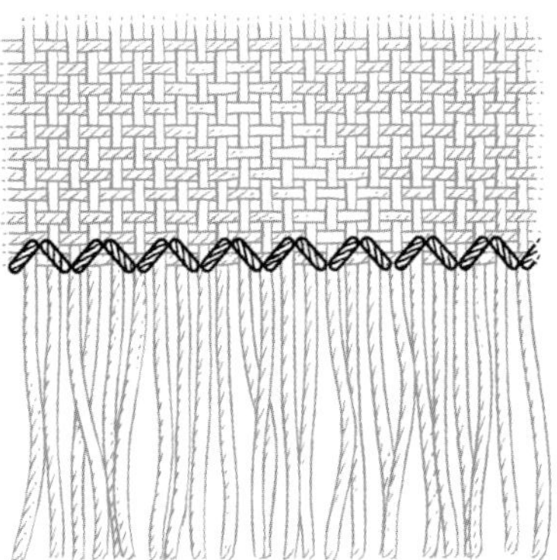

French-knot blanket

Evenly spaced French knots (page 52), stitched with yarn, are used to secure two layers of wool to create a blanket. Placed at equal intervals, the knots add a pleasing pattern and prevent the fabric from shifting. If you want to save the trouble of hemming, use wool felt.

MATERIALS basic sewing supplies, two 4-by-6-foot (1.2m × 1.8m) pieces of wool or other nonfraying fabric in contrasting colors (red and gray are shown), embroidery hoop, worsted-weight yarn in desired color (white is shown), darning needle

HOW-TO 1. Safety pin the layers of fabric together to keep them from shifting. To ensure the knots are evenly spaced, use a ruler and disappearing-ink fabric pen to mark dots in a grid. The dots for the blanket pictured are marked 8 inches (20.5cm) apart.

2. Place a section of the blanket in the embroidery hoop. Make French knots: Pass the threaded needle up from the blanket's back to the front through the marked dot, leaving a 2-inch (5cm) tail on the back. Keep the yarn taut with one hand, and use your other hand to wind it around the needle twice. Reinsert the tip of the needle into the fabric as close as possible to where it first emerged. Before passing the needle through the fabric, pull the yarn tight and be sure it is flush with the blanket. Pass the needle back through the blanket to create the knot. Secure on reverse and snip ends evenly.

felted-sweater patchwork blanket

Squares, rectangles, and triangles cut from a variety of ivory colored, machine-felted sweaters are pieced together to make a sweet blanket. The wool sweaters—some of which have cable or Aran-style patterns—were machine-washed in hot water and dried on high heat, allowing the fibers to pull together to produce a soft, thick felt. (For more on machine felting, see page 96.) For the patchwork, knits from sweaters of a similar weight and color work best; a variety of patterns adds visual and textural appeal.

MATERIALS basic sewing supplies, sweaters

HOW-TO Machine-wash and -dry the sweaters on high heat. (To protect both machines, wash and dry the sweaters in lingerie bags.) When you can cut a sweater and it doesn't fray, it is felted (you may need to wash and dry the sweaters several times). Cut out and arrange the pieces in a pleasing pattern to make a blanket (the one shown measures 3 ½ by 5 feet [1.1m × 1.5m]). Sew the pieces together with a ¼- to ⅜-inch (6–9mm) zigzag stitch. Do not overlap the pieces; instead, feed them side by side under the presser foot. Order the pieces so that those with hemmed edges form the perimeter of the blanket (otherwise, hem the edges to finish).

double-sided receiving blanket

Give new purpose to pretty fabric remnants by incorporating them into receiving blankets for a baby. They're super-easy to sew: Pair a lightweight natural fabric in an appealing pattern, such as a floral motif, polka dots, or seersucker, with thin flannel for warmth. Here, two blankets are stacked and tied together as a gift; the top corner of each is folded down to reveal the pattern on the reverse side.

MATERIALS basic sewing supplies, 1 yard (0.9m) of lightweight cotton fabric, 1 yard (0.9m) of cotton flannel

HOW-TO Cut two 36-by-45-inch (91cm × 114 cm) rectangles: one from the lightweight cotton, and the other from cotton flannel. Pin the pieces of fabric together, right sides facing. Machine-stitch the edges with a ½-inch (13mm) seam allowance, leaving a 3-inch (7.5cm) opening. Trim off the points of the corners. Turn the blanket inside out. Press the edges, then hand-sew the opening closed with a slipstitch (page 31).

PROJECT:

books

Between the covers of any book are stories. These can be literal, of course—as in the case of storybooks, journals, and novels—or figurative: After all, what are collections of recipes or photographs if not family narratives? Guest books, albums, gardening journals, and daily organizers, too, have tales to tell. And with hand-stitched and -crafted covers, they're sure to become treasured keepsakes.

Use time-tested techniques to fashion classic book covers from less-expected materials, including felt and oilcloth. For little hands, make soft books that gently introduce numbers and barnyard animal shapes. Or wrap a gardening journal with raw linen adorned with three-dimensional ribbon vegetables and fruits to create a sweet record of the seasons.

Terrific for weekend and evening crafting, these books make thoughtful gifts. So stock up on inexpensive journals and photo albums when you see them on sale, then tuck them away. When a gift-giving occasion arises, you'll be all set to create a truly personalized page-turner.

IN THIS CHAPTER: LEATHER NOTEBOOK AND CHECKBOOK COVERS — FELT BOOK JACKETS — GARDEN JOURNALS — OILCLOTH BOOK COVERS — APPLIQUÉD NUMBER BOOK

LEATHER NOTEBOOK AND CHECKBOOK COVERS (OPPOSITE): *Leather makes a durable and attractive covering for journals, checkbooks, and datebooks, and is available in a beautiful array of colors. The covers pictured are closed with a variety of materials, including snaps, ties, and elastic cord.*

WESTCOTT
JAMES L. GUBLER
40448 Sawgrass Court
Las Vegas, NV 89101
103
date
pay to the order of
$
dollars
memo
0000007028730386917592268 3 00103

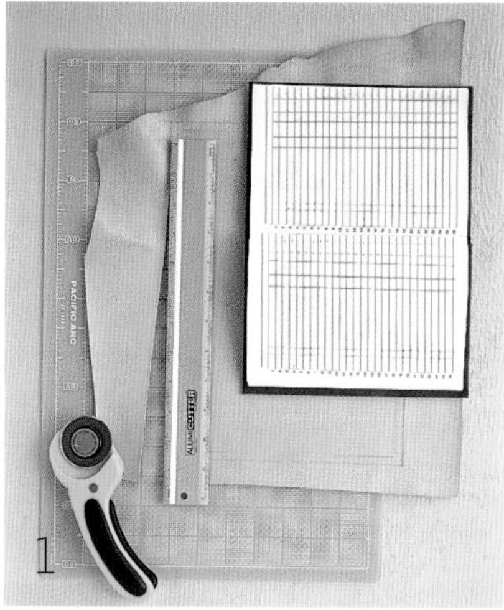

leather notebook and checkbook covers SEE PHOTO, PAGE 165

Leather conforms to different shapes, develops a soft, well-worn feel, and doesn't fray, so there's no need to hem the edges. Look for a leather hide that is 1⁄16 inch (1.6mm) or thinner, so that it can be fed through a home sewing machine. The best sources for leather are fabric stores, shoe-repair shops, and online retailers, where you can find a range of colors, thicknesses, textures, and perforated patterns.

MATERIALS basic sewing supplies; notebook or checkbook; colored leather hide (1⁄16 inch [1.6mm] or thinner); self-healing mat; no-slip ruler; rotary cutter; multipurpose cement; poly-cotton thread; leather needle; nonstick presser foot; leather hole punch (optional); snap kit or grommet kit, or elastic cording (optional); pinking shears (optional)

HOW-TO 1. Trace the notebook or checkbook onto the suede side of the leather, rolling it over to include the sides and the spine. (For checkbooks, add 2 inches [5cm] to the sides that will be folded to create a space for the pen loop.) Add 1⁄4 inch (6mm) to the perimeter for a seam allowance. Place the leather on a self-healing mat and hold it in place with the ruler; cut it out with a rotary cutter.

2. For a tie closure, cut two 1⁄8-inch-wide (3mm) strips of leather; cement one to each suede side of the leather. To create a front pocket, cut a rectangle of leather, center it on the front of the cover, and cement it on all but the top edge; let it dry. Before stitching, raise the tension according to your sewing machine's instructions, and make the stitches slightly longer than you would for regular fabric to prevent the leather from tearing (about 8 to 10 stitches per inch [2.5cm]); stitch the 3 sides of the pocket that you glued with a 1⁄8-inch (3mm) seam allowance. To make a pen loop for a checkbook, cut a 2-by-4-inch (5cm × 10cm) strip of leather; fold it lengthwise. Leaving a 1⁄2-inch (13mm) loop, cement the ends together; sew a line of reinforcing stitches. Cement the pen loop onto the spine. Cut 2 side flaps that will overlay three-fourths of the notebook or 3 inches (7.5cm) of the checkbook. Cement them on 3 sides; let dry.

3. Stitch the sides of the flaps you glued with a 1⁄8-inch (3mm) seam allowance. For a snap closure, use the hole punch to make small holes for the snap or grommet (as the kit requires); insert the snap or grommet. If you're using elastic cording, cut a piece twice the width of the notebook or checkbook. Slip it through a small hole punched through the bottom cover, then knot it, leaving the large loop on the outside to cinch it together. To create a band closure, use pinking shears to cut a thin strip of leather that will fit around your book; sew along the top and bottom edge in an alternating color and use the hole punch to pierce small holes for the snap (as the kit requires); insert the snap.

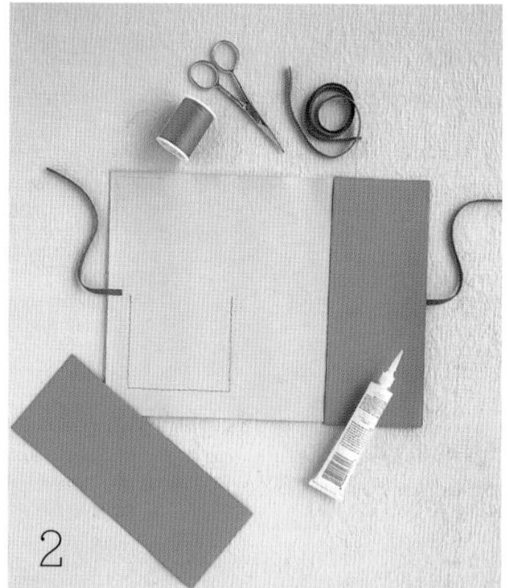

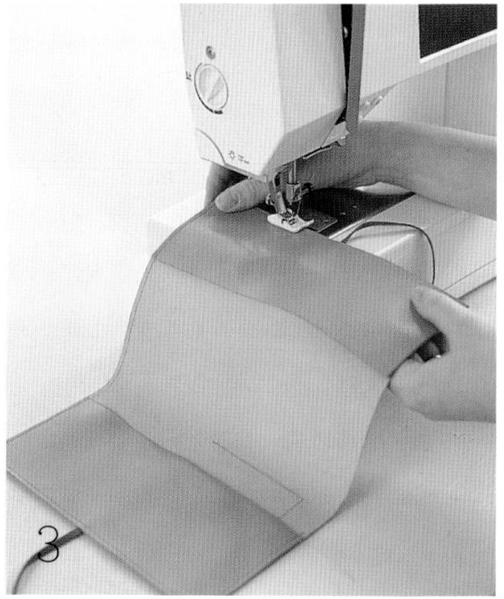

felt book jackets

Felt's soft texture and strong fibers make it a natural choice for book covers. The fabric is stiff enough to lend structure to a cover, but also quite pliable and forgiving so it won't pull or pucker while you're sewing. And because it requires no hemming, a felt book cover takes about half as long to sew as one made from other fabrics.

MATERIALS basic sewing supplies, journal or book, wool felt, size 14 needle, 100 percent polyester thread, elastic cord (optional), 1/4-inch (6mm) grommet kit (optional), buttons (optional), button-cover kit (optional)

HOW-TO Trace the journal onto the wrong side of the felt with tailor's chalk, rolling it over to include the sides and the spine, and extend each long side to enclose the front and back covers, as shown; add a 1/4-inch (6mm) seam allowance to all sides. Cut out the rectangle. Fold each short edge of the felt rectangle over to form a pocket that the book covers can slide into. Steam-iron the folds. Pin the top and bottom of each folded edge, and sew with a 1/4-inch (6mm) seam allowance. If you're using elastic cord for a closure, sew a button to one side of the felt cover, and a small loop of elastic cord to the inside edge of the opposite side. To create a band closure, cut a thin strip of felt that will fit around the book; mark where the button and buttonhole should be placed, sew on a felt-covered button (for instructions on covering buttons with a button-cover kit, see page 366), and make a slit for a buttonhole. To make a bookmark, cut a long, thin rectangle of felt with pinking shears; install a grommet in the top (following the grommet kit instructions) and tie a tassel to the grommet. The tassel is made from a 6-by-2-inch (15cm × 5cm) length of felt with a 1-inch (2.5cm) deep fringe cut along one side, then rolled tightly around a cord and secured with a few stitches. The other end of the cord is knotted through the grommet hole.

FELT BOOK BAND

This alternate felt button band is appropriate for a very special book, such as a wedding-guest book or keepsake journal. Cut a strip of felt long enough to wrap around the book and overlap it by 3 inches (7.5cm) or so (the one pictured is 3 inches [7.5cm] wide, or about one-third the height of the cover). Cut one end to be rounded; wrap the felt around the book. Position a button on top of the felt, approximately 1 inch (2.5cm) in from edge of the book; holding the button in place, carefully slide the band off the book. Sew on the button through both layers of felt. Slide the band onto the book.

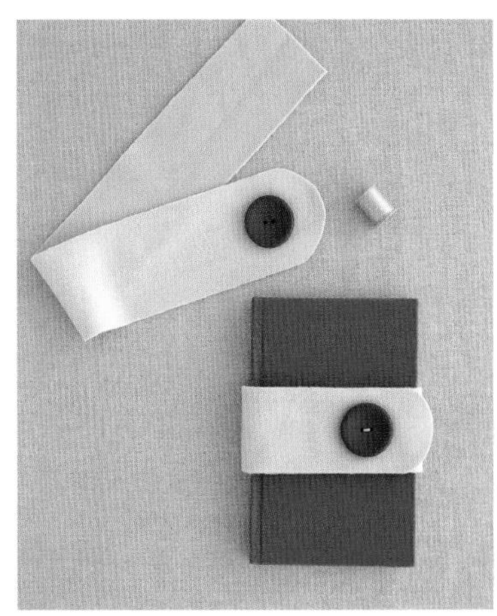

Rosemary

garden journals

Spruce up a pair of gardening journals with fabric jackets. These are created from a beige dish towel and orange linen. Plump fruits and vegetables are embroidered on top. For detailed ribbon-embroidery instructions, see pages 58–59.

MATERIALS basic sewing supplies, garden journals, linen dish towel or linen fabric, embroidery ribbon, embroidery needle, button and button-covering kit, wax twine

HOW-TO 1. Measure the height and length of the journal; for the length, measure the closed journal from edge to edge, around the spine. Add 4 inches (10cm) each to the height and length measurements. With a disappearing-ink fabric pen and a ruler, draw a rectangle with these dimensions on the fabric, and cut it out. Zigzag-stitch around all the edges; this will keep the fabric from unraveling.

2. Place the book in the center of the fabric and use a disappearing-ink fabric pen to make several marks along the top and bottom edges of the book. Remove the book; with the ruler, make a line 1/8 inch (3mm) below the bottom marks and 1/8 inch (3mm) above the top marks for the seam allowance. Fold the fabric in at these new lines, and press.

3. Fold the right edge of the fabric over 2 inches (5cm), and press. Slip the back cover of the journal into the folded flap and wrap the remaining length of the fabric over the front cover. Make several marks where the front edge of the book meets the fabric. Remove the book and press the fabric at the marks. Pin the right and left flaps down, and sew all along the top and bottom edges with a 1/8-inch (3mm) seam allowance.

4. For an embroidered cover, mark the placement of the fruits and vegetables with a disappearing-ink pen. Embroider your chosen designs, using the glossary at right and following the instructions on pages 58–59.

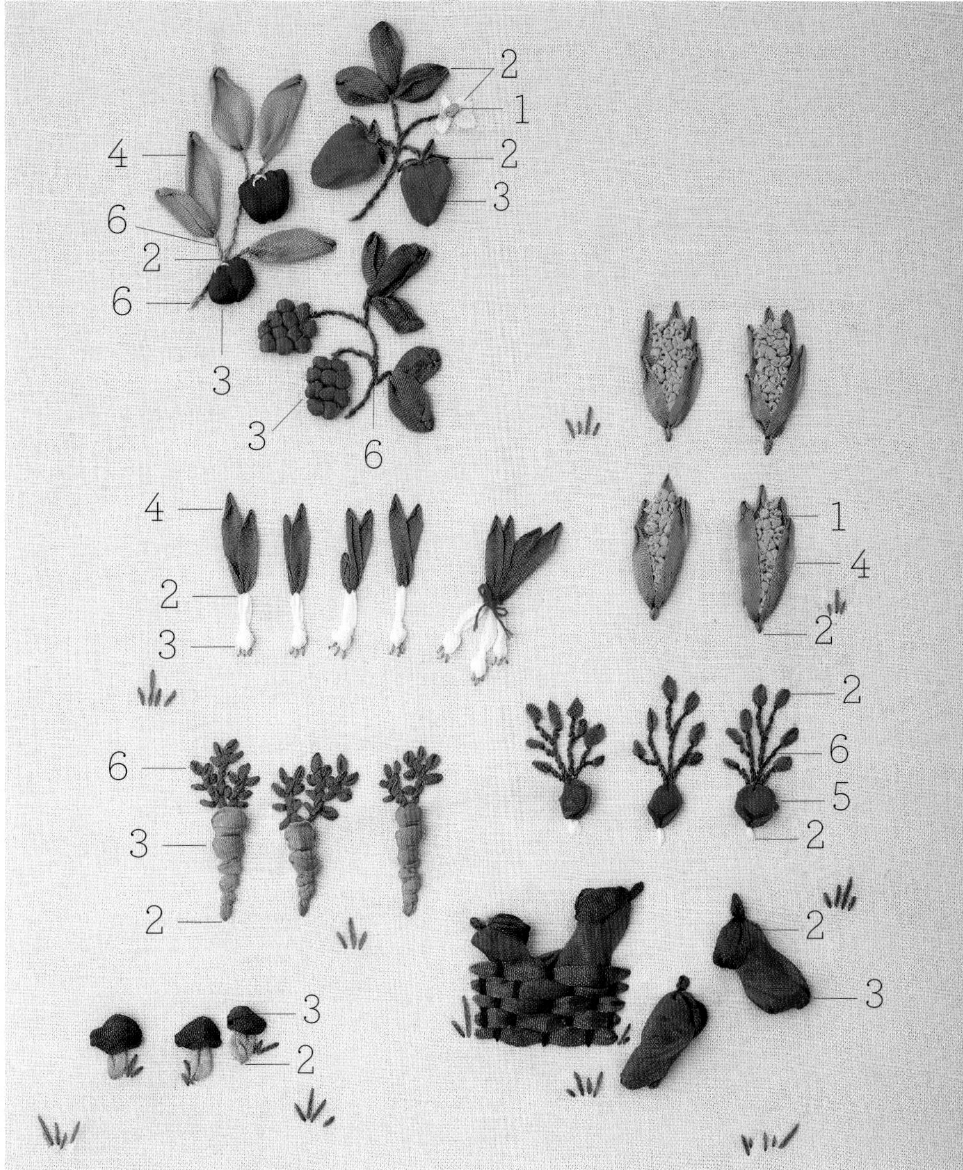

5. For a button closure, cover a button with an embroidered piece of linen (see page 366 for instructions on using a button-cover kit), and sew the button onto the front cover. Tie one end of wax twine around the base of the button, and then wrap the remaining twine around the book.

FRUIT AND VEGETABLE GLOSSARY

Six basic stitches yield an ample crop:

1. **FRENCH KNOT**
2. **STRAIGHT STITCH**
3. **PADDED STRAIGHT STITCH**
4. **RIBBON STITCH**
5. **PADDED RIBBON STITCH**
6. **STEM STITCH**

oilcloth book covers

Construct a set of durable oilcloth covers for cookbooks, crafts books, textbooks, or other volumes you'd like to keep safe from spills. You can use the same method with other waterproof materials, such as vinyl tablecloth fabric.

MATERIALS basic sewing supplies, books, oilcloth, paper clips

HOW-TO Measure the height and length of the book; for the length, measure the closed book from edge to edge, around the spine. Add 3/4 inch (2cm) to the height and 4 inches (10cm) to the length measurements. Using a disappearing-ink fabric pen and ruler, draw out a rectangle with these dimensions on the wrong side of the oilcloth, and cut out. Fold each short side in by 2 inches (5cm), and hold the oilcloth in place with paper clips. Machine-stitch across the top and bottom edges of the oilcloth cover, with a 1/8-inch (3mm) seam allowance. Unfold and insert book.

appliquéd number book

Practice your appliqué skills as you introduce numbers and a host of farmyard creatures to a child. The cotton counting book shown here features Swiss dot, calico, checked, and gingham appliqué shapes; the animals' features are embroidered. See page 41 for more detailed appliqué instructions, and page 48 for embroidery stitches.

MATERIALS basic sewing supplies, appliquéd number book templates, clear tape, assortment of patterned and solid cotton and felt fabrics, fabric glue, embroidery floss, cotton thread, tweezers, sharps (needles for making tiny stitches), embroidery scissors

HOW-TO Print the templates (see enclosed CD), and cut out. Measure and cut six 13-by-6 5/8-inch (33cm × 17cm) rectangles from solid fabric. With a disappearing-ink fabric pen, trace appliqué shapes onto patterned fabrics; cut out. Position and appliqué the numerals and designs on five rectangles, following the hand-turn method on page 41, and embroidering the details afterward; if you like, appliqué a design for the cover rectangle. Align "5" and "4" rectangles, with right sides facing. Machine-stitch around the perimeter, with a 1/8-inch (3mm) seam allowance and leaving a small opening on one side. Turn right-side out; slip-stitch (page 31) the opening closed. Repeat, pairing "2" and "3" rectangles, and "1" and the cover. To create a border around each page, zigzag-stitch along the edge in a contrasting color. To bind the book, place the cover facedown, then place "5" facedown, then "2" facedown on top, and machine-stitch the center seam through all the layers.

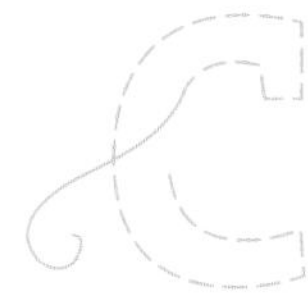

PROJECT:

clothing

Making your own clothing may seem old-fashioned, but there are plenty of modern reasons to do so. Style is one. By choosing fabrics, colors, and patterns that appeal to you, and adding distinctive details and trim, you can make skirts, dresses, pants, and other garments that you could never buy ready-made. Comfort is another. Sewing a garment allows you to fit it properly and adjust the height of the hem or length of the sleeves.

Most of the clothing projects that follow are straightforward and can be completed in a few hours. For adult garments, such as a wrap skirt and drawstring pants, making a muslin version of the pattern first will help you determine if it should be altered to fit. For kids' clothes, such as an adorable baby kimono and little girl's shirt dress, you should be able to skip this step.

Of course, crafting your own clothing doesn't always mean you need to start from scratch. In this chapter, you'll learn to add appliquéd designs to a store-bought shirt and to use fabric printing to embellish a sarong. Whether you choose to create a new garment or merely to embellish an existing one, you're sure to enjoy the chance to show off your personal style.

IN THIS CHAPTER: NO-SEW SCALLOPED WRAP SKIRT — EASY TUBE DRESS — A-LINE WRAP SKIRT — SIMPLE SARONG — SEA-PRINT SARONG — HAWAIIAN-PATTERN APPLIQUÉD ROBE — BABY KIMONO — GIRL'S SHIRT DRESS — BUTTERFLY-APPLIQUÉD SHAWL — FLOWER-APPLIQUÉD SHIRT — DRAWSTRING PANTS

NO-SEW SCALLOPED WRAP SKIRT (OPPOSITE): *Made of Ultrasuede, this skirt gets its curves from the outline of an oatmeal canister, and fastens at the back with a button.*

no-sew scalloped wrap skirt SEE PHOTO, PAGE 173

If you can sew on a button, you can make this skirt. It's cut from a long piece of cut-and-go Ultrasuede. You can either draw the skirt by hand, or use the pattern on the CD instead. Before cutting the skirt fabric, make a practice version with inexpensive muslin to test for size, then use that as a template to cut out the skirt.

MATERIALS basic sewing supplies; no-sew scalloped wrap skirt pattern; clear tape; 1 3/4 yards (1.6m) of 45-inch (114cm) wide muslin; 1 3/4 yards (1.6m) of heavyweight 45-inch-wide (114cm) Ultrasuede (for a skirt larger than size medium, you will need to buy 2 yards [1.8m]); 32-ounce (907g) oatmeal container; large button (for closure)

HOW-TO 1. If using the paper pattern, print the pieces (see enclosed CD), tape together, and cut out. Cut out a version of the pattern from the muslin, and skip to step 4. Otherwise, use the following instructions to create a muslin version without a pattern: On a flat surface, fold the muslin in half so it measures 31 by 45 inches (76cm × 114cm, or 36 by 45 inches if you are making a skirt larger than a size medium). Orient the fabric so that the fold is on your right-hand side. With a disappearing-ink fabric pen, mark 10 inches (25.5cm) up on the folded edge (from the lower right-hand corner), and draw a convex curved line from the point to the lower left-hand corner.

2. Mark a spot on the edge opposite the fold about 39 inches (99cm) up from the bottom. From that mark, draw a convex curved line to the upper right-hand corner (the other folded edge). Cut on the lines, rounding the lower left-hand corner. Wrap the skirt around your waist to fit. If the skirt is not big enough to overlap about 9 to 10 inches (23–25.5cm), repeat step 1 with a new piece of muslin, cutting a deeper curve from the bottom end.

3. Trace the oatmeal container to make shallow scallops along the edge (see illustration, below). Cut the scalloped edge through both layers at the waist. Fold back the top layer, and trace scallops around one end. Wrap the skirt around the waist to overlap; let the scalloped end drape.

4. Pin the finished muslin pattern (adjusted for size, if necessary) to the Ultrasuede fabric (folded in half, so it measures 31 by 45 inches [76cm × 114cm] or 36 by 45 inches [91cm × 114cm]). Mark the pattern with tailor's chalk. Cut out the fabric. Wrap the skirt around your waist to overlap; let the scalloped end drape. Mark the closure spot on the bottom layer with a pin. Sew the button on the marked spot. Snip a small slit in the top layer to serve as a buttonhole.

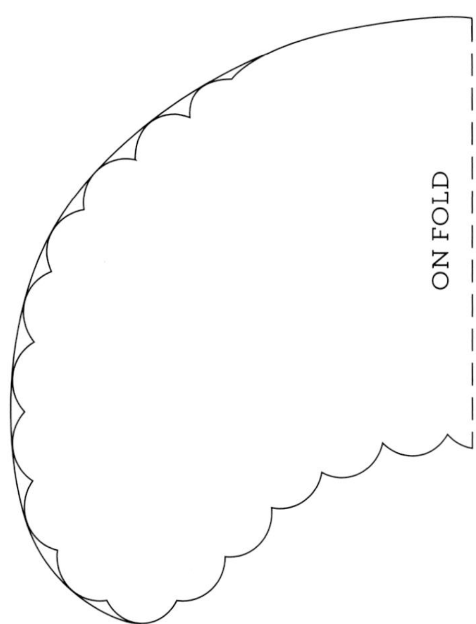

easy tube dress

With a mere 2 yards (1.8m) of fabric and a yard (0.9m) of cord, this chic, simple dress is a great project for beginning sewers, and it can be made in about an hour. If you're using striped material, make sure the pattern is vertical.

MATERIALS basic sewing supplies; about 2 yards (1.8m) 60-inch-wide (1.5m) fabric (you may need 4 yards [3.6m] if you're using a 45-inch-wide [114cm] bolt, depending on your measurements); 1 yard (0.9m) decorative cord, drapery rope, or ribbon

HOW-TO 1. Wash, dry, and press the fabric. Cut into 2 same-size rectangles. To determine the width, measure around your body at the widest point, add 7 inches (18cm), then divide in half. For length, measure from the top of your shoulder to the desired hemline; add 5 inches (12.5cm). Lay the rectangles together with right sides facing, and pin along long edges.

2. Use tailor's chalk to mark each long edge about 8 inches (20.5cm) from the top (for the armholes); on one side make another mark about 23 inches (58.5cm) from the bottom (for an ankle-length dress) to create a side slit. Starting at the top marks, machine-stitch down each side with a 1-inch (2.5cm) seam allowance, stopping at the slit mark on one side.

3. Press open the seam allowances, including the edges you have not sewn. At the armholes and slit, tuck the unfinished edges under 1/4 inch (6mm), press, and edge-stitch.

4. To create a channel, fold the front and back necklines over by 2 inches (5cm), wrong sides facing; press. Tuck the unfinished edges under 1/4 inch (6mm), press, and edge-stitch. Insert the cord through the channel, and tie. Fold the bottom hem over 1/2 inch (13mm), press, fold over 2 1/2 inches (6.3cm), press, and edge-stitch 1/8 inch (3mm) from the inner fold.

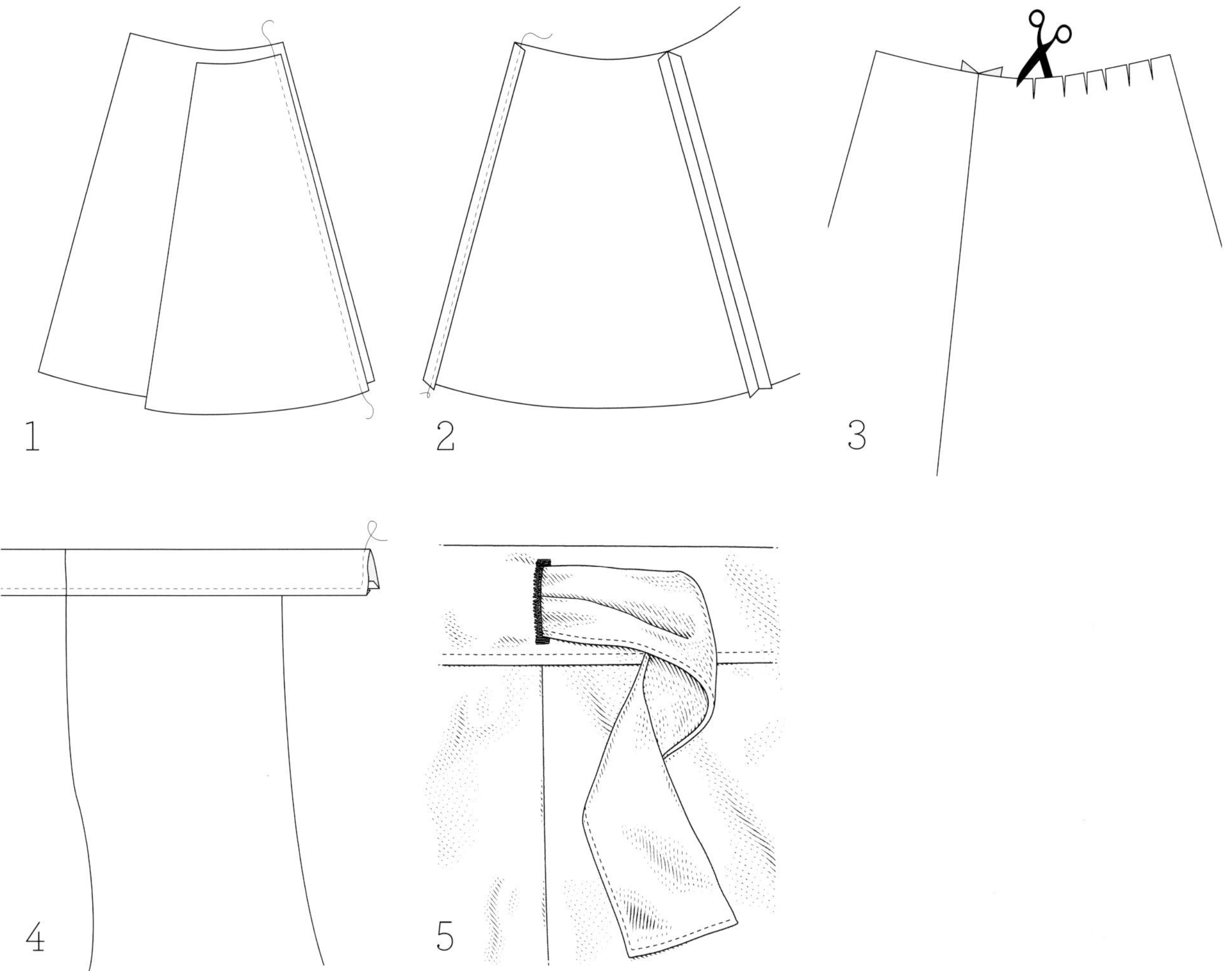

A-line wrap skirt

A wrap skirt retains the flattering shape of an A-line skirt, but doesn't require complicated darts or a zipper closure. With only five pattern pieces and just a few more seams, this skirt is easily sewn in a few hours. Choose a fabric that has a nice drape, but won't wrinkle easily.

MATERIALS basic sewing supplies, A-line wrap skirt pattern, clear tape, 3 yards (2.75m) medium-weight cotton

HOW-TO 1. Wash, dry, and press the fabric. Print the pattern pieces (see enclosed CD), tape together, and cut out the pattern, following the lines for your size. Fold the fabric lengthwise, wrong sides facing. Cut out the skirt pieces as directed on the pattern. Pin one side panel and center panel together, right sides facing. Sew the pieces together with a ½-inch (13mm) seam allowance. Press open the seam and finish the edges with a zigzag seam (page 36); press the seams open again. Repeat with the other side panel.

2. On the unfinished straight edge of the right front panel sew a double hem: Fold the edge over ¼ inch (6mm), press, fold again ¼ inch (6mm), press, pin, and edge-stitch. Repeat on the unfinished straight edge of left front panel.

3. To help the waistband lie flat, clip the curved top edge of the skirt, making ¼-inch (6mm) cuts and spacing the clips every ½ inch (13mm) (see "How to Sew Curves and Corners," page 35).

4. To create the waistband strap, join the waistband pieces: Pin pieces together, right sides facing, and sew together at one of the short ends with a ½-inch (13mm) seam allowance. Press the seams open. Fold and press each long edge of the waistband strap over ½ inch (13mm). Fold and press both short ends of the waistband strap over ½ inch (13mm). Fold the waistband strap in half, so that the long edges meet; press. Pin the waistband strap ½ inch (13mm) over the top edge of the skirt, aligning the waistband seam with the right side seam. Topstitch the entire length of the waistband strap ⅛ inch (3mm) from the bottom edge of the strap. Edge-stitch the ends of the strap.

5. Use a ⅛-inch (3mm) zigzag stitch to create a 1 ¾-inch (4.5cm) buttonhole (page 370) in the waistband strap above the left side seam. Use a small pair of scissors to cut open the hole. Double hem the skirt: Fold bottom edge over ¼ inch (6mm), press, fold over ¼ inch (6mm) again, press, pin, and edge-stitch.

simple sarong

Cover up with a breezy beach wrap. The one shown is fashioned from Indian cotton, cut from a 45-inch (114cm) bolt.

MATERIALS basic sewing supplies, cotton voile or other thin cotton fabric, 48-inch (122cm) length of ⅝-inch-wide (16mm) twill ribbon

HOW-TO To determine the length of cloth you'll need, measure from your waist to your ankle. For the width, measure around your hips, multiply that number by 2, and add 2 inches (5cm). Wash, dry, and press the fabric. Cut the fabric to the desired dimension. Double hem the short sides and the longer bottom edge: Fold each side over ½ inch (13mm), press, fold ½ inch (13mm) again, press, pin, and edge-stitch. To make the waistband, double hem the unfinished edge: Fold fabric over ½ inch (13mm), press, fold 1 inch (2.5cm), press, pin, and edge-stitch. To add ties, cut the twill tape in half, tuck one piece in each end of the waistband, and stitch in place.

sea-print sarong

Customize a handmade or store-bought sarong with printed motifs of seashells, sea stars, or fish. The sarong pictured is printed with a subtle and sophisticated tone-on-tone design, and finished with a hand-rolled hem, similar to the technique used for a handkerchief (page 246). For more on fabric printing, see page 87.

MATERIALS basic sewing supplies (optional); old towels; store-bought sarong or thin cotton fabric; fabric paint; sponge brush; practice fabric; seashells, sea stars, or rubber fish forms

HOW-TO If using a store-bought sarong, print on the fabric with a rubber sea star or other printing form as described on page 88. Let the paint set according to the manufacturer's instructions.
If making a sarong from scratch, cut the fabric to the desired dimensions, then print. Let the paint set, and finish the four sides of the fabric with a rolled hem (page 246), or finish as described for the simple sarong (above).

Hawaiian-pattern appliquéd robe

Inspired by the bold floral prints of Hawaiian quilts, this appliquéd linen robe makes a striking display, on or off.

MATERIALS basic sewing supplies, Hawaiian-pattern appliquéd robe template, store-bought linen robe, cotton fabric (for appliqué motif), appliqué needle

HOW-TO Print the template (see enclosed CD), enlarged to fit the size of the fabric square, and cut out. Wash, dry, and press the robe and fabric. Cut a square of fabric wide enough to span the robe's shoulders and drape it partway down each sleeve (the fabric used here was 20 inches [51cm] square). Fold the fabric, following the instructions on page 70 (see "Preparing to Cut the Appliqué Motif"). Lay the template on top of the folded fabric triangle, aligning the V of the template with the bottom-left corner. Trace the template with a disappearing-ink fabric pen. Pin fabric layers together inside the traced outline. Cut along the outline with sharp, pointed shears. Unfold fabric, and cut off one of the motif's 4 arms, discarding it. On a large work surface, position the motif on the robe, and pin in place. Baste 1/4 inch (6mm) inside the motif's perimeter with a 1/2-inch (13mm) running stitch (page 31). Using the appliqué needle, secure the motif to the robe, following the hand-turn appliqué instructions on page 41. Remove the basting stitches. Press.

Made from shirting fabric and trimmed with contrasting bias tape, these baby kimono shirts are soft against the skin. And they're comfortable and light enough to layer underneath winter clothes, as well. For beginning sewers, woven fabrics like these are easier to work with than knits.

baby kimono

Many features of traditional Japanese kimonos translate wonderfully to everyday baby clothes. Their wrap-style construction is ideal for babies, who dislike having clothing pulled over their heads. Short kimonos make lightweight, comfortable shirts, while longer ones work as dresses or coats. And the double layer of material across the chest will add extra warmth where a toddler needs it most.

MATERIALS basic sewing supplies, baby kimono pattern, clear tape, 1 yard (0.9m) of lightweight fabric (such as cotton shirting or lightweight wool), 2 yards (1.8m) single-fold bias tape, loop turner, 10 inches (25.5cm) of thin ribbon

HOW-TO 1. Print the desired size pattern pieces (see enclosed CD), tape together, and cut out. (If you are using a thick fabric, such as double-face wool, use the next size up.) Wash, dry, and press the fabric. Lay the fabric wrong-side up, pin the pattern pieces on top, and cut them out (a 3/8-inch [10mm] seam allowance is included in the pattern). Mark the dots on the fabric pieces with a disappearing-ink fabric pen. Make the ties: Cut a 21-inch (53.5cm) piece of single-fold bias tape. Open the tape, fold it in half, with right sides facing, and sew along the crease parallel to the fold. Trim close to the stitching. With a loop turner, turn it inside out; press. Cut into 3 equal pieces. Lay the main garment piece flat, wrong-side up, front toward you. Lift the fabric at angled cut at the shoulder; pin 2 ties at the dots, positioning as shown. Fold up the sleeve hems by 3/8 inch (10mm) twice; press, pin, and topstitch.

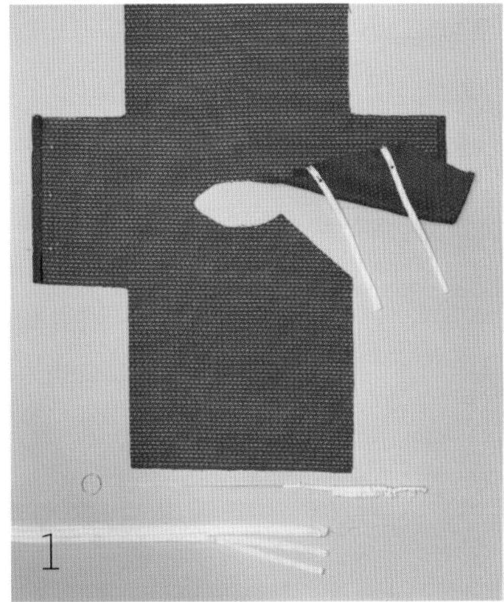

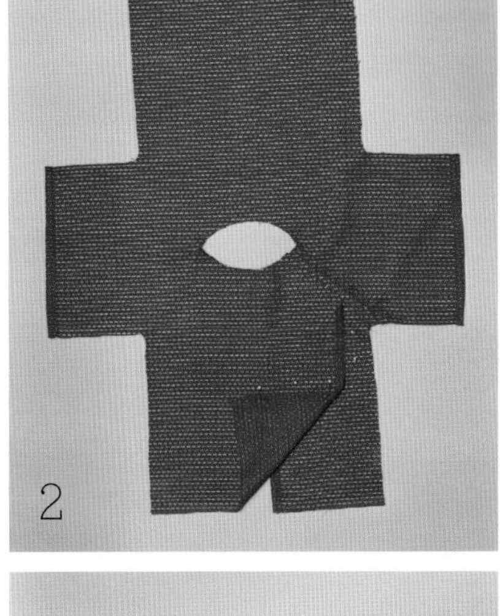

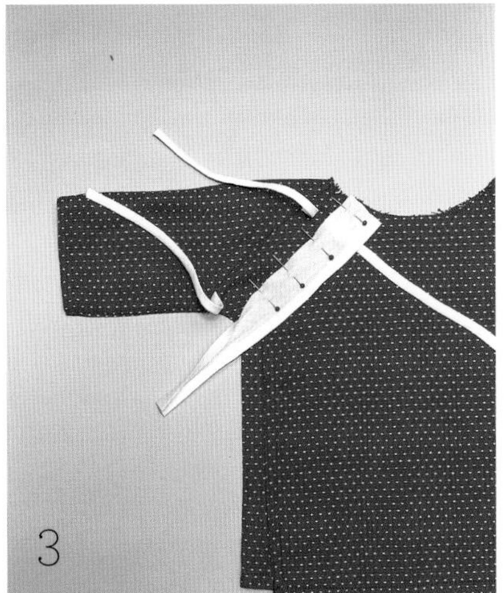

2. Lay the front-flap piece wrong-side up; fold the left side in by 3/8 inch (10mm) twice; press, pin, and topstitch. Place the front-flap piece on the main-garment piece over the right sleeve, right sides facing; align the angled shoulder edges, sandwiching in the ends of the ties, and pin. Stitch along the angled edge with a 3/8-inch (10mm) seam allowance. Zigzag-stitch the edges. Beneath the angled shoulder, fold the side edge of the main garment under twice by 3/8 inch (10mm); press, pin, and topstitch to the hem. Fold the kimono in half along the shoulders, right sides facing. Pin along the sides and the underside of the sleeves. On the left side (with the garment front facing you) at the dot under the arm, pin a 5-inch (12.5cm) length of ribbon. Hand-stitch another 5-inch (12.5cm) length of ribbon at the dot on the edge of the front flap (these become inner ties). Sew along the pinned edges with a 3/8-inch (10mm) seam allowance, catching the tie. Zigzag-stitch the edges. In the curves under each arm, make 5 cuts in the seam allowance without cutting through the straight stitching. Hem the kimono as the sleeves were hemmed. Turn it right-side out.

3. Pin the third 7-inch (18cm) tie at the dot on the angled edge of the garment front, as shown. Cut an 8-inch (20.5cm) piece of bias tape. Open, pin it to the angled edge, right sides facing, starting at the neck and aligning the edges as shown; sew along top crease, catching the tie. Fold tape over fabric edge, refold it at the crease, and hand-stitch it to the wrong side of the garment, sewing to the end of the tape. Press.

4. Trim away the point of the fabric extending beyond the angled edge of the front flap. Cut a 12-inch (30.5cm) piece of bias tape, and use it to cover the unfinished edge of the neckline as you did on the angled shoulder, turning the ends of the tape under to hem. Press.

To make the menswear bunny, see page 94.

girl's shirt dress

Mom's closet isn't the only source for a little girl's dress-up clothes; a dad or older brother's button-down shirt—or one bought specifically for the purpose—easily transforms into a lightweight shift dress that can be worn all year long. Choose bias tape in a complementary color for the trim and neck ties. The dress is designed to fit girls ages 4 to 8.

MATERIALS basic sewing supplies, girl's shirt dress pattern, clear tape, men's medium or large button-down shirt, 2 yards (1.8m) 1-inch (2.5cm) single-fold bias tape, 1/4 yard (22.8cm) shirting fabric (for ties), 1 yard (0.9m) 1/8-inch (3mm) elastic, safety pins

HOW-TO 1. Print the pattern pieces (see enclosed CD), tape together, and cut out. Lay the shirt flat and trace the pattern with a disappearing-ink fabric pen, following the higher neckline. Cut out; you will have a front and back piece. Trim the front neckline as shown on the pattern. Trim the dress length, if desired.

2. Pin the front and back pieces together, right sides facing, and sew along shoulders, under arms, and down sides, with a 1/2-inch (13mm) seam allowance. Notch under the arms. Press the seams open. Finish the seams with pinking shears or a zigzag stitch (page 36) to prevent fraying. If you shortened the length, finish the edge with a double-hem: Fold the unfinished edge over 1/4 inch (6mm), press, then fold over 1/4 inch (6mm), and press again; pin and edge-stitch.

3. Turn the dress right-side out. Fold a 16-inch (40.5cm) length of bias tape over the neckline and pin, turning under 1/2 inch (13mm) at each end. (If you wish to make your own bias tape with the shirting fabric, see page 369.) Stitch the tape 1/8 inch (3mm) from the edge. To make a tie, cut a 1-by-22-inch (2.5cm × 56cm) piece of bias tape. Fold in half, right sides facing so long edges, and stitch with 1/8-inch (3mm) seam allowance; use the loop turner to turn it right-side out. Cut a slit in the bias tape to the left of the button placket; attach a safety pin to the tie and thread all the way through the neckline, starting at the slit you just made. To finish the sleeves, fold an 11-inch (28cm) length of bias tape around each sleeve opening, turning under 1/2 inch (13mm) at each end, and pin. Stitch 1/8-inch (3mm) from the edge, leaving an opening where the tape meets at the base of the sleeve opening. To cinch the sleeves, attach a safety pin to a 11-inch (28cm) length of elastic and thread through the tape; cinch slightly. Trim the elastic so the ends overlap 1/2 inch (13mm), and stitch. Hand-sew opening shut.

butterfly-appliquéd shawl

Appliquéd butterflies flutter across a luxurious double-sided dupioni silk wrap. The shawl is sewn into a large tube with open ends, so that the appliqué stitches are hidden and the wrap has a full shape. For the butterflies, choose brocade and damask fabrics in colors and patterns that complement the shawl fabric.

MATERIALS basic sewing supplies; butterfly-appliquéd shawl template; assorted brocade and damask fabrics (for butterflies); 2 1/2 yards (2.3m) dupioni silk (for wrap)

HOW-TO 1. Print the template twice (see enclosed CD), and cut out; cut triangles from one butterfly piece. Trace both shapes onto brocade and damask with a disappearing-ink fabric pen. (Four butterflies were used for the wrap pictured.) Pin triangles onto butterfly bodies and appliqué with an 1/8-inch (3mm) seam allowance, following the instructions for the hand-turn method on page 41. For the wrap: Cut out a 43-by-90-inch (109cm × 231cm) rectangle from the dupioni silk. Pin the butterflies onto the fabric, keeping in mind that the finished wrap will be folded in half lengthwise. Appliqué the butterflies onto fabric, again using the hand-turn method.

2. Fold wrap in half, right sides facing, so long edges meet. Stitch long sides with an 1/8-inch (3mm) seam allowance to form a long tube. Turn right side out and double-hem short sides: Fold edges under 1/4 inch (6mm), press, fold again 1/2 inch (13mm), and press. Pin and edge-stitch. You could also use a rolled hem (page 37) to finish the short sides.

flower-appliquéd shirt

Give a store-bought cotton shirt a touch of handmade charm by adding a rose appliqué pattern. Use fabrics in a variety of prints and colors that will complement the shirt; here gingham, polka dot, and other patterned and solid blue fabrics combine to highlight a striped shirt. For more visually interesting effects, cut petals, leaves, and other parts of the flower from different fabrics.

MATERIALS basic sewing supplies, flower-appliquéd shirt template, store-bought shirt, assorted shirting fabrics (for rose and leaf motifs)

HOW-TO 1. Print the template (see enclosed CD) twice. Cut one of the templates around the outside of the motif. This outline will help determine placement on the shirt. With a disappearing-ink fabric pen, trace the motif onto the shirt; repeat as desired.

2. Cut out the individual pieces from the other template. Trace onto the shirting fabrics, adding a ⅛-inch (3mm) seam allowance; cut out. Pin pieces, as marked, onto the shirt and appliqué, following instructions for the hand-turn method on page 41. Keep in mind that when appliquéing small pieces, the shapes may not turn out as precise as those on the template, but the variation in each petal and leaf is part of the beauty of the hand-turn technique.

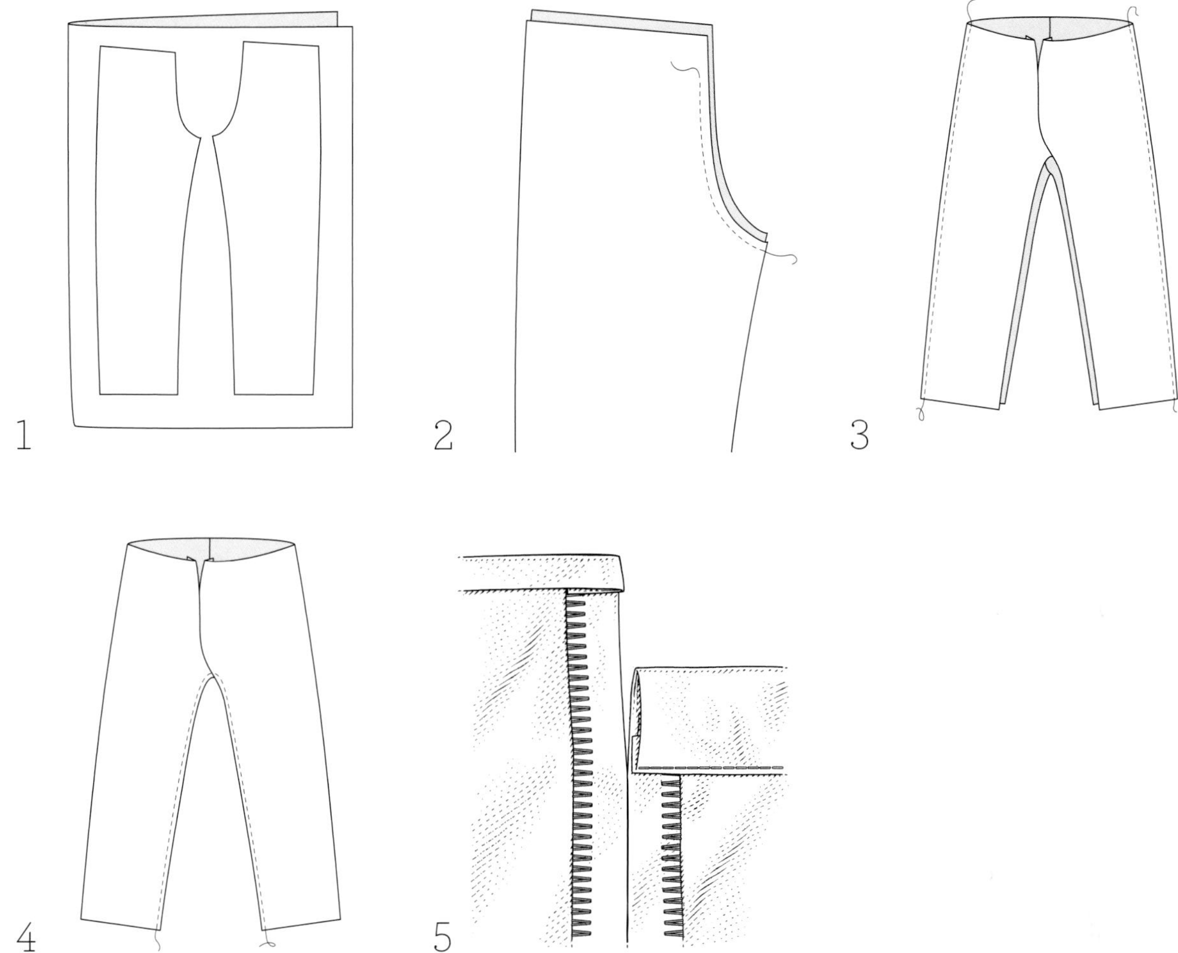

drawstring pants

Drawstring pants are one of the simplest and most comfortable pieces of clothing you can sew. Their easy form makes them suitable for all sizes and shapes. Use the pattern to sew pajama pants from flannel or cotton, or easy beachwear from lightweight linen. The pants pictured are made of lightweight seersucker.

MATERIALS basic sewing supplies, drawstring pants pattern, clear tape, 2 yards (1.8m) of fabric, 1 yard (.9m) twill tape, large safety pin

HOW-TO 1. Print the pattern pieces (see enclosed CD), tape together, and cut out. Wash, dry, and press the fabric. Cut out the pattern, following the lines for desired size. Fold the fabric, right sides facing, so that the fold is along the length of the fabric (selvages touching). Place the pattern pieces on the fabric, as shown above, and cut out the pieces.

2. Place the 2 front pieces together, right sides facing, and pin along the crotch seam; sew them together with a ½-inch (13mm) seam allowance, stopping 2 ½ inches (6.5cm) from the top. Press open the seam allowance and finish the edges with a zigzag stitch (page 36). Repeat with the left and right back-pant pieces, but sew all the way to the top.

3. Place the front and back pieces together, right sides facing; pin and sew the sides together with a ½-inch (13mm) seam allowance. Press open the seams, finish the edges with a zigzag-stitch, and press them open again.

4. Pin the front and back inseams together; sew with a ½-inch (13mm) seam. Press open the seam allowance, finish the edges with a zigzag stitch, and press them open again.

5. With the pants still inside out, create a channel around the waistband for a drawstring: Fold and press the top edge down ½ inch (13mm), then fold and press again 1 inch (2.5cm), and edge-stitch ⅛ inch (3mm) from the double fold's lower edge, making sure to stitch back and forth several times at the opening. Attach a safety pin to one end of the twill tape, and feed the tape through the channel. To hem the pants, put them on. Mark the hem you'd like, then make a mark 1 inch (2.5cm) below this initial mark. Cut away any fabric below the lower mark. Make a double hem: Fold edge over ½ inch, press, then fold over ½ inch (13mm) again. Press, pin, and edge-stitch.

PROJECT:

coasters

Spruce up a table—and protect it at the same time—with coasters that start out as colorful rounds and squares of fabric. Whether your style is modern and graphic, or vintage and romantic, these surface protectors require only tiny bits of fabric, making them perfect for quick projects and great for gift-giving. Bundle a dozen with ribbon for an easy housewarming or hostess gift.

Putting together a set of coasters provides a perfect excuse to indulge in patterns, color, and texture. Fabrics that might seem too bold or bright in large doses can delight the eye in small quantities. Remnants can be a fun place to start, as can scraps of oilcloth or felt. Quilting-supply shops, which sell tiny squares of fabric called "fat quarters," are another great source; the pieces are small, the prints are varied, and the colors tend to coordinate well with one another.

The sew and no-sew coasters on these pages can be made in minutes. Start with one set, but expect to soon find yourself inspired to start in on another.

IN THIS CHAPTER: OILCLOTH CUTOUT COASTERS — FOUR EASY FABRIC COASTERS: MACHINE-EMBROIDERED; FADED FLORAL FABRICS; FRINGED; RICKRACK-EDGED

OILCLOTH CUTOUT COASTERS (OPPOSITE): *Flowery waterproof coasters catch drips from icy cocktails. Here the pattern of the oilcloth—a large floral motif—dictates the shape of the coasters. Cut along the flower outlines to make coaster shapes. Place the shapes on another piece of oilcloth in a complementary color or pattern, wrong sides together; trace the shapes and cut out the backing. Working in a well-ventilated area or outdoors, spray the wrong sides lightly with spray-mount adhesive, and press them together. Machine-stitch along the edges, with a ¼-inch (6mm) topstitch. If desired, trim the edges with scalloping shears to finish.*

FOUR EASY FABRIC COASTERS

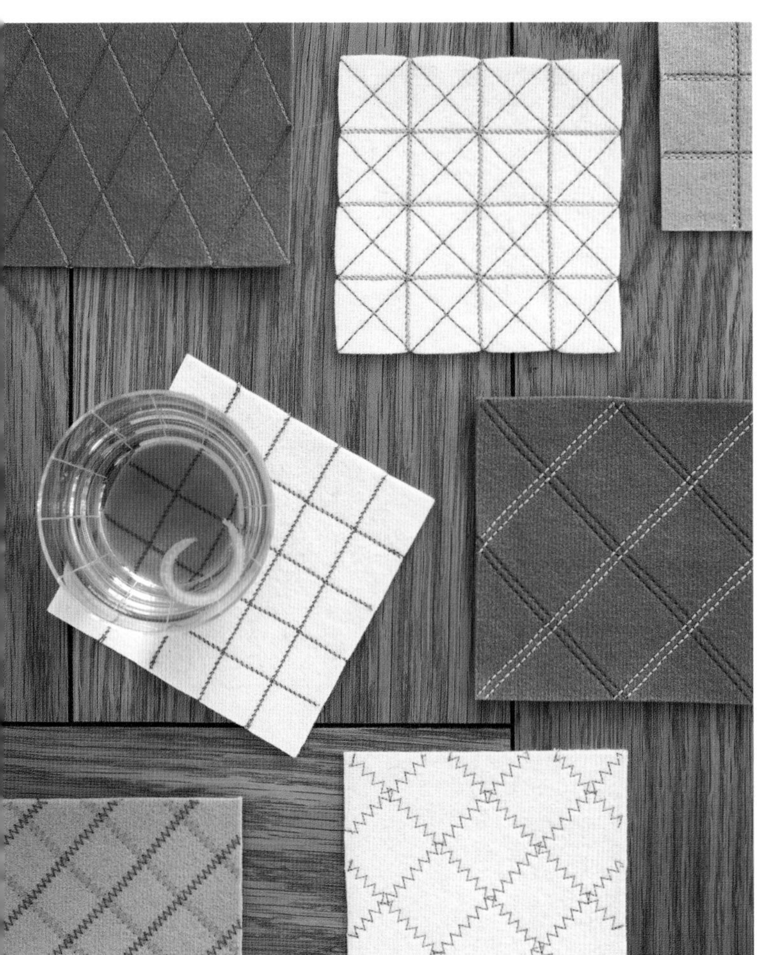

machine-embroidered

Machine embroider squares of wool felt to make coasters with straight and zigzag designs (page 60); both stitches are standard on any sewing machine.

MATERIALS basic sewing supplies; wool felt in one or more colors, cut into 5-inch (12.5cm) squares; ruler

HOW-TO On each square of felt, use a disappearing-ink fabric pen and ruler to mark a design in a grid. Machine-stitch along the markings one row at a time.

faded floral fabrics

Summery coasters and a tablecloth in shades of pink were bleached and overdyed using the methods described on page 80. You can use the same fabric for the coasters' top and backing, or choose a complementary solid fabric to make reversible coasters.

MATERIALS basic sewing supplies, bleached and overdyed floral cotton, solid cotton fabric for backing (optional)

HOW-TO Cut the fabric into 5-inch (12.5cm) squares. Pin and sew the squares together, right sides facing, with a 1⁄4-inch (6mm) seam allowance, leaving 2 inches (5cm) open on one side. Clip corners, and tuck the coasters right-side out; turn the open edge in and press. Topstitch around the perimeter, 1⁄8 inch (3mm) from the edges.

fringed

Hors d'oeuvres look especially festive when presented on fringed-fabric coasters in bright colors. You can make larger mats for plates of appetizers; use smaller coasters, like those shown above, for dainty bites.

MATERIALS scissors, ruler, disappearing-ink fabric pen, colored burlap or other loose-weave fabric

HOW-TO Measure and cut fabric into 3-inch (7.5cm) squares for small coasters, or 5-inch (12.5cm) squares for larger ones. To make the fringe, pull threads from the edges, making a ½-inch (13mm) border on all sides.

rickrack-edged

Plain linen napkins acquire an instant dose of cheer when red rickrack is attached on all sides with dots of fabric glue. A set of eight makes a winning holiday or hostess gift.

MATERIALS scissors, fabric coasters or cocktail napkins, ½-inch-wide (13mm) rickrack, fabric glue

HOW-TO Cut 4 pieces of rickrack, each the length of the coaster's side; make sure the ends match. Position the rickrack along the coaster's perimeter so that the corners meet. Dot the rickrack points on one edge with fabric glue; press into place on the wrong side of the fabric.

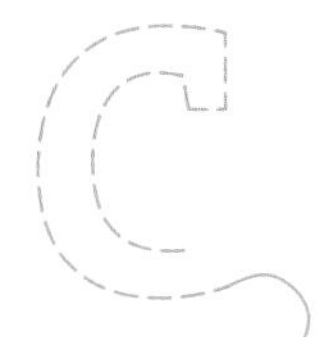

PROJECT:

cozies

Warmth: It's what we long for throughout the long winter months and on gusty days throughout the year. And it's what we crave when we're feeling sleepy or under the weather. Cozies, those low-tech heat-savers most often associated with pots of tea, let you trap warmth where you want it, and cushion delicate objects that need extra care. A cozy can be slipped over a hot-water bottle, popped over a boiled egg, or cradled in your hands. Every bit as comforting as their name implies, these soft, hand-stitched objects don't take long to make. So if you—or someone you know—could use a little tender loving care, don't hesitate to stitch up a cozy or two.

IN THIS CHAPTER: MENSWEAR WATER-BOTTLE COZY — PIE-WEIGHT HAND WARMER — CLUCKING-EGG COZY

MENSWEAR WATER-BOTTLE COZY (OPPOSITE): *Keep toasty with a hot-water bottle covered in wool menswear fabrics. An envelope opening on the front makes it easy to place the filled bottle inside the cozy.*

menswear water-bottle cozy

SEE PHOTO, PAGE 193

Whether it's chilly inside or out, a hot-water bottle slipped inside a soft cloth cover makes a comforting companion. The covers are small enough to sew with wool remnants and larger scraps. The cozy pictured was made for a two-quart (1.9-liter) water bottle from two complementary fabrics, but you could easily sew one with a single fabric.

MATERIALS basic sewing supplies, menswear water-bottle cozy pattern, clear tape, 1/2 yard (0.9m) wool fabric in 2 colors, seam binding, 2-quart hot-water bottle

HOW-TO Print the pattern pieces (see enclosed CD), and tape together. Cut out one front piece and one back piece from one of the wool fabrics; cut the other piece from another fabric. Fold seam binding over the straight edges of the front pieces; stitch in place, 1/8 inch (3mm) from edge. Lay front top piece right-side up, and fold straight edge up 1 inch (2.5cm). Press. Align back piece and 2 front pieces, right sides facing, so that front pieces overlap slightly. Pin and stitch around the perimeter with a 1/2-inch (13mm) seam allowance. Notch curves on either side of neck. Turn right-side out, and press flat. Slip the hot-water bottle through front flap.

pie-weight hand warmer

When you're building a snowman, shoveling the driveway, or taking a winter walk, your fingers will appreciate a toasty pair of hand warmers tucked into your coat pockets. Handmade pouches, filled with ceramic pie weights, can be made with a variety of 100 percent natural fabrics, such as the cashmere shown here. Do not use synthetic fabrics or blends, however, which can melt when heated in the microwave.

MATERIALS basic sewing supplies, about 1/4 yard (23cm) 100 percent natural fabric (such as wool or cashmere), ceramic pie weights, embroidery floss, embroidery needle

HOW-TO Cut out two 3-by-5-inch (7.5cm × 12.5cm) rectangles of fabric (or cut smaller or larger rectangles to fit hands of various sizes). Sew them together on 3 sides, with a 1/4-inch (6mm) seam allowance; clip the corners. Turn the bag right-side out; fill it with 1/2 cup (100ml) pie weights. Turn under the opening and pin, then blanket-stitch (page 49) on all sides with embroidery floss. To warm the pouch, place it in a microwave, set on high, for about 5 minutes. (Do not microwave longer, and never heat in a conventional oven.)

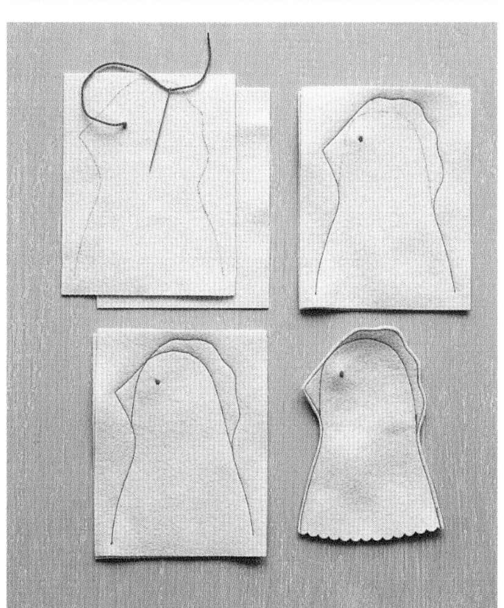

clucking-egg cozy

Brightly colored felt egg cozies shaped like hens should get brunch guests flocking to the table. Pop them onto hard- or soft-cooked eggs in egg cups, and position one at each place setting. They also make adorable take-home favors.

MATERIALS basic sewing supplies, clucking-egg cozy pattern, about 1/4 yard (23cm) (or large scraps) of felt in various colors, embroidery needle, embroidery floss, scalloping shears

HOW-TO Cut 2 pieces of felt to 3 1/2 by 5 inches (9cm × 12.5cm). Print two copies of the pattern (see enclosed CD), and cut out. Stack the felt pieces; lay one pattern on top. Trace the perimeter with a disappearing-ink fabric pen. Push a needle through the felt pieces to mark the eyes. Embroider the eyes with a needle and contrasting embroidery floss (sew through one layer of fabric at a time). Using a sewing machine and thread in a contrasting color, stitch through the felt layers, following the outline. Cut along the dotted line of the other pattern. Lay the pattern on one side of the cozy; trace the head. Stitch over the traced line. Cut out the shape, just outside the stitching, with fabric shears. Trim the bottom with scalloping shears.

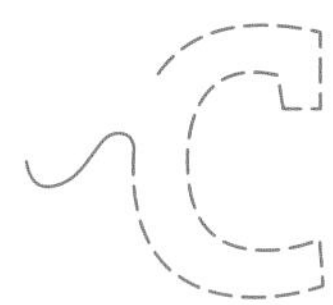

PROJECT:

curtains

Want to change the look of a room? Change the curtains! Select your fabric with the window size in mind. An oversized floral print or a bold stripe may suit a large area; a sweet print or gingham is nice in a smaller room. Consider the season, too. Lightweight spring and summer window treatments make a room feel fresh. Heavy weaves and textures look warm and welcoming as the cold draws near. You needn't look only to fabric by the yard; sheeting can be used to elegant effect.

Making curtains is not difficult. Seams are straight and few. And within the parameters of one simple shape, there are countless techniques to try: Sew a channel at the top, or a series of tabs. Give your curtains movement and shape with evenly spaced pleats, or fold and sew tiny horizontal tucks to create texture and pattern. You can even begin with ready-made curtains, adding details with trim, appliquéd shapes, ribbons, or stenciled patterns. When you're done, take a seat by an open window and watch as your newly made curtains dance gently in the breeze.

IN THIS CHAPTER: TWO-TONE LINEN VOILE CURTAINS — STENCILED CURTAINS — LINEN-EDGED SHEERS — RIBBON-STRIPED SHEERS — TUCKED-STRIPE CAFÉ CURTAIN — BUTTON-TAB CAFÉ CURTAIN — APPLIQUÉD CURTAIN — TWILL TAPE–EMBELLISHED CURTAIN — PINCH-PLEATED CAFÉ CURTAINS — TABLE-SKIRT CURTAINS

TWO-TONE LINEN VOILE CURTAINS (OPPOSITE): *Airy linen voile filters light beautifully. To make a pair, sew borders (use French seams) of dark yellow—a narrow strip on the top and along one side, with a wide border on the bottom—to each main pale-yellow panel. Double hem the bottoms and pinch-pleats (see page 206) at 6-inch (15.25cm) intervals to the tops. Hang with curtain pins.*

Two floral stencils, arranged agreeably askew, are used to decorate the borders of linen curtain panels. The same stencils embellish the pillow cover on a nearby chair.

1

2

3

4

stenciled curtains

This project requires several stages of painting: Be sure to complete all motifs in one color before moving on to the next. The painted curtains can be washed and steamed (or pressed). Use a small sheet of glass, a paint tray, or a paper plate as a palette. For more on stenciling, see page 89.

MATERIALS star flower template; bell flower template; full curtain template; scissors; 4 sheets of 8 1/2-by-11-inch (21.5cm × 28cm) waterproof paper; self-healing cutting mat; drafting tape; craft knife; 4 sheets of 11-by-17-inch (28cm × 43cm) vellum (for stencil placement); transparent tape; straight pins; 2 curtain panels made of linen or other natural fabric; palette; palette knife; 5 to 7 ounces (142–198.5g) each water-based permanent textile paint in yellow, red, dark green, light green, and white; colorless extender; natural sea sponges; double-sided tape

HOW-TO 1. Print each flower template (see enclosed CD) twice, and cut out. Affix each template to a sheet of waterproof paper. With drafting tape, secure one star flower template with waterproof paper backing to the cutting mat; cut out the flowers with a craft knife, excluding greenery. Remove the template from the waterproof paper, and discard it. Repeat with one bell flower template, cutting out only the flowers. On the second star flower template, cut out just the greenery. Tape the two cutout starred leaves onto a scrap of waterproof paper, and cut out the centers. Reserve (you will use the centers for leaf details later). Remove the template and discard it. Repeat with the second bell flower template, cutting out just the greenery. Tape the leaves onto a scrap of waterproof paper, and cut out the veins. Reserve. Remove and discard the template.

2. Print the full curtain template (see enclosed CD) onto vellum; arrange the sheets and tape them together. (Add or remove pages as needed, depending on the curtain size.) Position the vellum overlay along the curtain's inner edge, leaving an even border; secure with straight pins across the side. (As you stencil, remove the pins and insert others as needed to keep the vellum in place.)

3. Use the palette knife to mix one part yellow paint with one part colorless extender (mix an even amount of extender into all following paint colors). Align the star-shaped flower stencil (flowers cut out) under the vellum; fold back the vellum. Use a sponge to apply paint to the stencil. Let it dry 4 minutes. Unfold the vellum. Align the next set of yellow flowers under the vellum, varying the color placement by eye; paint. Repeat, flipping the stencil over as needed (make sure the reverse is dry), until the flowers are complete. Let dry. Repeat the process, using red paint until all the star-shaped flowers are complete.

4. Align the star-shaped flower stencil (greenery cut out) under the vellum; fold back vellum. Attach the inner cutouts of the leaves to the fabric with double-sided tape. Stencil as in step 3, using dark-green paint. Repeat, flipping the stencil as needed, until all star-flower leaves are complete. Repeat the process, using white paint and the bell-flower stencil (flowers cut out), then using light-green paint and the bell-flower stencil (greenery cut out), attaching the leaf veins to the fabric with double-sided tape before painting. Using the vellum overlay, repeat steps 2 to 4 to stencil the second panel. To set the paint, follow the manufacturer's instructions.

TIP
Diluting fabric paint with a colorless extender makes it translucent, allowing the fabric's color to show through, without thinning the paint's consistency.

linen-edged sheers

You'll need sheers at least 14 inches (35.5cm) higher than your windows; a linen band sewn at the bottom will extend the curtains to the floor.

MATERIALS basic sewing supplies, silk-organza sheers, linen, curtain rings

HOW-TO Add top linen trim: Cut a strip of linen equal to the width of the curtain plus 1 inch (2.5cm), and double the height of the top hemmed channel plus 1 inch (2.5cm). Fold in all edges 1/2 inch (13mm); press. Fold in half so long ends meet; press. Sandwich the strip over the curtain's channel; pin it in place, as shown, and stitch. Fold down top edge of curtain 14 inches (35.5cm); press. Sew rings to the fold about 6 inches (15cm) apart. Add bottom panel: Cut linen to width of sheer plus 2 inches (5cm), and height from windowsill to floor plus 4 inches (10cm). Fold 1/2 inch (13mm) along top edge; press. Pin folded edge to sheer, centering linen panel so there is a 1-inch (2.5cm) overhang on each side; stitch panel in place. Fold side edges 1/2 inch (13mm), then 1/2 inch (13mm) again; press, and stitch. Fold bottom edge up 1/2 inch (13mm), then 3 inches (7.5cm); press, pin, and stitch in place.

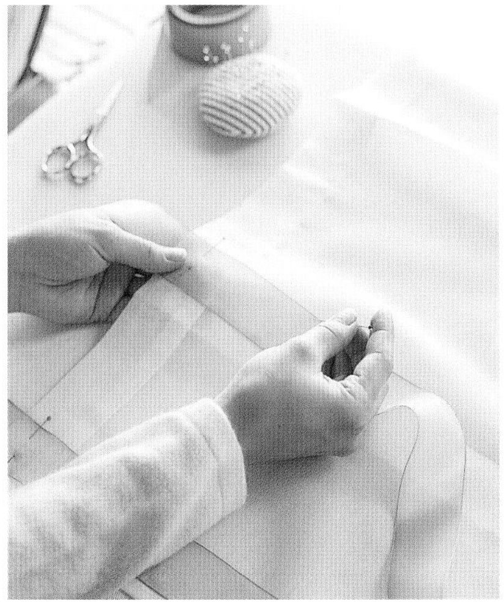

ribbon-striped sheers

Embellishing with ribbon is another quick and easy way to dress up plain window treatments. Here, organza ribbons create soft stripes on cotton-voile sheers. The ribbons are sewn to create tabs at the top of each curtain.

MATERIALS basic sewing supplies, cotton-voile sheers, wide organza ribbon

HOW-TO Fold the curtain lengthwise in accordion pleats of equal width (those shown are about 8 inches [20.5cm]); press creases. Measure the length of the curtain, and cut pieces of ribbon to the same length plus 10 inches (25.5cm). Center the ribbon over the creases, leaving 7 inches (18cm) at the top for curtain tabs and 3 inches (7.5cm) at the bottom for the hem; pin in place. Fold 3 inches (7.5cm) of the ribbon over at the bottom of the curtain; press. Fold 4 inches (10cm) of the ribbon over at the top to create the tabs (1 inch [2.5cm] of ribbon will overlap fabric); press. Stitch the curtains along the bottom and the top to secure the hem and the tabs. Stitch along both sides of the ribbons lengthwise.

tucked-stripe café curtain

Fold fabric and stitch in place to create decorative horizontal tucks. When measuring, decide how many tucks you want and how deep they will be. Multiply each tuck depth by 2, and add that number to your height measurement. For example, for each 1-inch (2.5cm) tuck, add 2 inches (5cm) of fabric.

MATERIALS basic sewing supplies, linen

HOW-TO Measure the fabric, adding 2 inches (5cm) to the width for side hems, and 3 inches (7.5cm) to the height for hems and channel; add extra inches to the height for tucks. Use a disappearing-ink fabric pen to mark horizontal lines to indicate tuck placement (they will be closer together once the tucks are made). To make a 1-inch (2.5cm) tuck, fold fabric along top horizontal line; press fold in place. Sew a horizontal line 1 inch (2.5cm) from fold. Unfold the fabric and press fold downward; crease is bottom edge of tuck, and stitch is top edge. Repeat with remaining tucks, working from top to bottom. Fold top edge under 1/2 inch (13mm), and hem. Fold remaining 3 sides 1/2 inch (13mm) and then 1/2 inch (13mm) again; stitch. Fold the top edge another 1 1/2 inches (3.8cm) to make a channel; edge-stitch.

DETERMINING FABRIC WIDTH

The width of your fabric will determine whether your curtains are flat and sleek or full and ruffled. A curtain that is the exact width of your window will be smooth, with no gathers or ruffles. In general, a curtain 1½ times the width of your window will give you an ideal amount of volume and movement. The wider the curtain in proportion to the window, the more gathered it will be.

button-tab café curtain

Tab-top curtains have a crisp appearance that is appropriate in any room. The purely decorative buttons are sewn in place atop the tabs to finish the curtains.

MATERIALS basic sewing supplies, silk taffeta, decorative buttons

HOW-TO Measure window frame; add one-eighth of the measurement to width to create soft folds, plus another 2 inches (5cm) to width for side hems. Add 3 inches (7.5cm) to height. Double-hem sides and bottom: Fold each edge ½ inch (13mm), then ½ inch (13mm) again. Press; edge-stitch. Sew a 1-inch (2.5cm) double hem at the top. Determine how many tabs you want (the curtain pictured has 10). Subtract 1 and divide the curtain's width by that number to determine placement. Mark intervals with pins. For tabs, cut twice as many 2 ½-by-9-inch (6.5cm × 23cm) strips of fabric as the number of buttons. Pin 2 strips of fabric together, right sides facing, and sew 3 sides with a ½-inch (13mm) seam allowance, leaving a short end open. Turn right-side out; press. Turn open edge under ½ inch (13mm); press and stitch. Repeat for remaining tabs. Stitch short ends of tabs to curtain, about 1 inch (2.5cm) from the top. Pin other short end to front, place button on top, and stitch both place.

appliquéd curtain

Delicate cotton flowers drift down a store-bought sheer curtain in the manner of snowflakes. Choose lightweight fabrics, such as eyelet and Swiss dot, for the appliqué pieces. Iron-on appliqué is an easy alternative to the hand-sewn method; fusible web adheres the motifs to the curtain. For more on iron-on appliqué, see page 43.

MATERIALS appliqué curtain template; cardstock; scissors or rotary cutter; cutting mat (optional); sheer silk organza curtain panels; disappearing-ink fabric pen; assorted lightweight white fabrics such as eyelet, cotton lace, and Swiss dot; fusible web; pencil; Teflon pressing sheets; ironing board and iron

HOW-TO 1. Print the template (see enclosed CD) twice onto cardstock, and cut out. Use scissors or a rotary cutter to cut inner pieces from one template. Trace templates onto curtain, using a disappearing-ink fabric pen, to indicate placement. Fuse webbing to wrong sides of cotton fabrics, leaving paper backing on. With a pencil, trace templates onto webbing's paper backing; cut out shapes.

2. Lay a Teflon pressing sheet on ironing board to keep the curtain from sticking. Remove paper backing and fuse shapes to curtain with an iron according to the manufacturer's instructions.

1

2

HANGING CURTAINS

To hang curtains, you can start by attaching rings: Some rings are made to be sewn on; others can be clipped to a curtain's top edge. Curtain pins, typically used with pleated curtains, slide into the curtain's hem for a nearly invisible appearance. You can mount a curtain rod with decorative finials on the wall above your window, or flush-mount the rod inside the window frame (for instructions, see page 206). Alternatively, a spring-loaded tension rod will fit inside a window frame and needs no mounting hardware. If your curtain has a channel, make sure it is wide enough to accommodate the rod you choose.

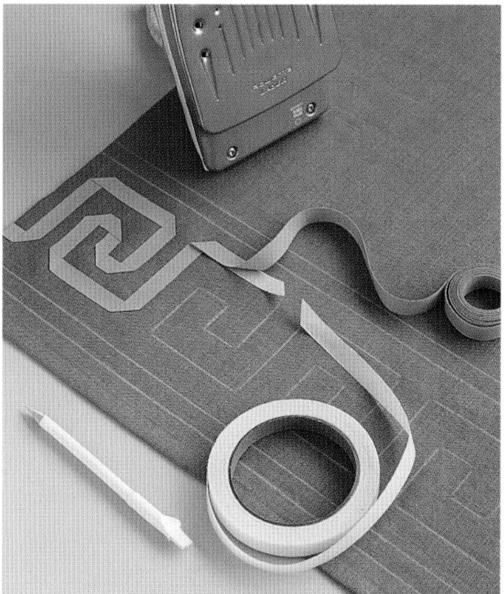

twill tape-embellished curtain

Adding a twill-tape border is an inexpensive way to update a simple linen curtain. A Greek key motif is pictured; any other geometric pattern would work as well. Start with a plain café curtain, either handmade or store-bought, without any gathers or pleats.

MATERIALS ruler, linen curtain (cotton and wool also work well), self-adhesive fusible tape, twill tape, scissors, iron

HOW-TO Using a ruler and a disappearing-ink fabric pen or chalk pencil, sketch the pattern onto the curtain. Use self-adhesive fusible tape to join the twill tape to the curtain in the desired pattern, working in one section at a time; press according to fusible tape manufacturer's instructions. At the corners, fold the twill tape at a 45-degree angle; cut the fusible tape at an angle to match, as shown. Repeat until the pattern is complete.

pinch-pleated café curtains

Loosely gathered pleats are pinched, then stitched in place to add sculptural depth to taupe wool crepe curtains. In this living room, the pleats echo the soft curves of the upholstery. They are hung instead from slender poles, flush-mounted inside the window frames (for how-to, see below).

MATERIALS basic sewing supplies, wool crepe, curtain rings

HOW-TO Measure the window frame; add extra width to the dimensions (for curtains to drape), and add 2 inches (5cm) to the width and 4 inches (10cm) to the height for the hems, plus extra fabric to the width for the pleats (each pleat pictured requires 6 inches [15cm] of fabric; the curtain pictured measures 2 ½ times the width of the window to accommodate the pleats and create a soft drape). Cut the fabric to the desired dimensions. Sew double hems on the sides and the bottom edge: Fold edge ½ inch (13mm), then ½ inch (13mm) again. Press; edge-stitch. Sew a double hem along the top edge: Fold edge 1 ½ inches (3.8cm), then 1 ½ inches (3.8cm) again; press and sew. Mark where you want your pleats to go: Determine the desired number of pleats, subtract 1, and divide the curtain's width by the resulting number; mark intervals with a disappearing-ink fabric pen. To create a triple pleat, gather the fabric into 3 folds (each 1 inch [2.5cm] deep), pinch them together, and hand-stitch where the fabric meets, parallel to the fold (see photo, right). Hand-stitch a few backstitches perpendicular to the folds to hold them together, 1 ½ inches (3.8cm) from the top. Stitch a curtain ring to the top of each cluster of folds.

HOW TO INSTALL A FLUSH-MOUNT BRACKET AND ROD

1. You will need a rod and bracket hardware—2 screws, 2 screw-through fittings, and threaded barrels that slip over the rod.

2. Mark the spot on one side of the frame where you want rod to hang. Measure from first mark to edge of sash and down to the base of frame; mark same spot on other side. Before you screw in fittings, hold up rod to marks to make sure it will be level. Center a fitting over one mark, and affix it to frame with a screw. Repeat on other side.

3. Slide the curtain onto the rod, and slip the barrel brackets onto each end.

4. Screw barrel brackets tightly onto fittings.

TABLE-SKIRT CURTAINS
A bright table skirt brings a lively accent to a rustic country kitchen. In this example, red and white ticking fabric was dyed a deep pink (for dyeing instructions, see page 79; for this color, use the basic dye bath formula with 3 teaspoons [15ml] red liquid dye and 3 teaspoons mauve dye), hemmed on all sides, and attached to brass rings. The skirt was slid onto a curtain rod that is screwed into the underside of the table. You can then use the same method to make matching café curtains for windows.

PROJECT:

decorative pillows

Pillows enliven any living space, their fabric delivering pops of color, texture, and pattern wherever it's needed. Fabrics such as damask and silk denote a more formal setting, whereas raw linen and soft cotton look more casual. Bold patterns and oversized embellishments look decidedly modern.

Pillow projects are satisfying for new and experienced sewers alike because their construction is simple, leaving you plenty of room to experiment with fabric, trim, and finishes. In short, pillows are small on effort and big on effect. In these pages, you'll discover how to sew a pillow cover from scratch, including instructions for three basic closures: slip-stitched, envelope, and zippered. You'll also learn a few more tailored finishes, such as Turkish corners and piped edges, as well as clever ways to embellish handmade and store-bought pillows.

IN THIS CHAPTER: SLIPSTITCHED PILLOW COVER — ENVELOPE-BACKED PILLOW COVER — ZIPPERED PILLOW COVER — DOUBLE FLANGES — RUFFLES — TURKISH CORNERS — PIPED EDGES — PILLOW TRIMMINGS — SEASHELL-PRINTED PILLOWS — WRAPAROUND PILLOW BANDS — NAPKIN PILLOW COVER — TUFTED CUSHION — PINCH-PLEATED PILLOW — WOVEN-WOOL PILLOW COVERS — BIRD-EMBROIDERED PILLOWS — FALLING-LEAF PILLOW COVERS — BOX PILLOWS AND CASES — CROSS-STITCH PILLOW COVER — TOOTH-FAIRY PILLOW — WEDDING-RING PILLOW — COUCHED PILLOW BANDS — HAND-APPLIQUÉD PILLOW COVERS — DRAWSTRING BOLSTER — SLIPSTITCHED BOLSTER — PIN-TUCK PILLOWS — EASY TUXEDO PIN-TUCK PILLOW

THREE BASIC PILLOW COVERS (OPPOSITE): *Pillow covers are among the simplest home accents to sew. A slipstitched cover (top), envelope-backed cover (middle) and zippered cover (bottom) can each be created in less than an hour.*

THREE WAYS TO MAKE A PILLOW COVER

These three simple finishing styles—a slipstitched closure, an envelope-backed closure, and a zippered closure—provide nice options for any sewn-from-scratch pillow project. Although the instructions are for square pillows, you can make rectangular pillow covers in the same fashion.

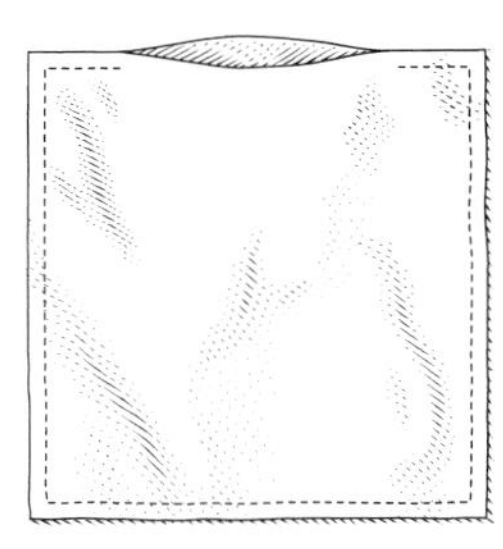

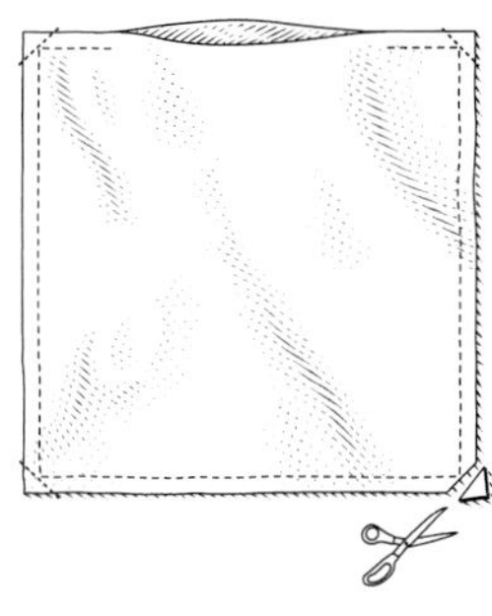

slipstitched pillow cover

For this streamlined style, the cover is closed with an invisible seam after inserting the pillow form. Because the closure is permanent, the cover is most appropriate for pillow forms that won't be washed. If you do need to wash the filled pillow—particularly if it's made of a delicate fabric, such as silk—have it dry-cleaned.

MATERIALS basic sewing supplies, pillow insert, fabric

HOW-TO 1. Add 1 inch (2.5cm) to the height and length of the pillow insert for the seam allowance. With a ruler and a disappearing-ink fabric pen, draw 2 squares of fabric with these dimensions; cut out squares.

2. Pin the squares together, right sides facing. On the top edge, make marks 3 inches (7.5cm) in from the right and left sides. Starting at one of the marks, sew along all the edges of the pillow with a ½-inch (13mm) seam allowance, leaving the space between the marks open.

3. Clip the corners and turn the pillow right-side out. Use a point turner or a closed pair of scissors to push the corners out. Press the edges of the pillow, turning the unfinished edges of the opening under ½ inch (13mm). Insert pillow form. Slipstitch (page 31) the opening shut.

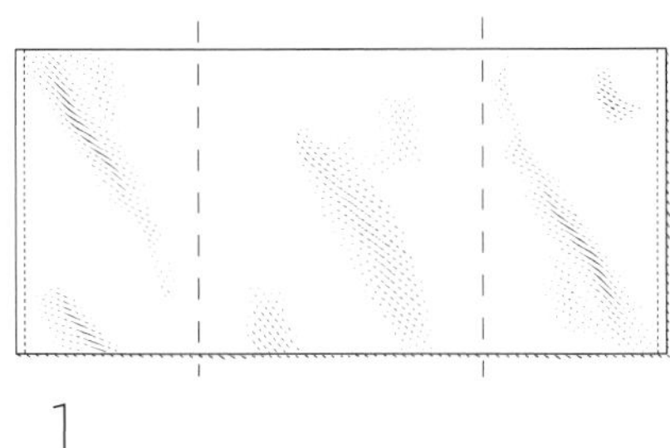

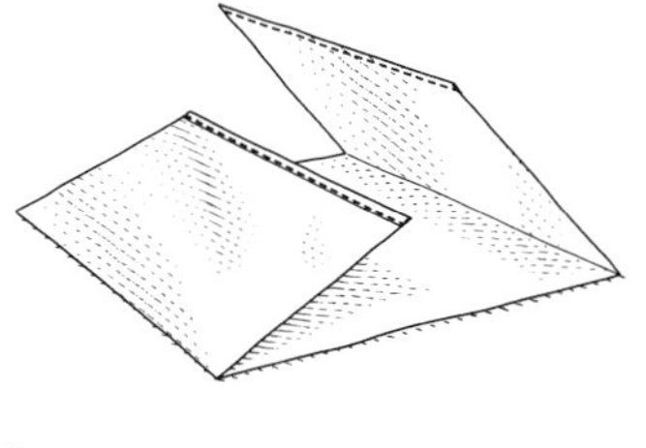

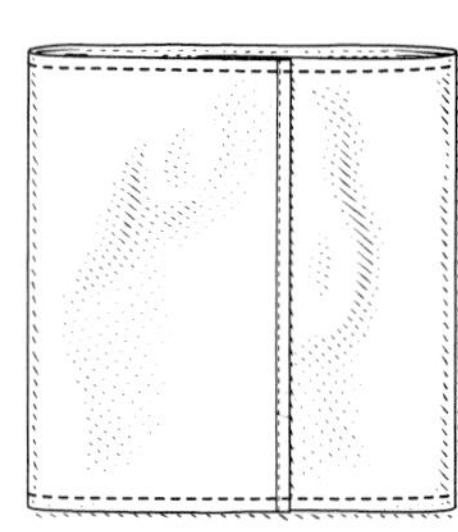

envelope-backed pillow cover

Creating an envelope backing is simple: One long rectangle of fabric is overlapped in the back to create the closure.

MATERIALS basic sewing supplies, pillow insert, fabric

HOW-TO 1. Measure the dimensions of your pillow. To determine the size rectangle you'll need, add 1 inch (2.5cm) to the height for the seam allowance, and multiply the length by 2, then add 6 inches (15cm). (For example, an 18-inch [45.5cm] pillow insert would require a 19-by-42-inch [48.5cm × 106.5cm] rectangle.) With a disappearing-ink fabric pen and a ruler, draw the dimensions of the rectangle onto your fabric; cut it out. Place the rectangle right-side down. Double hem the left and right edges: Fold each edge in ½ inch (13mm), press, then fold over again ½ inch (13mm), and press. Pin and edge-stitch ⅛ inch (3mm) from the inner fold.

2. Fold the left and right edges in, overlapping them by 4 inches (10cm). Measure the square to make sure it matches the dimensions of your pillow insert.

3. Pin the top and bottom edges and sew with a ½-inch (13mm) seam allowance. Turn the pillowcase right-side out. Use a point turner or a closed pair of scissors to push the corners out. Insert pillow.

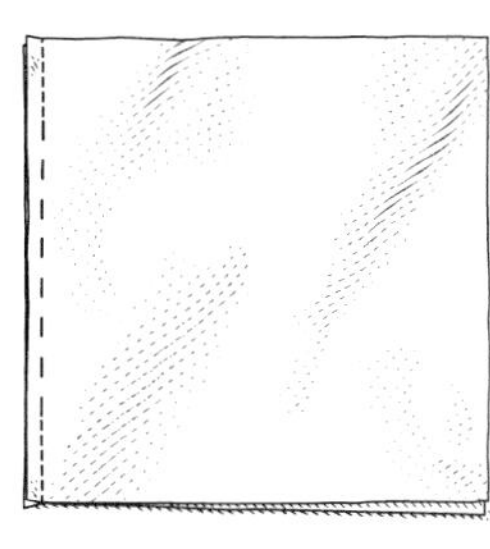

1

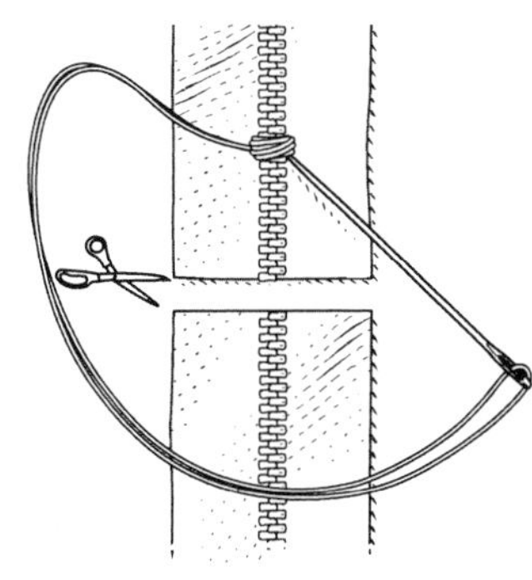

2

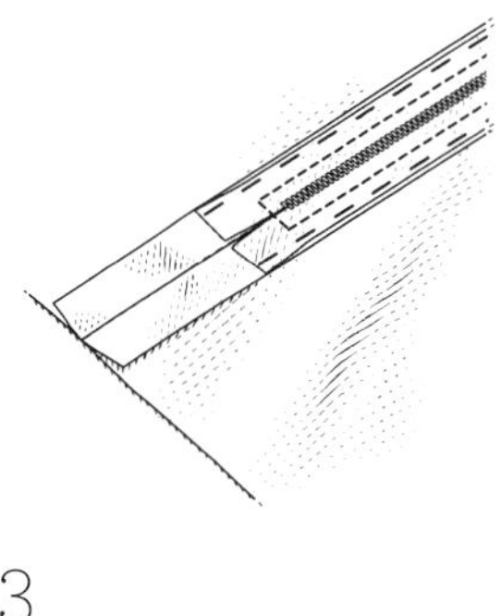

3

zippered pillow cover

Adding a zipper to a pillow cover makes it versatile; you can easily remove the insert to wash the cover, or replace it altogether. Use a zipper that is the exact length of or slightly longer than the pillow opening. A polyester coil zipper is a good choice because it is easy to shorten.

MATERIALS basic sewing supplies, pillow insert, fabric, zipper, zipper foot for sewing machine

HOW-TO 1. Add 1 inch (2.5cm) to the height and length of the pillow insert for the seam allowance. With a ruler and a disappearing-ink fabric pen, draw 2 squares of fabric with these dimensions; cut out squares. Pin the squares together, right sides facing. On one side make marks 3 inches (7.5cm) in from each edge. Starting at one edge, sew to the mark with a ½-inch (13mm) seam allowance; backstitch to secure. Repeat on the opposite edge. Set your machine to a basting stitch, and sew between the 2 marks (see dashed line; this is where you'll install the zipper). Press the seam open. With a disappearing-ink fabric pen, mark the seam allowance 3 inches (7.5cm) in from each edge (over your first marks).

2. If the zipper is longer than the pillow opening, mark the zipper the same length as the opening. Use a needle and thread to sew 5 to 10 times around the coils at the mark (this will prevent the zipper pull from slipping off the coils). Trim the zipper ½ inch (13mm) below the stitches.

3. Lay the zipper facedown on the opening seam, aligning the coils with the seam. Flip the zipper pull up, so that it can be moved down while you're sewing. Pin the zipper in place and use a needle and thread to baste the zipper tape to the seam allowance. Using the zipper foot, and starting 2 inches (5cm) from the top of the zipper, machine-sew around the zipper (about ⅛ inch [3mm] from coil), stopping 2 inches (5cm) from the top. Bring the zipper pull below the 2-inch (5cm) mark, and finish sewing around the top of the zipper, including the top edges. With a seam ripper, remove the basting stitches along the zipper tape, and from the opening. Unzip the zipper. Pin the front and back pillow pieces together, right sides facing, aligning the edges. Replace presser foot, then sew the remaining 3 sides with a ½-inch (13mm) seam allowance. Clip corners and turn the pillowcase right-side out. Use a point turner or a closed pair of scissors to push the corners out.

PILLOW INSERTS

In this book, you'll find that pillow covers are made to the exact size of their inserts. For an overstuffed look, make a pillow cover 1 to 2 inches (2.5–5cm) smaller than the insert; for a more relaxed look, make the cover slightly larger than the insert. The most common fillings for inserts are down and polyester batting. There are no industrywide standards for pillow sizing, but here are the measurements for the most common inserts you'll find in stores and online:

SQUARE Sizes range from 10 inches (25.5cm) to 36 inches (91cm) square. Most of the projects in this book call for square pillows, but you can adapt the instructions for any of the pillows below.

BOUDOIR These rectangular pillows are used to accent bed linens. They range from 12 by 16 inches (30.5cm × 40.5cm) to 14 by 36 inches (35.5cm × 91cm).

BOLSTER Shaped like a cylinder, bolsters can be used as armrests on a daybed or sofa and make comfortable neck pillows. They are measured by the diameter and length of the bolster, and standard inserts come in 4-, 8-, and 10-inch (10cm, 20.5cm, and 25.5cm) diameters and a variety of lengths. Common fillings include polyester batting and foam.

LUMBAR Long and rectangular, lumbar pillows are often used for lower back support while sleeping, and can replace the back cushions on a sofa. Sizes range from 14 by 18 inches (35.5cm × 45.5cm) to 14 by 36 inches (35.5cm × 91cm).

FOUR PILLOW-COVER FLOURISHES

The following finishing techniques will help produce handmade pillows with different outlines and decorative details.

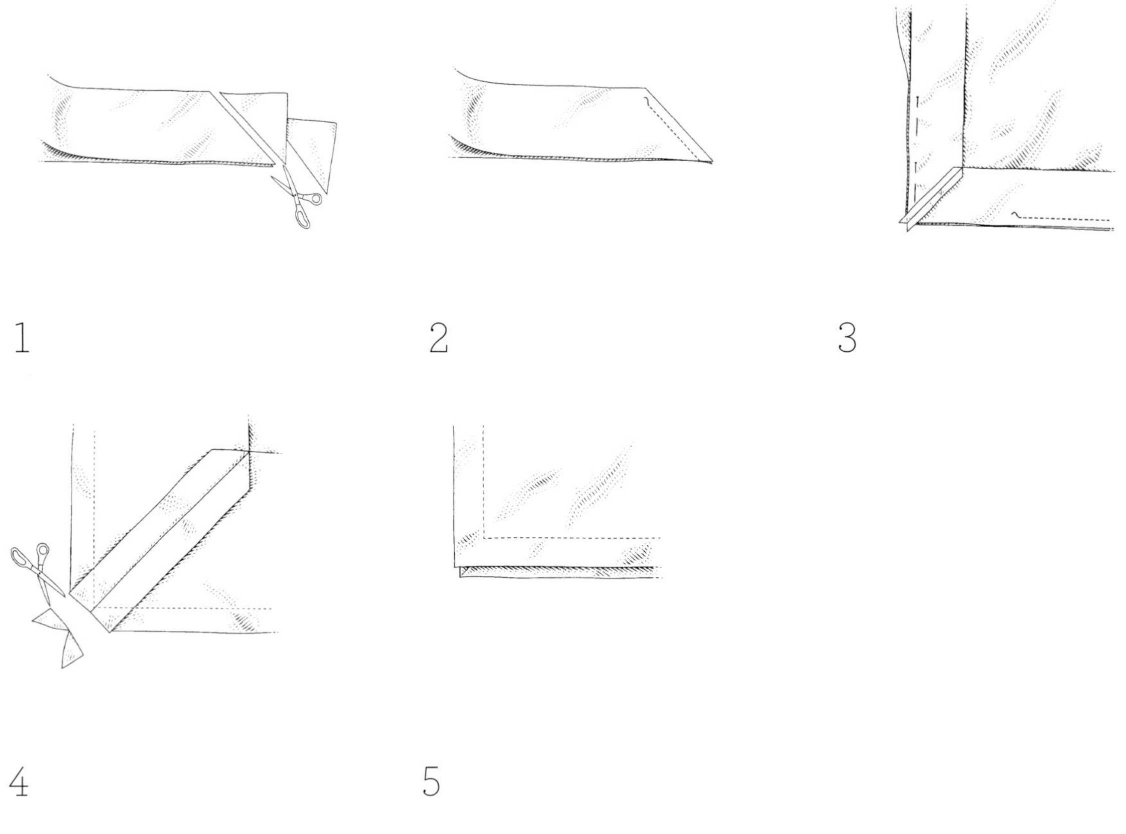

double flanges

Two extra projections of fabric—a double flange—emphasize the outline of a square or rectangular pillow cover. For an example, see pillow 4 on page 215.

1. Cut out 4 strips of fabric, each measured to fit one side of the pillow, plus an extra inch (2.5cm) for the seam allowance. Use a quilting ruler to mark both ends of each strip at 45-degree angles; trim away corners at the marks.

2. Line up the angled edges of 2 strips, right sides facing, and sew them together, as shown, with a ½-inch (13mm) seam allowance. Press the seam open. Repeat with the remaining strips to create a square or rectangular border.

3. With right sides facing, stitch the outer edge of the flange to the fabric for the front of the pillow cover, with a ½-inch (13mm) seam allowance.

4. Clip the corners, then add a bit of fabric glue to the center of the seam to prevent the flange from fraying. Press the flange open. Repeat steps 1 through 3, cutting and sewing additional strips of fabric for the back of the pillow.

5. Finish by stitching the front and back together at least ¼ inch (6mm) in from the unfinished edge of the flange, wrong sides facing, leaving an opening on one side for a pillow insert or batting. Stuff the pillow, and slipstitch the opening closed by hand.

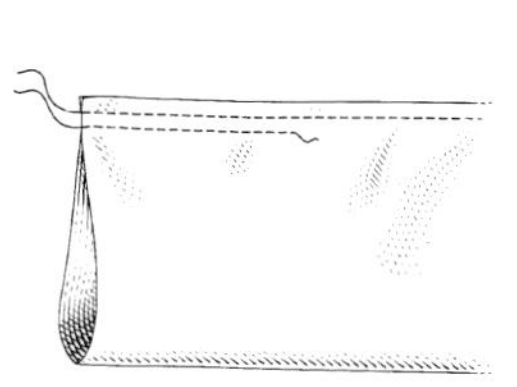
1

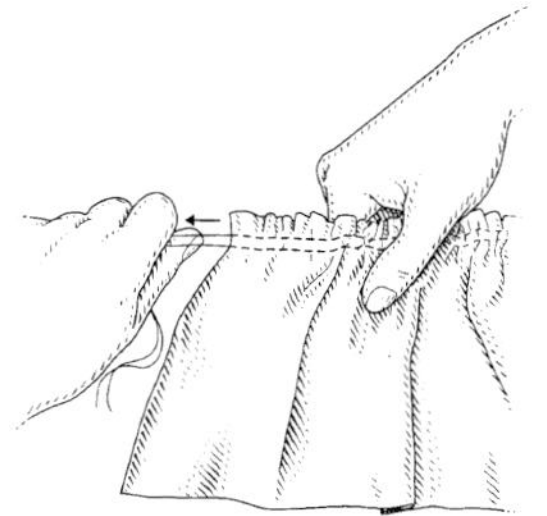
2

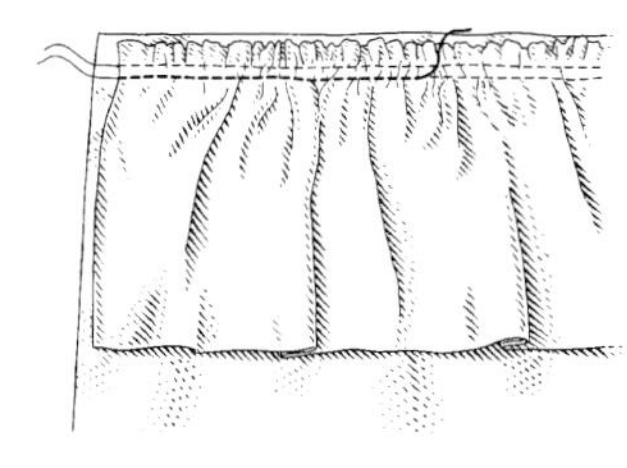
3

ruffles

Ruffles add softness and charm to a pillow cover's edges while at the same time defining its shape.

1. Begin with a piece of fabric 3 times as long as the perimeter of the pillow and twice as high as you want the ruffle to be, plus 1 inch (2.5cm) for seam allowance. Use one long piece or sew together several pieces, end to end. Fold the fabric in half, wrong sides facing, so long sides meet. Baste 1/4 inch (6mm) from the cut edge of the fabric, with a stitch length of about 3/16 inch (5mm). Make a second row in the same manner, 1/2 inch (13mm) in from the edge.

2. Ruffle the fabric: Pulling the threads from the bobbin side (underside), gather the fabric until it is one-third as long as it was. Knot the thread on both sides of the ruffle.

3. To attach the ruffle to the fabric for the front of the pillow, line up the sewn edge of the ruffle with the edge of the right side of the pillow fabric; pin in place, then stitch the 2 together along the second row of stitching, using normal tension and stitch length and a size 14 needle. To prevent the ruffle from bunching, use the tip of a seam ripper to adjust the gathers evenly as you sew. After the ruffle is sewn on, turn the unfinished ends under 1/2 inch (13mm), and slipstitch them together by hand. Line up the second side of the pillow with the first, right sides facing, and stitch along the edge again, leaving an opening for an insert or batting. Turn the fabric right-side out; insert the pillow, and slipstitch the opening closed by hand.

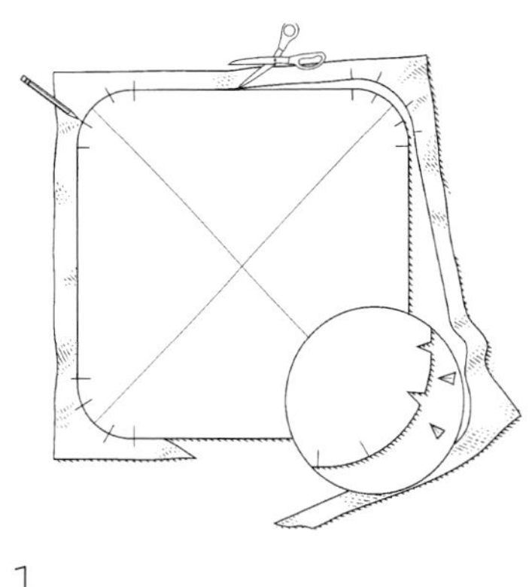
1

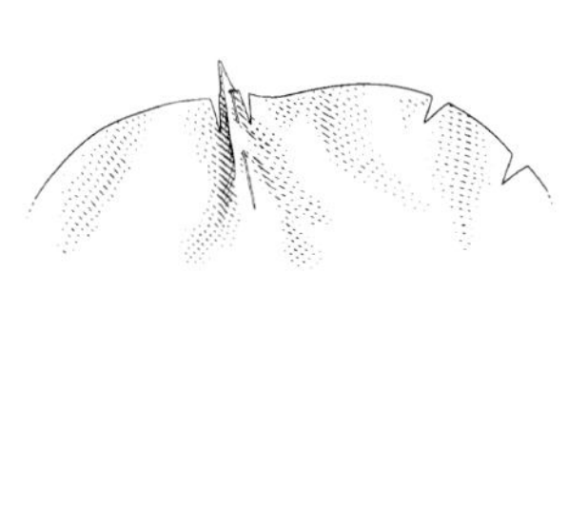
2

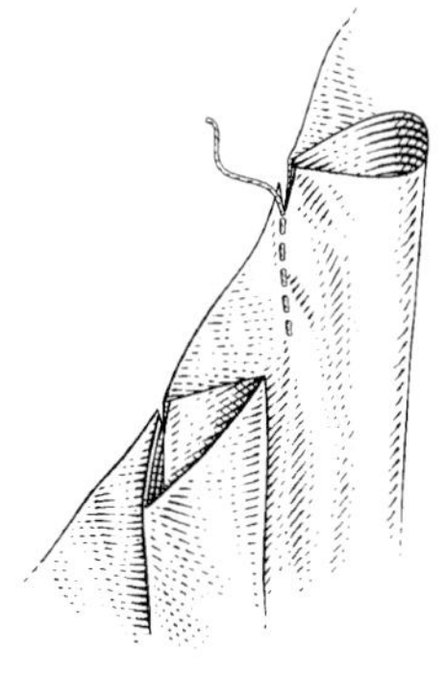
3

Turkish corners

Box pleats create pillow covers with rounded edges, called Turkish corners. For an example, see pillow 3 on page 215.

1. Make a template from a square of paper 1/2 inch (13mm) larger on all sides than the pillow insert; draw an X from corner to corner. Fold the square into quarters; cut around the unfolded corner to make 4 rounded corners. Unfold, and make 4 marks at each corner: two 1 1/2 inches (3.8cm) apart, on each side of the X. Use the template as a guide to cut out the fabric for the front and back pieces of the pillow, cutting notches at each mark.

2. For the front piece, line up the adjacent notches, then pin them together to make pleats. There will be 2 pleats at each corner. Repeat for back piece.

3. Stitch down each pleat 1/2 inch (13mm). Press pleats open, pressing them 1/2 inch (13mm) in from the edge of the fabric. Place front and back pieces of fabric together, right sides facing, lining up the pleats. Sew together with a 1/2-inch (13mm) seam allowance, leaving an opening for a pillow insert. Turn the fabric right-side out; insert the pillow, and slipstitch the opening closed by hand.

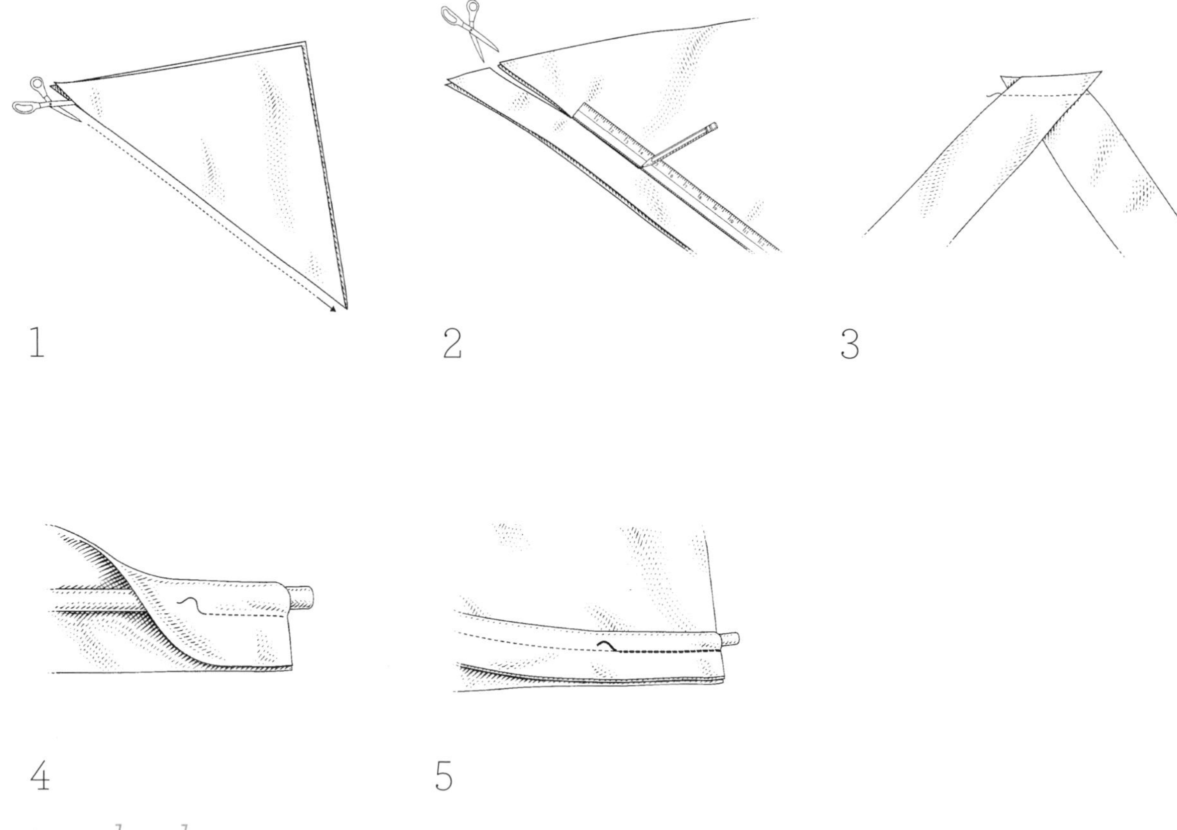

piped edges

A trim of piping (or welting) adds structure to the edges of a pillow cover. Made of fabric-wrapped cord, piping can also add a decorative detail when it contrasts with the color of the pillow fabric. You can find cord at fabric stores. For an example of piped edges, see pillow 1 on the opposite page. follow the steps below to make your own piping; skip to step 5 if using store-bought piping.

1. Cut strips of fabric to use for piping: Fold a piece of fabric in half diagonally, and then cut it along the fold into 2 triangles.

2. With both layers still stacked, use a ruler and a disappearing-ink fabric pen to mark 1 3/4 inches (4.5cm) in from the just-cut edge; cut. You will end up with 2 strips of fabric cut on the bias. Continue cutting strips until you have enough for the perimeter of your pillow.

3. Line up the ends of 2 strips, right sides facing, so they crisscross. Stitch the strips together along the top; press the seam open to create one long, even strip. Repeat with additional strips.

4. Place a length of piping cord on the wrong side of the strip. Fold the fabric over, and pin. Use a zipper foot to stitch along the cord.

5. To attach the piping, line up the edge of the piping fabric with the right side of the fabric for the front of the pillow cover; then stitch the 2 together, sewing over the previous stitching along the edge of the piping. Pin the back of the pillow to the front, right sides facing, and stitch along the edge of the piping again, leaving an opening for a pillow insert. Turn the pillow cover right-side out; insert the pillow, and slipstitch the opening closed by hand.

pillow trimmings

Trimmings add decorative detail to pillow covers. Rich fabrics in the same palette help coordinate an assortment of pillows and bring smart style to any living space.

1. BOLSTER WITH CORD TRIM In France, cylindrical cushions like this one often serve as bed pillows. They're also meant to provide structure along the back and sides of a sofa. Corded trim helps define the shape of this pale-gold silk-velvet example. For slip-stitched bolster how-to, see page 231.

2. BOLSTER WITH TASSELS An embroidered-taffeta cushion can be placed almost anywhere that needs dressing up. The bright floral-patterned fabric gives this bolster a boost; multicolored tassel trim adds a chic flourish.

3. SQUARE PILLOW WITH TURKISH CORNERS Box pleats give this silk-damask pillow softly rounded edges. Its large size (about 22 inches [56cm] square) makes it wonderful for resting against or holding (for instructions on making Turkish corners, see page 213). A double layer of caterpillar fringe creates a lush finish.

4. SQUARE PILLOW WITH A DOUBLE FLANGE A double flange edges the outline of a cotton chintz cushion. The flange is lined with persimmon satin fabric; its deep flame-orange color is picked up by a square of ribbon stitched to the front of the pillow and topped with white and gold trim. For instructions on making a double flange, see page 212.

seashell-printed pillows

Seashell prints help unify a collection of pillows made from various fabrics. The pillow covers can be store-bought or hand-sewn. If you are making them, print on the fabric before cutting it, so the pattern can continue all the way to the edge. Be playful in the design, with a mix of light and dark impressions, ordered and random patterns, or a graphic row of narrow Vs, made by inking only part of a large shell.

MATERIALS basic sewing supplies (optional), store-bought pillow cover or linen fabric, fabric paint, sponge brush, scallop shells, old towels, cotton or linen practice fabric

HOW-TO Print seashells onto the pillow cover or fabric using the fabric-printing technique on page 87. Experiment with a variety of sizes of scallop shells and printing techniques to create patterns that suit your taste. For the pillow pictured at the far left, small shells were printed in straight, symmetrical rows. The center three ridges of a large shell were used to create the wide band on the dark blue pillow. Medium-size shells helped create the evenly spaced design on the metallic silver pillow in the back. The peach pillow at front was stamped in an organic composition; to attain the lighter impressions, the shells were printed several times before re-inking. Finally, a minimalist column of small shells was printed down the center of the pillow at the far right. If you are making the pillow cover, choose the section of the printed fabric you like best for the front and back. Determine the type of cover you want to make (see page 210), and sew according to the instructions.

wraparound pillow bands

Ordinary sofa pillows take on more vibrant personalities with easy-to-assemble fabric bands. The bands shown here are made out of wool; their Velcro closures at the back let you swap them for lightweight bands when the weather warms. For a layered look, double up bands of different widths.

MATERIALS basic sewing supplies, loosely woven fabric (such as wool, cotton, or linen), iron-on Velcro strips

HOW-TO 1. Determine the length of the band by wrapping a measuring tape around the pillow; add 1 inch (2.5cm) to the measurement. Cut the fabric to that length and the desired width. Pull a few threads along the long edges to fringe the sides, if desired, or finish the long sides with a double hem (page 37).

2. Apply iron-on Velcro strips to the short sides, and fasten the bands in place around the pillows.

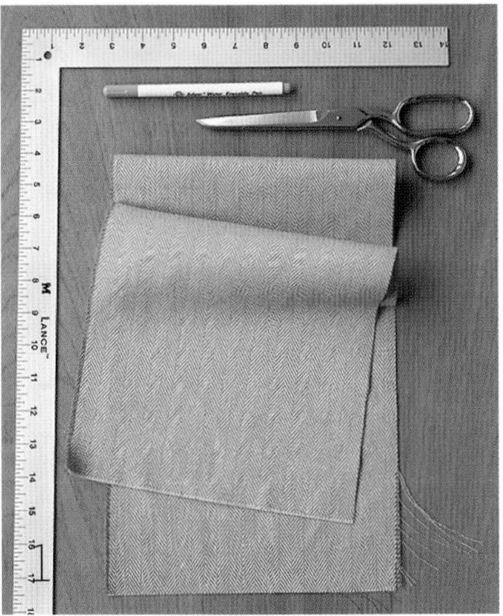

1

2

napkin pillow cover

Brighten any setting—indoors or out—with decorative pillows made from eye-catching cloth napkins. Use spares when their matches have been tossed or lost, or buy single napkins specifically for this purpose. The covers, which are a breeze to make, are fastened with a button, so they can be easily removed to wash. Make several using various hues and designs, and swap them whenever you want a quick change.

MATERIALS basic sewing supplies, 20-inch (51cm) square cloth napkin, 12- to 14-inch (30.5–35.5cm) pillow insert, button, decorative cord

HOW-TO Lay the napkin facedown, positioning it to resemble a diamond. Center the pillow insert on the napkin. Fold in 2 side points of the napkin to the middle, then fold up the bottom point. Tack the three triangles together at the center, and then sew about 2 inches (5cm) down on each side of the bottom flap. Stitch a button to the bottom flap near the point. Fold down the top flap; sew a loop of cord to the underside of the fabric to hold the button, ensuring that it fits snugly when closed.

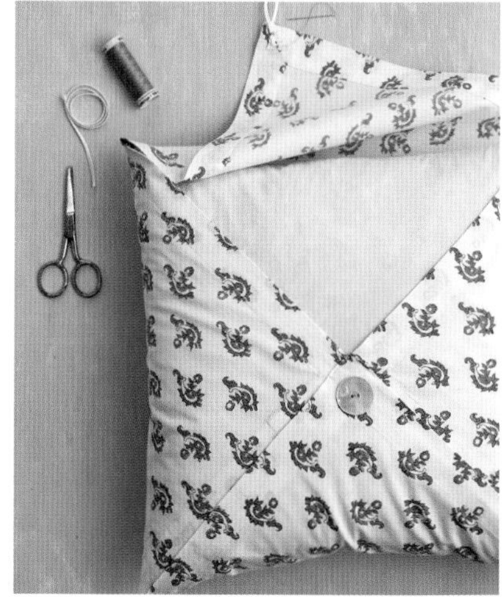

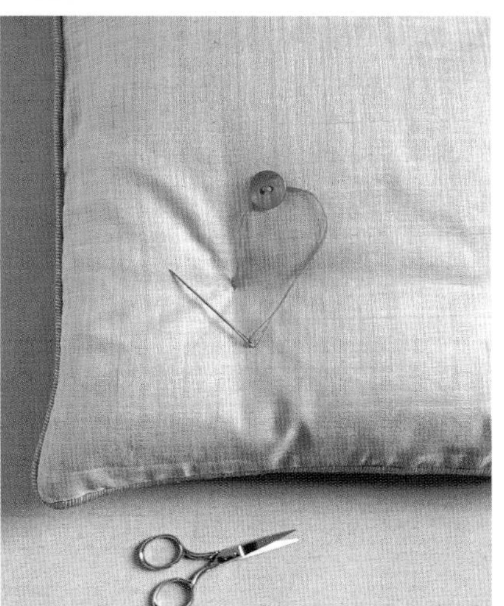

tufted cushion

Solid-colored pillows look more distinctive when embellished with pretty pom-poms or buttons. Adding them to both sides of a cushion will prevent the thread from straining the fabric and tearing. The tufting will keep the fill in the insert from shifting, so the pillow will rarely need to be fluffed.

MATERIALS basic sewing supplies, buttons or pom-poms, store-bought pillow cover with insert, upholstery thread, long upholstery needle

HOW-TO Mark the placement of the buttons or pom-poms on the pillow cover with a disappearing-ink fabric pen, then secure each embellishment with a double length of thread, passing through the pillow insert and inserting the needle into a matching button or pom-pom on the other side.

pinch-pleated pillow

Pinch pleats give pillow covers a subtle textural touch. Puckered folds such as these are easy to produce on store-bought pillows or handmade ones with a needle and thread; if you're creating your own cover, follow the instructions for one of the closures on page 210. Pinch-pleated covers look best when filled with smaller inserts, since the fabric needs room to slouch a bit.

MATERIALS basic sewing supplies, pillow cover, heavy-duty thread, pillow insert (slightly smaller than the cover)

HOW-TO Turn the pillow cover inside out. Using a disappearing-ink fabric pen and ruler, create a grid of evenly spaced dots on the cover (each dot will be the tip of a fold). Double-thread a needle with heavy-duty thread, and knot it. Pinch the fabric (see figure a). Pass the needle through the fold (the farther from the tip you stitch, the more puckered the fold will be); then pull it all the way around the fold. Pass the needle between the doubled threads, below the knot. Loop around twice; pass the needle under the loops (see figure b). Pull the thread tight; tie it off. Repeat for each marked dot. Turn the case right-side out and insert the pillow.

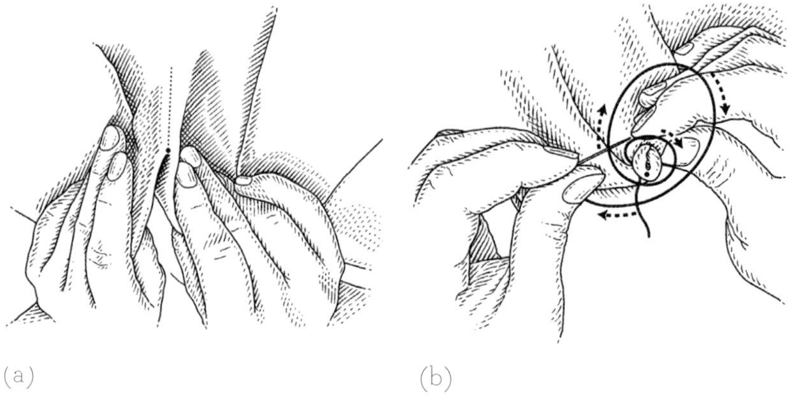

(a) (b)

woven-wool pillow covers

Weave a custom pillow cover from torn strips of soft Melton or double-faced wool. The front of the cover is made of woven strips over a solid piece of wool. The technique is easy and doesn't require much sewing; just be sure to be accurate when lining up and pinning the wool strips together. Make tone-on-tone pillow covers by weaving strips of the same color, or choose a base color and weave in a few strips of wool in a complementary hue.

MATERIALS basic sewing supplies, Melton or double-faced wool, pillow insert

HOW-TO 1. Measure the width and length of the pillow insert, add ½ inch (13mm) for seam allowance, and cut out two squares with these dimensions (one for the front piece and one for the back).

2. Divide the width of the square piece into equal segments; this will determine the width of the strips. Lay the remainder of the uncut fabric on a flat surface. Snip 1 inch (2.5cm) into the fabric from the selvage, then rip the strips along the width of the fabric with your hands. Cut enough strips to cover the width of the pillow, plus 1 inch (2.5cm) for seam allowance. You'll need an equal number of strips to cover the pillow vertically and horizontally.

3. Lay the front square of the pillow cover on a flat surface; working on top of the square, create an L shape with two strips, overlapping the ends. Working along the vertical strip, place a strip under and the next over the fabric, and so on, pinning as you go. Weave the remaining strips through the horizontal ones, pinning to secure. Sew the strips to the wool front piece; stitch around the square ½ inch (13mm) in from the unfinished edge.

4. Lay the front and back pieces together, wrong sides facing, and stitch ¼ inch (6mm) from the perimeter of the pillow cover, leaving an opening on one side. Insert pillow, and slipstitch (page 31) the opening closed.

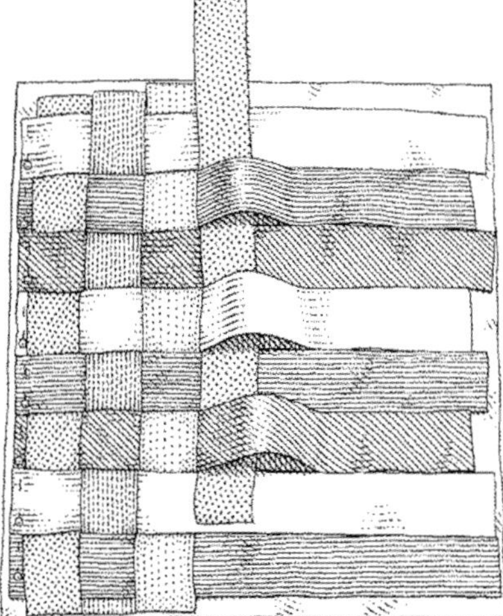

bird-embroidered pillows

White thread embroidered on colored fabric creates a modern effect. Here a Carolina wren was stitched onto aqua linen, a mountain bluebird onto brown linen. Choose your state's official bird or a personal favorite.

MATERIALS basic sewing supplies, bird template, store-bought pillow cover or linen fabric, pillow insert, transfer paper (white for dark fabric, dark for light fabric), ballpoint pen, embroidery floss, embroidery needle

HOW-TO 1. Print the template (see enclosed CD; adjust size, if necessary) and cut out. If you're making a pillow cover, you will need to embroider the front piece before finishing the pillow. If you're using a store-bought cover, only stitch through the front. Place transfer paper on top of the front of the pillow cover; place the bird pattern on top of the paper. Trace along the lines of the pattern with the ballpoint pen; the pressure will transfer the paper's ink onto the fabric.

2. Thread the needle with embroidery floss and chainstitch (page 48) over the transferred design.

3. If you're making the cover, finish according to the instructions on page 210.

falling-leaf pillow covers

Soft felt leaves are sewn onto pillow covers with details that mimic the midrib and veins of real foliage. This project combines elements of appliqué and machine embroidery. Attach the leaves before sewing the front and back pillow cover pieces together.

MATERIALS basic sewing supplies, falling leaf template, fabric for pillow (such as linen), pillow insert, wool felt, fabric glue

HOW-TO 1. Print the template (see enclosed CD), and cut out. Choose from the basic pillow designs on page 210, and cut out pieces to fit the pillow insert. Trace the template onto the felt with a disappearing-ink fabric pen, and cut out, using small scissors for detailed designs.

2. Position felt pieces in the desired pattern on the pillow cover, and attach them with fabric glue down the center (where the midrib would be). Machine-stitch a line down the center of the leaf to create a midrib. Machine-stitch V shapes: Starting at one edge of the leaf stitch to the midrib; pivot the pillow cover and sew back up the V. Repeat for the remaining Vs, using the pattern on the template as a guide. Repeat for the other leaves. Finish the pillow cover, following instructions on page 210.

box pillows and cases

It's a cinch to tailor store-bought pillows and covers so they have neat corners. A few simple stitches on a pillow insert and its existing cover are all that's needed to create the new shape. The box pillows are perfect for window seats or on benches, or even as pet beds (see page 272).

MATERIALS basic sewing supplies, pillow cover with removable insert

HOW-TO Remove a pillow from its cover, and turn the cover inside out. Make a box corner: At one pillow corner, gather and flatten the fabric to create a triangular flap; pin it in place, making sure the length of the triangle's base matches the desired depth of the finished pillow. Use a ruler and a disappearing-ink fabric pen to draw the stitch line on the pillow (the line should be perpendicular to the existing seam). Repeat on the other 3 corners of the pillow, as well as on the 4 corners of the case. Machine-stitch over the drawn lines (if there is a zipper, take care not to trap the pull in the corner of the case). Trim the corners of the pillow and case with pinking shears ½ inch (13mm) from the seam to finish, if desired. Turn the boxed pillowcase right-side out and insert the boxed pillow.

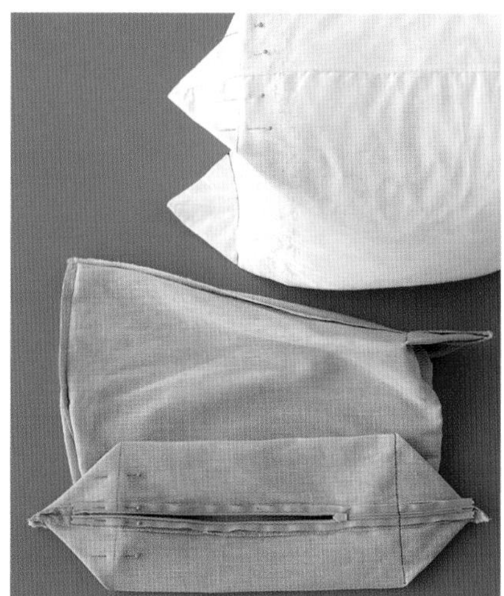

cross-stitch pillow cover

When rows of Xs are hand-embroidered with their ends touching, they create a handsome cross-stitch pattern. Here bold stripes or squares of fuzzy mohair yarn adorn a trio of decorative pillows in a modern setting. You can use this technique as easily on a store-bought pillow as on one made from scratch; just be sure the pillow cover is made of fabric with a loose weave. (For more on cross-stitch embroidery, see page 50.)

MATERIALS store-bought pillow cover or medium-weight loose-weave fabric (such as burlap or raw silk), pillow insert, mohair yarn, embroidery needle, embroidery hoop

HOW-TO 1. If you're making a pillow cover, choose from the basic pillow cover styles on page 210 and cut out front and back pieces to fit your pillow insert. (Embroider the front piece before finishing the pillow.) If you're using a store-bought cover, only stitch through the front.

2. Cross-stitch a design onto the front of the cover or the front square. Use the weave of the fabric as a guide, or grid, counting threads as you stitch (the height and width of each X should be equal). For small Xs, go up and over 5 threads; for large Xs, go up and over 10 threads.

3. If you're making the cover from scratch, finish according to the instructions on page 210. Insert the pillow.

tooth-fairy pillow

Sew a soft landing spot for the tooth fairy complete with a precious embroidered felt pocket. The miniature pillow is deliberately simple, so a child with very basic sewing skills can help make one.

MATERIALS basic sewing supplies, 1/4 yard (23cm) cotton fabric or remnants, felt, embroidery floss, embroidery needle, fill

HOW-TO 1. Cut 2 equal-size squares for the pillow. For the pocket, cut a smaller square out of the felt with pinking shears. Draw a design onto the felt with a disappearing-ink fabric pen; backstitch (page 48) over it with embroidery floss and needle. Machine-stitch the pocket to the pillow front on the sides and the bottom edge.

2. Pin the front and back pieces of the pillow together, right sides facing, and machine-stitch along 3 sides and halfway along the fourth with a 1/2-inch (13mm) seam allowance. Turn right-side out. Stuff the pillow with a generous amount of fill (see "About Fill," page 97), making sure it reaches well into the corners.

3. Fold the edges of the opening inward, pin, and slipstitch (page 31) to close.

wedding-ring pillow

Pretty printed fabrics, store-bought felt flowers, and short lengths of ribbon can be used to produce a variety of cheerful and lighthearted ring pillows. Look for great motifs in handkerchiefs, table linens, and pillowcases. This is a simple pillow to sew, making it an easy do-it-yourself detail for a bride, or a lovely handmade gift from a family member or bridesmaid.

MATERIALS basic sewing supplies, 1/4 yard (23cm) medium-weight cotton fabric or remnants, fill, thin ribbon or string, linen flowers (optional)

HOW-TO Cut the fabric into two 7-inch (18cm) squares. Sew the squares together, right sides facing, with a 1/2-inch (13mm) seam allowance; leave a 2-inch (5cm) opening on one side. Trim the corners (this will make them less bulky). Turn the pillow right-side out and stuff with fill (see "About Fill," page 97). Fold the edges of the opening inward, pin, and slipstitch to close (page 31). To attach the ribbon or string tie (to hold the rings for the ceremony), use a fabric tape measure to find the center of the pillow, then lay the ribbon flat at that spot; insert a threaded needle from the bottom of the pillow, pass it through the ribbon, and push it back through and out the bottom. Repeat, then knot. Sew on felt flowers, if using.

couched pillow bands

Couching, a technique that mimics the look of embroidery, involves arranging a piece of yarn or cord into a design and sewing it onto a piece of fabric. Here his-and-hers monograms are outlined on pillow bands (for instructions on making pillow bands, see page 217). Because of their small size, pillows are a good project on which to practice couching before moving on to larger canvases or more complicated items, such as bags, blankets, or bedskirts. To make a template, use your own handwriting, or look for letters in typography books, then photocopy to the desired size and cut out. Script-style letters work best with cord.

MATERIALS basic sewing supplies, letter template, pillow band, cord, fabric glue or liquid seam sealant

HOW-TO Pin a letter template to the pillow band, outline it with tailor's chalk or a disappearing-ink fabric pen, then lay the cording in place, and cut it to the precise length. Finish the ends with a dab of fabric glue or seam sealant (page 362) to keep them from unraveling. Pin the cording down all along the outline, then slipstitch it in place along both sides.

hand-appliquéd pillow covers

Gingko leaves and a stylized flowering stem are appliquéd by hand onto solid-colored pillowcases. Use the templates provided, or look for designs in botanical books and from nature to turn into templates. (For more on creating your own templates, see page 40.)

MATERIALS basic sewing supplies, hand-appliquéd pillow covers templates, 2 store-bought linen pillow covers or linen fabric, 2 pillow inserts, assorted linen and velvet fabrics (for appliqué shapes). metallic cord (for knobbed botanical motif), transfer paper (optional), tracing wheel (optional)

HOW-TO 1. Print the template pieces (see enclosed CD), and cut out. If making your own pillow, follow the directions on page 210. Trace the templates onto the appliqué fabric with a disappearing-ink fabric pen; cut out.

2. For the ginkgo leaf motif: Trace the templates onto the pillow cover with a disappearing-ink fabric pen to mark placement. Baste in place, then appliqué the cutouts with a ⅛-inch (3mm) seam allowance, following the hand-turn method on page 41.

3. For the knobbed botanical motif: Pin 2 lengths of cord in place on the pillow cover. Slipstitch them to the cover, following the directions for couching on the opposite page. With a disappearing-ink fabric pen, trace templates onto the pillow fabric. Appliqué the ovals on top of the cord in descending size order.

A variety of bolsters made from dyed cotton ticking have thin or thick stripes of green, beige, lavender, or blue (for instructions on dyeing, see page 77). Side panels were sewn to the main panel to make perpendicular stripes on the drawstring-cinched ends.

drawstring bolster

Bolsters of any size make comfortable additions to a daybed or window seat, serving as back supports, armrests, and neck pillows.

MATERIALS basic sewing supplies; bolster pillow insert; dyed cotton ticking or other medium-weight fabric, such as cotton or linen; cotton cord; safety pin

HOW-TO 1. Measure the circumference and length of the pillow insert; add 1 inch (2.5cm) to both (for a ½-inch [13mm] seam allowance). Use tailor's chalk to draw a rectangle on the fabric with these dimensions, as shown below. (For striped fabric, such as ticking, draw the rectangle so that the lines will run the length of the bolster.) To create the side panels, draw 2 smaller rectangles; the length should match the short side of the larger rectangle (the circumference of the bolster plus 1 inch [2.5cm] for the seam allowance) and the width should be equal to half the diameter of the bolster. (For striped fabrics, the lines should run parallel to the long edges.) Cut out all the pieces.

2. Machine-stitch the long sides of the small rectangles to the short edges of the large rectangle, right sides facing (with a ½-inch [13mm] seam allowance); press seams open.

3. Fold the rectangle in half, right sides facing, so long edges meet, and sew the long sides together, with a ½-inch (13mm) seam allowance, stopping 2 ½ inches (6.35cm) from each end. Press seams open, including the ends.

4. To create channels for the drawstrings, double hem each end: Fold over ½ inch (13mm), press, fold over 1 inch (2.5cm), press. Pin and edge-stitch; turn cover right-side out.

5. To cover the exposed ends of the pillow insert, cut circles of the fabric the same size as the bolster's ends. Zigzag-stitch around the raw edge to prevent unraveling. Lay the circles onto the ends of the bolster inserts, and tack in place with a few stitches around the rim.

6. Attach a length of cotton cord to a safety pin, and thread it through one of the channels, being careful not to pull it all the way through. Repeat on the other side. Insert the bolster. Pull drawstrings taut, and tie.

BOLSTER BODY

cut 1 piece

circumference + 1 inch

length of bolster + 1 inch

BOLSTER SIDE PANELS

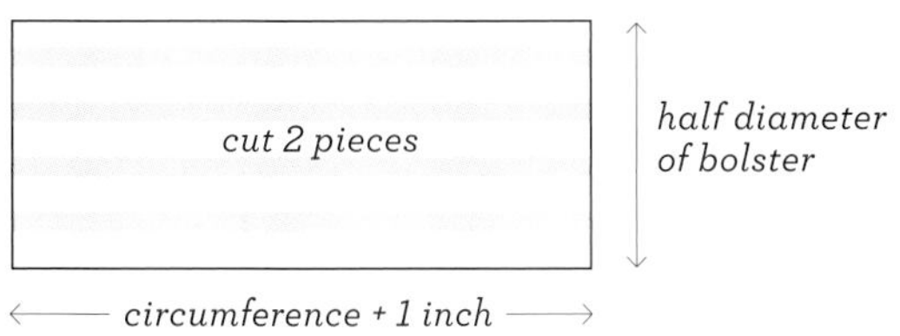

SLIPSTITCHED BOLSTER

A more traditionally constructed bolster cover is finished with a slipstitched closure. Piping or tassel trim may be added to the ends (page 215), if desired.

1. Measure the circumference and length of the bolster. Add 1 inch (2.5cm) to each measurement for the seam allowance. With a disappearing-ink fabric pen and a ruler, draw a rectangle with these dimensions (the circumference will be the width) onto the fabric. Cut it out.

2. Using a compass, draw a circle onto a piece of paper that is 1 inch (2.5cm) wider than the bolster's circumference. Cut out the pattern and use it as a guide to cut 2 circles from the fabric for the end pieces.

3. To create the body of the pillow, fold the rectangle in half lengthwise, right sides facing. Along the long unfinished edge, make a mark 3 inches (7.5cm) in from the right and left sides. Sew from one side to the mark, and backstitch to secure. Repeat on the opposite side. Leave the center of the long edge open. To attach piping, refer to the instructions on page 214, basting the piping to the body of the pillow.

4. Pin the round pieces to the body piece, right sides facing, and sew together with a ½-inch (13mm) seam allowance. Turn the cover right-side out. Insert the bolster pillow and slipstitch the cover closed by hand.

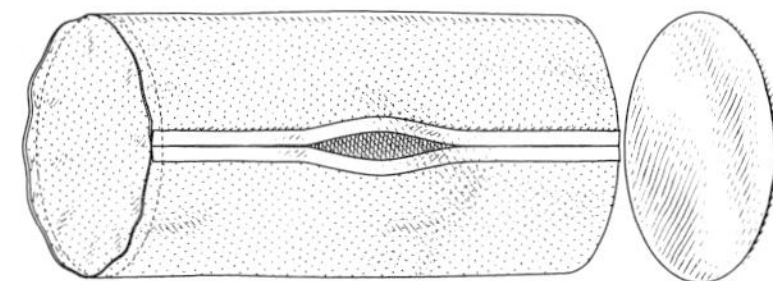

pin-tuck pillows

Pin-tuck patterns are easily created with slim, straight folds sewn into fabric. You can produce either free-form or methodical designs with pin-tucking. Both work well with any lightweight fabric; the examples shown are made from cotton broadcloth. Use a piece of fabric several inches larger than you think you might need; you can always trim any excess after making the tucks.

MATERIALS basic sewing supplies, cotton broadcloth or other lightweight fabric, pillow insert

HOW-TO Determine the style of pillow closure you'd like to make (page 210), and cut out front and back pieces. Cut the front piece larger to accommodate the pin-tucks; about 1/4 inch (6mm) extra fabric will be needed for each 1/8-inch (3mm) pin-tuck. (It may help to draw out the design on paper to determine the number of pin-tucks, and whether they will be horizontal or vertical.) Lay out the material on a work surface, right-side down. Fold the fabric over; the fold's crease will be the ridge of the tuck. To ensure an even fold, use a ruler to check that the fold is the same distance from the edge of the fabric, or the preceding fold, along its entire length (see photo, below). Press the fold flat, and stitch 1/8 inch (3mm) from the edge. Repeat for remaining pin-tucks. As additional pin-tucks are added, puckers and slight bulges will probably develop—don't worry about them. These irregularities are part of the charm. Once all of the pin-tucks are sewn, finish the pillow according to the directions on page 210.

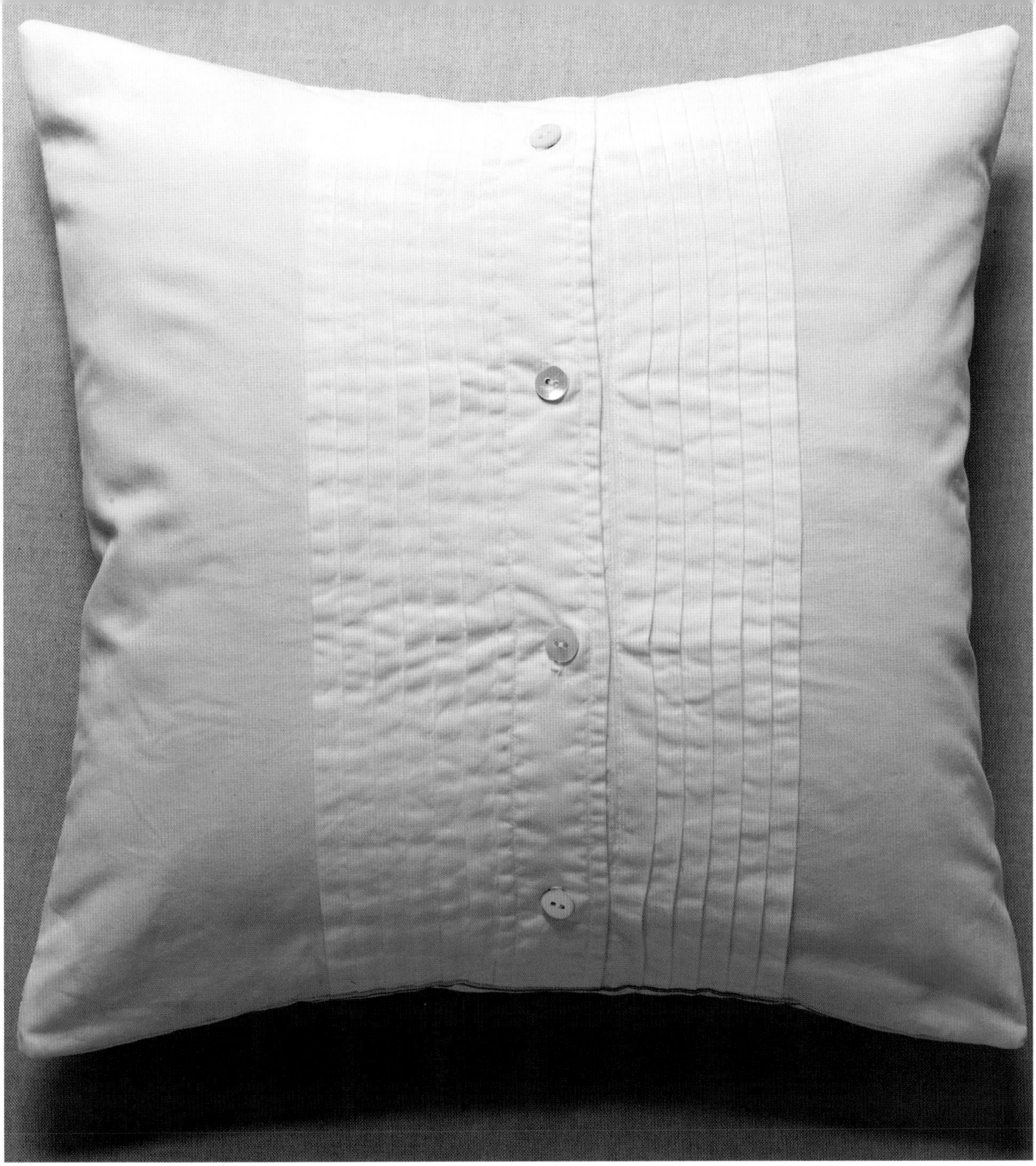

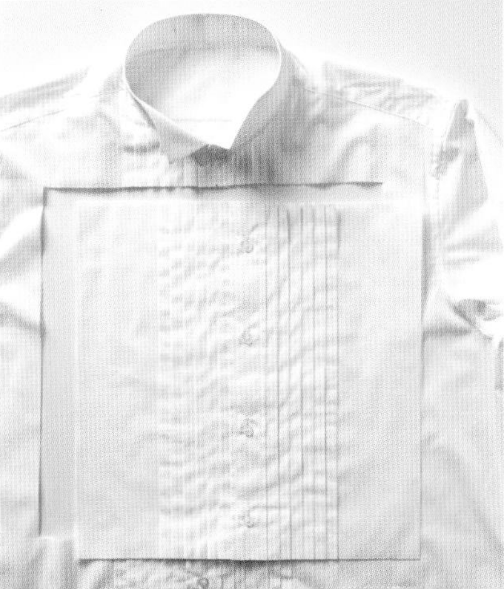

easy tuxedo pin-tuck pillow

Turn a tuxedo shirt into a pillow cover as an easy way to mimic pin-tucking by hand. The buttons at the front of the shirt also act as the opening for the pillow, so you don't need to make your own closure. This is an exceptionally easy project for those new to sewing.

MATERIALS basic sewing supplies, tuxedo shirt, 12-inch pillow insert

HOW-TO Lay the shirt flat on an ironing board or towel, and press. Using a ruler and disappearing-ink fabric pen, mark a 13-inch (33cm) square, making sure to center the square around the folds and the buttons on the front of the shirt. Cut out the square from the front and back of the shirt. (If desired, you can cut a square from a different fabric for back of pillow.) Place the squares together, right sides facing, and sew all edges with a ½-inch (13mm) seam allowance. Clip corners. Turn the pillowcase right-side out through the opening at the front and insert the pillow form; button to close.

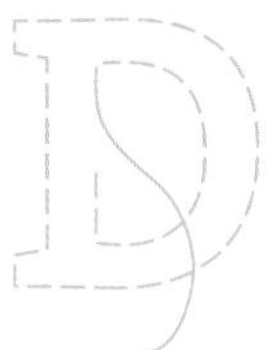

PROJECT:

dolls

A doll often becomes a child's best friend—and why not? It's always there, night or day, and can be counted on for security and comfort. The handmade dolls on these pages are deliberately simple in design, but while their facial expressions are neutral and their body shapes plain, they will surely come alive in the arms of a baby or small child. In fact, their simplicity is meant to encourage imagination and creativity. The dolls are modeled after examples from the Waldorf educational model, founded by Rudolf Steiner; you may hear similar ones referred to as Waldorf dolls, or Steiner dolls. Like their original inspiration, they are constructed entirely of natural materials, such as cotton and wool, and their hair is made of wool, mohair, or bouclé yarn. You can personalize the doll with your choice of hairstyle, skin and eye color, and clothing fabric. Create one that resembles a particular child, or sew a few dolls that are completely different and uniquely charming. For the body, consider using fabric from a garment a baby has outgrown; it will make the doll instantly familiar and that much more meaningful.

This project requires only basic sewing skills. Instructions and a template are provided, but feel free to improvise. After all, a handmade doll is much more than a gift; it's an expression of the person who lovingly crafted it.

HAND-SEWN DOLLS (OPPOSITE): *These small fabric dolls are big on personality and charm. Yarn is used for the varied hairstyles. Embroider bangs directly to the head with a satin stitch; use longer strands for the rest, or trim for a cowlick. For curly short hair, embroider mohair directly to head, and brush slightly. For long hair, use strands of wool or cotton. For pigtails, use heavy-gauge wool yarn; tie with more of the same. Alpaca works for straight hair. Bouclé has curls built in; loops are clipped to make spiky hair.*

hand-sewn dolls

MATERIALS basic sewing supplies, doll clothing template, 10-by-18-inch (25.5cm x 45.5cm) piece of washable fabric (for clothing), nearly 10-inch (25.5cm) square of cotton jersey (for skin), wool batting, embroidery floss (for eyes and mouth), embroidery needle, yarn (for hair; see caption, page 234)

HOW-TO 1. Print the template (see enclosed CD), and cut out. Fold the body fabric end to end, right sides facing. Lay the template on the fabric with the shoulders on the fold, and cut it out along the solid lines; pin. From the skin fabric, cut a 3-by-7-inch (7.5cm x 18cm) strip (for the head) and four 2-inch (5cm) squares (for the hands and feet).

2. Starting at the bottom outer edge of one leg, stitch up the side to the end of the arm, with a ¼-inch (6mm) seam allowance. Repeat on the other side of the body. Sew the inner edges of the legs. Notch curves on the body, as shown. Fold the head rectangle in half lengthwise; pin. Starting at the fold, stitch a curved shape across the short end, as shown, and continue stitching down the open side; snip away any excess fabric, keeping a ⅛-inch (3mm) seam allowance. Turn both pieces right-side out.

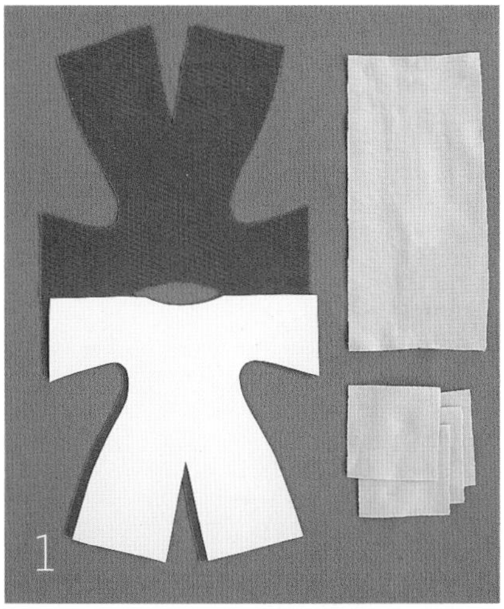

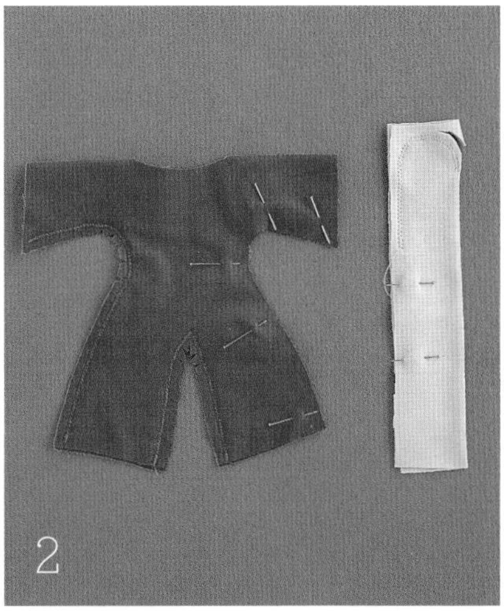

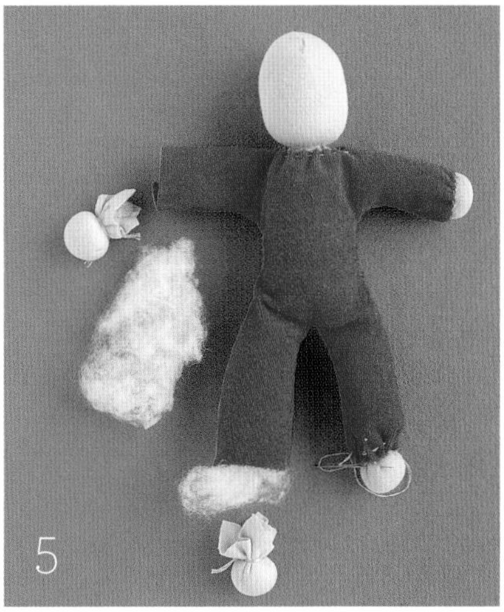

3. Cut three 2-by-7-inch (5cm × 18cm) strips of batting; lay them in a star shape, as shown. Roll more batting into a 2-inch (5cm) ball; place it on the star. Bring the strips up and around the ball; use a chopstick and your fingers to push the batting inside the head. The head should be firm; add more batting if necessary, smoothing with your fingers.

4. Tie thread the same color as the skin around the head below the ball to create a neck. Stitch the bottom opening closed. For the hands and feet, place a 1-inch (2.5cm) ball of batting on each square; bundle, tying with thread to secure.

5. Stuff the body, but not as firmly as the head. Use a running stitch (page 31) to tighten the neck opening. With a doubled length of skin-colored thread, slipstitch the head to the body, folding under the unfinished edge. Repeat for the hands and feet: first tighten the openings with a running stitch, then attach each piece with the slipstitch.

6. Use pins to mark the placement of the features. To keep the hair in place, secure the loops of yarn with anchoring stitches, as shown. For features, insert a needle threaded with embroidery floss through the back of the head and come out at a pin. Stitch the features; the needle should exit at the back of the head. Tie off the thread.

7. Snip the loops. Use your fingers to sculpt and smooth the face. Hand-wash doll in mild detergent and warm water; air-dry.

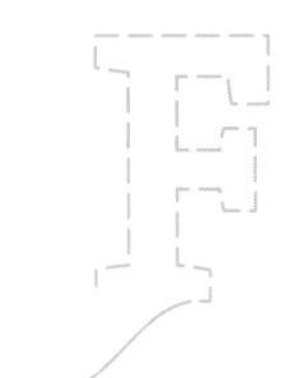

PROJECT:

flowers

In the hands of a clever crafter, scraps and strips of fabric are easily transformed into exotic flora. If you find inspiration in the infinite variety and lovely hues of flowers and blooming trees, bring your ideas to life using fabrics and ribbons in all manner of textures, patterns, or colors. Inexpensive notions, such as buttons and vibrant rickrack trim, can be made into other playful fabric-flower projects. Once the blossoms are complete, use them to add dimension to clothing or to create party-perfect decorations: Dot a baby's spring outfit with sweet (but sturdy) rickrack daisies, dress up a special-occasion outfit with an elegant boutonniere, or set out a vase full of everlasting branches "in bloom" at a party. To get started, study the forms and instructions on the pages that follow, keeping an eye to the natural world for clues to a flower's composition. Whatever your choices, these hand-worked blossoms are sure to bring a sunny exuberance to everything that they touch.

IN THIS CHAPTER: FLOWERING BRANCHES — COVERED-BUTTON BOUTONNIERE — RICKRACK FLOWERS

FLOWERING BRANCHES (OPPOSITE): *A bunch of branches wrapped in seam binding and bedecked with fabric flowers makes a striking alternative to a traditional floral arrangement. Here the shapely branches arc over a display of party favors topped with fabric flowers in the same shades. To decorate favors, wrap each small box with layered ribbons or a strip of fabric, and glue a single fabric blossom on top.*

flowering branches SEE PHOTO, PAGE 239

Adorn branches with fabric flowers to resemble a spray of quince blossoms. Use branches from your own yard, or purchase them from a nursery or florist. Floral wire, tape, and artificial stamens can be found at crafts stores. For flowers, opt for lightweight cotton fabrics, which can be easily torn along the fabric's grain, or use a length of grosgrain ribbon.

MATERIALS basic sewing supplies, ½-inch (13mm) lightweight cotton fabric or grosgrain ribbon, liquid seam sealant, artificial stamens, tacky glue, tree branches, ½-inch-wide (13mm) seam binding

HOW-TO 1. For fabric flowers, tear the cotton into 1-inch (2.5cm) strips and cut them 8 inches (20.5cm) long. For ribbon flowers, cut ribbon 4 inches (10cm) long. Using thread in a matching color (knot the end), sew a running stitch (page 31) lengthwise along one edge of the strip or ribbon, leaving the needle in the fabric until you've stitched the entire length.

2. Slide the fabric or ribbon along the thread, drawstring style, to gather; pull taut.

3. Keeping the thread taut, bring the ends of the fabric or ribbon together, right sides facing, and sew; backstitch a couple times to secure. Snip off any excess fabric or ribbon, and apply seam sealant to the cut edges to prevent unraveling. Fold a few artificial stamens in half, then insert them into the center of the flower so the stamen heads emerge just a bit; add a dab of tacky glue to secure them, and let them dry.

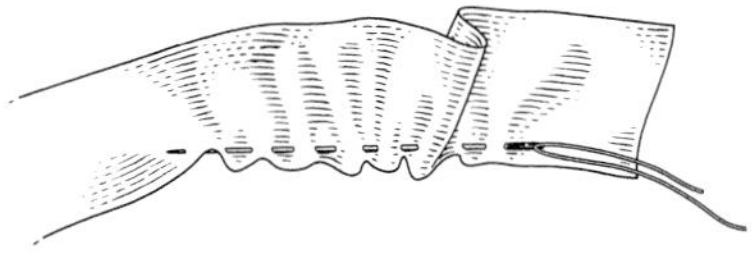

1

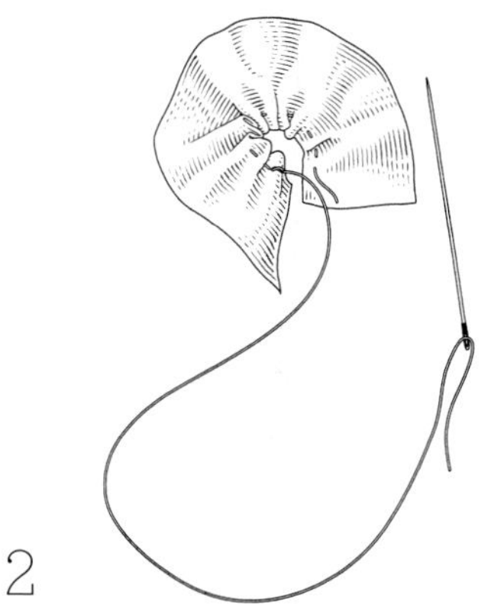

2

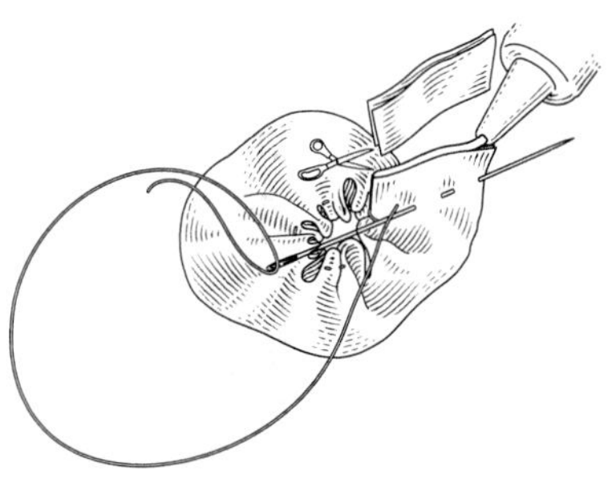

3

WRAPPING BRANCHES

Tie a piece of seam binding to the bottom of each branch. Pulling slightly to keep binding tight, wrap it around the branch, overlapping by about a third (see photo, above). When you reach the end of the branch, tie a knot, and trim any excess to create a "leaf." If you run out of seam binding midbranch, tie the end to the branch and trim; then tie on a new ribbon, and continue wrapping (secure all knots with a dab of tacky glue beneath them). Glue flowers to branch.

1

2

3

covered-button boutonniere

Create a wearable bouquet by mixing fabric-covered buttons in different sizes, hues, and patterns; a linen leaf completes the look. For more on covering buttons with fabric, see page 366.

MATERIALS basic sewing supplies, covered button kit, solid or patterned linen or other medium-weight fabric (for buttons and leaf), fusible web, floral wire, floral tape, thin ribbon in 2 colors, straight pin

HOW-TO 1. For the leaf, layer 2 pieces of fabric, wrong sides facing, with fusible web and floral wire between them; press to fuse. Draw a leaf shape and cut out; wrap the stem with floral tape.

2. Cover buttons with fabric, following the kit's instructions. For each blossom, slip the floral wire up through the button shank; wrap around one side and then the other to make a figure 8; twist around the stem, and wrap with floral tape.

3. Bind the bouquet's stems with fragments of floral tape. Tie thin ribbons around the stems; trim the ends. Pin to lapel.

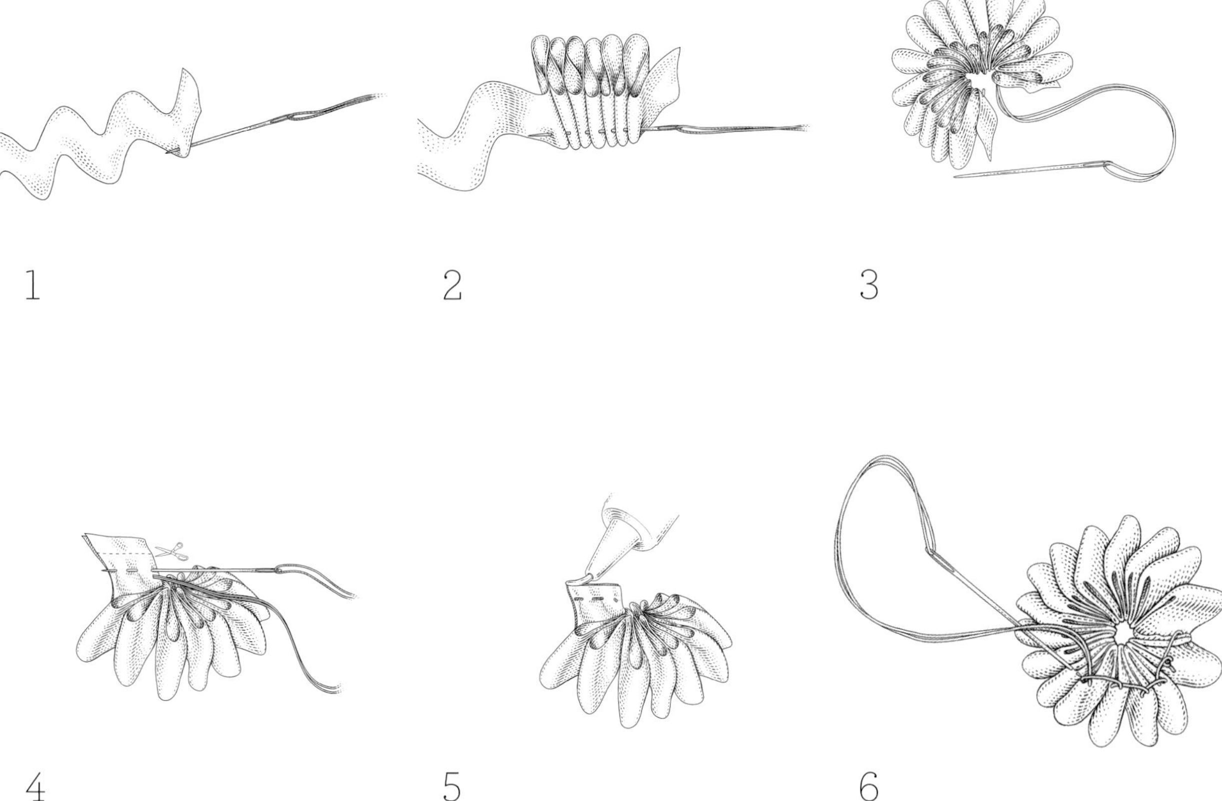

rickrack flowers

Abundant rickrack blossoms brighten any wardrobe. The flowers pictured on the opposite page decorate kids' clothing, but you can also embellish adult garments and accessories. Clockwise from top left: An oversize purple blossom, glued to a button cover to make it removable, adorns a simple white frock. A boy's lightweight jacket gets a boost of formality from a double-blossom boutonniere in two colors. Rickrack stems spring up from the hem of a coat, anchoring a garden of assorted flowers. Tiny white daisies made from narrow rickrack are sprinkled across a baby's romper; instead of stamens, the flowers' centers consist of embroidered French knots (page 52).

MATERIALS basic sewing supplies, rickrack, liquid seam sealant, artificial stamens, tacky glue

HOW-TO 1. Count 16 points along the lower edge of the rickrack; snip with the cut edges pointing upward. Thread a 10-inch (25.5cm) length of thread through a needle, and tie the end into a very large knot.

2. Pass the needle through the bottom points of the rickrack, as shown, gathering them together and allowing them to collect on the needle. (The rickrack will tend to spin on your needle; be sure to keep it upright as you work.)

3. After all the points have been gathered onto the needle, hold them together in a bunch as you draw the thread through. Still holding the points together, pass the needle back through the first fold and let go of the points as you pull the thread tight. Determine which side will be the front of the flower, and fold the edges toward the back. (Illustrations are for a flower with cupped petals; for bowed petals, fold the cut edges toward the other side.)

4. Sew the unfinished edges of the cut ends together, right sides facing, as shown. Cut away any excess rickrack; do not cut the thread yet.

5. Dab liquid seam sealant on the cut edges to stop the rickrack from fraying.

6. Put your thumb in the center of the bloom, fanning out the petals. Using the same length of thread, backstitch through the top of the loop of each petal on the wrong side, as shown. Secure the thread by slipping it under the stitches, and cut. Rearrange the petals with your fingertips. Fold a few stamens in half, then insert into the center flower so the stamen heads emerge just a bit. Add a dab of tacky glue to secure; let dry.

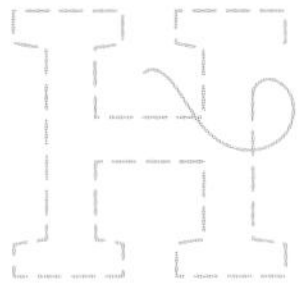

PROJECT:

handkerchiefs

Handkerchiefs, those light and airy squares of cloth, hint at an elegant past. But handkerchiefs can be useful in modern life, too. Tucked into a purse or pocket, they provide a more refined alternative to a humdrum packet of tissue.

A stack of handmade hankies makes a thoughtful gift for even a hard-to-shop-for loved one. Sewing a set from scratch takes little time, and their diminutive size and uncomplicated forms make them an ideal project for those new to needlecraft. The same rolled hem-finishing technique used for handkerchiefs can also be applied to a larger project made of delicate fabric, such as a sarong or shawl.

Embroidering store-bought hankies is a lovely way to personalize them. The fact that they are already hemmed gives you a head start. Look for vintage examples at thrift shops, tag sales, and flea markets—or even in your attic or at the back of dresser drawers.

IN THIS CHAPTER: EMBROIDERED HANDKERCHIEFS — ROLLED-HEM HANDKERCHIEFS

EMBROIDERED HANDKERCHIEFS (OPPOSITE): *Equipped with a few basic embroidery supplies, you can create charming hand-stitched handkerchiefs. Practically any image can be embroidered. Buy an iron-on transfer design from a crafts store, or trace an image from a clip-art book onto paper with a heat-transfer pencil. Press the image directly onto the fabric. Initials take on varying weights, depending on the stitch. Here a Scottie dog is made with satin stitches and stem stitches, and a paper clip from stem stitches in metallic silver thread. For more on basic embroidery stitches, see page 48.*

For Jodi
Jonathan

rolled-hem handkerchiefs

Because they're small and require just a needle and thread, making rolled-hem hankies is good practice for someone new to sewing. Don't worry if the handkerchiefs end up slightly asymmetrical or if your stitches are a little uneven—this will only add to their homespun appeal. Choose soft cotton or linen fabric; you should be able to make four hankies from ½ yard (45.5cm). Use a thread color that blends with the background of the fabric, or choose a contrasting color to add decorative detail.

MATERIALS basic sewing supplies, ½ yard (45.5cm) lightweight linen or cotton shirting fabric, self-healing mat (optional), rotary cutter (optional)

HOW-TO 1. Wash, dry, and press the fabric. Lay the fabric on a flat surface, wrong-side up. With a ruler and tailor's chalk, mark a 12 ½-inch (32cm) square. Cut out the square with scissors, or lay the fabric on a self-healing mat and cut it with a rotary cutter, using the ruler as a guide.

2. Thread a needle: You'll need about 55 inches (139.5cm) of thread to go around the outer edge; if this is too cumbersome, use several pieces that are 18 inches (45.5cm) long. With the fabric still wrong-side up, roll 1⁄4 inch (6mm) of the top edge of the square toward you (you may want to moisten your finger to help catch the fabric). Roll the hem tightly, so that it won't unravel when washed.

3. Insert the threaded needle into one end of the rolled edge, guiding the needle out near the base of the rolled hem, about 1⁄2 inch (13mm) from where you inserted the needle. Catch a few threads of the main part of the fabric just below the edge of the rolled hem (figure a). Make larger stitches if you'd like them to show on the right side. Pull the thread through the fabric and insert the needle back into the roll slightly to the left of where the thread first came out. Repeat stitches along one side of the handkerchief (figure b), spacing about 1⁄2 inch (13mm) apart and stopping about 1⁄2 inch (13mm) from the end. To make the corner, tightly roll the perpendicular hem to match the first hem. Roll tightly to create an even edge. Stitch the corner down, and continue stitching around the perimeter, tightly rolling the remaining edges as you go, and stitching down each corner. At the last corner, make several tiny knots just under the rolled hem.

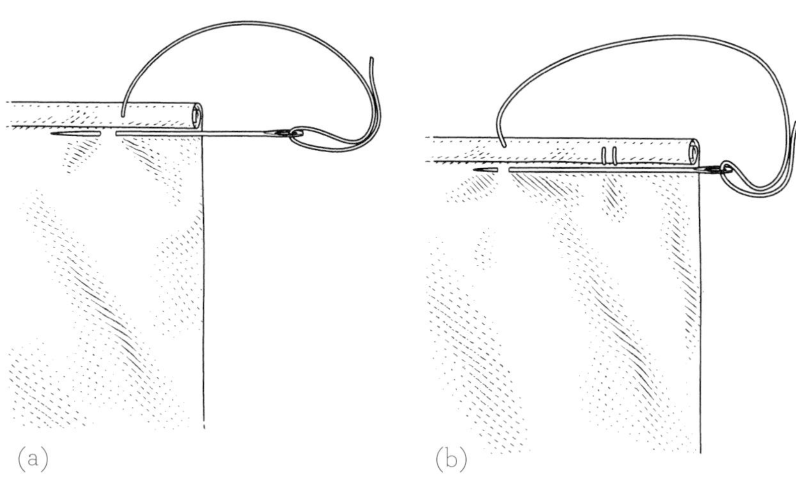

RIBBON-EMBROIDERED HANDKERCHIEFS

A trio of colorful cosmos adorn a linen handkerchief. To duplicate them, embroider with fine ribbon in various widths and shades and a combination of stitches—overlapping straight stitches for the petals, French knots for the centers, ribbon stitches for the leaves, and stem stitches for the stems. For a glossary of ribbon-embroidery stitches, see page 58.

PROJECT:

nursery

The mere prospect of a new baby awakens an impulse to create. Sweet, one-of-a-kind project ideas leap to mind. And there emerges a newfound desire to sew, quilt, and embroider. Whether it's toys, clothing, or bedding that call to you as projects, the idea is to welcome the little one home. Visit a fabric store to find inspiration in the delicate calico prints, playful notions and trim, and soft, natural fabrics you'll find there. Or gradually create an adorable suite of nursery accessories, using the projects that you find here. Whether you decide to make a quilted patchwork crib bumper, a happy and colorful garland, or an iron-on appliqué growth chart, you're sure to end up with a nursery that's equally pleasing for parent and child.

IN THIS CHAPTER: SCALLOPED CANOPY — QUILTED CRIB BUMPER — GROWTH CHART — SIMPLE FELT GARLAND — SHIRT-POCKET ORGANIZER — CHANGING-TABLE CURTAINS

SCALLOPED CANOPY (OPPOSITE): *A store-bought crib canopy, topped with a sewn-on scalloped felt crown border, makes a darling addition to a nursery. To make one, print the scallop template (see enclosed CD), and trace it to cut a 4-inch-wide (10cm) strip of felt—the length of the felt strip should equal the circumference of the canopy's ring. Cut out the scalloped edge, then sew the short ends of the felt together, using a zigzag stitch, to make a crown shape. Sew a length of scalloped-edge ribbon in a contrasting color along the top edge. To attach, sew one set of ribbons to the felt crown and one set to the canopy; tie crown to canopy ring. Hang canopy according to manufacturer's instructions; for safety, remove it once the baby is able to stand.*

quilted crib bumper

Line a newborn's crib with a lovingly stitched patchwork bumper. This example, made from a combination of new and vintage fabrics, will fit a standard 27-by-52-inch (68.5cm × 132cm) crib. Make sure the bumper extends all the way around the inside of the crib, and that it can be fastened securely to the slats. Include ties at the corners, and at least one on each long side; the ties should be no longer than 6 inches (15cm). When the baby begins to stand, remove the bumper.

MATERIALS basic sewing supplies, kraft paper, lightweight cotton in a variety of complementary patterns for the inside of the bumper (about 1 3/4 yards [1.6m] total), 1 3/4 yards (1.6m) fabric (such as quilted cotton) for the outside of the bumper, rotary cutter, cutting mat, extra-loft cotton batting; 8 1/2 yards (7.8m) of 1/2-inch-wide (13mm) trim

HOW-TO 1. From kraft paper, make a 10 1/2-by-9 1/2-inch (26.5cm × 24cm) template; use it to cut 18 rectangles from the lightweight cotton fabrics with a rotary cutter and cutting mat. Cut the fabric for the outside of the bumper into two 10 1/2-by-52 1/2-inch (26.5cm × 133cm) and two 10 1/2-by-27 1/2-inch (26.5cm × 70cm) rectangles. Cut the batting into four 9 1/2-by-51 1/2-inch (24cm × 131cm) and four 9 1/2-by-26 1/2-inch (24cm × 67.5cm) rectangles (for a double layer). Cut the trim into twelve 12-inch (30.5cm) lengths for ties (they will be folded in half), and one 4 1/2-yard (4m) strip for piping.

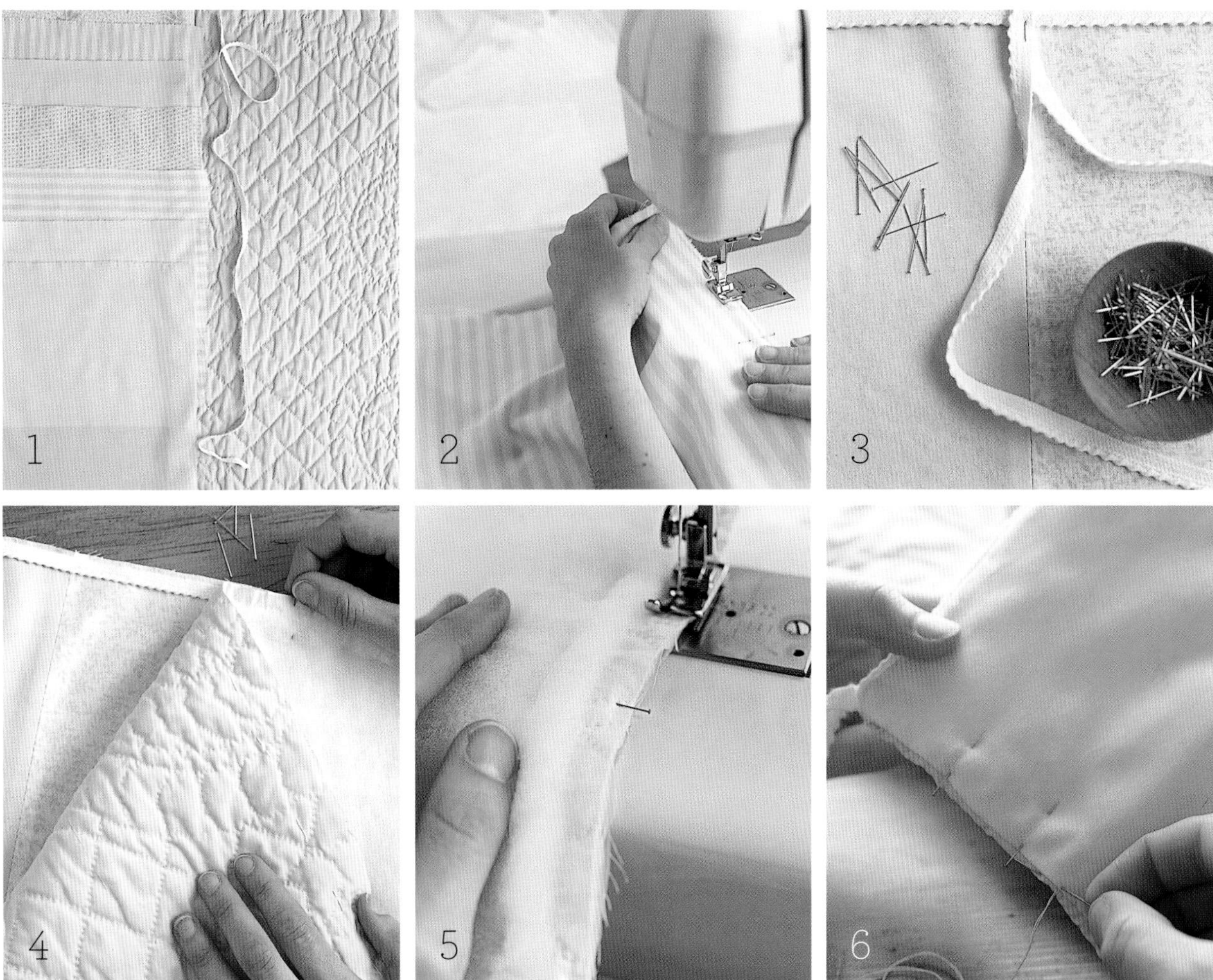

2. Arrange the patches in the desired order. Pin the long sides together, right sides facing; sew into one long panel. Measure against the inside of the crib as you go; panels that fall on the short sides of the crib will need a seam allowance of about 1/4 inch (6mm); those on the long sides, 1/2 inch (13mm). Press the seams flat. (For more on patchwork, see page 66.)

3. With the patchwork panel right-side up, lay the 4 1/2 yards (4.1m) of trim for the piping along the top edge; pin it in place. Stitch with a long zigzag along the edge. Remove the pins. Measure and mark the placement for the ties (at the top and bottom end corners of the crib, and 2 at the top on each long side where the bumper meets the crib slats). Cut 2 ties in half; pin a halved tie to the piping at each top and bottom end corner. Fold the remaining ties in half; pin them in place where marked at the top of the piping. Tack the ties with a zigzag stitch.

4. Pin 2 layers of batting to the wrong side of the outer rectangles; hand-baste near the edge (this will keep it from shifting). Make one long panel: Pin the short sides of the outer rectangles together, alternating sizes. Sew with a 1/4-inch (6mm) seam allowance. Lay the patchwork panel right-side up; place the solid-color panel, right-side down, on top. Pin on 3 sides, leaving one short side open (make sure the ties are sandwiched inside and the loose ends won't stray into the seam).

5. Sew together on pinned sides with a 1/4-inch (6mm) seam allowance, catching the piping trim and the folded ends of the ties in the stitching. Remove the basting stitches. Carefully remove all the pins. Turn the bumper right-side out; press the edges flat.

6. Tuck in the unfinished edges of the open side, pin, and slipstitch the opening closed. Remove the pins. Press the edges flat.

growth chart

Record your children's rapid growth with a crafty handmade chart featuring iron-on appliqué numbers. The shapes are cut from printed cotton pieces and affixed with fusible web.

MATERIALS basic sewing supplies, growth chart number templates, Homasote fiberboard (see box, page 264), 2 yards (1.8m) canvas, cotton quilting fabric (for numbers), yardstick, fusible web, fine-point permanent marker, embroidery floss, embroidery needle, staple gun, drill, screws, washers

HOW-TO 1. Have a piece of Homasote fiberboard cut to 14 by 63 inches (35.5cm × 160cm). Cut a 20-by-69-inch (51cm × 175.2cm) piece of canvas. With a yardstick and a disappearing-ink fabric pen, draw horizontal lines 3 inches (7.5cm) from the top and bottom edges. Measure 12 inches (30.4cm) up from the center of the bottom line and mark; this will be your 1-foot (30.5cm) mark when the chart is hung. From this mark, measure and mark subsequent feet. Make numbers: Using a word-processing program, print 5-inch-tall (12.5cm) block numbers from 1 to 5; alternatively, print number templates (see enclosed CD) and enlarge to 5 inches (12.5cm) tall. Cut out five pieces of fusible web slightly bigger than numbers. With the marker, trace numbers onto right sides of web; flip web over and trace outlines onto paper backing (numbers will be backward). Press webbing to wrong sides of 5-by-7-inch (12.5cm × 17.7cm) pieces of fabric, and cut out numbers.

2. Remove paper backing and press numbers to chart, aligning top of each number to its corresponding foot (30.5cm) mark. Working up from top of each number, use a disappearing-ink fabric pen to mark evenly spaced intervals (the ones shown are 1 3/4 inches [4.4cm] apart); stitch a 1/2-inch (13mm) line at each mark. Align top and bottom lines on canvas with top and bottom edges of Homasote; wrap fabric around board and secure to the back with a staple gun. Hang chart flush with the floor: Drill a hole in each corner, and screw chart to the wall, with a washer in between each screw and the chart.

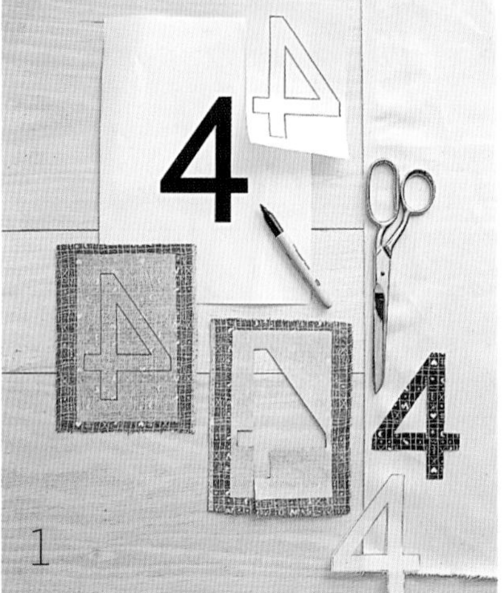

1

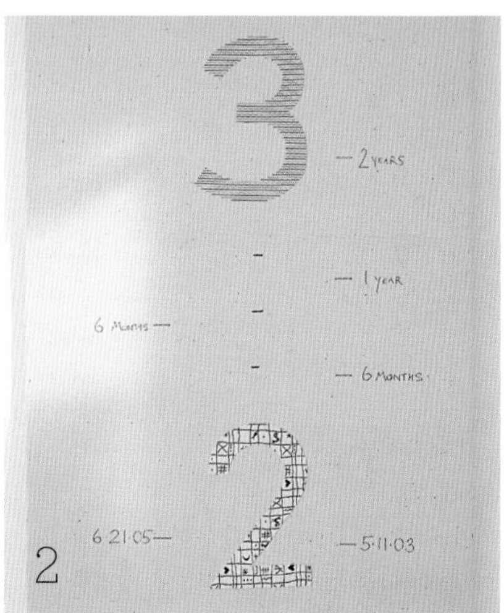

2

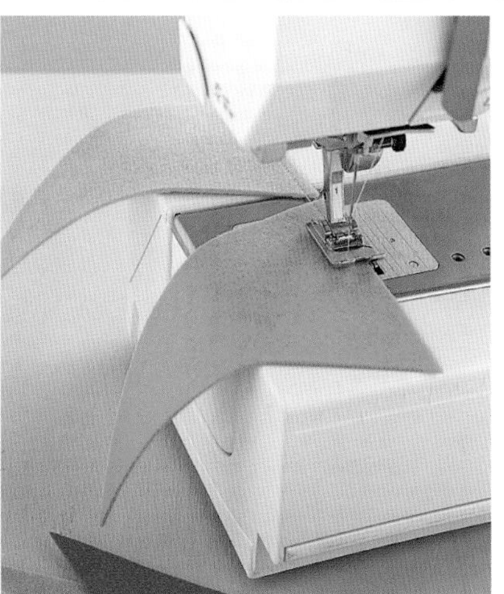

simple felt garland

Babies will love staring at the shapes and bright colors of this easy-to-make felt garland. Hang the banner above the crib, where a baby can study the cheery forms. Make sure it stays well beyond the baby's reach, and remove it once the baby can stand up.

MATERIALS basic sewing supplies, kraft paper, felt in a variety of colors, heavy-duty thread, nails or wall hooks

HOW-TO Cut out a kraft paper triangle about 5 inches (12.5cm) wide and 7 inches (18cm) long; use it as a template to trace and cut out as many felt triangles as you need. Sew the triangles together, corner to corner, with one long straight stitch. There is no need to overlap the flags; the thread will hold them together. Hang the ends from nails or hooks in the wall.

shirt-pocket organizer

A hanging quilt made from retired button-down shirts holds favorite small toys and accessories. Hang the quilt low enough that it's accessible to a child. Make all nine squares from shirts, or incorporate patches made from coordinating cotton fabric.

MATERIALS basic sewing supplies, button-down shirts with pockets, 1 yard (0.9m) cotton shirting (or 1 ½ yards [1.4m] if the fabric is less than 45 inches [114cm] wide), 4 buttons, fusible interfacing, ¼-inch-thick (6mm) cotton batting, dowel, wall hooks

HOW-TO Cut nine 11-inch (28cm) squares from shirts, with pockets centered. For variety, use a seam ripper to remove the pockets, and sew them onto different shirt squares. Pin the top row of squares together, right sides facing; sew with a ½-inch (13mm) seam allowance. Repeat with the middle and bottom rows. Press open all seams. Sew the 3 rows together and press the seams open. Cut out the border pieces: one bottom piece (2 ½ by 34 inches [6.5cm × 86cm]), 2 side pieces (2 ½ by 31 inches [6.5cm × 79cm] each), and one top piece (3 by 34 inches [7.5cm × 86cm]). Add 4 vertical buttonholes (page 370) to the top border piece, spacing evenly, ½ inch (13mm) down from the top edge. Do not open them; sew a button over each one. Sew the border pieces to the patchwork body, sewing the sides first, then the top and bottom pieces. Make the tabs: Cut 4 strips of shirting fabric, each 4 by 5 inches (10cm × 12.5cm). Fold a strip in half lengthwise; stitch the long edges together. Turn the tab right-side out, center the seam, and press. Repeat with the remaining strips. Fold each tab in half so that the short ends meet, with the seam on the inside. Pin each folded tab over a button (on the right side of the quilt), loop end down and unfinished edges aligned with the raw top edge of the quilt. Cut one piece each of fusible interfacing and shirting fabric measuring 34 by 34 ½ inches (86cm × 87.5cm). Press the interfacing onto the wrong side of the quilt front. Pin the shirting fabric to the quilt front, right sides facing. Sew edges together with a ½-inch (13mm) seam allowance, leaving a 24-inch (61cm) opening at the bottom. Turn the quilt right-side out. To quilt, insert a 33-by-33 ½-inch (84cm × 85cm) piece of batting into the opening. Tack through all the layers at the corners of each square piece. Slipstitch the quilt closed. Use the dowel and wall hooks to hang the organizer.

changing-table curtains

A changing table is rigged with blue linen flaps reminiscent of sails; snaps help hold them out of the way when you need to reach items on the hidden shelves.

MATERIALS basic sewing supplies, changing table, wooden lattice strips, linen, snaps and snap kit, double-sided tape, staple gun or nails, screws, screwdriver

HOW-TO Measure underside of table on front and sides; cut 2 lattice strips for each measurement. Measure distance from underside of table to floor and add 2 inches (5cm). Cut one fabric panel for each side and a pair for front (add 1 inch [2.5cm] to side edges for hems). Make double hems on sides and bottom edges: Fold fabric ½ inch (13mm), press, then ½ inch (13mm) again; press, then stitch in place. Using snap pliers, attach male halves of snaps to top outer corners of front panels, about 2 inches (5cm) from unfinished edge. Fold midpoint of each inside edge up to meet male half at top outer corners; attach a female half to this point. Add female halves to bottom corners for weight, and add snaps for decoration, if desired. Sandwich tops of panels between lattice strips using double-sided tape. Staple or nail each pair of strips together, and screw to underside of table on front and sides.

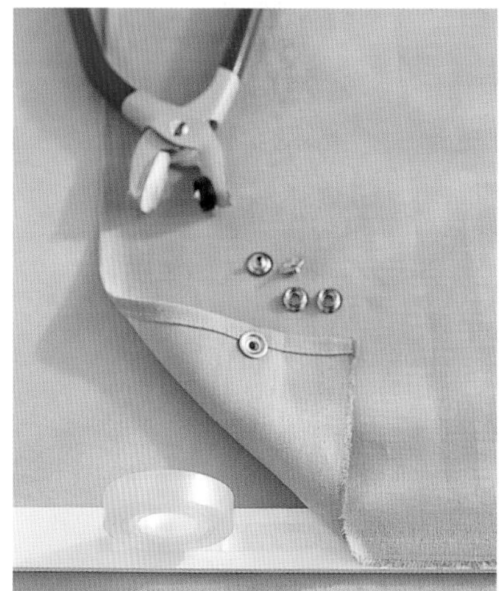

PROJECT:

organizers

When it comes to organizing, think inside—and outside—of the box. Create attractive fabric liners and covers for bins, cartons, and other clutter containers to hold photographs, crafts supplies, kitchen tools, toys, or any other small items that tend to "disappear" if not corralled properly.

Handy pocketed projects of all kinds will bring order to every room in the house. An ottoman cover with gusseted pockets holds the television remote and a notebook. There's also a pocketed wall unit, as well as a couple of bulletin board projects that have as much to do with inspiration as they do with organization. After all, any bulletin board can serve as a mirror of sorts, reflecting our lives in its ever-changing display of to-do lists, feel-good photos, and family artwork.

Find an area that needs some order, then get started. There's something so pleasing about knowing where things are when you need them—and something just as satisfying about having a place to put them once you're done.

IN THIS CHAPTER: FABRIC-TOPPED STORAGE BOXES — VELVET-LINED JEWELRY BOXES — FABRIC-WRAPPED ACCORDION FOLDERS — RIBBON-STRIPED BULLETIN BOARD — FALLING-LEAVES FELT BOARD — LEATHER COIN PURSE — WRAPAROUND BULLETIN BOARD — POCKETED OTTOMAN COVER — MULTIPLE-POCKET BULLETIN BOARD

FABRIC-TOPPED STORAGE BOXES (OPPOSITE): *Organizing stores and home centers abound with storage boxes in solid colors and basic shapes. Dress up the box tops with swatches of patterned fabrics to create a more visually interesting arrangement.*

Of Empire
GREAT IDEAS
Fear and Trembling
GREAT IDEAS
Oslo
Cairo
Zurich
Prague
Madrid

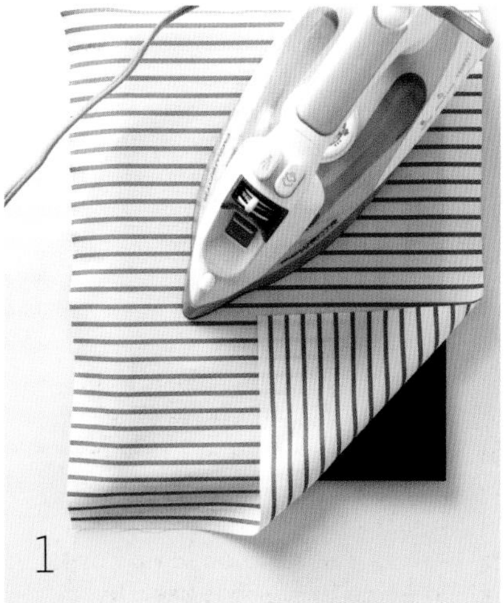

1

2

fabric-topped storage boxes

SEE PHOTO, PAGE 257

Men's cotton suiting fabric in a limited range of colored stripes was used to cover the tops of the boxes shown on the preceding page; the resulting organizers are handsome and streamlined. You can follow the same instructions to adorn boxes in other prints and patterns, such as florals, polka dots, or gingham, to suit your decorating style.

MATERIALS striped cotton shirting fabric, storage box with lid, ruler, fusible web, scissors, iron

HOW-TO 1. Measure the length and width of the lid; add the height of the lid plus ½ inch (13mm) to each measurement, and cut a piece of shirting fabric to these dimensions. Press fusible web to the wrong side of the fabric, following manufacturer's instructions; trim excess. Peel off paper backing and center the fabric on the lid. Press, following manufacturer's instructions.

2. Cut a notch in each corner of the fabric (the corner of each notch should be ¼ inch [6mm] from the corner of the lid).

3. Fold and press one side, then its opposite; repeat for remaining sides. Fold edges inside lid and adhere to the underside of the lid with the tip of the iron.

3

velvet-lined jewelry boxes

A Shaker-style oval wooden box lined with velvet ribbon holds smaller variations of itself, romantic repositories for family heirlooms or other favorite baubles. The exteriors of the small boxes were first brightened with milk paint, a coating typically used by American rustic-furniture makers. Lining the boxes (available at crafts stores and online) isn't difficult, but it does require precision and time.

MATERIALS fine-grit sandpaper, oval Shaker-style wooden craft box or heart-shaped box, milk paint (optional; salmon is pictured), velvet ribbon (its width should match the height of the box; 3/8 inch [10mm] is shown), lay-flat paste (such as Yes! Paste), small paintbrush, archival mat board, scissors, craft knife, lining fabric (pink silk satin is shown), fabric glue

HOW-TO 1. Lightly sand the exterior of the craft box; wipe it clean. Apply 2 coats of milk paint, if desired.

2. Measure the inside perimeter of the box, and cut the ribbon to this length. (If the box is deeper than the ribbon is wide, cut 2 lengths; if shallower, trim the ribbon to fit.)

3. With a small paintbrush, apply paste to the inside wall of the box. Align the edge of the ribbon to the top rim, and press so it adheres smoothly and the ends abut cleanly. (If 2 lengths are needed, align the first one to the bottom edge, then glue the second ribbon on top, aligned with the top edge.) Let dry completely.

4. Trace the bottom of the box onto archival mat board. Cut 1/8 inch (3mm) inside the line. Test to see that the mat board oval (or heart) fits into box; trim as needed with a craft knife. Place the board on the wrong side of the lining fabric, and cut an oval (or heart) 1/4 inch (6mm) wider all around. Apply fabric glue to the board, and affix it to the reverse side of the fabric. Smooth the fabric. Glue down the cloth edging on the back side. When dry, fit the panel, fabric side up, inside the box.

fabric-wrapped accordion folders

Add a splash or two of color and texture—as well as orderly storage space for paperwork—to a home office by covering accordion folders with pretty fabrics. The folders are a mainstay of office-supply stores. Use any durable fabric in an eye-pleasing style, and secure with ties made from ribbon or twill tape.

MATERIALS accordion folders, ribbon or twill tape, scissors, tape, mat board, fabric (linen, woven silk, and wool are shown), fusible web, small paintbrush, white craft glue, canned goods or other heavy objects

HOW-TO Remove any ties or flaps from the folders. For a small one, cut a ribbon long enough to tie around the folder and into a bow; tape its midpoint to the back of the folder. For a large folder, tape a 12-inch-long (30.5cm) ribbon to the top of the front and another to the back. Cut mat board ¼ inch (6mm) larger than the front of the folder on all sides. Cut fabric 1 inch (2.5cm) larger than the mat. Affix the fabric to the mat with fusible web, following the manufacturer's instructions. Brush glue on the fabric-covered board and attach it to the folder. Repeat on opposite side. Weight the folder down with canned goods; let dry for at least 2 hours.

ribbon-striped bulletin board

Twill tape in a colorful array of hues creates stripes that brighten a workspace while holding reminders and mementos neatly in place.

MATERIALS Homasote fiberboard (see box, page 264); fabric, such as canvas or linen; staple gun; twill tape or seam binding in multiple colors; pushpins

HOW-TO Have a ½-inch (13mm) thick piece of Homasote fiberboard cut to the dimensions you want. Cut a piece of fabric to fit around the fiberboard, with 2 ½ inches (6.5cm) extra on all sides. Lay the fiberboard on top of the fabric, then use a staple gun to affix the fabric securely to the board: pull the fabric taut, then staple one side in place. Continue on opposite side, pulling fabric taut each time, then on remaining two sides. Stretch the twill tape or seam binding over the length of the board, tacking it down at the top and bottom with pushpins. Turn the board over, and staple the ends of the tape to the back of the board; take out the pushpins and trim the overhang.

falling-leaves felt board

Tuck cards, notes, and keepsakes behind subtle leaf silhouettes. The leaves are partially cut from a double layer of medium-weight felt; a piece of sky-blue felt was fused to a creamy off-white piece on the board shown. If you prefer, use a single layer of heavyweight felt; just make sure it's sturdy enough to hold papers and other items in place. Cover the board first with background fabric, and keep in mind that it will show through the cutout edges.

MATERIALS falling leaves template; Homasote fiberboard (see box, page 264); 2 pieces medium-weight felt; background fabric; fusible web (optional); disappearing-ink fabric pen; craft knife; staple gun

HOW-TO Print the template pieces (see enclosed CD), and cut out. Have a piece of Homasote cut to desired size. Cut 2 pieces of felt and one piece of background fabric 2 inches (5cm) larger than the board on all sides. Cover the fiberboard with the background fabric as described on page 265. Sandwich fusible web between 2 pieces of felt (if you are using heavyweight felt, skip this step); press. Lay the fused felt, facedown, on a work surface. With a disappearing-ink fabric pen, trace the leaves onto the felt in a random pattern (make sure the leaves don't fall within the 2-inch [5cm] border). Using a craft knife, partially cut out the leaves. Lay the fiberboard on top of the felt, and use a staple gun to affix the felt securely behind the board, working on one side at a time.

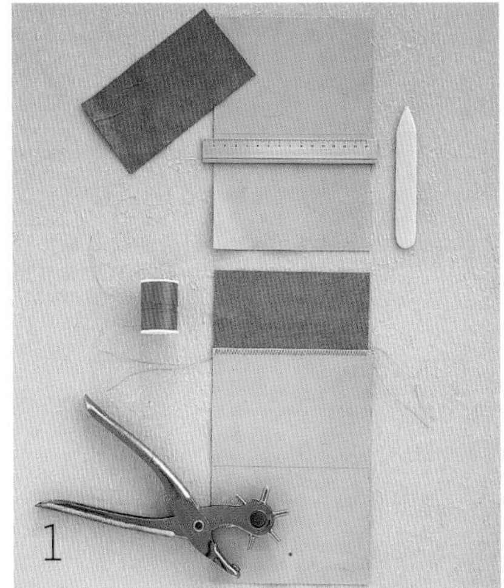

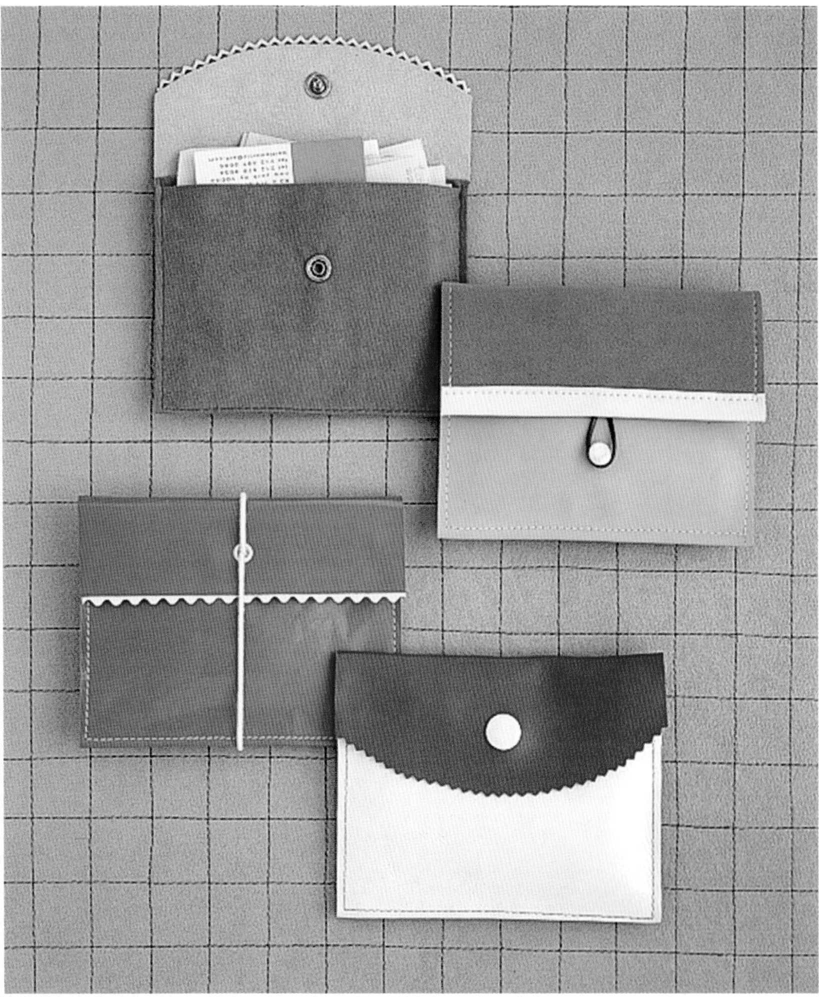

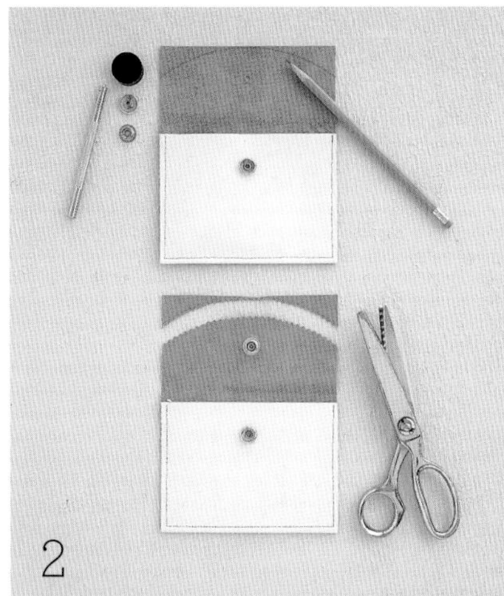

leather coin purse

Small leather purses crafted in bright colors are easy to spot in a crowded handbag. Each of these basic patterns can be dressed up with fanciful trims and a snap, a length of elastic, or a button. For a purse in a single color, cut parts from one piece of leather; for one with a different colored flap, cut the top third from another piece and allow 1/4-inch (6mm) excess to overlap the main section.

MATERIALS basic sewing supplies; leather coin purse template; scissors; leather; no-slip ruler; rotary cutter; cutting mat; bone folder; multipurpose cement; sewing machine equipped with a nonstick foot and a leather needle; sturdy poly-cotton thread; leather hole punch; snap kit, grommet kit, or elastic cording; pinking shears.

HOW-TO 1. Print the template (see enclosed CD), and cut out. Trace the template onto the suede side of the leather, and use a rotary cutter to cut out the shape on the cutting mat. (Always use a ruler to hold the leather in place and to guide your cutting or scoring.) Score the lower fold with the bone folder. Attach the colored flap (if using) to the main piece: Apply a strip of multipurpose cement along its overlapping edge, and then press it in place. Let it dry 2 to 3 minutes; then zigzag-stitch over that line. Use the hole punch to pierce small holes for the snap or grommet (as the kit requires).

2. Install the snap or grommet. At the scored line, fold the purse. Cement the sides together, and allow to dry, then stitch around the edges, backstitching the ends. If desired, use pinking shears to trim the flap.

3. If you're using elastic cording, cut a piece twice the width of the purse. Slip both ends through the bottom hole and knot them, leaving the large loop on the outside.

wraparound bulletin board

Covered in pink canvas and framed by molding, the bulletin board that wraps these walls makes a striking—and practical—bedroom detail. The things that hang on it can change as quickly as a child's interests. Choose fabric that is lightweight enough to fold flat at the corners and will hide pinholes well. This project is best completed by two people, since the large boards can be difficult to maneuver.

MATERIALS Homasote fiberboard; fabric (cotton canvas is shown; the amount will depend on the size of the boards); staple gun; hammer; 1-inch (2.5cm) finishing nails; 2 1/2-inch-wide (6.5cm) molding, mitered for corners; 3/8-inch (10mm) grosgrain ribbon; fabric glue

HOW-TO 1. Determine where you want the boards to go, how large they will be, and how many you will need (Homasote is available in 4-by-8-foot [1.2m × 2.4m] sheets); subtract the board's thickness at the room's corners, and allow some space for the fabric.

ABOUT HOMASOTE

Homasote fiberboard is a lightweight, inexpensive board made from recycled paper fibers. It's sold in 4-by-8-foot (1.2m × 2.4m) sheets at lumberyards and some hardware stores, usually in 1/2-inch (13mm) thickness (5/8-inch [16mm] and 3/4-inch [2cm] thicknesses are sometimes available); have someone at the lumberyard cut it to size. Keep in mind that fabric is typically available in widths ranging from 44 inches (112cm) to 60 inches (152.5cm); cut fiberboard within these dimensions to avoid having seams on your finished board.

1

2

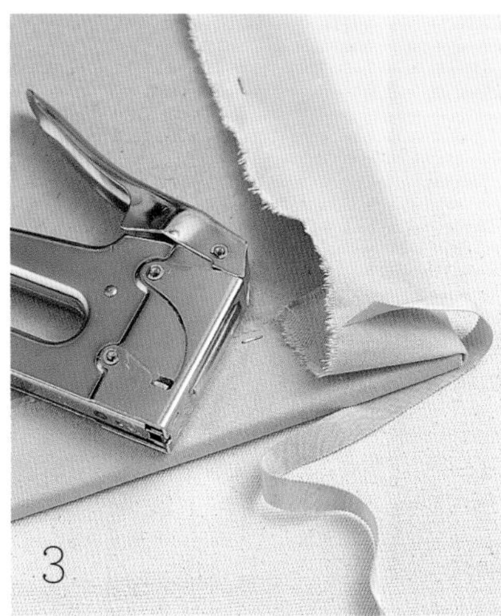
3

4

5

2. Cut fabric 3 inches (7.5cm) larger than Homasote on all sides; lay it facedown. Center the Homasote over the fabric. Use a staple gun to affix the fabric to the back of the board, following the instructions at right.

3. Cut 2 ribbons to go across the long sides of the board and around to the back; they will cover the finishing nails that hang the board at top and bottom. Staple one end of each ribbon to the back of the board. Pull the fabric taut; staple the other end.

4. Before putting the boards on the walls, first install the molding, using the finishing nails. Space the molding so it will sit tight against the top and bottom edges of the boards. Place the board between pieces of molding. It's easier if one person holds the board while the other hammers the nails through the board into the wall.

5. As you nail the board in place, lift the ribbon slightly so it's out of the way. Nail the board to the wall along the top and bottom, inserting nails at roughly 1-foot (30.5cm) intervals; if you can find the studs, nail into them. Be sure to hammer the nail heads flush. Once you've hammered all the nails, glue the ribbons into place over them, using a thin line of fabric glue.

COVERING A BOARD WITH FABRIC

When covering a bulletin board with fabric, use the following technique to ensure a smooth finish: Lay the fiberboard on top of the fabric. Wrap one edge of the fabric around the board and secure it with a staple in the center. Pull the fabric taut, and staple it on the opposite side. Repeat with the other two sides. Continue stapling, working toward the corners and adding staples in pairs on opposite sides. At the corners, fold the fabric to make it as flat as possible: Staple one side all the way to the corner, then fold the perpendicular side on top of it; pull it taut, and staple.

pocketed ottoman cover

An ottoman slipcover equipped with deep gusseted pockets provides a discreet place to stow everyday items.

MATERIALS basic sewing supplies, upholstery fabric (the yardage will depend on the size of the ottoman; wool is shown), ottoman

HOW-TO 1. Make the cover: Measure the ottoman, then cut a single piece of fabric large enough to cover 2 sides plus the top, adding 1 inch (2.5cm) to the width and several inches (7.5–10cm) to the length. Cut 2 fabric pieces large enough to cover the remaining sides of the ottoman, adding an inch (2.5cm) to the width and several inches (7.5–10cm) to the length. Zigzag-stitch all unfinished edges to prevent fraying.

2. Stitch the long fabric pieces to one side piece, right sides facing, with a ½-inch (13mm) seam allowance. You will need to sew along each side, stopping ½ inch (13mm) before each end to allow for seam allowance, then pivot the fabric before moving on to the next side (see "How to Sew Curves and Corners," page 35). Repeat with other side piece. Turn the ottoman cover right-side out and topstitch the seam edges.

3. Finish the bottom edge: With the cover right-side out, fold the bottom edge under a few inches (5–7.5cm), and pin. Turn the folded edge up about 1 inch (2.5cm), and pin. Edge-stitch around the perimeter. Remove pins.

4. Make 2 gusseted pockets: For each, cut the fabric 2 inches (5cm) longer and several inches (7.5–10cm) wider than the desired pocket. Double hem the top: Fold top edge under ½ inch (13mm), press, then fold another 1¼ inches (3.2cm), and press. Topstitch twice: ⅛ inch [3mm], then 1 inch [2.5cm] from the edge. Fold the bottom and the right edges under ¼ inch (6mm). Pin, and stitch the right edge to the ottoman cover. Fold the fabric to create right and left accordion-style folds; pin pleats in place. (If the pocket will be holding a thick object, test to make sure it will fit.) Trim the left edge to fit, fold it under ¼ inch (6mm), and press. Stitch it to the cover. Stitch the bottom edge. Press the pocket to crease; remove the pins. Repeat to make second pocket.

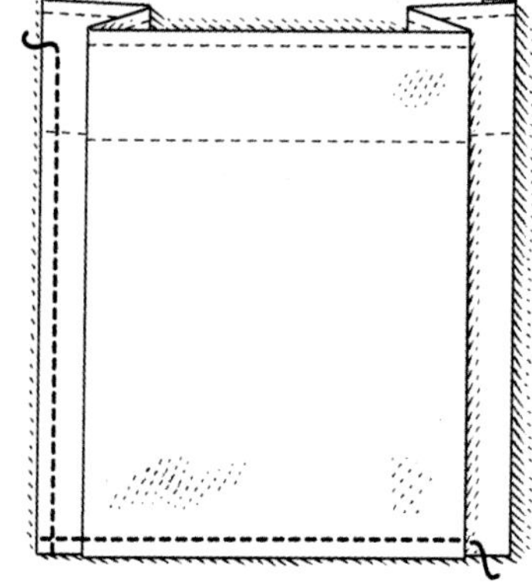

multiple-pocket bulletin board

Make room on your desk by relocating small items to a cloth-covered bulletin board outfitted with flat and pleated pockets. A deep flat pocket holds papers and file folders, while pleated pockets corral pens.

MATERIALS basic sewing supplies, ½-inch-thick (13mm) Homasote fiberboard, cut to desired size; colored canvas (amount will depend on the size of your board; you will need enough to cover the board, plus extra for pockets); ribbon or seam binding; fabric glue

HOW-TO 1. Wrap the board with canvas and tape in place while you mark the placements of the desired pockets, using a disappearing-ink fabric pen.

2. Add pockets: Remove canvas from the board, and place the pockets where indicated. To make a flat pocket (figure a): Cut the fabric slightly wider and 2 inches (5cm) longer than the desired pocket. Double hem the top: Fold over ½ inch (13mm), press, then 1¼ inches (3.2cm), and press. Topstich twice: ⅛ inch [3mm], then 1 inch [2.5cm] from the edge. Fold the remaining edges under ¼ inch (6mm), and stitch in place to the board cover. To make a pleated pocket (figure b): Choose the contents of the pocket, and arrange them on the fabric. Cut the fabric slightly longer and a few inches (7.5–10cm) wider than the items. Stitch a double seam at the top. Fold the bottom and right edges under. Stitch the right edge to the board cover. Place the first item next to the right edge; hold it in place as you stitch a seam on the left side of the item, using a zipper foot. Repeat with the remaining items. Trim the left edge to fit, and finish it with a flat pocket for scissors or another pleated pocket. With the items in place, stitch the bottom, folding the excess fabric at the bottom to pleat. Once the pockets are in place, cover the board with the fabric, stretching it taut and stapling it to the back to secure. Finish the sides by affixing the ribbon or seam binding with fabric glue.

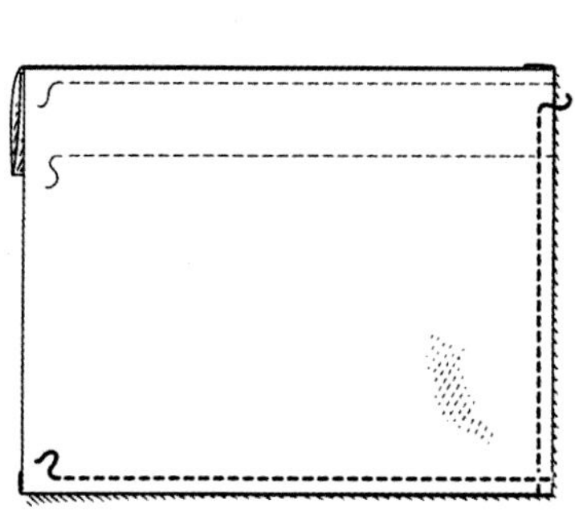

(a)

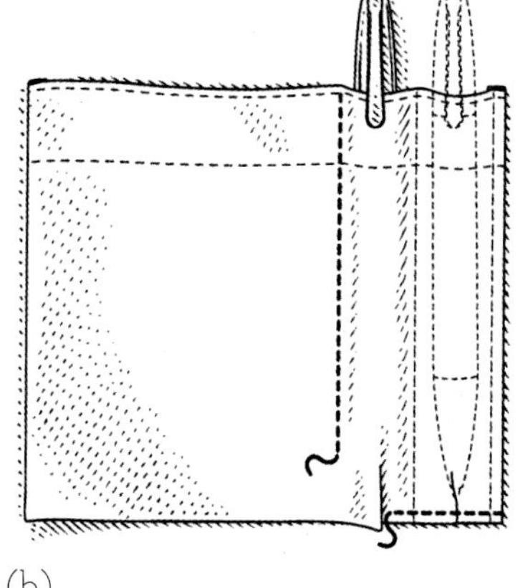

(b)

PROJECT:

pets

Spoil your pet with hand-sewn clothes, toys, pillows, and more. Making pet projects is an ideal way to expand your crafting knowledge without having to worry about precision: If the stitching isn't exactly straight, chances are that your sweet puppy or playful kitten won't mind a bit. And if one stuffed fabric toy quickly becomes a favorite, you can easily make several more in different sizes, colors, and textures. Some of the projects in this chapter can be stitched by hand in next to no time at all; others require a sewing machine. Either way, you're sure to be pleased at how nicely these projects come together—and how much attention they'll get.

IN THIS CHAPTER: QUILTED DOG JACKET — CATNIP FISH ON A POLE — SIMPLE DOG BED — ULTRASUEDE DOG COAT — MENSWEAR MICE

QUILTED DOG JACKET (OPPOSITE): *Martha's beloved French bulldogs, Francesca and Sharkey, wear handsome weatherproof coats made from quilted coated linen.*

quilted dog jacket SEE PHOTO, PAGE 269

Outfit your canine companion with a custom-made jacket. Coated linen lends a sheen to these coats and also makes them water-resistant; a fleece fabric lining keeps the dog warm and cozy. The jackets are sized for small dogs, about 13 inches (33cm) in length from neck to tail, but the pattern can be easily adjusted to fit slightly larger dogs by lengthening the straps.

MATERIALS basic sewing supplies, quilted dog jacket pattern, ½ yard (55cm) coated linen for top, ½ yard (45.5cm) fleece for underside, spray adhesive, 25 inches (63.5cm) of Velcro strips, ½-inch-wide (13mm) bias tape

HOW-TO Print the pattern pieces (see enclosed CD), tape together, and cut out. Secure each piece of linen to each piece of fleece with spray adhesive, right sides out, then stitch as described for box-quilted fabric (page 372; omit batting). Using the pattern pieces as guides, cut out the body, the strap, and the collar pieces from the quilted fabric. Cut a 12-inch (30.5cm) strip of Velcro hook fastener into two 3 ½-inch (9cm) pieces and two 2 ½-inch (6.5cm) pieces. Cut a 13-inch (33cm) strip of Velcro loop fastener into two 2 ½-inch (6.5cm) pieces and two 4-inch (10cm) pieces. When attaching the strips, stitch around the perimeter of each Velcro strip; refer to the diagram below for placement. Sew the two 3 ½-inch (9cm) hook strips to the belly strap. Before stitching the two 4-inch (10cm) Velcro loop strips to the coat body, sew them together along their long sides. Sew the remaining loop strips to the linen side of the collar and the remaining hook strips to the opposite tab of the collar on the fleece side. Cut a piece of bias tape to go around the outer curve of the collar. Pin it in place, then stitch. To attach collar to the coat: Pin the collar, linen side up, to the linen side of the coat. Stitch ¼ inch (6mm) from the edge. Remove the pins. Cut a piece of bias tape to go around the edge of the body piece, plus 1 inch (2.5cm). Beginning at the tip of one of the neck flaps, pin it in place. Fold under ½ inch (13mm), leaving ½ inch (13mm) overlapping. Stitch it in place with a fold-over finish (page 369). Remove the pins. Cut a piece of bias tape to go around the edge of the belly strap, plus 1 inch (2.5cm). Pin in place. Fold under ½ inch (13mm), leaving ½ inch (13mm) overlapping. Stitch it in place with a fold-over finish, and remove the pins. Attach the belly strap to the body piece.

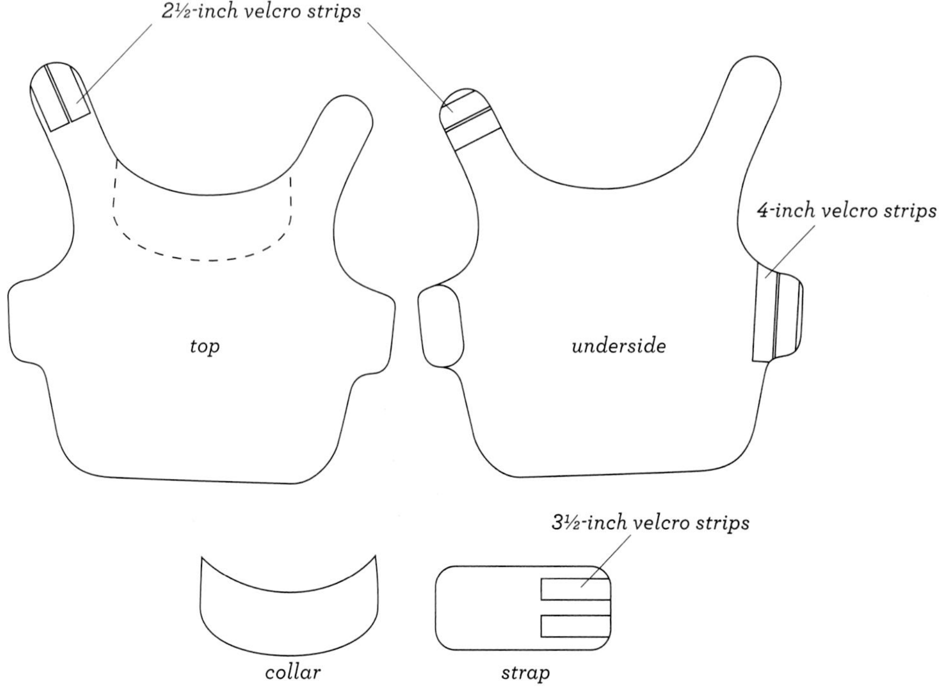

catnip fish on a pole

Handmade pet toys, like this fish on a pole, are often more sturdy (and adorable) than store-bought varieties, and they make great gifts. Use dried catnip, as fresh catnip is susceptible to mold.

MATERIALS basic sewing supplies, catnip fish on a pole pattern, fabric, fusible interfacing (optional), funnel, dried catnip, heavy-duty thread, 3-foot (91cm) wooden dowel, craft glue, embroidery floss, embroidery needle

HOW-TO Print the pattern (see enclosed CD), and cut out. Pin 2 pieces of fabric together, wrong sides facing (if the fabric is thin, fuse it to the interfacing to strengthen it). Trace the pattern onto the pinned fabric using a disappearing-ink fabric pen; stitch on top of the tracing, leaving a 1-inch (2.5cm) opening at the fish's tail. Cut out the fish with pinking shears, staying close to the stitching without cutting into it. Using a funnel, fill the fish with catnip. Slipstitch the opening to close. Sew one end of 2 1/2 feet (76cm) of heavy-duty thread to the mouth. Tie the other end to the dowel, and secure the knot with a dab of craft glue. Embroider the eyes with satin stitches (page 48).

simple dog bed

This soft bed, suitable for small dogs, such as the pug shown, is made from two dish towels and a piece of upholstery foam. Velcro fasteners make it easy to remove for washing.

MATERIALS basic sewing supplies, 2 same-size dish towels, 2-inch-thick (5cm) foam (cut 4 inches [10cm] shorter and narrower than the towels), iron-on Velcro fasteners

HOW-TO Lay the towels on top of each other, right sides facing. Pin and sew on two long sides with a ½-inch (13mm) seam allowance. Turn the case right-side out, and insert the foam. Fold the ends as if you were wrapping a gift box, and mark placement of Velcro fasteners on open ends of each side. Remove case, and iron Velcro fasteners in place. Reinsert foam, and secure ends.

Ultrasuede dog coat

This super-easy dog coat is made up of just a few rounded rectangles—a wide one for the body and two thin ones for straps. And because it's constructed of Ultrasuede, there's no hemming involved. If your dog is bigger than the French bulldog shown, enlarge the fabric as necessary: Measure your dog from neck to tail and side to side and adjust the length and width of the body piece. Lengthen the straps. If you're uncertain of the fit, make a test pattern first with muslin or pattern paper. If your dog is still growing, you can replace the straps with longer ones later.

MATERIALS basic sewing supplies, ½ yard (45.5cm) of Ultrasuede (for a 20-pound [9kg] dog), 4 large buttons

HOW-TO Cut the fabric into a 14-by-11-inch (35.5cm × 28cm) rectangle and two 1½-inch-wide (3.8cm) straps, 13 and 14 inches (33cm and 35.5cm) long. Round the corners. Drape over the dog. With a pen, mark placement of buttons to hold the straps, across the lower neck and behind the front legs. Sew the buttons onto the body piece, and cut slits in the straps for buttonholes.

1

2

4

3

menswear mice

Treat a kitty to a game of cat-and-mouse with a few dapper fabric toys. There's no mistaking these critters for the real thing—they're constructed from brightly colored suiting and shirting fabrics.

MATERIALS basic sewing supplies; menswear mice pattern; assorted menswear fabrics such as wool suiting, cotton shirting, corduroy, and cotton velvet; fusible web; loop turner; fill; embroidery floss; embroidery needle

HOW-TO 1. Make body: Print the pattern pieces (see enclosed CD), and cut out. Using the pattern as a guide, cut out one bottom piece and one side piece from the same or different fabric. Flip pattern and cut out another side piece. Working on the bias (cutting the fabric diagonally), cut a 1-by-4-inch (2.5cm × 10cm) strip for a tail. For ears, adhere 2 different fabrics together with an iron and fusible web, following manufacturer's instructions. Using pattern, cut out ears from fused fabric.

2. Fold tail in half lengthwise, right sides facing; stitch with a ¼-inch (6mm) seam allowance, leaving ends open. Turn tail right-side out using a loop turner. Pin body pieces together, right sides facing; stitch with a ¼-inch (6mm) seam allowance, leaving a 1-inch (2.5cm) opening at the back.

3. Turn body right side out, and stuff with fill. Insert tail into opening; slipstitch opening closed. Knot end of tail.

4. Fold ears in half and attach to body with small hand stitches. Mark placement of eyes with pins, then embroider eyes and nose using backstitches (page 31).

PROJECT:

pincushions

Even if they weren't so practical, handmade pincushions would still be considered adorable. Part of a playful crafts tradition, these utilitarian objects have long been sewn in familiar three-dimensional shapes—fruits and vegetables, crowns, hats, and animals—each one rendered in whimsical style. Someone new to sewing can easily create one of these clever and compact objects by hand; there's no complicated stitching involved. Try an heirloom-tomato design rendered in cotton, or a felt strawberry leaf. These novelties can be created in sizes that are as big or as small as you like. Mix and match inexpensive calicos or solids in tonal hues, or make the most of bits of felt or remnants you have at home. And when you're finished, keep one nearby; as you embark on other sewing projects, it will serve as an instant reminder of your ever-increasing skill with a needle and thread.

IN THIS CHAPTER: HEIRLOOM-TOMATO PINCUSHIONS — STRAWBERRY PINCUSHIONS — MASON-JAR SEWING KIT — FELT-LEAF NOTIONS

HEIRLOOM-TOMATO PINCUSHIONS (OPPOSITE): *A bumper crop of pincushions in different sizes and fabrics is both pretty and practical. Scraps of patterned and solid fabric—including scarlet corduroy, red-and-white gingham, and plum velvet—create a naturally diverse palette for a whole harvest's worth of cushions.*

heirloom-tomato pincushions

SEE PHOTO, PAGE 277

These sewing-box staples are just as sweet as garden-grown tomatoes, and you don't have to wait until summer to enjoy them. For pincushions with symmetrical shapes, begin at step 1; start at step 3 for cushions with the uneven contours common in heirloom varieties.

MATERIALS basic sewing supplies; heirloom-tomato cap template; cotton or any other medium-weight fabric (such as corduroy or velvet); cotton or polyester fill; large embroidery needle; perle cotton; scraps of green felt (for caps); fabric glue

HOW-TO 1. Cut a rectangle of fabric on the bias that's twice as long as it is wide (the yellow tomato—3 1/8-inch 8cm] diameter when finished—required a 10-by-5-inch [25.5cm × 12.5cm] piece). With the fabric facing right-side up, fold it in half as shown, and join the ends with a 1/4-inch (6mm) seam allowance. Sew a running stitch (page 31) around the top edge; tightly pull the thread to cinch the fabric, and secure with a few backstitches.

2. Turn the pouch right-side out. Stuff with fill (cotton is firmer than polyester). Sew a running stitch around the open end; pull the thread to cinch the fabric. Tack it shut with a few stitches, and knot. To flatten, double-thread the embroidery needle with the perle cotton, and pull it through the "core" a few times. Mimic a tomato's fluted details by wrapping the thread around the cushion and back through the core several times. Knot the thread at the top to finish.

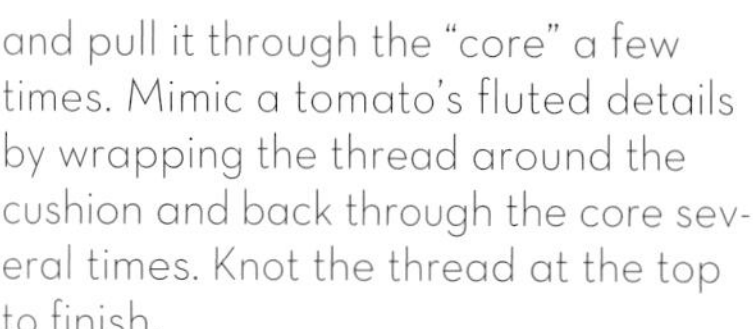

3. For an heirloom-style tomato, cut a circle of fabric (the red one—3 1/2-inch [9cm] diameter when finished—required a 10-inch [25.5cm] diameter circle). With the fabric wrong-side up, hand-sew a running stitch around the perimeter. Place batting in the center of the fabric, and gather the fabric into a pouch around it. Stuff with more batting, then pull the thread to cinch; tack with fluted stitches and knot. Flatten the cushion and apply details, as described in step 2.

4. For the cap, trace the template (see enclosed CD) onto green felt with a disappearing-ink fabric pen, and cut it out. Using a needle threaded with a single length of perle cotton, sew and knot a loop onto the cap. Glue the cap to the top of the pincushion.

1

2

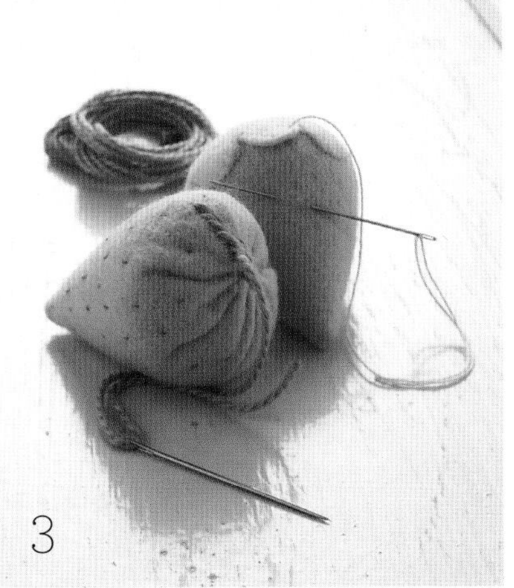

3

strawberry pincushions

Small strawberry-shaped pincushions are especially easy to make, and when filled with emery or fine sand they will sharpen the needles and pins they are holding. The cushions here are made from ribbon remnants, shirting fabric, and felt—which works well because its edges don't fray.

MATERIALS basic sewing supplies, strawberry pincushion pattern, fabric (such as cotton or felt) or ribbon remnants, felt for cap (optional), small jar or bottle, fine sand or emery, fabric glue (optional), #3 perle cotton (optional), embroidery needle, embroidery floss

HOW-TO 1. Print the pattern (see enclosed CD), and cut out. (The strawberries here range from 1 to 2 inches [2.5-5cm].) Trace the cone piece onto the fabric, and cut out. If desired, trace the strawberry cap piece onto a piece of felt with a disappearing-ink fabric pen, and cut out. Sew the fabric into a cone shape with the right sides together, stitching along one edge.

2. Hand-sew a loose, even running stitch (page 31) along the top of the cone. Before cinching the top, place the cone in the small jar or bottle to balance it, and fill it with fine sand or emery. Pull the thread taut, and stitch it closed.

3. If you're using the felt cap, attach it first with a drop of fabric glue in the center; slipstitch the edges. Or use perle cotton and long stem stitches to create "leaves" (for more on embroidery stitches, see page 48). Sew and knot a loop at the top as a handle. Embroider berry seeds with one or 2 strands from a length of embroidery floss, using a single stitch or a French knot.

Mason-jar sewing kit

Mason jars have long served busy home canners and gardeners. Make one doubly useful by converting its lid into a pincushion and the container below into a sewing kit.

MATERIALS Mason jar with a two-part lid, thick cardboard, a compass, linen or cotton fabric, cotton or polyester fill, hot-glue gun

HOW-TO 1. Separate the lid's sealer and screw cap. Trace the sealer's circumference onto cardboard; add 1 inch (2.5cm) to that circle's diameter, and, using a compass, draw another circle on the fabric. Cut out both circles.

2. Make a plump cushion by stuffing fill between the fabric and the cardboard. Turn the screw cap upside down, and apply hot glue to the inside edge of the rim; quickly press the assembled cushion into the lid, until the cloth side protrudes smoothly above the screw cap's opening and the cardboard is flush against the rim. Apply hot glue around the edge of the cardboard backing; fold over any excess fabric, easing as necessary, and press down. Glue the top of the sealer to the cardboard for a neat finish. Fill the jar with sewing or craft supplies, and top with the pincushion lid.

1

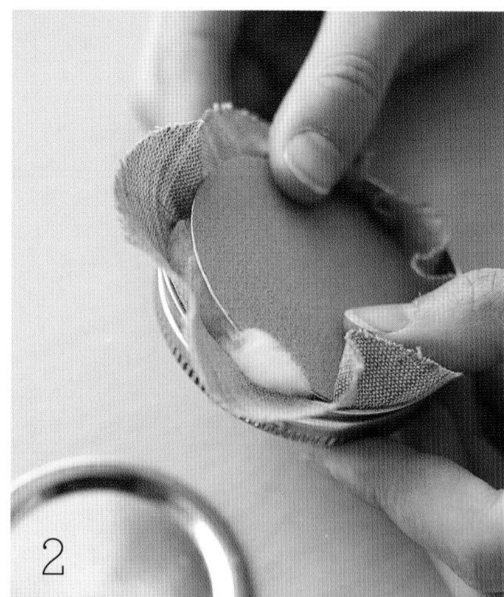

2

felt-leaf notions

A few autumn-inspired felt pieces keep sewing tools handy any time of year—and making them doesn't require a single stitch. A matching set—needle book, scissors holder, and pincushion (presented with decorative pins)—makes a lovely gift for a crafter.

MATERIALS basic sewing supplies, fabric inkpad with white ink, leaf-shaped rubber stamps, colored felt, muslin, clear-drying fabric glue, small funnel, sand

HOW-TO 1. Stamp white-ink leaf images onto the colored felt: Make 3 images for a needle book; 2 images for a scissors holder or a pincushion. To set the ink, cover the felt with muslin and press with a medium setting. Let ink dry, then cut out shapes.

2. For a needle book "stem," cut a 3-by-¼-inch (7.5cm × 5mm) felt strip. Glue it to the base of one leaf. Glue a second leaf to the first at the base; repeat with a third leaf, and glue the other end of the felt strip to the top. For the scissors holder, glue 2 leaves together along the edges, leaving an opening at the stem end. For the pincushion, glue leaves together along outer edges, leaving a small opening; let dry. Using the funnel, pour sand into the opening until the pouch is almost full; seal the opening with more glue.

1

2

PROJECT:

pot holders

Humble pot holders are surprisingly evocative. Their fabrics, often cotton prints softened by time and repeated washings, have an instantly nostalgic, comforting allure. These kitchen favorites can be updated easily next time you have a little creative energy. Gather fabrics that suit your kitchen palette and please your eye. Charming heart-shaped holders (as shown, opposite) add whimsy to a kitchen, and let you piece fabric, patchwork-style, and trim it with seam binding, so you'll gain experience in more than one technique as you work.

For the most heat-resistant pot holder, choose the best-quality batting you can find. Washable wools and sturdy cottons have natural insulating qualities and make for wonderfully soft holders. Or skip the batting and use quilted heat-resistant fabric, the kind used to cover ironing boards. The appeal of pot holders is timeless, so stitch up more than a few: they're sure to make much-appreciated gifts.

IN THIS CHAPTER: HEART-SHAPED POT HOLDER — DOUBLE-POCKETED POT HOLDER

HEART-SHAPED POT HOLDERS (OPPOSITE): *Patchwork heart-shaped kitchen helpers in assorted red-and-white patterns have homespun appeal. The pot holders are pieced together from quilting fabric and trimmed with bias tape; pockets keep hands protected from hot pots and pans.*

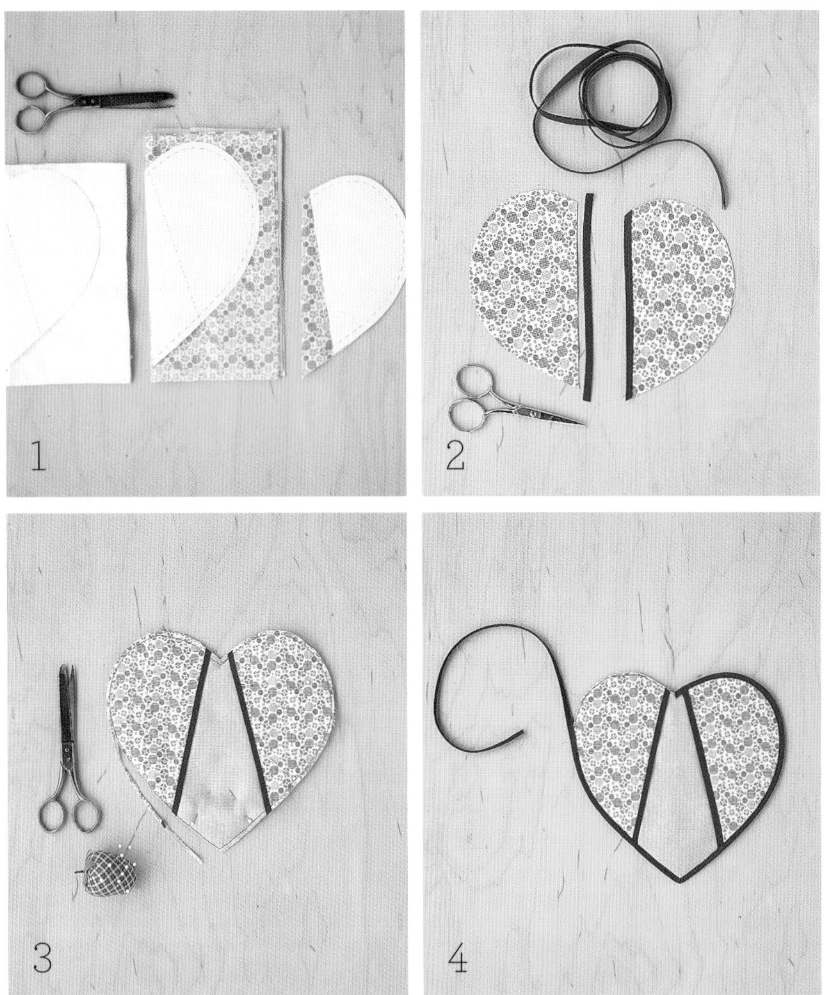

heart-shaped pot holder SEE PHOTO, PAGE 283

Make one of these winsome kitchen helpers from pieces of fabric in the same pattern, or use various designs in complementary colors.

MATERIALS basic sewing supplies, heart-shaped pot holder pattern, ½ yard (45.5cm) cotton batting, ½ yard (45.5cm) cotton fabric, 1 yard (0.9m) bias tape

HOW-TO 1. Print three copies of pot holder pattern (see enclosed CD). Cut one along the solid line for the fabric hearts, one along the inner dotted line for the batting, and the third along the diagonal line for the fabric pockets. Stack 3 layers of cotton batting and fold them in half; align the batting template's straight edge with the fold, and cut it out. Fold 3 stacked 12-inch (30.5cm) squares of cotton fabric in half; align the heart template's straight edge with the fold, and cut it out. Lay the pocket template on one folded fabric heart; cut on the diagonal line.

2. Pin bias tape in place along the straight edges of the pockets and sew; back-stitch the ends.

3. Layer the pieces, starting with a fabric heart (face down), batting, another fabric heart (face up), and pockets (face up); pin. Sew along the outside edge, with a ¼-inch (6mm) seam allowance. Trim the edge as close to the stitching as possible.

4. Sew the bias tape to the heart, starting at the top center and folding the ends under. Sew a 5-inch (12.5cm) piece of bias tape, ends turned under, into a loop. Pin and stitch to pot holder.

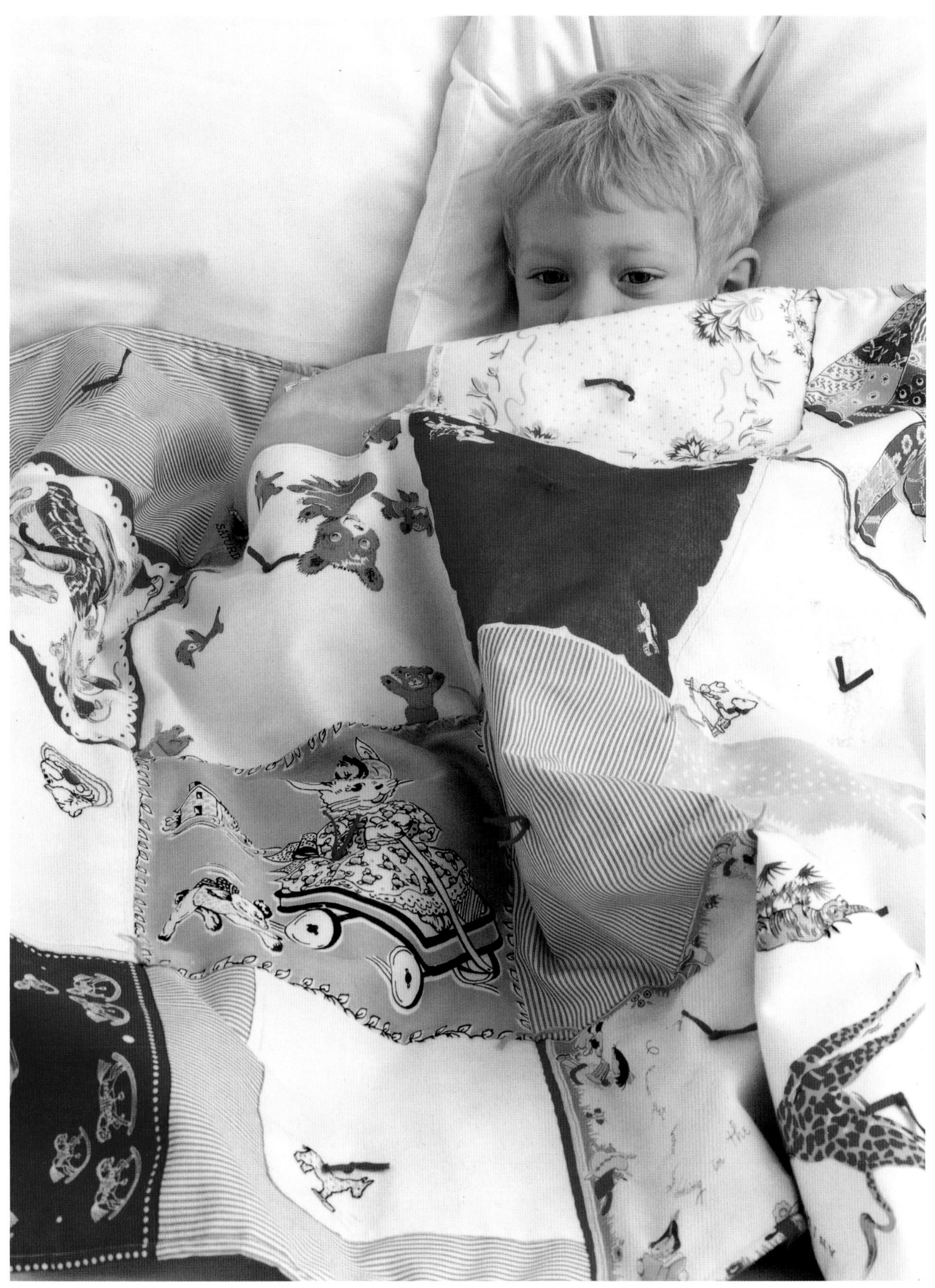

vintage-handkerchief quilt SEE PHOTO, PAGE 287

You will need twenty 8-inch (20.5cm) square hankies to complete this project. If you have any hankies that are larger than 8 inches (20.5cm) square, cut them down. To use hankies that are smaller than 8 inches (20.5cm), first stitch each one onto an 8-inch (20.5cm) square of cotton fabric. For more on the basics of making a patchwork quilt, see page 66.

MATERIALS basic sewing supplies; twenty 8-inch (20.5cm) square handkerchiefs; 35-by-42-inch (89cm × 106.5cm) batting; 35-by-42-inch (89cm × 106.5cm) cotton fabric (for backing; red ticking was used here); white cotton fabric (optional); 4 1/4 yards (3.9m) of 3/8-inch-wide (10mm) ribbon, cut into fifty 3-inch (7.5cm) pieces; large-eyed needle

HOW-TO 1. Arrange handkerchiefs into five rows of four squares each. Machine-sew the 4 squares in each row together, right sides facing, with a 5/8-inch (16mm) seam allowance, then sew the long sides of the rows together, right sides facing, with a 5/8-inch (16mm) seam allowance. Press all the seams open.

2. Lay the top layer on the batting (if the handkerchiefs are very thin, insert a layer of white cotton underneath), and baste together in a spiral pattern, working from the center outward (this will prevent puckering). Cut off any excess batting. Pin together the patchworked handkerchiefs and the cotton backing with right sides facing. Sew the perimeter with a 1/2-inch (13mm) seam allowance, leaving an 8-inch (20.5cm) opening. Clip corners. Remove pins, turn the quilt right-side out, and slipstitch the opening closed. Topstitch around the perimeter of the quilt 3/4 inch (2cm) from the edge.

3. To hold the layers together, tuft with ribbon ties: Thread a 3-inch (7.5cm) piece of ribbon through the large-eyed needle; pass the needle through all three layers and back up again, then tie a double knot. Place a ribbon tie at all four corners and the center of each square. To finish, remove the basting stitches, and press the quilt flat around the edges.

1

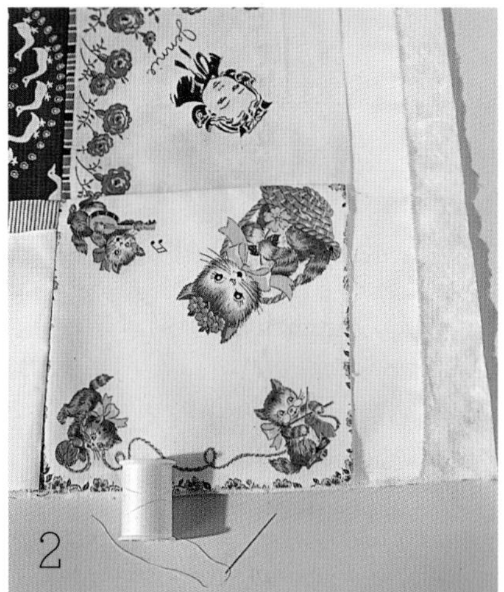

2

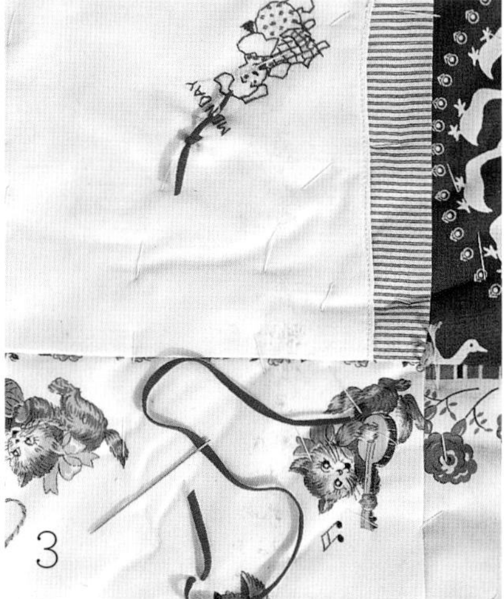

3

menswear patchwork throw

Patches of menswear fabrics in several hues are easily fashioned into a handsome throw blanket. For visual interest, the fabrics can vary in type and color, but they should be of similar weight. The finished patchwork blanket measures 64 by 88 inches (163cm × 223.5cm). For more on patchwork quilting, see page 66.

MATERIALS basic sewing supplies; rotary cutter; ruler; self-healing cutting mat; assorted menswear fabrics, such as wool, flannel, corduroy, and cotton velvet; 4 yards (3.6m) cotton flannel (for insulation); 4 yards (3.6m) cotton shirting fabric (for backing); wool yarn (for ties); darning needle

HOW-TO 1. With the rotary cutter, ruler, and cutting mat, measure and cut rectangles from menswear fabrics for patchwork. The blanket shown includes rectangles that are 4, 8, and 10 inches (10 cm, 20.5cm, and 25.5cm) wide; their lengths vary. Arrange rectangles to form desired pattern, aligning same-width patches in rows. Pin rectangles together, right sides facing, then sew with a ½-inch (13mm) seam allowance to complete each row. Press all seams open. Pin together rows of patches, right sides facing, and sew with a ½-inch (13mm) seam allowance. Press all seams open. Cut flannel and shirting each to finished quilt size, with a ½-inch (13mm) seam allowance on all sides (you may have to connect more than one piece to achieve the desired width). Layer and pin fabric pieces together: patchwork right-side up, backing right-side down, then flannel. Stitch around perimeter with a ½-inch (13mm) seam allowance, leaving a 12-inch (30.5mm) opening on one side. Clip corners, and turn quilt right-side out. Slipstitch the opening shut. Press quilt flat around the edges.

2. With yarn, make ¼-inch (6mm) tufting stitches at various intersections all over quilt (keep the pattern random rather than ordered): Poke the needle through the quilt along one seam, ⅛ inch (3mm) from an intersecting point; bring the needle back up ⅛ inch (3mm) from intersecting point on the other side. Tie a square knot; trim ends.

state bird-embroidered quilt

Thirty embroidered birds perch on a quilt of crisp white linen. Some states celebrate the same bird, so only twenty-eight species are honored with state designations (two are repeated on the quilt). Templates for all of them are included on the enclosed CD. A single stitch—the chainstitch—was used for all the birds, and just one color of thread for each one, giving them an appealing graphic quality. The finished quilt is made of thirty embroidered squares plus twenty-six plain squares that are incorporated to form a border; it fits a full-size bed and measures 72 1/2 by 82 1/2 inches (184cm × 209.5cm). A mockingbird graces the throw pillow.

MATERIALS basic sewing supplies, state bird templates, 5 1/3 yards (4.9m) of 60-inch-wide (152.5cm) white linen fabric, dark transfer paper, ballpoint pen, embroidery floss (in multiple colors), embroidery hoop, 12 1/2-inch (32cm) square quilting ruler, rotary cutter, 5 yards (4.5m) of 60-inch-wide (152.5cm) linen fabric in a contrasting color for the back and the border (green was used for the quilt shown), 2 full-size sheets of cotton batting (90 by 96 inches [229cm × 244cm] each)

HOW-TO 1. Cut out thirty 14-inch (35.5cm) squares of white linen. Photocopy the templates (see enclosed CD) so that each is 7 to 8 inches (18–20.5cm) tall (for 30, you will have to use two birds twice). Place a linen square right-side up, and top with a sheet of dark transfer paper. Place the bird pattern on top; trace the lines of the bird pattern with a ballpoint pen.

2. Secure the linen square in the embroidery hoop. Thread a needle with embroidery floss. Using the chainstitch (page 48), embroider each square.

3. After you've finished stitching, place the square quilting ruler over an embroidered square, and use the grid to center the embroidered bird. With a rotary cutter, trim each of the edges to 12 1/2 inches (32cm). Repeat with the remaining squares. For the border, cut out 26 plain 12 1/2-inch (32cm) square pieces. Lay out the quilt, 8 rows long by 7 columns wide, arranging the birds as you desire (in the center, 6 rows and 5 columns) with a white border around the entire perimeter.

4. Sew the squares together to make columns (you will have 7 columns of 8 when you're done), right sides facing, with a 1 1/4-inch (3cm) seam allowance; press open the seams. Sew the strips to one another: Begin by sewing 2 adjacent strips together, first pinning at points where horizontal seams meet to align the squares' corners exactly. Sew together 2 sets of 2 strips and one set of 3. Sew the 2 sets of 2 to each other, and then sew that piece to the set of 3. Press open all seams.

5. Cut the 5 yards (4.5m) of contrasting color fabric in half lengthwise. Sew the long sides together with right sides facing, with a 1/2-inch (13mm) seam allowance, to make a piece about 90 by 120 inches (229cm × 305cm); press the seam flat. Lay out the quilt parts, starting with the colored fabric wrong-side up. Top with 2 layers of batting and the embroidered squares, right-side up. Attach a safety pin just inside each side of each square, piercing through the quilt, batting, and colored-cloth backing. Trim the batting to the size of the front piece. Machine-stitch along each square's seams through all the layers (called "stitching in the ditch"); remove the pins. Trim the colored cloth to extend 2 inches (5cm) beyond the sewn squares. To create the quilt's colored border, fold the colored cloth 1/2 inch (13mm) all around; press. Fold over the remaining 1 1/2 inches (3.8cm); press. Topstitch all around.

tablecloth quilt

A vintage floral linen tablecloth makes a stylish top for a handmade quilt. One piece of medium-weight linen in a complementary color is folded up and over the top to create the backing and the border. Tufts of embroidery floss pass through the center of each flower.

MATERIALS basic sewing supplies, tablecloth, cotton batting (cut to the same size as the tablecloth), linen (about 2 inches [5cm] longer on all sides than the tablecloth), embroidery floss (for tufting), embroidery needle

HOW-TO 1. Layer the three pieces: top layer right-side up, bottom layer right-side down, and batting in between. Safety-pin together, starting in the center and working toward the edges, smoothing as you go. Secure with tufting at regular intervals: Send an embroidery needle threaded with two strands of floss through all three layers from the top; bring it back up again 1/8 inch (3mm) away. Knot, and trim the ends to 1 inch (2.5cm). Repeat with two more strands in almost the same spot, then repeat tufting all over quilt. Trim the excess bottom layer of fabric, leaving a 1 1/2-inch (3.8cm) border all around.

2. Fold the edge of the border fabric over 1/2 inch (13mm), and press. Fold the remaining inch (2.5cm) over the top layer, press, and pin. Continue folding and pinning around the perimeter. At the corners, tuck the fabric into itself neatly, creating the effect of a mitered corner, as shown below. Edge-stitch the border in place. Hand-stitch the flaps of fabric at the corners to secure. Remove pins.

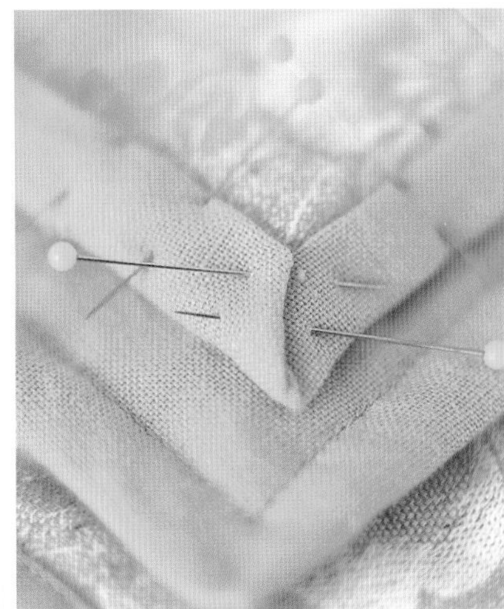

FOUR UNEXPECTED BED COVERINGS

vintage-linen patchwork coverlet

Arranging the hand towels, napkins, and pillowcases that make up this coverlet is like putting a puzzle together—except there's no right or wrong way to do it. Just move them around until you find the combination you like best. Vintage pieces in shades of white and flax with red monograms and embroidery help coordinate the eclectic collection. All the pieces are sewn onto a thick, vintage linen sheet, which establishes the size of the coverlet. Start by laying the linens out on a sheet (or another panel of fabric), so they're flush with the edges. Pin them all in place, then stitch around the exposed edges of all the linens, leaving the fringes to dangle freely. If desired, change the top thread to match each piece, and stitch ball fringe into the seams along two sides of the coverlet.

dyed-ticking patchwork quilt

Vintage ticking is cut up and dyed (page 77) in delicate shades of lavender and pink to produce a quilt that looks like a treasured hand-me-down. Some of the 10-inch (25.5cm) squares are made of pieces in two or three different colors (remember to include a seam allowance when factoring the sizes of pieces that are combined to form one square). The patchwork of squares is sewn to a white linen backing and a layer of cotton batting; then the whole thing is turned right-side out (so the batting remains tucked inside) and topstitched around the edges. Embroidery floss is tied at the corners of each square to keep the layers together and prevent the batting from shifting. For more on patchwork quilting, see page 66.

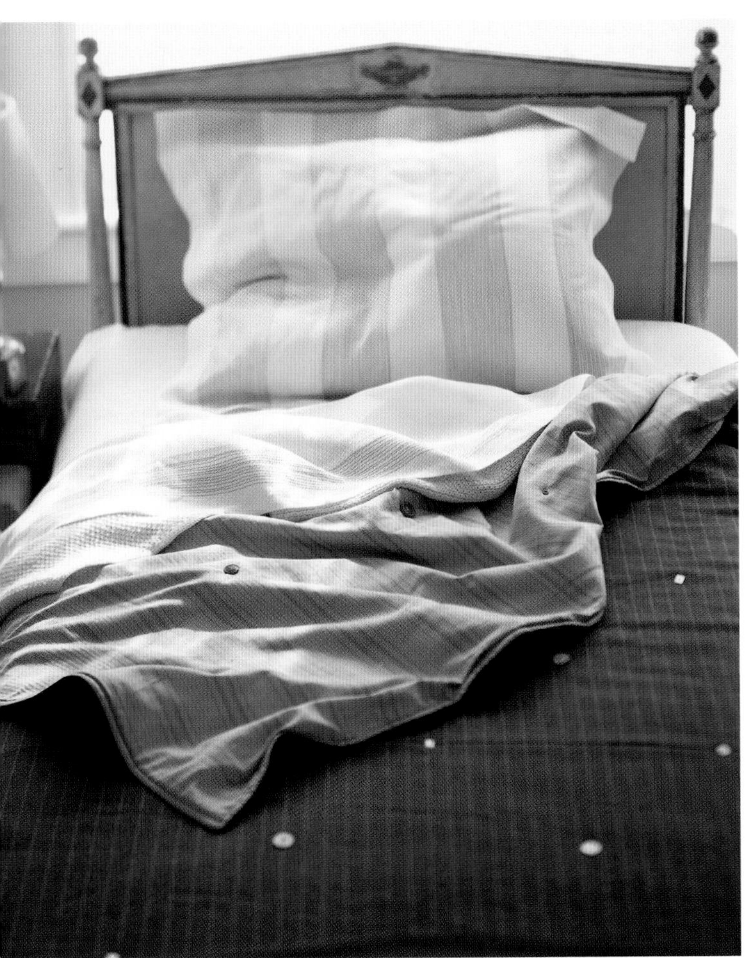

quilted suiting coverlet

This chalkboard-stripe wool coverlet has a silk lining, like a well-tailored suit jacket (but is a lot less formal). Its construction is that of a quilt, with two layers of batting sandwiched between the top and bottom fabrics. Rather than securing the finished quilt with yarn or ribbon ties, it is tufted with vintage buttons—white mother-of-pearl ones on the wool side, anchored with dark buttons on the silk side.

denim patchwork quilt

Eye-catching quilt rectangles, cut from gently worn jeans, cotton ticking fabric, and cotton dish towels, make up this pleasantly surprising patchwork bed cover. It is similar to the menswear patchwork throw on page 289, in that patches of the same width are sewn into rows, and then the rows are joined to make the top. To find an interesting mix of materials to work with, scour antiques shops, yard sales, thrift stores, flea markets, and your own closet for old jeans and denim scraps in different washes and textures. Include a few pieces of new denim, too—buy it by the yard from a fabric store. Once the patchwork pieces are sewn together, line the quilt with cotton batting, and back with cotton flannel.

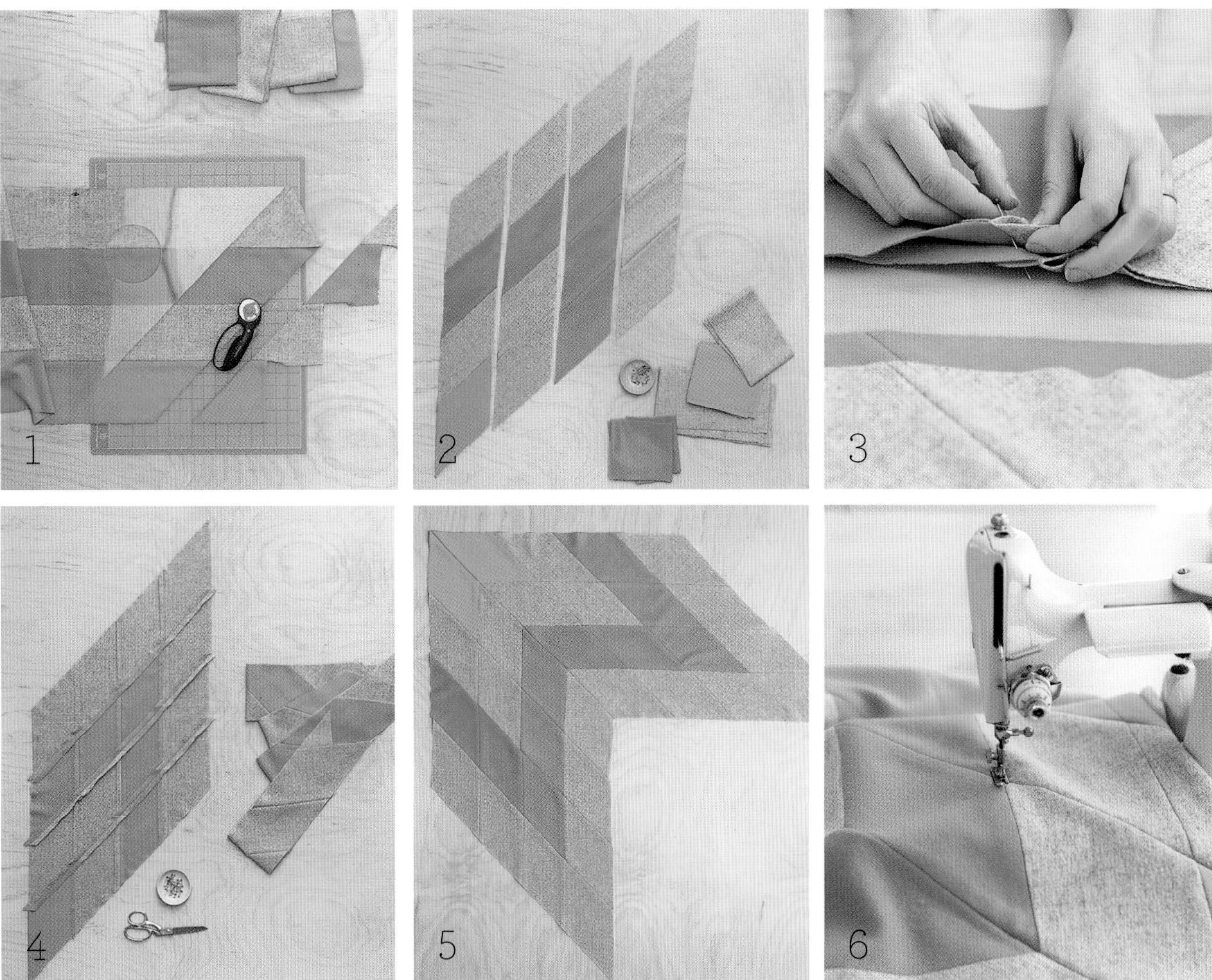

star-pattern patchwork coverlet

An eight-pointed star radiates from the center of this bold bed cover. The diamonds are made from wool strips cut on an angle. Machine-stitching highlights the stars and secures the queen-size coverlet's two layers. (Unlike in the other projects in this chapter, there is no batting used here.) For more on star-pattern patchwork, see page 68.

MATERIALS basic sewing supplies, 3 ⅓ yards (3m) pale-gray medium-weight wool, 1 ⅔ yards (1.5m) chartreuse medium-weight wool, ⅓ yard (30.5cm) blue medium-weight wool, plastic 45-degree angle, 7 ⅔ yards (7m) dark-gray medium-weight wool

HOW-TO 1. Cut 5 ¾-by-60-inch strips (14.5cm × 152.5cm): 2 blue, 10 chartreuse, and 20 pale gray. Pin and sew together 8 sets of 4 strips (see color sequence in photo), with a ½-inch (13mm) seam allowance, arranged in this order: (1) blue, gray, chartreuse, gray; (2) 2 gray, 1 chartreuse, 1 gray; (3) 3 chartreuse, 1 gray; (4) 4 gray. Repeat. Stagger the strips to align along a 45-degree angle. Using a plastic angle as a guide, cut through the strips every 7 ½ inches (19cm).

2. Eight 4-strip, 16-diamond points make one lone star. After cutting and sewing together 32 of the 4-diamond strips, lay out the entire design before stitching together the star's 8 points with a ½-inch (13mm) seam allowance.

3. To prevent the strips from shifting, pin them at the tips and corners of the diamond before stitching.

4. With the pins in place, sew the strips together to create a 16-piece diamond. You have now completed one-eighth of the star pattern. Repeat, making 7 more 16-piece star points.

5. Stitch together 2 of the 8 star points you have just completed. Refer to the star-pillow patchwork instructions on page 69 to assemble the star and its background. Six 28-inch (71cm) squares of dark-gray wool are needed for the coverlet's front side; you will cut 2 in half to form triangles.

6. Pin the front atop a 93-inch (236cm) square of dark-gray wool for the backing (you will have to join 2 pieces to make the square), right sides facing. Stitch the perimeter, leaving a 12-inch (30.5cm) opening; clip corners, and turn the quilt right-side out. Use safety pins to keep the layers together as you finish. Machine-stitch through the seams of the center star to the coverlet's edges and along the outlines of the blue, chartreuse, and pale-gray stars. Remove pins.

PROJECT:

shades

Shades enhance a room's style while managing the flow of natural light. And they present a delightful opportunity to dress up any window, no matter its size. In this chapter, you'll learn how to make shades from scratch, as well as ways to perk up store-bought varieties. Some of the projects require dowels or other hardware that's easy to find at any home center or drapery-supply store.

First, consider how much light you want to block. Drapery and upholstery fabrics work best for heavy shades. For an airy, translucent look, try voile, linen, or broadcloth. And keep the type of room in mind as you plan a design. Roman shades look lovely in living and dining rooms. Casual fold-up linen shades bring sweetness to a nursery, kitchen, or guest room.

Enjoy the wide range of options and experiment with styles to suit different surroundings. After all, a shade that is made by hand and hung with care is sure to give any room a more custom look—and a very welcoming air.

IN THIS CHAPTER: CLASSIC ROMAN SHADE — BILLOWY ROMAN SHADE — LONDON SHADE — EASY STENCILED SHADE — VINE-STENCILED SHADE — BUTTON-UP WINDOW SHADE — CREWELWORK ROMAN SHADES

CLASSIC ROMAN SHADE (OPPOSITE): *Simple, chic, and very versatile, Roman shades (there are three kinds to choose from in this chapter) suit any style of décor. This cotton-sateen shade features vertical ribbon stripes; blackout lining keeps the sun at bay.*

classic Roman shade SEE PHOTO, PAGE 299

The most basic Roman shades have dowels sewn in to give them structure, while allowing for gentle folds when raised. They can be mounted inside window frames for a neat and tidy appearance.

MATERIALS basic sewing supplies, cotton sateen or other medium-weight fabric, blackout fabric, 1/4-inch (6mm) dowels (cut to the width of the shade), strips of cotton muslin or lining fabric (4 3/4 inches [12cm] high each, cut to the shade's width plus 3/4 inch [2cm]), 2-by-1-inch (5cm X 2.5cm) wooden batten (cut to the width of the shade), staple gun, brass or plastic rings, cord lock, screw eyes, shade lift cord, cord condenser, cord pull

HOW-TO 1. Determine the size you want the shade to be, then add 4 inches (10cm) to the width and 8 1/2 inches (21.5cm) to the length (see right). Cut the shade and the lining fabric to size. Cut additional 4-by-5-inch (10cm X 12.5cm) pieces of shade fabric to cover the ends of the batten. Lay the shade fabric right-side down. Fold and press 2-inch (5cm) hems on the long sides and the bottom edge. Unfold. Fold the bottom corners in as shown; press. Refold the hems. Slipstitch the corners, mitering them and leaving a 1/4-inch (6mm) opening on one side for a dowel. Hem the sides and the bottom edge by hand (or by machine if you don't mind visible stitches).

2. Lay the lining right-side down. Fold and press 2 3/8-inch (6cm) hems on the long sides and the bottom edge. Pin the lining on the shade, wrong sides facing, so the shade shows on the long sides and the bottom edge. Slipstitch the lining to the shade on the hemmed sides.

3. The dowel pockets should be evenly spaced at intervals of 8 to 12 inches (20.5-30.5cm), depending on how far apart you want the folds to be. Once you've decided how to space the dowels, determine the position of the bottom pocket: Divide the size of the intervals by 2, and add 1 (for example, if you're spacing dowels 12 inches [30.5cm] apart, the bottom pocket should be 7 inches [18cm] from the bottom of the shade). Starting from the bottom pocket, measure positions of the other dowels; mark them on the back of the shade with a disappearing-ink fabric pen. The top pocket should be at least 10 inches (25.5cm) from the top of the shade. Sew cotton strips as shown: Fold them in half lengthwise, wrong sides facing; press (see top strip). Machine-stitch a double hem on the long edge (see middle strip): Fold edge 3/8 inch (10mm), then 3/8 inch (10mm) again, then press and edge-stitch in place. At one short side, fold, press, and machine-stitch a 3/8-inch (10mm) double hem (see bottom strip).

4. Pin the folded long edges of the dowel pockets along the pen marks; machine-stitch along the folded edge. Insert dowels in each pocket, and slipstitch a 3/8-inch (10mm) double hem. Insert a dowel into the mitered corner's opening at the bottom edge. Slipstitch closed.

5. Draw a line 6 1/2 inches (16.5cm) below the top of the shade. Wrap the batten ends in small pieces of shade fabric, and staple. Position the batten as pictured; staple in place. Roll and staple the batten until the edge covers the marker line.

6. Stitch the rings to the hemmed edge of the pockets, forming 3 columns: one up the center and the others each 2 inches (5cm) from a long side. Attach the cord lock (to merge the cords) to the batten 1/2 inch (13mm) in from its edge on the side where the strings will fall. Attach a screw eye to the batten at the top of the remaining ring rows. In each row, starting at the bottom of the shade, tie the end of a length of cord to the lowest ring. Thread the cord through the rings in that row, through the screw eyes at the top, then through the cord lock. Thread the loose ends through the cord condenser; knot them below, trim 2 of the cords, and pull the condenser down to cover the knot. Cut the remaining cord so that it hangs two-thirds of the way down the shade. Thread through the cord pull and tie a knot to secure. Screw the wooden batten directly into the window frame.

DETERMINING SHADE SIZE

For inside-mounted shades, which sit flush within the window frame, measure the width and height of your window (inside the frame), then subtract 1 inch (2.5cm) from the width and ½ inch (13mm) from the height. This should be the size of your completed shade. When cutting fabric, add the appropriate number of inches to the width and height as instructed in the project instructions. Use a carpenter's rule or a steel tape measure, rather than a fabric tape measure, when measuring windows. If you're making multiple shades, measure each window, even if you think they are the same size.

ABOUT BLACKOUT FABRIC

A synthetic-blend fabric with a rubberlike film sandwiched inside, blackout lining blocks light and provides insulation. You'll find it at hardware stores, fabric stores, and home centers.

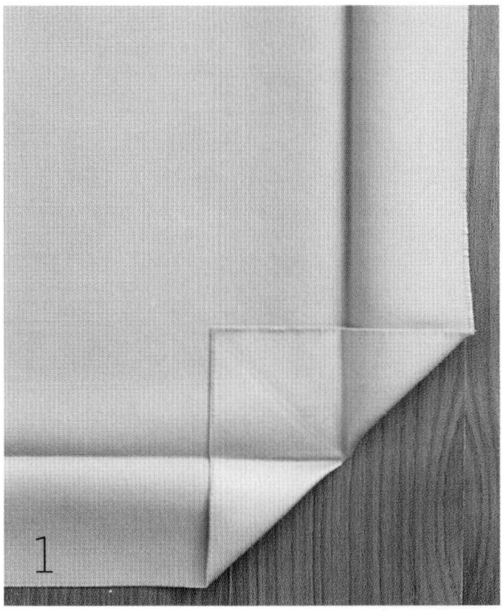

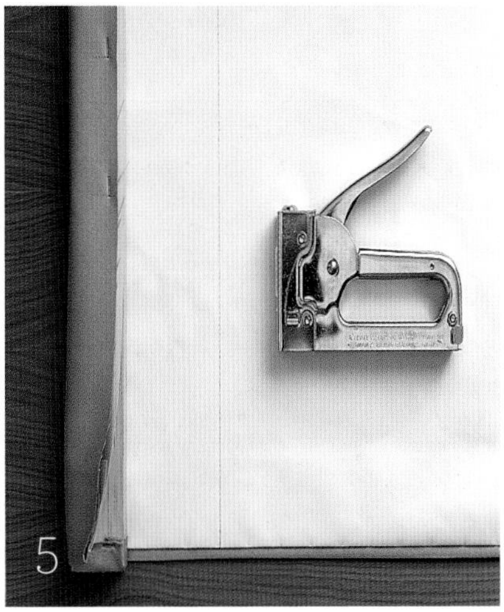

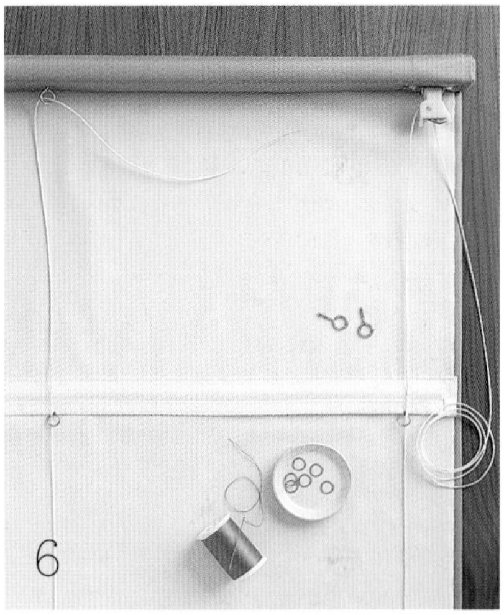

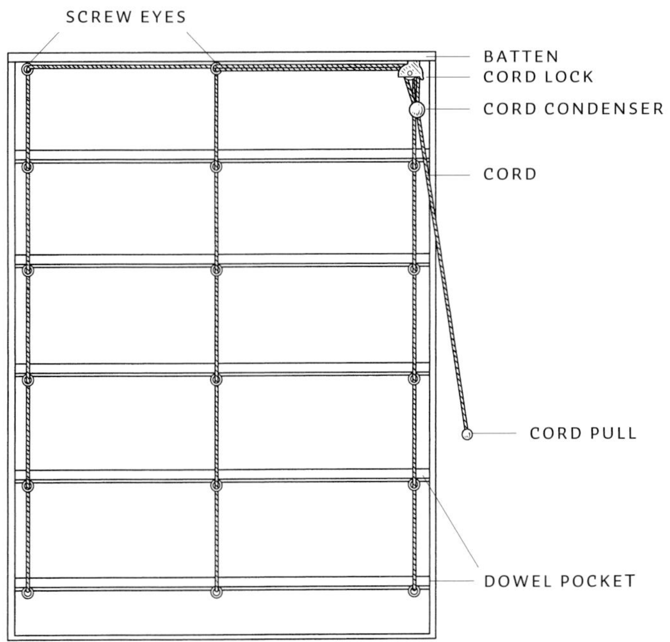

SHADE HARDWARE

Choose smooth nylon cord that will slide easily through the rings. The length of the cord and the number of rings you'll need will depend on your shade size. A cord lock keeps the shade in place when it's raised. After the cords have been threaded through it, you can pull them to one side to lock the shade in place or move them to the other side to release it. A cord condenser merges multiple cords into one; tie all the cords in a knot, trim the ends off all but one, and hide the knot inside the condenser. Don't forget to add a decorative pull to give your cord a finished look. You'll find these products at drapery-supply stores and home centers, and from online retailers.

BILLOWY ROMAN SHADE *A less formal variation of the classic Roman shade, this linen shade has no lining and calls for just a single dowel in the hem. Rather than additional pockets, the folds in the shade are formed by cords threaded through brass rings stitched directly to the back of the fabric. Use a disappearing-ink fabric pen to mark rows every 8 to 12 inches (20.5–30.5cm), as you would for a classic Roman shade. Stitch brass rings to the shade in two columns, each a couple of inches in from a long side. Thread the cord through the rings, lock, and tassel, then knot it before mounting the shade.*

London shade

This elegant shade, made of patterned fabric with deep bottom pleats, suits a more traditional decorating style. It is designed to remain partially raised, accentuating its lovely form. Use a lightweight cotton liner (instead of blackout fabric) to let sunlight draw attention to the print.

MATERIALS basic sewing supplies, patterned cotton or other medium-weight fabric (for shade), plain light-weight cotton (for lining), 1/4-inch (6mm) dowel, brass rings, 2-by-1-inch (5cm × 2.5cm) wooden batten (cut to the width of the shade), staple gun, cord lock, cord condenser, screw eyes, shade lift cord, cord pull

HOW-TO 1. Determine the size you want your shade to be (see sidebar, page 300), then add 16 inches (40.5cm) to the width and 18 1/2 inches (47cm) to the length. Complete steps 1 and 2 of the Classic Roman Shade (page 300). Fold the fabric to create a 3-inch-wide (7.5cm) pleat along each long side of the fabric; press and pin. Cut a dowel long enough to fit between the pleats. Insert the dowel through the opening in the bottom hem, slide it between the pleats, and hand-sew a running stitch around it to keep it in place.

2. Hand-stitch the rings in 4-inch (10cm) intervals along the rear fold of each pleat. Attach batten and cording as described on page 300. Pull the cords so the bottom 10 inches (25.5cm) of the shade are gathered (the bottom hem will be drawn up the back side, thus concealing it). Slide the cords through the lock and condenser. Tie a knot, trim 2 cords, and slide the condenser over the knot. Take out the pins (the pleats will be held in place by the batten and the dowel). Attach the pull, mount the shade, and arrange the gathers.

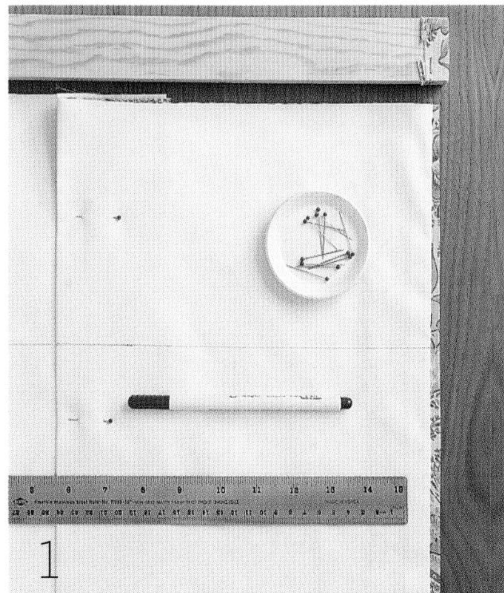

1

2

easy stenciled shade

Stenciling a store-bought fabric roller shade adds decorative detail in just a few foolproof steps. Stencils designed for borders or walls work best; using a paint roller is quicker than using a brush or sponge.

MATERIALS fabric roller shade, ruler, pencil, stencil, spray adhesive, paint roller, acrylic paint, paint tray

HOW-TO Lay out the fabric shade on a table. Using a ruler and pencil, mark where the stencil will go; the pattern top should align with the shade bottom, since you'll paint from bottom to top. Lightly mist the stencil back with spray adhesive; affix to the shade. Paint over the stencil with the roller and acrylic paint. Remove the stencil, and let the paint dry. Use the stencil's registration marks to match the pattern's repeat. For more on stenciling, see page 89.

vine-stenciled shade

Painted white vines wind down a gray roller shade; the light-colored pattern shows up best on a blackout shade. For a palette, use a piece of window glass, a paint tray, or even a paper plate. For more on stenciling, see page 89.

MATERIALS roller shade, vine stencil, ruler, drafting tape, pencil, natural sea sponge, 5 to 7 ounces (141–198g) white acrylic paint, palette, palette knife

HOW-TO Measure the width of the roller shade and stencil. Determine how many stencil repetitions will fit across shade, leaving even spaces between columns and on outer edges. Using tape, block off space between columns and outer edges. The stencil should fit snugly into columns. Place stencil in far-left column, shifting it 1 to 2 inches (2.5–5cm) below shade's bottom edge for a wraparound effect. Using a pencil, mark registration holes at stencil's top edge (erase pencil marks once paint is dry). Pat sponge in a dab of paint, then apply paint to stencil. Let dry for 2 to 3 minutes. Shift stencil up, aligning it with registration holes and marking new ones; paint. Repeat until column is complete, then repeat for remaining columns, flipping stencil over (make sure reverse is dry) so adjacent motifs mirror each other.

button-up window shade

This handsome cotton shade is quickly and easily sewn. It can be raised to two heights to adjust the amount of light.

MATERIALS basic sewing supplies, cotton ticking, raw linen or other coordinating medium-weight fabric, twill tape, 6 buttons

HOW-TO Measure the inside of the window frame, add ½ inch (13mm) to the width and ½ inch (13mm) to the length, and use those dimensions to cut two equal-size pieces, one of ticking and one of linen (your finished shade will be ½ inch [13mm] smaller than the window frame). Place ticking and linen on a work surface, right sides facing. Cut three 4-inch (10cm) lengths of twill tape for loops. Position the loops on the bottom edge of the shade—one on each end, ½ inch (13mm) from edge, and one in the center—and sandwich them between linen and ticking, with loops facing inward and raw edges of twill tape and fabric aligned; pin in place. Sew around perimeter of shade with a ½-inch (13mm) seam allowance, leaving a few inches open along top edge. Turn curtain right-side out, and slip-stitch opening closed. To make the curtain-rod channel, top-stitch shade ¼ inch (6mm) from top edge. Make a second seam across the top, 1½ inches (3.8cm) from the first. Open the channel's side seams with a seam ripper. Hand-sew two rows of buttons—three at the top and three halfway down the shade—to the shade so they align with the loops.

CREWELWORK ROMAN SHADES *The trim lines of Roman shades allow them to look right at home in modern as well as traditional settings. Crewelwork, a kind of richly textured embroidery that has remained popular over hundreds of years, looks thoroughly contemporary when sewn into a pair of neatly tailored kitchen window shades. For instructions on making a Roman shade,* *see page 300.*

PROJECT:

slippers

Satisfy the desire to slip into something more comfortable. Hand-craft slippers in warm, cozy fabrics, such as wool felt, that will keep toes snug in any weather. And do so easily thanks to the simple patterns here, which include snuggly styles for both adults and kids.

As you create slippers, you'll practice and perfect a variety of crafting techniques, including sewing, embroidery, monogramming, and cut-work. And you'll fashion the footwear from pliable soft fabrics in wonderful fabrics that make you think of the wearer. This is a wonderful process, not only because it demystifies shoe-making, but because the fundamentals of slipper construction can be learned so quickly that you will soon be able to use what you've learned to create slipper designs of your own.

IN THIS CHAPTER: MONOGRAMMED SLIPPERS — NATURE-INSPIRED FELT SLIPPERS — FELT BABY SHOES

MONOGRAMMED SLIPPERS (OPPOSITE): *Personalize a pair of store-bought boiled-wool slippers with hand-stitched monograms. To make them, first embroider initials on to felt labels, fabric-covered buttons (see page 366 for instructions on covering buttons), or directly on the slippers themselves. Chainstitches, satin stitches, and French knots are used to embellish the slippers shown (for more on embroidery stitches, see page 48).*

EHS
EHS

nature-inspired felt slippers

Slippers adorned with cutout butterflies and leafy branches are sure to brighten chilly mornings.

MATERIALS basic sewing supplies, nature-inspired slipper pattern, wool felt (in 2 colors for branch slippers, 2 or more colors for butterfly slippers), fusible web, pencil, craft knife, fabric glue (optional)

HOW-TO BRANCH SLIPPERS: print the pattern in the desired size (see enclosed CD), and cut out. Cut equal-size rectangles of the top color (tan is pictured), the inside color (orange is pictured), and the fusible web (leaving one side of the paper backing on), each large enough for 2 slipper tops. Place the fusible web, paper side up, on top of tan felt. Place the slipper-top patterns side by side on top of the webbing.Trace with a pencil, marking notches A and B as indicated on the pattern. Place the branch pattern on one traced slipper top, using the marked points to position it correctly; trace. Repeat on the second slipper top, flipping the branch pattern to trace a mirror image. Using a craft knife, cut out the branch designs (slice through the webbing). Carefully remove paper backing from webbing, keeping edges aligned. Place the orange-felt rectangle on the webbing, and flip the layers over. Press, following manufacturer's instructions. Lay the slipper-top patterns on the tan side of fused felt, and align notches A and B. Trace with a disappearing-ink fabric pen. Cut out slipper tops, cutting through the notches. Fuse together another rectangle of tan and orange felt for soles. Lay the patterns for both soles side by side on the fused fabric; trace and cut out. Machine-sew closed the vertical seam at the back of each slipper top with a zigzag stitch (do not overlap the fabric; instead, align at the edges and stitch). Pin one slipper top to one sole, tan sides out. Starting at the heel, sew around the perimeter, with a 1/4-inch (6mm) seam allowance. Repeat to finish the second slipper.

BUTTERFLY SLIPPERS: print pattern pieces in desired size, and cut them out. Cut equal rectangles of cream felt, white felt, and fusible web, each large enough to accommodate 2 slipper tops. Fuse layers together, following manufacturer's instructions. Trace slipper-top patterns onto cream side of fused felt; cut out. Trace butterfly patterns onto different shades of felt and cut them out. Pin butterflies to the cream sides of the slipper tops (or use fabric glue). Stitch along the midline of each butterfly to secure. Machine-sew closed the slipper tops in back; sew to the soles as described for branch slippers.

felt baby shoes

Cradle an infant's feet with a pair of hand-sewn felt booties. Rickrack trim and punched-hole borders add subtle detailing. Fasten the straps with buttons, snaps, or an elastic band. If you like, choose felt in a contrasting color for the soles.

MATERIALS basic sewing supplies; felt baby shoes pattern; felt (in one or 2 colors); mini hole punch (optional); rick-rack or other trim (optional); fabric glue (optional); buttons, snaps, or 3/8-inch-wide (10mm) elastic

HOW-TO 1. Measure baby's foot from heel to toe. Print pattern pieces (see enclosed CD), resizing to fit baby's foot, adding 1/8 inch (3mm) all around for a seam allowance. Trace the pattern pieces onto the felt with a disappearing-ink fabric pen; cut out. For a punched-hole border, punch holes following the dotted line on the pattern. To make the heel, fold the top piece in half and stitch the straight edge shut with a 1/8-inch (3mm) seam allowance.

2. Pin the top, wrong-side out, to the sole; sew the pieces together. Turn the shoe right-side out. If desired, glue rickrack on the outside or inside rim of the instep. Sew a button or half a snap onto one strap of the shoe; make a small slit for a buttonhole or sew the other piece of the snap on the opposite strap. Repeat with the second shoe. To make slip-ons, square off the ends of the straps. Sew a 1-inch (2.5cm) length of elastic to the ends of the straps (on the inside).

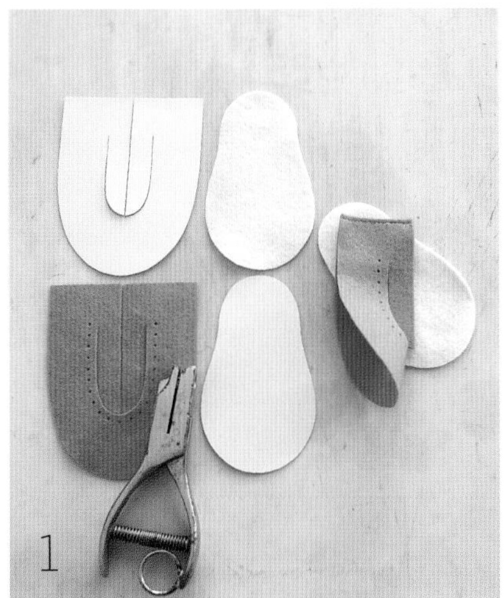

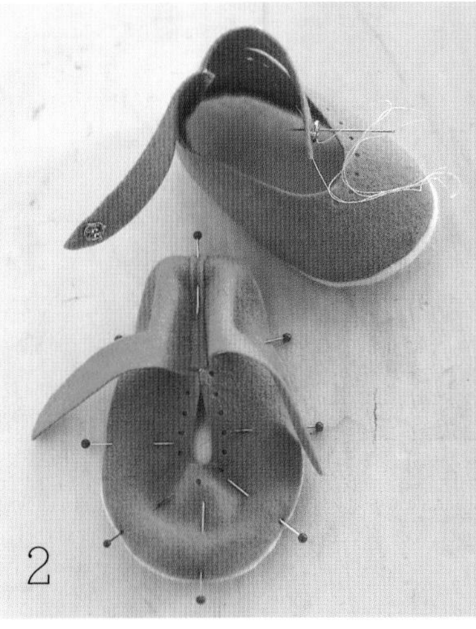

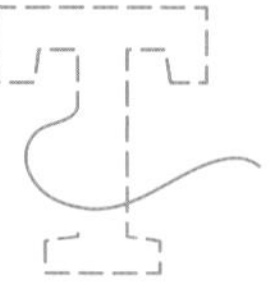

PROJECT:

table linens

Drape any table in fabric, and expectations rise. Suddenly the dining room becomes a destination. Whether it's a tablecloth, place mats, a runner, or cloth napkins, something about adorning a table with fabric makes sharing a meal feel more special.

To create a look, whether formal or casual, everyday or holiday, turn to yardage and remnants of material that speak to the season in which you're serving, or the style of your home. Solid and patterned fabrics work equally well. And if you're up for a particularly creative project, you can even enhance yardage by printing it or dyeing it yourself. Table linens are, in many respects, the easiest of sewing projects given their straight lines and basic shapes. But they can also be the most beautiful, making them lovely offerings as gifts.

IN THIS CHAPTER: EYELET TABLE RUNNER — BASIC LINEN NAPKINS — FEATHER-STAMPED NAPKINS — FOUR EASY NAPKIN PROJECTS: FADED FLORALS; OMBRÉ; DYED TICKING; BUTTON EMBROIDERY — BIAS-TAPE TABLE RUNNER — ULTRASUEDE LEAF PLACE MATS — FRINGED TABLE RUNNERS — DRAWN-THREAD TABLE RUNNERS — BATIK TABLE LINENS — BLEACH-BATIK TABLE LINENS — LINEN TABLECLOTH — JAPANESE-EMBROIDERED TABLE LINENS — MACHINE-EMBROIDERED PLACE MATS — BLOCK-PRINT TABLE LINENS — RAFFIA-EMBROIDERED PLACE MATS — DOILY TABLECLOTH — LEATHER TABLE MATS

EYELET TABLE RUNNER (OPPOSITE): *Eyelet adds beauty to any surrounding; here it makes a dining room feel fresh, crisp, and light. A length of cotton-voile oval eyelet, usually sold in 45-inch (114cm) widths, makes an almost-instant table runner. Just hem the ends or cut around the stitching on a disk pattern, as shown. Layered over a linen tablecloth, the runner creates a graceful play of color and texture.*

basic linen napkins

Making napkins from scratch is simple: The ones shown are 20 inches (51cm) square and have mitered corners for a neat finish. Begin by preshrinking the fabric: Wash, dry, and press. Once you've mastered the basic skills required for this project, you can apply them to making a tablecloth with mitered corners.

MATERIALS basic sewing supplies, 23-inch (58.5cm) square of fabric (for each napkin; peach-colored linen is shown)

HOW-TO 1. Press 2 folds into each side of the fabric square; the first fold is ½ inch (13mm) wide; the second is 1 inch (2.5cm). Unfold the second crease. Fold one corner in so the second crease lines up, as shown. Press.

2. Unfold the corner, and refold on a diagonal with right sides together. Stitch along the crease made by the folded corner. Repeat with the remaining corners.

3. Trim the points from the corners to ¼ inch (6mm), tapering as shown. Press the seams open and the corners flat.

4. Turn all 4 corners inside out (which is actually right-side out); press again.

5. Stitch down the fold all the way around, so you have a seam 1 inch (2.5cm) from the edges.

STANDARD NAPKIN SIZES

COCKTAIL: *8 by 6 ½ inches (20.5cm X 3 16.5cm)*

LUNCHEON: *10 by 10 inches to 13 by 13 inches (25.5cm square–33cm square)*

DINNER: *20 by 20 inches to 24 by 24 inches (51cm square–61cm square)*

feather-stamped napkins

For this modern table setting, one small feather was used to stamp delicate, wispy impressions on a hemstitched linen napkin; the motif is repeated on the place card. This technique works equally well on any type of cotton or linen fabric, and on heavy paper, such as card stock. You will need an ink pad with ink designed for use on fabric and a brayer for printing (for more on fabric printing, see page 87). Feathers are available at crafts and fishing-gear stores.

MATERIALS feathers (natural mallard duck feathers are shown), fabric-safe ink pad in metallic gold or brown, scrap paper (for blotting), tweezers, napkins, brayer

HOW TO Place a feather on the ink pad; place a piece of scrap paper on top. Flip, then press with fingertips. With tweezers, remove feather from paper. Place the feather, ink side down, on the napkin (or any other surface on which you wish to print). Lay a fresh piece of scrap paper over the feather, then carefully roll brayer over the surface. Remove the feather with tweezers. Let dry. Check manufacturer's instructions to see if fabric ink needs to be heat-set with an iron.

FOUR EASY NAPKIN PROJECTS

faded florals

The same floral fabric can be used to create a tablecloth and napkins in two different shades. Here a hand-sewn tablecloth was faded to a golden hue; the napkins were faded, then tinted (or "overdyed") with a mixture of tangerine and scarlet dyes. (The other napkins shown were sewn from solid red material.) Follow the instructions on page 80 to fade and overdye the fabrics. These have simple double hems on each side, rather than mitered corners.

ombré

Basic linens dyed in ombré patterns dress up the dining room table. Here, shades of coral embellish a napkin (and a coordinating rice-paper place card), echoing the nearby floating anemone blossoms. To dye tops and bottoms, begin by folding each napkin in half horizontally. Pin through the top layer to mark the shade levels. Stack 2 pinned napkins, securing them with binder clips at the folded edges. Dye according to the instructions on page 77.

dyed ticking

Handmade ticking napkins with pale-green stripes takes on new charm when dyed a series of luscious rainbow colors. There's no sewing required for this project; just fringe the unfinished edges (for a more secure finish, see fringe how-to, page 319). Be sure to make the fringe before dyeing the fabric so that the threads easily absorb the color. The napkins shown were dyed according to the instructions on page 77; the amount of adjusted dye used was, from top to bottom: yellow (1 1/2 teaspoons [7.5ml] yellow plus 1/2 teaspoon tan [2.5ml]; orange (1 teaspoon [5ml] tangerine); red (1/4 teaspoon [1.3ml] scarlet); pink (1/2 teaspoon [2.5ml] mauve); lavender (1/2 teaspoon [2.5ml] purple). After using the napkins, machine-wash on the gentle cycle or hand-wash them.

button embroidery

It takes only a few stray buttons and some embroidery floss to transform plain napkins into a harvest of whimsical linens. Arrange the buttons and mark their places with a disappearing-ink fabric pen, then sew on the first button, using matching thread. Lightly mark out a design (such as leaves and stems for fruits and vegetables) with the disappearing-ink fabric pen. Stitch along the pen marks, using embroidery floss and a classic chainstitch (see pages 48–49 for basic embroidery stitches) or a stem stitch, which works well when outlining. For the leaves, use a satin stitch, making straight (not slanted) stitches, each touching the next, across the width of the leaf.

bias-tape table runner

The runner shown is 86 inches (218.5cm) long; you can add or subtract leaves as needed.

MATERIALS basic sewing supplies, bias-tape table runner template, linen (celadon, mint, and lemon are shown), 1/2-inch-wide (13mm) single-fold bias tape

HOW-TO Print the template (see enclosed CD), and cut out. Cut 27 leaves from the linen. With bias tape, bind the raw edge along one side of each leaf, tip to tip: Slip tape over the edge, pinning to secure. Stitch 1/8 inch (3mm) in from the tape's edge, making sure needle passes through underside of tape. There is no need to finish the tape ends. Bind the opposite side of each leaf, covering the unfinished edges at the tips with an overlap finish: Cut bias tape 1 inch (2.5cm) longer than the side of the leaf, slip over edge, and pin. Stitch in place, stopping about 1 inch (2.5cm) before you reach the end. Open the bias tape like a book; fold under 1/2 inch (13mm) at end. Close tape, and stitch in place. Arrange the leaves in your desired pattern; pin, and hand-stitch together.

Ultrasuede leaf place mats

All you need is a pair of scissors and a good dose of spring fever to produce big-leaf place mats from Ultrasuede fabric. Ultrasuede, which is available at most fabric and craft stores, is machine washable and doesn't fray, so sewing is unnecessary. This design alternates between fabric in two shades of green to set an inviting table for lunch.

MATERIALS Ultrasuede leaf place mats template, Ultrasuede (about 1 1/2 yards [1.4m] for 6 place mats), pencil, scissors

HOW-TO Print the template (see enclosed CD), and cut out. Lay the template over a large piece of Ultrasuede. Trace the shape onto the fabric with a pencil, and cut it out with scissors.

fringed table runners

A few lengths of bright yellow loose-weave linen, fringed at both ends, are evenly spaced and placed perpendicular to a dining table for an easy, bold, modern table setting.

MATERIALS basic sewing supplies, 2 yards (1.8m) of loose-weave linen (for each runner)

HOW-TO 1. Wash, dry, and press the linen. Cut the linen to the desired length, adding 2 inches (5cm) at either end for fringing. Trim the fabric to the desired width (at least 26 inches [66cm]; enough space for a place setting, plus allowance for hems). Sew a line across the runner, 2 inches (5cm) from each short end.

2. Pull out individual strands from one long side of the runner to the other up to the sewn lines. Make a double hem on the long sides: Fold over each side 1/2 inch (13mm), and press, then fold over another 1/2 inch (13mm). Edge-stitch the hems in place.

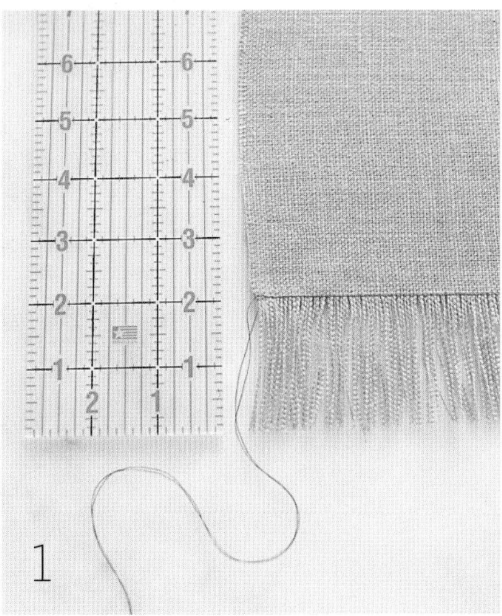
1

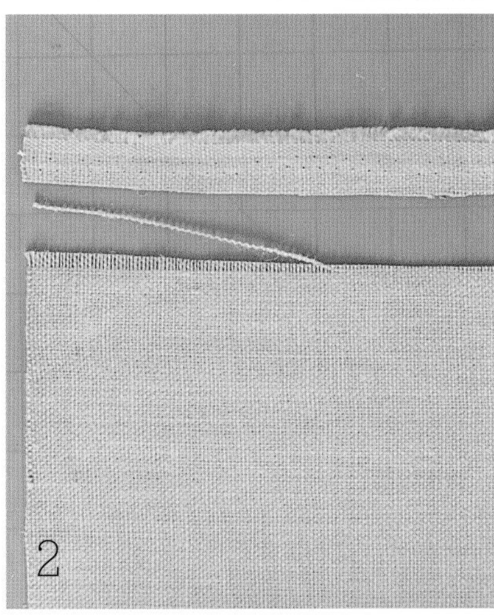
2

drawn-thread designs

When you pull a thread from a woven textile, such as linen, the fabric remains intact—with a gap left by the missing strand. This technique can be used to create decorative patterns. The basic method involves removing thread from the weave's warp (running lengthwise) or weft (running crosswise), or both ways. Even large expanses of fabric can be altered in this manner. A more complex process, called drawing in, replaces pulled threads with new ones (or ribbons) to produce contrasting stripes (see "Drawing in Ribbons," opposite). The thread to be inserted is tied to the one being removed, so that as you "draw out" the old, you "draw in" the new. Drawing in is easiest to accomplish with small pieces of cloth. Use new, unwashed, unironed linen or cotton fabric with a smooth, even weave and strong threads. (Buy an extra foot [30.5cm] of material so you can practice this technique before starting a drawn-thread project.) Six-strand cotton embroidery floss is the best candidate for drawing in. You can also pull the strands apart to make thinner stripes.

drawn-thread table runner

Both drawn-out and drawn-in threads embellish this fringed red linen table runner (opposite, top). A detail (opposite, bottom) shows the thin stripes filled with white embroidery floss; wider stripes are left empty. Two ends of the runner are fringed (page 319) to incorporate both the white floss and the red linen into the border.

MATERIALS basic sewing supplies, red linen table runner, white embroidery floss, darning needle

HOW-TO 1. Plan your decorative pattern on the runner, then measure from the side of the fabric piece to mark where you want to place a line of color. Pull out the thread from the unfinished edge at that spot.

2. Use six-strand embroidery floss, doubled on insertion. If the channel you've made in the fabric is too small for floss, pull out an adjacent thread or two. Cut a piece of floss twice the length of the cloth plus an extra inch (2.5cm); fold it in half to make a loop for insertion. Begin to pull out the next thread. Tie this guide thread tightly to the loop of floss.

3. Locate the other end of the guide thread and pull it out gently, easing the looped floss through with your fingers.

4. Use a darning needle to smooth out any threads that bunch up as you proceed.

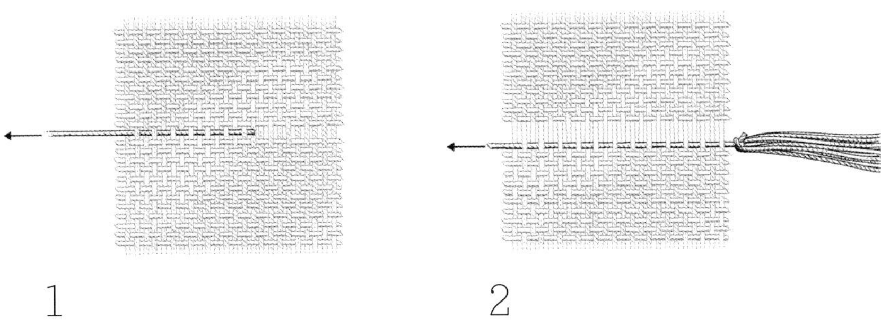

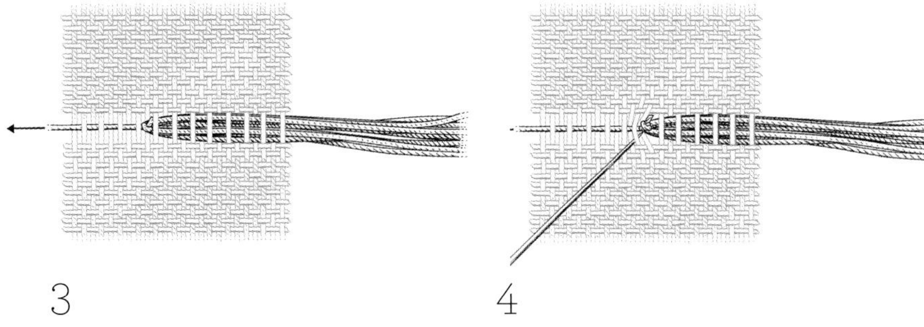

DRAWING IN RIBBONS

Using the technique described at left, you can also draw in ribbons in different colors and thicknesses for interesting effects. Cotton embroidery fabric, called Aida cloth, is ideal for this kind of drawn-thread work. It is evenly woven of sturdy double threads, which are easy to count for exact placement of stripes. You want a snug fit, so remove threads from the fabric until the channel is just wide enough to accommodate the ribbon. Tie the new thread to a loop of ribbon. As you pull out the other end of this guide thread, keep the loop of ribbon from twisting by feeding the lower strand through two fingers.

batik table linens

Cotton table linens and hand-sewn seat-cushion covers (stuffed with batting) are stippled with a pleasing array of dots and rings. The relief pattern was produced by dipping small kitchen items into melted wax, then stamping them onto white table linens, which were then dyed. For the tablecloth, you will need a basin large enough to dye the fabric evenly.

MATERIALS nonreactive basins or bins, rubber gloves, beeswax or paraffin, dye (periwinkle and coffee-brown were used for the linens shown), 54-inch (137cm) square tablecloth, cloth napkins, cotton yardage (for cushions; optional), batting, graph paper, double boiler, kraft paper, item(s) to stamp (such as cake-decorating tips and wooden dowels), twill tape

HOW-TO Follow instructions for batik (page 78) to make patterns on the tablecloth using melted beeswax, cake-decorating tips, and wooden dowels. Dye the tablecloth periwinkle blue. Make a similar pattern on cloth napkins, using the same stamping tools and coffee-brown dye. Finally, make seat cushions with fabric dyed a lighter shade of periwinkle blue. To construct cushions, start by measuring the width and length of the seat. Add a ½-inch (13mm) seam allowance on all sides, and cut 2 pieces of batik-dyed fabric to that measurement. Cut one piece of batting to the seat dimensions (without adding a seam allowance). Pin the 2 pieces of fabric, right sides facing, and sew all 4 sides, with a ½-inch (13mm) seam allowance and leaving an 8-inch (20.5cm) opening on one side. Turn the seat cushion right-side out, and press it flat. Insert the batting and slip-stitch the opening closed. To make ties for each cushion, you will need 2 pieces of ¼-inch (6mm) twill tape (the ones shown were decorated with a dotted batik pattern, using wooden dowels). Fold the tape in half, then hand-sew the folded end to the back edge of the cushion, about 2 inches (5cm) from the corner edge.

To give a tablecloth and napkin set as a gift, tie it with batik-dyed cotton ribbon; simple twill tape will accept dye, too.

bleach-batik table linens

Here, a bleach pen with a metal tip creates the look of batik (page 78) on blue linens. The technique works best for natural fibers.

MATERIALS bleach-batik table linens template, gel bleach pen, ½-millimeter screw-on metal applicator tip (optional), colored cotton canvas, water-soluble dressmaker's pencil

HOW-TO Fit the bleach pen with the tip (this makes it easier to draw a clean, thin line). Hem canvas into 16-inch (40.5cm) square napkins and a 12-inch (30.5cm) wide runner (store-bought linens will also do). Test a discreet area to make sure the fabric reacts well to the bleach. Use the dressmaker's pencil to mark a grid on the fabric; where the lines intersect, create a 2-inch (5cm) square, as shown at left. With the pen, draw a four-point flower within each square and add dotted lines between the flowers (use the template on the enclosed CD as a guide). Let the bleach set until the pattern has faded to the desired shade, about 20 minutes. To rinse, lay the fabric flat in a shallow pan of water and gently agitate; let it stand until the color dissolves (work in sections for the runner). Be careful not to let the bleach "land" in other spots on the fabric. Gently wash the linens by hand.

Linen voile drapes beautifully when covering a table, indoors or out. Here three linen panels—two white, one ecru—are joined to make a long tablecloth with rickrack sewn into the seams. Hems with pockets hold pebbles or other weights to keep the cloth in place on breezy days.

MATERIALS basic sewing supplies; 2 panels of white linen voile, each 28 ½ inches (71cm) wide and 94 inches (239cm) long; one panel of ecru linen voile, 14 inches (5.5cm) wide and 94 inches (239cm) long; pebbles (or other weights); 3 yards (2.75m) prewashed rickrack

HOW-TO 1. Baste around the outside of all panels, ¼ inch (6mm) from the edge. Fold the hems inward along the baste lines; press flat. Fold all 4 hems on the ecru panel inward again, press, and edge-stitch. Fold, press, and edge-stitch 3 hems on each white panel, leaving one long side of each panel unstitched. Fold the fourth hem of each white panel inward by 4 inches (10cm); press.

2. To create the pockets, topstitch a seam perpendicular to the fold, beginning 4 inches (10cm) from either corner. Topstitch the hem between the pockets.

3. Pin the rickrack along the long, narrow-hemmed side of one white panel, overlapping the rickrack onto the front side of the panel by no more than ⅛ inch (3mm), and folding it under ¼ inch (6mm) at each end. Topstitch. Pin and topstitch the other edge of the rickrack to the ecru panel, as shown. Repeat on the other side.

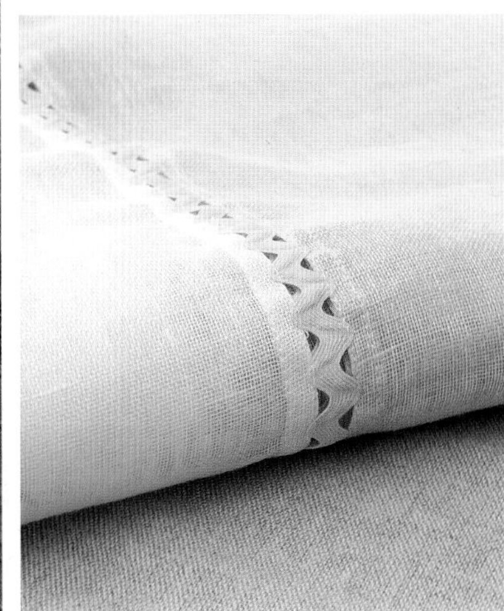

JAPANESE-EMBROIDERED TABLE LINENS *Finely detailed, hand-embroidered patterns lend visual interest to a serene table setting. Here, a variety of sashiko patterns (see the enclosed CD; shown here, clockwise from top left: hiyokuigeta, koushiawabe, koushitsunagi, and shippoutsunagi) were produced on gray and white linen place mats, in colors carefully chosen to complement the palette of the Japanese tableware. To make similar place mats, cut two pieces of linen to desired size; embroider a pattern on one piece, following the sashiko instructions on page 55. Combine the top (embroidered) piece to the backing with the French seam method (page 36). You can use the same color for both pieces, or choose fabric in a complementary color for the backing.*

machine-embroidered place mats

Even the smallest embroidered details can give table linens a nuanced elegance. Here, a machine-embroidered hem transforms plain napkins into place mats that can serve as a casual alternative to a tablecloth. Many stitches typically used for utilitarian purposes—such as for hemming or preventing fraying—are pretty enough to create embellishments (for more on machine embroidery, see page 60). This project requires fabric stabilizer to secure the stitches in place as you work (for more on stabilizer, see page 363).

MATERIALS basic sewing supplies, cloth napkins, fabric stabilizer

HOW-TO Measure in about 2 inches (5cm) from the edge of the napkin; mark a line that is parallel to the hem. Using a sewing machine and fabric stabilizer, create a wide border by stitching 3 rows of honeycomb stitches very close together. Measure up 1 more inch (2.5cm), and stitch 2 more rows of honeycomb close together. Remove the stabilizer. Drape the mats so the decorative border hangs over the edge of the table.

block-print table linens

Leaves stamped and scattered on a runner and napkins give a nod to autumn. Follow the instructions below to make block-printed table linens in any motif you like; for more on block printing, see page 88.

MATERIALS block-print table linens template (optional); graphite pencil; tracing paper; artist's carving block (available at crafts stores and online); bone folder; linoleum cutter; wide brush; transparent, water-based fabric paint (that sets with an iron); paper towels; scrap paper; linen table runner and napkins; mild, alcohol-free detergent

HOW-TO 1. Print the template (see enclosed CD), and cut out, or draw your own. With a graphite pencil, trace the design onto tracing paper. Place the tracing paper, marked side down, on the artist's carving block. Rub the wide edge of a bone folder over the paper to transfer the design. Use a linoleum cutter with a V-shaped attachment to outline the design and add veins as desired. Switch to a U-shaped attachment to carve out larger areas around the design, which should be recessed about ⅛ inch (3mm).

2. With a wide brush, cover the design with a thick layer of fabric paint. Paint with uniform strokes (brushstrokes will be visible on the fabric), avoiding any veins. If the paint pools in the crevices, soak up the excess with the corner of a paper towel. Practice printing on scrap paper first, then print on fabric. Apply fresh paint each time you use a block. If you're using a new paint color, clean the block first with a damp cloth and, if necessary, the detergent. Let dry, about 15 minutes. Set the paint with an iron, according to the manufacturer's instructions. The pieces may be machine-washed and -dried.

raffia-embroidered place mats

Use several strands of raffia and a large-eyed needle to add geometric designs to solid-colored, open-weave place mats.

MATERIALS basic sewing supplies; a large-eyed needle (designed for ribbon or crewel); place mat or large napkin made of an open-weave fabric (such as cotton, linen, raffia, or straw); raffia in desired colors

HOW-TO 1. Using a disappearing-ink fabric pen, draw a row of diamond shapes (the ones shown are 1 1/2 by 1 1/2 inches [3.8cm × 3.8cm]) along the bottom of a place mat. Draw an additional diamond shape at the top left of the place mat.

2. Thread the large-eyed needle with raffia, knotting it before embroidering a design using a detached chainstitch.

3. Starting with the first diamond, draw a threaded needle up through A. Draw the needle down through A, creating a loop. Holding the loop, gently use your fingers to flatten and spread out the raffia.

4. Draw the needle up through B, inside the loop (as shown, far left). Pull the loop taut. Bring the needle down through B, outside the loop (as shown, near left).

5. Working on one side of the diamond at a time, repeat steps 3 and 4, creating a stitch from A to D; C to D; and then C to B.

6. Stitch the remaining diamonds onto the place mats. When stitching several in a row, connect them: Always use point D of the preceding diamond as your new point B. Knot the stitches on the underside of the mat to finish. Spot-clean the mats as needed.

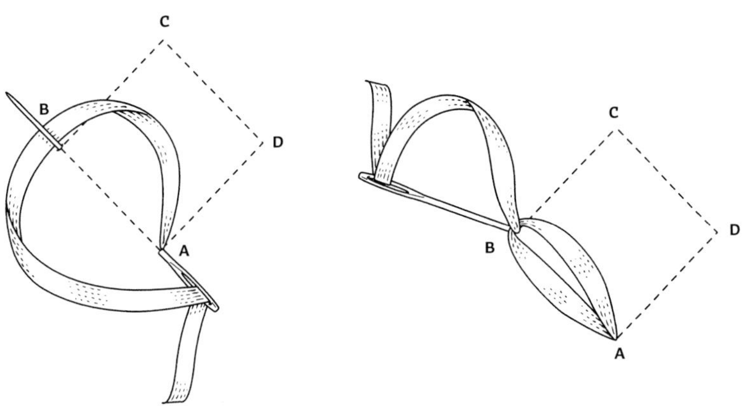

doily tablecloth

A winter table setting evokes drifts of snow with a table cover made from rows of stitched-together doilies. You will need enough same-size doilies to cover the surface of your table, with a 12-inch (30.5cm) overhang on each long side.

MATERIALS basic sewing supplies, cloth doilies (8-inch [20.5cm] ones are shown)

HOW-TO On a work surface, lay 2 cloth doilies side by side, barely touching. Using a needle and white thread, attach the doilies with 3 or 4 slipstitches, knotting the stitches on the reverse side. Repeat to attach additional doilies, one at a time, in a single row until the row is long enough to accommodate the table width and both overhangs. Position another doily beside the first doily in the completed row; lay the doilies flat to make sure there are no ripples. Attach the doilies as directed above. Lay the next doily in the second row. Attach it to first doily in the second row and to the corresponding doily in the first row. Repeat to attach additional doilies, one at a time, to complete the second row. Continue adding rows until tablecloth is complete.

leather table mats

Giant leather place mats, each made from six pieces of lambskin that were sewn together, topstitched, and given a canvas backing, are a modern and fashionable twist on a traditional tablecloth. To help ward off stains, treat the mats with a protectant spray.

MATERIALS basic sewing supplies, leather table mats template, machine needle for leather, double-sided tape, ballpoint pen, rotary cutter, ruler, bone folder, leather adhesive

HOW-TO 1. Print the template pieces (see enclosed CD), and cut out. Cut out leather pattern pieces: Adhere the paper pattern to the "good" side of the leather, avoiding imperfections or very thin areas, with bits of double-sided tape (not pins). Trace with a ballpoint pen, then cut out, using scissors for curves and a rotary cutter and ruler for straight lines. Cut 2 of pattern A, then flip template over and cut 2 more pieces so that you have 4 total (2 are mirror images). Cut 2 leather pieces using pattern B. To make the backing, fold canvas in half; use pattern C to cut a piece of canvas, making sure to line up the marked edge with the folded edge of the canvas. Unfold.

2. Match up one B leather piece and 2 opposing A pieces so that the sides marked "a" are next to each other and place them "good" sides together. Hold pieces together with small pieces of tape (not pins), no more than 1/4 inch (6mm) from edge of the leather.

3. Using the leather needle and a heavy-fabric setting, sew pieces together with a 1/2-inch (13mm) seam allowance (take care not to stretch or pull the leather as you sew). Smooth flaps open with the bone folder and glue flaps open with leather adhesive (as shown). Topstitch 1/8 inch (3mm) from both sides of the seam. Repeat steps 2 and 3 with remaining leather pieces.

4. Lay canvas pattern C on top of leather mat, "good" sides together. Sew together, with a 1/2-inch (13mm) seam allowance all around. Leave a 10-inch (25.4cm) opening along the side marked "B" in the template. Turn project inside out through the opening so that the "good" sides are showing. Tuck in 1/2 inch (13mm) of excess fabric from the 10-inch (25.4cm) opening and topstitch 1/4 inch (6mm) from the edge around the entire mat.

PROJECT:

upholstery

Fabric softens a room's lines, adds layers of texture, and establishes the character of the space. In the form of upholstered and slipcovered furniture, a fabric's color and pattern can transform even ordinary examples into artistic focal points. Of course, upholstered furniture is functional, as well; for example, slipcovers give new life to old favorites and protect them from wear and tear.

You needn't be daunted at the prospect of do-it-yourself upholstery. Here, "upholstery" is loosely defined, and includes simple chair cushions and slipcovers, as well as slightly more involved projects. The techniques range from sewing straight seams to beginners' upholstery methods that require not much more than a staple gun and some batting or foam. No matter what your experience level, you'll surely acquire new skills as you go, discovering and adapting methods that can be applied to a multitude of furniture projects throughout your home.

IN THIS CHAPTER: BASIC DAYBED COVER — UPHOLSTERED DINING CHAIR — CUSHION-TOP BLANKET CHEST — PADDED HEADBOARD — UPHOLSTERED COFFEE TABLE — SLIPCOVERED PATIO DAYBED — REUPHOLSTERED CAMP STOOLS — EASY CHAISE CUSHIONS — HAWAIIAN-PATTERN STENCILED CUSHIONS — FITTED ARMCHAIR SLIPCOVERS — VELVET CHAIR SKIRT — SLIPCOVERED END TABLE — OMBRÉ HEADBOARD COVER — SIMPLEST BED FRAME SLIPCOVER — CREWELWORK HEADBOARD COVER

BASIC DAYBED COVER (OPPOSITE): *A formal fabric set against a rustic backdrop is unexpectedly stylish. This Mission daybed is covered with an Arts and Crafts–style silk damask. The cushion shows one side of the pattern; the pillow, its reverse.*

basic daybed cover SEE PHOTO, PAGE 333

Although its scale may seem daunting, sewing a daybed cover is not at all complicated—six rectangles are simply sewn together to form a box shape.

MATERIALS basic sewing supplies, daybed frame, upholstery foam, upholstery-weight fabric

HOW-TO Measure the length and width of the daybed frame; have a piece of 4- to 6-inch-thick (10–15cm) foam cut to size (or carefully cut it yourself with a large serrated knife or saw). From the fabric, you will need to cut one top piece and one bottom piece (width by length), 2 short side pieces (width by height), and 2 long side pieces (length by height). Add 1 inch (2.5cm) to the length, width, and height measurements of each for seam allowances; using these measurements, cut out the fabric. With a ½-inch (13mm) seam allowance, sew all four side pieces together, end to end and right sides together, alternating between long-side and short-side pieces to make one long strip. Sew the open ends together to make a four-sided box. Press seams open. Pin the side (box) piece to the top piece, right sides together (match the long and short sides); sew with a ½-inch (13mm) seam allowance. Press seams open. To turn a corner, leave the machine's needle down; lift the presser foot. Rotate the fabric. Lower the presser foot and continue sewing. Pin the side piece to the bottom piece, right sides together with a ½-inch (13mm) seam allowance. Sew three sides, leaving one short side open. Press seams open. Turn right-side out. Insert the foam: Bunch the fabric and pull it over the foam to enclose completely. Reach inside the cover and adjust the foam and fabric as needed, making sure the corners fit snugly. Slipstitch the open edge shut.

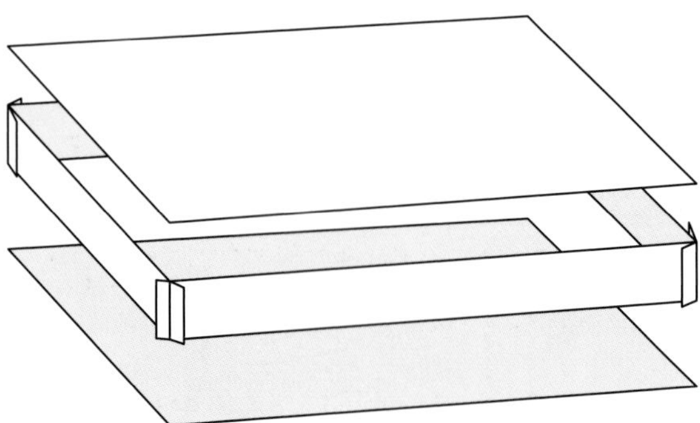

ABOUT UPHOLSTERY SUPPLIES

+ Upholstery foam is sturdy, comfortable, and easy to work with. You can buy foam in precut sizes or have it cut to size; look for it at fabric or upholstery-supply stores, or from online retailers. It is sold according to density.

+ Cotton or polyester batting, which comes in a variety of thicknesses, adds a layer of softness and loft; several projects in this chapter use ½-inch-thick (13mm) batting.

+ For furniture with a distinctive shape or curved edges, make a pattern out of muslin before cutting your fabric. This will help you get the best fit.

+ A staple gun is indispensable for securing fabric in place; staples come in a variety of sizes.

+ For some projects, you may wish to cover visible staples with upholstery trim; a variety of flat trim is available at fabric and upholstery-supply stores. You may also consider using decorative upholstery nails, available at many fabric and hardware stores; use a tack hammer, also available at hardware and upholstery-supply stores, to drive the nails.

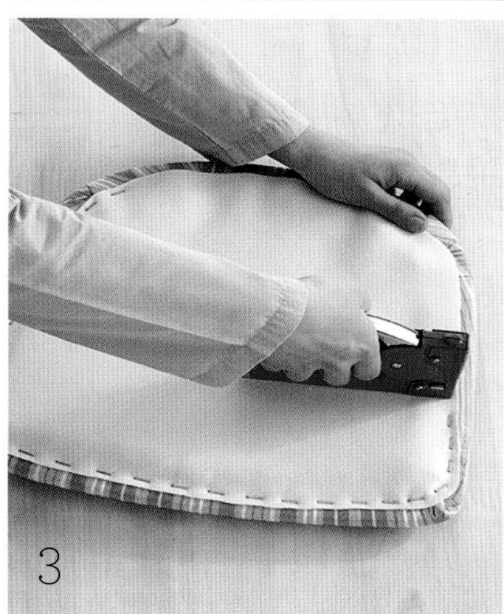

upholstered dining chair

With some fabric and a staple gun, it's easy to update a set of upholstered dining chairs. You can also use this technique to transform a hodgepodge collection of chairs into a coordinated set with matching seat covers.

MATERIALS basic sewing supplies, chair, upholstery-weight fabric for seat (about ⅔ yard [61cm] per chair), felt for underside (about ⅔ yard [61cm] per chair), screwdriver, 1-inch-thick (2.5cm) foam (see "Upholstery Supplies," opposite), cotton batting, staple gun

HOW-TO 1. Unscrew the seat from the chair's frame. Remove the cover and the padding until you hit the middle board; reserve the board. Cover the seat: Trace the board onto 1-inch (2.5cm) thick foam; cut foam about ⅛ inch (3mm) larger than the outline on all sides. Cut the batting and upholstery fabric 2 inches (5cm) larger than the seat on all sides. Cut a piece of felt 1 inch (2.5cm) smaller than the outline on all sides. Stack fabric (facedown), batting, foam, and board, in that order.

2. Attach the fabric and batting to the board with a staple in the center of the front side; pull the fabric and batting taut and staple the center of the back side. Repeat with the left and right sides. Continue stapling, working toward the corners and adding staples in pairs on the opposite sides. Round the corners by pleating the fabric and the batting.

3. Staple the felt to the underside to cover the exposed edges. Screw the chair seat back into the frame with the original hardware.

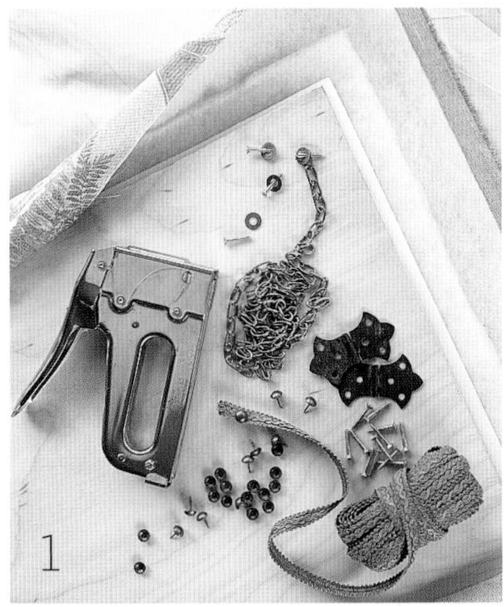
1

2

3

cushion-top blanket chest

An upholstered plywood lid transforms a large cedar planter into a blanket chest that doubles as a bench. Planters such as this one are widely available at home centers and garden-supply stores. They are a natural choice for storing linens, since cedar is durable and absorbent, and cedar's pleasant, musky scent discourages moths. If you use a different-size planter, cut the plywood to the planter's length and to its width plus 1 inch (2.5cm); adjust other materials accordingly.

MATERIALS 5-by-2 1/2-by-2-foot (152.5m × 76cm × 61cm) cedar garden planter, 1 quart (0.9l) each of latex primer and paint, paintbrush, 5-foot-by-2-foot-1-inch (152.5cm × 61cm × 2.5cm) piece of 3/4-inch (2cm) plywood, scissors, spray-mount adhesive, 5-foot-by-2-foot-1-inch (152.5cm × 61cm × 2.5cm) piece of 1-inch (2.5cm) upholstery foam, 5-foot-8-inch-by-2-foot-9-inch (172.5cm × 84cm) piece of cotton batting, 3 yards (2.7m) upholstery fabric (toile is shown), staple gun, 3 yards (2.7m) of upholstery trim, decorative upholstery nails, tack hammer, 5-foot-1-inch-by-2-foot-2-inch (155cm × 66cm) piece of canvas (for underside of lid), 2 to 4 decorative hinges, 1/2-inch (13mm) screws (for hinges and chain), string, wire cutters, 4-foot (1.2m) small-link chain, 2 washers (slightly wider than the link of chain)

HOW-TO 1. Prime and paint the outside and top edge of the cedar planter (latex semigloss is used here), leaving interior unfinished. Working in a well-ventilated area, spray-mount the foam to the plywood, centering so the overhang is even all the way around; top the foam with the batting. Cover both layers with upholstery fabric. Wrap the fabric around the edge of the lid, turning under 1 inch (2.5cm) and pulling the fabric taut; staple it in place: For an even finish, secure the fabric on one side with a staple in the center. Pull fabric taut, and staple the opposite side. Continue stapling, working toward the corners and adding staples in pairs on opposite sides.

2. Position the trim along the outside edge of the plywood board; secure with upholstery nails, using a tack hammer to drive them through the fabric into the wood. Space the nails as desired. To finish the underside of the lid, turn under and press flat a 1-inch (2.5cm) hem along the edges of the canvas. Spray the back of canvas with adhesive and affix to plywood, covering the staples; reinforce it with upholstery nails.

3. Attach the seat with the hinges, securing to the chest and the plywood lid with 1/2-inch (13mm) screws. Make a safety chain: Open the lid to a 90-degree angle plus 2 inches (5cm). With a piece of string, measure the distance from the midpoint of the planter's width to halfway up the width of the lid. With wire cutters, cut the small-link chain this length; attach with 1/2-inch (13mm) screws and washers.

padded headboard

It's much easier than you might think to make your own upholstered headboard. Here, a padded insert adds a pillowy center to a vintage wooden headboard. Matelassé, a textured fabric commonly used for bedding, gives it a luxurious appearance. This technique works for any headboard with molding that creates a "frame" around a recessed area. Because the plywood required is fairly thin, avoid staples that are more than 1/4 inch thick (6mm), which could poke through the fabric. Paint the headboard before upholstering, if desired.

MATERIALS scissors, headboard with a recessed panel, 1/4-inch-thick (6mm) plywood, 1/2-inch-thick (13mm) batting, spray-mount adhesive, upholstery-weight fabric (such as matelassé), staple gun with 1/4-inch (6mm) staples, Velcro strips

HOW-TO 1. Cut plywood about 1/4 inch (6mm) smaller than the recessed area of the headboard. Cut 2 pieces of batting: The first should be about 3 inches (7.5cm) smaller on all sides than the plywood to create a raised center; the second piece should be the same dimensions as the plywood. Using spray-mount adhesive, affix the smaller piece of batting, then the larger piece, to the plywood. Cut a piece of fabric about 3 inches (7.5cm) larger than the plywood on all sides. Lay the board with the batting side down on top of the fabric (right-side down). Wrap fabric around board and attach with a staple in the center of the top edge; pull the fabric and the batting taut and staple the center of the bottom edge. Repeat with the left and right sides. Continue stapling, working toward the corners and adding staples in pairs on opposite sides.

2. Staple Velcro strips along the perimeter of the recessed area on the headboard and along the perimeter of the back of the fabric board. Position the fabric board against the headboard, and attach.

1

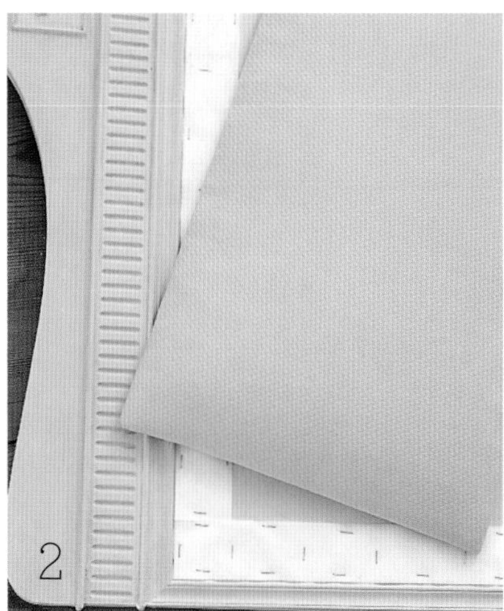

2

upholstered coffee table

This handsome table was originally an ottoman; it was found at a flea market and reupholstered in heavy chenille fabric. To make one like it, you will also need decorative upholstery nails and a tack hammer for the nailhead trim, plus black fabric to hide the stapled edges underneath.

MATERIALS basic sewing supplies, ottoman, upholstery-weight fabric (chenille is shown), plain black cotton or other light-weight fabric, cotton batting, staple gun, decorative upholstery nails, tack hammer

HOW-TO Remove the original fabric. Measure the width and length of the ottoman's top. Add the cushion height plus 3 inches (7.5cm) to all sides, and cut the fabric to this dimension. Center the fabric right-side down on the ottoman, and mark the 4 corners of the top with tailor's chalk. Pin the fabric together snugly at the corner seams; mark the seam lines with tailor's chalk. Remove the fabric. Sew the corners along the tailor's chalk lines. Trim excess fabric from the corners. Turn the cover right-side out, and press. Cut a piece of batting to fit the ottoman's top; place batting on ottoman. Slip the cover over it. Turn the ottoman upside down, and pull the fabric to the underside. Carefully cut away the fabric around the legs. Staple the fabric in place: For the most even finish, secure the fabric on one side with a staple in the center. Pull the fabric taut, and staple the opposite side. Continue stapling, working toward the corners and adding staples in pairs on opposite sides. Cut a piece of black fabric to the dimensions of the underside of the ottoman. Fold under 1/2 inch (13mm) on all sides, and press it flat. Staple in place. Hammer decorative upholstery nails around the perimeter of the stool.

slipcovered patio daybed

A smart-looking slipcover transfers a camp cot into a fetching daybed. The cover's construction is basic: A boxy cushion trimmed in coordinating piping rests atop a skirted slipcover made from the same pattern. Choose fabric designed for outdoor use, such as Sunbrella®. You may use store-bought piping or handmade. Look for a camp cot at camping-supply stores. If desired, paint the frame to complement the fabric.

MATERIALS basic sewing supplies, camp cot, 4-inch-thick (10cm) foam, outdoor upholstery fabric, coordinating outdoor upholstery fabric for piping and ties, piping cord, outdoor upholstery fabric for lining

HOW-TO 1. Measure the length and width of the cot; have foam cut to size. Cut daybed cover pieces as described for Basic Daybed Cover (page 334); sew the four side pieces together to make a box shape, as described, and press seams open. Measure the perimeter of the top piece; multiply this number by 3 to determine how much piping you'll need (the daybed pictured has piping on the top and bottom edge of the cushion as well as along the skirt's bottom edge). Make the piping (see page 373 for instructions). Pin and machine-baste the piping, using a zipper foot, to the right sides of the top and bottom pieces, facing inward, with the cord ½ inch (13mm) from the edge; clip the corners. Sew the side piece to the top piece, right sides together, with the piping sandwiched in between. Repeat with the bottom piece, leaving one short end open. Insert the foam into the daybed cover; slipstitch the opening closed.

2. Make the skirted slipcover: Cut a piece of fabric the same length and width as the cot (do not add a seam allowance, since the piece should end up slightly smaller than the cot). Subtract 1 inch from the cot's length and width; using these measurements, cut out the skirt side pieces from upholstery fabric and lining: You should have two long sides and two short sides in each fabric, each 9 ½ inches (24cm) high. Cut two long pieces of piping and two short pieces to match skirt dimensions. Pin upholstery fabric and lining pieces right sides together, with piping sandwiched in between along the bottom edge (the piping should be facing inward, with raw edges aligned). Using a zipper foot and with a ½-inch (13mm) seam allowance, stitch around sides and bottom edge of each skirt piece. Turn pieces right-side out. Sew the unfinished sides to the top piece, right sides together, with a ½-inch (13mm) seam allowance. Press the seam allowances to the inside of the skirt.

3. Make the ties: Cut eight 13-by-2-inch (33cm × 5cm) strips of fabric. Turn under one short end ½ inch (13mm) and stitch. Fold the long edges inward ½ inch (13mm) so they meet in the center; fold the strip in half lengthwise. Edgestitch closed. Repeat to make remaining strips. Hand-stitch the ties to the skirt sides, 3 inches (7.5cm) from the top. Tie the slipcover to the cot; top it with the daybed cushion.

reupholstered camp stools

Camp stools can provide extra outdoor seating for guests or serve as side tables. Here a half-dozen stools were updated with cotton fabric in place of the original seat covers. You'll find inexpensive wooden stools at camping-supply stores. The stools shown were treated with milk paint before attaching new covers; you can also use latex paint (see the stools on the opposite page for examples).

MATERIALS basic sewing supplies; camp stool; sandpaper (optional); paint (optional); paintbrush (optional); cotton ticking or other durable fabric, such as canvas; staple gun

HOW-TO 1. Remove the original canvas seat from the stool. If you are painting the stool, sand and paint it before putting on a new cover. Using the original seat as a template, trace a new seat from cotton ticking; add ½ inch (13mm) to all sides and cut it out. Fold the edges under ½ inch (13mm) and stitch ¼ inch (6mm) from edge.

2. With a staple gun, fasten one end of the new seat cover to one side of the stool; wrap it around the crossbar twice, then wrap it around the other crossbar and staple in place.

1

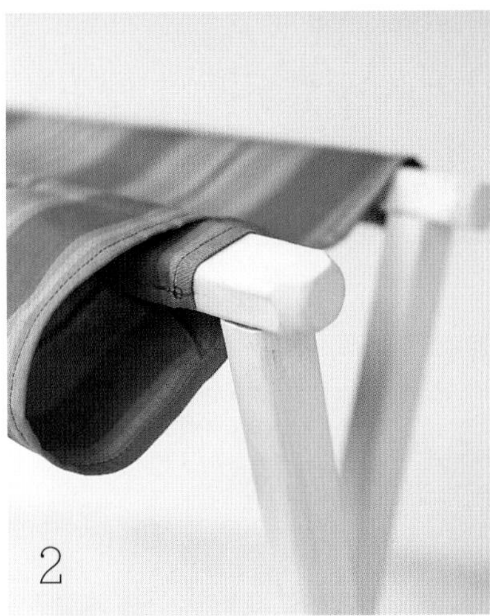

2

easy chaise cushions

Instead of settling for a print that's not quite right, make your own outdoor chaise cushions out of extra-comfy (yet inexpensive) pillows and the fabric of your choice. For each seat, you'll need four bed pillows and waterproof fabric designed for outdoor use, such as Sunbrella. The fabric will protect the pillows from moisture, but it's best to keep the cushions inside between uses.

MATERIALS basic sewing supplies, 2 ½ yards (2.3m) outdoor upholstery fabric, twill tape, 4 polyester-filled bed pillows (22 by 18 inches [56cm × 45.5cm])

HOW-TO Cut a 46-by-77-inch (117cm × 195.5cm) piece of fabric. Fold the fabric in half, right sides facing, so long sides meet, and sew the two short ends shut with a ½-inch (13mm) seam allowance. Turn the fabric right-side out. Using a disappearing-ink fabric pen and a ruler or yardstick, mark horizontal lines to divide the fabric into four equal parts; pin, and sew. Cut sixteen 12-inch (30.5cm) lengths of twill tape; hand- or machine-stitch two pair to each opening, 6 inches (15cm) from each horizontal seam. Insert the pillows, and tie to enclose.

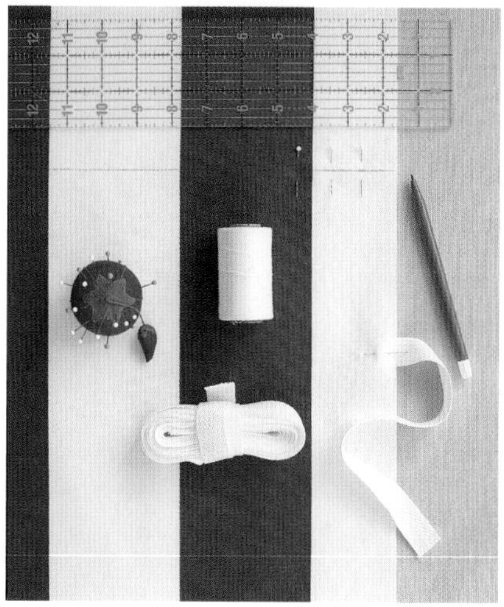

Hawaiian-pattern stenciled cushions

Stenciled floral motifs patterned after Hawaiian quilts enliven a pair of store-bought lounge cushions. Use the template provided, or apply the same technique with the stencil of your choice. (For more information on stenciling, see page 89.)

MATERIALS Hawaiian-pattern stenciled cushions template, ruler or measuring tape, cushion to be embellished, masking tape or painter's tape, waterproof paper, self-healing cutting mat, craft knife, natural sponge, fabric paint

HOW-TO Determine the size you want your motif to be. Choose and print the template (see enclosed CD), resizing as necessary, and cut out. Lightly mark guidelines on the cushion cover with a disappearing-ink fabric pen and ruler or measuring tape. Tape the template to waterproof paper (you may have to tape several pieces together). Place on a self-healing mat and cut out the stencil with a craft knife; discard template. Position the stencil on the cushion, using lines as guides; tape it in place. Dab the sponge in the fabric paint, then gently dab the paint onto the cushion. Let dry for a few minutes, then carefully remove stencil.

fitted armchair slipcovers

A neoclassical-style chair gets a makeover with cotton-velvet panels cut to fit the armrests, seat, and back.

MATERIALS basic sewing supplies, chair, muslin (for pattern), cotton velvet or other upholstery fabric, thin ribbon

HOW-TO Drape muslin over chair seat and trim to the desired shape, cutting curved edges at corners. The cover shown extends ½ inch (13mm) below the cushion underneath. Lay two pieces of velvet, right sides together; place the muslin on top. Add ½ inch (13mm) all around the muslin, and cut out fabric. With a ½-inch (13mm) seam allowance, sew velvet pieces together, clipping corners and leaving 8 inches (20.5cm) open in the back. Turn right-side out, and slipstitch shut. Topstitch around perimeter, ¼ inch (6mm) from edge. Cut eight 8-inch (20.5cm) pieces of ribbon, trimming on the diagonal. Tack ribbons to the corners of the slipcover; tie in place. Trace armrest shape onto muslin, adding ½ inch (13mm) all around; cut out. Place two pieces of velvet right sides together and cut out armrest pieces (four total). With a ½-inch (13mm) seam allowance, sew each set of two armrest pieces together, leaving a small opening. Turn right-side out, and slipstitch shut. Topstitch ¼ inch (6mm) from edge. Tack eight 8-inch (20.5cm) pieces of ribbon onto armrest pieces; tie in place. Measure height and width of the seat back cushion; add 1 inch (2.5cm) to the height and 1 inch (2.5cm) to each measure. With a ½-inch (13mm) seam allowance, sew each set of two pieces together, right sides facing, leaving an 8-inch (20.5cm) opening. Turn right-side out, and slip-stitch shut. Topstitch around perimeters, ¼ inch (6mm) from edge. Tack ribbons to the tops of both pieces, 2 inches (5cm) from the edges. Drape slipcover over the seat back; tie in place.

velvet chair skirt

A fitted cover in textured velvet gives a sharp look to the seat of an open-back chair. Velcro fasteners allow the cover to be easily attached or removed; the fasteners are sewn to tabs at the back corners for a tailored fit.

MATERIALS basic sewing supplies, chair, muslin (for seat pattern), velvet or other upholstery fabric, 1-inch-wide (2.5cm) Velcro tape

HOW-TO Using muslin, make a template of the seat's top; add 1/2 inch (13mm) all around for seam allowances. Measure the width of the seat's back edge along cushion from the outside of one leg to the outside of the other; add 2 inches (5cm) for hems and cut a 6 1/2-inch-wide (16.5cm) strip of fabric to this length. (The finished skirt shown is 5 inches [12.5cm] high; cut a wider or narrower strip, if you prefer.) Measure the front section: Start at the inside edge of one back leg, wrap the measuring tape around the front of the seat, and end at the inside edge of the other back leg. Add 1 inch (2.5cm) for hems and cut a 6 1/2-inch-wide (16.5cm) strip to this length. Using a ruler and tailor's chalk, draw a line to mark the center of each piece (on the wrong side); you will use this as a guide when aligning pieces. Sew double hems on the short sides of the back piece: Fold fabric 1/2 inch (13mm), then 1/2 inch (13mm) again; edge-stitch. Fold the short sides of the front piece under 1/2 inch (13mm) and stitch. Double hem the bottom edges of the back and front pieces: Fold 1/2 inch (13mm), then 1/2 inch (13mm) again; edge-stitch. Clip curved portions of the seat top around back rest, and fold under 1/2 inch (13mm); topstitch 1/8 inch (3mm) from the folded edge. Using your center lines as a guide, align the back piece to the back edge of the seat top, right sides together; stitch from the inside edge of one back-rest curve to the inside edge of the other. Fold the unsewn edges (bottom tabs) under 1/2 inch (13mm), and stitch. Cut two 4 3/4-inch (12cm) strips of Velcro. Sew the Velcro pieces to the back tabs. Align the front piece and the front edge of the seat, right sides together, and pin; stitch from the one leg, around the front of the chair, to other leg. Fold the unsewn edges (top tabs) under 1/2 inch (13mm), and stitch. Sew the remaining Velcro pieces to the front tabs. Slip the skirt over the chair seat and fasten the Velcro pieces to secure.

slipcovered end table

With a plum-colored slipcover tied in place to protect its cushioned top, a tall Victorian stool makes a fine bedside table. The small black tray provides a firm surface for a reading lamp and other bedside necessities.

MATERIALS basic sewing supplies, stool or small table, upholstery-weight fabric, small plate or round lid (for drawing rounded corners), ½-inch-wide (13mm) bias tape, grommet kit, 1 yard (0.9m) cotton or silk cord

HOW-TO Measure the length and width of the stool's top; add 4 inches (10cm) to all sides. Cut a piece of fabric to this dimension. To make a rounded corner, find a lid or dessert plate (make sure it fits into the corner of the fabric) to trace the round edge onto the fabric. Repeat for all corners. Cut along the trace line. Measure the perimeter of the fabric; add 1 inch (2.5cm). Cut a piece of bias tape to this length. Fold the tape evenly over the unfinished edge of the fabric, pinning in place as you go. Sew through the tape and the fabric, keeping the tape even and making sure that the stitching goes through all three layers, ⅛ inch (3mm) from the edge of the tape. Fold the tape under ½ inch (13mm) where the ends meet, and stitch in place. To place the grommet holes, fold each corner on the diagonal. Mark a spot on both sides of the folded fabric that is approximately 3 inches (7.5cm) from the bottom edge and 1 inch (2.5cm) from the fold. Mark two more spots, each 2 inches (5cm) from the fold. Install a grommet (see page 370) at each spot, four to a corner. Thread an 8-inch (20.5cm) length of cord through each set of grommet holes. Tie knots in the ends to keep the cord from sliding through. Tie the cord together to hold the slip-cover in place.

ombré headboard cover

This monochromatic bedroom features a headboard of sky-blue linen dyed in an ombré pattern (page 82), with pillowcases to match. The amount of fabric you will need depends on its width and the size of your headboard; if possible, use fabric that is 60 inches (152.5cm) wide.

MATERIALS basic sewing supplies, plain upholstered headboard, linen or other upholstery-weight fabric, binder clips, noniodized salt, fabric dye, soda ash fixer

HOW-TO Measure the headboard. For the back piece, add 1 inch (2.5cm) to the width and 1 1/2 inches (3.8cm) to the height; cut out a piece of fabric to these dimensions and set it aside (this piece will not be dyed). Cut another piece of fabric 8 inches (20.5cm) wider on each side and 8 inches (20.5cm) longer on one side than the headboard: After dyeing, this piece will be cut into the front, top, and side pieces. Lay out the fabric horizontally on a large work area, and make four vertical accordion folds. Pin through all layers in horizontal rows to mark the shade levels, which should be parallel to the long end when fabric is unfolded. Fold down the remaining fabric, and secure with binder clips to keep it out of the dye solution. Dye according to ombré instructions (page 78). When the fabric has dried, cut it into front, top, and side pieces (add 1/2 inch [13mm] on all sides to the headboard measurements for seam allowances), keeping the dye pattern aligned. Sew two side pieces to the top piece, using a 1/2-inch (13mm) seam allowance. Sew the side piece to the front and back pieces. Double hem the bottom edge: Fold 1/2 inch (13mm), then 1/2 inch (13mm) again, and edge-stitch. Pull the slipcover over the headboard.

simplest bed frame slipcover

Panels of brown-and-white cotton ticking sewn along the top rails of a bed frame follow the profiles of the head- and footboard. The panels are tied at the sides, emphasizing the crisp look of the room.

MATERIALS basic sewing supplies, bed frame, kraft paper, pencil, cotton ticking, linen or other medium-weight fabric

HOW-TO For a headboard with a level top, simply drape fabric over the headboard, cut it to fit, and hem the edges. If you're using a headboard with an angled top, like the one shown, make a template first: Lay the headboard on a piece of kraft paper and trace to make a template; add ½ inch (13mm) to the top for seam allowances and 1 inch (2.5cm) to each side and bottom edge for hems. Cut out the template, then use it to cut out the front and back pieces of the headboard cover. Measure the length and width of the headboard's top, adding 2 inches (5cm) to the length for hems and 1 inch (2.5cm) to the width for seam allowances. Cut a strip of fabric to these dimensions, for the top piece. Pin and sew together the top piece to the front and back pieces, right sides together, with ½-inch (13mm) seam allowances. Double hem the sides and the bottom edges: old ½ inch (13mm), then ½ inch (13mm) again; press and edge-stitch. Press seams open. Make the ties: Cut eight 12-by-2-inch (30.5cm × 5cm) strips of fabric. Turn under one short end ½ inch (13mm) and stitch. Fold the long edges inward ½ inch (13mm) so they meet in the center; fold the strip in half lengthwise. Machine-stitch ⅛ inch (3mm) from the edge. Repeat with the remaining strips. Hand-stitch the ties to the slipcover front and back; tie to secure the slipcover.

CREWELWORK HEADBOARD COVER: *Since fabric yardage is not always wide enough to cover a large headboard, the slipcover shown here was sewn from a duvet cover patterned with leafy crewelwork. The embroidered fabric's distinctive pattern and texture make luxurious bedroom accents. To make one like it, measure the front, back, sides, and top of a headboard; cut pieces ½ inch (13mm) larger on all sides for seam allowances. Sew the side pieces and top together to make one long strip. Baste piping to the front and back pieces; sew to the side-top piece. Double hem all along the bottom edge, and slip the cover over the headboard.*

PROJECT:

wall décor

Walls adorned with fabric-based artwork provide a pleasing counterpoint to other decorative home accents and details. Indeed, the fibers in these framed pieces—linen, velvet, wool, cotton, and felt—bring a sense of softness to any room. And using techniques such as three-dimensional ribbon embroidery or appliqué brings additional textural elements into play.

All of the projects in this chapter combine fabric, notions, and needlework, and all can be adapted by changing the colors and textures you choose; they include keepsake wall art for a nursery, an embroidered letter sampler, and a star-patterned design that speaks to quilting (but takes a fraction of the time needed to complete a bed cover). Best of all, because of their size, the projects are portable. You can work on them while curled up in a chair, sitting on the bus or train, or any time you have a few spare minutes and are feeling creative.

IN THIS CHAPTER: RIBBON-EMBROIDERED WALL HANGINGS — FARMYARD APPLIQUÉ WALL HANGING — EMBROIDERED LETTER SAMPLER — FRAMED PATCHWORK STAR

RIBBON-EMBROIDERED WALL HANGINGS (OPPOSITE): *A grouping of picture-perfect plants, created with embroidery tools and thin ribbon, was inspired by pressed and framed flowers, popular decorations in the Victorian era. Shown, clockwise from left, are magnolia, delphiniums, cosmos, ferns, dogwood, lily of the valley, daffodils, and hydrangea. (All the flowers shown here are also shown in detail on page 58 in the embroidery technique section.) Start with a piece of linen slightly larger than your frame. Make a rough drawing of the flower design on the linen with a disappearing-ink fabric pen. Embroider the flowers, using the instructions and the glossary on page 58 for inspiration. For thin stems, use embroidery floss; embroider thick stems with embroidery ribbon. When finished, frame the embroidered linen (see page 353 for instructions).*

ZIM · MARTIN FLOWERS SIMON AND SCHUSTER
OUR NORTHERN SHRUBS
KEELER
SCRIBNERS
THE TREES OF NORTH-EASTERN AMERICA

farmyard appliqué wall hanging

Decorate a baby's or small child's room with this scene of a bucolic farmyard, complete with linen sky and grass, trees that sprout gingham checks and polka dots, and a soft felt-and-corduroy menagerie. Three appliqué techniques are used here: the classic hand-turn method covered on page 41, another method that incorporates freezer paper to produce a stiff edge for folding over the seam allowance, and another that uses Mylar to make precise shapes (such as circles).

MATERIALS basic sewing supplies, farmyard appliqué wall hanging templates, frame, green and blue linen, brown ribbon, assorted fabrics for appliqué motifs, freezer paper, spray starch, small paintbrush, heat-resistant Mylar

HOW-TO 1. Cut a piece of blue linen to fit your frame. Following the hand-turn appliqué method on page 41, appliqué a strip of green linen to the blue linen to create a grass field. Appliqué brown ribbon to the linen for tree trunks. Print the templates (see enclosed CD; adjust size, if desired), and cut out. If using felt or other nonwoven fabrics, trace template directly onto fabric; cut out. (These don't fray, so no seam allowance is needed; simply slip-stitch the felt designs to the background.) For all other fabrics, first cut shape from freezer paper: trace the templates onto the shiny side of the paper, and cut out. Place freezer paper backing, shiny side down, on wrong side of fabric; press with medium-heat dry iron.

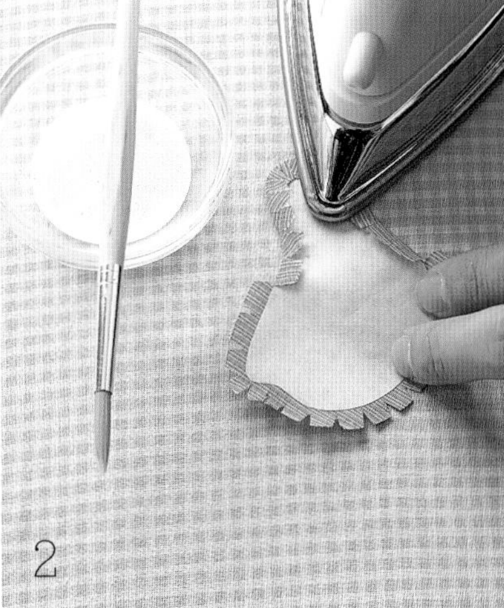

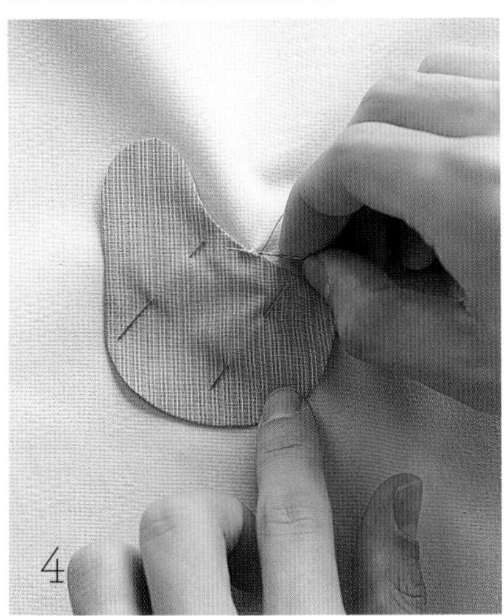

2. Draw a 1/4-inch (6mm) seam allowance around the shape; cut fabric along seam allowance. At curves, cut slits at 3/8-inch (10mm) intervals around seam allowance. Cut extra slits around concave areas to ensure smoothness. Notch convex areas to prevent pleating. For outside corners, cut slits at 45-degree angle to reduce bulk. For inside corners, cut a single slit at a 45-degree angle. Spray some starch into a bowl; brush on to seam allowance to stiffen. With medium-heat dry iron, fold seam allowance over freezer paper and press (if shape has curves and corners, turn under points first). If freezer paper sticks to fabric, lower iron temperature.

3. For perfect circular treetops and tractor wheels, trace the round templates onto Mylar; cut them out. Lay the Mylar on the wrong side of the fabric; trace with a disappearing-ink fabric pen, adding a 1/4-inch (6mm) seam allowance. Cut out. Baste around the seam allowance; tug on the thread until the fabric gathers around the shape without puckering; knot the end. Brush starch onto the seam allowance, Press it flat; let it cool. Remove the basting stitches and remove the Mylar.

4. Mark the placement of the appliqué pieces onto the background with a disappearing-ink fabric pen. Pin center of shapes to background fabric. With thread, sew around perimeter (not through freezer paper, if using) with a slipstitch as follows: Pull knotted thread up through folded edge of appliqué, not background fabric. Pick up a thread or two from background fabric slightly under appliqué. Insert needle back into folded edge of appliqué 3/16 inch (5mm) from previous stitch; pull thread through. Continue around shape, leaving a small opening.

5. Remove pins; carefully remove freezer paper, if using, and stitch opening closed.

HOW TO FRAME FABRICS

To frame a fabric-based wall hanging, you'll need a frame; acid-free foam-core board cut to fit the size of the frame; and acid-free tape. (Using acid-free materials will help keep your artwork from deteriorating in the frame over time.) Have the foam core cut to size at a framing store; look for acid-free tape at most art-supply, crafts, and organizing stores. Stretch the fabric over the foam core, making sure the design is centered and the grain of the fabric is parallel to the edge of the foam core. Use acid-free tape to secure the fabric to the back of the foam core. Insert the mounted work into the frame, then insert and lock the back of the frame.

embroidered letter sampler

Traditionally, alphabet samplers were created by young women learning to embroider letters and numbers, which they would later use to monogram linens. Today, a sampler makes a charming decoration, particularly in a child's room. If you're embroidering on white linen, work with multiple colors of floss (seven were used here). On black or another dark-colored linen, use one tone, such as white or ecru floss, to re-create the charm of an old-time chalkboard.

MATERIALS basic sewing supplies, pen, paper, transfer paper, heat-transfer pencil, linen, frame, large embroidery hoop (optional), embroidery floss, embroidery needle

HOW-TO 1. Write letters on a plain piece of paper to desired size (it may be helpful to work on a grid), or download a favorite copyright-free font. Trace the mirror images of the letters onto transfer paper with the heat-transfer pencil. Cut the linen to fit the frame with a border all around. With the transfer paper facedown, press the letters onto the linen. Fit the fabric right-side up in the hoop, if using.

2. Cut an 18-inch (45.5cm) length of embroidery floss, and split the 6 threads into 3 pair. Stem-stitch (page 48) each letter. Don't knot the ends of the floss or they will leave marks in the linen: Instead, secure with a few tiny backstitches, or pull through at least 1 inch (2.5cm) of the floating threads on the back of the fabric. Clip the ends of the floss carefully. Start and end each length this way. Have the sampler professionally framed, or frame it yourself, following the instructions on page 353.

1

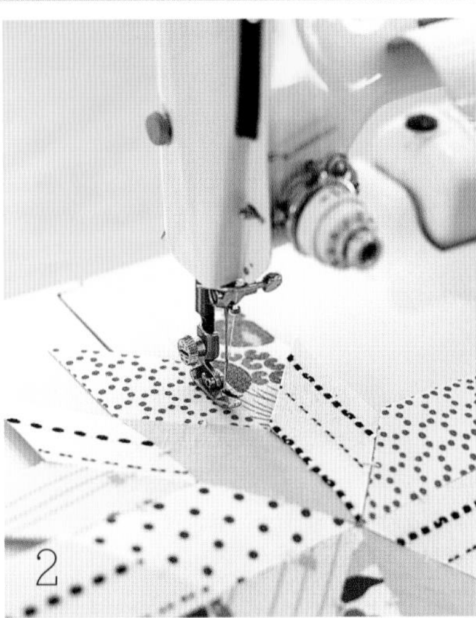

2

framed patchwork star

Crafted in the manner of traditional star pattern–quilted bedcovers, this framed patchwork looks right at home in a modern setting. For more on star-pattern quilting, see page 68.

MATERIALS basic sewing supplies; solid and patterned medium-weight fabric scraps (such as poly-cotton blend, medium-weight wool, or cotton shirting fabric); medium-weight fusible web; plastic 45-degree angle; rotary cutter; self-healing cutting mat; fabric glue; background fabric (such as linen)

HOW-TO 1. Back scraps of fabric with medium-weight fusible web (affixed with a hot, dry iron). Mark the backs of the fabric scraps with vertical lines spaced 2 inches (5cm) apart. Then, with the angle as a guide, mark a second set of lines every 2 inches (5cm) across the first set, creating diamond shapes (as shown). (For a 24-inch (61cm) square frame, you will need 48 diamonds.) Place fabric on a cutting mat and, using a ruler as a guide, cut along the lines with the rotary cutter.

2. Once all the pieces are cut, lay them on a work surface, and, starting at the center, arrange them as you wish. Stitch the pieces together by machine or by hand. Glue the finished star to the background of your choice, then frame (see page 353). Or ask a professional framer to "float" it in front of a linen-covered board (as shown).

XYZ

tools and materials

The items that follow are those that experienced sewers and fabric crafters reach for most often. If you are new to sewing, there's no need to purchase everything on this list. Instead, reference it when a project calls for something unfamiliar.

NEEDLES AND PINS

HAND-SEWING NEEDLES

SEWING NEEDLE An all-purpose sewing needle of medium size with a small eye is invaluable for hand-sewing. Needle sizes are numbered: 1 is the largest, and 12 the smallest. Sharps are the most common hand-sewing needles; use blunt, or ball-point, needles for knit fabrics.

QUILTING NEEDLE Its short length and sharp point are ideal for making small stitches; the narrow eye ensures the needle passes smoothly through multiple layers. Quilting needles are sometimes called "betweens," and come in sizes 7 (largest) through 12 (smallest).

APPLIQUÉ NEEDLE An appliqué needle should be thin in order to slide easily through the fabric and leave nearly invisible holes.

CREWEL NEEDLE Used for embroidering crewelwork on tightly woven fabric, these needles have sharp tips for piercing fabric, and long eyes to make threading yarn easier. They come in sizes 1 (largest) through 10 (smallest).

CHENILLE NEEDLE These needles have sharp points for embroidering on tightly woven fabric. Their large eyes make them a good choice for ribbon embroidery.

MILLINER'S NEEDLE Also called straw needles, milliners' needles are long and thin with small eyes. They are commonly used for appliqué, and for making long basting stitches when sewing.

TAPESTRY NEEDLE A tapestry needle's blunt point allows it to push between the fibers of loosely woven fabrics, ensuring that the fibers won't snag or break, and allowing for evenly spaced stitches. Use it for embroidery, especially cross-stitch. Needles range in size from 13 (largest) to 26 (smallest).

UPHOLSTERY NEEDLE This large, sharp needle easily pierces heavy-duty fabrics such as canvas or other thick upholstery fabrics.

SASHIKO NEEDLE When embroidering in the Japanese style of sashiko (see page 55), gather a series of running stitches on this extra-long needle before passing it through the cloth.

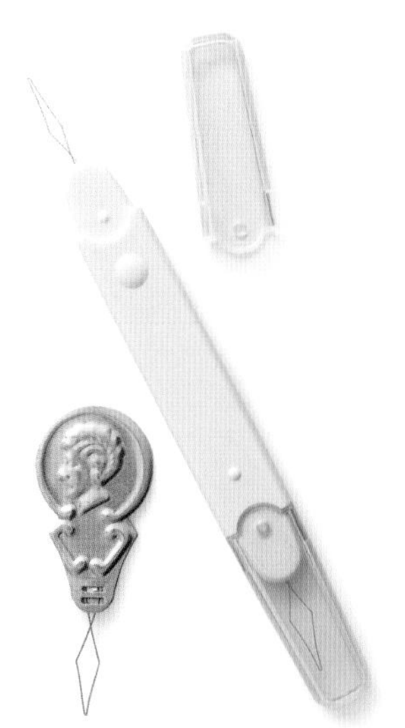

NEEDLE THREADERS

A needle threader guides thread through a needle's tiny eye. The one pictured on the right has two threaders, one standard and one extra-fine. For more on how to use a needle threader, see page 28.

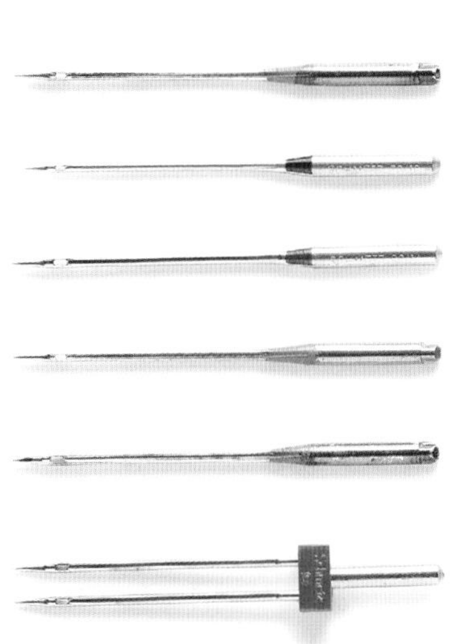

MACHINE NEEDLES

Machine needles come in different styles and shapes; use the size that corresponds to the weight of the fabric you are sewing (unlike for hand-sewing needles, the smaller the number, the finer the needle; 12 is a common all-purpose size). A sharp-point needle is best for woven fabrics, and a blunt point for knit fabrics. Twin needles sew rows of parallel lines. Change needles frequently—after every eight hours of sewing, or when you begin a new project—since a dull needle can damage fabric.

PINS

Different lengths, thicknesses, and head styles of pins are designed for various projects. Colorful ball-head pins are easy to see; however, plastic ball-head pins can melt when ironed (glass ball-head pins or metal flat-head pins will not melt). Long flower-head pins lie flat with the fabric, and are even easier to see. Dressmaker's pins, which are roughly 1¹⁄₁₆ inch to 1½ inches (2.8–3.8cm) long, are useful for almost any project. Choose short pins for detailed work such as appliqué, since you can place many of them close together; long pins are best for piecing together multiple layers of fabric, as when quilting. While most pins are sharp, blunt pins are available for pinning knit fabrics. Pins also vary in thickness: Choose fine pins for sheer, delicate fabrics, and thicker ones for heavier fabrics.

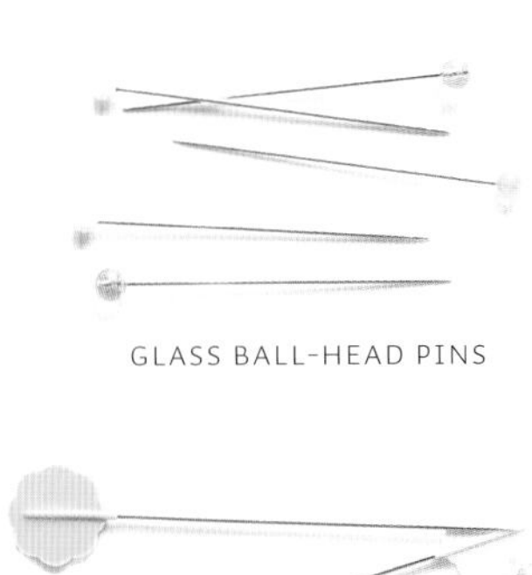

GLASS BALL-HEAD PINS

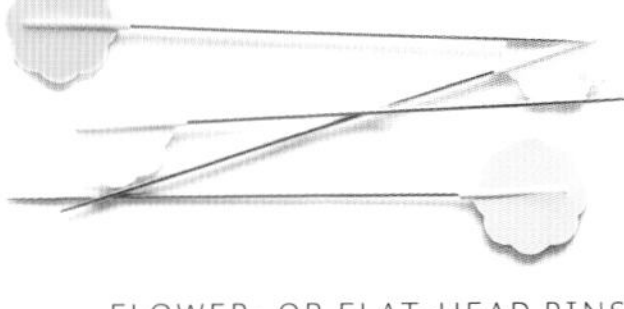

FLOWER- OR FLAT-HEAD PINS

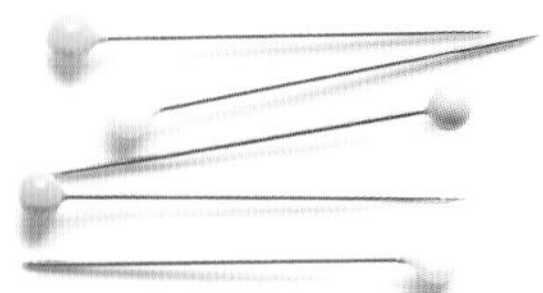

PLASTIC BALL-HEAD PINS

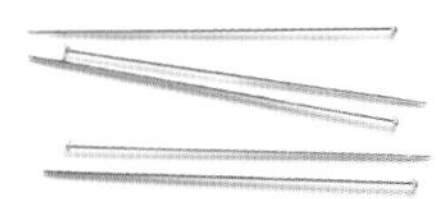

LONG DRESSMAKER'S PINS

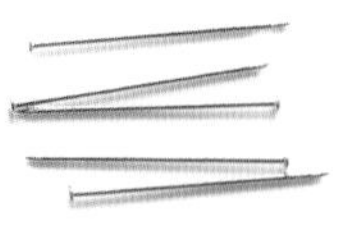

MEDIUM DRESSMAKER'S PINS

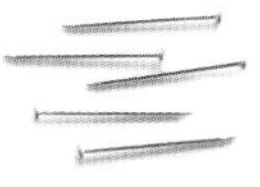

SHORT DRESSMAKERS' PINS

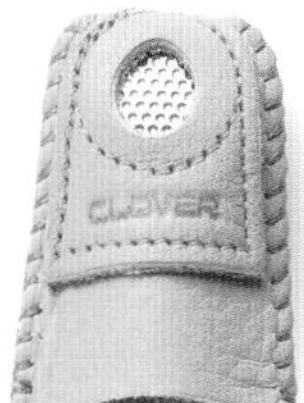

COIN THIMBLE

THIMBLE

THIMBLES

Wear a thimble on the index or middle finger of your sewing hand, and use it to push the needle through the fabric. Traditional thimbles are made of metal, but leather versions, such as the "coin thimble" pictured (above left), are considered more comfortable by some home sewers.

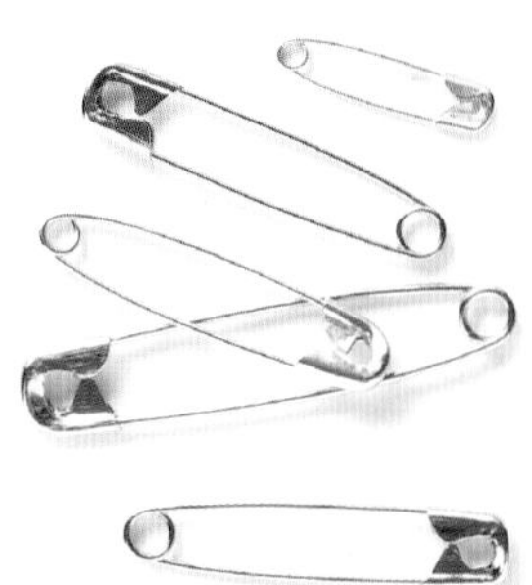

SAFETY PINS

Available in a variety of sizes, shapes, and materials, safety pins hold fabric in place. Use them to secure quilting layers and to thread ribbon or cord through a channel.

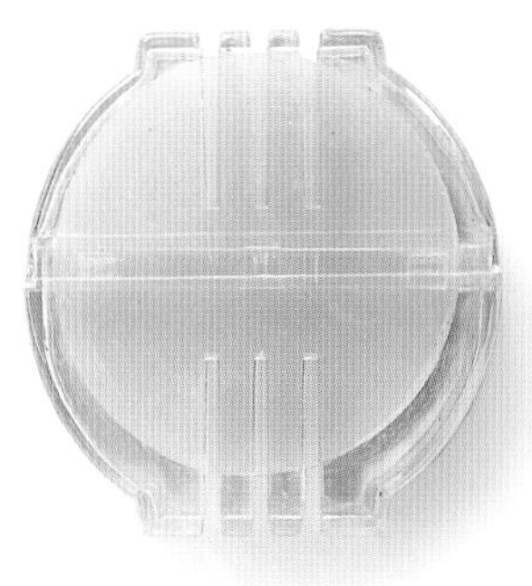

WAX

As you sew, if your thread tangles and knots easily, run it across a disk of beeswax to give it a tangle-resistant coating.

MEASURING TOOLS

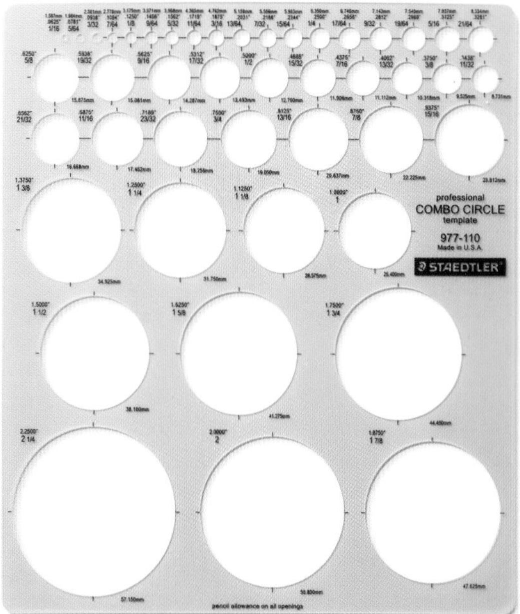

CIRCLE TEMPLATE

Use this tool, available at crafts and office-supply stores, to mark perfect circles on fabric for appliqué, embroidery, or stenciling. It's also handy for rounding off corners.

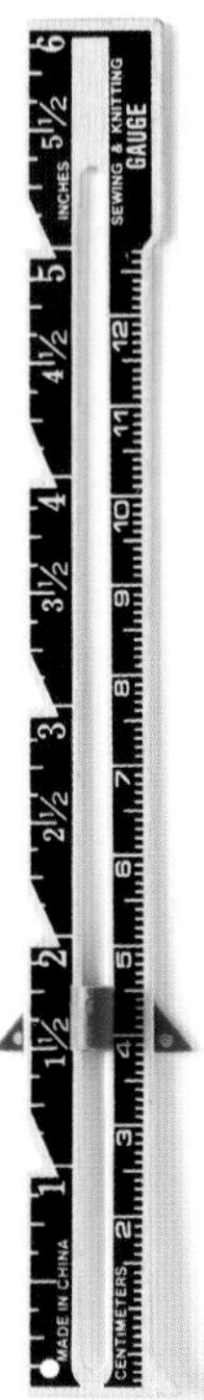

SEAM GAUGE

When sewing a hem or seam, stop periodically and measure it with a seam gauge to ensure that it is even.

FLEXIBLE TAPE MEASURE

This indispensible sewing tool can follow three-dimensional or curved lines to produce accurate measurements; use it to take body measurements.

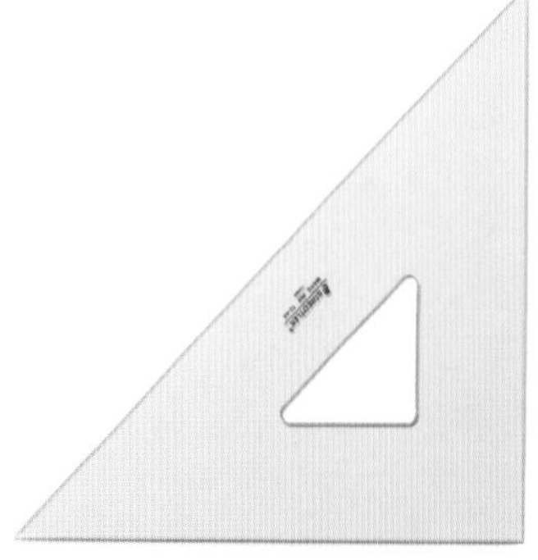

TRIANGLE

A triangle helps you make perfectly square right angles and diagonal lines. This is especially critical when cutting rectangular pieces of fabric for pillows or when squaring the corners of a quilt or blanket.

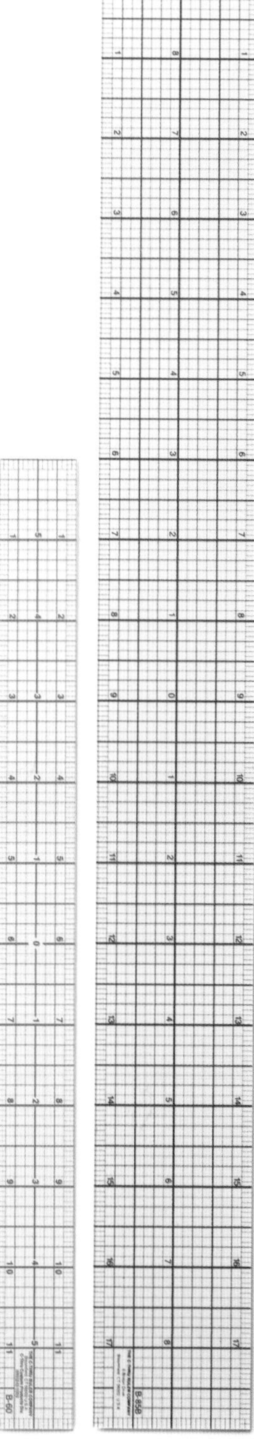

RULERS

Use a ruler to measure dimensions of fabric, or to draft patterns on paper, on a flat work surface. A transparent ruler allows you to see the fabric or paper and any markings underneath; it is also useful for quilting, and is sometimes called a quilting ruler.

MARKING AND PATTERN-MAKING TOOLS

HEAT-TRANSFER PENCIL AND HOT-IRON TRANSFER PEN

Pencils and pens such as these are used to mark designs for embroidering: A design is first drawn on paper, then transferred to the fabric when ironed. Once the lines are applied, they cannot be erased or washed out, so be sure to cover them completely with stitches.

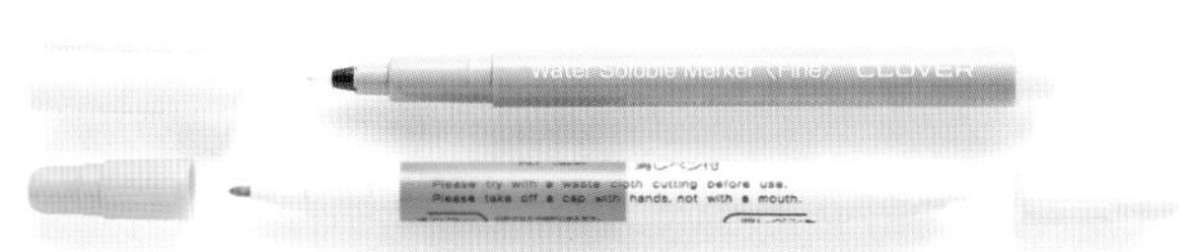

DISAPPEARING-INK FABRIC PENS

There are two types of disappearing-ink fabric pens: A water-soluble pen is used to mark fabrics that can be washed; an air-soluble pen is better for fabrics that shouldn't get wet (the bottom pen has an eraser on one end). Whichever pen you choose, be sure to test it on a small scrap of fabric, as the ink may leave permanent marks on some fabrics.

CHALK PENCILS

Chalk pencils are used to mark lines on fabric when tracing a pattern or template. They are usually white, but are also available in colors such as blue, yellow, or pink. The chalk comes off when the fabric is washed or dry-cleaned; some pencils (top) have a stiff plastic brush at one end for removing the chalk. An artists' pastel pencil (center) also works well; they are sold at art-supply or sewing-supply stores.

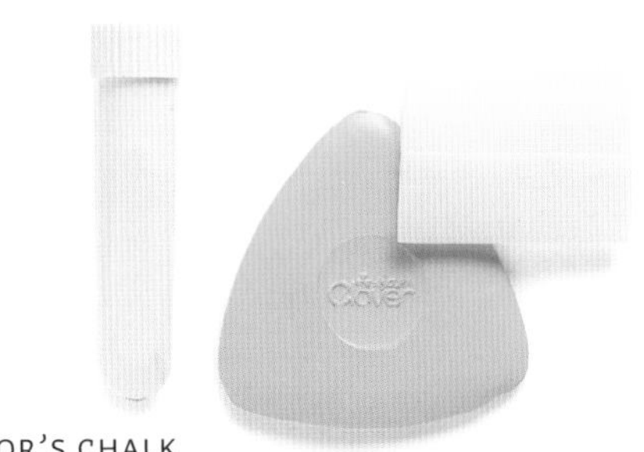

TAILOR'S CHALK

Chalk pens and wedges are the traditional tools for marking fabric, especially for tailoring and altering. A chalk pen (pictured, left) is filled with chalk dust, which brushes off easily (and can be refilled); wedges or blocks of chalk (pictured, center and right) have sharp edges for marking clean lines.

TRANSFER PAPER

Also known as dressmaker's carbon, this paper is used to transfer a design onto fabric for embroidery or appliqué. It comes in several colors; use a shade that will show up clearly. A general rule is dark paper for light fabrics, white paper for dark fabrics.

TRACING WHEEL

To transfer an image from transfer paper to fabric, press firmly along the lines you wish to mark with a tracing wheel. The wheel is nimble enough to follow curved lines. Use a spoked wheel for medium- to heavy-weight fabrics, and a plain wheel for delicate materials. You can also use a ballpoint pen.

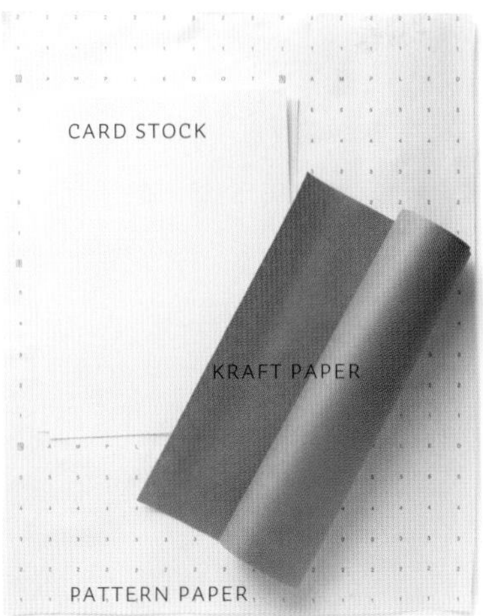

CARD STOCK, KRAFT PAPER, AND PATTERN PAPER

Many sewing projects require a pattern or a template. In such cases, specialized papers may be easier to work with than regular paper. Pattern paper can be pinned to fabric without creating bulk; look for paper with a grid to help you measure and draw accurately. Sturdy card stock and kraft paper work well for templates that will be traced.

CUTTING TOOLS

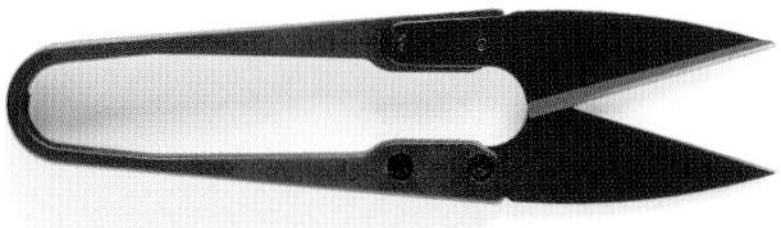

THREAD CLIPS

ALL-PURPOSE SCISSORS

HOT-FORGED STEEL FABRIC SHEARS

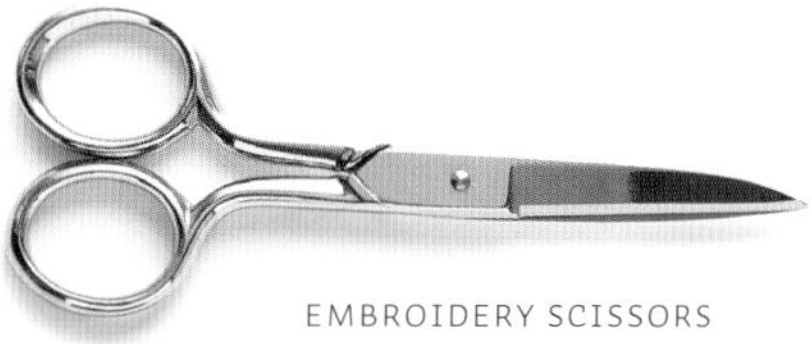

EMBROIDERY SCISSORS

SEAM RIPPER

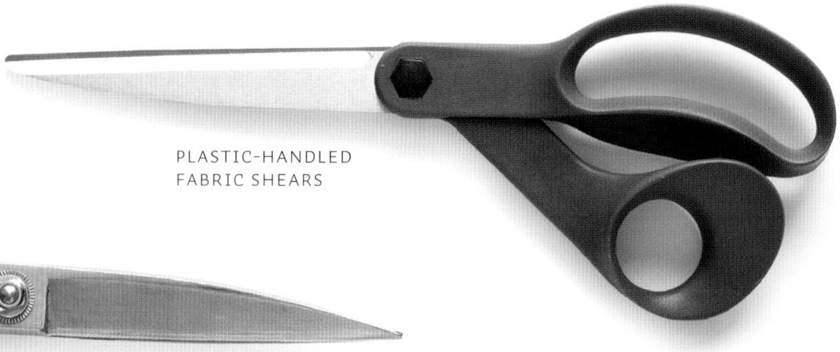

PLASTIC-HANDLED FABRIC SHEARS

BENT-HANDLED FABRIC SHEARS

THREAD CLIPS

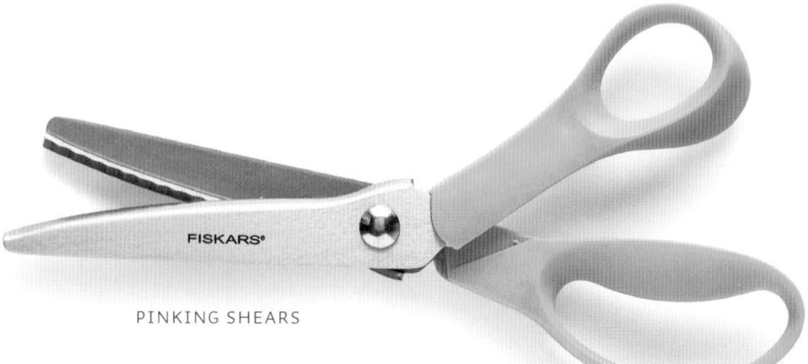

PINKING SHEARS

SMALL ALL-PURPOSE SCISSORS

ALL-PURPOSE SCISSORS

Using scissors to cut paper dulls them, so it's important to have a specified pair of inexpensive all-purpose scissors on hand for cutting paper templates and patterns. Do not use these scissors for cutting fabric, as their dull edges can snag the cloth.

FABRIC SHEARS

Use shears to cut fabric and trim such as bias tape, ribbon, and piping. If you are new to sewing, you may want to start with an inexpensive pair of shears with plastic handles (pictured, center). However, if you are a dedicated sewer, choose hot-forged steel shears (pictured, right, near top), in which each blade and handle piece is forged from one continuous piece of steel; these shears are more durable and will last a lifetime if properly cared for. When buying shears, test them first to see if the shape and weight are comfortable in your hand. Do not use fabric shears to cut paper; it's a good idea to label them "fabric only" or keep them in your sewing box so family members won't use them for other crafts. Sharpen shears regularly: You can buy a sharpener from a sewing store, or take your shears to a professional sharpener. Some manufacturers will also sharpen shears for you.

EMBROIDERY SCISSORS

Small, slender scissors are perfect for cutting embroidery thread, floss, and yarn. Their size allows you to make precise cuts close to the fabric. They also fit inside the diameter of many embroidery hoops and under stitches that you want to snip and remove due to errors. They are also useful for trimming small pieces of fabric for appliqué, or clipping and notching along seam allowances.

BENT-HANDLED FABRIC SHEARS

The angled handle on these shears facilitates cutting that is laid out on a flat surface such as a work table (the flatter the fabric, the more accurate your cuts will be). While a pair of basic fabric shears are sufficient for most sewing projects, you may find a pair of bent-handled shears useful if you sew frequently, and especially if you are often cutting out clothing pieces or other large shapes.

THREAD CLIPS

A thread nipper, which may have a finger loop (pictured, bottom left) but can also come without one (pictured, top right), is a spring-loaded clipper whose short blades easily snip stray threads.

SEAM RIPPER

As its name indicates, a seam ripper is used to safely remove unwanted stitches without damaging the surrounding fabric.

PINKING SHEARS

The zigzag edges of pinking shears cut a sawtooth edge on fabric. This edge is used either to prevent fraying or for decoration. If possible, test shears in the store to make sure the pattern is uniform and the shears are easy to handle.

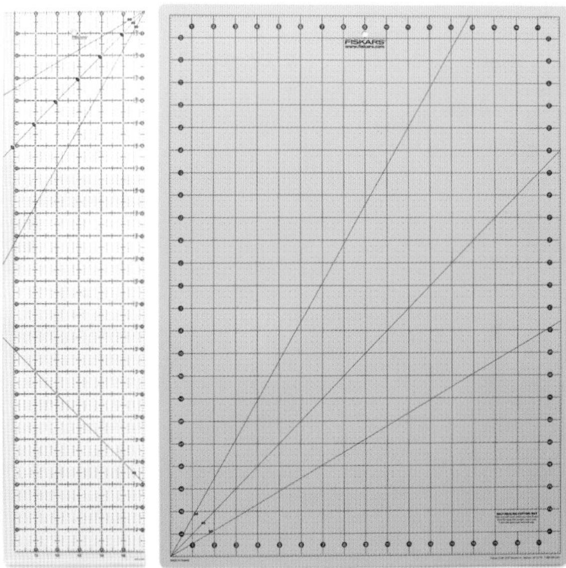

CUTTING MAT WITH ACRYLIC RULER

When cutting repeated straight lines, such as when making squares for patchwork projects, it is best to use a rotary cutter (see right), along with an acrylic ruler (above left) and a cutting mat (above right). The thick acrylic guides the blade of the cutter; the self-healing cutting mat protects your work surface from damage. Diagonal lines on the mat and ruler help you create diamond and triangle shapes from fabric.

ROTARY CUTTER

Available in a variety of blade sizes, from 18 to 60 millimeters in diameter, rotary cutters can be a better option than scissors for cutting precise shapes. Larger blades will cut through fabric more easily and can cut through several layers at once; smaller blades are useful for cutting rounded lines. A switch on the handle retracts the blade for safety. Choose a cutter with a handle that is comfortable to use; the handles come in several different styles.

ADHESIVES

FUSIBLE TAPE AND WEB

Fusible tape and web are used to fuse pieces of fabric together without sewing; heat from an iron bonds the tape or web to the fabric. Use tape for small work, such as hems, and web, which is available in sheets by the yard, for larger pieces. Web is available in different weights; choose the weight that corresponds to the thickness of your fabric and desired thickness of your project.

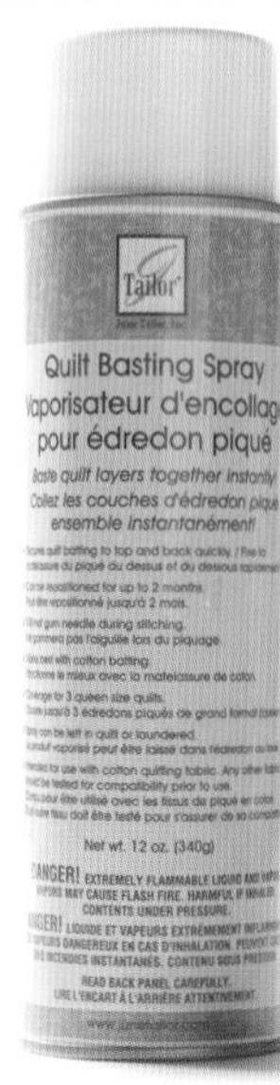

QUILT BASTING SPRAY

Available at fabric and quilting-supply stores, basting spray holds layers of fabric and batting together as you quilt, eliminating the need for hand-basting. You can wash it out after you are finished assembling the quilt, or let it dissipate over time. Some brands may be used on all types of fabric and batting; others are meant to be used only on 100% cotton (check the label).

CRAFT GLUE

Plain white glue, available at crafts stores, is useful for many crafting projects. Diluted glue can also stop fabric edges from fraying.

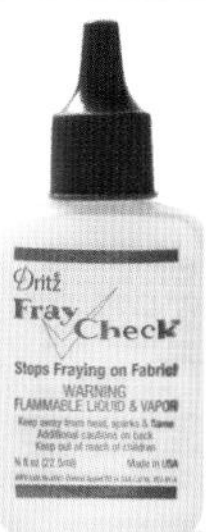

LIQUID SEAM SEALANT

As an alternative to hemming or cutting with pinking shears, you can apply this to the edges of cut fabric and ribbons to keep them from fraying.

TEMPORARY FABRIC ADHESIVE

Use temporary adhesive to bond fabric to batting, stabilizer, patterns, or other fabric; it dissipates after about four to six months, or it can be washed out.

TACKY GLUE

Because it is thicker and generally more adhesive than craft glue, tacky glue is a good choice for many fabric crafts.

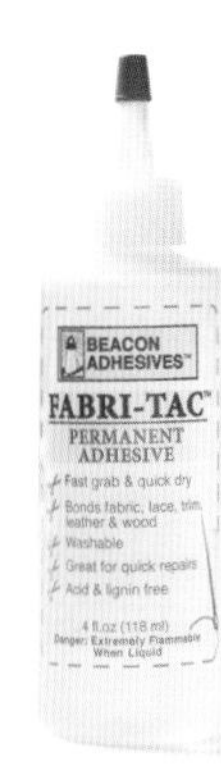

PERMANENT FABRIC ADHESIVE

Use this to glue trim to fabric. The clear gel is washable, although it can be removed by dry-cleaning. For best results, prewash and press fabrics before gluing.

FABRIC GLUE

Use it for no-sew projects, or for quick repairs, such as fixing a hem. The fine tip allows for precise application. Once the glue dries (in 24 hours), the fabric can be machine-washed and -dried.

MISCELLANEOUS

BODKIN AND LOOP TURNER

Use a bodkin (center) to thread a piece of cord, ribbon, or elastic through a channel. In a pinch, a safety pin can be used as a bodkin: Pin through the cord or ribbon, then guide the pin through the channel. Use a loop turner (bottom) to turn a long, thin channel inside out, when making ties, straps, or the tail for a stuffed animal.

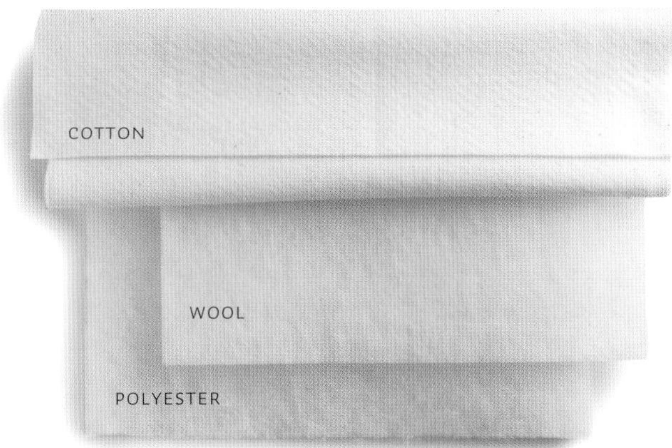

BATTING

A layer of batting adds softness and warmth to a quilt, or padding to upholstered projects. Batting can be made of cotton, wool, or polyester, and comes in a variety of thicknesses (this is known as its loft), from 1/8 inch to 2 inches (3mm–5cm). For more on types of batting, see page 64.

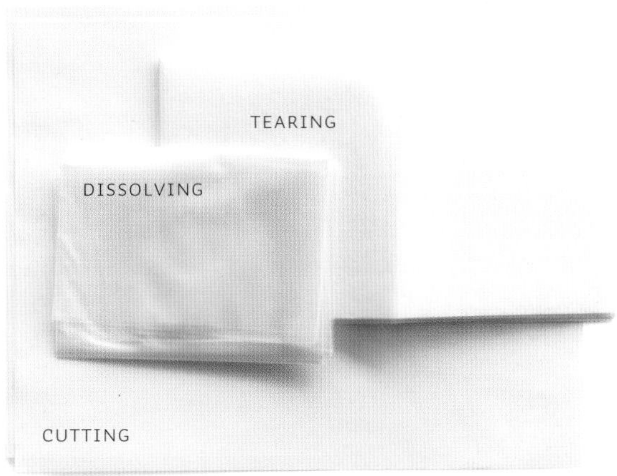

FABRIC STABILIZERS

When embroidering by machine, a fabric stabilizer provides a secure foundation for the stitches, and keeps the embroidered fabric from stretching, which could distort the pattern. After embroidering, some or all of the stabilizer is removed: The most common types of stabilizer are removed either by cutting, tearing, or dissolving (in water or with a hot iron).

TWEEZERS

A pair of tweezers can help you pick up small items, such as tiny pieces of fabric (used for appliqué or other embellishments), stray threads, buttons, or beads.

EMBROIDERY HOOP

Use a hoop to keep fabric taut while you embroider, to prevent buckling and keep fabric free of your working hand. To use, sandwich fabric between the hoop's two rings, and tighten the screw. Remove hoop when you stop stitching to avoid leaving a mark on the fabric. Hoops are made of wood and plastic, and come in many sizes.

POINT TURNER

A point turner, made of wood or plastic, helps you create sharp corners when making pillows or linens with mitered corners; use it to push the corner into shape.

TRIM

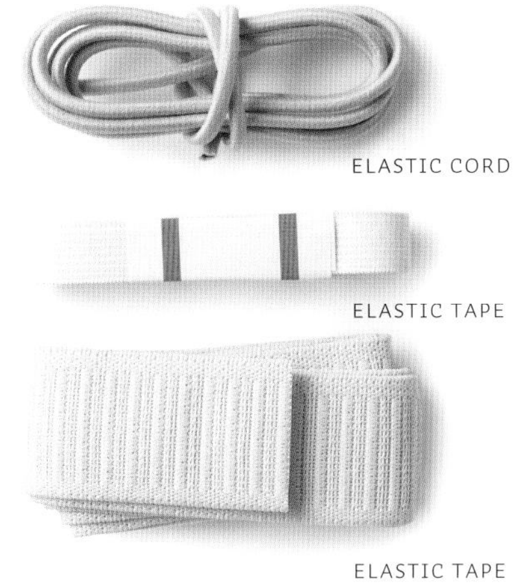
ELASTIC CORD

ELASTIC TAPE

ELASTIC TAPE

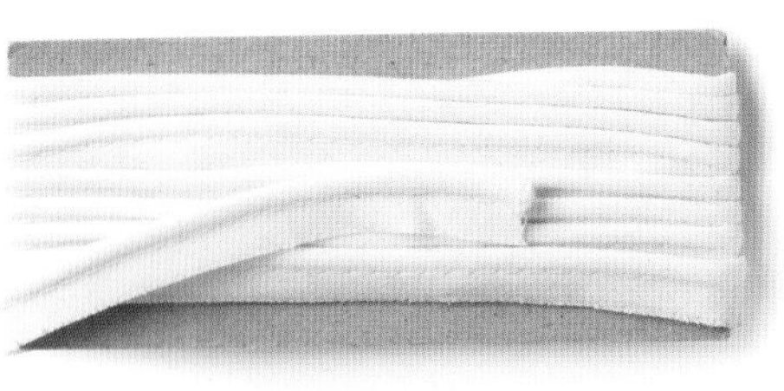

PIPING

DECORATIVE PIPING

TWILL TAPE

CORD

SEAM BINDING

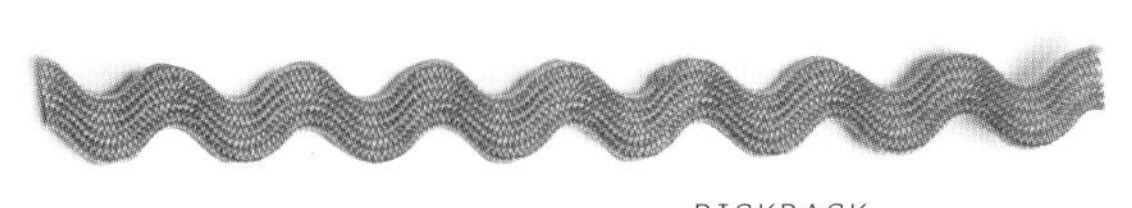
RICKRACK

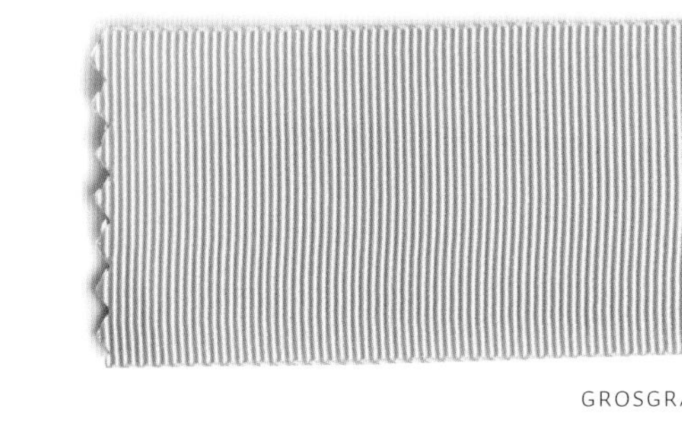
GROSGRAIN RIBBON

ELASTIC Cord or tape can be bought by the yard or in packages; tape is available in a variety of widths. Elastic is most commonly used for clothing, such as in a waistband or puffed sleeves.

PIPING Use piping around the edges of upholstery projects, pillows, and even clothing for a finished look. While the size and texture may vary, all piping has a flat tape edge. Sew along this flat edge, as close to the piping as possible; use a zipper foot for best results. You can also make your own piping, by covering piping cord (sometimes called welting) with the fabric of your choice (see page 373 for instructions).

WEBBING Cotton and nylon webbing—available in assorted widths and colors—make sturdy handles for bags, or for any application that requires a durable strap. Nylon webbing is stronger than cotton.

TWILL TAPE Like twill fabric, twill tape has a diagonal weave, which makes it resistant to stretching and tearing. It can be used to reinforce seams for durability, to make ties for clothing such as drawstring pants, or as decoration.

CORD Use cord for ties, drawstrings, or other decorative touches. It comes in a nearly infinite variety of colors, textures, and widths, and can be made of cotton, silk, or synthetic materials.

SEAM BINDING Lightweight and inexpensive, seam binding is used to cover raw edges inside garments. It can also be used to secure a hem.

RICKRACK This trim has a distinctive zigzag shape, and can be found in many widths and colors. Its playful appearance makes it well suited to embellishing clothing for a child or baby, or for trimming linens such as tea towels or coasters.

GROSGRAIN RIBBON Characterized by its ribbed texture, grosgrain ribbon makes a lovely adornment on almost any craft or sewing project—try it as trim around a waistband or as handles for a purse.

BIAS TAPE

Made from strips of folded fabric, bias tape creates a binding for raw fabric edges quickly and easily. It is made from fabric that has been cut on the bias, or diagonally, so it conforms to curved seams without puckering. Use bias tape to finish curved hems, create functional details such as loops for hanging potholders, or decorate everyday items. A bias-tape maker creates single-fold bias tape; store-bought tape can be single-fold or double-fold (folded lengthwise a second time). The second crease aligns easily with fabric edges. Bias tape is sold in a variety of solid colors and is widely available, typically in 3- or 4-yard (2.75m or 3.6m) packages.

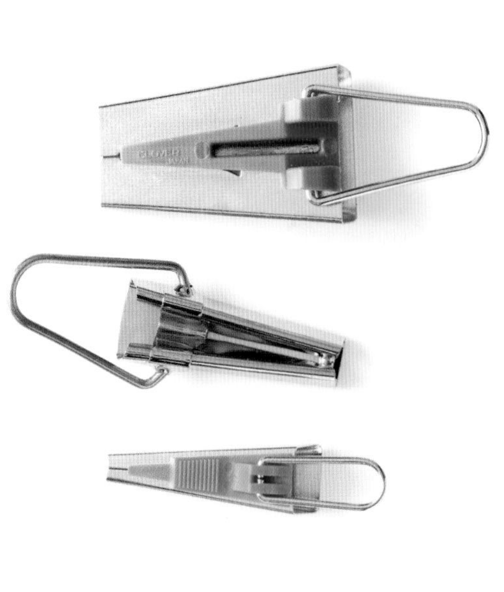

BIAS TAPE MAKER

Instead of using store-bought bias tape, you can create your own from almost any woven fabric using a bias-tape maker. Bias-tape makers come in a range of sizes, creating strips of fabric ¼ inch to 2 inches (6mm–5cm) in width. For instructions on how to make bias tape, see page 369.

CLOSURES AND FASTENERS

HOOK AND EYE

Standard hooks and eyes come in several sizes, from 0 (smallest) to 3 (largest). They are usually black, white, or nickel-plated. Eyes can be round (top) or straight (bottom); use a round one for adjacent edges and a straight eye for an overlapping edge. For more on sewing on a hook and eye, see page 372.

BUTTONS

You'll find buttons made out of plastic, wood, leather, glass, mother-of-pearl, and other materials; older buttons may be made from bone or Bakelite. Nearly every fabric store sells an array of buttons; you can also find vintage ones at antique stores and flea markets, and from online retailers. For instructions on attaching buttons, see pages 370–371.

COVERED BUTTONS

A covered-button kit allows you to create customized shank buttons. To use one, cut circles of fabric larger than the buttons (the kit should come with a template). Some buttons rely on teeth to hold fabric in place (above left); other kits come with a ring and pusher (above right) to press the pieces together.

SEW-ON SNAPS

As their name implies, these snaps are sewn directly to fabric. Because they are not decorative, they are generally hidden, sewn on with small, nearly invisible stitches. For more on how to sew on a snap, see page 371.

PUNCHED SNAPS

These fasteners are punched onto fabric with a tool rather than sewn into place; punched-snap kits are sold at fabric and crafts stores.

GROMMET KIT

With a grommet kit, you can easily punch holes in any heavyweight fabric, such as canvas or vinyl, that you wish to hang. The holes are then sealed with metal (usually brass). Grommet kits are available at crafts stores and hardware stores (grommets are also sold separately). For instructions on installing a grommet, see page 370.

ZIPPERS

A zipper is composed of a set of teeth or coils that interlock when closed. A tab, called a slider, opens and closes the zipper. Zippers can be constructed of metal or plastic, and come in different styles. Metal chain zippers are commonly used for pants. A pattern will specify the length of zipper required; if you cannot find the correct length, you can shorten a plastic coil zipper.

INVISIBLE An invisible zipper, used for clothing such as skirts and dresses, does not show when the zipper is shut.

PLASTIC CHAIN These come in many colors, to match many fabrics. They are commonly used for bags and jackets as they are chunky and heavier.

PLASTIC COIL A plastic coil zipper is an excellent all-purpose zipper; use it for pillows or some clothing. Rather than the molded plastic or metal teeth or a chain zipper, its teeth are made from tiny coils, making them more pliable than other styles.

METAL CHAIN Use a metal-chain zipper for jeans and other pants; its stark appearance can also be used for decorative effect.

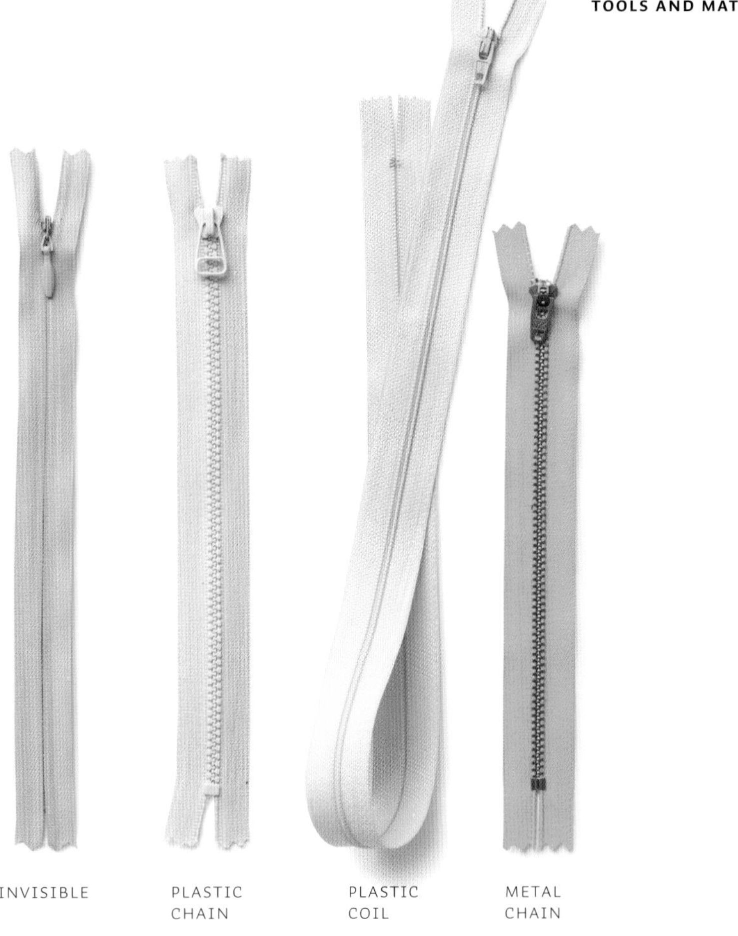

INVISIBLE　PLASTIC CHAIN　PLASTIC COIL　METAL CHAIN

PRESSING TOOLS

IRON

Use an iron to press fabric before cutting and sewing, and to press seams open. When pressing seams, hold the iron down for a few seconds, then lift it up; do not slide it along the seam. An iron is also used to fuse web to fabric and to transfer markings from a hot-iron transfer pen or heat-transfer pencil.

IRONING BOARD

Choose a lightweight, sturdy ironing board with adjustable height and a padded surface. If you have space in your home, opt for a larger ironing board, which can accommodate big projects; a full-size ironing board is generally about 4 ½ feet (1.4m) long and 12 to 18 inches (30.5–45.5cm) wide. Fit your board with a nonstick cover to keep delicate fabrics from sticking.

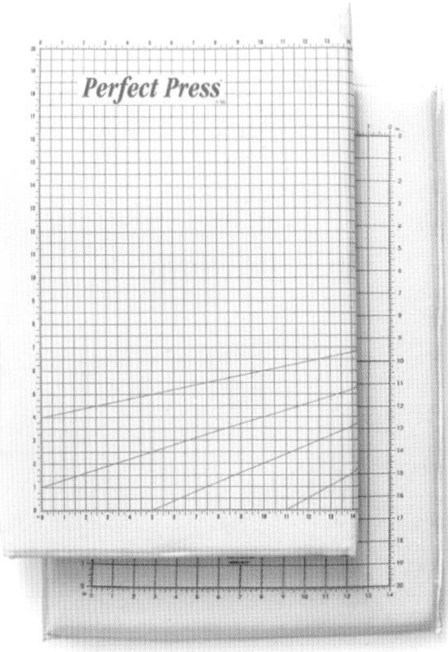

IRONING PAD

If you don't have room for an ironing board, or if you simply don't want to take it out for every project, an ironing pad is a good alternative. You can spread it out on any flat work surface, such as a large table. A large pad works well for ironing wide pieces of fabric; use a smaller pad for ironing cut pieces and small seams.

XYZ

tips and extra techniques

In addition to knowing the basic sewing and fabric craft techniques, familiarizing yourself with a few other essential skills will ensure the best outcome for your projects. Following are more than a dozen hints, tips, and step-by-step instructions to help guide you in your efforts.

how to select a sewing machine

Working with the right sewing machine is crucial, so choose wisely. There are three types of sewing machines available for use in the home: mechanical, electronic, and embroidery. The most basic (and generally least expensive) models are mechanical and rely on manual knobs and dials. Electronic machines (also called computerized) have more power and the capability to carry out additional functions. Embroidery machines are hybrids that have all the functionality of a regular sewing machine, but can also be used to create embroidery, using special attachments.

Begin by deciding which features you need. If you plan to do a lot of quilting, for example, look for a machine that comes with dual feed or an even feed foot. These will move the top and bottom layers of fabric simultaneously, instead of just the bottom, which helps when matching patterns or sewing together fabrics of different weights.

Stores that specialize in sewing machines have the best selection, and they often allow you to test out their products. (Even though many department stores carry several models, you may not have the opportunity to test them.) Some large fabric stores also sell machines. Bring a few types of fabric with you so you can test the machines, and try out at least three models. Check tension with silky fabrics, and determine the potential for snagging with chiffon. Use heavy fabrics to gauge needle penetration; multiple layers will give you a feel for the ease of stitching. To test how well each model works for quilting, bring projects in various stages to determine if the machine gets tripped up on seams or batting. Don't forget to load and wind the bobbin, and change the needle and foot to see how easy it is to work with the machine in general.

When you are shopping and comparing, inquire about the length of the warranty and about the parts and labor that are covered. Find out how the store handles repairs. Will they be done locally? Are the parts made in the United States, or will they have to be imported? You want to be sure repairs will be fast and affordable.

MECHANICAL

ELECTRONIC

EMBROIDERY

how to make bias tape

Bias-tape makers, which come in a variety of sizes, create strips of fabric 1/4 inch (6mm) to 2 inches (5cm) wide. Use a medium-weight woven fabric, such as quilting cotton or linens. These instructions are for making single-fold bias tape; store-bought double-fold tape is folded lengthwise a second time.

1. Start with 1 yard (0.9m) of fabric. With a chalk pencil and a clear quilting ruler, mark strips at 45-degree angles, one beside the next. (To determine the width of the strips, see the instructions that come with the bias-tape maker.) Cut out strips.

2. To create longer lengths of bias tape for larger projects, join strips end to end as follows: Place two strips, right sides facing and diagonal ends aligned, at a 90-degree angle. Stitch in place with a 1/2-inch (13mm) seam allowance, backstitching to secure. Press open with an iron. Snip corners.

3. Feed one end of fabric into the bias-tape maker, pulling 1 to 2 inches (2.5–5cm) of fabric through the other side. Pin bias tape to ironing board to hold it in place. Press. Continue to pull strip through bias-tape maker, pressing as you go.

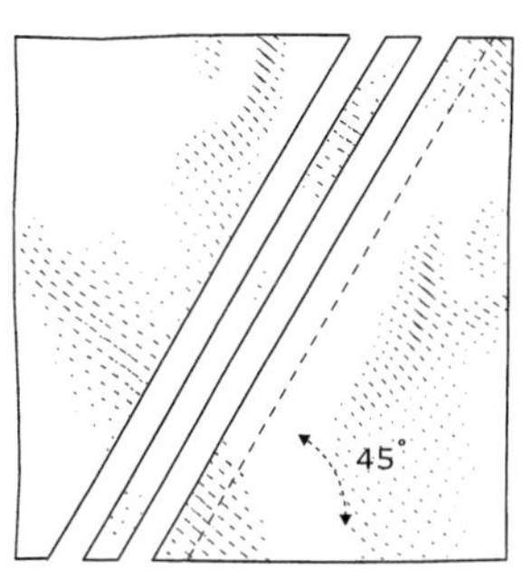

1

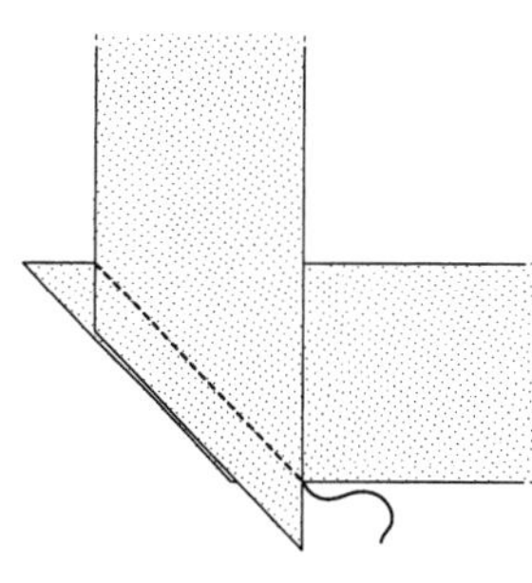
2

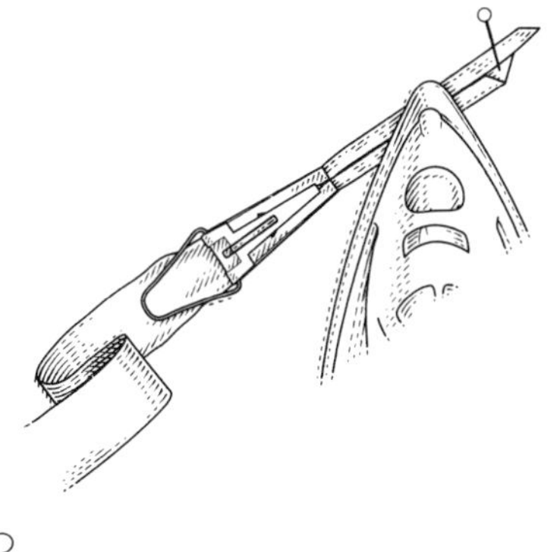
3

how to finish bias tape ends

The shape of your completed project will determine the method you choose to finish the ends of the bias tape: Use the fold-over finish when binding only one edge; the overlap finish is used for continuous binding.

1. ONE-STEP BINDING To bind raw edges or embellish seams, slip bias tape over the edge of the project. Pin to secure. Stitch 1/8 inch (3mm) in from tape's edge, making sure needle passes through underside of tape.

2. FOLD-OVER FINISH Cut bias tape 1/2 inch (13mm) longer than required. Stop stitching about 1 inch (2.5cm) before the tape's end. Open the bias tape like a book; fold end over the edge of the project's fabric. Close bias tape, and stitch in place.

3. OVERLAP FINISH Cut bias tape 1 inch (2.5cm) longer than required. Stop stitching about 1 inch before reaching the end of the project. Open the bias tape like a book; fold under 1/2 inch (13mm) at end. Close bias tape, and stitch in place.

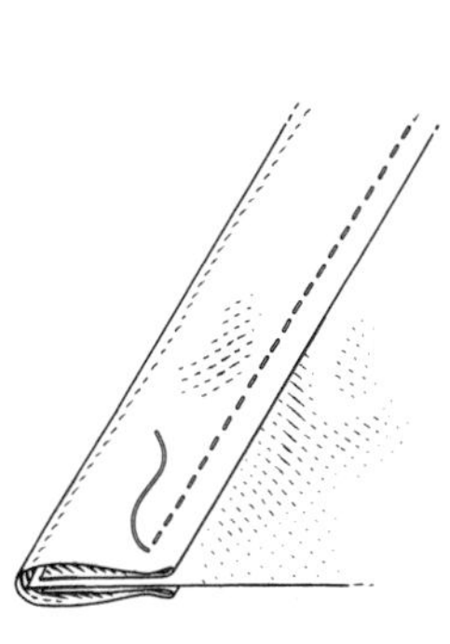
1

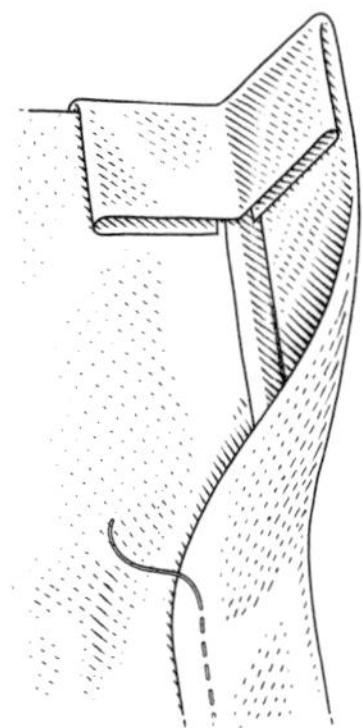
2

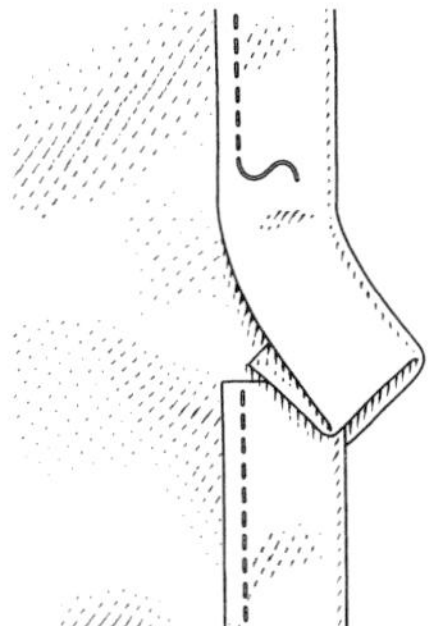
3

how to install a grommet

A grommet has two parts: the grommet (with a raised post in the center), and the washer. In addition to those pieces, a grommet kit (available at crafts and hardware stores) will include a hardwood backer (to protect the work surface), a hole cutter, a punch, and an anvil. You will also need a wooden or rubber mallet and a hammer. To install a grommet, mark the position of the grommet with a small X on the wrong side of the fabric. With fabric right-side down on the hardwood backer, place the hole cutter over the mark, and hit with a mallet. Insert the grommet into the hole through the right side of fabric; set the grommet on the anvil. Place the washer over the grommet, on the wrong side of the fabric. Insert the punch into the hole in the grommet. Strike the punch with a hammer until the washer and grommet are secured.

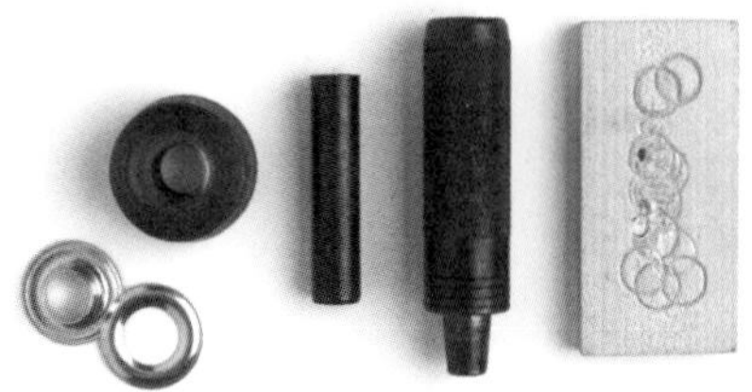

how to machine-sew a buttonhole

First, measure the buttons to determine the size buttonhole you will need: The length of the buttonhole (not including the finished ends, called bar tacks) should equal the diameter plus the thickness of the button. Set your sewing machine to its buttonhole stitch accordingly. It's a good idea to practice first, using the same number of fabric layers that will be in the finished product. After stitching, place a pin at each end of the buttonhole to mark the bar tacks. With small, sharp scissors, cut the fabric in the center of the buttonhole, stopping just before you reach the bar tacks.

If your machine does not have a buttonhole stitch, use a zigzag stitch. Mark the length of the button hole, and set the machine to a narrow to medium stitch width and a length between 0 and 1. Sew along one side of the marked line (do not sew over the line). At the end of the marked line, increase the stitch width to about double the original width and make a few stitches to create a bar tack. Leave the needle in the fabric, raise the presser foot, and pivot the fabric. Decrease the stitch width again, and sew along the opposite side of the marked line, making sure not to sew over the first row of zigzag stitches. Make another bar tack at the end of the marked line. Use small, sharp scissors to carefully cut the buttonhole open.

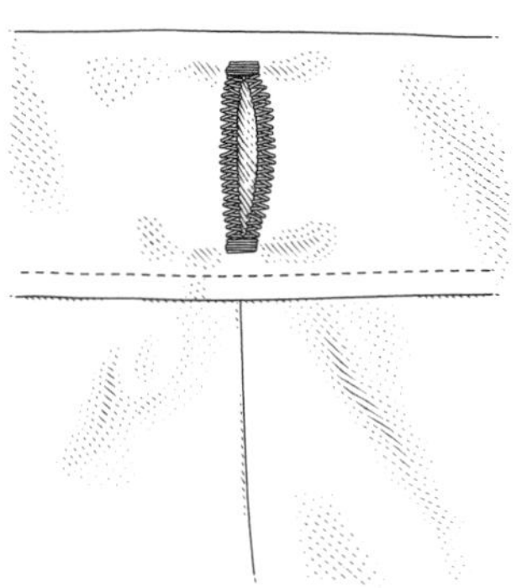

how to sew on a flat button

Mark button placement with a chalk pencil. Pass the needle through the fabric and through one hole in the button. Place a toothpick across the top of the button. Bring the needle down through the second hole (if using a four-hole button, continue back up and down through the third and fourth holes). Repeat, making about six stitches. Remove the toothpick, and lift the button slightly—the extra thread creates a shank that will allow room for the fabric that will close around it (this is especially important when sewing buttons onto heavy coats or other bulky garments). Wrap thread tightly around the shank, then slip the needle through one of the stitches and pull tight to secure.

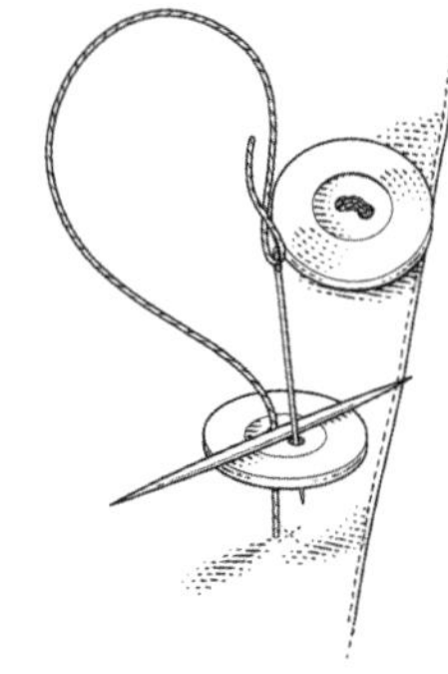

how to sew on a shank button

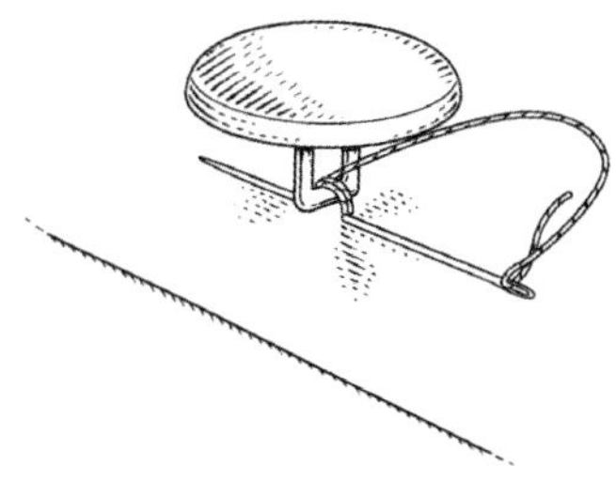

Often, shank buttons are reinforced with a flat button, stitched to the inside of the garment; use any 2- or 4-hole button in a size and color appropriate to your garment. As you sew on the button, tug the thread only until it is snug—not taut or tight. This will ensure that the button has enough give to slip easily through the buttonhole. Mark button placement with a chalk pencil. With a needle and a single strand of knotted thread, pick up a small amount of fabric at the mark; gently pull thread until the knot settles on top of the marked spot. Work two small stitches close to the mark. Pass the needle to the inside of the garment and through the flat button. Then return through the button's opposing hole, coming out at your anchor stitches. Slip the needle through the shank. Slide the button down the thread's length, aligning the shank's hole with the direction of the buttonhole. Pass the needle back through the garment and out through the flat button. Repeat five times. Tightly wrap the thread three times around the base of the shank, and snip thread. To knot, slip the needle through one of the stitches; pull tight.

how to sew on a snap

A sew-on snap is made up of two parts: the ball-stud (the outie) and the socket-stud (the innie). As you sew, be sure to pick up only the top layer of fabric so your stitches won't show on the outside of your garment.

1. With a chalk pencil, mark the position for the ball-stud. With a needle and a 12-inch (0.3m) length of knotted single thread, pick up the top layer of fabric, and pull the thread until the knot sits on the mark. Slip the needle through a hole in the ball-stud; slide it down the thread, holding it firmly in place on the fabric. Pass the needle down and over the ball-stud's edge, and then back up through a hole. Repeat, working about four stitches in each of the four holes. To finish, backstitch, knot, and snip thread. Snap the ball-stud and socket stud together.

2. Overlap your garment pieces. Pass a pin through the center of the closed snap, and mark where it emerges. Using the pin as a guide, mark placement for the socket-stud.

3. Unsnap the two parts, and stitch the socket-stud in place using the same technique as you used for the ball-stud.

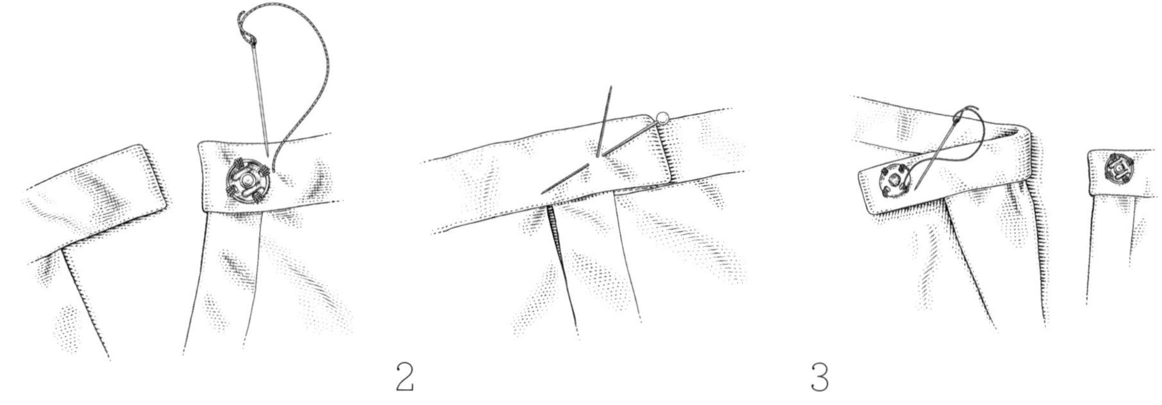

how to sew on a hook and eye

As you sew, pick up only small bits of fabric so your stitches won't show on the outside of your garment.

1. Mark the placement for the hook and eye. Position the hook on the inside of the garment, about 1/8 inch (3mm) from the edge. To keep it in place, stitch twice over the hook's "neck." Stitch into and over the hook's loops. Knot, and snip thread.

2. Place the eye on in a corresponding position. Its loop should extend over the garment's edge. Make one stitch on either side of the eye to keep it in place.

3. Stitch into and over the eye's two loops. Knot, and snip thread.

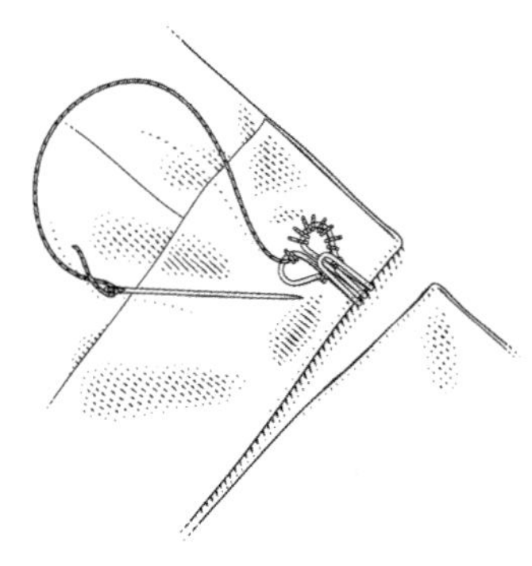

1

2

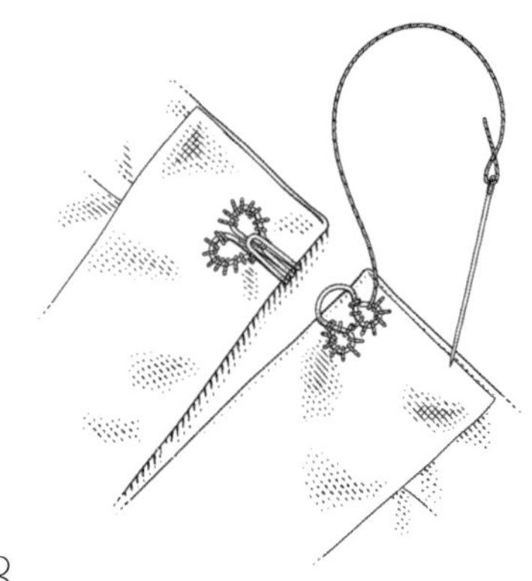

3

how to make quilted fabric

Start with two square or rectangular pieces of fabric (make sure the fabric is big enough to accommodate your finished project; place pattern pieces or templates on top to be sure). Place one piece of fabric wrong-side up on a flat surface in a well-ventilated area; spray it with quilt basting adhesive. Immediately place an equal size piece of batting on the sticky side of the fabric; flip over. Working from the center out, smooth fabric to remove any ripples or creases. Repeat by attaching another piece of fabric, wrong side down, to the other side of the batting. With a ruler and tailor's chalk or a disappearing-ink fabric pen, mark a grid on the fabric: Diagonal lines will result in a diamond pattern; horizontal and vertical lines will create a box-quilt pattern. To prevent fabric from puckering, sew along all the lines in the same direction; repeat with perpendicular lines, again sewing in one direction.

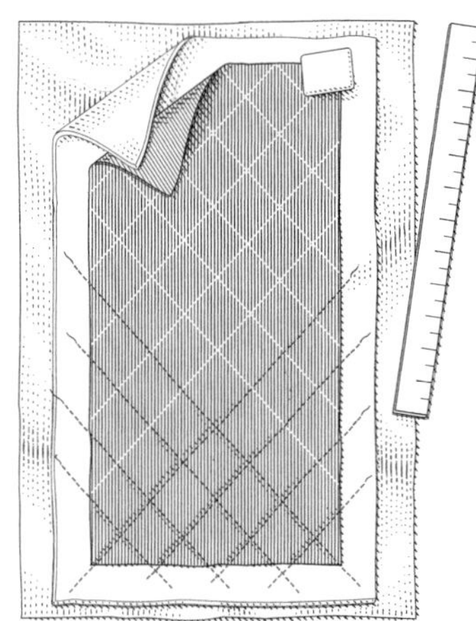

how to fix a fallen hem

Turn the pant leg inside out. Start and end your repair about 1/2 inch (13mm) on either side of the fallen hem. Some of the stitching will show, so use a thread that matches the garment. You don't have to knot the thread for mending; to secure it in the fabric, use a short backstitch: Piercing only the folded inner edge of the fabric, insert the needle in the hem, below the seam, and pull it out to make a 1/8-inch (3mm) stitch. Then reinsert the needle through the same stitch, and repeat once more. The thread is now secure. Just above the hem, insert needle through fabric from right to left. Make the smallest possible stitch; it will show on the right side of the garment. Insert needle through the inside of the hem, to the left of the first stitch. Bring thread up and make a tiny stitch above the hem. Repeat, working from right to left. Continue stitching up and down the hemline until the rip is closed. As you sew, keep the tension of the thread slightly loose; pulling it too tight could break it or pucker the fabric. When finished, secure the hem with a short backstitch, as at the start.

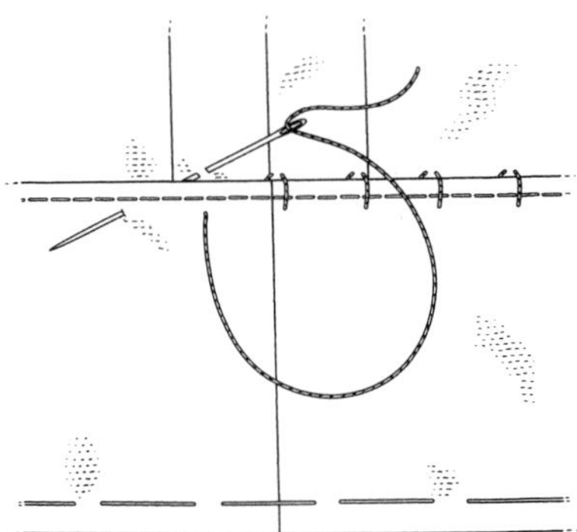

how to repair a ripped seam

Use this method when a seam is ripped, but the garment is not torn. Do not pull tightly as you stitch, as this will cause the fabric to pucker.

Turn the garment inside out, and with a pin or seam ripper, remove any stray threads. Pin the seam back together, aligning the edges. Use an 18-inch (0.4m) length of single knotted thread in a matching color. Backstitch (see "How to Fix a Fallen Hem," opposite), overlapping the intact stitching by about 1/2 inch (13mm) and following the original stitching line along the seam allowance. Continue, ending about 1/2 inch (13mm) into the intact stitching at the other end. Knot; snip thread.

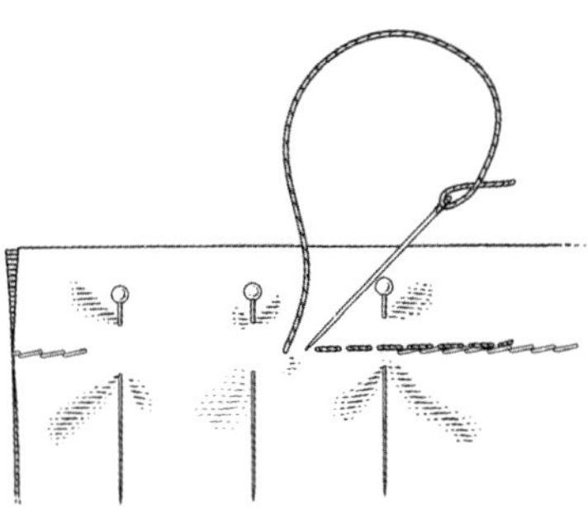

how to make piping

You will need woven fabric and piping cord (sometimes called welting). Cut fabric on the bias into 2-inch-wide (5cm) strips (for 1/4-inch [6mm] piping cord; cut wider strips for larger piping). To join strips into a longer piece, place two strips, right sides facing and diagonal ends aligned, at a 90-degree angle. Stitch in place with a 1/2-inch (13mm) seam allowance, backstitching to secure. Press open; snip corners. Fold strip, right side out, around piping cord, with raw edges aligned. Using the zipper foot on your sewing machine, stitch along the length of the strip as close to the cording as possible to ensure a snug fit. Trim raw edges to 1/2 inch (13mm) from seam.

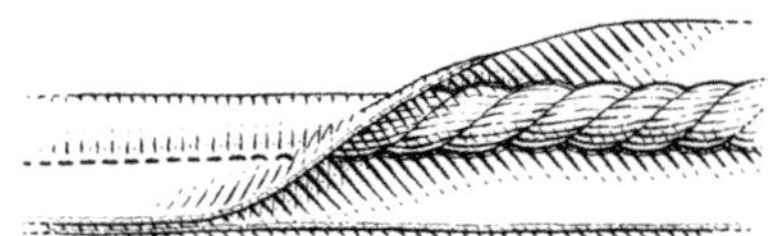

how to patch a hole

Some stitches will be visible, so be sure your thread matches the fabric color. You will need matching fabric for the patch.

1. With small scissors, cut the hole into a clean square or rectangle. This will make the repair neater and easier. Trim any loose threads. At each corner of the square hole, cut a 1/4-inch (6mm) notch at a 45-degree angle. Turn the material inside out; fold the square's 1/4-inch (6mm) edges onto material's wrong side, and press them flat.

2. With fabric scissors, cut out the patch material; measure and cut out a square that's about 1/2 inch (13mm) bigger all around than the hole you're repairing.

3. With the material still inside out, position patch fabric on top of hole. If using a material with obvious grain, like denim, be sure to match up the patch and shirt so the grain lines are all going the same way. Turn material right-side out, and pin patch in place. Slip-baste the patch in place from the outside of the shirt. Starting anywhere on the square, make a 1/4-inch (6mm) stitch down through the patch fabric, push the needle up and out, catching the folded edge of the hole; continue all around hole, and remove pins.

4. Turn the garment inside out. Fold back the 1/2-inch (13mm) excess of patch fabric, so it's flush with the folded edge of the hole. Insert the needle down through the folded edge of the patch (only one layer of fabric), then stitch up diagonally through the folded edge of the material, joining the two fabrics. Continue this stitch in a uniform manner all around the square. Make several short backstitches at each corner to further secure patch and fabric. The stitch will be slightly visible on the front of the garment.

5. To finish off the edges of the patch inside the garment, use the short backstitch described in "How to Fix a Fallen Hem" (opposite). Cut off the tips of the four corners of the patch at 45-degree angles. Fold back edges 1/4 inch (6mm). Stitch the edge to the shirt, picking up only one or two threads with each stitch. Press patch when finished.

cd patterns and templates

On the following pages, you'll find thumbnail images of all the patterns and templates included on the enclosed CD, in the order in which they appear in the book.

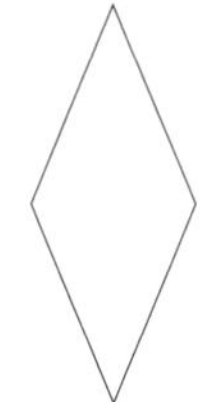

QUILTING AND PATCHWORK
STAR-PATTERN PATCHWORK

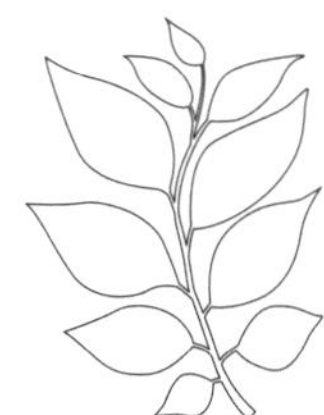

PRINTING
BLOCK PRINT BRANCH

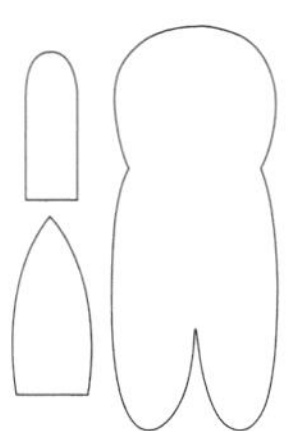

ANIMALS
MENSWEAR BUNNY

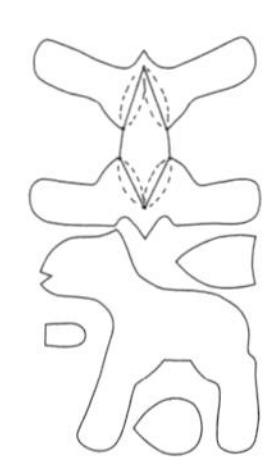

ANIMALS
FELTED LAMB

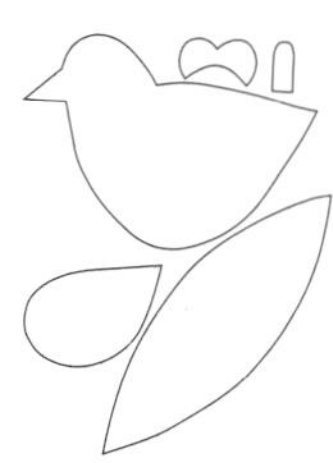

ANIMALS
FELTED CHICKEN

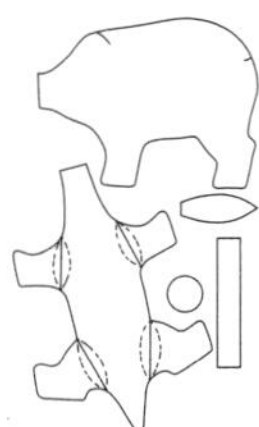

ANIMALS
FELTED PIG

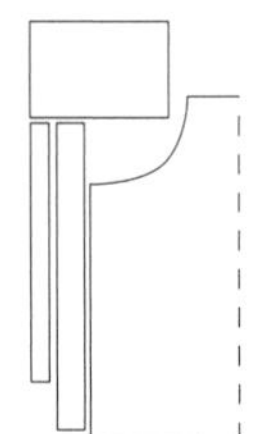

APRONS
BASIC LINEN APRON

APRONS
CRAFTER'S APRON

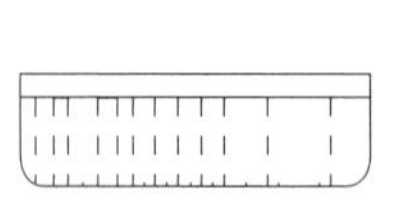

APRONS
CRAFTER'S APRON POCKET

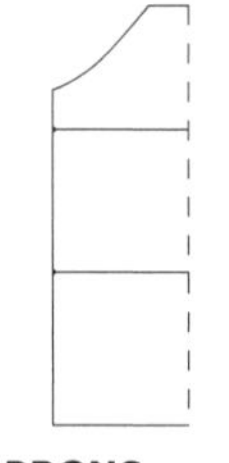

APRONS
BAKER'S APRON

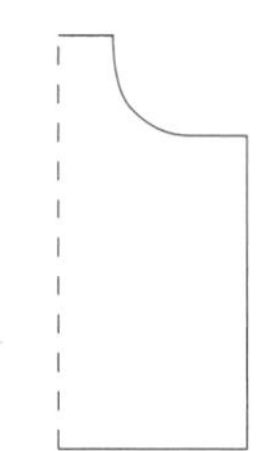

APRONS
FAUX-BOIS GARDENER'S APRON

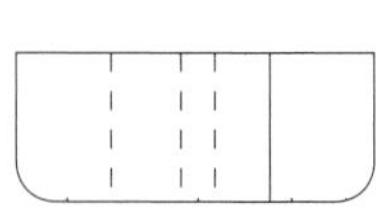

APRONS
FAUX-BOIS GARDENER'S APRON POCKET

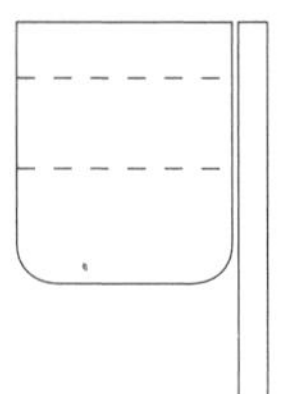

BAGS
MULTICOMPARTMENT BAG

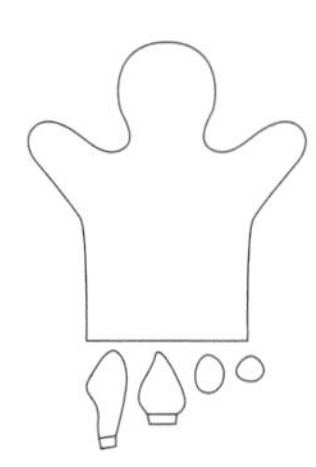

BATH LINENS
WASHCLOTH PUPPETS

BED LINENS
FRENCH-KNOTTED BORDERS

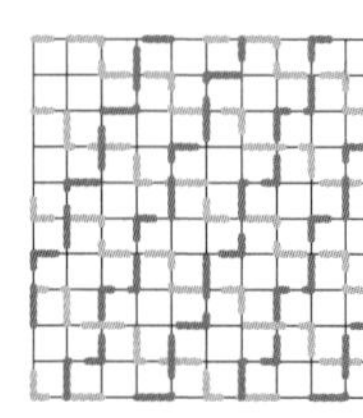

BED LINENS
SASHIKO-EDGED PILLOWCASES

BED LINENS
APPLIQUÉD DUVET COVER AND PILLOWCASES

BIBS
APPLE-EMBROIDERED BIB

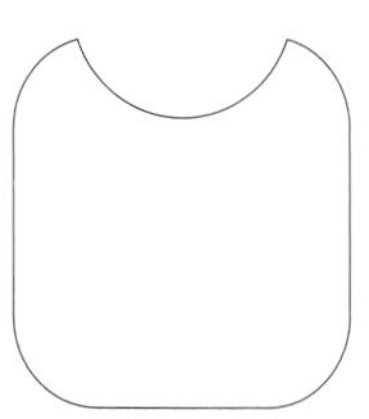

BIBS
BIAS TAPE–EMBELLISHED BIB

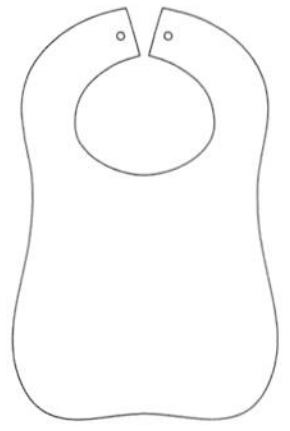

BIBS
OILCLOTH POCKETED BIB

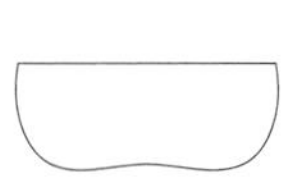

BIBS
OILCLOTH POCKETED BIB POCKET

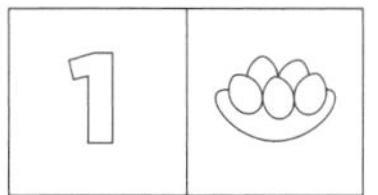

BOOKS
APPLIQUÉD NUMBER BOOK: 1

BOOKS
APPLIQUÉD NUMBER BOOK: 2

BOOKS
APPLIQUÉD NUMBER BOOK: 3

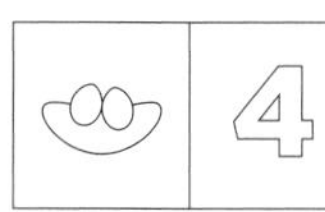

BOOKS
APPLIQUÉD NUMBER BOOK: 4

BOOKS
APPLIQUÉD NUMBER BOOK: 5

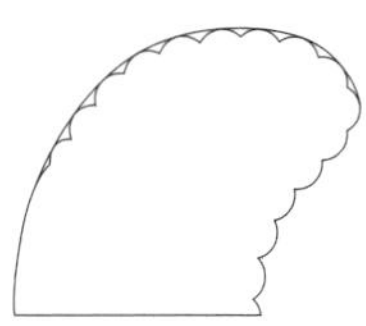

CLOTHING
NO-SEW SCALLOPED WRAP SKIRT

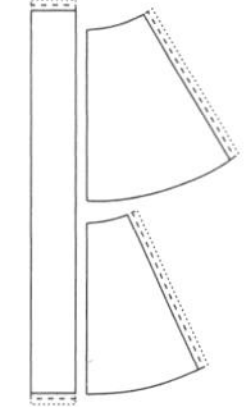

CLOTHING
A-LINE WRAP SKIRT (3 SIZES)

CLOTHING
HAWAIIAN-PATTERN APPLIQUÉD ROBE

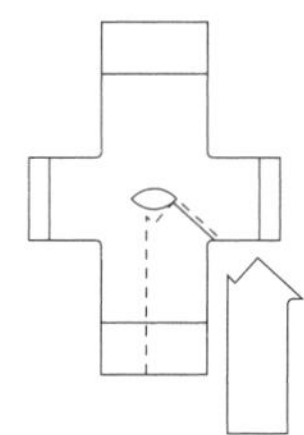

CLOTHING
BABY KIMONO (6 SIZES)

CLOTHING
GIRL'S SHIRT DRESS

CLOTHING
BUTTERFLY-APPLIQUÉD SHAWL

CLOTHING
FLOWER-APPLIQUÉD SHIRT

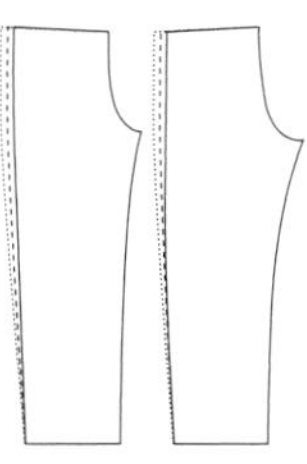

CLOTHING
DRAWSTRING PANTS (3 SIZES)

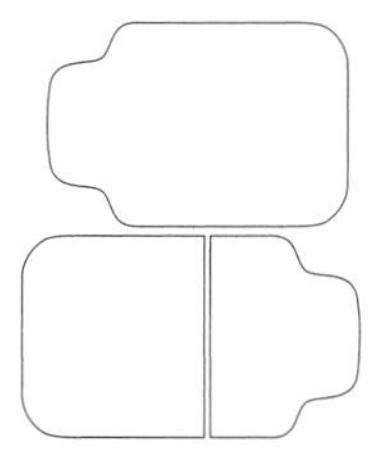

COZIES
MENSWEAR WATER-BOTTLE COZY

COZIES
CLUCKING-EGG COZY

CURTAINS
STENCILED CURTAINS: STAR FLOWER

CURTAINS
STENCILED CURTAINS: BELL FLOWER

CURTAINS
STENCILED CURTAINS: FULL CURTAIN

CURTAINS
APPLIQUÉD CURTAIN

DECORATIVE PILLOWS
BIRD-EMBROIDERED PILLOWS

black-capped chickadee

purple finch

western meadowlark

cardinal

blue hen chicken/rhode island red

scissor-tailed flycatcher

eastern bluebird

mockingbird

brown thrasher

nene

roadrunner

yellowhammer

lark bunting

mountain bluebird

carolina wren

american goldfinch

california gull

california quail

wood thrush

ruffed grouse

baltimore oriole

american robin

hermit thrush

brown pelican

cactus wren

common loon

willow ptarmigan

ring-necked pheasant

DECORATIVE PILLOWS
FALLING-LEAF PILLOW COVERS

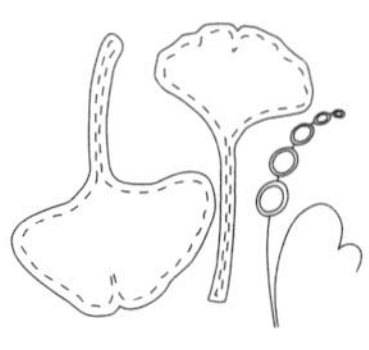
DECORATIVE PILLOWS
HAND-APPLIQUÉD PILLOW COVERS

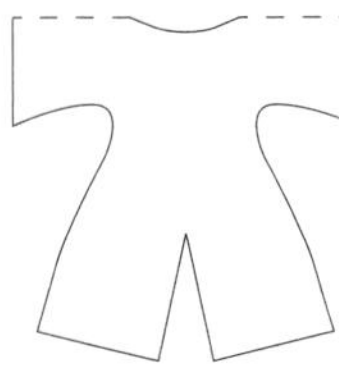
DOLLS
DOLL CLOTHING

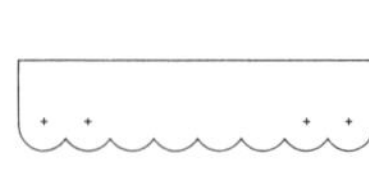
NURSERY
SCALLOPED CANOPY

NURSERY
GROWTH CHART

ORGANIZERS
FALLING-LEAVES FELT BOARD

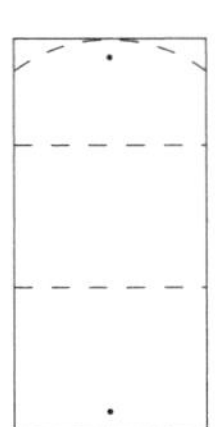

ORGANIZERS
COIN PURSE

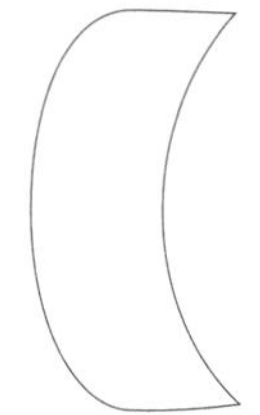

PETS
QUILTED DOG JACKET COLLAR

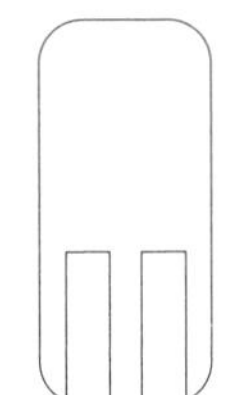

PETS
QUILTED DOG JACKET STRAP

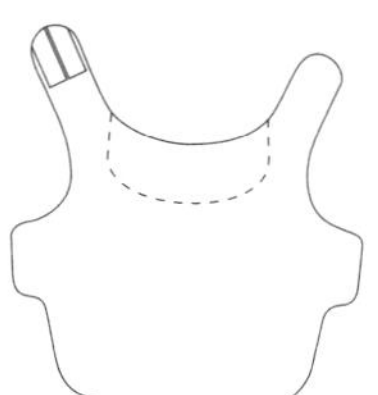

PETS
QUILTED DOG JACKET TOP

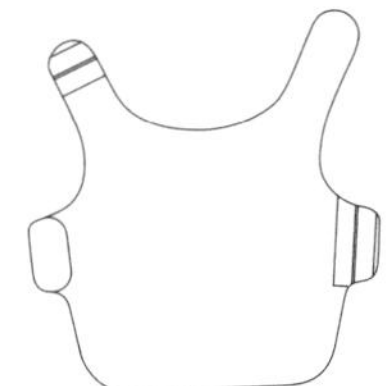

PETS
QUILTED DOG JACKET UNDERSIDE

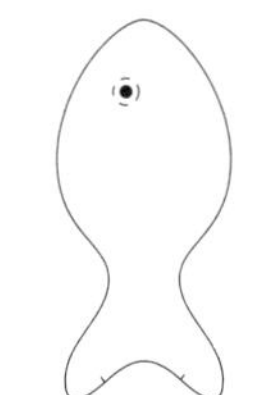

PETS
CATNIP FISH ON A POLE

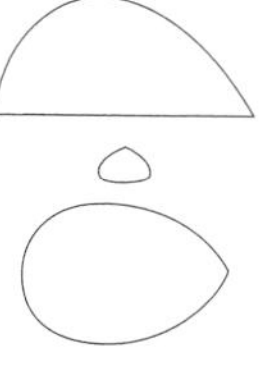

PETS
MENSWEAR MICE

PINCUSHIONS
HEIRLOOM-TOMATO PINCUSHIONS

PINCUSHIONS
STRAWBERRY PINCUSHIONS

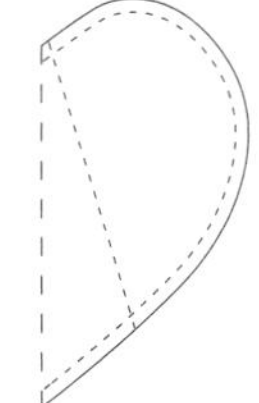

POT HOLDERS
HEART-SHAPED POT HOLDER

QUILTS AND PATCHWORK
STATE BIRD–EMBROIDERED QUILT

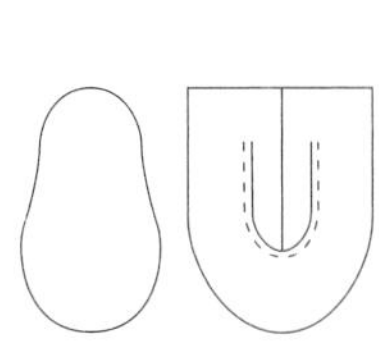

SLIPPERS
FELT BABY SHOES

SLIPPERS
NATURE-INSPIRED SLIPPERS: BRANCH DESIGN (VARIOUS SIZES)

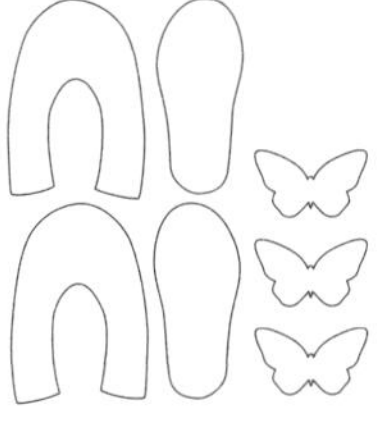

SLIPPERS
NATURE-INSPIRED SLIPPERS: BUTTERFLY DESIGN (VARIOUS SIZES)

TABLE LINENS
BIAS-TAPE TABLE RUNNER

TABLE LINENS
ULTRASUEDE LEAF PLACE MATS

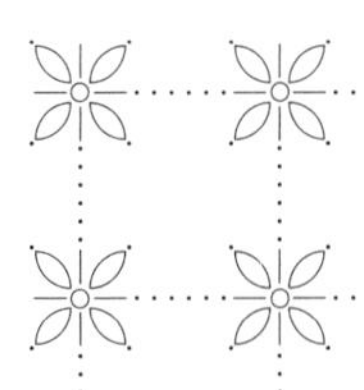

TABLE LINENS
BLEACH-BATIK TABLE LINENS

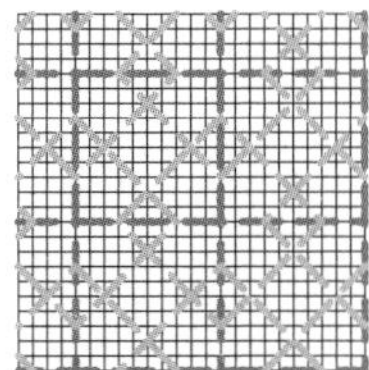

TABLE LINENS
HIYOKUIGETA JAPANESE-EMBROIDERED TABLE LINENS

TABLE LINENS
KOUSHIAWABE JAPANESE-EMBROIDERED TABLE LINENS

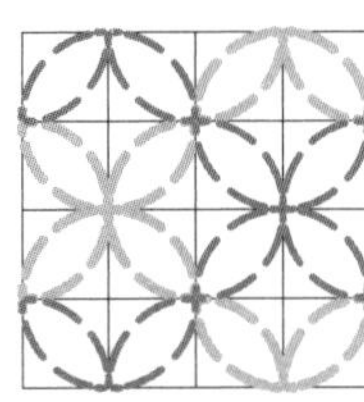

TABLE LINENS
SHIPPOUTSUNAGI JAPANESE-EMBROIDERED TABLE LINENS

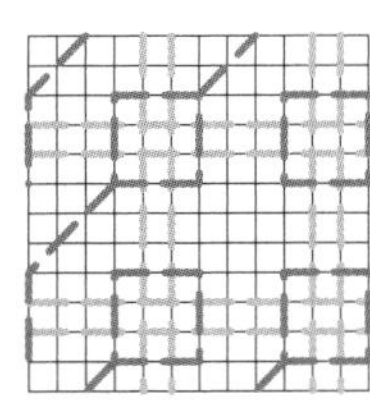

TABLE LINENS
KOUSHITSUNAGI JAPANESE-EMBROIDERED TABLE LINENS

TABLE LINENS
BLOCK-PRINT TABLE LINENS

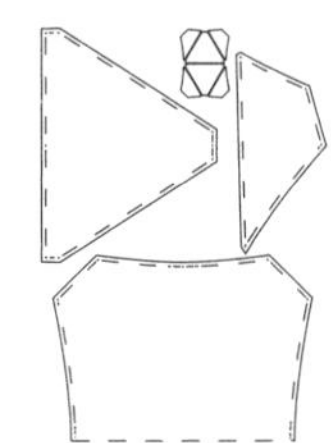

TABLE LINENS
LEATHER TABLE MATS

UPHOLSTERY
HAWAIIAN-PATTERN STENCILED CUSHIONS: GINGER FLOWER

UPHOLSTERY
HAWAIIAN-PATTERN STENCILED CUSHIONS: NAUPAKA FLOWER

UPHOLSTERY
HAWAIIAN-PATTERN STENCILED CUSHIONS: OHI'A LEHUA FLOWER

WALL DÉCOR
FARMYARD APPLIQUÉ WALL HANGING

sources

The following is a list of the vendors our editors turn to again and again for craft and sewing supplies, fabric, trim, notions, and other essentials. The list beginning on page 380 contains sourcing information specific to the projects in this book. All addresses, phone numbers, and websites verified at the time of publication are subject to change.

basic craft supplies

BLICK ART MATERIALS
800-828-4548
dickblick.com

CREATE FOR LESS
866-333-4463
createforless.com

JOANN FABRIC AND CRAFT STORES
888-739-4120
joann.com

MARTHA STEWART CRAFTS
marthastewart.com/shop

MICHAELS
800-642-4235
michaels.com

sewing supplies and notions

ACME NOTIONS
acmenotions.com

CLOTILDE
800-545-4002
clotilde.com

CLOVER
800-233-1703
clover-usa.com

CREATE FOR LESS
866-333-4463
createforless.com

JOANN FABRIC AND CRAFT STORES
888-739-4120
joann.com

JUNE TAILOR
262-644-5288
junetailor.com

PURL PATCHWORK
147 Sullivan Street, New York, NY 10012
212-420-8798
purlsoho.com

SINGER SEWING COMPANY
800-474-6437
singerco.com
For product information on the SINGER sewing machines used in this book, and a special offer exclusively for you, please visit www.singerco.com/martha

STEINLAUF AND STOLLER INC.
239 W. 39th Street, New York, NY 10018
212-869-0321
steinlaufandstoller.com

quilting supplies
including fabric, batting, quilt basting spray, quilting thread, and quilting needles

CLOTILDE
800-545-4002
clotilde.com

CREATE FOR LESS
866-333-4463
createforless.com

PURL PATCHWORK
147 Sullivan Street, New York, NY 10012
212-420-8798
purlsoho.com

fabric
including basic and specialty fabrics, felt, and oilcloth

A CHILD'S DREAM COME TRUE
800-359-2906
achildsdream.com
Felt in a large selection of colors and sizes

B&J FABRICS
525 7th Avenue, New York, NY 10018
212-354-8150
bandjfabrics.com

FABRIC TALES
fabrictales.com
Japanese printed fabrics

GLOBAL LEATHERS
212-244-5190
globalleathers.com
Leather and leather tools

GRAY LINE LINEN
260 W. 39th Street, New York, NY 10018
866-585-4636
graylinelinen.com

KARMA KRAFT
karmakraft.com
Custom-printed fabric

MAGIC CABIN
888-623-3655
magiccabin.com
Wool felt in a large selection of colors

MOOD FABRICS
225 W. 37th Street, 3rd floor
New York, NY 10018
212-730-5003
moodfabrics.com

NEAR SEA NATURALS
877-573-2913
nearseanaturals.com
Organic cotton, wool, and other sustainable fabrics

OILCLOTH INTERNATIONAL
323-344-3967
oilcloth.com

PURL PATCHWORK
147 Sullivan Street, New York, NY 10012
212-420-8798
purlsoho.com
Quilting cotton in a large selection of prints and solids

REPRO DEPOT FABRICS
reprodepot.com
Vintage cotton fabric reproductions

SPOONFLOWER
919-321-2949
spoonflower.com
Custom-printed fabric

THE SILK TRADING COMPANY
888-745-5302
silktrading.com
Decorator fabrics for upholstery and drapery

TANDY LEATHER FACTORY
817-872-3200
tandyleatherfactory.com
Leather and leather tools

trim

Ribbons, cord, and other trim; custom clothing labels

DAYTONA TRIMMING
251 W. 39th Street, New York, NY 10019
212-354-1713
daytonatrim.com

HYMAN HENDLER & SONS
21 W. 38th Street, New York, NY 10018
212-840-8393
hymanhendler.com

JKM RIBBON & TRIMS
jkmribbbon.com

M&J TRIMMING
1008 6th Avenue, New York, NY 10018
800-965-8746
mjtrim.com

MOKUBA NEW YORK
55 W. 39th Street, New York, NY 10018
212-869-8900
mokubany.com

NAMEMAKER
800-241-2890
namemaker.com
Custom labels for clothing and quilts

TINSEL TRADING
1 W. 37th Street, New York, NY 10018
212-730-1030
tinseltrading.com

dyeing and printing supplies

Including fabric dyes, color fixers, natural dyes, fabric paint, soft-carve blocks, linoleum cutters, and stencils

BLICK ART MATERIALS
800-828-4548
dickblick.com

DHARMA TRADING
800-542-5227
dharmatrading.com

EARTHUES
206-789-1065
earthues.com

upholstery supplies

Including foam, upholstery fabric, upholstery thread, decorative nails, and tools

DIY UPHOLSTERY SUPPLY
662-280-0020
diyupholsterysupply.com

ZARIN FABRICS
314 Grand Street, New York, NY 10002
212-925-6112
zarinfabrics.com

buyer's guide

Items that do not appear below are no longer available from our original sources. Most projects can be completed with similar fabrics—choose colors and patterns that best suit your style. If you are still unable to locate a tool or material, try searching online; you should be able to find everything you need to complete all of the projects in this book.

animals

MENSWEAR BUNNY, PAGE 93: Similar WOOL SUITING FABRIC, from New York Elegant Fabrics, 222 W. 40th Street, New York, NY 10018, 212-302-4980 or nyelegantfabrics.com. Similar COTTON SHIRTING FABRIC, from B&J Fabrics, 525 7th Avenue, New York, NY 10018, 212-354-8150 or bandjfabrics.com.

aprons

BASIC LINEN APRON, PAGE 103: 60"-wide Judy LINEN in natural (#30), from Grayline Linen, 260 W. 39th Street, New York, NY 10018, 866-585-4636 or graylinelinen.com.

CRAFTER'S APRON, PAGE 105: CANVAS in Green, from B&J Fabrics, 525 7th Avenue, New York, NY 10018, 212-354-8150 or bandjfabrics .com. LEATHER in Light Gray, from Global Leathers, 212-244-5190 or globalleathers.com.

CHILD'S OILCLOTH APRON, PAGE 107: OILCLOTH in yellow mini gingham and solid white, both from Oilcloth International, 323-344-3967 or oilcloth.com.

DISH-TOWEL APRON, PAGE 108: Color-band DISH TOWELS (DTL-CBA), set of 12 in six colors, from Barrett House, 800-432-5776 or barrett-house.com. 25mm-wide TWILL TAPE (#5600) in Teal (#56), from Mokuba New York, 55 W. 39th Street, New York, NY 10018, 212-869-8900 or mokubany.com.

ADJUSTABLE APRON, PAGE 108: Similar APRON (#5707468) in Dijon, from Williams-Sonoma, 877-812-6235 or williams-sonoma .com.

BAKER'S APRON, PAGE 109: Striped COTTON, from B&J Fabrics, 525 7th Avenue, New York, NY 10018, 212-354-8150 or bandjfabrics.com.

FAUX-BOIS GARDENER'S APRON, PAGE 110: 1" D-RINGS, from CreateForLess, 866-333-4463 or createforless.com. Wood-grain OILCLOTH, from Bell'occhio, 10 Brady Street, San Francisco, CA 94103, 415-864-4048 or bellocchio.com. CANVAS in Gray, from B&J Fabrics, 525 7th Avenue, New York, NY 10018, 212-354-8150 or bandjfabrics.com.

bags

FABRIC-POCKET TOTE BAG, PAGE 113: 30mm TWILL TAPE (#10016) in Yellow (#60), from Mokuba New York, 55 W. 39th Street, New York, NY 10018, 212-869-8900 or mokubany.com. Similar 17"-by-19" CHILD'S APRON (#0153-NAT) in Natural from Bag-Works, 800-365-7423 or bagworks.com.

RAFFIA-EMBROIDERED TOTE, PAGE 115: Recycled cotton CANVAS TOTE BAG, by Ecobags, from amazon.com. Matte finish RAFFIA caps in Coral (SM008), Pale Yellow (SM033), White (SM030), and Mint (SM018), from Raffit Ribbons, raffit.com. Matte rayon RAFFIA in Daffodil (#749DA) and Orange (#749OR), by Wraphia, from Nashville Wraps, 800-547-9727 or nashvillewraps.com.

BASIC CANVAS TOTE, PAGE 116: 61"-wide Definitive Natural CANVAS (#1591), from Near Sea Naturals, 877-573-2913 or nearseanaturals.com.

APPLIQUÉD SEA-PRINT TOTE, PAGE 117: TEXTILE COLORS (#01208) in Scarlet Red and White, by Jacquard, from Blick Art Materials, 800-828-4548 or dickblick.com. White finger STARFISH, 3" to 4" (#2500-653), set of 6; and White knobby STARFISH 3" to 4" (#2520-653), set of 10; white knobby STARFISH, 4" to 6" (#2520-654), set of 6; white knobby STARFISH, 6" to 8" (#2520-656); all from seashellco.com, 954-565-2300. My TOTE, large with round handle, (#4945247162202), from Muji, muji.us.

MINIATURE FELT PURSES, PAGE 118: WOOL FELT, 9"x12" or 18" square, from Magic Cabin, 888-623-3655 or magiccabin.com. WOOL-AND-RAYON FELT in various colors, by National Nonwovens, 800-333-3469 or woolfelt.com.

EMBROIDERED FELT HANDBAG, PAGE 119: Similar Designer Diamond SEWING AND EMBROIDERY MACHINE, from Husqvarna Viking, husqvarnaviking.com.

IRON-ON SILHOUETTES, PAGE 120: SILHOUETTES from *Silhouettes: A Pictorial Archive of Varied Illustrations*, by Carol Belange Grafton (Dover, 1979; ISBN #0486237818), 800-223-3130 or doverpublications.com. 9-oz. CANVAS TOTE (BS121), from CheapTotes.com, 888-387-1181. 10"x12" flat TOTE in Natural (#0011-NAT), and 19"x12½"x5½" LARGE GUSSET TOTE in Natural (#2666-NAT), from BagWorks, 800-365-7423 or bagworks.com. TWILL TAPE (#10016) in Green (#17), from Mokuba New York, 55 W. 39th Street, New York, NY 10018, 212-869-8900 or mokubany.com.

LABELS AND MONOGRAMS, PAGE 120: 15" square CANVAS BAG in White, from Innovative Greetings, ingreetings.com. 12¾"x12½" x2" CANVAS TOTE BAG (IN-14/117), set of 12 assorted colors, from Oriental Trading, 800-228-2269 or orientaltrading.com. 13½"x13½"x4" TOTE in Natural (#2667-NAT), from BagWorks, 800-365-7423 or bagworks.com. Similar 10"x11"x4" TOTE in natural (#03523990), by BagWorks, from CreateForLess, 866-333-4463 or createforless.com. Light FABRIC TRANSFERS (#3271), set of 6, and Dark FABRIC TRANSFERS (#3279), set of 5, from Avery, 800-462-8379 or avery.com.

EMBROIDERED CIRCLES, PAGE 121: 20" canvas UTILITY BAG (#315), by McGuire-Nicholas, from Texas Tool Totes, 877-663-5038 or texastooltotes.com. Metallic PERLE COTTON THREAD (MD700315) in Silver (#5283), by DMC, from Herrschners, 800-713-1239 or herrschners.com. 100% BAMBOO YARN (XS-32) in Gray, and similar natural HEMP/SILK YARN in Natural White (XS-12), from Habu Textiles, 212-239-3546 or habutextiles.com. Pure Silk DK YARN in purple by Debbie Bliss, and Cotton Glace YARN in Amethyst, by Rowan, from Katonah Yarn, 120 Bedford Road, Katonah, NY 10536, 914-977-3145 or katonahyarn.com.

OMBRÉ, PAGE 121: 18"x14"x4" Island TOTE in Natural (#0401-NAT), from BagWorks, 800-365-7423 or bagworks.com.

DRAWSTRING POUCHES, PAGE 122: Similar COTTON SHIRTING FABRIC, from New York Elegant Fabrics, 222 W. 40th Street, New York, NY 10018, 212-302-4980 or nyelegant fabrics.com. Similar WOOL SUITING FABRIC, Rosen & Chadick, 561 7th Avenue, 2nd Floor, New York, NY 10018, 212-869-0142 or rosenandchadickfabrics.com.

CROSS-STITCH SILHOUETTE TOTE, PAGE 123: Off-white BURLAP, from B&J Fabrics, 525 7th Avenue, New York, NY 10018, 212-354-8150 or bandjfabrics.com. 15mm TWILL TAPE (#5600), from Mokuba New York, 55 W. 39th Street, New York, NY 10018, 212-869-8900 or mokubany.com. DMC #8 PERLE COTTON THREAD in black (#310), pale blue (#747), and brown (#801), from Daytona Trimming, 251 W. 39th Street, New York, NY 10018, 212-354-1713 or daytonatrim.com. Similar 40"-wide Natural BURLAP FABRIC (BURNAT), from onlinefabric store.net, 866-232-8907.

OILCLOTH LUNCH BAG, PAGE 124: OILCLOTH in assorted patterns and colors, from Oilcloth International, 323-344-3967 or oilcloth.com.

APPLE-PRINT BAG, PAGE 125: TEXTILE COLORS (#01208), by Jacquard, from Blick Art Materials, 800-828-4548 or dickblick.com. Similar canvas totes in a selection of styles from BagWorks, 800-365-7423 or bagworks.com.

MULTICOMPARTMENT BAG, PAGE 127: Similar Wrights extra-wide double-fold BIAS TAPE in Light Blue and Dark Grey, from Jo-Ann Fabric and Craft Stores, 800-525-4951 or joann.com. Similar Amy Butler printed FABRIC available from Purl Patchwork, 147 Sullivan Street, New York, NY 10012, 212-420-8798 or purlsoho.com. Cotton CANVAS in Blue, Green, and Gray, from B&J Fabrics, 525 7th Avenue, New York, NY 10018, 212-354-8150 or bandjfabrics.com.

bath linens

MACHINE-EMBROIDERED BATH SET, PAGE 129: Similar Simply Cord SHOWER CURTAIN in White, similar Low Twist TOWELS, and similar Solid Cotton BATH MAT, all by the Martha Stewart Collection, from Macy's, 800-289-6229 or macys.com. Thread in a large selection of colors, by Gutermann, from Greenberg & Hammer, 535 8th Avenue, New York, NY 10018, 800-955-5135 or greenberg-hammer .com.

LINEN SHOWER CURTAIN, PAGE 130: Similar 60"-wide Judy LINEN in colors #37, #41, and #56, from Grayline Linen, 260 W. 39th Street, New York, NY 10018, 866-585-4636 or graylinelinen.com.

BIAS TAPE–EMBELLISHED TOWELS, PAGE 131: Similar Low Twist TOWELS, by the Martha Stewart Collection, from Macy's, 800-289-6229 or macys.com. FABRIC for towels: Paul, by Liberty of London, from B&J Fabrics, 525 7th Avenue, New York, NY 10018, 212-354-8150 or bandjfabrics.com. 50mm (2") BIAS-TAPE MAKER (#464/50), from Clover, 800-233-1703 or clover-usa.com. Similar WASHCLOTH by Yves Delorme, from ABC Carpet & Home, 212-473-3000 or abchome.com.

RAIN SLICKER SHOWER CURTAIN, PAGE 134: MATTE VINYL and lightweight LAMINATED DENIM, from B&J Fabrics, 525 7th Avenue, New York, NY 10018, 212-354-8150 or bandjfabrics.com.

REVERSIBLE-BORDER SHOWER CURTAIN, PAGE 136: Similar Simply Cord SHOWER CURTAIN in White, by the Martha Stewart Collection, from Macy's, 800-289-6229 or macys .com. Lime-green GINGHAM and CORDUROY FABRIC, from B&J Fabrics, 525 7th Avenue, New York, NY 10018, 212-354-8150 or bandjfabrics.com. Buttons, from Daytona Trimming, 251 W. 39th Street, New York, NY 10018, 212-354-1713 or daytonatrim.com.

EYELET SHOWER CURTAIN, PAGE 137: Similar modern open EYELET, from B&J Fabrics, 525 7th Avenue, New York, NY 10018, 212-354-8150 or bandjfabrics.com.

bed linens

FADED SHEET SET, PAGE 139: Similar 19th century Double Pinks FABRICS from ReproductionFabrics.com, 800-380-4611. Floral FABRICS, by Liberty of London, from B&J Fabrics, 525 7th Avenue, New York, NY 10018, 212-354-8150 or bandjfabrics.com.

EYELET OVERLAY, PAGE 140: Similar EYELET from B&J Fabrics, 525 7th Avenue, New York, NY 10018, 212-354-8150 or bandjfabrics.com.

EYELET PILLOWCASES, PAGE 141: Cotton organdy-bordered EYELET, from B&J Fabrics, 525 7th Avenue, New York, NY 10018, 212-354-8150 or bandjfabrics.com. 58" Shamrock cotton-voile EYELET, from New York Elegant Fabrics, 222 W. 40th Street, New York, NY 10018, 212-302-4980 or nyelegantfabrics.com.

ZIGZAG EMBROIDERY, PAGE 142: Similar 280 Thread Count Simple Care SHEET SETS, by the Martha Stewart Collection, from Macy's, 800-289-6229 or macys.com.

SHELL-STAMPED, PAGE 142: Similar 400 Thread Count Diamond Embroidered Stitch SHEETS, and similar Trousseau Garden QUILT or Solid Diamond Stitch QUILT, by the Martha Stewart Collection, from Macy's, 800-289-6229 or macys.com.

FRENCH-KNOTTED BORDERS, PAGE 143: Similar BLANKET in cotton fleece (#2750) in Cinnamon, similar double-size Paintbrush Flannel BEDDING (#00012) in Cranberry: flat and fitted SHEETS and PILLOWCASES, all from Garnet Hill, 800-870-3513 or garnethill.com. Six-strand EMBROIDERY FLOSS (#117), in orange (#741), brown (#433), and green (#905), from DMC, 800-275-4117 or dmc-usa.com.

RICKRACK TRIM, PAGE 143: Assorted RICKRACK, from Daytona Trimming, 251 W. 39th Street, New York, NY 10018, 212-354-1713 or daytonatrim.com. 22"x33" crystal-white hemstitched standard PILLOWCASE (UCRY.P33), similar 12"x18" crystal-white hemstitched boudoir SHAM (UCRY.S1620), and flat and fitted TWIN SHEETS, from Celtic Linens, celticlinens.com.

LINEN PILLOWCASES, PAGE 144: Colored LINEN, from B&J Fabrics, 525 7th Avenue, New York, NY 10018, 212-354-8150 or bandjfabrics.com. Similar Natural LINEN (on small pillow), from Mecox Gardens, 631-287-5015 or mecoxgardens.com.

MENSWEAR BEDDING SET, PAGE 145: Spa queen-sized FLAT SHEET (#3438201) in White Orchid, Spa standard PILLOWCASES (#3438201) in White Orchid, and Oxford queen-sized FITTED SHEET (#2963577) in Blue, from Ralph Lauren, 888-475-7674 or ralphlauren.com. Similar COTTON SHIRTING FABRIC, from Rosen & Chadick, 561 7th Avenue, 2nd Floor, New York, NY 10018, 212-869-0142 or rosenandchadickfabrics.com.

RUNNING STITCH–EMBROIDERED BEDDING, PAGE 148: Similar 280 Thread Count Simple Care SHEET SETS, by the Martha Stewart Collection, from Macy's, 800-289-6229 or macys.com. Similar 100% COTTON (for pillows) and WOOL CASHMERE (for blanket), from Mood Designer Fabrics, 225 W. 37th Street, New York, NY 10018, 212-730-5003 or moodfabrics.com. Six-strand EMBROIDERY FLOSS (MD700117) in Medium Antique Violet (#3041), by DMC, from Herrschners, 800-713-1239 or herrschners.com. Similar 100% silk tram YARN (NS-28), from Habu Textiles, 212-239-3546 or habutextiles.com.

SASHIKO-EDGED PILLOWCASES, PAGE 149: SASHIKO KIT, from Purl Patchwork, 147 Sullivan Street, New York, NY 10012, 212-420-8798 or purlsoho.com.

bibs

APPLE-EMBROIDERED BIB, PAGE 153: Six-strand EMBROIDERY FLOSS in a selection of colors, by DMC, from Herrschners, 800-713-1239 or herrschners.com.

BIAS TAPE–EMBELLISHED BIB, PAGE 154: FABRIC for bibs: Nancy Ann (top) and Capel (bottom), by Liberty of London, from B&J Fabrics, 525 7th Avenue, New York, NY 10018, 212-354-8150 or bandjfabrics.com.

OILCLOTH POCKETED BIB, PAGE 155: OILCLOTH in solid pink, solid white, orange gingham, similar doily in orange, and mums in white, from Oilcloth International, 323-344-3967 or oilcloth.com.

blankets

EMBROIDERY-EDGED BASIC BLANKET, PAGE 157: Raspberry WOOL CASHMERE, from B&J Fabrics, 525 7th Avenue, New York, NY 10018, 212-354-8150 or bandjfabrics.com. Similar handknit COTTON YARN by Rowan, from Purl, 137 Sullivan Street New York, NY 10012, 212-420-8796 or purlsoho.com.

RIBBON-BORDER BLANKET, PAGE 159: 36mm Rayon Grosgrain RIBBON in color #16, and 50mm Rayon Grosgrain RIBBON in color #43, from Shindo, 152 W. 36th Street, New York, NY 10018, 212-868-9311 or shindo.com.

FRINGED THROW, PAGE 160: 58" Yellow MOHAIR, from New York Elegant Fabrics, 222 W. 40th Street, New York, NY 10018, 212-302-4980 or nyelegantfabrics.com. Similar Flore-14 MOHAIR YARN, by Joseph Galler, from Purl, 137 Sullivan Street, New York, NY 10012, 212-420-8796 or purlsoho.com.

FRENCH-KNOT BLANKET, PAGE 161: Orange WOOL FABRIC, from Rosen & Chadick, 561 7th Avenue, 2nd Floor, New York, NY 10018, 212-869-0142 or rosenandchadickfabrics.com. Gray WOOL FELT, from B&J Fabrics, 525 7th Avenue, New York, NY 10018, 212-354-8150 or bandjfabrics.com. "Sinful" CASHMERE YARN, in natural (#20093), by Classic Elite; 978-453-2837 or classiceliteyarns.com.

DOUBLE-SIDED RECEIVING BLANKET, PAGE 163: Similar COTTON PRINTS and COTTON FLANNEL, from Purl Patchwork, 147 Sullivan Street, New York, NY 10012, 212-420-8798 or purlsoho.com.

books

LEATHER NOTEBOOK AND CHECKBOOK COVERS, PAGE 166: Similar 3-Piece QUILTING SET (#95237097, includes 45mm rotary cutter, 18"x24" cutting mat, 6"x24" acrylic ruler cutter), from Fiskars, 866-348-5661 or fiskarscrafts.com. 3½"x5" Floral-pattern Parker NOTECARD, from Carrot & Stick Press, 866-595-5333 or carrotandstickpress.com. ROTARY CUTTER, by Olfa, from Beverly's Fabrics, 831-684-4220 or beverlys.com. 12" Alumicutter RULER (#1312), from Alumicolor, 800-624-9379 or alumicolor.com. Similar "Bond Cement 527" GLUE from New York Beads, 1026 Sixth Avenue, New York, NY 10018, 212-382-2994 or beadson5th.com.

FELT BOOK JACKETS, PAGE 167: Similar tapestry WOOL YARN in ecru (#700486), by DMC, from Herrschners, 800-713-1239 or herrschners.com. SCALLOPING SHEARS, by Fiskars, from Jo-Ann Fabric and Craft Stores, 888-739-4120 or joann.com. GROMMET KIT by Dritz, from Steinlauf and Stoller, 877-869-0321, steinlaufandstoller.com. Similar 3-inch organdy RIBBON, from Midori, midoriribbon.com.

GARDEN JOURNALS, PAGE 168: Silk EMBROIDERY RIBBON in a selection of colors, from YLI, 800-296-8139 or ylicorp.com. Hand-dyed 100% silk EMBROIDERY RIBBON in a selection of colors, from River Silks, 877-944-7444 or riversilks.com. Packed washable EMBROIDERY FLOSS in a selection of colors, from Mokuba New York, 55 W. 39th Street, New York, NY 10018, 212-869-8900 or mokubany.com. Six-strand EMBROIDERY FLOSS in a selection of colors, by DMC, from Michaels, 800-642-4235 or michaels.com. SEAM BINDING in a selection of colors, from Daytona Trimming, 251 W. 39th Street, New York, NY 10018, 212-354-1713 or daytonatrim.com.

OILCLOTH BOOK COVERS, PAGE 170: OILCLOTH in orange gingham and orange orchids patterns, from Oilcloth International, 323-344-3967 or oilcloth.com.

clothing

NO-SEW SCALLOPED WRAP SKIRT, PAGE 173: ULTRASUEDE Soft in Executive Grey, from Field's Fabrics, 800-678-5872 or fieldsfabrics.com.

A-LINE WRAP SKIRT, PAGE 176: Similar Printed 53"-wide Tana Lawn COTTON FABRIC, by Liberty of London, from Purl Patchwork, 147 Sullivan Street, New York, NY 10012, 212-420-8798 or purlsoho.com.

SEA-PRINT SARONG, PAGE 178: 58"-wide COTTON BATISTE in pink, from New York Elegant Fabrics, 222 W. 40th Street, New York, NY 10018, 212-302-4980 or nyelegantfabrics.com. TEXTILE COLOR (#01208) in Scarlet Red, by Jacquard, from Blick Art Materials, 800-828-4548 or dickblick.com. White finger STARFISH, 6" to 8" (#2500-656), set of 6, from seashellco.com, 954-565-2300.

HAWAIIAN-PATTERN APPLIQUÉD ROBE, PAGE 179: Similar LINEN BATHROBE in white, from Linen Dreams, 512-358-1542 or linendreams.com. HANDKERCHIEF LINEN in Dark Sage, from Grayline Linen, 260 W. 39th Street, New York, NY 10018, 866-585-4636 or graylinelinen.com.

BABY KIMONO, PAGE 180: Feather-wale CORDUROY and red-and-white striped COTTON SHIRTING FABRIC, from B&J Fabrics, 525 7th Avenue, New York, NY 10018, 212-354-8150 or bandjfabrics.com. 54" stretch COTTON SATEEN, from New York Elegant Fabrics, 222 W. 40th Street, New York, NY 10018, 212-302-4980 or nyelegantfabrics.com. Polka-dot SILK, from Rosen & Chadick, 561 7th Avenue, 2nd Floor, New York, NY 10018, 212-869-0142 or rosenandchadickfabrics.com. SEAM BINDING, from Mokuba New York, 55 W. 39th Street, New York, NY 10018, 212-869-8900 or mokubany.com.

BUTTERFLY-APPLIQUÉD SHAWL, PAGE 184: SILK SHANTUNG in Silver, from B&J Fabrics, 525 7th Avenue, New York, NY 10018, 212-354-8150 or bandjfabrics.com. Similar BROCADE FABRIC from New York Elegant Fabrics, 222 W. 40th Street, New York, NY 10018, 212-302-4980 or nyelegantfabrics.com.

FLOWER-APPLIQUÉD SHIRT, PAGE 185: Similar COTTON SHIRTING, from New York Elegant Fabrics, 222 W. 40th Street, New York, NY 10018, 212-302-4980 or nyelegantfabrics.com.

DRAWSTRING PANTS, PAGE 186: Similar 43"-wide COTTON SEERSUCKER, from Jo-Ann Fabric and Craft Stores, 888-739-4120 or joann.com.

coasters

OILCLOTH CUTOUT COASTERS, PAGE 189: OILCLOTH in assorted patterns and colors, from Oilcloth International, 323-344-3967 or oilcloth.com.

MACHINE-EMBROIDERED, PAGE 190: 18" square FELT in Celery, Melon, and White, from Magic Cabin, 888-623-3655 or magiccabin.com.

FADED FLORAL FABRICS, PAGE 190: Floral FABRICS, by Liberty of London, from B&J Fabrics, 525 7th Avenue, New York, NY 10018, 212-354-8150 or bandjfabrics.com. Anti-Chlor BLEACH NEUTRALIZER, from PRO Chemical & Dye, 800-228-9393 or prochemical.com. DYE LIQUID, from Rit, 866-794-0800 or ritdye.com.

FRINGED, PAGE 191: Similar 60" WOOL-CASHMERE BLEND in light-pink, 44" RAW SILK in green or yellow, 58" orange BURLAP, and similar 60" WOOL-CASHMERE BLEND in dark pink, from New York Elegant Fabrics, 222 W. 40th Street, New York, NY 10018, 212-302-4980 or nyelegantfabrics.com.

RICKRACK-EDGED, PAGE 191: ½" scarlet RICKRACK (#29) from Daytona Trimming, 251 W. 39th Street, New York, NY 10018, 212-354-1713 or daytonatrim.com.

cozies

MENSWEAR WATER-BOTTLE COZY, PAGE 193: Similar WOOL SUITING FABRIC, from Rosen & Chadick, 561 7th Avenue, 2nd Floor, New York, NY 10018, 212-869-0142 or rosenandchadickfabrics.com. Classic single-ribbed HOT WATER BOTTLE in ivory, by Fashy, from amazon.com.

CLUCKING-EGG COZY, PAGE 195: 18" square WOOL FELT in Shell, Aqua, and Peas, from Magic Cabin, 888-623-3655 or magiccabin.com.

curtains

STENCILED CURTAINS, PAGE 199: 84"x50" opaque Belgian linen CURTAIN PANELS in Honey (13020128HONY), from Restoration Hardware, 800-762-1005 or restorationhardware.com. 11"x17" ADVENTURE PAPER (for stencils), 10 sheets, from waterproof-paper.com. Sheer trace VELLUM (#901417), by Borden & Riley, from Village Supplies, 708-824-1402 or artstuff.net. TEXTILE COLORS (JACTC8) in #123 White, #102 Goldenrod, #103 Orange, and #106 True Red (for flowers), and #117 Emerald Green, #112 Sapphire Blue, and #122 Black (for leaves), by Jacquard, from Dharma Trading, 800-542-5227 or dharmatrading.com.

LINEN-EDGED SHEERS, PAGE 200: Silk organza DRAPERY, from Restoration Hardware, 800-762-1005 or restorationhardware.com. Similar 60"-wide Barry LINEN in Mint from Grayline Linen, 260 W. 39th Street, New York, NY 10018, 866-585-4636 or graylinelinen.com. CURTAIN RINGS, from Zarin Fabrics, 314 Grand Street, New York, NY 10002, 212-966-6690 or zarinfabrics.com.

RIBBON-STRIPED SHEERS, PAGE 201: Voile Sheer DRAPE in White, from Pottery Barn, 888-779-5176 or potterybarn.com. 36mm aqua RIBBON (SIC-123), from Shindo, 152 W. 36th Street, New York, NY 10018, 212-868-9311 or shindo.com.

TUCKED-STRIPE CAFÉ CURTAIN, PAGE 202: LINEN/RAYON BLEND, from B&J Fabrics, 525 7th Avenue, New York, NY 10018, 212-354-8150 or bandjfabrics.com.

BUTTON-TAB CAFÉ CURTAIN, PAGE 203: SILK TAFFETA, from B&J Fabrics, 525 7th Avenue, New York, NY 10018, 212-354-8150 or bandjfabrics.com. Similar BUTTONS from M&J Trimming, 1008 Sixth Avenue, New York, NY 10018, 800-965-8746 or mjtrim.com. ⅜" ALUMINUM ROD, from Greentex Upholstery Supplies, 236 W. 26th Street, New York, NY 10001, 212-206-8585.

APPLIQUÉD CURTAIN, PAGE 204: Silk organza DRAPERY, from Restoration Hardware, 800-762-1005 or restorationhardware.com. Similar EYELET from B&J Fabrics, 525 7th Avenue, New York, NY 10018, 212-354-8150 or bandjfabrics.com.

TWILL TAPE–EMBELLISHED CURTAIN, PAGE 205: FUSIBLE STRIPS by Steam A Seam 2 and DRESSMAKER'S MARKING PENCIL, by Dritz, from sewandquilt.com, 360-757-1812. Assorted colors and sizes of TWILL TAPE, from Shindo, 152 W. 36th Street, New York, NY 10018, 212-868-9311 or shindo.com.

PINCH-PLEATED CAFÉ CURTAINS, PAGE 206: WOOL CREPE, from B&J Fabrics, 525 7th Avenue, New York, NY 10018, 212-354-8150 or bandjfabrics.com. Similar ⅜" Polished Brass ROD (#01136291), similar pair of ⅜" 2-Part Barrel BRACKETS (#01115637), and similar ¾" Diameter "No-sew" Eyelet Café RINGS (#00127167), all from Gracious Home, 800-338-7809 or gracioushome.com.

TABLE-SKIRT CURTAINS, PAGE 207: Red-striped TICKING, from Joe's Fabric Warehouse, 102 Orchard Street, New York, NY 10002, 212-674-7089 or joesfabric.com. Similar brass RINGS from New York Beads, 1026 Sixth Avenue, New York, NY 10018, 212-382-2994 or beadson5th.com. ½" brass-plated aluminum or steel ROD (#70003-063), and ½" brass BARREL BRACKETS (#732-63), from Zarin Fabrics, 314 Grand Street, New York, NY 10002, 212-966-6690 or zarinfabrics.com.

decorative pillows

PILLOW TRIMMINGS, PAGE 215: Similar MOHAIR in Rio, Edith SATIN in Coral (for flange lining), and Molly FABRIC in Chamomile (for bolster), from The Silk Trading Co., 888-745-5302 or silktrading.com. Similar PILLOW INSERTS in various sizes from The Company

Store, 800-323-8000, or thecompanystore.com. Double-faced Satin RIBBON (#1100) in Rust (#9), from Mokuba New York, 55 W. 39th Street, New York, NY 10018, 212-869-8900 or mokubany.com. Similar assorted trims from Tinsel Trading, 1 W. 37th Street, New York, NY 10018, tinseltrading.com.

SEASHELL-PRINTED PILLOWS, PAGE 216: TEXTILE COLORS (#01208) in Scarlet Red, White, and Yellow Ochre, by Jacquard, from Blick Art Materials, 800-828-4548 or dickblick.com.

TUFTED CUSHION, PAGE 219: Similar silk Hayward PILLOWS in various colors, from Crate & Barrel, 800-967-6696 or crateandbarrel.com.

PINCH-PLEATED PILLOW, PAGE 220: 20"x20" Napoli vintage LINEN in Flax and Pewter, and 15"x15" in Plum Frost, from Libeco Home, libecohomestores.com.

BIRD-EMBROIDERED PILLOWS, PAGE 222: Oxford green LINEN, from B&J Fabrics, 525 7th Avenue, New York, NY 10018, 212-354-8150 or bandjfabrics.com. Similar 2-sided dark-brown WAXED LINEN, from NY Elegant Fabrics, 222 W. 40th Street, New York, NY 10018, 212-302-4984 or nyelegant.com.

FALLING-LEAF PILLOW COVERS, PAGE 223: Similar WOOL FELT, from from A Child's Dream Come True, 800-359-2906 or achildsdream.com.

CROSS-STITCH PILLOW COVER, PAGE 225: LINEN BURLAP and LINEN UPHOLSTERY FABRIC in stone, from B&J Fabrics, 525 7th Avenue, New York, NY 10018, 212-354-8150 or bandjfabrics.com. Similar RAW SILK from New York Elegant Fabrics, 222 W. 40th Street, New York, NY, 212-302-4980 or nyelegantfabrics.com. Yellow lace MOHAIR YARN, from School Products, 1201 Broadway, New York, NY 10001, 212-679-3516 or schoolproductsyarns.com. Kidsilk haze MOHAIR YARN in Majestic (#589) and similar yarn: Loet Sale Kidlin in Tomato Red, from Purl, 137 Sullivan Street, New York, NY 10012, 212-420-8796 or purlsoho.com.

TOOTH-FAIRY PILLOW, PAGE 226: 9"x12" or 18" square WOOL FELT, from Magic Cabin, 888-623-3655 or magiccabin.com. WoolFelt WOOL-AND-RAYON FELT in various colors, by National Nonwovens, 800-333-3469 or woolfelt.com.

WEDDING-RING PILLOW, PAGE 227: Linen FLOWERS in small (AP854) and large (AP855), from Tinsel Trading, 1 W. 37th Street, New York, NY 10018, tinseltrading.com. Bird-print HANDKERCHIEF by Sukie, sukie.co.uk. ¼" cream RIBBON (REF726/6), from Tinsel Trading, 1 W. 37th Street, New York, NY 10018, tinseltrading.com. "White Dove" LINEN in Citrus (#4002-02), from Victoria Hagan Home, 212-888-3241 or victoriahaganhome.com. Similar ⅜" double-faced satin RIBBON in cream, from Mokuba New York, 55 W. 39th Street, New York, NY 10018, 212-869-8900 or mokubany.com.

COUCHED PILLOW BANDS, PAGE 228: Similar CORD, from M&J Trimmings, 1008 Sixth Avenue, New York, NY 10018, 212-391- 9072 or mjtrim.com.

HAND-APPLIQUÉD PILLOW COVERS, PAGE 229: 54"-wide Belgian LINENS in North Sea (P533) and Water Green (P336), from B&J Fabrics, 525 7th Avenue, New York, NY 10018, 212-354-8150 or bandjfabrics.com. COTTON VELVET in Chartreuse and Salmon, and 58"-wide metallic LINEN (L522) in silver, from New York Elegant Fabrics, 222 W. 40th Street, New York, NY 10018, 212-302-4980 or nyelegantfabrics.com. Antique metallic spindle cord (SIC-9518), size small in color #4, from Shindo, 152 W. 36th Street, New York, NY 10018, 212-868-9311 or shindo.com.

DRAWSTRING BOLSTER, PAGE 231: Lavender, light-green, and blue thin-striped TICKING, from Joe's Fabric Warehouse, 102 Orchard Street, New York, NY 10002, 212-674-7089 or joesfabric.com. Similar Blue striped TICKING, from Zarin Fabrics, 314 Grand Street, New York, NY 10002, 212-966-6690 or zarinfabrics.com. 9" cylindrical FOAM, similar 6" cylindrical FOAM, and 4" cylindrical FOAM, from Economy Foam & Futons, 56 W. 8th Street, New York, NY 10011, 212-475-4800 or economyfoamandfutons.com.

PIN-TUCK PILLOWS, PAGE 232: COTTON BROADCLOTH, from B&J Fabrics, 525 7th Avenue, New York, NY 10018, 212-354-8150 or bandjfabrics.com.

dolls

HAND-SEWN DOLLS, PAGE 235: DOLL-SKIN COTTON FABRIC in five colors (#815001), and WOOL STUFFING (#816501), from Magic Cabin, 888-623-3655 or magiccabin.com.

flowers

FLOWERING BRANCHES, PAGE 239: Yellow (FL413) and white (FL422) STAMENS, from Tinsel Trading, 1 W. 37th Street, New York, NY 10018, tinseltrading.com. 45" pink Pimatex STRETCH COTTON, and 60" HEAVY MUSLIN, from B&J Fabrics, 525 7th Avenue, New York, NY 10018, 212-354-8150 or bandjfabrics.com. Similar Raining dots FABRIC in Daffodil Yellow (AVSHO4YE), by Michele Wojeicki for Avlyn, from equilter.com, 877-322-7423. Similar Tana Lawn Sarah's Secret Garden FABRIC in Hot Pink, by Liberty of London, from Purl Patchwork, 147 Sullivan Street, New York, NY 10012, 212-420-8798 or purlsoho.com. ⅞" and 1½" grosgrain RIBBONS (color #001), from Hyman Hendler & Sons, 21 W. 38th Street, New York, NY 10018, 212-840-8393 or hymanhendler.com. ½" SEAM BINDING, from Sil Thread, 257 W. 38th Street, New York, NY 10018, 212-997-8949. 30mm cotton double-face SATIN TAPE (SIC-147), from Shindo, 152 W. 36th Street, New York, NY 10018, 212-868-9311 or shindo.com. 1" ridged SATIN RIBBON (MAKO) and ⅝" white grosgrain RIBBON, from Hyman Hendler & Sons, 21 W. 38th Street, New York, NY 10018, 212-840-8393 or hymanhendler.com. 15mm pleated SATIN RIBBON (#0492) in white (#2), 15mm natural COTTON RIBBON (#1502), and 20mm SILK-TAFFETA RIBBON (#1549) in sheer white (#1), from Mokuba New York, 55 W. 39th Street, New York, NY 10018, 212-869-8900 or mokubany.com. ½" SEAM BINDING and FABRIC GLUE, by Magna-Tac, from Sil Thread, 257 W. 38th Street, New York, NY 10018, 212-997-8949. 50mm grosgrain RIBBON (#8900), in yellow (#60), from Mokuba New York, 55 W. 39th Street, New York, NY 10018, 212-869-8900 or mokubany.com.

COVERED-BUTTON BOUTONNIERE, PAGE 241: Half-ball COVERED BUTTON KITS, in size 24 (#86590624), set of 5; size 30 (#27650309), set of 4; and size 45 (#40700618), set of 3; all by Dritz, from CreateForLess, 866-333-4463 or createforless.com. 54" Leaf-print FABRIC in glenjade by Liberty; and dark-blue LINEN, from B&J Fabrics, 525 7th Avenue, New York, NY 10018, 212-354-8150 or bandjfabrics.com. 7mm picot TAFFETA RIBBON (#1548), in navy (#19) and light blue (#25), from Mokuba New York, 55 W. 39th Street, New York, NY 10018, 212-869-8900 or mokubany.com. 28-gauge 7" STEM WIRE (#47969960), 50 pieces, by Fibre Craft; FUSIBLE WEB (#70143631) by Steam-a-Seam; and 60' FLORAL TAPE in Light Green (#09028275), by Panacea; all from CreateFor Less, 866-333-4463 or createforless.com.

RICKRACK FLOWERS, PAGE 242: RICKRACK in various sizes and colors, from Daytona Trimming, 251 W. 39th Street, New York, NY 10018, 212-354-1713 or daytonatrim.com. Similar FLORAL STAMENS, from Tinsel Trading Company, 1 W. 37th Street, New York, NY 10018, tinseltrading.com.

handkerchiefs

EMBROIDERED HANDKERCHIEFS, PAGE 245: Similar pure cotton HANDKERCHIEF in White from Brooks Brothers, 800-274-1815 or brooksbrothers.com. Six-strand EMBROIDERY FLOSS in a selection of colors, by DMC, from Herrschners, 800-713-1239 or herrschners .com.

RIBBON-EMBROIDERED HANDKERCHIEFS, PAGE 247: Silk EMBROIDERY RIBBON in a selection of colors, from YLI, 800-296-8139 or ylicorp.com. Hand-dyed 100% silk EMBROIDERY RIBBON in a selection of colors, from River Silks, 877-944-7444 or riversilks.com. Packed washable EMBROIDERY FLOSS in a selection of colors, from Mokuba New York, 55 W. 39th Street, New York, NY 10018, 212-869-8900 or mokubany.com. Six-strand EMBROIDERY FLOSS in a selection of colors, by DMC, from Michaels, 800-642-4235 or michaels.com. SEAM BINDING in a selection of colors, from Daytona Trimming, 251 W. 39th Street, New York, NY 10018, 212-354-1713 or daytonatrim.com.

nursery

QUILTED CRIB BUMPER, PAGE 250: Assorted COTTON FABRICS for bumper, from B&J Fabrics, 525 7th Avenue, New York, NY 10018, 212-354-8150 or bandjfabrics.com. Additional FABRICS and BATTING, from The City Quilter, 133 W. 25th Street, New York, NY 10001, 212-807-0390 or cityquilter.com. PIPING and TIES, from Daytona Trimming, 251 W. 39th Street, New York, NY 10018, 212-354-1713 or daytonatrim.com.

SIMPLE FELT GARLAND, PAGE 253: 18" WOOL FELT, from Magic Cabin, 888-623-3655 or magiccabin.com.

organizers

FABRIC-TOPPED STORAGE BOXES, PAGE 257: Similar COTTON SHIRTING, from New York Elegant Fabrics, 222 W. 40th Street, New York, NY 10018, 212-302-4980 or nyelegant fabrics.com. Similar Gustav CD/DVD/VIDEO BOX (#9491569), Similar "Sverker" A3 LETTER BOX (#934145601) in dark grey, and Johan archive FILE BOX (#954145601) in dark grey, by Bigso, from organize.com, 800-600-9817.

VELVET-LINED JEWELRY BOXES, PAGE 259: 9³/₈"x6½"x4" oval unfinished SHAKER BOX #5 (#13G11), from Shaker Workshops, 800-840-9121 or shakerworkshops.com. Oval wood CHEESE BOX (BOX9402), in four sizes; and mini round CHEESE BOX (BOX9403), by Nicole Crafts, from A.C. Moore, acmoore.com. Similar ³/₈" antique VELVET RIBBON, from Hyman Hendler & Sons, 21 W. 38th Street, New York, NY 10018, 212-840-8393 or hymanhendler .com. MILK PAINT in Salmon, from Old Fashioned Milk Paint, 866-350-6455 or milkpaint .com. SILK SATIN in Pink, SILK TAFFETA in Orange and Salmon, and DUPIONI SILK in Brown, from B&J Fabrics, 525 7th Avenue, New York, NY 10018, 212-354-8150 or bandjfabrics.com.

FABRIC-WRAPPED ACCORDION FOLDERS, PAGE 260: 9mm, 12mm, and 20mm cotton herringbone TWILL TAPE (SIC-146, color #35), from Shindo, 152 W. 36th Street, New York, NY 10018, 212-868-9311 or shindo.com. Similar Woolen TWEED and similar SILK, from Mood Designer Fabrics, 225 W. 37th St, New York, NY 10018, 212-730-5003 or moodfabrics.com. Accordion letter-size EXPANDING FILE (#119099), from Staples, 800-378-2753 or staples.com.

FALLING-LEAVES FELT BOARD, PAGE 262: 60"-wide, 100% WOOL FELT from B&J Fabrics, 525 7th Avenue, New York, NY 10018, 212-354-8150 or bandjfabrics.com.

LEATHER COIN PURSE, PAGE 263: Assorted LEATHER Skins in White, Gold Finch (#5884), Haze (#5947), Regal Blue (#5749), Tanager (#5879), Perruche (#5928), Imperial Red (#5588), Mallard (#5944), and Pomme (#5933), from Kaufman Shoe Repair Supplies, 346 Lafayette Street, New York, NY 10012, 212-777-1700. Pink LEATHER, from Leather Impact, 256 W. 38th Street, New York, NY 10018, 212-302-2332 or leatherimpact.com. Revolving PUNCH PLIER (#72), from USA Hardware, 763-417-0094 or usahardware.com. Similar BONE FOLDER, by Martha Stewart Crafts, from Michaels, 800-642-4235 or michaels.com. PINKING SHEARS, by Fiskars, from Jo-Ann Fabric and Craft Stores, 888-739-4120 or joann.com. SNAP-ALL SETTER (#8108-01), from Tandy Leather Factory, tandyleatherfactory .com. 15mm urushi leather TRIM (#1511) in white (#2), similar white RICKRACK, ELASTIC CORD (#7404) in white (#2), 2mm SUEDE TRIM (#1509) in blue, and 5mm urushi leather TRIM (1511) in white (#2), from Mokuba New York, 55 W. 39th Street, New York, NY 10018, 212-869-8900 or mokubany.com. Gripper PLIER KIT for assorted snaps (CDL523 080049), by Dritz, from Jo-Ann Fabric and Craft Stores, 888-642-4235 or joann.com.

WRAPAROUND BULLETIN BOARD, PAGE 264: Pink COTTON CANVAS, from B&J Fabrics, 525 7th Avenue, New York, NY 10018, 212-354-8150 or bandjfabrics.com.

MULTIPLE-POCKET BULLETIN BOARD, PAGE 267: COTTON CANVAS, from B&J Fabrics, 525 7th Avenue, New York, NY 10018, 212-354-8150 or bandjfabrics.com.

pets

QUILTED DOG JACKET, PAGE 269: LAMINATED LINEN in Orange and Blue, from B&J Fabrics, 525 7th Avenue, New York, NY 10018, 212-354-8150 or bandjfabrics.com. 58"-wide FLEECE in Brown (#7000-06), from onlinefabricstore.net, 866-232-8907. LINEN in Brown and Taupe (for bias tape), from Grayline Linen, 260 W. 39th Street, New York, NY 10018, 866-585-4636 or graylinelinen.com.

CATNIP FISH ON A POLE, PAGE 271: Air erasable MARKING PEN (Q328), from ThreadArt, 800-504-6867 or threadart.com. Certified organic CATNIP from Pet Food Express, petfoodexpress.com.

ULTRASUEDE DOG COAT, PAGE 273: ULTRASUEDE SOFT in Morning Sky, from Field's Fabrics, 800-678-5872 or fieldsfabrics .com. Salmon BUTTONS, by Tender Buttons, 143 E. 62nd Street, New York, NY 10065, 212-758-7004.

MENSWEAR MICE, PAGE 274: Similar WOOL SUITING, from New York Elegant Fabrics, 222 W. 40th Street, New York, NY 10018, 212-302-4980 or nyelegantfabrics.com. Similar COTTON SHIRTING, from B&J Fabrics, 525 7th Avenue, New York, NY 10018, 212-354-8150 or bandjfabrics.com.

pincushions

HEIRLOOM-TOMATO PINCUSHIONS, PAGE 277: Similar 8-piece HAWAIIAN QUILTING NEEDLE SET (#47904424), by Clover, from CreateForLess, 866-333-4463 or createforless .com.

STRAWBERRY PINCUSHIONS, PAGE 279: Six-strand cotton EMBROIDERY FLOSS (MD700117) in dark coral (#349), light coral (#352), white (#B5200), and light mustard (#3822), and PERLE COTTON in similar very light pistachio green (#369), and forest green (#989), all by DMC, from Herrschners, 800-713-1239 or herrschners.com. 60" red cotton mini stripe SHIRTING FABRIC, from Rosen & Chadick, 561 7th Avenue, 2nd Floor, New York, NY 10018; 212-869-0142 or rosenandchadick fabrics.com. 18" square WOOL FELT in red, melon, white, and shell, from Magic Cabin, 888-623-3655 or magiccabin.com.

MASON-JAR SEWING KIT, PAGE 280: Similar GLUE GUN and ALL-PURPOSE SCISSORS, by Martha Stewart Crafts, from Michaels, 800-642-4235 or michaels.com.

FELT-LEAF NOTIONS, PAGE 281: 2¾"-by-1¾" INK PAD in frost white, by ColorBox, from The Ink Pad, 22 8th Avenue, New York, NY 10014, 212-463-9876 or theinkpadnyc.com. 18" square WOOL FELT, in Cranberry, Pumpkin, and Salmon, from Magic Cabin, 888-623-3655 or magiccabin.com. Unique Stitch ADHESIVE, by Dritz, from Jo-Ann Fabric and Craft Stores, 888-642-4235 or joann.com. Plain CRAFT SAND from Affordable Crafts, 423-623-5006 or gelstuff.com.

pot holders

HEART-SHAPED POT HOLDER, PAGE 283: Assorted printed-cotton FABRICS from B&J Fabrics, 525 7th Avenue, New York, NY 10018, 212-354-8150 or bandjfabrics.com. Crib-size select cotton BATTING, from The City Quilter, 133 W. 25th Street, New York, NY 10001, 212-807-0390 or cityquilter.com. Assorted ½" BIAS TAPE, by Wright's, from Greenberg & Hammer, 535 8th Avenue, New York, NY 10018, 800-955-5135 or greenberg-hammer .com.

DOUBLE-POCKETED POT HOLDER, PAGE 285: QUILTED IRONING BOARD COVER and similar 54"-wide Tavern TICKING (#CIW113 6004253) in Wedgwood, by Waverly, from Jo-Ann Fabric and Craft Stores, 888-642-4235 or joann.com.

quilts and patchwork

VINTAGE-HANDKERCHIEF QUILT, PAGE 287: Rocking-horse HANDKERCHIEF (#003220Io), from Westfalenstoffe, westfalenstoffe.com. Similar 3mm RIBBON (SIC-147) in color #42 from Shindo, 152 W. 36th Street, New York, NY 10018, 212-868-9311 or shindo.com. Red TICKING FABRIC, from B&J Fabrics, 525 7th Avenue, New York, NY 10018, 212-354-8150 or bandjfabrics.com. Similar 3-Piece QUILTING SET (#95237097, includes 45mm rotary cutter, 18"x24" cutting mat, 6"x24" acrylic ruler cutter), from Fiskars, 866-348-5661 or fiskarscrafts.com.

MENSWEAR PATCHWORK THROW, PAGE 289: Similar WOOL SUITING, from Rosen & Chadick, 561 7th Avenue, 2nd Floor, New York, NY 10018, 212-869-0142 or rosenandchadick fabrics.com and from New York Elegant Fabrics, 222 W. 40th Street, New York, NY 10018, 212-302-4980 or nyelegantfabrics.com.

STATE BIRD–EMBROIDERED QUILT, PAGE 291: Assorted EMBROIDERY HOOPS, from Jo-Ann Fabric and Craft Stores, 888-642-4235 or joann.com. Fine-line WATER ERASABLE MARKING PEN (NT455), from Ginger's Needleworks and Quilting, 337-232-7847 or quiltknit .com. Six-strand EMBROIDERY FLOSS in a large selection of colors, by DMC, from Herrschners, 800-713-1239 or herrschners .com. TRANSFER PAPER, in Red, Blue, Yellow, White, or Graphite, from Saral Paper, 212-223-3322 or saralpaper.com. Yellow LINEN from B&J Fabrics, 525 7th Avenue, New York, NY 10018, 212-354-8150 or bandjfabrics.com.

DYED-TICKING PATCHWORK QUILT, PAGE 294: TICKING, from Zarin Fabrics, 314 Grand Street New York, NY 10002, 212-966-6690 or zarinfabrics.com.

QUILTED SUITING COVERLET, PAGE 295: 60"-wide gray WOOL with pinstripe, from Rosen & Chadick, 561 7th Avenue, 2nd Floor, New York, NY 10018, 212-869-0142 or rosenandchadickfabrics.com. 54"-wide chechi stripe TAFFETA in yellow/gray, from The Silk Trading Co., 888-745-5302 or silktrading.com.

DENIM PATCHWORK QUILT, PAGE 295: Assorted DENIM, from B&J Fabrics, 525 7th Avenue, New York, NY 10018, 212-354-8150 or bandjfabrics.com.

STAR-PATTERN PATCHWORK COVERLET, PAGE 296: Similar WOOL in pale gray from Paron Fabrics, 206 W. 40th Street, New York, NY 10018, 212-768-3266 or paronfabrics.com. Similar ALL-PURPOSE SCISSORS, by Martha Stewart Crafts, from Michaels, 800-642-4235 or michaels.com.

shades

CLASSIC ROMAN SHADE, PAGE 299: FUSIBLE WEB (#70143631), by Steam-a-Seam, from CreateForLess, 866-333-4463 or createforless .com. BLACKOUT DRAPERY LINING FABRIC, from Beacon Fabric and Notions, 8331 Epicenter Boulevard, Lakeland, FL 33809, 800-713-8157 or beaconfabric.com. ½" brass SHADE RINGS, set of 100, shade lift CORD, CORD LOCK, small hourglass CORD TASSEL, and round wooden CORD CONDENSER, from draperysewingsupplies.com at Heavenly Home, 877-874-2202.

BILLOWY ROMAN SHADE, PAGE 302: Yellow Irish LINEN from Rosen & Chadick, 561 7th Avenue, 2nd Floor, New York, NY 10018, 212-869-0142 or rosenandchadickfabrics.com.

LONDON SHADE, PAGE 303: Similar 2½" CORD CLEATS from draperysewingsupplies .com at Heavenly Home, 877-874-2202. RING TAPE from Zarin Fabrics, 314 Grand Street, New York, NY 10002, 212-966-6690 or zarinfabrics.com.

EASY STENCILED SHADE, PAGE 304: Calypso ROLLER SHADE in Cornsilk (#843), from Smith + Noble, 800-248-888 or smithandnoble.com. WHIZZ ROLLER Set (#76380) and similar Modern Master STENCIL set from Janovic Plaza, 718-786-4444 or janovic.com.

VINE-STENCILED SHADE, PAGE 305: Custom ROLLER SHADE, from Smith & Noble, 800-248-8888 or smithandnoble.com. 4½"x18" Spencer Eddy House vine STENCIL (#352B2), from M. B. Historic Décor, 888-649-1790 or mbhistoricdecor.com.

slippers

NATURE-INSPIRED FELT SLIPPERS, PAGE 310: 72"-wide 40% wool FLAMEPROOF FELT in Smoke Tan (#5315), from Central Shippee, 800-631-8968 or thefeltpeople.com. 8"x12" HOLLAND WOOL in Salmon, Flesh, Soft White, Rose, and Tea Rose, from A Child's Dream Come True, 800-359-2906 or achildsdream .com.

FELT BABY SHOES, PAGE 311: 18" square WOOL FELT, from Magic Cabin, 888-623-3655 or magiccabin.com. RICKRACK, from Daytona Trimming, 251 W. 39th Street, New York, NY 10018, 212-354-1713 or daytonatrim.com. 1/16" circle HOLE PUNCH, by Martha Stewart Crafts, from Michaels, 800-642-4235 or michaels.com. Six-strand EMBROIDERY FLOSS in a large selection of colors, by DMC, from Herrschners, 800-713-1239 or herrschners .com.

table linens

EYELET TABLE RUNNER, PAGE 313: 100% cotton voile oval EYELET FABRIC, from B&J Fabrics, 525 7th Avenue, New York, NY 10018, 212-354-8150 or bandjfabrics.com.

FEATHER-STAMPED NAPKINS, PAGE 315: Metallic STAMP PAD in Gold, by Encore, from Paper Presentation, 800-727-3701 or paperpresentation.com. Ancient Page Dye INKPAD in Chocolate, by Clearsnap, from Frantic Stamper, 877-242-3726 or frantic stamper.com. Mallard DUCK FEATHERS: Natural (SI0188) and lemon-dyed (SI0189), from Orvis, 888-235-9763 or orvis.com.

FADED FLORALS, PAGE 316: Floral FABRIC, by Liberty of London, from B&J Fabrics, 525 7th Avenue, New York, NY, 10018, 212-354-8150 or bandjfabrics.com.

OMBRÉ, PAGE 316: Similar LINEN NAPKIN in White (#404899), from Crate & Barrel, 800-996-9960 or crateandbarrel.com.

DYED TICKING, PAGE 317: TICKING, from Joe's Fabric Warehouse, 102 Orchard Street, New York, NY 10002, 212-674-7089 or joesfabric.com.

BUTTON EMBROIDERY, PAGE 317: Similar small purple BUTTONS, from Greenberg & Hammer, 535 8th Avenue, New York, NY 10018, 800-955-5135 or greenberg-hammer .com.

ULTRASUEDE LEAF PLACE MATS, PAGE 318: ULTRASUEDE FABRIC in assorted colors, from Edinburgh Imports, 310-320-8151 or edinburghimports.com.

DRAWN-THREAD DESIGNS, PAGE 320: HANDKERCHIEF LINEN, from B&J Fabrics, 525 7th Avenue, New York, NY 10018, 212-354-8150 or bandjfabrics.com. Six-strand EMBROIDERY FLOSS (#117) in white, from DMC, 800-275-4117 or dmc-usa.com.

DRAWN-THREAD TABLE RUNNER, PAGE 321: Belgian linen mesh, from B&J Fabrics, 525 7th Avenue, New York, NY 10018, 212-354-8150 or bandjfabrics.com.

BATIK TABLE LINENS, PAGE 322: 24"x24" linen HANDKERCHIEF (#2724.HSI) and 54" square linen hemstiched TABLECLOTH (#700), from Ulster Linen, 631-859-5244 or ulsterlinen .com.

BLEACH-BATIK TABLE LINENS, PAGE 323: 100% cotton CANVAS in Wedgwood, from B&J Fabrics, 525 7th Avenue, New York, NY 10018, 212-354-8150 or bandjfabrics.com. ½mm stainless steel APPLICATOR TIP, by Jacquard, from New York Central Art Supply, 62 Third Avenue, New York, NY 10003, 800-950-6111 or nycentralart.com.

LINEN TABLECLOTH, PAGE 324: LINEN, from B&J Fabrics, 525 7th Avenue, New York, NY 10018, 212-354-8150 or bandjfabrics.com.

JAPANESE-EMBROIDERED TABLE LINENS, PAGE 326: SASHIKO KIT, from Purl Patchwork, 147 Sullivan Street, New York, NY 10012, 212-420-8798 or purlsoho.com.

BLOCK-PRINT TABLE LINENS, PAGE 328: LINEN MESH GRYNING in White with beige selvedges, from Just Scandinavian, 161 Hudson Street, New York, NY 10013, 212-334-2556 or justscandinavian.com.

RAFFIA-EMBROIDERED PLACE MATS, PAGE 329: Matte rayon RAFFIA in Daffodil (#749DA), by Wraphia, from Nashville Wraps, 800-547-9727 or nashvillewraps.com. Matte finish RAFFIA SOLOS in in White (SM030), from Raffit Ribbons, raffit.com.

DOILY TABLECLOTH, PAGE 330: Similar 8" Cluny white DOILIES, from Lartisana, lartisana.com.

LEATHER TABLE MATS, PAGE 331: Eco-Flo LEATHER WELD (#2655-01) from Tandy Leather Factory, tandleatherfactory.com. Diamond LAMBSKIN in Aqua and Pear, from Global Leathers, 212-244-5190 or globalleathers.com.

upholstery

BASIC DAYBED COVER, PAGE 333: Blumen DAMASK (#462870), by Dagobert Peche, from Maharam, 800-645-3943 or maharam.com.

UPHOLSTERED COFFEE TABLE, PAGE 339: Similar CHENILLE FABRIC on large footstool and similar SILK FABRIC on smaller footstool, from ABC Carpet & Home, 212-473-3000 or abchome.com.

REUPHOLSTERED CAMP STOOLS, PAGE 341: Similar Pangean COMFORT STOOL (#222P) by Byer of Maine, from Barre Army Navy Store, 800-448-7965 or vtarmynavy.com. Similar MILK PAINT in Snow White, from Old Fashioned Milk Paint, 866-350-6455 or milkpaint .com.

EASY CHAISE CUSHIONS, PAGE 342: Sunbrella OUTDOOR FABRIC, from Glen Raven, 336-221-2211 or sunbrella.com for stores.

HAWAIIAN-PATTERN STENCILED CUSHIONS, PAGE 343: 11"x17" ADVENTURE PAPER (for the stencils), from waterproof-paper.com. 3" natural silk SEA SPONGES, from Florida Sponge Company, floridasponges.com. TEXTILE PAINT (JACTC8) in 123 White, 112 Sapphire Blue, and 116 Apple Green, and 100 COLORLESS EXTENDER, by Jacquard, from Dharma Trading, 800-542-5227 or dharmatrading.com.

FITTED ARMCHAIR SLIPCOVERS, PAGE 344: Lilac VELVET, from The Silk Trading Co., 888-745-5302 or silktrading.com.

OMBRÉ HEADBOARD COVER, PAGE 347: Yarn-dyed LINEN (color #8), from Grayline Linen, 260 W. 39th Street New York, NY 10018, 866-585-4636 or graylinelinen.com.

wall décor

RIBBON-EMBROIDERED WALL HANGINGS, PAGE 351: Silk EMBROIDERY RIBBON in a large selection of colors, from YLI, 800-296-8139 or ylicorp.com. Hand-dyed 100% silk EMBROIDERY RIBBON in a large selection of colors, from River Silks, 877-944-7444 or riversilks.com. Packed washable EMBROIDERY FLOSS in a large selection of colors, from Mokuba New York, 55 W. 39th Street, New York, NY 10018, 212-869-8900 or mokubany .com. Six-strand EMBROIDERY FLOSS in a large selection of colors, by DMC, from Michaels, 800-642-4235 or michaels.com. SEAM BINDING in a large selection of colors, from Daytona Trimming, 251 W. 39th Street, New York, NY 10018, 212-354-1713 or daytonatrim .com.

index

Page numbers in italics indicate illustrations.

A

Accordion folders, fabric-wrapped, 260
Acrylic grid ruler, 28, *29*
Adhesives, 362
Adjustable apron, 108
A-line wrap skirt, *176*, 177
All-purpose dyes, 76, *76*
Alternative hems, 37
Animals project, 92–102
Apple-embroidered bib, *153*
Apple-print bag, 125
Appliqué, 39
 by hand, 41
 iron-on, 43
 quilting, 70–71
 by sewing machine, 42
 supplies, 40
Appliquéd curtain, 204
Appliquéd duvet-cover, *150*, 151
Appliquéd number book, 171
Appliquéd pillowcases, *150*, 151
Appliquéd pillow covers, 229
Appliquéd robe, Hawaiian-pattern, 179
Appliquéd sea-print tote, 117
Appliquéd shawl, butterfly, 184
Appliquéd shirt, flower, 185
Appliqué needle, 356
Aprons, 102–111
 adjustable, 108
 baker's, 109
 basic linen, *103*, 104
 child's oilcloth, *106*, 107
 crafter, 105
 dish-towel, 108
 faux-bois gardener's, 110–111
Area, for sewing, 20–21
Armchair slipcovers, fitted, 344
Asanocha, *56*, 57

B

Baby kimono, *180*, 181
Baby shoes, 311
Backstitch, 31, 48
Bags, 112–127
 apple-print, 125
 appliquéd sea-print tote, 117
 canvas tote, 116
 cross-stitch silhouette tote, 123
 drawstring, 122
 embroidered circles on, 121
 fabric-pocket tote, *113*, 114
 felt embroidered handbag, 119
 iron-on silhouette, 120
 labels on, 120
 miniature felt, *118*, 119
 monograms on, 120
 multicompartment, 127
 oilcloth lunch, *124*, 125
 ombré, 121
 pillowcase, 126
 raffia-embroidered tote, 115
Baker's apron, 109
Band, book, 167
Bands, pillow
 couched, 228
 wraparound, 217
Basic canvas tote, 116
Basic cottons, 12
Basic daybed cover, *333*, 334
Basic linen apron, *103*, 104
Basic supplies, 28, *29*
Basin, for dyeing, 76, *76*
Basting spray, 362
Bath linens, 128–137
 bath mat, 135
 bias tape-embellished towels, 131
 embroidered set, *129*, 130
 hooded towel, 133
 shower curtain
  eyelet, *137*
  linen, 130
  rain slicker, 134
  reversible border, 136
 washcloth puppets, 132
Bath mat, ribbon-bordered, 135
Batik, 78–79
Batik table linens, 322
Batting, 64, 363
Bed, dog, 272
Bed frame slipcover, 348
Bed linens, 138–151
 appliquéd, *150*, 151
 duvet cover, *146*, 147
 embroidered, 142
 eyelet overlay, 140
 eyelet pillowcases, 141
 faded sheet set, *139*
 flat-sheet duvet, 147
 French-knotted borders, 143
 linen pillowcases, 144
 menswear bedding set, 145
 rickrack trim, 143
 running stitch-embroidered, 148
 sashiko-edged pillowcases, 149
 shell-stamped, 142
Beeswax, 28, *29*
Bent-angled fabric shears, *360*, 361
Bias tape, 64, *64*, 365
Bias tape–embellished bib, 154
Bias tape–embellished towels, 131
Bias tape maker, 365
Bias-tape table runner, 318
Bibs, 152–155
 apple-embroidered, *153*
 bias tape–embellished, 154
 oilcloth pocketed, 155
Big stitches, 54, *54*

Bird-embroidered pillows, 222
Bird-embroidered quilt, state, *290*, 291
Blanket chest, cushion top, *336*, 337
Blankets, 156–163
  double-sided receiving, 163
  embroidery-edged, *157*, 158
  felted-sweater patchwork blanket, 162
  French-knot, 161
  fringed throw, 160
  menswear patchwork throw, 289
  ribbon-border, 159
Blanket stitch, 49
Bleach-batik table linens, 323
Bleaching, 80, *81*
Blended all-purpose thread, 19
Blind hemstitch, *60*
Block-printing, 88
Block-print table linens, 328
Bobbin, *32*, 33
Bobbin case, *32*, 33
Bobbin cover, *32*, 33
Bobbin winder, *32*, 33
Bobbin winder tension disk, *32*, 33
Bodkin, 363
Bolsters, *230*, 231
Books, 164–171
  appliquéd number, 171
  checkbook cover, *165*, 166
  felt jackets, 167
  garden journals, *168*, 169
  leather notebook cover, *165*, 166
  oilcloth covers, 170
Boutonniere, covered-button, 241
Boxes
  fabric-topped storage, *257*, 258
  velvet-lined jewelry, 259
Box pillows, 224
Bracket, flush-mount, 206
Branches
  flowering, *239*, 240
  wrapping, 240
Breaks, 21
Brick pattern, 54, *54*
Brushes, craft, 86, *86*
Bulldog, sock, 100
Bulletin board
  multiple-pocket, 267
  ribbon-striped, 261
  wraparound, 264–265
Bunny, menswear, 94
Butterfly-appliquéd shawl, 184
Button covers, 366
Button embroidery napkins, 317
Buttonhole stitch, *60*
Buttons, 366
Button tab café curtain, 203
Button-up window shade, 306, *307*

C

Café curtain
  button-tab, 203
  pinch-pleated, 206
  tucked stripe, 202
Calico, 13
Camp stools, reupholstered, 341
Canopy, scalloped, *249*
Canvas, 12
Canvas tote, 116
Card stock, 359
Cardstock templates, 40
Cashmere, 16
Catnip fish, 271
Chainstitch, 48
Chair, 21
Chair, dining, 335
Chair skirt, velvet, 345
Chaise cushions, 342
Chalk, tailor's, 28, *29*, 359
Chalk pencil, 28, *29*, 359
Chambray, 12
Chamomile, 77
Changing-table curtains, 255
Checkbook cover, *165*, 166
Chenille needle, 356
Chicken, felted, 96
Chicken scratch, 54, *54*
Child's oilcloth apron, *106*, 107
Circle running stitch, 54, *54*
Circles, embroidered, 121
Circle template, 358
Classic Roman shade, *299*, 300–301
Clipping corners, 35
Clipping curves, 35
Closed overlock stitch, *60*
Closures, 366
Clothing, 172–187
  A-line wrap skirt, *176*, 177
  baby kimono, *180*, 181
  butterfly-appliquéd shawl, 184
  drawstring pants, *186*, 187
  easy tube, 175
  flower-appliquéd shirt, 185
  girls shirt dress, *182*, 183
  Hawaiian-pattern appliquéd robe, 179
  no-sew scalloped wrap skirt, *173*, 174
  sarong, 178
Clucking-egg cozy, 195
Coasters, 188–191
  faded floral fabric, 190
  fringed, 191
  machine-embroidered, 190
  rickrack-edged, 191
Coat, dog, 273
Coated linen, 15
Coffee table, upholstered, 339
Coin purse, leather, 263
Color, thread, 19
Compuiter-aided embroidery, 61
Cookie cutter, 79

Coordinated sheet duvet cover, *146*, 147
Copying, in appliqué, 40
Cord, elastic, *364*, 365
Corduroy, 12
Corners, 35
Cotton(s)
  basic, 12
  batting, 64
  patterned, 13
Cotton all-purpose thread, 19
Cotton velvet, 12
Cotton voile, 12
Cotton web, *364*, 365
Couched pillow bands, 228
Covered-button boutonniere, 241
Coverlet
  star-pattern patchwork, *296*, 297
  suiting quilted, 295
  vintage-linen patchwork, 294
Covers
  bobbin, *32*, 33
  book, 170
  button, 366
  checkbook, *165*, 166
  daybed, *333*, 334
  duvet, *146*, 147
  leather notebook, *165*, 166
  ombré headboard, 347
  ottoman, 266
  pillow
    basic, *209*
    box, 224
    cross-stitch, 225
    doubled flanged, 212
    envelope-backed, 210
    falling leaf, 223
    hand appliquéd, 229
    napkin, 218
    piped edged, 214
    ruffled, 213
    slipstitched, 210
    Turkish cornered, 213
    woven wool, 221
    zippered, 211
  water-bottle, *193*, 194
Cozies, 192–195
  clucking egg, 195
  menswear water-bottle, *193*, 194
  pie-weight hand warmer, 194
Crafter's apron, 105
Craft glue, 362
Craft knife, 86, *86*
Craft paintbrushes, 86, *86*
Crewel needle, 356
Crewelwork headboard cover, *349*
Crib bumper, 250–251
Cross-stitch, 50–51, *60*
Cross-stitch patterns, 51
Cross-stitch pillow covers, 225
Cross-stitch silhouette tote, 123
Curtains, 196–207
  appliquéd, 204
  bracket, 206
  button-tab café, 203
  changing-table, 255
  floral stenciled, *198*, 199
  hanging of, 204
  linen-edged sheer, 200
  pinch-pleated café, 206
  ribbon-striped sheer, 201
  rod, 206
  shower
    eyelet, *137*
    linen, 130
    rain slicker, 134
    reversible border, 136
  table-skirt, *207*
  tucked-stripe café, 202
  twill-tape embellished, 205
  two-tone linen voile, *197*
Curves, 35
Cushions
  chaise, 342
  designated, 22
  Hawaiian-pattern stenciled, 343
  tufted, 219
Cushion-top blanket chest, *336*, 337
Cutting, of fabric, 30
Cutting area, 21
Cutting mat, 361
Cutting tools, *360*, 361

D

Dachshund, sock, 100
Dalmatian, sock, 100
Damask linen, 15
Damask silk, 14
Daybed, slipcovered patio, 340
Daybed cover, *333*, 334
Decorative pillows, 208–233
  bird-embroidered, 222
  box, 224
  easy tuxedo pin-tuck, 233
  pinch-pleated, 220
  pin-tuck, 232
  seashell-printed, 216
  tooth-fairy, 226
  tufted, 219
  wedding ring, 227
Denim, 12
Denim patchwork quilt, 295
Designated pincushions, 22
Diagonal stitch, 54, *54*
Dining chair, 335
Disappearing-ink fabric pen, 28, *29*, 359
  in appliqué, 40, *40*
  in embroidery, 46, *46*
Dish
  magnetic pin, 23
  porcelain, *20*
Dish-towel apron, 108
Dog bed, 272
Dog coat, 273
Dog jacket, *269*, 270
Dogs, sock, *99*, 100–101
Doily tablecloth, 330
Dolls, 234–237
Dotted Swiss, 13
Dotted zigzag stitch, *60*
Double flange pillow finishing, 212
Double-pocketed pot holder, 285
Double-sided receiving blanket, 163
Dowel, 79
Drafting tape, 86, *86*
Drawn-thread designs, 320
Drawn-thread table runner, 321
Drawstring bolsters, *230*, 231
Drawstring pouch, 122

Drawstring pants, *186*, 187
Dress
easy tube, 175
girl's shirt, *182*, 183
Drop cloths, 76, *76*
Drying, of fabric, 30
Duvet cover, *146*, 147
Dyed-ticking napkins, 317
Dyed-ticking patchwork quilt, 294
Dyeing, 75
batik, 78–79
by hand, 77
ombré, 82–83
overdyeing, 80
protection for, 76
supplies, 76
test batch for, 76
Dyes, 76, *76*, 77

E

Easy chaise cushions, 342
Easy stenciled shade, 304
Easy tube dress, 175
Easy tuxedo pin-tuck pillow, 233
Echo quilting, 70–71
Edge stitches, 34
Elastic cord, *364*, 365
Embroidered bib, *153*
Embroidered circles, on bags, 121
Embroidered felt handbag, 119
Embroidered handkerchief, *245*
Embroidered letter sampler, 354
Embroidered tote, 115
Embroidery, 45
computer-aided, 61
floss, 46, *46*, 64, *64*
by hand, 47, *47*, 48–49
hoops, 46, *46*, 363
machine, 60
ribbon, 58–59
supplies, 46, *46*
yarn, 64, *64*
Embroidery-edged basic blanket, *157*, 158
Embroidery scissors, *360*, 361
End table, slipcovered, 346
Envelope-backed pillow cover, 210
Equipment, 21
Eyelet, 13
Eyelet overlay, 140
Eyelet pillowcases, 141
Eyelet shower curtain, *137*
Eyelet table runner, *313*

F

Fabric
for dyeing, 76
for quilting, 65
Fabric framing, 353
Fabric glue, 362
Fabric inkpad, 86, *86*
Fabric paint, 86, *86*
Fabric pen, 28, *29*, 359
in appliqué, 40, *40*
in embroidery, 46, *46*
Fabric-pocket tote bag, *113*, 114
Fabric preparation, 30
Fabric shears, 64, *64*, *360*, 361
Fabric sides, 30
Fabric stabilizers, 363
Fabric-topped storage boxes, *257*, 258
Fabric-wrapped accordion folders, 260
Faded floral fabric coasters, 190
Faded floral napkins, 316
Faded sheet set, *139*
Fading, 80, *81*
Falling-leaf pillow covers, 223
Falling-leaves felt board, 262
Farmyard appliqué wall hanging, 352–353
Fasteners, 366
Faux-bois gardener's apron, 110–111
Feed dogs, *32*, 33
Felt, 17
Felt baby slippers, 311
Felt board, falling-leaves, 262
Felt book band, 167
Felt book jackets, 167
Felted chicken, 96
Felted lamb, 95
Felted pig, 97
Felted-sweater patchwork blanket, 162
Felted-wool animals, 95–97
Felt garland, 253
Felt handbag, embroidered, 119
Felt-leaf notions, 281
Felt purse, miniature, *118*, 119
Felt slippers, nature-inspired, 310
Fiber-reactive dyes, 76, *76*
Fill, for stuffed animals, 97
Finishing knots, 31
Finishing seams, 35
Fishbone stitch, 49
Fitted armchair slipcovers, 344
Flannel, 12, 16
Flat-sheet duvet, 147
Floral coasters, faded, 190
Floral napkins, faded, 316
Floral stenciled curtains, *198*, 199
Floss, embroidery, 46, *46*
Flower-appliquéd shirt, 185
Flowering branches, *239*, 240
Flowers, 238–243
covered-button boutonniere, 241
rickrack, *242*, 243
Flush-mount bracket, 206
Flush-mount rod, 206
Flywheel, *32*, 33
Foam tools, 86, *86*
Folders, fabric-wrapped accordion, 260
Foot controller, *32*, 33
Framed patchwork star, 355
Framing fabrics, 353
Freestyle running stitch, 54, *54*
French knot, 52, *53*, *58*
French-knot blanket, 161
French-knotted borders, 143
French seam finish, 36
Fringed coasters, 191
Fringed table runner, 319
Fringed throw, 160
Fundoutsunagi, *56*, 57
Furnishings, 21
Fusible tape, 362
Fusible web, 40, *40*, 362

G

Garden journals, *168*, 169
Garland, 253
Gingham, 13
Gingham batik, 79
Girl's shirt dress, *182*, 183
Glass-head pins, 64, *64*
Gloves, for dyeing, 76, *76*
Glue, fabric, 362
Grain, fabric, 30
Grid ruler, 28, *29*
Grommets, 366
Grosgrain ribbon, *364*, 365
Growth chart, 252

H

Hanahishigata, *56*, 57
Hanakikkou, *56*, 57
Hand appliqué, 41
Handbag
  bias tape-trimmed, 127
  felt embroidered, 119
Hand-drawn stuffed creatures, 98
Hand dyeing, 77
Hand embroidery, 47, *47*, 48–49
Handkerchief linen, 15
Handkerchiefs, 244–247
Hand needles, 28, *29*, 64, *64*
Hand-rolled hem, 37
Hand-sewing needles, 40, *40*, 356
Hand-sewn dolls, *235*, 236–237
Hand stitches, 31
Hand warmer, pie-weight, 194
Hanging, of curtains, 204
Hawaiian-pattern appliquéd robe, 179
Hawaiian-pattern stenciled cushions, 343
Headboard, padded, 338
Headboard cover
  crewelwork, *349*
  ombré, 347
Heart-shaped pot holders, *283*, 284
Heat-transfer pencil, 46, *46*, 359
Heavy-duty thread, 19
Heirloom tomato pincushions, *277*, 278
Hem sewing, 37
Hemstitch, *60*
Herringbone, 16
Herringbone cross-stitch, 50
Hishimoyou, *56*, 57
Hiyokuigeta, 57, *57*
Hiyokuigeta place mat, *326*
Homasote, 264
Homespun linen, 15
Honeycomb stitch, *60*
Hooded towel, 133
Hook and eye, 366
Hoops, embroidery, 46, *46*, 363
Hot-iron transfer pen, 359

I

Icing tip, 79
Inkpad, fabric, 86, *86*
Inserts, pillow, 211
Intersecting grid running stitch, 54, *54*
Invisible hem, 37
Invisible thread, 19
Invisible zipper, 367
Iron, 367
Ironing board, 367
Ironing pad, 367
Ironing station, 21
Iron-on appliqué, 43
Iron-on silhouette bag, 120

J

Jacket
  book, 167
  quilted dog, *269*, 270
Japanese sashiko, 55
Jewelry boxes, 259
Journals, garden, *168*, 169
Jujitsunagi, 57, *57*

K

Kimono, baby, *180*, 181
Knife
  craft, 86, *86*
  palette, 86, *86*
Knots
  finishing, 31
  French, 52, *53*, *58*
Koushiawabe place mat, *326*
Koushitsunagi, 57, *57*
Koushitsunagi place mat, *326*
Kraft paper, 76, *76*, 359

L

Labels, on bags, 120
Lace, 13
Lamb, felted, 95
Lazy-daisy stitch, 49
Leather, 17
Leather coin purse, 263
Leather notebook cover, *165*, 166
Leather table mats, 331
Letter sampler, embroidered, 354
Lighting, 21
Linen apron, *103*, 104
Linen-edged sheer curtains, 200
Linen leaf, *56*, 57
Linen napkins, 314
Linen pillowcases, 144
Linens, 15
  bath, 128–137
  bed, 138–151
  table, 312–331
Linen shower curtain, 130
Linen tablecloth, *324*, 325
Linen voile curtains, two-tone, *197*
Liquid seam sealant, 362
London shade, *302*, 303
Long and short stitch, 49
Loop turner, 363
Lunch bag, oilcloth, *124*, 125

M

Machine-embroidered bath set, *129*, 130
Machine-embroidered coasters, 190
Machine-embroidered place mats, *326*, 327
Machine embroidery, 60
Machine embroidery thread, 19
Machine felting, 97
Machine needles, 357
Magnetic pin dish, 23
Magnetic pin organizers, 23
Marking hem, 37
Marking tools, 359
Mason-jar sewing kit, 280
Mat
  cutting, 361
  self-healing
    in printing, 86, *86*
    in quilting, 64, *64*

Materials, 356–367
Measuring spoons, 76, *76*
Measuring table, 22
Measuring tools, 358
Menswear bedding set, 145
Menswear bunny, 94
Menswear mice, *274*, 275
Menswear patchwork throw blanket, 289
Menswear water-bottle cozy, *193*, 194
Menu screen, *32*, 33
Mesh linen, 15
Metal chain zipper, 367
Metallic thread, 19
Mice, menswear, *274*, 275
Milliner's needle, 356
Miniature felt purse, *118*, 119
Mohair, 16
Monogrammed slippers, *309*
Monograms, on bags, 120
Multicompartment bag, 127
Multiple-pocket bulletin board, 267
Muslin, 12

N

Napkin pillow cover, 218
Napkins
  button embroidery, 317
  dyed-ticking, 317
  faded floral, 316
  feather-stamped, 315
  linen, 314
  ombré, 316
Natural dyes, 77
Natural sponge, 86, *86*
Nature-inspired felt slippers, 310
Needle clamp, *32*, 33
Needles
  appliqué, 356
  chenille, 356
  crewel, 356
  embroidery, 46, *46*
  hand, 28, *29*, 64, *64*, 356
  milliner's, 356
  quilting, 356
  sashiko, 356
  sewing, 356
  sewing machine, 28, *29*, *32*, 33, 357
  tapestry, 356
  upholstery, 356
Needle threader, 28, *29*, 357
Noniodized salt, 76, *76*
Nonreactive basin, 76, *76*
No-sew scalloped wrap skirt, *173*, 174
Notebook cover, leather, *165*, 166
Number book, appliquéd, 171
Nursery, 248–255
  changing-table curtains, 255
  growth chart, 252
  quilted crib bumper, 250–251
  scalloped canopy, *249*
  shirt-pocket organizer, 254
  simple felt garland, 253
Nylon web, *364*, 365

O

Oilcloth, 17
Oilcloth apron, *106*, 107
Oilcloth book covers, 170
Oilcloth-cutout coasters, *189*
Oilcloth lunch bag, *124*, 125
Oilcloth pocketed bib, 155
Ombré bag, 121
Ombré headboard cover, 347
Ombré napkins, 316
Ombré pattern, 82–83
Organization, 21
Organizers
  fabric-topped storage boxes, *257*, 258
  fabric-wrapped accordion folders, 260
  falling-leaves felt board, 262
  leather coin purse, 263
  multiple-pocket bulletin board, 267
  pin, 23
  pocketed ottoman cover, 266
  project, 256–267
  ribbon-striped bulletin board, 261
  shirt-pocket, 254
  velvet-lined jewelry boxes, 259
  wraparound bulletin board, 264–265
Organza, 14
Ottoman cover, 266
Oval scallop stitch, *60*
Overdyeing, 80
Overedge stitch, 34
Overlay, eyelet, 140
Overlock stitch, *60*

P

Padded headboard, 338
Padded ribbon stitch, 59
Padded straight stitch, 59
Paint, fabric, 86, *86*
Paintbrushes, 86, *86*
Palette, 86, *86*
Palette knife, 86, *86*
Pants, drawstring, *186*, 187
Paper
  kraft, 76, *76*, 359
  transfer, 40, *40*, 46, *46*, 359
  waterproof, 86, *86*
Paper templates, 40
Pastry cutter, 79
Patchwork, 63
Patchwork projects, 286–297
  denim patchwork quilt, 295
  framed star, 355
  menswear throw blanket, 289
  star-pattern patchwork coverlet, *296*, 297
  vintage handkerchief quilt, *287*, 288
  vintage-linen patchwork coverlet, 294
Patchwork quilt, 66–67
Patchwork repair, 72–73
Patio daybed, 340
Patterned cottons, 13
Pattern-making tools, 359
Pattern pinning, 30
Patterns
  batik, 79
  cross-stitch, 51
  ombré, 82–83
  quilting, 68–69
Pen
  fabric, 28, *29*, 359
    in appliqué, 40, *40*
    in embroidery, 46, *46*
  hot-iron transfer, 359
Pencil
  chalk, 28, *29*, 359
  heat-transfer, 46, *46*, 359
Permanent adhesive, 362
Pets, 268–275
  catnip fish on pole, 271
  dog bed, 272
  dog coat, 273
  dog jacket, *269*, 270

menswear mice, *274*, 275
Pie-weight hand warmer, 194
Pig, felted, 97
Pillow bands
couched, 228
wraparound, 216
Pillowcase bag, 126
Pillowcases
appliquéd, *150*, 151
eyelet, 141
linen, 144
sashiko-edged, 149
Pillow covers
basic, *209*
box, 224
cross-stitch, 225
doubled flanged, 212
envelope-backed, 210
falling leaf, 223
hand appliquéd, 229
napkin, 218
piped edged, 214
ruffled, 213
slipstitched, 210
Turkish cornered, 213
woven wool, 221
zippered, 211
Pillow inserts, 211
Pillows, decorative, 208–233
bird-embroidered, 222
box, 224
easy tuxedo pin-tuck, 233
pinch-pleated, 220
pin-tuck, 232
seashell-printed, 216
tooth-fairy, 226
tufted, 219
wedding ring, 227
Pillow trimmings, 215
Pinch-pleated café curtains, 206
Pinch-pleated pillow, 220
Pincushions, 22, 28, *29*, 276–281
felt-leaf, 281
heirloom tomato, *277*, 278
Mason jar, 280
strawberry, 279
Pin dish, magnetic, 23
Pinking shears, 28, *29*, 36, *360*, 361
Pinning, 30
Pin organizer, 23
Pins, 28, *29*, 64, *64*, 357
Pin-tuck pillows, 232
Piped edge pillow covers, 214
Piping, *364*, 365
Place mats
machine-embroidered, *326*, 327
raffia-embroidered, 329
Ultrasuede, 318
Plastic chain zipper, 367
Plastic coil zipper, 367
Plastic covering, 76, *76*
Pocketed bib, oilcloth, 155
Pocketed ottoman cover, 266
Pocket organizer, 254
Point turner, 28, *29*, 363
Polar fleece, 17
Polka dot, 13
Poly-cotton blend batting, 64
Polyester batting, 64
Polyester thread, 19
Poplin, 12
Porcelain dishes, *20*
Pot holders, 282–285
double-pocketed, 285
heart-shaped, *283*, 284
Pouch, drawstring, 122
Presser foot, *32*, 33
Pressing, of fabric, 30, 367
Prewashing, 76
Printing, 85
supplies, 86
Projects
animals, 92–102
bags, 112–127
bath linens, 128–137
bed linens, 138–151
bibs, 152–155
blankets, 156–163
books, 164–171
clothing, 172–187
decorative pillows, 208–233
dolls, 234–237
flowers, 238–243
handkerchiefs, 244–247
nursery, 248–255
organizers, 256–267
pet, 268–275
pincushions, 276–281
pot holders, 282–285
shades, 298–307
slippers, 308–311
stuffed animals, 92–102
table linens, 312–331
upholstery, 332–349
wall décor, 350–356
Protection, for dyeing, 76
Puppets, washcloth, 132
Purse, miniature felt, *118*, 119

Q

Quilt basting spray, 362
Quilted crib bumper, 250–251
Quilted dog jacket, *269*, 270
Quilter's ruler, 64, *64*
Quilting, 63
appliqué, 70–71
echo, 70–71
fabric, 65
needle, 356
patchwork, 66–67
pattern, 68–69
repair, 72–73
stitch, 65
supplies, 64
thread, 19, 64, *64*
Quilts, 286–297
denim patchwork, 295
dyed-ticking patchwork, 294
state bird-embroidered, *290*, 291
tablecloth, *292*, 293
vintage-handkerchief, *287*, 288
Quilt stitch, 54, *54*

R

Raffia-embroidered place mats, 329
Raffia-embroidered tote, 115
Rain slicker shower curtain, 134
Raw silk, 14
Repair, of patchwork quilt, 72–73
Reupholstered camp stools, 341
Reverse stitch button, *32*, 33
Reversible-border shower curtain, 136
Ribbon, grosgrain, *364*, 365

Ribbon-border blanket, 159
Ribbon-bordered bath mat, 135
Ribbon-embroidered handkerchief, 247
Ribbon-embroidered wall hangings, *351*
Ribbon embroidery, *58*, 58–59
Ribbon embroidery stitches, 59
Ribbon stitches, *58*, 59
Ribbon-striped bulletin board, 261
Ribbon-striped sheer curtains, 201
Rickrack, *364*, 365
Rickrack-edged coasters, 191
Rickrack flowers, *242*, 243
Rickrack trim, 143
Robe, appliquéd Hawaiian-pattern, 179
Rod, flush-mount, 206
Rolled-hem handkerchiefs, 246–247
Roman shade, *299*, 300–301
Rotary cutter, 64, *64*, 361
Round hem, 37
Rubber gloves, 76, *76*
Rubber stamps, 86, *86*
Ruffled pillow covers, 213
Ruler, 358
  grid, 28, *29*
  quilter's, 64, *64*
Running stitch, 31, 54
Running stitch–embroidered bedding, 148

S

Safety, sewing machine, *32*, 33
Safety pins, 64, *64*, 357
Salt, 76, *76*
Sarong
  sea-print, 178
  simple, 178
Sashiko, 55
Sashiko-edged pillowcases, 149
Sashiko needle, 356
Satin, 14
Satin stitch, 48
Scalloped blanket stitch, 49
Scalloped canopy, *249*
Scallop satin stitch, *60*
Scissors
  all-purpose, *360*, 361
  embroidery, *360*, 361
  small pointed
    in appliqué, 40, *40*
    in quilting, 64, *64*
Seam binding, *364*, 365
Seam-finishing techniques, 36
Seam gauge, 28, *29*, 358
Seam ripper, 28, *29*, *360*, 361
Seam sealant, 362
Seam sewing, 35
Sea-print sarong, 178
Sea-print tote, appliquéd, 117
Seashell-printed pillows, 216
Sea sponge, 86, *86*
Seersucker, 13
Self-healing mat
  in printing, 86, *86*
  in quilting, 64, *64*
Seven treasures, 57, *57*
Sewing
  hem, 37
  seams, 35
Sewing area, 20–21
Sewing kit, Mason-jar, 280
Sewing machine, *32*, 33
Sewing machine appliqué, 42
Sewing machine needles, 28, *29*, 357
Sewing needle, 356
Sewing shears, 28, *29*
Sewing style, 20
Sewing supplies, basic, 28, *29*
Sewing table, 21
Sew-on snaps, 366
Shades, 298–307
  button-up window, 306, *307*
  classic Roman, *299*, 300–301
  London, *302*, 303
  stenciled, 304
  vine-stenciled, 305
Shantung, 14
Shawl, appliquéd butterfly, 184
Shears
  bent-angled, *360*, 361
  fabric, 64, *64*, *360*, 361
  pinking, 28, *29*, 36, *360*, 361
  sewing, 28, *29*
Sheer curtains
  linen-edged, 200
  ribbon-striped, 201
Sheet set, faded, *139*
Shell-stamped bedclothes, 142
Shippoutsunagi, 57, *57*
Shippoutsunagi place mat, *326*
Shirt, flower appliquéd, 185
Shirt dress, girl's, *182*, 183
Shirting, 13
Shirt-pocket organizer, 254
Shower curtain
  eyelet, *137*
  linen, 130
  rain slicker, 134
  reversible border, 136
Sides, fabric, 30
Silhouette tote, cross-stitch, 123
Silks, 14
Simple felt garland, 253
Simple sarong, 178
Simplest bed frame slipcover, 348
Sizing, appliqué, 40
Skirt
  A-line wrap, *176*, 177
  no-sew scalloped wrap, *173*, 174
Slide plate, *32*, 33
Slipcovered end table, 346
Slipcovered patio daybed, 340
Slipcovers
  bed frame, 348
  fitted armchair, 344
Slippers, 308–311
  baby, 311
  monogrammed, *309*
  nature-inspired felt, 310
Slipstitch, 31
Slipstitched bolster, 231
Slipstitched pillow cover, 210
Small pointed scissors
  in appliqué, 40, *40*
  in quilting, 64, *64*
Snaps
  punched, 366
  sew-on, 366
Sock bulldog, 100
Sock dachshund, 100
Sock Dalmatian, 100
Sock dogs, *99*, 100–101
Solid zigzag stitch, *60*
Space constraints, 20–21

Specialty fabrics, 17
Sponge, natural, 86, *86*
Spool, 79
Spool pin, *32*, 33
Spoons, for dyeing, 76, *76*
Stabilizers, fabric, 363
Stamped floral curtains, *198*, 199
Stamping, 87
Stamping tools, 79
Stamps, 86, *86*
Star, framed patchwork, 355
Starburst decorative stitch, *60*
Star-pattern patchwork, 68–69
Star-pattern patchwork coverlet, *296*, 297
State bird–embroidered quilt, *290*, 291
Stem stitch, 48, *58*, 59
Stenciled curtains, floral, *198*, 199
Stenciled cushions, Hawaiian pattern, 343
Stenciled shade
  easy, 304
  vine, 305
Stenciling, 89
Stitches
  embroidery, 48–49
  hand, 31
  machine, 34
Stitching corners, 35
Stitching curves, 35
Stitch-length selector, *32*, 33
Stitch selector, *32*, 33
Stitch-width selector, *32*, 33
Stools, reupholstered camp, 341
Storage boxes, fabric-topped, *257*, 258
Straight stitch, 34, *58*, 59, *60*
Strawberry pincushions, 279
Stripe, 57, *57*
Striped curtains
  sheer ribbon, 201
  tucked café, 202
Stuffed animals project, 92–102
Style, sewing, 20
Suiting quilted coverlet, 295
Supplies
  appliqué, 40
  basic, 28, *29*
  dyeing, 76
  embroidery, 46, *46*
  printing, 86
  quilting, 64

T

Table
  coffee, upholstered, 339
  end, slipcovered, 346
  measuring, 22
  sewing, 21
Tablecloth
  doily, 330
  linen, *324*, 325
Tablecloth quilt, *292*, 293
Table linens, 312–331
  batik, 322
  bias-tape table runner, 318
  bleach batik, 323
  block-print, 328
  button embroidery napkins, 317
  doily tablecloth, 330
  drawn-thread, 320
  drawn-thread table runner, 321
  dyed-ticking napkins, 317
  faded floral napkins, 316
  feather-stamped napkins, 315
  fringed table runner, 319
  leather table mats, 331
  linen napkins, 314
  linen tablecloth, *324*, 325
  machine-embroidered place mats, *326*, 327
  ombré napkins, 316
  raffia-embroidered place mats, 329
  Ultrasuede place mats, 318
Table mats, leather, 331
Table runner
  bias-tape, 318
  drawn-thread, 321
  eyelet, *313*
  fringed, 319
Table-skirt curtains, *207*
Tacky glue, 362
Tailor's chalk, 28, *29*, 359
Take-up lever, *32*, 33
Tape
  bias, 64, *64*
  drafting, 86, *86*
  fusible, 362
Tape, twill, *364*, 365
Tape measure, 28, *29*, 358

Tapestry needle, 356
Task lighting, 21
Tea leaves, 77
Templates
  appliqué, 40
  printing, 86, *86*
Temporary fabric adhesive, 362
Tension regulator, *32*, 33
Terry cloth, 12
Test batch, in dyeing, 76
Thimble, 28, *29*, 357
Thread, 28, *29*
  appliqué, 40, *40*
  embroidery, 46
  quilting, 64, *64*
  types of, *18*, 19
Thread clips, *360*, 361
Thread color, 19
Threader, 28, *29*, 357
Thread guides, *32*, 33
Throat plate, *32*, 33
Throw, fringed, 160
Throw blanket, patchwork menswear, 289
Ticking, 13
Tomato pincushions, *277*, 278
Tools, 356–367
Tooth-fairy pillow, 226
Topstitches, 34
Tortoise shell, *56*, 57
Tote
  appliquéd sea-print, 117
  canvas, 116
  cross-stitch silhouette, 123
  multipocketed, *113*, 114
  raffia-embroidered, 115
Towel
  bias tape–embellished, 131
  hooded, 133
Tracing wheel, 40, *40*, 359
Transfer paper, 40, *40*, 46, *46*, 359
Triangle, 358
Trim, *364*
Trimmings, pillow, 215
Triple straight stitch, *60*
Tube dress, easy, 175
Tucked-stripe café curtain, 202
Tufted cushion, 219
Turkish corners, 213
Tuxedo pin-tuck pillow, 233

Tweed, 16
Tweezers, 28, *29*, 363
Twill, 12
Twill tape, *364*, 365
Twill tape–embellished curtain, 205
Two-tone linen voile curtains, *197*

U

Ultrasuede, 17
Ultrasuede dog coat, 273
Ultrasuede leaf place mats, 318
Upholstery, 332–349
  bed frame slipcover, 348
  chaise cushions, 342
  coffee table, 339
  crewelwork headboard cover, *349*
  cushion-top blanket chest, *336*, 337
  daybed cover, *333*, 334
  dining chair, 335
  fitted armchair slipcovers, 344
  Hawaiian-pattern stenciled cushions, 343
  ombré headboard cover, 347
  padded headboard, 338
  reupholstered camp stools, 341
  slipcovered end table, 346
  slipcovered patio daybed, 340
  velvet chair skirt, 345
Upholstery linen, 15
Upholstery needle, 356
Upholstery thread, 19

V

Velvet, 14
Velvet, cotton, 12
Velvet chair skirt, 345
Velvet-lined jewelry boxes, 259
Vine-stenciled shade, 305
Vintage-handkerchief quilt, *287*, 288
Vintage-linen patchwork coverlet, 294
Voile, cotton, 12

W

Wall décor, 350–356
  embroidered letter sampler, 354
  farmyard appliqué wall hanging, 352–353
  framed patchwork star, 355
  ribbon-embroidered wall hangings, *351*
Wall hangings
  farmyard appliqué, 352–353
Wall hangings, ribbon-embroidered, *351*
Washcloth puppets, 132
Washing, of fabric, 30
Water-bottle cozy, menswear, *193*, 194
Waterproof paper, 86, *86*
Wax, 28, *29*, 78, 357
Web
  cotton, *364*, 365
  fusible, 40, *40*
  nylon, *364*, 365
Wedding-ring pillow, 227
Wheel, tracing, 40, *40*, 359
Windowpane wool, 16
Wood block, 79
Wool batting, 64
Wools, 16
Woven-wool pillow covers, 221
Wraparound bulletin board, 264–265
Wraparound pillow bands, 217
Wrapping branches, 240
Wrap skirt
  A-line wrap skirt, *176*, 177
  no-sew scalloped, *173*, 174

Y

Yarn, embroidery, 64, *64*

Z

Zigzag-embroidered bedclothes, 142
Zigzag stitch, 34, *60*
Zigzag-stitch finish, 36
Zippered pillow cover, 211
Zippers, 367

projects by technique

APPLIQUÉ

Appliquéd Curtain, 204
Appliquéd Duvet Cover and Pillowcases, 150–151
Appliquéd Number Book, 171
Appliquéd Sea-Print Tote, 117
Butterfly-Appliquéd Shawl, 184
Couched Pillow Bands, 228
Falling-Leaf Pillow Covers, 223
Farmyard Appliqué Wall Hanging, 352–353
Flower-Appliquéd Shirt, 185
Growth Chart, 252
Hand-Appliquéd Pillow Covers, 229
Hawaiian-Pattern Appliquéd Robe, 179

DYEING

Batik Table Linens, 322
Bleach-Batik Table Linens, 323
Dyed Ticking Patchwork Quilt, 294
Dyed Ticking Napkins, 317
Faded Floral Coasters, 190
Faded Floral Napkins, 316
Faded Sheet Set, *139*
Ombré Headboard Cover, 347
Ombré Napkins, 316
Ombré Tote Bag, 121
Table-Skirt Curtains, *207*

EMBROIDERY

Apple-Embroidered Bib, *153*
Bird-Embroidered Pillows, 222
Button-Embroidered Napkins, 317
Cross-Stitch Pillow Cover, 225
Cross-Stitch Silhouette Tote, 123
Embroidered Circle Bag, 121
Embroidered Felt Handbag, 119
Embroidered Handkerchiefs, *245*
Embroidered Letter Sampler, 354
Embroidery-Edged Basic Blanket, *157*, 158
Falling-Leaf Pillow Covers, 223
French Knot–Bordered Bed Linens, 143
French-Knot Blanket, 161
Fringed Throw, 160
Garden Journals, 168–169
Japanese-Embroidered Table Linens, *326*
Machine-Embroidered Bath Set, *129*
Machine-Embroidered Coasters, 190
Machine-Embroidered Place Mats, 327
Monogrammed Slippers, *309*
Raffia-Embroidered Place Mats, 329
Raffia-Embroidered Tote, 115
Ribbon-Embroidered Handkerchiefs, 247
Ribbon-Embroidered Wall Hangings, *351*
Running Stitch-Embroidered Bedding, 148
Sashiko-Edged Pillowcases, 149
State Bird–Embroidered Quilt, 290–291
Tooth-Fairy Pillow, 226
Zigzag-Embroidered Bed Linens, 142

NO-SEW

Apple-Print Bag, 125
Block-Print Table Linens, 328
Covered-Button Boutonniere, 241
Cushion-Top Blanket Chest, 336–337
Drawn-Thread Table Runner, 320–321
Easy Stenciled Shade, 304
Eyelet Shower Curtain, *137*
Eyelet Table Runner, *313*
Fabric-Topped Storage Boxes, *257*, 258
Fabric-Wrapped Accordion Folders, 260
Falling-Leaves Felt Board, 262
Feather-Stamped Napkins, 315
Felt-Leaf Notions, 281
Fringed Coasters, 191
Hawaiian-Pattern Stenciled Cushions, 343
Iron-On Silhouette Bags, 120
Labeled and Monogrammed Bags, 120
Mason-Jar Sewing Kit, 280
No-Sew Scalloped Wrap Skirt, *173*, 174
Ombré Tote Bag, 121
Padded Headboard, 338
Ribbon-Striped Bulletin Board, 261
Rickrack-Edged Coasters, 191
Sea-Print Sarong, 178
Shell-Stamped Bed Linens, 142
Twill Tape–Embellished Curtain, 205
Ultrasuede Leaf Place Mats, 318
Upholstered Dining Chair, 335
Velvet-Lined Jewelry Boxes, 259
Vine-Stenciled Shade, 305
Wraparound Bulletin Board, 264–265

PRINTING

Apple-Print Bag, 125
Appliquéd Sea-Print Tote, 117
Block-Print Table Linens, 328
Easy Stenciled Shade, 304
Feather-Stamped Napkins, 315
Hawaiian-Pattern Stenciled Cushions, 343
Sea-Print Sarong, 178
Seashell-Printed Pillows, 216
Shell-Stamped Bed Linens, 142
Stenciled Curtains, 198–199
Vine-Stenciled Shade, 305

QUILTING AND PATCHWORK

Denim Patchwork Quilt, 295
Dyed-Ticking Patchwork Quilt, 294
Felted-Sweater Patchwork Blanket, 162
Framed Patchwork Star, 355
French-Knot Blanket, 161
Hawaiian-Pattern Quilted Pillow, 70–71
Menswear Patchwork Throw, 289
Patchwork Memory Quilt, 66–67
Quilted Crib Bumper, 250–251
Quilted Dog Jacket, *269*, 270
Quilted Suiting Coverlet, 295
Shirt-Pocket Organizer, 254
Star-Pattern Patchwork Coverlet, 296
Star-Pattern Patchwork Pillow, 68–69
State Bird–Embroidered Quilt, 290–291
Tablecloth Quilt, 292–293
Vintage-Handkerchief Quilt, *287*, 288
Vintage-Linen Patchwork Coverlet, 294

SEWING

A-Line Wrap Skirt, 176–177
Adjustable Apron, 108
Appliquéd Number Book, 171
Baby Kimono, 180–181
Baker's Apron, 109
Basic Canvas Tote, 116
Basic Daybed Cover, *333*, 334
Basic Linen Apron, *103*, 104
Basic Linen Napkins, 314
Batik Table Linens, 322
Bias Tape–Embellished Bib, 154
Bias Tape–Embellished Towels, 131
Bias-Tape Table Runner, 318
Billowy Roman Shade, *302*
Bleach-Batik Table Linens, 323
Box Pillows and Cases, 224
Butterfly-Appliquéd Shawl, 184
Button-Tab Café Curtain, 203
Button-Up Window Shade, 306
Catnip Fish on a Pole, 271
Changing-Table Curtains, 255
Child's Oilcloth Apron, 106–107
Classic Roman Shade, *299*, 300–301
Clucking-Egg Cozy, 195
Coordinated-Sheet Duvet Cover, 146–147
Crafter's Apron, 105
Crewelwork Headboard Cover, *349*
Crewelwork Roman Shades, *307*
Cross-Stitch Pillow Cover, 225
Dish-Towel Apron, 108
Doily Tablecloth, 330
Double-Pocketed Pot Holder, 285
Double-Sided Receiving Blanket, 163
Drawstring Bolster, 230
Drawstring Pants, 186–187
Drawstring Pouches, 122
Easy Chaise Cushions, 342
Easy Tube Dress, 175
Easy Tuxedo Pin-Tuck Pillow, 233
Embroidered Felt Handbag, 119
Embroidery-Edged Basic Blanket, *157*, 158
Envelope-Backed Pillow Cover, *209*, 210
Eyelet Overlay, 140
Eyelet Pillowcases, 141
Fabric-Pocket Tote Bag, *113*, 114
Faded Floral Fabric Coasters, 190
Faux-Bois Gardener's Apron, 110–111
Felt Baby Shoes, 311
Felt Book Jackets, 167
Felted-Wool Animals, 95–97
Fitted Armchair Slipcovers, 344
Flat-Sheet Duvet, 147
Flowering Branches, *239*, 240
Fringed Table Runners, 319
Fringed Throw, 160
Garden Journals, 168–169
Girl's Shirt Dress, 182–183
Hand-Drawn Stuffed Creatures, 98
Hand-Sewn Dolls, *235*, 236–237
Heart-Shaped Pot Holders, *283*, 284
Heirloom-Tomato Pincushions, *277*, 278
Hooded Towel, 133
Leather Coin Purse, 263
Leather Notebook and Checkbook Covers, *165*, 166
Leather Table Mats, 331
Linen Pillowcases, 144
Linen Shower Curtain, 130
Linen Tablecloth, 324–325
Linen-Edged Sheers, 200
London Shade, 303
Menswear Bedding Set, 145
Menswear Bunny, *93*, 94
Menswear Mice, 274–275
Menswear Water-Bottle Cozy, *193*, 194
Miniature Felt Purses, 118–119
Multicompartment Bag, 127
Multiple-Pocket Bulletin Board, 267
Napkin Pillow Cover, 218
Nature-Inspired Felt Slippers, 310
Oilcloth Book Covers, 170
Oilcloth Cutout Coasters, *189*
Oilcloth Lunch Bag, 124–125
Oilcloth Pocketed Bib, 155
Ombré Headboard Cover, 347
Pie-Weight Hand Warmer, 194
Pillowcase Bag, 126
Pin-Tuck Pillows, 232
Pinch-Pleated Café Curtains, 206
Pinch-Pleated Pillow, 220
Pocketed Ottoman Cover, 266
Quilted Dog Jacket, *269*, 270
Rain Slicker Shower Curtain, 134
Reupholstered Camp Stools, 341
Reversible-Border Shower Curtain, 136
Ribbon-Border Blanket, 159
Ribbon-Bordered Bath Mat, 135
Ribbon-Striped Sheers, 201
Rickrack Flowers, 242–243
Rickrack-Trim Pillowcases, 143
Rolled-Hem Handkerchiefs, 246–247
Sashiko-Edged Pillowcases, 149
Scalloped Canopy, *249*
Sea-Print Sarong, 178
Simple Dog Bed, 272
Simple Felt Garland, 253
Simple Sarong, 178
Simplest Bed Frame Slipcover, 348
Slipcovered End Table, 346
Slipcovered Patio Daybed, 340
Slipstitched Bolster, 231
Slipstitched Pillow Cover, *209*, 210
Sock Dogs, *99*, 100–101
Strawberry Pincushions, 279
Tooth-Fairy Pillow, 226
Tucked-Stripe Café Curtain, 202
Tufted Cushion, 219
Two-Tone Linen Voile Curtains, *197*
Ultrasuede Dog Coat, 273
Upholstered Coffee Table, 339
Velvet Chair Skirt, 345
Washcloth Puppets, 132
Wedding-Ring Pillow, 227
Woven-Wool Pillow Covers, 221
Wraparound Pillow Bands, 217
Zippered Pillow Cover, *209*, 211

photography credits

WILLIAM ABRANOWICZ 130, 144, 157, 197, 249, 255, 264, 265, 287, 288, 324–325, 338, 348

SANG AN 22 (bottom), 23 (bottom), 113, 114, 120, 135 (top), 153, 155, 170, 194 (bottom), 280, 317 (right), 330 (top)

STEFANO AZARIO 242

JAMES BAIGRIE 227, 272, 342

CHRISTOPHER BAKER 228, 309, 311

HARRY BATES (illustrations) 31, 34, 36, 37, 40, 48–50, 52, 54, 58, 59, 65, 95–97, 101, 104 (right), 115, 116, 125, 158, 159, 160, 177 (#5), 187 (#5), 210–214, 220, 221, 231 (right), 240, 243, 247, 266, 267, 301, 321, 329, 334, 369–373

JUSTIN BERNHAUT 22 (top), 220

ANDREW BORDWIN 336, 337

ANITA CALERO 223, 239, 262, 310 (top)

EARL CARTER 200, 201

GEMMA COMAS 58, 163, 168, 169, 247, 351

SUSIE CUSHNER 232

CARLTON DAVIS 167 (top)

REED DAVIS 28, 151 (right)

PIETER ESTERSOHN 333

FORMULA Z/S 260

RICHARD FOSTER 215

SCOTT FRANCES 296, 304 (top)

LAURIE FRANKEL endsheets, 1, 13, 17, 24¬–25, 32, 47 (bottom), 90–91, 167 (bottom)

DANA GALLAGHER 77, 81, 139, 145 (top), 182, 190 (right), 193, 207, 230, 233 (top), 274, 294 (right), 295 (right), 316 (left), 317 (left), 354

GENTL & HYERS 171, 173, 273, 352, 353

ALISON GOOTEE 127, 131, 154, 318 (top)

CATHERINE GRATWICKE 60, 129, 142 (left), 190 (left), 327

JOHN GRUEN 23 (top), 65

FRANK HECKERS 66, 67, 180, 181

RAYMOND HOM 11, 12, 18, 26, 38, 71, 94, 122 (bottom 2), 145 (bottom 2), 176, 183, 194 (top), 233 (bottom), 258, 275, 285 (bottom 2), 289 (bottom 2), 356–367

MATTHEW HRANEK 105, 109, 110, 319, 331

LISA HUBBARD 51, 78, 79, 123, 147, 160, 225, 292–293, 294 (left), 295 (left), 318 (bottom 2), 322

GABRIELLE IMPERATORI-PENN 277, 278

DITTE ISAGER 87, 117, 178 (bottom), 216

KARL JUENGEL 111, 370

DEAN KAUFMAN 175

KELLER & KELLER 202, 203, 206

YUNHEE KIM 217, 241

YOSHIHARU KOIZUMI 2, 4, 55–57, 149, 326

SIVAN LEWIN 98

STEPHEN LEWIS 99, 254, 271

STEVEN MCDONALD 135 (bottom)

MAURA MCEVOY 52, 53, 72, 73, 108 (top 2), 143, 161, 191 (right), 315 (top)

JAMES MERRELL 68, 69, 222, 290, 291, 297, 355

ELLIE MILLER 30, 88, 195, 218 (top), 219, 328

JOHNNY MILLER 6, 14–16, 29, 40, 44, 46, 62, 64, 74, 76, 83, 84, 86, 89, 93, 103, 116, 122 (top), 159, 186, 199, 209, 218 (bottom), 240, 246, 257, 259, 285 (top), 289 (top), 305 (bottom), 310 (bottom), 315 (bottom), 330 (bottom)

LAURA MOSS 224, 269

AMY NEUNSINGER 35, 314

HELEN NORMAN 178 (top), 250, 251, 323, 340

JANNE PETERS 41–43, 150, 151 (left 2), 184, 185, 204, 229

ERIC PIASECKI 82, 108 (bottom 2), 121 (right), 205, 221, 252, 261, 266, 267, 299, 301, 303, 307, 316 (right), 347, 349

SABINE PIGALLE 320, 321

DAVID PRINCE 279, 306

MARIA ROBLEDO 95, 162

FRANCE RUFFENACH 132

DAMIAN RUSSELL 344, 345

JOSEPH SCAFURO 325

CHARLES SCHILLER 191 (left), 281

ANNIE SCHLECHTER 125, 133, 165, 166, 235–237, 253, 263

KATE SEARS 54, 121 (left), 126, 148

MARK SEELEN 302

MATTHEW SEPTIMUS 283, 284

SIMON UPTON 61

MIKKEL VANG 70, 179, 198, 305 (top), 343

JONNY VALIANT 115, 329

WILLIAM VAN RODEN 174, 177 (#1–4), 187 (#1–4)

WILLIAM WALDRON 146

SIMON WATSON 50, 106, 107, 124, 189, 339, 346

WENDELL T, WEBBER 20, 134, 136, 142 (right)

ANNA WILLIAMS 47 (top), 118, 119, 137, 140, 141, 226, 245, 313, 341

JAMES WORRELL 304 (bottom)

Photos on page 368 courtesy of Singer